EXPLORING HUMAN DEVELOPMENT

EXPLORING HUMAN DEVELOPMENT

INTERDISCIPLINARY READINGS

edited by

HAROLD W. BERNARD
Oregon State System of Higher Education

WESLEY C. HUCKINS
Wright State University

Allyn and Bacon, Inc.

BOSTON

Second printing ... May, 1973

Library of Congress Catalog Card Number: 74–159769 √

Printed in the United States of America

Contents

Preface

ONLY FIVE YEARS have passed since this book's predecessor, *Readings in Human Development,* was published, yet there are topics of concern today that were rare at the earlier time, such as the threat of pollution in the atmosphere, genetic engineering, and the effects of malnutrition on mental development. In other areas, previously existing concerns have been accelerated: youth's quest for identity, growing belief in the unused potential of mankind, meaningful education for the culturally different, and dangers of population explosion. These interests are reflected in the choice of articles for inclusion in this volume. In still other areas, topics that have long been recognized as needing emphasis have continued to generate interest and discussion. In such matters we have retained articles that are still recognized as being classics of pertinency and succinctness.

Professional colleagues have given us advice on articles which they and their students have liked or disliked in the first collection of readings, and such advice has influenced our choices. The most gratifying clues to new articles meriting inclusion have come from our own students. They report having been stimulated to read more widely in such journals as were available and have made many recommendations regarding current pieces from various sources. Many of these students have gratuitously asserted that their enthusiasm for journals has increased because of exposure to readings.

We have tried to select the writing of authors who are well known and respected for their contributions to some phase of human development. Prominence was not, however, the sole criterion of selection. Many of the selections concisely and clearly present a point of view or a unique aspect of development that seems to merit the attention of a student.

Various aspects of development receive preponderant attention, even though the articles are contained in different sections. One such concept relates to the environmental stimulation of intellectual potential, especially the importance of appropriate early stimulation. Another aspect, closely related, yet of still more pervasive influence because it affects personality, ambitions, education, and attitudes, is socioeconomic status. This topic merits the attention it gets partly because of its far-reaching influence and also because of its relation to recent federal legislation and activity in local communities and schools. We must also admit to some partiality in the selection of articles relating to the self-concept. This is so pervasive in relation to success with one's peers, to school achievement, and to general mental health that no apologies are made for its frequent mention.

Without preplanning, we find that these readings are interdisciplinary —as the study of human development should be. Articles come from journals in sociology, social work, psychology, education, and biological science.

The editors have made a few observations on each selection. This is done not to convince or persuade the reader but to acquaint him with the process of reading critically. This may best be done by reacting from a frame of reference; by weighing each statement against a position and by taking a stand as a criterion for verification, modification, or rejection. Such a process requires active reader involvement. Reading becomes more a dialogue with the author than either a passive ingestion or an automatic rejection of his ideas. As the reader becomes conscious of the part he plays in choosing, organizing, and reorganizing information, his responsibility for his own intellectual development and for the structure of his opinions and attitudes becomes more apparent to him.

The readings are divided into three parts: Developmental Perspectives, Phases of Development, and Developmental Forces. These three parts are subdivided into fourteen sections to make the correlation with the textbooks on human development and educational psychology an easier task.

As we have studied these articles, first for the matter of tentative choice and then to write introductory comments, we have found new points and ideas missed on the first reading. Hence, we suggest that the student, after reading the articles that appear later in the book, return to earlier articles which have points of similarity to see if their relevance has increased. He may find a pertinence and an application on second or third reading that previously had evaded him. Because his knowledge and understanding have increased, he may be able to recombine some of the ideas and concepts he has gained into a unique and more valuable approach. This is the essence of intellectual development. While an exact reconstruction is of scant value, something different may open the way to new answers and new interpretations. Each individual, because he is unique, offers a new hope and another possibility for novel and more illuminating perceptions and ideas.

Harold W. Bernard
Wesley C. Huckins

part one

DEVELOPMENTAL PERSPECTIVES

THE MOST amazing aspect of human development might be the matter of potential. Other animals are born with clear-cut limitations on what they might become. Other animals are born with greater capacity for self-care, and their rapid development makes the period of "childhood" dependency quite short. Man, by way of contrast, is quite helpless; slow but continuous development makes him dependent for a long period of time. One result of this lack of ready-made response and its slow maturation is that man is more adaptable than other creatures. He possesses fascinating potential because of plasticity, modifiability, and responsiveness to environment.

The first part of this book of readings deals with various perspectives on man's potential for development. It includes: (1) the expanding role of science and its visions for the better use of potential; (2) how behavior potential begins to be shaped by genetic and prenatal factors; (3) the orderliness and dependability of development expressed in encompassing principles; (4) ways in which human potential may be utilized to better advantage—i.e., teaching-learning relations; and (5) the central aspect of plasticity, adaptiveness, and potential—or the capacity for the development of intelligence. But in this respect no student, if he really is to study human development, can afford to be unconcerned with the manner in which people gain and test ideas, for this determines the way in which men interact with environmental factors and genetic endowments in shaping what they will become.

The first selections for this book present different theoretical approaches to the study of psychology and human development. This is done purposefully because an idea is a necessary antecedent in the pursuit of knowledge. Some sort of idea and the hypotheses and assumptions that are generated lie behind most of the theories that now are accepted. These, in turn, provide bases for generating, stating, and testing new ideas. Neither the proven theory nor the idea is apt to have happened in the absence of the other—they are interdependent. Despite this relationship, however, the gap between theory-based hypotheses and accepted facts sometimes is wide indeed and it is well for those

1

who study psychology to appreciate this. Sometimes it is difficult in those disciplines concerned with human behavior to distinguish one from the other. In the genesis of a concept into dependable knowledge it is not always easy to discern, precisely, the status of the idea. On the basis of his experience, a psychologist may believe a certain thing to be true. He may write and speak of his belief, but the idea will not be accepted among his fellows until he can furnish proof that it works or does what he claims it can do.

This skepticism among psychologists exists for several reasons. First, psychology is a relatively new discipline. It has existed in a formal and recognized sense for less than a century, since the opening of the first psychological laboratory by Wilhelm Wundt in 1879. The status and acceptance accorded to the physical sciences are yet to be gained by psychology. While it would not be justifiable to say that psychologists try harder, it may be permissible to suggest that they are less convinced, and under more compulsion to defend, to explain, and to justify what they say. A second reason for the "show me" attitude of psychologists lies with the differences in basic attitude and orientation among them. As Bruce indicates in selection 1, both points of view and consequent ethical concerns vary considerably among the three identified approaches. There are advantages in these varied approaches. Criticism and discourse are generated and checks and balances are provided. Statements are challenged and validating research is demanded and promoted. An example of this process can be found in the article by Williams (selection 8), who challenges psychologists to extend their boundaries if they aspire to a complete science. A third reason why psychology and psychologists should, and must, question the ideas they generate can be found in the nature of the work in which they are involved. They are concerned primarily with humanity rather than with objects or with animals. When errors can hurt people, ethical considerations and meticulous attention to the development of principles and techniques become increasingly important.

There are a number of ways in which people in general and psychologists in a formal sense function to test the validity of their ideas. And in a way the reader presently is involved in one of these. This is the process of *publication*—of sharing ideas and of inviting and promoting discourse about them. The author, in effect, says, "this is what I think, and what represents the present state of my belief," and in support of his argument he may cite others whose ideas are similar. Through these actions he invites the reaction and comment that force him to clarify, to modify and change, or perhaps to discard the ideas he started with. He becomes involved in the process of getting agreement concerning the applicability and value of his thinking. This process is known as *consensual validation*. Much of this book, and many other human development publications, constitutes an example of this process. The reader should look for instances of its use in these readings and other situations. He should learn how to employ the consensual validation process himself and how to provide criticism, feedback, and assistance for others as they use it.

Another way of validating ideas and hypotheses is merely to try them to see if they work. This is the *pragmatic,* or what Coffield (selection 3) calls the R-R, approach. It tests ideas in actual situations and assesses their value in terms of results. There may be a range all the way from a trial-and-error, haphazard approach to a carefully planned study. As with the other approaches for validating ideas, however, there are advantages and disadvantages. Because results are gained in real situations, they generally are pertinent and the question of whether or not they may be transferred or generalized tends to arise less often. An example of this approach can be found in the article by Staffieri (selection 30). He was concerned about the attitudes which prepubescent boys have toward their own physiques so he dealt directly with boys of this age and their reactions. Contrast this with what needs to be done to relate Harlow's (selection 46) research with monkeys to human development. Although his findings probably are pertinent and although valuable insights appear to have been gained, certainty depends upon a replication with human babies in similar situations. Can you imagine many mothers allowing this?

This brings into focus some of the disadvantages of what we have chosen to call the *pragmatic* approach. (1) It takes a long time. Humans mature slowly. If one wishes to determine the effects of childhood behaviors upon the same person as an adult, he must observe for several decades. (See selection 31 by Moss and Kagan.) (2) Humans are difficult to study. Their freedom cannot be curtailed without their consent and they sometimes refuse to act predictably from sheer perversity. (3) The control of conditions or variables that may affect results is not always feasible outside the laboratory. When a number of conditions, any one of which might be a causal factor, exist at the same time, it is difficult to attribute results to any specific one and it is difficult to replicate the exact situation so that the same outcome can be expected again.

Another way of validating ideas, one that avoids the above disadvantages, is the *laboratory,* experimental, or (in Coffield's terminology) S-R *approach.* In it animals often, but not always, are substituted for the more difficult to control human subjects. Conditions and variables can be regulated and results can be assessed in terms of the presence or absence of specific factors. The drawback here, of course, is that it is not always possible to generalize from animals to humans and from controlled laboratory conditions to situations in the world outside. Hence, no one approach, and perhaps no combination of approaches, completely fills the bill (selection 3).

The process of validating ideas is not an easy one. It is difficult to set up experiments that will yield results acceptable to all, or perhaps even to the majority, of psychologists. Discriminating reading in the area of psychology and human development is not an easy task. It is not always possible to tell when a writer is speculating, when he speaks from a recognized theory, whether he is reporting the findings and ideas of others, or whether he has facts and experiments to substantiate the points he is making. Although no authors in the professional journals of human development can be expected deliberately to mislead a reader, being misled is, as much or more, the responsibility of the reader. It is he who is responsible for the clarity and pertinence of his own thinking and it is he who determines the degree of credence he will attach to what he reads.

Some attention to the following suggestions may prove helpful in increasing the power to read in a discriminating fashion. (1) Opinions and ideas contained in articles printed in professional journals usually are more acceptable than those in popular and nonprofessional magazines. (2) If the author has cited others of the same opinion and if he has indicated similar research, his ideas probably merit consideration. (3) The ideas and projects generated by authors of recognized professional status and reputation naturally command confidence. (4) Conclusions based upon data gathered from careful observation merit consideration and generate acceptance. (5) Results and procedures of experiments conducted to test specific hypotheses possess comparatively high credibility for the situation in which they were gained. Their application, however, depends upon the degree of similarity between laboratory and actual conditions. (6) Although the validity of the conclusions obtained from an experimental study usually is dependent upon a number of factors, the reader is urged to pay particular attention to the following: How well was the study designed to answer the question, i.e., prove or disprove a stated hypothesis? How well were the possible causal agents or variables controlled so that the reasons for results could be determined? To what degree do the derived conclusions appear to be justified by the study?

Bruce (selection 1), Caldwell and Richmond (2), Otto (4), and Maslow (5), using different perspectives, deal with the role and use of science in capitalizing upon unrecognized and unappreciated potential. A few years ago parents frowned upon, if they did not prohibit, their children's wasting time on the improbable trash of Buck Rogers. Now men do suspend themselves in space, walk on the moon, steam through icebergs. Bruce describes the three broad points of view under which most psychological theories and systems can be classified. It will help the reader's orientation and understanding if he asks himself as he reads, "Could the ideas presented by this writer be classified as stimulus response, psychoanalytic, or humanistic, or do they combine elements of all three? Kagan (selection 25) represents the combination approach. He speaks of learning attitudes toward self and sex roles from parents in early childhood via social reinforcement. And he substantiates what he has to say with documentation and research. Examples of most, if not all, of the ways of validating ideas and elements of each of the three forces in psychology can be found in this one selection. Caldwell and Richmond expand the listing of theories to include those primarily concerned with human development. They make it clear that if we are to capitalize upon man's potential for flexible, competent behavior, a safe take-off is requisite. This requisite is provided in the form of soundly based theories of child-rearing. Current theories are evaluated and the authors also suggest ways in which evolving theories may be tested and refined.

Otto suggests a number of things about human potential that have seemed improbable but are now regarded as routine function. He leaves the reader in suspense and with the hope that other breakthroughs in capitalizing on potential are close at hand. His article and the one by Williams constitute examples of the process of publication and discourse. There will be reactions and comments suggesting that some of the statements they make are unsubstantiated; but as we have indicated, these are a necessary prelude to formulating and testing relevant hypotheses.

Maslow emphasizes a phenomenon about which we need to be warned periodically—the tendency to categorize and to think in either-or postulations. Hence, he emphasizes that he is not a behavioristic, a pro-Freudian, or a humanistic psychologist but is some of all of these, because each emphasizes some important aspect of behavior and development. In addition, perhaps it should be said *mainly,* he emphasizes the need for scientists to take a value orientation. Instead of regarding a fact merely as a fact, it is necessary to see good and bad information. Data are good if they help one to actualize potential. The editors are pleased to present this first group of articles because they help to show the role that theory and even speculation play in the development of credible and valid ideas. The selections help to show how the actualization of ideas through scientific experimentation contributes to the self-actualization of people and the development of human potential.

The second set of articles by Lederberg, Sontag, Williams, and Dayton (selections 6 through 9) invite a close look at what takes place in the course of human development even before birth. Science, functioning in the realm of agriculture, has—in just the past ten, twenty, fifty years—made amazing advances: Faster growing, more nutritious, more disease-resistant wheat and rice are being created from season to season. Chickens that produce eggs at a continuous and rapid rate are replaced in batches of thousands by chickens who lay eggs still more competently. And there are cattle whose purpose in life, much like Al Capp's schmoos, seems to be solely that of pleasing man's palate. Scientific feats, perhaps still more amazing, seem to be possible in terms of modification of the genetic building blocks of humans.

Lederberg suggests that instead of relying mainly upon natural genetic potential, there is the possibility and likelihood of man's being able to improve that potential. IQ's of 350, self-shearing heads of hair are possibilities. He doesn't mention it, but how about persons with built-in humanitarianism who would make war impossible? Life can be improved even without change in genetic structure. Sontag (selection 7) indicates that there is much we know that is not fully used, and much we do not know that could be used, about how to provide an optimum environment for fetal development. The challenges are not exclusive; we can do both: improve the potential and use more effectively the potential now possessed.

All is not well on the developmental front. It seems that with our humanitarian ideals there is a tendency to perpetuate defect. There is no longer an evolutionary process of survival of the fittest—at least as far as western culture is concerned. There are problems of identity—who really is who, or what—as the successful use of organ transplants becomes commonplace. There are problems of overpopulation. Perhaps science can teach us how to grow enough food for limitless numbers or how to develop organisms that use food much more economically than we do now. But how to dispose of the waste we create is as much of a menace as it was in the days of Roman power or Grecian splendor. Specifically, man becomes a victim of his own inventions and conventions—he becomes a matter of his own making. Selected examples are presented by Williams and Dayton (selections 8 and 9) who are saying that man is much less than he needs be. Gaining new knowledge is a laudable pursuit, but an equally great challenge is to practice what we already know.

Opinions differ regarding just how much of development is due to hereditary and congenital factors as opposed to the molding influence of environment. There is agreement, though, on the principle that both play some role in an interactive process. The matter of how, how much, and under what conditions principles of development function is dealt with in representative articles by Anastasiow, Ames and Ilg, and Piaget (selections 10 through 12). The three articles in the section entitled "Principles of Development" deal with questions which just seem to refuse to be answered satisfactorily. The problem of nature-nurture presumably was laid to rest by a publication of the National Society for the Study of Education in a Yearbook, *Nature and Nurture: Their Influence upon Intelligence,* published in 1928. The question did, indeed, lie dormant for a number of years, but Jensen revived it in full vigor forty years later.

Ames and Ilg illustrate the value of studying developmental principles by showing the regularity and predictability of human change. Their article, which emphasizes the up-down, forward-back nature of progress, should be helpful to teachers and parents. It should remind them that a child who once achieves a skill does not then irrevocably possess it. The article should remind them that comparisons between children are not just unfair—they are cruel. One child might just be on the regressive end of a forward thrust while the other might be on the leading edge.

Piaget, like the nature-nurture controversy, is not a newcomer to this intellectual territory. His publications, postulations, and pronouncements have been translated, interpreted, and reinterpreted by numerous educators and psychologists. We shall let him speak for himself and content ourselves with saying we're glad we can present one of his most recent explanations of cognitive development.

Newspapers, magazines, radio, and television tell us daily that all is not well with education—the foremost, formally organized institution for cultural transmission. It is not enough to tell ourselves that criticisms of education are perennial. Two major factors make the dilemma more pressing today than ever before. One is the fact that, more than ever, an attempt is being made to educate all children to the maximum of their potential. It no longer suffices to have an educational system that reaches only those who come to school with built-in motivation. Ways must be found to make the process of education challenging enough and relevant enough to capitalize upon the heterostatic impulses to grow and become that all normal children have. The second factor that alters the teaching-learning dilemma is that children are different today from what they previously have been. Whatever the explanation might be—the pervasiveness of TV in the lives of those now of school age; or the passage of the struggle for survival to a search for fulfillment; or the discontent of the young with the older generation's accomplishment; or the shift from authoritarian control in homes and schools to permissiveness; or the belief that the young are now primarily role oriented rather than goal oriented, or . . . —the fact is that pupils today are different from what they have been. The old approaches, the tested remedies, and the sage advice no longer work so effectively as they once did in teaching-learning transactions.

The articles by Bigge and Gagné (selections 13 and 14) offer some postulations regarding what might be done. Certainly, with as complex a phenomenon as effective teaching-learning transactions, it is not possible to provide conclusive solutions. These articles do provide some insights into what might become more productive approaches.

Because man is not so circumscribed in his behavior as other animals by ready-made responses—because of his plasticity—*culture* is a major factor in determining what he will become. Culture includes customs, mores, family, government, schools, technology, etc.; it also includes that sub-aspect called socioeconomic class. Social class grants privilege and opportunity to some and imposes restrictions and deprivations on others. Students of human development will have their appreciation of the toughness, variability, plasticity, and creativity of man increased by a study of the impact of socioeconomic class.

Social class is evaluated by such criteria as the kind and location of the homes in which people live, the amount and source of their income, the extent and nature of their education, the attitudes they have toward themselves and others, and, of course, the kinds of behavior that evolve from such forces as are herein listed. It follows that understanding human development necessitates the study of the ramifications of socioeconomic class. Several articles imply that culture does more than influence behavior—it molds the content and structure of the brain. Meyer (selection 5) states that we are also wasting the nascent talent of both lower and upper middle class young people. Havighurst (selection 16) suggests some things that might change the existing pattern of wasting human potential.

If one takes the view that the most prominent feature of man's distinctiveness is intelligence (which is the view of the editors), then nothing can be more fascinating than the study of the potential and the means of cultivating intelligence. The pessimistic view, held by a diminishing number of scholars, is that we are born with intelligence: "Genius will out." "You can't make a silk purse out of a sow's ear." A somewhat more optimistic view is that we are born with the potential for the development of intelligence. A number of pundits indicate that typically man uses, or develops, only a small part of his intellectual potential—a mere five to ten per cent is the guess of some. The most sanguine scholars propose that we are not born with intelligence, nor are we born just with the potential for the development of intelligence. Upon whatever the human has in the way of hereditary and congenital intellectual equipment it is possible, through a salubrious environment, to build both additional power *and* potential.

Krech (selection 17) presents the latter hopeful view. Penfield (selection 19) postulates that through neglect to use one's potential at an early age, certain aspects of intelligence tend to become atrophied. Brown (selection 18) shows how language development indicates how complex the operation of the brain is and how language and intelligence are interdependent—if not quite equivalent. Guilford (selection 20) has, in the editors' opinions, presented in his theory of the structure of intelligence the most exciting thing that has come down the pike in recent years. Unfortunately this theory cannot be adequately presented in a short article, but some of the titillating implications are presented in this selection.

Science and human development

1.

Three forces in psychology and their ethical and educational implications

PAUL BRUCE

The editors hope that users of this volume of readings will exercise the ability to read in a discriminating manner. Some frame of reference for organizing, classifying, and interpreting information is necessary in order to do this. Generally, the more sense a concept makes, the easier it is to learn, the longer it will be remembered, and the more effectively it will be used. In addition, the more organized knowledge he possesses, the more the reader will be able to make sound choices between those things he wishes to learn and those which may not merit his time and effort. One needs to read with an open mind but he cannot afford to accept all that which is printed. He must screen contradictory ideas if his thinking is to have power, direction, and coherence.

The article by Bruce provides a frame of reference. Three broad forces in psychology are identified and, as suggested, may be used as a sort of classification for the reading of subsequent selections. Some words of caution are in order: (1) Some articles will fit nicely with one or another of the emphases. (2) Numerous articles and the thinking of many psychologists will reflect elements of all three. (3) There will be diversity among authors who might be identified with any one of the described orientations.

In addition to the three phase system of psychology, Bruce introduces the matter of ethical considerations—a force often neglected in scientific investigations.

PRACTICALLY ALL strands of our society are being influenced by theories and research from the field of psychology. Probably the most blatant example of this influence is seen in the women's magazines which month after month headline lead articles by "experts" advising and analyzing the psychological

Educational Forum, 30:277–285, 1966. Reprinted by permission of Kappa Delta Pi, An Honor Society in Education. Paul Bruce, Associate Professor, San Diego (California) State College.

problems of our day: sex, marriage, child-rearing, narcotics, alcoholism, etc. Even more significant than this is the more subtle influence psychology is having in such fields as advertising (*à la* Vance Packard's *The Wastemakers*), human engineering in industry, psychotherapy and counseling, and, of course, in our schools. Maybe one measure of this impact is the amount of critical attention psychology (in the name of mental health) is getting from the ultra-conservative elements who, indeed, find the influence from psychology to be threatening the status quo of a bygone era.

The point I want to make is that if through psychology humans can be influenced in certain directions, then the ethical problem arises of evaluating these directions in terms of their being desirable or not. And if through psychology the process of education toward certain goals becomes more effective, then it becomes imperative that these goals and the determination of these goals be carefully evaluated.

Now, the typical psychologist (or I might better say the typical scientific psychologist) does not like to admit the ethical implications of his discipline; he prefers to don the robes of scientific impartiality and limit his consideration to the quest for truth as he finds it. But I don't think we should let him get away with this. We need to face up to the ethical implications ourselves, and we need to ask the psychologist to face up to the ethical implications of their theories and research and even to take a stand regarding them.

To illustrate and further define this issue, I want to discuss three forces or schools of influence in psychology today and indicate the ethical and educational implications of their formulations as I see them. These are associationism—particularly as represented by reinforcement (S-R) theory; Freudianism or classical psychoanalytic theory; and the third force which is relatively new and has no consistent label as yet, but goes under the names of humanistic psychology, perceptual psychology, existential psychology or neo-Freudianism. I will present these three schools of thought briefly as theoretical models and ask the reader to realize, as with everything else, that the adherents and practitioners who represent these models modify the theory to fit their own needs and perceptions.

ASSOCIATIONISM

Associationism in psychology developed during the latter part of the nineteenth century out of the thinking of such philosophers as Herbart, who described the mind as a complex of isolated sensations, ideas, thoughts, decisions, and feelings bound together by the process of association. With the aid of a new interest in the use of animals for observation and experimentation, psychologists, first under the leadership of E. L. Thorndike, developed theories of behavior most familiarly represented by the stimulus-response formula. Thus, Thorndike proposed that every new idea, every new feeling or sensation is a response to a preceding idea, feeling, or sensation. Under this system, memory or learning was explained as a series of stimulus-response connections, particular stimuli calling forth the specific responses. Various laws or principles of learning were developed which explained the establishment of a bond or association between stimulus and response. For example, reward or punishment, repetition, need satisfaction, reinforcement, conditioning, etc., were postulated as effecting learning and could be used to elicit certain desired behavior patterns.

This school of thought has persisted though modified and developed, and today it remains the most popular theory (at least among scientific and academic psychologists) and perhaps the most influential force representing psychology in society today. In our schools and colleges, the prevalent use of repetition as in drills (e.g., write each spelling word five times); the use of workbooks and tests which provide the stimulus and require the student to provide the "right" response which is subsequently approved or disapproved; the extensive use of a system of rewards and penalties (as in the way grades are typically given); all of these reflect the influence of this school of thought. More recently a whole new medium has been developed and is currently being promoted—that of programed learning or more popularly termed teaching machines. Based primarily on B. F. Skinner's reinforcement theory (a refinement of associationism), programed learning involves the careful presentation and division of the subject matter into extremely small units so that the student is frequently rewarded by correct answers and can move along independently at his own pace.

In advertising, political campaigns, public relations programs, etc., the principle of conditioning is used very effectively. Briefly, the principle of conditioning states that if a stimulus and response are associated enough times together, this association will be learned. Thus, if you hear a brand name associated with a product enough times, you will automatically think of the brand whenever you think of the product; and if the terms "liberal," "socialist," "civil libertarian," "progressive education," "life adjustment," are associated with the concept of the Communist menace enough times, then these labels and those to whom they apply become tainted with the same attitudes ascribed to Communism.

Thus, when addressing themselves to the problems and issues of our times, these psychologists, believing that people's behavior to be a result of the forces exerted upon them, find their answers in terms of the manipulation of these forces. The ethical problem implicit in this system, of course, is that somebody, other than the persons affected, must decide the desired direction the behavior is to take. This necessarily calls for a "great man" philosophy of dealing with people—somebody who knows where the people should go. This system calls for leaders who are supermen of a sort, skilled in the manipulation of forces to get people to behave in the ways desired by the knowing few.

And so in schools, for example, we have developed specialists and experts who are determining what the children should learn in the various subject areas, and other experts who are predigesting what will be programed in the teaching machines. In the Midwest they now have airborne educational television by which one *expert* teacher can serve schools in six states (7000 school districts; over five million children); meaning that where used, all the children are getting the *same* presentation of the *same* curriculum at the *same* time!

One of my students wrote the following, which perhaps overstates the kind of teaching which follows from this system wherein learning is thought to result from having students respond to well-ordered stimuli:

> Teaching too often becomes the process of carrying, pulling, showing, and assisting pupils along to the end of the course. *Teachers* do the reading, the explaining, the thinking, the talking, the appreciating, the devising, the planning; the problems are *teacher*-worked, the reasons are *teacher* thought-out; the beautiful is *teacher*-selected. All the pupils do is to remain passive, to listen, to copy, to memorize, and finally to recite or to write at a stated time what they have managed to cull out of an extended dictation!

B. F. Skinner, a prominent scientist from this force in psychology, wrote a novel some years ago entitled *Walden Two* in which he gives a fictional account of what he regards as a Utopian community in which the learnings of the behavioral sciences are fully utilized in all aspects of life— marriage, child rearing, ethical conduct, work, play, and artistic endeavor. Skinner's conception of paradise is a large rural colony where democracy is replaced by behavioral engineering. The common theme of this novel and of some of his other treatises is that the psychologist possesses the means of social control and must use these means effectively for the welfare of society. Let me quote what Skinner has his hero say in this novel:

> Well, what do you say to the design of personalities? Would that interest you? The control of temperament? Give me the specifications, and I'll give you the man! What do you say to the control of motivation, building the interests which will make men most productive and most successful? Does that seem to you fantastic? Yet some of the techniques are available, and more can be worked out experimentally. Think of the possibilities! . . . Let us control the lives of our children and see what we can make of them. . . .[1]

In another paper Skinner elaborates the implications of his theories; he states,

> We must accept the fact that some kind of control of human affairs is inevitable. We cannot use good sense in human affairs unless *someone* engages in the design and construction of environmental conditions which affect the behavior of men. . . .[2]

As you can see, Skinner's projection of his system is garbed in benevolence; however, the ethical question still remains as to who is to determine the *desired* direction behavior should take. And presumably this molding of human behavior would be the function of the schools, and we ask if this is the function we want education to perform.

CLASSICAL PSYCHOANALYSIS

If associationism is the most popular force among academic and scientific psychologists, Freudianism (classical psychoanalysis) has been the most influential among the clinical psychologists, and psychotherapists and counselors. Although few accept the theories exactly as Freud postulated them (which would be impossible anyway, since Freud modified and even contradicted his own theories throughout his lifetime), yet the main tenor of his system remains and poses some ethical questions.

Psychoanalysis originated in the field of medicine as a result of attempts to find some cure for the neuroses and in revolt against the dominant somatic or physiological explanations which were popular in the nineteenth century. Some psychiatrists were becoming convinced that such causal factors as brain lesions were not to be found in their patients, and they began to substitute such factors as emotional stress, weakness of will, suggestibility, and irrational habits as explanations. Soon hypnotism was introduced and accepted by some elements of the medical profession particularly when dealing with such neurotic conditions as hysteria. It was on this medical scene with an interest in neurology that Freud began his productive but controversial practice in Vienna. Influenced by the French schools in Paris under Charcot and later in Nancy under Janet, Freud built up a practice dealing primarily with hysteric patients, experimenting with hypnosis and eventually, giving this up, developing his own techniques and corresponding theoretical formulations.

The point I want to bring out in this very brief historical sketch is that psychoanalytic theory originated and was developed as a result of studying and treating mentally disturbed, upper-class Europeans during a period referred to as the Victorian era. In other words, Freud's sampling from which he drew his conclusions was anything but representative of the human race.

With his medical background, it is not surprising to learn that Freud believed that the nature of man is essentially biological; man is born with certain instinctual drives which can (though they frequently don't) work themselves out as a person grows. Freud classified the instincts under two main headings: the *life* instincts (*Eros*) and the *death* instincts (*Thanatos*). The life instincts include hunger, thirst, and sex, the latter being considered the most driving. The principle operating here is the pleasure principle or self-gratification. The death instincts include hate, aggressiveness, and self-destruction.

According to Freud, the *psyche* is divided horizontally into *conscious* and *unconscious;* and vertically into what he labels the *id, ego,* and *super-ego.* Gradually the child's unconscious fills with things forgotten or suppressed because they are unpleasant, and more importantly, with emotions and drives which are too painful to be tolerated in the consciousness. The *id,* entirely unconcious, is the most primitive and concerned only with the gratification of drives. The *ego,* almost entirely conscious, develops from experience and reason, interacts with the environment and acts as a check on the *id.* The *superego,* largely unconscious, is the restraining force, the conscience, and consists of the attitudes and moral codes absorbed unwittingly in childhood. Neuroses, then, result from a lack of harmony among the *id, ego,* and *superego.* Neuroses can develop as a result of lack of gratification of the instinctual drives (the *id*), or as a result of a weak *ego* structure and thus poor reality contact, or as a result of a too severe *superego,* which is the product of too strenuous socialization of the child at the hands of harsh, punitive parents.

In spite of the magical, fable-like quality of the theory, its distinctive, widely-accepted contribution to our understanding of human behavior is the significance the theory attributes to the unconscious.

The ethical implications of this theory are of greater or lesser significance depending on how literally we accept its assumptions and principles. Probably the most crucial implication stems from the proposition concerning the instinctual drives. Freud wrote,

> . . . Men are not gentle, friendly creatures wishing for love, who simply defend themselves if they are attacked, but . . . a powerful measure of desire for aggression has to be reckoned as part of their instinctual endowment. The result is that their neighbor is to them not only a possible helper or sexual object, but also a temptation to them to gratify their aggressiveness, . . . to seize his possessions, to humiliate him, to cause him pain, to torture and to kill him; . . . who has the courage to dispute it in the face of all the evidence in his own life and in history?[3]

According to this view, man's *finer* sentiments and strivings are only sublimations of animal instincts which lurk beneath the surface of his civilized veneer.

If this be the nature of man, then we cannot look to nature to provide us answers to our ethical question—the definition of good and evil. Traditional Christian doctrine provides an out with its supernatural definition of good and evil. But Freud rejected religion and referred to it as the "mass obsessional neurosis," and deplored society's religion-based concept of morality. Furthermore, denial, or even worse, restriction of man's nature (as viewed by Freud) leads to mental illness indicating we cannot look to the antithesis of the Freudian assumption for a solution.

Interestingly enough, much of the recent clamor against permissiveness and "life adjustment" in the schools (neither of which ever existed to any great extent in actual school practice) has been misdirected when "Progressive education" and John Dewey are blamed. (Dewey argued for an experimental, experience-centered, activity, problem-solving approach to education.) Actually the permissive, life adjustment emphasis stems largely from the Freudian influence whereby parents and teachers are admonished not to thwart or deny the expression of a child's instinctual drives or else his *psyche* will become crippled and pave the way for adult neuroses.

On the other hand, acceptance of the Freudian notion of the inherent primitive, animalistic, aggressive nature of the child leads many teachers and administrators to be preoccupied with the problem of control and discipline sometimes to the exclusion of concern over the learning process.

Another implication derives from the deterministic nature of the theory. The underlying causal factors of behavior are primarily unconscious and irrational. Man's motives are something other than they appear on the surface, and his thinking is easily distorted by inner desires and passions of which he is not aware. How then, with the minimizing of man's rational powers, with the denial of free will, can the individual be held responsible for his actions or behavior? Anna Russell catches the spirit of the problem posed by Freud's psychic determinism when she sings in her "Psychiatric Folksong,"

> At three I had a feeling of
> Ambivalence toward my brothers,
> And so it follows naturally,
> I poisoned all my lovers.
> But now I'm happy; I have learned
> the lesson this has taught;
> That everything I do that's wrong,
> Is someone else's fault.[4]

This view (shared with associationism) that man is the product of forces beyond his control, undercuts the basic convictions underlying democracy and democratic relations among men. Democracy just doesn't make sense (and wouldn't work) unless man is basically free, and active (and not just reactive), and capable to some degree of making rational choices and decisions and being responsible for his actions.

THIRD FORCE: HUMANISTIC PSYCHOLOGY

Throughout the development of psychology as a formal discipline during the past 60–75 years a number of psychologists have started rebellions of some importance against what they considered the dominant deterministic and analytic trends in psychology represented by associationism and psychoanalysis. Until recently, these psychologists did not represent a unified system or school. In the last few years, however, these various groups have been coalescing into an increasingly comprehensive theory of human na-

ture, into what Abraham Maslow calls a "Third Force." This group includes the so-called neo-Freudians who emphasize man's nature as being
primarily social and cultural rather than biological or instinctual; the Gestalt or field theorists who emphasize man's interaction with his environment as a unitary function which cannot be understood in a piecemeal
fashion, as they claim the associationists would have us do; the organismic
psychologists who, like the Gestaltists, insist on considering the individual
as a whole; the perceptual psychologists and existential psychologists who
emphasize the uniqueness and integrity of the individual and of his very
personal and unique interpretation of his life and environment. As all of
these movements place great significance on the individual human being
and on distinctively human qualities (as opposed to animalistic or mechanistic qualities of the other two forces discussed above) the label *Humanistic
Psychology* seems appropriate.

In contrast to the other two forces, many of the propositions of this
third force stem from a study of man (as opposed to animals) and a study
of psychologically healthy (rather than neurotic or sick) men. For example,
A. H. Maslow, although beginning his career in the study of abnormal psychology, developed his present theories while studying psychologically
healthy people and while studying the healthiest experiences and moments
(which he called peak experiences) in the lives of average people.

Basic to this humanistic force in psychology is the conviction that man
is essentially *good* if permitted to develop his natural humanistic qualities.
Only when his nature is distorted by pathological conditions, rejecting parents, constant failure and rebuff, or a repressive culture does man become
aggressive and cruel. *Good* in this context is equated with *nature,* thus anything conducive to bringing out man's inner nature is desirable. *Bad* or abnormal is anything that frustrates or blocks or denies the essential nature
of man. Putting it another way, Maslow equates what we *ought* to be with
what we *can* be, and he states further that by substituting the concept of
what one *can* become for the term *ought* or *should,* the matter becomes open
to empirical, scientific investigation.[5]

Space does not permit me to be more definitive regarding the inner
nature (and thus what would be defined as desirable) in man. Writers such
as A. Combs, A. Maslow, and C. Rogers do this well in their writings.[6]
Suffice it to say that research being done in anthropology, psychiatry, sociology as well as psychology is coming up with some consistent findings. For
example, there is widespread agreement that the following are characteristics of psychologically healthy (self-actualized) people: they can be described as loving, self-accepting, well integrated, fully functioning, creative,
autonomous, reality-centered, adaptable, among other characteristics.

The other two forces we have discussed have built systems describing
man as he *is.* Humanistic psychology has added the dimension of looking at
what man can *become*—a look at not only the *actualities* but the *potentialities* as well. Also in contrast to the other two forces which look upon man

as *reactive* to the forces in the environment or to the *psyche,* humanistic psychology looks upon man as being active and having the capacity, at least to some degree, to evaluate and choose. While agreeing that human behavior is influenced by the environment and culture, humanistic psychology emphasizes that the ultimate effect of the environment and culture is in large part determined by the individual's unique view and attitudes of these external factors. That is, I am influenced by my world as I see it, not as you or anyone else sees it nor as the world may *really* be.

This view of man as having a large potential for freedom is consistent with the democratic conviction that the ordinary man given access to factual information *can* evaluate public issues with some degree of objectivity and rationality rather than as a robot conditioned to think and behave in certain ways. It is assumed that the freedom granted by democracy to the individual to make decisions is not just an illusion.

Similarly, the view of man as free and active is basic to a philosophy of education which emphasizes the development of young adults capable of rational problem solving, creativity, and critical evaluation. Applying the insights of this force in psychology (compared to those of associationism), teaching would involve facilitating learning rather than directing learning; it would involve uncovering new vistas rather than covering what is already known; it would involve asking pertinent questions rather than telling what is already thought out; it would involve helping children learn rather than making children go through the motions of learning.[7]

Obviously, the ethical implications of this third force are part and parcel of the system it proposes. Unlike the other two forces, it does not beg the question of values. A commitment to a criterion for determining value—that which corresponds to basic human nature—underlies the entire movement. Some will claim that this takes the movement out of the jurisdiction of science. Maslow argues otherwise. He claims that the scientific approach can and should be used to develop greater understanding of man's basic nature, and thus a science of values *is* possible. Erich Fromm writes:

> The thesis is that values are rooted in the very conditions of human existence; hence that our knowledge of these conditions, that is of the "human situation," leads us to establishing values which have objective validity; this validity exists only with regard to the existence of man; outside of him there are no values.[8]

In summary, let me make this observation. The diverse views of human nature as neutral, evil, or good have important ethical and educational implications. Whichever view one accepts, it is apparent that man is a highly educable creature and that his development for good or evil can be greatly influenced by environmental conditions. But here agreement ends. If man is by nature hostile and aggressive, society through the school must shape him by exerting stringent controls; if, on the other hand, man's natural tendencies are for good, society through the school can best achieve its

purposes by structuring the environment in such a way as to allow the
child considerable freedom for creativity and self-development.

NOTES

1. B. F. Skinner, *Walden Two* (New York: Macmillan, 1948), p. 243.
2. B. F. Skinner, "Freedom and the Control of Men," *American Scholar*, 25:47–65, Winter, 1955–56, p. 56.
3. S. Freud, *Civilization and its Discontents* (London: Hogarth Press, 1930), pp. 85–6.
4. Quoted in O. H. Mowrer, "Sin, the Lesser of Two Evils," *American Psychologist*, 15:301–4, 1960, p. 301.
5. A. H. Maslow, *Motivation and Personality* (New York: Harper and Brothers, 1954), p. 344.
6. See the 1962 Yearbook of the Association for Supervision and Curriculum Development (N.E.A.), *Perceiving, Behaving, Becoming*, which includes papers on this topic by Combs, Kelley, Maslow, and Rogers.
7. Adapted from A. W. Combs and D. Snygg, *Individual Behavior* (New York: Harper and Brothers, 1959), Rev. Ed., pp. 401–2.
8. In A. H. Maslow, ed., *New Knowledge in Human Values* (New York: Harper and Brothers, 1959), p. 151.

2.

The impact of theories of child development

BETTYE M. CALDWELL
JULIUS B. RICHMOND

This article applies parts of the theoretical framework described as "Three Forces in Psychology" in the first selection to the development of children. It and Bigge's article (selection 14) can be used by the reader to develop a more comprehensive framework for understanding psychology and human development.

Caldwell and Richmond describe theories and, in addition, they theorize about theories. They suggest the direction that future theorizing may take and they recognize certain limitations; e.g., the better our knowledge, the less theorizing is necessary and the more the

Children, 9:73–78, March–April, 1962. Bettye M. Caldwell, Research Associate; Julius B. Richmond, Professor and Chairman, Department of Pediatrics, College of Medicine, State University of New York at Syracuse.

theorist must responsibly justify any position he takes. As these authors indicate, a good theory not only generates hypotheses leading. to experimentation and research; it also is sufficiently dynamic to absorb new facts into its explanatory structure.

It is worth noting that theories tend to mirror the times and the culture in which they are developed and how much they, in turn—through the thinking and discourse they generate—help to remold and shape subsequent culture. Both psychoanalysis and behaviorism have had a tremendous impact upon the attitudes of people and the manner in which they live. The reader should be able to find much evidence of the influence of Freud and Watson as he continues with this book.

IT IS appropriate, on this 50th Anniversary of the Children's Bureau, to discuss the impact of child-development theories on child care in the United States, for no agency has had a greater influence on the gradual improvement of child health and the translation of child-development theory into practice than the Children's Bureau.

Direct improvements of the physical health of children are easier to assess than indirect benefits from educational programs. Yet in this area of indirect influence, the Children's Bureau has played a major role. The two pamphlets, "Prenatal Care" and "Infant Care" have over the years reached more American families than any comparable publications, thus serving as the major interpreters of child development theories. If one knew none of the direct research studies and none of the writings of the system makers, one could read successive editions of "Infant Care" and infer the prevailing theoretical approaches of each time period.

But even before the Children's Bureau, there were theories about the nature of the child and attempts to persuade parents to act toward their children in some particular way. Generally these theories were based on *a priori* assumptions rather than on any data and were theologically toned. An example is the doctrine of innate depravity which asserted that the child was inherently evil and that the main duty of parents and educators was to eradicate this depravity.

Probably each major theory which left any mark on the history of ideas had to be attuned to its era—a little bit, but not too far, ahead of its time. Thus intellectual prerevolutionary France was receptive to Rousseau's challenge of the doctrine of innate depravity with his assertion that the child is inherently good until corrupted by society. In postrevolutionary America, when rigid self-discipline and industry were required to subdue the frontier, theories which stressed obedience, discipline, and submission to adult authority found acceptance.

In every era there are two kinds of "experts" about child behavior—those who publish and those who do not. Every parent has his or her theory about how children develop. This theory may remain at the level of proverbs or cultural maxims ("Spare the rod and spoil the child"), may involve broad generalizations lacking behavioral referents ("Just give them love and security"), or may propose precise hypotheses about genetic in-

fluence on behavior or the relative efficacy of reward or punishment for inducing learning.

These implicit theories are important determinants of parental action
and reaction. For example, a "spare the rod" theory makes it unnecessary
for the parent to make a fresh decision about how to handle a particular
type of behavior each time it occurs; it also insulates the parent from guilt
about behaving punitively toward his child.

TWENTIETH CENTURY THEORIES

During the 20th century, three theoretical systems about child development have made major inroads into the personal learning theories of American parents: the behavioristic (or social learning); the maturational; and
the psychoanalytic.

Social Learning Theories

While the work of several theorists could be cast into the framework
of social learning theory, John B. Watson had the greatest influence in this
direction. Watson's concept of infancy was essentially a Lockean *tabula
rasa*—an amorphous bit of behavior potential to be shaped by the learning
opportunities experienced by the infant. His psychological theories appeared
at a time in the history of ideas when most complex types of emotional experience were attributed to the expression of instincts.

Convinced as he was that emotions were acquired throughout the
learning process, Watson used naive subjects, infants, to test his hypotheses. He designed and executed a number of ingenious experiments which
demonstrated that many fears could be acquired and subsequently eliminated through conditioning. From these experiments he concluded that
most forms of complex behavior were the result of concatenations of reflexes and simple response systems associated through conditioning.

Such a view of the child places an awesome degree of power into the
hands of parents and other "teachers." A completely malleable infant be-
speaks an omnipotent training agent. Watson wasted no time in extrapolating from the laboratory to home and school and in communicating his ideas
directly to parents. His widely read publications had considerable influence
on recommendations made to parents about child care. The 1928 edition of
"Infant Care," always the best statement of current professional ideas, relied
heavily upon Watsonian suggestions about shaping behavior, such as developing habits of regularity, dependability, independence, and self-reliance.

Watson attempted to put to pasture many sacred cows of child development literature, including mother love and the importance of encouraging
emotional dependency between parents and children. His language was too
pungent to escape caricature. Witness this example:

There is a sensible way of treating children. Treat them as though they were young adults. Let your behavior always be objective and kindly firm. Never hug and kiss them, never let them sit in your lap. If you must, kiss them once on the forehead when they say good night. Shake hands with them in the morning. Give them a pat on the head if they have made an extraordinarily good job of a difficult task. Try it out. In a week's time you will find how easy it is to be perfectly objective with your child and at the same time kindly. You will be utterly ashamed of the mawkish, sentimental way you have been handling it.[1]

Unfortunately publishers have no standard code for reporting whether an author wrote a particular passage with tongue in cheek. Therefore, an author must expect to be taken literally and to live with the implications of his words as written. In recent years Watson and his theories of conditioning have been felled by the impact of just such statements as the above. The reactions of his critics have ranged from vilification to mere ridicule, and feeling still runs high. Several modern theorists, however, notably Skinner,[2] Miller and Dollard,[3] and Rotter,[4] have significantly advanced social learning theory and have extended our knowledge about the limits of external manipulation and control of infant and child behavior.

Maturational Theory

This system is represented by the writings of Arnold Gesell.[5-8] A prolific and at times poetic writer, Gesell also recognized the journalistic principle that one picture is worth a thousand words and copiously illustrated his books with pictorial samples of child behavior. Although perhaps referred to more often for his methods of developmental diagnosis and cinema-analysis and for the norms of behavioral development which he and his students accumulated over the years, Gesell was nonetheless an important formulator of a theory of child behavior.

Gesell's theory of development is relatively simple yet, in some ways, more global than other more complex theories. The key concept is that of *maturation* or growth. It is a theory of intrinsic development, of an infant's maturation proceeding from both the human and the individual nature of the infant.

Implicit in the concept of maturation is self-regulation of growth. Gesell urged recognition of this principle in every aspect of development from the establishment of infant feeding schedules to the acquisition of moral values. Acceptance of the principle by parents calls for a certain considerateness, an "alert liberalism," to use Gesell's phrase. Infants, as well as older children, are entitled to certain courtesies, to being regarded as "people." A passionate regard for the individual was, Gesell maintained, crucial to a truly democratic orientation to life.

A corollary of this stress on the importance of the individual is the concept of individual differences. Yet, paradoxically, it is here that Gesell seems to have been most generally misinterpreted and, indeed, almost to have courted misinterpretation. This stems from the organization of most of his books in terms of ages and stages of behavior. Indeed, the books' typography—the capitalization of each age period as though personified—conduces to such misinterpretation. For example:

> THREE is a kind of coming-of-age . . . You can bargain with THREE and he can wait his turn . . . FOUR (and half past) tends to go out of bounds . . . FIVE is a SUPER-THREE with a socialized pride in clothes and accomplishments, a lover of praise.[6]

About this approach Gesell and Ilg say:

> We regard the formal concept of chronological age and the functional concept of maturity level as indispensable both for practical common sense and for the science of child development. In the guidance of children it is absolutely necessary to consider the age values of behavior and the behavior values of age. The reader is warned, in advance, however, that *the age norms are not set up as standards and are designed only for orientation and interpretive purposes.* . . . The prevalence and significance of individual variations are recognized at every turn.[6]

Perhaps these occasional warnings do not carry enough weight to counterbalance the continued stress on ages and stages in development throughout childhood and adolescence.

With respect to the timing of the maximum impact of the three major theories we are discussing, Gesell followed Watson and preceded Freud. Nevertheless, many of Gesell's most popular publications came out during the period of popularization of psychoanalytic thought. Gesell did not seem to be a man for polemics, however, and he seldom bothered to take notice of other points of view. His books deal largely with the presentation of his own material. He quotes other researchers only when their studies relate to his interest. In the four Gesell books reviewed for this article, there are only two references to Freud. Gesell was more concerned with developmental congruences than interpersonal conflicts, with eye-hand coordination and prehension than emotional cathexes. Even in the volume *Youth*,[8] "sex" is indexed in terms of "differences" and not of preoccupations and problems.

Watson is quoted once in these four Gesell works, but anonymously as "a distinguished behaviorist" and the source of the quote is not in the reference list. However, in isolated articles, Gesell occasionally opposed certain points important in behavioristic doctrine, as he did when he suggested[9] that the conditioned reflex theory promised too much and threatened too much, and that maturation protected the infant from certain chance conditionings.

In reflecting on the impact of Gesell's work one must not overlook the influence of distribution.

Until the appearance of the amazing Spock volume,[10] Gesell's writings were probably more widely disseminated than any other full-length book on child development. Furthermore, Gesell, like Watson, was persuaded of the obligation to present child development material directly for parental consumption. Knowledge about infants and young children, he said, "must extend into the homes of the people; for the household is the 'cultural workshop' where human relationships are first formed."

Psychoanalytic Approach

The theoretical formulations of psychoanalysis and the body of empirical data collected to test the hypotheses have provided perhaps the most significant and pervasive influence on child-development theories and child-rearing practices in recent decades. By clinically reconstructing the life history of the adult or child through therapeutic efforts, psychoanalysts have developed theoretical formulations concerning the meaning of interaction of the infant or young child with his environment. It is understandable that, in a scientific era, a theory explaining the development in all its subtleties (unconscious and conscious) would capture widespread attention.

The complexities of psychoanalytic theory are difficult to distill into a few paragraphs. Unlike the maturation theory, psychoanalytic theory has undergone many revisions and is continuously modified. Classical (or Freudian) psychoanalysis and the neo-Freudian formulations differ in many respects.

Psychoanalysis is generally referred to as a biological theory of personality; yet the biological drives are manifested entirely in a social context. From the standpoint of the developing child, this context is mainly the family group. Unless basic drives (instincts) are gratified during early interactions with the parents—primarily the mother—the child moves forward from infancy with some degree of fixation at this earlier stage and somewhat impaired in adaptability. Or, if gratification at succeeding stages of development is insufficient, the child falls back on earlier patterns of behavior (regression) for gratification.

The concepts of fixation and regression are based on a sequence of stages in development. Thus personality development progresses from oral to anal stages in early life and then to a sequence of genital stages—oedipal, latent, adolescent, and mature. Experiences during each period are conceived of as affecting character traits of later life.

During the "oral period" in infancy, for example, it is thought the child develops feelings about accepting things and the mother's manner of giving them. Erickson[11] has postulated that from the totality of experiences in this period, the individual develops a basic sense of trust in people—or else a lack of trust which hampers his ensuing development. During the period of acquisition of bowel and bladder control when the child must integrate contradictory impulses of retention and elimination, traits related to orderliness, punctuality, and thrift are thought to develop.

The awareness of genital differences and feelings brings with it even more complex integrative tasks. Personality begins to take shape in more recognizable form, and characteristic modes of dealing with adaptive problems (mechanisms of defense) become evident. The relationship of the individual's later feelings and character traits to earlier experiences suggests that manipulation of these experiences in a "healthy" direction may favorably influence later development. This assumes agreement on a desirable mature model toward which to strive. Chronic failure of the parents to provide for the gratification of the basic drives is likely to result in permanent personality distortions remediable only through a kind of regrowth process via the therapeutic relationship.

These formulations have been theoretically enticing and have provided many hypotheses for investigation by workers in the field of child development as well as for child-care workers in various disciplines interested in the prevention of emotional disorders. Many psychoanalytic concepts have been embraced as guides to child rearing by parents concerned with raising "emotionally healthy" children. However, a review of the experimental literature[12] indicates that no specific relationships between early experiences and later development can be established at the present time.

There is growing recognition among psychoanalytic investigators that the application of knowledge gained from psychoanalysis in preventive efforts must be approached cautiously. The objective of psychoanalytic investigation as stated by Erickson[11] a decade ago remains valid:

> Psychoanalysis today is implementing the study of the ego, the core of the individual. It is shifting its emphasis from the concentrated study of the conditions which blunt and distort the individual ego to the study of the ego's roots in social organization. This we try to understand not in order to offer a rash cure to a rashly diagnosed society, but in order to first complete the blueprint of our method.

To pursue these objectives, psychoanalytic research workers are departing from the predominant use of reconstructive interview or play techniques to the greater use of direct observation of development (as indicated by the current interest in research in mother-infant interaction), experimental approaches (animal and human), and cross-cultural studies. Also, more intensive and objective studies of psychoanalytically oriented interviews are being developed.

IMPLICATIONS FOR TODAY

The fact that different theories can flourish contemporaneously validates Knapp's observation[13] that man is a "recalcitrant and reluctant experimental subject." Yet these theories of child development are not contradictory or mutually exclusive. All are concerned with learning, with the interaction of organism and environment. They all highlight different facets of behavior and use different conceptual systems. And, undoubtedly, they are all a little bit right.

From all of them one can infer that parents wield an awesome degree of power in shaping the lives of their children. Even maturational theory, with its emphasis upon the growth integrity of the young organism, its inherent potential for healthy development, implies that the parent can inhibit or distort this growth potential. With greater awareness of the implications of their caretaking activities, some parents have shown signs of what might be loosely termed a midcentury parental neurosis: an over-determination to seek suggestions for child rearing as insurance of healthy development for their children.

Professional workers in the field of child care (pediatricians and other health workers, psychologists and child welfare workers) have not been immune to these pressures. They have sometimes advocated as universally desirable such programs as "natural childbirth," rooming-in of the newborn with the mother at the hospital, breast feeding, and permissive or self-regulating patterns of child care. To their credit, psychoanalysts have not been in the forefront of these movements. Rather, these movements have often represented misinterpretation or premature application of psychoanalytic principles. Recently they have been placed in a more appropriate perspective, as doctrinaire approaches to "prevention" have been given up in favor of the more traditionally eclectic orientation of child-care professions—except perhaps by social work which has remained heavily committed to psychoanalytic theory.

Guidance in child rearing will probably become increasingly professionalized in the United States in the years to come. The child-care professions, therefore, must face up to the challenge of providing services for parents even with incomplete knowledge. If these services are to be provided for families, adequate professional personnel must be made available. The specific professions to provide this personnel, the appropriate distribution, and the organization of services are issues with which we as a nation have not yet come to terms. The current ferment about the "new pediatrics" and concern with the directions in which this profession should move educationally and in practice suggests the need for planning constructively for all kinds of child-care services.

Since the launching of Sputnik in 1957, we have awakened to our responsibilities to fulfill our potentialities as a democratic nation. The resultant emphasis on academic achievement has the same over-determined emphasis which other child-rearing formulae have had in previous years. While we must strive for full intellectual development of our children, this need not be at the expense of their social and emotional growth. If it is, we may inhibit the learning we seek to foster.

IMPLICATIONS FOR FUTURE THEORIES

What thoughts can now be projected about the child development theories of the future? Undoubtedly they will continue to be prevalent both at the scientific level and as part of each individual's general philosophy. The individual theories will change only as rapidly as cultural changes occur, and presumably those cultural changes will be at least in part a function of the rapidity of scientific change. However, we will make a few predictions about the characteristics of heuristic child development theories of the future:

1. Extrapolation from research data will not be so extreme.

The science of behavior has matured into a more conservative, slightly subdued stage. Professionals in the field have themselves matured somewhat. Also the interdisciplinary origin of many of the reasonably stable parts of child development knowledge is conducive to conservatism.

The young Watson, with little knowledge of genetics and its constitutional limitations upon adaptability of the organism, could assert that he could take any four healthy infants and make them whatever type of adult he wished. The somewhat provincial Freud, unaware of the nascent body of data from cultural anthropology, could assume that the memories and fantasies of individuals from a fairly narrow sociocultural context represented universal attributes. Today's theorists are no longer permitted the luxury of being uninformed about work in any area of knowledge which might limit the predictions from a given theoretical system. With greater availability of information which might make predictions hazardous, the theories themselves will become more cautious about specific predictions.

2. Future theories of child behavior will be concerned with a broader time spectrum.

The view of the child as a miniature adult is outmoded. But in its place has come with too much finality a view of the child almost as an eternal child. The child *is* a future adult, as he is a future adolescent and a future senescent. The 6-month-old baby who experiences a certain type of mothering will presumably carry some residual of that experience with him at age 3 or 13. Since each type of later experience may modify the nature of residual, such differences need to be fully explored. Useful child development theories of the future will be concerned with predictions which span wide segments of the developmental curve, not just one narrow section.

3. Future theories of child behavior will be related to broader aspects of social theory and philosophy.

A point already stressed in this paper is that each enduring or influential child development theory related to powerful currents of social history.

Within the past few decades even the seemingly remote physical sciences have had to face such a relationship. There is now less talk about a separation of science from values. Certainly in the field of child development no such separation is possible. We rear children to fit into a particular culture, on the basic premise that the culture is somehow "good" or at least acceptable.

The past two decades have seen considerable sniping at Watson for the naiveté of his theories, with an occasional implication that he was heartless and cruel for denouncing mother love and the child-rearing practices of most parents. Such criticism fails to recognize that Watson was far more explicit than most theorists about the behavioral attributes he wished to foster. He concludes one of his books[1] with a formal apologia to critics who have taken him to task for having no "ideals" for bringing up children, commenting perceptively that different programs of care fit different civilizations. Then he describes briefly the kind of child he had in mind when making his child-rearing suggestions, the kind he considered best adapted to the changing America of the late twenties:

> We have tried to sketch in the foregoing chapters a child as free as possible of sensitivities to people and one who, almost from birth, is relatively independent of the family situation . . . Above all, we have tried to create a problem-solving child. We believe that a problem-solving technique (which can be trained) plus boundless absorption in activity (which can also be trained) are behavioristic factors which have worked in many civilizations of the past and which, so far as we can judge, will work equally well in most types of civilizations that are likely to confront us in the future.[1]

Undoubtedly, many persons would not agree with Watson's goals, but it is to his credit that he attempted to relate his theory to the social milieu.

4. Future theories of child development will not attempt to answer (or predict) everything about child development for all time. They will modestly relate themselves to one sociocultural group—until something is proven to have universal relevance—and for a finite scientific era.

New discoveries can outmode existing theories overnight. For example, future research on behavioral genetics might drastically modify many of the assumptions underlying research on the effects of specific parent practices on child behavior. Any heuristic theory will be quick to incorporate new data, thus building a more stately theoretical structure. Victor Hugo's tribute to the power of an idea whose time has come might well apply in reverse here, for nothing is more effete than a theory that has outlived its time.

REFERENCES

1. Watson, J. B.: Psychological care of infant and child. Allen and Unwin, London. 1928.

2. Skinner, B. F.: Science and human behavior. Macmillan, New York. 1953.
3. Miller, N. E.; Dollard, J.: Social learning and imitation. Yale University Press, New Haven. 1953.
4. Rotter, J. B.: Social learning and clinical psychology. Prentice-Hall, New York. 1954.
5. Gesell, A., and others: The first five years of life. Harper and Bros., New York. 1940.
6. Gesell, A.; Ilg, Frances L.: Infant and child in the culture of today. Harper and Bros., New York. 1943.
7. ———: The child from five to ten. Harper and Bros., New York. 1946.
8. Gesell, A.: Youth—the years from ten to sixteen. Harper and Bros., New York. 1956
9. ———: Maturation and infant behavior pattern. *Psychological Review,* July 1929.
10. Spock, B. M.: The common sense book of baby and child care. Duell, Sloan, and Pearce, New York. 1946.
11. Erikson, E.: Childhood and society. Norton and Company, New York. 1950.
12. Richmond, J. B.; Caldwell, Bettye M.: Child rearing practices and their consequences. In press.
13. Knapp, P.: Symposium: expression of emotions in man. Annual meeting, American Association for the Advancement of Science, 1960.

3.

Research methodology: a possible reconciliation

K. E. COFFIELD

This selection has been included in these readings as a natural next step to the process of theorizing in the validation of ideas. The author contrasts two basic ways of testing the hypotheses which arise from good theories. He indicates the ways in which these approaches complement each other and he shows the part that each can play in the investigation of development.

It is important to the reader's developing system for understanding psychology and human development that he grasp the sequential relationship of this article to the preceding selections and also that he stick with this one until he is pretty sure that he gets the message. The editors suggest that maximum value can be gained by referring back from time to time as research-based selections are encountered in order

American Psychologist, 25(No. 6):511–516, June, 1970. K. E. Coffield, University of Alabama at Huntsville.

to use this article to critique and to understand the experimental designs involved.

One more suggestion: this is not the type of reading one can do with a part of his mind elsewhere; and it is not the kind of reading one does just to fulfill an assignment. An ounce of understanding here may prevent a pound of befuddlement later. This is basic information for the student who really is serious about reading psychology with understanding.

PSYCHOLOGICAL RESEARCH, at its least, is a difficult and exacting enterprise. At its best, variables are identified and controlled to the extent that stable predictions can be made. Yet, throughout the history of psychological experimentation, there have been a number of methodological frustrations that have plagued this venture. In attempting to arrive at a solution, empirical effort has divided itself into two apparently divergent camps. One such group maintains that the more traditional procedures of formal experimentation must be followed, while a second group points out that nature does not always allow for such rigorous examinations. In this paper, the rationale underlying each will be examined, working toward a possible reconciliation of the two methodologies.

Before proceeding into the respective arguments, it should be indicated that the basic distinction between these two approaches is not new. Cronbach (1957) indicates that the argument has flown under many flags. At one time, it was experimental versus genetic. With the impact of such investigators as Stern and Binet being felt, there was the contrast of general versus individual psychology. In 1913, Yerkes saw the potential in all of correlational psychology and classified the techniques available at that time under the single title of comparative psychology. Dashiell (1939) contrasted the experimental with the clinical method, whereas Bindra and Scheier (1954) replaced the clinical term with psychometric. Cronbach himself seems to have made the final step, however, by contrasting the experimental with correlational techniques.

The respective names employed make little difference in the issue at hand. For the sake of communication, the terminology presented by Bindra and Scheier will be accepted, as it seems to describe the contrast quite well. Response–response (R–R) laws, generalizations, etc., will be used interchangeably with psychometric method; and stimulus–response (S–R) laws, etc., will be interchanged with experimental.

In order to amplify the contrast between these two approaches and to clearly point out some of the more salient issues involved, the following additional points might well be considered. (*a*) Psychological investigators up to the time of Lewin's (1935) revolutionary thinking had been moderately content to follow Aristotelian logic. With this logic, these investigators were, in the main, quite content to place empirical emphasis on frequency of occurrence, statistical validation, and the standardization of some particular phenomena. Lewin rejected this logic in favor of a Galileian approach. Following this, great stress was placed on both individual differences and individuality. As a consequence, Lewin gave heavy emphasis to psychometric thinking and added the formal scholar sanction to the distinction that was growing rapidly in psychology.

Second, it should be indicated that science progresses to the extent that it can gain control over the variables in any empirical situation. This is a point that has been debated widely by researchers following their respective orientations, with each maintaining that their procedures for control, etc., are the most precise ones.

Third, and still a point of additional debate, is the issue of prediction. It is granted that near the heart of any science is the ability to predict in contingent situations. It will be pointed out below, however, that the debate raised concerning prediction by these two respective approaches may be only a pseudo-issue and one that can be resolved rather easily.

Fourth, Spence (1963) has made the case that it is possible to divide the empirical data of psychology into three classes. These classes, she points out, are the response variables, the stimulus variables, and the physiological variables. Due to what is apparently a lack of physiological knowledge on the part of most psychologists, the primary empirical interest seems to have been given over to one or the other of these variables. It is not agreed, however, that such a major issue needs to be made over these two remaining variables per se. In both cases, the investigators are interested in the final dependent variable of behavior, but they have arrived at this end point in a different fashion. The methodologies employed may vary, but in both cases the rigors of scientific control will have been exercised in order to understand this dependent variable. At this point, a brief examination and discussion of the aims of each of these procedures seems well in order.

The aim of the experimental procedure is to analyze specific contingent relationships having held constant all relevant variables other than the ones of particular interest. Experimentation assumes the isolation of a phenomenon from all other cross-phenomena. It assumes that all relevant variability has been brought under control, and any variation that does exist either will be unimportant or will be covered within the statistical design employed. Through such control, the experimenter is now ready to introduce the specific condition in which he is interested. He now is ready to vary the independent variable in some systematic fashion.

From this description, four conditions become apparent concerning experimentation. First, an exerted attempt is made to isolate the particular phenomena in question (Dashiell, 1939). Second, having isolated it, some change is made either in the environmental or internal conditions of the subject or both. Third, the variations may now become defined in terms of the experimental operations and become variables by virtue of the fact that experimental conditions can be changed (Bindra & Scheier, 1954). Fourth, no attempt is made to isolate and study individual qua individual (Dashiell, 1939). There may be an attempt to study groups with a given characteristic, but these groups will be subjected to different experimental conditions. This point will be modified later, where it will be indicated that by accepting such a position as this, concerning individual behavior, perhaps the traditional experimentalist loses as much as he gains.

As has been indicated, the use of the experimental method is greatly dependent on *experimenter ingenuity* in such things as hypothesis formation, variation selection, and control. The question might be asked as to how he can possibly gain all of his needed information. Here the answer most often given is that the experimenter gains his ideas from the theory out of which he is working. From theory he is able to deduce a given cause-and-effect relationship that he puts to an experimental test. This may be one of the strongest arguments for experimental research that can be given. The experimentalist is, in this case, typically working out of some "fairly tight" theoretical framework that, to a very large extent, is "directing" the ongoing research program. In addition, the conclusions generated from a piece of research can be fitted into some general theoretical scheme, as opposed to remaining a bit of descriptive data in "free-floating space."

Extrapolating from Cronbach (1957), the following seem to summarize the major strengths of experimental methodology: (*a*) it is more coherent, as the variables are clearly specified, defined, and brought under control. (*b*) The more traditional experimental methodology is used to investigate the manipulations of the experimenter rather than those of nature. (*c*) It emphasizes the results of environmental change and its effect on task performance. (*d*) Its emphasis is on between-treatment variance, and thus it studies only the variance as it occurs among treatments. (*e*) The individual differences that do occur within a treatment can be handled statistically by error variance. (*f*) The respective experimental hypotheses are derived from some theoretical basis, and the empirical results are worked into the theoretical structure.

Psychometric, or R–R, methodology has created a great deal of debate within the confines of psychological research. Almost every possible criticism seems to have been leveled against it at one time or another. Before discussing some of these attacks, however, it would be well to examine the working structure of R–R methodology.

Kimble and Garmezy (1963) oversimplify the R–R issue somewhat, but do present a very easily understood account. They maintain that in an $R_1 - R_2$ statement, the R_1 refers to behavior in one standard situation, such as a test. This behavior is used to estimate the person's probable behavior, R_2, in some other situation. Dashiell, going in a somewhat different direction, maintains that the central interest of this approach is in the individual as a *unique human being* and in his natural and social habitat.

Spence (1963), on the other hand, presents a more accurate picture of R–R methodology. She is quite willing to grant that one form of R–R investigation does occur as Kimble and Garmezy (1963) and Dashiell (1939) have indicated. With this, there is no debate. This is the form of investigation, however, that makes up the basis of diagnostic testing. Psychometric research represents another issue, and some very clear separation should be made between the two.

As a diagnostic device, the clinician is typically interested in immediate utility. His interest must be in Dashiell's "unique human being." The clinician can "afford," for the sake of his prime interest, to allow the environmental conditions to play a secondary role. Thus, it is granted that there is this side of an R–R *investigation*.

There is still another form and that is R–R *research*, which needs more careful attention. Bindra and Scheier maintain that in psychometric research no attempt is made to change the individual subject. The investigator simply has some characteristic that he wishes to study. Subjects are selected who possess this quality, and it is assumed that it will remain relatively constant throughout the investigation. Any variations that are needed concerning this quality are obtained by selecting subjects who differ in respect to the particular characteristic observed at different levels.

In any event, the investigator is observing behavior in various controlled situations and comparing the performance that he finds in one situation with those of another, for example, Rorschach performance with IQ measures, etc. Spence (1963) points out that the details of these respective conditions may well have been arrived at following the more traditional S–R laws. The R–R research in question, however, is aimed toward a greater understanding of some particular aspect of behavior as observed in a "fixed" test situation. This is a research procedure that accepts manifest individual differences, observed in formal testing, and attempts to demonstrate how these behaviors will be expressed in various situations. By the very nature of the technique itself, there are variables being manipulated in the R–R design. These are variables that have been demonstrated on the level of some psychometric procedure, which derive their meaning from the particular psychometric operations employed.

By understanding this rather subtle point concerning the control of variables within the psychometric treatment, some of the confusion concerning personality research should be clarified (Bindra & Scheier, 1954). A great deal of personality research deals with psychometric variables being defined in terms of individual differences. This has led many S–R experimentalists to believe that personality research is concerned with individual differences per se, rather than with variables and their interrelations. In addition, this has led to some confusion between personality research and clinical diagnosis where, in the latter case, the concern is with the individual case. The use of the individual who possesses a given characteristic in personality research is only one means of studying a given variation, and is not considered as an end in itself. As in other scientific investigations, personality investigations are greatly concerned with specific variables. The questions being asked by the personality researcher seem to be better suited, however, to psychometric procedures, and, thus, for the moment a great deal of research is produced following this methodology. Guilford (1961), in speaking of factor-analytic studies, stated the case quite well as follows:

> I should like to add here that the fact that we have an elaborate computational procedure for treating data does not relieve us of the necessity of observing the ordinary requirements of experimental logic and experimental controls [p. 2].

From these comments, it is possible to see that R–R investigations can meet some of the common criticisms given by the more experimentally oriented investigator. It is also possible to observe that these two methodologies may not be quite as divergent as some have envisioned. At this point, it would be well to examine a few of the common criticisms of R–R methodology to see if something of a "straw man" may not have been established.

Bergmann and Spence (1944) and Spence (1944) have raised a typical series of such criticisms concerning the R–R procedure. These include the following: (*a*) much of the information gained in personality is of the R–R form (Bergmann & Spence, 1944). (*b*) Too much of the human element or "human yardstick" in an R–R design is used in making pertinent judgments concerning the Rs given (Bergmann & Spence, 1944). (*c*) The most interesting laws of contemporary psychology undoubtedly take the form in which the stimulus and response variables occur (Bergmann & Spence, 1944). (*d*) It does not allow for the level of prediction one might hope for in science, but is directed more toward a description of conditions as they currently exist or have existed (Spence, 1944).

For each of the criticisms, it is possible to point out the following in rebuttal:

1. With regard to this as a procedure in gaining information in personality research, it can only be indicated that this is certainly not an argument against R–R methodology. It may be an argument against personality theorists or the current questions being asked, but not the R–R design that is in question. Beyond this, it should be pointed out that personality research is not limited to any single methodology. In fact, a great deal of successful personality research has been accomplished following a strict S–R design (Bindra & Scheier, 1954). The questions asked and the variables studied by the investigator, rather than the particular phase of psychology with which one identifies, would seem to be the deciding factor as to the procedure employed.

2. It is said that there exists too much of the human element in making pertinent judgments concerning the Rs given in the R–R design. Here, there are at least two issues to be considered. First, there is the matter of too much human element which needs clarification. If this is a statement that there is too much of the human element being investigated, it is possible to counter with the proposition that there are those who maintain that psychologists are moving far too slowly in studying this human element. As

psychologists, the progress is not being made rapidly enough for the many other disciplines that must have the information. The learning researcher, for example, continues his work on the lower organisms, while the practicing classroom teacher literally does not know how her pupils learn. Or, the speech therapist begs for information from our motivation researcher on the dynamics of stuttering, for example, while he goes on his way demonstrating how to arouse a public need for some late-model soap product. Is this the human element to which Bergmann and Spence refer? If they are saying that the tests employed to judge this human element are poor, then again this is not an argument against the method. Indeed, Allport made the case for a number of years that these tests should play a more secondary role, while a more direct approach to the individual should be encouraged. Finally, there are many psychologists, both historically as well as currently, who would make a case for psychology as a study of only the human element and nothing more. If, however, reference is being made here to the experimenter as the "human element," then it should be pointed out that in all empirical effort this element plays a salient part. This was described above as "experiment's ingenuity." This criticism, then, becomes a criticism of all empirical work and not any single methodology.

Now let us consider the second phase of the criticism concerning the researcher's "making pertinent judgments concerning the Rs given." This again cannot be a criticism leveled at the R–R system alone. Any research procedure must depend on some investigator to make a decision. This may be a decision concerned with the equipment, design, the variables involved, and that final dependent variable under question. By its very nature, this cannot be a criticism leveled exclusively at any single research method. The human element enters all experimentation.

3. It has been said that the S–R laws are the most interesting. This is certainly not a criticism, but a value judgment, and should be recognized for what it is. No further comment is required.

4. The R–R procedure does not allow for the level of prediction one might hope for in science, but is directed more toward a description of conditions as they currently exist or have existed. Here, again, at least two separate criticisms seem to be implied. Concerning the latter, that of description of conditions, it is possible to observe that much of science today seems to look on some basic description of conditions in an unfavorable light. Psychology is no exception. If an investigator is capable of developing some complex descriptions of a given situation at a respectable level of significance, his work typically is not given the attention that it deserves. Rather, it is often identified as being superficial and most probably devoid of any "real value."

Perhaps the time is again right for a review of the aims of any science. Kaplan (1964) has made the case quite well that these aims still remain that of description, prediction, and control. Must we not have this descriptive information, and does this not represent at least some part of the vital information or foundation of the particular science itself? One might be hard put to dismiss descriptive research quite as easily as Spence (1944).

As for prediction, it might be asked just where these predictions come from in both the S–R and R–R situations. In the S–R situation, prediction is made from some environmental condition. In the R–R statement, the prediction comes from some aspect of behavior taken from a previous test or measurement situation. In both cases, that which is predicted is always behavior. If we assume that in both situations the condition that allows for prediction is the behavior of our organisms under like conditions (in their respective treatments), then we have a common basis for comparison. Under all conditions, a great deal of individual variation will still be observed. Even the learning theorists, the most ardent of S–R theorists, will grant that this individual difference does occur (Spence, 1963). In granting this, however, he is forced to conclude that the observed behavior is a function of more than the immediate stimulus situation. To predict accurately, he must have more information than that given to him by the simple treatment itself. Short of this, he loses precision in his prediction. He does not have the additional information concerning the individual organism that the R–R investigator is attempting to gain. Thus, it is altogether possible to show how the criticizer now becomes open to his own criticism. It is also possible to demonstrate from the above argument how the two methodologies might complement each other.

Before examining this complementary relationship, it would be well to summarize some of the major strengths of R–R methodology, as was done for the S–R procedure. Again by extrapolating from Cronbach (1967), some of these strengths seem to be the following: (*a*) in using this methodology, in most cases, it is possible to investigate the variations between individuals, groups, etc., that already exist, maintaining that this variation is important to study. (*b*) Following this system, it is possible to study what man has not learned to control or can never hope to control. (*c*) Emphasis is placed more on test construction and its accuracy and less on theory. (*d*) The findings of R–R methodology often have immediate utility, not the least of which lies in guiding experimentation.

This last point takes us directly to a discussion of how these two procedures may be used to complement each other. Bindra and Scheier (1954) point out that it is altogether possible to combine these two different techniques. The experimental procedure could be employed to advantage with psychometric research. Used jointly, they could help to explain most of the intraindividual variation found in successive testing. Psychometric aid could be given to experimental research in certain problems where a range of variation is needed that the experimental procedure cannot encompass, that is, in working with extreme-anxiety subjects.

Even in 1939, Dashiell thought he detected signs of combining these two methodologies for the good of psychological research. After making a rather strong case demonstrating the then current separation of S–R and R–R methodologies, Dashiell (1939) maintained that "we can discern at the present moment *signs of a developing rapprochement* even here [p. 17]." As evidence for this move, he cites: (*a*) the then current interdivisional cooperative research programs between the two major disciplines of clinical and experimental psychology; (*b*) the experimental study of neurosis in sub-human species; (*c*) the work of Murray (1938) at Harvard concerning a complex study of 51 college-age subjects; (*d*) Hull's (1936–38) seminar at Yale discussing psychoanalytic concepts, with an attempt being made to put these doctrines into well-accepted laboratory principles; (*e*) Lewin's (Brown & Lewin, 1937) work on motivation which had proven to be "without instruments of brass yet nonetheless experimental [p. 17]"; (*f*) the study of abnormal persons, not as patients, but as representative of disease classifications; and (*g*) the newer areas of child development and experimentation concerning the developing organism.

There is precedent, then, for a combination of these two approaches for the good of psychological research. Spence (1963) has gone to some length to demonstrate how this combination can be accomplished. Briefly, her argument is as follows: Those working from an S–R design must be concerned with individual differences, for they must observe all of their organisms under like experimental conditions. She believes that this S–R formulation can be modified to take these individual differences into account. By incorporating the physiological variables, the S–R formula would become $R = f(S, O)$. Still a second and more common way of knowing these individual differences would be to expand the formula to include other relevant information gained in previous situations. By doing this, the formula now becomes $R_1 = f(S, R_2)$. The subscripts would indicate the individual difference variable as measured independent of the behavior being predicted.

It would be possible to expand this formulation to include the past experience of the organism interacting with the current situation. In this case, the formulation would become $R = f(S_{past}, S_{present})$. In dealing with human organisms, however, we cannot manipulate these past conditions to suit our empirical needs. To circumvent this, those organisms are selected for study that have had certain experiences in their life history, and these are relevant to the situation in which we are interested. The formula now becomes $R_1 - R_2$! Spence (1963) points out that in animal work it is altogether possible to manipulate these historical variables, gaining the needed control in this fashion. With the human organism, this becomes both an ethical and a legal problem, and such manipulation is impossible. There is some serious question here, following the present thinking, that Spence (1963) may have stopped short in her own argument. In R–R research, just this kind of manipulation is done. Those individuals who have had certain experiences are isolated for intensive study. This is done, however, within the confines of the psychometric framework, and little ethical or legal problem is encountered. That is, following the above formulation, those individuals who do manifest a particular kind of behavior may be selected for experimental study where variables can be controlled, etc. By gaining this information, it then becomes more probable to predict subsequent responses in certain conditions. Thus, the reconciliation of these two approaches becomes that of additional information given to the experimenter germane to each of his subjects in any experimental treatment. With this information, prediction becomes more precise and experimental rigor intensified out of the additional information which is relevant to the past acquisitions of the unique subjects. It should be noted, however, that many investigators to date remain less concerned with these past variables than they are with the effects of the present variables on future behavior. They fail to take into account that which any organism brings into any experimental situation. They seem more concerned with the effects of the present situation as it relates to later acquisition of certain response patterns.

Having said this, however, it should become rather clear that both R–R and S–R laws have a definite place in psychological investigation. R–R laws are invaluable for greater understanding of the details which lie behind individual variation. Cronbach (1957) has stated the case quite well, and we can do no better than to use his work as summary:

> It is not enough for each discipline to borrow from the other. Correlational psychology studies only variance among organisms; experimental psychology studies only variance among treatments. A united discipline will study both of these, but it will also be concerned with the otherwise neglected interactions between organismic and treatment variables. Our job is to invent constructs and to form a network of laws which permits prediction. From observations we must infer a psychological description of the situation and of the present state of the organism. Our laws should permit us to predict, from this description, the behavior of organism-in-situation [pp. 681–682].

REFERENCES

Bergmann, G., & Spence, K. W. The logic of psychological measurement. *Psychological Review,* 1944, **51,** 1–24.

Bindra, D., & Scheier, I. H. The relation between psychometric and experimental research in psychology. *American Psychologist,* 1954, **9,** 69–71.

Cronbach, L. J. The two disciplines of scientific psychology. *American Psychologist,* 1957, **12,** 671–684.

Dashiell, J. F. Some rapprochements in contemporary psychology. *Psychological Bulletin,* 1939, **36,** 1–24.

Guilford, J. P. Factorial angles to psychology. *Psychological Review,* 1961, **68,** 1–20.

Kaplan, A. *The conduct of inquiry.* San Francisco: Chandler, 1964.

Kimble, G. A., & Garmezy, N. *Principles of general psychology.* New York: Ronald, 1963.

Lewin, K. *Dynamic theory of personality.* New York: McGraw-Hill, 1935.

Spence, J. T. Learning theory and personality. In J. M. Wepman & R. W. Heine (Eds.), *Concepts of personality.* Chicago: Aldine, 1963.

Spence, K. W. The nature of theory construction in contemporary psychology. *Psychological Review,* 1944, **51**, 47–68.

4.

New light on the human potential

Herbert A. Otto

A reader in the field of human development may go two ways: (1) his concern may be with understanding others or (2) he may pose questions about himself and his development.

The author of this selection describes a situation that is both challenging and disturbing. It is nice to know that men possess great amounts of unrealized potential, and that there are almost unlimited possibilities for human improvement. It is nice, also, for anyone to know that he himself has many as yet untapped and undeveloped capabilities—until he begins to wonder what limits realization. To a considerable extent, dissatisfaction and frustration are both cause and result of unrealized potentials. One may begin to face up to the fact that much of the living, experiencing, and growing of which he is capable is passing him by. He may begin to be aware that for time and energy spent, he is getting only a fraction of the possible return. In terms of his potential for living, he may be half dead. Finally, he may attempt, as the author does, to find some explanations and some reasons for his own inability to actualize self and to live fully.

Whether or not the reader agrees with the author concerning the cultural conditions he lists as reasons or limiting factors for the realization of human potential, such charges as pathologically oriented culture, negative conditioning, and man's estrangement from man furnish food for thought. The editors agree that the problem exists and that the quest for answers must be unremitting. We hope to enlist others in the search.

William James once estimated that the healthy human being is functioning at less than 10 per cent of his capacity. It took more than half a century

Saturday Review, 52(No. 51):14–17, December 20, 1969. Copyright 1969 Saturday Review, Inc. Herbert A. Otto, Chairman, National Center for the Exploration of Human Potential, La Jolla, California.

before this idea found acceptance among a small proportion of behavioral scientists. In 1954, the highly respected and widely known psychologist Gardner Murphy published his pioneering volume *Human Potentialities*. The early Sixties saw the beginnings of the human potentialities research project at the University of Utah and the organization of Esalen Institute in California, the first of a series of "Growth Centers" that were later to be referred to as the Human Potentialities Movement.

Today, many well-known scientists such as Abraham Maslow, Margaret Mead, Gardner Murphy, O. Spurgeon English, and Carl Rogers subscribe to the hypothesis that man is using a very small fraction of his capacities. Margaret Mead quotes a 6 per cent figure, and my own estimate is 5 per cent or less. Commitment to the hypothesis is not restricted to the United States. Scientists in the U.S.S.R. and other countries are also at work. Surprisingly, the so-called human potentialities hypothesis is still largely unknown.

What are the dimensions of the human potential? The knowledge we do have about man is minimal and has not as yet been brought together with the human potentialities hypothesis as an organizing force and synthesizing element. Of course, we know more about man today than we did fifty years ago, but this is like the very small part of the iceberg we see above the water. Man essentially remains a mystery. From the depths of this mystery there are numerous indicators of the human potential.

Certain indicators of man's potential are revealed to us in childhood. They become "lost" or submerged as we succumb to the imprinting of the cultural mold in the "growing up" process. Do you remember when you were a child and it rained after a dry spell and there was a very particular, intensive earthy smell in the air? Do you remember how people smelled when they hugged you? Do you recall the brilliant colors of leaves, flowers, grass, and even brick surfaces and lighted signs that you experienced as a child? Furthermore, do you recall that when father and mother stepped into the room you *knew* how they felt about themselves, about life, and about you—at that moment.

Today we know that man's sense of smell, one of the most powerful and primitive senses, is highly developed. In the average man this capacity has been suppressed except for very occasional use. Some scientists claim that man's sense of smell is almost as keen as a hunting dog's. Some connoisseurs of wines, for example, can tell by the bouquet not only the type of grape and locality where they were grown but even the vintage year and vineyard. Perfume mixers can often detect fantastically minute amounts in mixed essences; finally there are considerable data on odor discrimination from the laboratory. It is also clear that, since the air has become an overcrowded garbage dump for industrial wastes and the internal combustion engine, it is easier to turn off our sense of smell than to keep it functioning. The capacity to experience the environment more fully through our olfactory organs remains a potential.

It is possible to regain these capacities through training. In a similar manner, sensory and other capacities, including visual, kinesthetic, and tactile abilities, have become stunted and dulled. We perceive less clearly, and as a result we feel less—we use our dulled senses to close ourselves off from both our physical and interpersonal environments. Today we also dull our perceptions of how other people feel and we consistently shut off awareness of our own feelings. For many who put their senses to sleep it is a sleep that lasts unto death. Again, through sensory and other training the doors of perception can be cleansed (to use Blake's words) and our capacities reawakened. Anthropological research abounds with reports of primitive tribes that have developed exceptional sensory and perceptive abilities as a result of training. Utilization of these capacities by modern man for life-enrichment purposes awaits the future.

Neurological research has shed new light on man's potential. Work at the UCLA Brain Research Institute points to enormous abilities latent in everyone by suggesting an incredible hypothesis: The ultimate creative capacity of the human brain may be, for all practical purposes, infinite. To use the computer analogy, man is a vast storehouse of data, but we have not learned how to program ourselves to utilize these data for problem-solving purposes. Recall of experiential data is extremely spotty and selective for most adults. My own research has convinced me that the recall of experiences can be vastly improved by use of certain simple training techniques, provided sufficient motivation is present.

Under emergency conditions, man is capable of prodigious feats of physical strength. For example, a middle-aged California woman with various ailments lifted a car just enough to let her son roll out from under it after it had collapsed on him. According to newspaper reports the car weighed in excess of 2,000 pounds. There are numerous similar accounts indicating that every person has vast physical reserve capacities that can be tapped. Similarly, the extraordinary feats of athletes and acrobats—involving the conscious and specialized development of certain parts of the human organism as a result of consistent application and a high degree of motivation—point to the fantastic plasticity and capabilities of the human being.

Until World War II, the field of hypnosis was not regarded as respectable by many scientists and was associated with stage performances and charlatanism. Since that time hypnosis has attained a measure of scientific respectability. Medical and therapeutic applications of hypnosis include the use of this technique in surgery and anesthesiology (hypnoanesthesia for major and minor surgery), gynecology (infertility, frigidity, menopausal conditions), pediatrics (enuresis, tics, asthma in children, etc.), and in dentistry. Scores of texts on medical and dental hypnosis are available. Dr. William S. Kroger, one of the specialists in the field and author of the well-known text *Clinical and Experimental Hypnosis,* writes that hypnotherapy is "directed to the patient's needs and is a methodology to tap the 'forgotten assets' of the *hidden potentials* of behavior and response that so often lead to new learnings and understanding." (My italics.) As far as we know now, the possibilities opened by hypnosis for the potential functioning of the human organism are not brought about by the hypnotist. Changes are induced by the subject, utilizing his belief-structure, with the hypnotist operating as an "enabler," making it possible for the subject to tap some of his unrealized potential.

The whole area of parapsychology that deals with extrasensory perception (ESP), "mental telepathy," and other paranormal phenomena, and that owes much of its development to the work of Dr. J. B. Rhine and others is still regarded by much of the scientific establishment with the same measure of suspicion accorded hypnosis in the pre-World War II days. It is of interest that a number of laboratories in the U.S.S.R. are devoted to the study of telepathy as a physical phenomenon, with research conducted under the heading "cerebral radio-communication" and "bio-electronics." The work is supported by the Soviet government. The reluctance to accept findings from this field of research is perhaps best summarized by an observation of Carl C. Jung's in 1958:

(Some) people deny the findings of parapsychology outright, either for philosophical reasons or from intellectual laziness. This can hardly be considered a scientifically responsible attitude, even though it is a popular way out of quite extraordinary intellectual difficulty.

Although the intensive study of creativity had its beginnings in fairly recent times, much of value has been discovered about man's creative potential. There is evidence that every person has creative abilities that can be developed. A considerable number of studies indicate that much in our educational system—including conformity pressures exerted by teachers, emphasis on memory development, and rote learning, plus the overcrowding of classrooms—militates against the development of creative capacities. Research has established that children between the ages of two and three can learn to read, tape record a story, and type it as it is played back. Hundreds of children between the ages of four and six have been taught by the Japanese pedagogue Suzuki to play violin concertos. Japanese research with infants and small children also suggests the value of early "maximum input" (music, color, verbal, tactile stimuli) in the personality development of infants. My own observations tend to confirm this. We have consistently underestimated the child's capacity to learn and his ability to realize his potential while *enjoying* both the play elements and the discipline involved in this process.

In contrast to the Japanese work, much recent Russian research appears to be concentrated in the area of mentation, with special emphasis on extending and enlarging man's mental processes and his capacity for learning. As early as 1964 the following appeared in *Soviet Life Today,* a U.S.S.R. English language magazine:

The latest findings in anthropology, psychology, logic, and physiology show that the potential of the human mind is very great indeed. "As soon as modern science gave us some understanding of the structure and work of the human brain, we were struck with its enormous reserve capacity," writes Yefremov (Ivan Yefremov, eminent Soviet scholar and writer). "Man, under average conditions of work and life, uses only a small part of his thinking equipment. . . . If we were able to force our brain to work at only half its capacity, we could, without any difficulty whatever, learn forty languages, memorize the large Soviet Encyclopedia from cover to cover, and complete the required courses of dozens of colleges."

The statement is hardly an exaggeration. It is the generally accepted theoretical view of man's mental potentialities.

How can we tap this gigantic potential? It is a big and very complex problem with many ramifications.

Another signpost of man's potential is what I have come to call the "Grandma Moses effect." This artist's experience indicates that artistic talents can be discovered and brought to full flowering in the latter part of the life cycle. In every retirement community there can be found similar examples of residents who did not use latent artistic abilities or other talents until after retirement. In many instances the presence of a talent is suspected or known but allowed to remain fallow for the best part of a lifetime.

Reasons why well-functioning mature adults do not use specific abilities are complex. Studies conducted at the University of Utah as a part of the Human Potentialities Research Project revealed that unconscious blocks are often present. In a number of instances a person with definite evidence that he has a specific talent (let's say he won a state-wide contest in sculpture while in high school) may not wish to realize this talent at a later time because he fears this would introduce a change in life-style. Sometimes fear of the passion of creation is another roadblock in self-actualization. On the basis of work at Utah it became clear that persons who live close to their capacity, who continue to activate their potential, have a pronounced sense of well-being and considerable energy and see themselves as leading purposeful and creative lives.

Most people are unaware of their strengths and potentialities. If a person with some college background is handed a form and asked to write out his personality strengths, he will list, on an average, five or six strengths. Asked to do the same thing for his weaknesses, the list will be two to three times as long. There are a number of reasons for this low self-assessment. Many participants in my classes and marathon group weekends have pointed out that "listing your strengths feels like bragging about yourself. It's something that just isn't done." Paradoxically, in a group, people feel more comfortable about sharing problem areas and hang-ups than they do about personality resources and latent abilities. This is traceable to the fact that we are members of a pathology-oriented culture. Psychological and psychiatric jargon dealing with emotional dysfunction and mental illness has become the parlance of the man in the street. In addition, from early childhood in our educational system we learn largely by our mistakes—by having them pointed out to us repeatedly. All this results in early "negative conditioning" and influences our attitude and perception of ourselves and other people. An attitudinal climate has become established which is continually fed and reinforced.

As a part of this negative conditioning there is the heavy emphasis by communications media on violence in television programs and motion pictures. The current American news format of radio, television, and newspapers—the widely prevalent idea of what constitutes news—results from a narrow, brutalizing concept thirty or forty years behind the times and is inimical to the development of human potentials.

THE news media give much time and prominent space to violence and consistently underplay "good" news. This gives the consumer the impression that important things that happen are various types of destructive activities. Consistent and repeated emphasis on bad news not only creates anxiety and tension but instills the belief that there is little except violence, disasters, accidents, and mayhem abroad in the world. As a consequence, the consumer of such news gradually experiences a shift in his outlook about the world leading to the formation of feelings of alienation and separation. The world is increasingly perceived as a threat, as the viewer becomes anxious that violence and mayhem may be perpetrated on him from somewhere out of the strange and unpredictable environment in which he lives. There slowly grows a conviction that it is safer to withdraw from such a world, to isolate himself from its struggles, and to let others make the decisions and become involved.

As a result of the steady diet of violence in the media, an even more fundamental and insidious erosion in man's self-system takes place. The erosion affects what I call the "trust factor." If we have been given a certain amount of affection, love, and understanding in our formative years, we are able to place a certain amount of trust in our fellow man. Trust is one of the most important elements in today's society although we tend to minimize its importance. *We basically trust people.* For example, we place an enormous amount of trust in our fellow man when driving on a freeway or in an express lane. We trust those with whom we are associated to fulfill their obligations and responsibilities. The element of trust is the basic rule in human relations. When we distrust people, they usually sense our attitude and reciprocate in kind.

The consistent emphasis in the news on criminal violence, burglarizing, and assault makes slow but pervasive inroads into our reservoir of trust. As we hear and read much about the acts of violence and injury men perpetrate upon one another, year after year, with so little emphasis placed on the loving, caring, and humanitarian acts of man, we begin to trust our fellow man less, and we thereby diminish ourselves. It is my conclusion the media's excessive emphasis on violence, like the drop of water on the stone, erodes and wears away the trust factor in man. By undermining the trust in man, media contribute to man's estrangement from man and prevent the full flourishing and deeper development of a sense of community and communion with all men.

Our self-concept, how we feel about ourselves and our fellow man and the world, is determined to a considerable extent by the inputs from the physical and interpersonal environment to which we are exposed. In the physical environment, there are the irritants in the air, i.e., air pollution plus the ugliness and noise of megapolis. Our interpersonal environment is characterized by estrangement and distance from others (and self), and by the artificiality and superficiality of our social encounters and the resultant violation of authenticity. Existing in a setting that provides as consistent inputs multiple irritants, ugliness and violence, and lack of close and meaningful relationships, man is in danger of becoming increasingly irritated, ugly, and violent.

As work in the area of human potentialities progressed, it has become ever clearer that personality, to a much greater degree than previously suspected, functions in response to the environment. This is additional confirmation of what field theorists and proponents of the holistic approach to the study of man have long suspected.

Perhaps the most important task facing us today is the regeneration of our environment and institutional structures such as school, government, church, etc. With increasing sophistication has come the recognition that institutions are not sacrosanct and that they have but one purpose and function—to serve as a framework for the actualization of human potential. It is possible to evaluate both the institution and the contribution of the institution by asking this question: "To what extent does the function of the institution foster the realization of human potential?"

Experimental groups consistently have found that the more a person's environment can be involved in the process of realizing potential, the greater the gains. It is understandable why scientists concerned with the study of personality have been reluctant to consider the importance of here-and-now inputs in relation to personality functioning. To do so would open a Pandora's box of possibilities and complex forces that until fairly recently were considered to be the exclusive domain of the social scientist. Many scientists and professionals, particularly psychotherapists, feel they have acquired a certain familiarity with the topography of "intra-psychic forces" and social workers now realize that over and beyond keeping up with de-functioning of the personality.

It is significant that an increasing number of psychologists, psychiatrists, and social workers now realize that over and beyond keeping up with developments in their respective fields, the best way to acquire additional professional competence is through group experiences designed for personal growth and that focus on the unfolding of individual possibilities. From this group of aware professionals and others came much of the initial support and interest in Esalen Institute and similar "Growth Centers" later referred to as the Human Potentialities Movement.

Esalen Institute in Big Sur, California, was organized in 1962 by Michael Murphy and his partner, Dick Price. Under their imaginative management the institute experienced a phenomenal growth, established a branch in San Francisco, and is now famous for its seminars and weekend experiences offered by pioneering professionals. Since 1962 more than 100,000 persons have enrolled for one of these activities.

The past three years have seen a rapid mushrooming of Growth Centers. There are more than fifty such organizations ranging from Esalen and Kairos Institutes in California to Oasis in Chicago and Aureon Institute in New York. The experiences offered at these Growth Centers are based on several hypotheses: 1) that the average healthy person functions at a fraction of his capacity; 2) that man's most exciting life-long adventure is actualizing his potential; 3) that the group environment is one of the best settings in which to achieve growth; and 4) that personality growth can be achieved by anyone willing to invest himself in this process.

Human potentialities is rapidly emerging as a discrete field of scientific inquiry. Exploring the human potential can become the meeting ground for a wide range of disciplines, offering a dynamic synthesis for seemingly divergent areas of research. It is possible that the field of human potentialities offers an answer to the long search for a synthesizing and organizing principle which will unify the sciences. The explosive growth of the Human Potentialities Movement is indicative of a growing public interest. Although there exist a considerable number of methods—all designed to tap human potential—work on assessment or evaluation of these methods has in most instances not progressed beyond field testing and informal feedback of results. The need for research in the area of human potentialities has never been more pressing. The National Center for the Exploration of Human Potential in La Jolla, California, has recently been organized for this purpose. A nonprofit organization, the center will act as a clearing house of information for current and past approaches that have been successful in fostering personal growth. One of the main purposes of the center will be to conduct and coordinate basic and applied research concerning the expansion of human potential.

Among the many fascinating questions posed by researchers are some of the following: What is the relationship of body-rhythms, biorhythms, and the expansion of sensory awareness to the uncovering of human potential? What are the applications of methods and approaches from other cultures such as yoga techniques, Sufi methods, types of meditation, etc.? What is the role of ecstasy and play vis-à-vis the realizing of human possibilities? The exploration of these and similar questions can help us create a society truly devoted to the full development of human capacities for love, joy, creativity, spiritual experiencing. This is the challenge and promise of our lifetime.

5.

Music education and peak experience

ABRAHAM H. MASLOW

*The title of this article may be misleading because it is more about life
and living than it is about music education. The author of this selection has had much to do with redirecting the emphases of psychology.
The more traditional approaches have stressed the study of the psychologically unhealthy person in order to bring him up to par or
average. Maslow has urged, as he does here, the study of the extra
healthy, the superior person, the one who is most capable of peak
experiences. He believes that this approach will provide concepts of
what men can become and what kind of conditions they must structure in order to help themselves to get there.*

*In contrast to the behavioristic and psychoanalytic explanations,
which tend to describe human behavior in terms of reacting to, and
being determined by, social and biological stimuli, the humanistic or
"third force" in psychology emphasizes that people can exert some
control over what behavior will be. Further, the humanistic psychologist believes that individuals can become self-directing and that, in
some measure, they can choose what they will become. Whereas the
older concepts see human behavior as mostly reactive, the more recent
explanation endorsed by the author of this article sees man as also
able to function in an enactive or proactive manner: that is, as capable
of choosing how he wishes things to be and then operating to make
them happen. He, "This Good Person," can be described as the self-
evolving, responsible-for-self, self-actualizing individual. This, we think,
should be the goal of human development. But one caution: theories
of human behavior are not necessarily mutually exclusive. The reader
is not forced totally to renounce the insights of conditioning, association, and psychoanalysis because he finds another view more compatible with his beliefs and attitudes. Man is both proactive and reactive.*

SOMETHING BIG is happening. It's happening to everything that concerns
human beings. Everything the human being generates is involved, and
certainly education is involved. A new *Weltanschauung* is in the process
of being developed, a new *Zeitgeist,* a new set of values and a new way of
finding them—certainly a new image of man. There is a new kind of
psychology, presently called the humanistic, existential, third-force psychology, which at this transitional moment is certainly different in many im-

Music Educators Journal, 54(No. 6):72–75, 163–171, February, 1968. Abraham H. Maslow, late Professor of Psychology, Brandeis University.

portant ways from the Freudian and behavioristic psychologies, the two great comprehensive, dominating psychologies.

To sketch this briefly and to indicate that I am talking about a life philosophy, the beginning of a new century, it is evident that there are new conceptions of interpersonal relationships. There is a new image of society. There is a new conception of the goals of society, of all the social institutions, and of all the social sciences, which are a part of society. There is a new economics, for instance, a new conception of politics. I have written in the past several years of revolutions and have tried to apply these revolutions to religion, to science, and to work. There is a newer conception of education popping along that I will mention briefly, because it will be the background for my iconoclastic ideas about music, music education, and creativeness.

First, I would mention psychologies of learning. If one took a course or picked up a book in the psychology of learning, most of it, in my opinion, would be beside the point—that is, beside the "humanistic" point. Most of it would present learning as the acquisition of associations, of skills and capacities that are *external* and not *intrinsic* to the human character, to the human personality, to the person himself. It is a matter of picking up coins or keys or possessions or something of the sort in order to pick up reinforcements and conditioned reflexes that are, in a certain, very profound sense, expendable. It does not really matter if one has a conditioned reflex; if I salivate to the sound of a buzzer and then this extinguishes, nothing has happened to me; I have lost nothing of any consequence whatever. We might almost say that these extensive books on the psychology of learning are of no consequence, at least to the human center, to the human soul, to the human essence.

Generated by this new humanistic philosophy is also a new conception of learning, of teaching, and of education. Stated simply, such a concept holds that the function of education, the goals of education—the human goal, the humanistic goal, the goal so far as human beings are concerned—is ultimately the "self-actualization" of a person, the becoming fully human, the development of the fullest height that the human species can stand up to or that the particular individual can come to. In a less technical way, it is helping the person to become the best that he is able to become.

Such a goal involves very serious shifts in what we would teach in a course in the psychology of learning. It is not going to be a matter of associative learning. Associative learning in general is certainly useful, extremely useful for learning things that are of no real consequence. And many of the things we must learn are like that. If one needs to memorize the vocabulary of some other language, he would learn it by sheer rote memory. Here, the laws of association can be a help. Or if one wants to learn all sorts of automatic habits in driving, responding to a red signal light or something of the sort, then conditioning is of consequence. It is important and useful, especially in a technological society. But in terms

of becoming a better person, in terms of self-development and self-fulfill-
ment, or in terms of "becoming fully human," the great learning experiences are very different.

In my life, such experiences have been far more important than classes,
listening to lectures, memorizing the branches of the twelve cranial nerves
and dissecting a human brain, or memorizing the insertions of the muscles,
or the kinds of things that one does in medical schools, in biology courses,
or other such courses.

Far more important for me have been such experiences as having a
child. Our first baby changed me as a psychologist. It made the behaviorism I had been brought up in look so foolish that I could not stomach
it any more. It was impossible. Having a second baby, and learning how
profoundly different people are even before birth, made it impossible for me
to think in terms of the kind of learning psychology in which one can teach
anybody anything. Or the John B. Watson theory of, "Give me two babies
and I will make one into this and one into the other." It is as if he never
had any children. We know only too well that a parent cannot make his
children into anything. Children make themselves into something. The best
we can do and frequently the most effect we can have is by serving as
something to react against if the child presses too hard.

Another profound learning experience that I value far more highly
than any particular course or any degree that I have ever had was my personal psychoanalysis: discovering my own identity, my own self. Another
basic experience—far more important—was getting married. This was
certainly far more important than my Ph.D. by way of instructiveness. If one
thinks in terms of the developing of the kinds of wisdom, the kinds of
understanding, the kinds of life skills that we would want, then he must
think in terms of what I would like to call *intrinsic* education—*intrinsic*
learning; that is, learning to be a human being in general, and second, learning to be this particular human being. I am now very busily occupied in
trying to catch up with all the epiphenomena of this notion of intrinsic
education. Certainly one thing I can tell you. Our conventional education
looks mighty sick. Once you start thinking in this framework, that is, in
terms of making a good human being, and if then you ask the question
about the courses that you took in high school, "How did my trigonometry
course help me to become a better human being?" an echo answers, "By
gosh, it didn't!" In a certain sense, trigonometry was a waste of time.
My early music education was also not very successful, because it taught a
child who had a very profound feeling for music and a great love for the
piano *not* to learn it. I had a piano teacher who taught me that music is
something to stay away from. And I had to relearn music as an adult, all
by myself.

Observe that I have been talking about ends. This is a revolution that
is a repudiation of nineteenth-century science and of contemporary professional philosophy, which is essentially a technology and not a philosophy

of ends. I have rejected thereby, as theories of human nature, positivism, behaviorism, and objectivism. I have rejected thereby, the whole model of science and all its works that have been derived from the historical accident that science began with the study of nonpersonal, nonhuman things, which in fact had no ends. The development of physics, astronomy, mechanics, chemistry, and biology was in fact impossible until it had become value-free, value-neutral, so that pure descriptiveness was now possible. The great mistake that we are now learning about is that this model, which developed from the study of objects and of things, has been illegitimately used for the study of human beings. It is a terrible technique. It has not worked.

Most of the psychology on this positivistic model, on this objectivistic, associationistic, value-free, value-neutral model of science, as it piles up like a coral reef or like mountains and mountains of small facts about this and that, was certainly not false, but merely trivial. I would like to point out here that in order not to sell my own science short, I think we do know a great deal about things that *do* matter to the human being, but I would maintain that what has mattered to the human being that we have learned has been learned by nonphysicalistic techniques, by the humanistic science techniques of which we have become more conscious.

In speaking of the world situation at the opening ceremonies of a recent Lincoln Center Festival, Archibald MacLeish said in part:

> . . . What is wrong is not the great discoveries of science—information is always better than ignorance, no matter what information or what ignorance. What is wrong is the belief behind the information, the belief that information will change the world. It won't. Information without human understanding is like an answer without its question— meaningless. And human understanding is only possible through the arts. It is the work of art that creates the human perspective in which information turns to truth. . . .

In a certain sense I disagree with MacLeish, although I can understand why he said this. What he is talking about is information *short of this new revolution,* short of the humanistic psychologies, short of the conceptions of the sciences that not only repudiate the notion of being value-free and value-neutral, but actually assume as an obligation, as a duty, the necessity for discovery of values—the empirical discovery, demonstration, and verification of the values that are inherent in human nature itself. This work is now busily going on.

What Mr. MacLeish said was appropriate for the era from 1920 to 1930. It is appropriate today if one doesn't know about the new psychologies. "And human understanding is only possible through the arts." That *was* true. Fortunately, it is no longer true. It now is possible to gather information that can contribute to human understanding, that carries imbedded within it value hints, vectorial and directional information, information that goes someplace instead of just inertly lying there like flapjacks.

"It is the work of art that creates the human perspective in which information turns to truth." I deny that, and we had better argue about that. We must have some criteria for distinguishing good art from bad art. They do not yet exist in the realms of art so far as I know. They are beginning to exist, and I would like to leave one hint, an empirical hint. A possibility is beginning to emerge that we would have some criteria for discriminating good art from bad art.

If your situation is like mine, you know that we are in a complete and total confusion of values in the arts. In music, you try to prove something about the virtues of John Cage as against Beethoven—or Elvis Presley. In painting and architecture similar confusion is present. We have no shared values anymore. I don't bother to read music criticism. It is useless to me. So is art criticism, which I have also given up reading. Book reviews I find useless frequently. There is a complete chaos and anarchy of standards. For instance, the *Saturday Review* recently carried a favorable review of one of Jean Genet's crummy books. Written by a professor of theology, it was total confusion. It was the approach that Evil now has become Good because there is some kind of paradox while playing with words: if evil becomes totally evil, then it somehow becomes good, and there were rhapsodies to the beauties of sodomy and drug addiction which, for a poor psychologist who spends most of his time trying to rescue people from the anguish of these kinds of things, were incomprehensible. How can a grown man recommend this book as a chapter in ethics and a guide to the young?

If Archibald MacLeish says that works of art lead to the truth, Archibald MacLeish is thinking about particular works of art that Archibald MacLeish has picked out, but ones his son might not agree with. And *then,* MacLeish really has nothing much to say. There is no way of convincing anybody about this point. I think this could be some symbol of the way in which I feel that we are at a turning point. We are moving around the corner. Something new is happening. There are discernible differences— and these are not differences in taste or arbitrary values. These are empirical discoveries. They are new things that have been found out, and from these are generated all sorts of propositions about values and education.

One is the discovery that the human being *has higher needs,* that he has instincts—like needs, which are a part of his biological equipment— the need to be dignified, for instance, and to be respected, and the need to be free for self-development. The discovery of higher needs carries with it all sorts of revolutionary implications.

Secondly, the point I have already made about the social sciences: many people are beginning to discover that the physicalistic, mechanistic model was a mistake and that it has led us . . . where? To atom bombs. To a beautiful technology of killing, as in the concentration camps. To Eichmann. An Eichmann cannot be refuted with a positivistic philosophy or science. He just cannot; and he never got it until the moment he died. He didn't know what was wrong. As far as he was concerned, nothing was wrong; he had done a good job. He *did* do a good job, if you forget about the ends and the values. I point out that professional science and professional philosophy are dedicated to the proposition of forgetting about the values, excluding them. This, therefore must lead to Eichmanns, to atom bombs, and to who knows what!

The great discoveries Freud made, we can now add to. His one big mistake, which we are correcting now, is that he thought of the unconscious merely as undesirable evil. But unconsciousness carries in it also the roots of creativeness, of joy, of happiness, of goodness, of its own human ethics and values. We know that there is such a thing as a healthy unconscious as well as an unhealthy one. And the new psychologies are studying this at full tilt. The existential psychiatrists and psychotherapists are actually putting it into practice. New kinds of therapies are being practiced.

So we have a good conscious and a bad conscious—and a good unconscious and a bad unconscious. Furthermore, the good is real, in a non-Freudian sense. Freud was committed by his own positivism. Remember, Freud came out of a physicalistic, chemicalistic science. He was a neurologist. And a sworn oath that is in print called for a project to develop a psychology that could be entirely reduced to physical and chemical statements. This is what he dedicated himself to. He himself disproved his point. And about this higher nature that I claim we have discovered and that, of course, exists, the question is, how do we explain it? The Freudian explanation has been reductive. Explain it away. If I am a kind man, this is a reaction formation against my rage to kill. Somehow, the killing is more basic than the kindness. And the kindness is a way of trying to cover up, repress, and defend myself against realizing the fact that I am truly a murderer. If I am generous, this is a reaction formation against stinginess. I am really stingy inside. This is a very peculiar thing. Somehow there is the begging of the question that is so obvious now. Why did he not say, for instance, that maybe killing people was a reaction formation against loving them? It is just as legitimate a conclusion and, as a matter of fact, more true for many people.

But to return to the principal idea, this exciting new development in science, this new moment in history. I have a very strong sense of being in the middle of a historical wave. One hundred and fifty years from now, what will the historians say about this age? What was really important? What was going? What was finished? My belief is that much of what makes the headlines is finished, and the growing tip of mankind is what is now growing and will flourish in a hundred or two hundred years, if we manage to endure. Historians will be talking about this movement as the sweep of history, that here, as Whitehead pointed out, when you get a new model, a new paradigm, a new way of perceiving, new definitions of the old words, words which now mean something else, suddenly, you have an illumination, an insight. You can see things in a different way. That, for instance, as one of the consequences generated by what I have been talking about, is flat denial. Empirical, mind you. I am not being pious, or arbitrary, or *a priori,* or wishful. This is an empirical denial of the Freudian contention of a necessary, intrinsic, built-in opposition between the needs of the individual and the needs of society and civilization. It just is not so. We now know something about how to set up the conditions in which the needs of the individual become synergic with, not opposed to, the needs of society, and in which they both work to the same ends. This is an empirical statement, I claim.

Another empirical statement is about the peak experiences. This is the most dramatic and probably the most relevant for this particular audience. We have made studies of peak experiences by asking groups of people and individuals such questions as, What was the most ecstatic moment of your life? Or as one investigator asked, Have you experienced transcendent ecstasy? One might think that in a general population, such questions might get only blank stares. Apparently, the transcendent ecstasies had all been kept private, because there is no way of speaking about them in public. They are sort of embarrassing, shameful, not scientific—which, for many people, is the ultimate sin.

In our investigations of peak experiences, we found many, many triggers, many kinds of experiences that would set them off. Apparently all people, or almost all people, have peak experiences, or ecstasies. The question might be asked in terms of the single, most joyous, happiest, most blissful moment of your whole life. You might ask questions of the kind I asked. How did you feel different about yourself at that time? How did the world look different? What did you feel like? What were your impulses? How did you change if you did? I want to report that the two easiest ways of getting peak experiences (in terms of simple statistics in empirical reports) are through music and through sex. I will push aside sex education, as such discussions are premature—although I am certain that one day we will not giggle over it, but will take it quite seriously and teach children that like music, like love, like insight, like a beautiful meadow, like a cute baby, or whatever, that there are many paths to heaven, and sex is one of them, and music is one of them. These happen to be the easiest ones, the most widespread, and the ones that are easiest to understand.

For our purposes in identifying and studying peak experiences, we can say it is justified to make a list of these kinds of triggers. The list gets so long that it becomes necessary to make generalizations. It looks as if any experience of real excellence, of real perfection, of any moving toward the perfect justice or toward perfect values tends to produce a peak experience. Not always. But this is the generalization I would make for the many kinds of things that we have concentrated on. Remember, I am talking here as a scientist. This doesn't sound like scientific talk, but this is a new kind of science. A dissertation will soon be published which will show that out of this humanistic science has come, I would say, one of the real childbearing improvements since Adam and Eve. It is a dissertation on peak experiences in natural childbirth. And this can be a potent source of peak experiences. We know just how to encourage peak experiences; we know the best way for women to have children in such a fashion that the childbearing mother is apt to have a great and mystical experience, a religious experience if you wish—an illumination, a revelation, an insight. That is what they call it, by the way, in the interviews—to simply become a different kind of person because, in a fair number of peak experiences, there ensues what I have called "the cognition of being."

We must make a new vocabulary for all these untilled, these unworked problems. This "cognition of being" means really the cognition that Plato and Socrates were talking about; almost, you could say, a technology of happiness, of pure excellence, pure truth, pure goodness, and so on. Well, why *not* a technology of joy, of happiness? I must add that this is the only known technique for inducing peak experiences in fathers. It had occurred to us, as my wife and I had first gotten to these surveys in college students, that many triggers were discovered. One of them was that while women talked about peak experiences from having children, men didn't. Now we have a way to teach men also to have peak experiences from childbirth. This means, in a certain condensed sense, being changed, seeing things differently, living in a different world, having different cognitions, in a certain sense some move toward living happily ever after. Now these are data, various paths to mystical experiences. I think that I had better pass them by as they are so numerous.

For our purposes, let's proceed to music in this relation. So far, I have found that these peak experiences are reported from what we might call "classical music." I have not found a peak experience from John Cage or from an Andy Warhol movie, from abstract expressionistic kind of painting, or the like. I just haven't. The peak experience that has reported the great joy, the ecstasy, the visions of another world, or another level of living, have come from classical music—the great classics. Also I must report to you that this melts over, fuses over, into dancing or rhythm. So far as this realm of research is concerned, there really isn't much difference; they melt into each other. I may add even, that when I was talking about music as a path to peak experiences, I included dancing. For me they have already melted together. The rhythmic experience, even the very simple rhythmic experience—the good dancing of a rumba, or the kinds of things that the kids can do with drums: I don't know whether you want to call that music, dancing, rhythm, athletics, or something else. The love for the body, awareness of the body, and a reverence of the body—that kind of thing that gets mixed in there—these are clearly good paths to peak experiences. These in turn are good paths (not guaranteed, but statistically likely to be good paths) to the "cognition of being," to the perceiving of the Platonic essences, the intrinsic values, the ultimate values of being, which in turn is a therapeutic-like help toward both the curing-of-sicknesses kind of therapy and also the growth toward self-actualization, the growth toward full humanness. In other words, peak experiences often have consequences. They can have very, very important consequences. Music and art in a certain sense can do the same; there is a certain overlap. They can do the same there as psychotherapy, if one keeps his goals right, and if one knows just what he is about, and if one is conscious of what he is going toward. We can certainly talk, on the one hand, of the breaking up of symptoms, like the breaking up of clichés, of anxieties, or the like; or on the other hand, we can talk about the development of spontaneity, and of courage, and of Olympian or God-like humor and suchness, sensory awareness, body awareness, and the like.

Far from least, it happens that music and rhythm and dancing are excellent ways of moving toward the discovering of identity. We are built in such a fashion that this kind of trigger, this kind of stimulation, tends to do all kinds of things to our autonomic nervous systems, endocrine glands, to our feelings, and to our emotions. It just does. We just do not know enough about physiology to understand why it does. But it does, and these are unmistakable experiences. It is a little like pain, which is also an unmistakable experience. In experientially empty people, which includes a tragically large proportion of the population, people who do not know what is going on inside themselves and who live by clocks, schedules, rules, laws, hints from the neighbors—other-directed people—this is a way of discovering what the self is like. There are signals from inside, there are voices that yell out, "By gosh this is good, don't ever doubt it!" This is a path, one of the ways that we try to teach self-actualization and the discovery of self. The discovery of identity comes via the impulse voices, via the ability to listen to your own guts, and to their reactions and to what is going on inside of you. This is also an experimental kind of education that, if we had the time to talk about it, would lead us into another parallel educational establishment, another *kind* of school.

Mathematics can be just as beautiful, just as peak-producing as music; of course, there are mathematics teachers who have devoted themselves to preventing this. I had no glimpse of mathematics as a study in aesthetics until I was thirty years old, until I read some books on the subject. So can history, or anthropology (in the sense of learning another culture), social anthropology, or palaeontology, or the study of science. Here again I want to talk data. If one works with great creators, great scientists, the creative scientists, *that* is the way they talk. The picture of the scientist must change. The image of the scientist, which most high school kids have, as one who never smiles, who bleeds embalming fluid rather than blood, and whom the high school girls are horrified by and wouldn't want to marry. "Marry one of those monsters who will do experiments on my babies?" they might think. This conception of scientists is giving way to an understanding of the creative scientist, and the creative scientist lives by peak experiences. He lives for the moments of glory when a problem solves itself, when suddenly through a microscope he sees things in a very different way, the moments of revelation, of illumination, insight, understanding, ecstasy. These are vital for them. Scientists are very, very shy and embarrassed about this. They refuse to talk about this in public. It takes a very, very delicate kind of a midwife to get these things out, but I have gotten them out. They are there, and if one can manage to convince a creative scientist that he is not going to be laughed at for these things, then he will blushingly admit the fact of having a high emotional experience from, for example, the moment in which the crucial correlation turns out right. They just don't talk about it, and as for the usual textbook on how you do science, it is total nonsense.

My point here is that it is possible that if we are conscious enough of what we are doing, that is if we are philosophical enough in the insightful sense too, we may be able to use those experiences that most easily produce ecstasies, that most easily produce revelations, experiences, illumination, bliss, and rapture experiences. We may be able to use them as a model by which to reevaluate history teaching or any other kind of teaching.

Finally, the impression that I want to try to work out—and I would certainly suggest that this is a problem for everyone involved in arts education—is that effective education in music, education in art, education in dancing and rhythm, is intrinsically far closer than the core curriculum to intrinsic education of the kind that I am talking about, of learning one's identity as an essential part of education. If education doesn't do that, it is useless. Education is learning to grow, learning what to grow toward, learning what is good and bad, learning what is desirable and undesirable, learning what to choose and what not to choose. In this realm of intrinsic learning, intrinsic teaching, and intrinsic education I think that the arts, and especially the ones that I have mentioned, are so close to our psychological and biological core, so close to this identity, this biological identity, that rather than think of these courses as a sort of whipped or luxury cream, they must become basic experiences in education. I mean that this kind of education can be a glimpse into the infinite, into ultimate values. This intrinsic education may very well have art education, music education, and dancing education at its core. (I think dancing is the one I would choose first for children. It is the easiest for the two-, three-, or four-year-old children—just plain rhythm.) Such experiences could very well serve as the model, the means by which perhaps we could rescue the rest of the school curriculum from the value-free, value-neutral, goal-less meaninglessness into which it has fallen.

section ii

The beginnings of development

6.

Humanics and genetic engineering

JOSHUA LEDERBERG

With this selection, if not previously, it may occur to the reader that an increasing number of ways of influencing human development are just in the offing and may become possibilities within a few years. To the environmental and social controls, considered in preceding readings, this selection adds the thought of modifying the genetic endowment of germ-cell structure from which the human being grows and which helps to determine future physical and intellectual competencies.

As these concepts are considered, it may be well to bear in mind that the choice to become involved in human and environmental engineering already has been made. Man, consciously or unconsciously, has been tampering with nature's balances for years. Even if he wished to do so at this point, he couldn't quit. For every control instigated, more controls become necessary. So it is that with medical technology more individuals with defective genes survive and the possibilities of passing on the affliction increase. So it is that insecticides or birth control pills solve one problem and create others.

We wonder, what additional human engineering demands and problems will be generated by the ability to fuse four separate human eggs into a single embryo, or by the technique of growing complete organs and perhaps carbon copies of individuals from small fragments cut from them? Chances are increasing that most readers will live to see the possible clinical application of these experimentally tested technological developments and will be faced with the consequent problems.

HUMANICS IS DEFINED in the dictionary as the scientific study of human nature. It tells something of our past traditions that the word is an unfamiliar one; but the subject it describes is inevitably caught up in the recent rush of progress in experimental biology. In particular, dramatic advances in our knowledge of the biochemistry of deoxyribonucleic acid (DNA) and

Reprinted with permission from the *1970 Britannica Yearbook of Science and the Future.* Copyright © 1969 by Encyclopaedia Britannica, Inc. Joshua Lederberg, Department of Genetics, Stanford University School of Medicine.

of its function as the material basis of heredity have provoked much new speculation about the application of this new knowledge to man and his problems. (See *1969 Britannica Yearbook of Science and the Future,* Feature Article: "The Language of Life.") As a result of these advances, we anticipate better tools to mitigate disease, to improve agriculture, and to exploit microorganisms in industry.

We must also visualize, however, the impact of genetic engineering on humanics, which includes the possible modification of human nature toward previously unattainable ideals. Phrases like "genetic programming" or "genetic engineering" may conjure up the Frankensteinian image of a mad scientist or a technocratic dictator pushing the buttons that will control an assembly line of babies produced to order for service as infantrymen or storm troopers or docile subjects. Some may even imagine that their own genes may somehow be subjected to alteration at someone else's command or, alternatively, that they will have unlimited options to create any manner of offspring they wish—perhaps a child who might grow up as an athletic prodigy with an IQ of 350 and a head of hair that automatically shears itself at regular intervals. Actually, our present knowledge of genetic science is not the obvious limiting factor for the furtherance of such aims. Rather, we lack the necessary insight into the essential biochemistry, developmental biology, psychology, and social dynamics of these phenomena. And indeed, were we to gain such insight, genetic engineering would probably be a redundant tool in competition with many other ways of influencing human development and behavior. To avoid the distorted view of genetic engineering that is all too prevalent in contemporary journalism, the topic must be examined within a broader view of man's evolutionary history and of the impact of established institutions on human biology.

UNCONSCIOUS GENETIC ENGINEERING

Genetic engineering has, nevertheless, been an important element in human cultural progress. The beginnings of agriculture depended on the remarkable insight that the seeds of a given plant would beget others like it. Early agricultural man, in his development of crops like Indian corn and wheat, accomplished technical miracles that have still to be surpassed by contemporary plant science. This kind of "biological engineering"—to produce reliable food crops from wild grasses—achieved a phenomenal result without the benefit of profound insight into the mechanism of heredity or the chemistry of DNA. The prescientific domestication of animals such as the dog likewise speaks for an uncanny shrewdness on the part of early man.

We have no way of knowing whether prehistoric man consciously applied similar principles to guiding his own evolution by selective breeding. In many subhuman primates the social hierarchy does give a dominant male privileged access to receptive females during their intervals of maximum fertility. With the development of democratic ideals, however, the very concept of compulsory selective breeding as a method of engineering human improvement has been discredited as a violation of elementary human rights. Nevertheless, the whole social fabric constitutes a pattern of genetic engineering of human qualities more or less consciously intended to prevent deviance from the established norms of a given community. Racial characteristics may just as likely have been conserved by cultural discrimination against deviants and strangers who displayed differences in these obvious features. Other customs, like monogamy, primogeniture, prohibitions against incest, nationalism, war, and commerce have played their part in the de facto policy of genetic engineering of the human species.

Very few new techniques for genetic engineering have been firmly established, although there are many important innovations in early prospect. Genetic analysis has, however, helped to expose the actual practices just summarized, and to point out that they do constitute a pragmatic social policy of human reproduction, whether or not this was arrived at by conscious legislation.

GENETIC DISEASES

The principal utility of genetics in modern medicine is in diagnosis, now applicable to many specific genetic diseases with great precision, mainly by the use of biochemical and of microscopic methods. It is often possible to counsel the parents in a family where a rare disease has cropped up about the prospects of a similar anomaly occurring again in future children. Since many parents will respond to discouraging advice by not taking chances, this kind of genetic counseling is a de facto form of selective breeding. Its principal benefit, however, is intended to promote the integrity of the family and to prevent the conception of children likely to suffer from a serious defect. A by-product of genetic counseling in this situation is to reduce the frequency of defective genes in the next generation.

Because certain deleterious genes can also be detected in the hybrid carrier state, some individuals may use this information in their selection of mates. As yet, we have no reliable statistical information on the subject, but it is doubtful that any significant number of people take genetic factors into account when they fall in love and marry. From a population-genetic point of view, selective mating does not help to eliminate a deleterious gene from the population; it merely postpones the overt occurrence of defective offspring. Since future generations may well be better equipped to repair a genetic defect than we are at the present time, selective mating can hardly be called an imprudent policy.

The genetic diseases to which such considerations apply are each quite rare, but there are enough of them to warrant the spreading practice of genetic diagnosis in order to furnish significant information to a considerable proportion of the population. The average human being carries the equivalent of eight or ten potentially harmful genetic defects, all of which are usually masked in the hybrid condition. Although most of these defects are not now recognizable by biochemical analysis, studies of DNA specificity and of cell fusion are beginning to revolutionize our approach to these problems.

Cell cultures from specimens of blood or from tiny fragments of skin have enhanced the diagnosis of many genetic diseases. More recently, this technique has also been applied to cells obtained from the amniotic fluid that surrounds the developing fetus. By this method the occurrence of a serious genetic disease in a young fetus can be diagnosed and the mother may request a therapeutic abortion so as to avoid bearing a severely crippled or retarded child.

A number of genetic diseases can now be detected prenatally. Of these cystic fibrosis, a metabolic disorder in children, is undoubtedly the most prevalent and, therefore, statistically the most important. Its incidence, however, is too rare to recommend the routine examination of amniotic fluid in every pregnancy. On the other hand, the carrier state for cystic fibrosis can also be determined in the parents, and fetal examination would be indicated if there is already one chance in four that the fetus may be diseased. While the elimination of fetuses having this serious genetic disease may appear to be a negative approach, this procedure should be weighed against the assurance that can be given parents of being able to nurture a child free from disease on future attempts. Eventually, a better understanding of the biochemistry of cystic fibrosis may lead to methods of treatment so effective that the disease would no longer be the serious burden to the young child that it is today.

In many respects, mongolism, or Down's syndrome, is more serious than cystic fibrosis because of its severe mental retardation. Prenatal examination can reveal the extra chromosome that causes the condition. Down's syndrome occurs in one of about 600 births, but certain individuals have a chromosome pattern that predisposes them to a much higher frequency of afflicted progeny. For such mothers, and mothers with pregnancies at advanced ages, a prenatal examination of fetal cells is especially indicated.

Paradoxically, additional conceptions undertaken to compensate for an eliminated fetus will tend to increase the frequency of the deleterious gene in the population. For example, the child with cystic fibrosis was, until recently, not likely to survive until reproductive age and, therefore, did not contribute to the gene pool of the following generation. Also, the diseased child tended to displace a potential sibling whose odds are two in three of being a carrier for the gene and who would eventually contribute to the gene pool. If, however, our objective in this kind of medicine is to alleviate unnecessary human distress, then we should focus our attention on the reduction of the disease, rather than on the elimination of the gene for it. In spite of the obvious natural selection against it, the gene's very capacity to survive in the human population indicates that it might also carry some still unexplained and even beneficial function in human fitness.

SELECTIVE BREEDING

Another characteristic (one hesitates to call it a disease) that can be diagnosed by prenatal examination is the sex of the fetus. Improved determination of fetal sex at an early age, and the development of drugs to induce a voluntary abortion that is essentially indistinguishable from induced menstruation may make individual control of the sex of the offspring technically plausible. The use of abortion for this purpose, however, would probably be repugnant to most people. If there are biases favoring one or the other sex, we should, perhaps, be giving more attention to rectifying a social order that fosters such discrimination.

Germinal choice, which is another approach to selective breeding, has been advocated strongly by Julian Huxley and the late Hermann J. Muller. Their scheme would provide for the banking of sperm from preferred men in cold storage for later voluntary use in artificial insemination. Real problems arise, of course, in the identification of preferred males, even some years posthumously, and in the social environment in which the qualities of one versus another potential sire are publicly touted.

However bizarre these schemes for selective breeding may appear, the present world does exhibit a wide disparity in the number of offspring produced by different parents. In some sense, our other social policies establish the pattern for these discrepancies. Yet, we know too little of human genetics to sustain an informed criticism (or approval!) of that pattern. It is much more difficult not to be alarmed at some examples of negative family planning in relation to parents' ability to provide each child with the parental care that should be his birthright. On the other hand, we have still to devise compulsory schemes that can discourage overbreeding where it demeans a child's rights without at the same time creating an unacceptable invasion of the personal freedoms of the parents.

EXPERIMENTS IN GENETIC INTERVENTION

Let us now consider some of the more speculative proposals for genetic intervention that are founded on experiments with laboratory animals and plants. It is not easy, however, to set clear boundaries for the subject of genetic intervention. Since one could postulate that the right set of genes could forestall the possibility of a disease developing in a person, any disease can then be said to have a genetic aspect. Preventive measures, such as the Sabin vaccine for polio, can be regarded as an artificial replacement of the human genes that are unequal to this one of life's challenges. We do not know, however, whether any living human beings already contain genetic factors for resistance to polio virus. If they did, the comparison of resistant and sensitive individuals would put the genetic aspect of this kind of medicine into sharper focus.

The same point can be made even more vividly by considering the global disease called malnutrition, which is usually regarded as a dietary insufficiency stemming from a lack of appropriate amino acids in the available food. But, because no known human beings have the necessary built-in genes to accomplish the internal synthesis of the required amino acids and vitamins, malnutrition can also be regarded as a pan-human genetic defect. By contrast, most plant species and many microorganisms are well endowed with the necessary genes for the biosynthesis of these materials.

It is not inconceivable that some humans already possess those genes needed for effective internal synthesis of amino acids. This idea, in fact, now appears somewhat less fanciful than it did with the recent discovery that, among the world's adult population, probably only Caucasians usually have the genes needed for the formation of lactase, an enzyme for the digestion of milk sugar. On the other hand, many samples of Negroes and of Orientals tested as adults lacked this capacity and tended to be intolerant of milk.

One conceivable approach to solving the problem of malnutrition would be the attempt to find and selectively breed those individuals whose genetic endowment may possibly enable internal synthesis of amino acids. Or we may solve this genetic deficit by producing proper food and distributing it to those who need it, thus accomplishing the same purposes as selective breeding.

It is clear that the growth of the human brain is retarded by either maternal malnutrition or malnutrition of the newborn, or both. It is also sad to have to report that malnutrition is practiced on a large scale as a central process in the world political system. One does not have to grow babies in bottles, as Aldous Huxley envisaged in *Brave New World,* in order to achieve a separation of human capacities into alphas and gammas. We can merely contrive to feed some mothers and deny others.

The brain, in its growth, must be subject to some explicit regulation from external stimuli. This is an urgent item on the humanicist's agenda. We need powerful tools to deal, on the one hand, with obvious defects that cry out to be corrected and, on the other, with the possible enhancement of human intellectual ability. The closest parallel to this in present practice is the care that physicians take to be sure that pregnant mothers do not suffer from thyroid deficiency.

GENETICS AND TRANSPLANTS

Another approach to the modification of an established genetic makeup is the transplantation of the tissue or organ from another individual. When the indication for such a transplant is a failing heart or kidney, obviously the operation is not a compensation for a genetic defect. The message is clearer, however, when the indication is a metabolically insufficient pancreas—say diabetes, though the primary lesion may be elsewhere—or a congenital deficiency in some other endocrine gland.

Tissue transplantation is still seriously impeded by two factors: the phenomenon of tissue rejection based on genetic incompatibility of different individuals, and the serious difficulty of obtaining viable organs for transplant. Fundamental genetic studies on the determination of the protein structure of antibodies and of tissue antigens may be expected to eliminate the first obstacle. As for organ supply, a thorough understanding of tissue rejection may make it possible to use animal organs for transplant purposes. (See *1969 Britannica Yearbook of Science and the Future*, Feature Article: "New Parts For Old: The Latest Medical Adventure.") One approach that would allow the use of animal organs would be the early inoculation of infants with purified pooled antigens representing the tissue specificities of potential future organ donors.

Transplantation, in the sense of mixing cells of different origin into one organism, can be done experimentally at very early stages of embryological development. Already, as many as four different mouse eggs, representing eight different parents, have been fused to form a single embryo that matured into a single adult mouse. This procedure has great theoretical interest because of its potentiality for incorporating complementary advantages from a variety of different parental strains.

EXPERIMENTS WITH MICROORGANISMS

Except for a calculated choice of parentage, intelligent design plays a limited role in controlling the genetic makeup of an individual. In microorganisms, however, it is now possible to introduce specific new genetic information in a much more controlled fashion. But such experiments still have considerable random components, and usually it is not possible to instruct one particular cell to adopt a specific new genotype. Instead, a large number of cells are exposed to DNA that has been contrived to have the desired characteristics. One out of many cells may incorporate the foreign DNA and with it some new characteristic. The occasional cell that responds in the appropriate fashion can then be separated from the other cells.

The great force of recent work in molecular biology stems from the use of relatively simple experimental materials, such as viruses and bacteria. The direct manipulation of individual genes within the chromosomes in cells of higher organisms, however, presents formidable and possibly insuperable technical difficulties. Nevertheless, we can foresee the use of viruses to mediate the transmission of specific genetic information. This process of viral transduction was first described in 1951 by Norton D. Zinder and Joshua Lederberg for bacteria of the *Salmonella* group.

Contemporary work with animal viruses by a number of other workers now strongly suggests that these viruses may also be capable of introducing genetic information in the cells that they infect. For example, the SV-40 virus of monkeys, which as far as is known is harmless in man, leaves a number of copies of its DNA sequences in the chromosomes of cells infected in tissue culture. This suggests that viral DNA can be engineered and that synthetic viruses can be used for the modification of genetic defects. For example, it should soon be technically feasible to attach the genetic DNA that codes for the enzyme phenylalanine hydroxylase, which functions in the liver of normal men and animals, to the DNA of SV-40 virus. The inoculation of an infant with such a hybrid virus would be expected to alleviate the disease phenylketonuria.

Man has, in fact, been practicing a similar form of genetic engineering for quite some time. When Edward Jenner discovered the vaccination against smallpox, he introduced the use of a variant virus to compensate for a "genetic defect" shared by all mankind; namely, our inherent sluggishness in producing antibodies against the smallpox virus. The projected design for the use of more carefully engineered viruses to generate specific enzymes shows an obvious parallel to this long-established medical procedure.

This approach to genetic engineering also has the advantage that, in all likelihood, the genetic information carried by such viruses is not incorporated in the sex cells for transmission to the next generation. This is a purely empirical observation: to be sure of keeping future options open, this limitation of virogenetic effect to somatic tissues must be carefully verified in every case. At this writing, only one important technical difficulty remains, that of attaching specific segments of DNA from totally unrelated sources. However, enzymes discovered in 1968 for rejoining DNA molecules broken in just one strand are already being used as essential reagents in research.

The theoretical possibility of virogenic attachment to chromosomes and propagation to further generations cannot be completely determined without empirical study. If we do not keep a vigilant lookout on the effects of viruses—whether used for vaccination against disease, for genetic repair, or as infectious agents in our environment—we may be in for some unpleasant surprises. Because the use of viruses for vaccination purposes has not been generally associated with the alarms of "genetic engineering," these agents do not receive the close attention they deserve in view of their biological potentialities. At the very least, viruses used for vaccination should be chemically purified and identified as having only the one desired species of DNA or RNA (ribonucleic acid). This standard has not yet been adopted by the pharmaceutical industry, nor has it been included in the regulations enforced by governments.

The extraordinary specificity of pairing by the two strands of a DNA molecule has opened the way for studying biological specificity, mainly by molecular hybridization. The specific reagent in these experiments is a solution of DNA single strands prepared from reference material. For some purposes, this DNA may be incorporated into a culture medium of solid agar or attached to the surface of filter membranes. When exactly complementary strands of DNA, or sometimes of RNA, are added, conventional double-stranded DNA structures will be re-formed and can be detected by a variety of different methods. Some of these methods are so sensitive that it may be possible to discern even single nucleotide differences between a reference and an unknown in a sample. These procedures will, undoubtedly, be instrumental for the isolation of specific-gene DNA, an objective which has already been achieved to a limited extent. Molecular hybridization also furnishes a method of distinguishing from each other the messenger-RNAs produced by different cells.

VEGETATIVE PROPAGATION

Other advances in cell biology have opened up some additional technical possibilities for the evasion of genetic scrambling that now invariably accompanies sexual reproduction. The propagation of new plants from cuttings is a familiar experience in horticulture. In lower animals such as earthworms, vegetative reproduction is a common occurrence; missing organs can regenerate spontaneously in small fragments cut from the previous individual. One might speculate that deeper insights into the mechanisms of this embryological development could lead to similar phenomena, even in man, but these are remote prospects indeed!

An alternative approach is offered by experiments in frogs, in which the existing nucleus of a fertilized egg was displaced and the egg renucleated with a nucleus from a tissue cell of a mature frog. The purpose of these experiments was to determine whether tissue differentiation was invariably associated with a permanent loss of developmental functions in the cell nucleus. Apparently this is not always true, for some nuclei of adult tissue cells are capable of supporting the total development of a new frog from a renucleated egg. From a genetic point of view, however, the new frog was vegetatively propagated from the mature tissue because it carries exactly the same set of genetic information.

Groups of individuals derived by vegetative propagation and having identical genetic constitutions are called "clones." The prospect of producing genetically homogeneous groups of individuals presents some interesting issues; in addition, it is a way of propagating a genotype already tested in one generation for further trial in a second. We already have a foretaste of the properties of a clone in the behavior of identical twins.

Clonal propagation would afford an otherwise unavailable opportunity for certain humanic experiments, in the same sense that efforts to optimize a child's education are experiments. Without such tests it is unlikely that

we will ever be able to know the extent to which the performance of acknowledged geniuses or athletic stars are manifestations of unusual genetic
endowment.

The technical limitation to human cloning is mainly the much smaller
size of mammalian eggs when compared with the egg of a frog, but, almost
certainly, this is not an insuperable difficulty. There may be, however, other
obstacles based on differences in the biology of the frog egg and that of the
human that are not yet known.

Within the last few years, it has been discovered that tissue cells can
be made to fuse with one another in the presence of certain virus-derived
particles. These cells thus form "vegetative hybrids" that can originate from
such widely distinct species as fish and human. The technique has already
become quite important in the analysis of the genetic functions carried by
different human chromosomes, which can be tested for their ability to
make up for known defects in other animal cells.

Vegetative hybridization and the use of the hybrid cells to renucleate
an egg open the door to another form of genetic engineering—hybrid plants
or animals containing some or many chromosomes from distant species.
Crop improvement is the most obvious area for applying this technique. In
fact, many Soviet workers have made far-reaching claims for the efficacy of
graft-hybridization in plant improvement, but most of these claims defy re-
producibility and credibility. Perhaps for this reason the whole subject has
been virtually ignored by Western geneticists, who may thereby have missed
some kernel of useful innovation. [The concept of fusing plant cells for
breeding purposes has been taken up in recent works by Professor E. C.
Cocking and his associates at the University of Nottingham. See *Nature,*
225:1016 (Mar. 14) 1970.]

THE FUTURE OF GENETIC ENGINEERING

When we approach functions as complex as human intelligence and
sympathy, we must be quite humble about our capacity to unravel the components of heredity and environment. Certainly, there is no gene that can
ensure the ideal development of a child's brain without reference to tender
care and inspired teaching. The paths to intelligence can be deviated at
many points—for example, the child born deaf was for all practical purposes an idiot until we learned the special techniques needed to teach him.
These considerations suggest that the main role of genetic science may be
to sharpen perceptions of how to engineer the environment for the optimum
development of existing genetic types. When we have reached some mastery
of this challenge, we can more reasonably advocate the extension of genetic
engineering beyond the repair of the most obvious and urgent forms of
genetic defect.

IN DEFENSE OF GENETIC ENGINEERING

Humanics, the understanding of human nature, is rightly viewed as the capstone of Western culture. Scientific insight is, however, a challenge to traditional thought and authority in at least two ways. It amplifies the power for good or harm that men can inflict on one another, when we are already on the brink of failure to contain massive aggression. Perhaps even more embarrassingly, it reveals existing flaws in the providence and justice of our social institutions—like the world arrangements that leave so many human beings underfed and uneducated.

Many thoughtful critics have questioned whether we are socially and morally prepared to cope with such newly emerging powers as genetic engineering. Some go so far as to advocate explicit restraints on technological development in this field, a plea that is readily translated into diffidence about financial support for basic biological research. The straw man has even been erected that pictures scientists (but which ones?) as demanding that we put into practice everything that is technologically possible, without regard to the human consequences.

Such absurdities should not require discussion, but insofar as they do, they have a positive answer. The consequences of ignorance are no less frightening, perhaps more unpredictable than those of scientific understanding. When we contemplate large-scale technological applications in any sphere, we need a wide range of scientific knowledge to analyze their consequences. Restraints on research in genetic science might restrain sophisticated genetic engineering, but they will make even more plausible the crude efforts of those who advocate the legalized involuntary sterilization of the "unfit" and deprive us of many urgently needed advances in medicine and in agriculture.

Sharply limited military research would never have uncovered the genetic hazards of radioactive fallout. The euphenic point of view may upset some people who do not know how to handle the responsibility of choice for the quality of their offspring, but our present uninformed choices, like those that lead to global malnutrition and mental retardation for millions of infants, are also a policy. Man may have lived in a paradise of submissive ignorance before he ate from the tree of knowledge, but human civilization began just then and there is no return.

This is not to shrug off the perversion of science. Brute force is the overriding instrument of authority, but the most totalitarian governments will exploit more subtle weapons to secure the peaceful cooperation of their subjects. The "control of the mind" by chemicals is the usual cliché one thinks of here, but Aldous Huxley himself pointed out that the scientific techniques portrayed in *Brave New World* were intended as a parody of existing institutions. Is it less intrusive on a human personality to indoctrinate a child in a given set of religious beliefs than it would be to "program" his genes? (Usually, the answer is "yes"—if the religion is the right one.)

But dictators will not stop at propaganda; they will use genetic engineering too, if they have the wit and if they stay in power long enough. The only answer is to strengthen our democratic institutions, of which public education to make informed critical judgment is the most crucial. We should also minimize the intrusion of government in any aspect of individual reproductive policy. It is incredible to think that, until recently, many states had laws that interfered with the dissemination of information about family planning. It is equally incredible that most states still interfere with the private decision of a mother to abort an unwanted pregnancy.

The self-awareness that characterizes man is part of his unique capacity for cultural evolution. During the past 100,000 years, this has completely overtaken his biological evolution. Biological change during this period is not only much less important than the cultural, but is itself deeply influenced by self-awareness, as illustrated by the rapid differentiation of the races with respect to obvious features as opposed to the deeper elements of humanity. Self-awareness may also impede substantive biological change unless we can learn to assimilate a view of the human future that allows for variety, experimentation, and change. What is quite new is that we are now scientifically aware of evolution and must take on the burden of conscious choice about its future directions.

The most important ethical inference from the fact of human evolution is that we are still perfectible. It is one of the least debatable of human purposes that our posterity should be wiser than we are, and above all for deciding the direction of the species. This principle puts a high premium on preserving the flexibility of decision for future generations, to make the fewest irreversible decisions. It is arguable whether evolutionary commitments are less reversible than cultural ones, but we would still prefer euphenic and somatic modifications to those that committed the whole species to a new genotype. On the other hand, we should not confuse global shifts (for which war is already more pertinent than eugenics) with isolated experiments in genetic engineering, any more than we would confuse global indoctrination with efforts at educational experimentation.

FOR ADDITIONAL READING:

Dobzhansky, T., *Mankind Evolving* (Yale University Press, 1964).

Haynes, R. H., and Hanawalt, P. C. (eds.), "The Molecular Basis of Life," *Readings from the Scientific American* (Freeman, 1968).

Lederberg, Joshua, "Experimental Genetics and Human Evolution," *Beyond Left and Right: Radical Thought for Our Times,* ed. by Richard Kostelanetz (Morrow, 1968).

Lederberg, Joshua, "Orthobiosis: The Perfection of Man," *Nobel Symposium XIV: The Place of Value in a World of Facts* (Wiley Interscience, in press).

Lerner, I. M., *Heredity, Evolution and Society* (Freeman, 1968).

Platt, J. R., "The New Biology and the Shaping of the Future," *The Great Ideas Today 1968* (Encyclopaedia Britannica, 1968).

Ramsey, P., *Fabricated Man: the Ethics of Genetic Control* (Yale, 1970).

Sonneborn, T. M. (ed.), *The Control of Human Heredity and Evolution* (Macmillan, 1965).

AUDIOVISUAL MATERIALS FROM ENCYCLOPAEDIA BRITANNICA EDUCATIONAL CORPORATION:

Films: *DNA: Molecule of Heredity; Gene Action; Laws of Heredity.*

7.

Implications of fetal behavior and environment for adult personalities

LESTER W. SONTAG

For a long time psychologists argued the point of whether a person is what he is because of what he learns or because of his genes. The conclusion, of course, has been that the two factors are mutually deterministic. With the development of the humanistic or existential point of view, a third determinant has been added. This is the individual himself and his ability to influence his own development through choices and decisions.

The research reported by Sontag indicates that this process of mutual determination begins much earlier than has been thought to be possible. The infant at birth appears to be considerably more than a blank page. Maternal emotions as well as maternal physical health may have influenced or taught the neonate to be irritable and even neurotic. Hence, when one speaks of preschool education, he may have to consider fetal sensitivity to stimuli and ways of using this to promote mental health and emotional stability for infants.

Sontag tells us that cardiac lability or stability can be measured and that this may have certain implications for personality develop-

Annals of *The New York Academy of Sciences,* 134:782–786, 1966. Copyright © 1966 by The New York Academy of Sciences; reprinted by permission. Lester W. Sontag, Fels Research Institute, Yellow Springs, Ohio.

This research was supported in part by Research Grant HD-00868 from the National Institutes of Health, United States Public Health Service.

ment. Does it indicate a fetus more receptive to stimuli and presage a greater capability for learning? Certainly, it shows that genetic differences begin to influence response tendencies very early in development. What are the implications for human development and for the concepts of genetic and social engineering discussed in the previous selections?

UNTIL RECENTLY, most *in vivo* studies of the human fetus have been designed to assess through electrocardiographic tracings its state of viability and to predict its survival chances. However, a number of studies, both in laboratory animals and in human beings, have been designed to explore the vulnerability of the fetus to changes in his environment. Environmental changes which have been explored include changes in the mother's emotional state, the introduction of drugs and toxic substances, the use of sounds of different frequencies both on the fetus and as a matter of changing the maternal environment.

Ader and Conklin[1] have demonstrated that pregnant rats fondled for 10 minutes a day during pregnancy produced offspring which at maturity were less "neurotic" than the offspring of continually caged mothers. Lieberman[2] has mimicked emotional stress in mice by the injection of hydrocortisone, epinephrine and norepinephrine and has produced "neurotic" mice. W. R. Thompson[3] has demonstrated that the production by a conflictual situation of a neurosis in pregnant rats resulted in offspring which showed "neurotic" characteristics at adolescence. W. D. Thompson and Sontag[4] have demonstrated that audiogenic seizures induced in pregnant white rats at the ninth and tenth day of pregnancy resulted in offspring which at adolescence exhibited a poorer pattern of maze learning than did controls. In most of these experiments, neurotic behavior was assessed by measurements of frequency of urination and defecation and by open field tests.

The remainder of my paper I shall devote to the work carried on at the Fels Research Institute for the Study of Human Development in the years from 1932 to the present. It was designed to explore the behavior of the human fetus, its developmental progress, individual differences, capabilities, perceptions and responses to stimuli in a normal situation during the last four months of pregnancy. It was designed also to measure certain characteristics of fetal behavior and the environment, as represented by the mother, and its relationship to postnatal behavior and even adolescent and adult behavior, although the extended life span of human beings makes the latter objective an exotic and almost impossibly ambitious one.

FETAL MOVEMENT

Our original work on fetal movement was done on a group of 60 or so house subjects, or "living-in" subjects, and 200 extramural subjects whose fetal activity was measured for a period of two hours a week. During this two-hour period each week, some 60 or 70 samples of heart rate in 10-beat segments were recorded. We started our fetal movement study with an apparatus consisting of four rubber bags sewed into a cloth container, each connected with a tambour and a recording drum. Over this group of rubber bags, which corresponded to the four quadrants of the abdomen, we placed a plaster of Paris cast which had been made especially for the subject and was replaced with a new one each week as the fetus grew. This system was then inflated with air to the pressure of a few millimeters of water. When a movement of the fetus occurred, air in one bag was subjected to increased pressure by a presenting elbow, knee, head or what not, with a corresponding decrease in pressure in another bag. This combination of four bags and four tambours permitted us to rule out the constantly present respiratory movements of the mother. After using this equipment for a time, we began simultaneously having the mother record, by a system of buttons which activated kymograph pens, the periods during which she felt activity. We found the correlation between the mother's recording and the mechanically recorded samples was well above 0.8. Because we wanted access to the abdomen at frequent intervals to make heart rate recordings, we, therefore, eventually discarded the mechanical recording device for fetal activity. We discovered early that there were three differential types of fetal activity: (1) the sharp kicking or punching movement of the extremities which increase steadily from six months to birth; (2) a squirming or writhing slow movement which is at its maximum frequency during the third to fourth month before birth and declines steadily from there on until birth; and (3) a sharp, convulsive movement which others have described as a fetal hiccup or spasm of the diaphragm. Such fetal hiccups occurred in 33 of 48 subjects.

As anyone who has ever concerned himself with the care of pregnant women knows, there is a tremendous individual difference in activity level between different fetuses. It occurs not only as the fetuses of one woman are compared with another, but from one fetus to another in succeeding pregnancies of the same woman. Women say, "This one is not going to be anything like little Mary. She hardly kicked at all. This one is kicking all the time." Such statements are literally almost true.

These differences in fetal activity level appear to be predictive of the degree of activity, restlessness and, sometimes, resistance to handling, etc. of the infants during the first year of life. Richards and Nelson[5] have also found that the active fetuses are more advanced at six months than are the relatively inactive ones as measured by their performance on the Gesell tests. This increased motor development may possibly be the product of greater prenatal activity or it may be another expression of it at a later stage of development. There is also a small but significant correlation between the body type of the newborn infant as expressed as weight over length cubed and the level of activity as measured during the last two months of pregnancy. This finding seems reasonable since calories used in exercise will not be stored as fat.

SOUND

There has been no adequate exploration of the ability of the fetus to perceive sound, and the way it may react to various kinds of sound. In the 1920's a German investigator reported a number of cases of expectant mothers who complained that they could not go to symphony concerts because of the greatly intensified activity level of the babies they were carrying. Another reported a case of an expectant mother who found that the applause of the audience at the symphony caused such extreme fetal activity that it was painful. When a small block of wood is placed over the abdomen of a woman eight months pregnant and a doorbell clapper is permitted to strike at the rate of 120 vibrations per second, there is, in about 90 per cent of cases, an immediate and convulsive response on the part of the fetus. The response is in the form of violent kicking and moving. There is also an increase in heart rate. This increased heart rate occurs even when, in a small percentage of cases, there is no movement response. This startle reflex is, we believe, the same response as is the Moro reflex after birth.

MATERNAL EMOTIONS

One of the early observations we have made seems particularly germane in terms of the animal experimental work which I have described earlier. It is, that severe maternal emotions, during the last trimester of pregnancy at least, do cause an immediate and profound increase in the activity level of the fetus. We were, as a matter of pure fortune, presented with several examples of this situation. In one instance a young woman carrying her first baby, which we had been studying weekly in terms of activity and heart rate level, took refuge at the Fels Institute building one evening because her husband had just suffered a psychotic break and was threatening to kill her. She was terrified, felt alone and did not know where to turn for help. She came into the Institute, and we gave her a bed and room for the night. When she complained after a few minutes conversation that the kicking of her fetus was so violent as to be painful, we proceeded to record the activity level. It was more than ten-fold what it had been in the weekly sessions prior to this incident. Another case came to our attention when a woman we had been studying, lost her husband in an automobile accident. Again, the violence of the activity and the frequency of movement of the fetus increased by a factor of more than ten. During the period of ten years, we managed to collect eight such dramatic incidents, all showing the same phenomena of extreme increase in fetal activity in response to grief, fear and anxiety. Children of such mothers (who suffered their emotional trauma late in pregnancy and not early) showed, of course, no congenital defect. In general, they were, however, irritable, hyperactive, tended to have frequent stools, and three of them had marked feeding problems.

FETAL HEART RATE

Every physician is aware, of course, that there are continuous variations in heart rate during rest in individuals of almost any age, although this variability does tend to decrease with extreme age. A part of this great fluctuation, or lability, is associated with respiration. It is the sinus arrhythmia for respiration. The remainder, however, is not. The degree of this variation from second to second seems to be characteristic of each individual. A boy who has a high lability score at age 6 will also have a high lability score at 16 or 26. Lacey and Lacey[6] of our laboratories have studied such phenomena in a considerable number of children and adults. Lacey and coauthors[7] have studied possible relationships between this physiological variable and certain personality variables. Using three-hour interviews as a basis for rating a variety of personality characteristics, they found that the level of dependency material was much greater in labiles than in stabiles. A sex difference was apparent in their material. Cardiac labile males were more reluctant to depend on love objects, and they had more conflict over dependency than did the stabiles. They were more compulsive, indecisive and introspective. We have no explanation, of course, for these relationships. That these physiological correlates do exist, however, is fascinating. They make the question of what part of the incorporation of life experiences is a matter of the experiences themselves and what part is determined by gene-determined, or prenatally acquired physiological characteristics.

This suggestion that there may be a physiological component of personality or behavior brings to the fore the question of whether this constitutional gene-determined characteristic is really gene-determined or whether it is the result of differences in fetal environment. Differences in cardiac lability may very well be an indicator of the differences in physiological operation which are accountable for a part of the differences in behavior patterns and personality of individuals.

The above findings have led us to become interested in whether large fluctuations in *fetal* heart rate are related to the degree of lability and stability of the heart rate of the *adult*. Unfortunately, the problem is a difficult one for many reasons. To have the same individual and the same data available on him during his eighth fetal month and his twentieth year presents problems. If, then, we compound these problems by the fact that the fetus is an uncooperative research subject and will not rest while we take his heart rate, the magnitude of the problem is obvious. We do have a few preliminary figures which are much more intriguing than conclusive. On 12 fetuses (which are now adults), we have 400 or more short samples of fetal heart rate although not necessarily at rest. By calculating the standard deviation of the heart rate for each fetus from these 10-beat samples, we arrive at a measure of its variability, a measure comparable to a considerable degree to the variability of heart rate measured on these individuals as adults. It is possible, therefore, to make some comparison of the variability of heart rate of these individuals as 8-month fetuses with the resting variability of their heart rates at age 20 years. The scatter diagram of the lability of heart rate of fetuses, plotted against the lability of the heart rate of the individuals as adults, is most interesting. There is a 5:5 and 1:1 distribution. Because the number of cases is so small, a rho of 52 significant at the 0.05 level of confidence is suggestive rather than conclusive in indicating that there is a tendency for cardiac labiles during fetal life to be cardiac labiles in adult life. On the basis of the correlation between physiological variables in the form of cardiac lability-stability and personality variables already described, we are interested, then, in seeing whether certain aspects of personality in adults may be predicted from a constitutional factor measurable during the fetal period.

Another individual difference in autonomic nervous system functions is the degree of cardiac rate response to a stress situation. Lacey and Lacey[6] have found that cardiac response to different kinds of stress in a given individual is comparable. One individual does vary, of course, tremendously from another, however, in the degree of response that he exhibits. Lacey and his coauthors[7] have found that there are also personality correlates; in this instance, there are differences in cognitive style, or ways of thinking and perceiving between strong reactors and weak. In general, these strong and weak cardiac reactors exhibit differences in perception of affect. In picture test situations, the strong reactors tend to attribute emotion or feeling to the human figure and the situations which they are viewing. They also tend to exhibit much more imagination in what they see or what they describe. They project feeling and emotion into the pictures. The low reactors, in addition, show evidence of a much higher degree of emotional and behavioral control in all kinds of situations. They are less likely to act out their emotions than high reactors are.

Fetuses differ in their response to a stress situation. In the instance of the sound stress applied with a door knocker, there was a marked difference between fetuses both in degree of cardiac acceleration and movement. We are currently interested in and are studying the relationship of the magnitude of this response during the eighth and ninth fetal months to responses to stress situations many years after the individual has emerged into the world. I am not in the position to give you any data which I would consider significant at this time. Perhaps, it is worth while, however, to tell you what we are trying to do.

SUMMARY

I have described some variables in the fetus which can be measured without severely disturbing him or damaging him. I have called attention to certain responses the fetus makes to his maternal, or outside, environment. I have indicated that there are some prenatal predictors of early postnatal environment or behavior, and that there very possibly may be predictors of some behavior or personality at a much later age. These observations are necessarily different as is the methodology from that used in the animal experiments quoted, but both are designed to assess the effects of prenatal environment on the behavior of the offspring.

REFERENCES

1. Ader, R. and P. Conklin. 1963. Handling of pregnant rats: Effects on emotionality of their offspring. Science **142**:411–412.
2. Lieberman, M. 1963. Early developmental stress and later behavior. Science **141**:824–825.
3. Thompson, W. R. 1957. Influence of prenatal and maternal anxiety on emotionality of their offspring. Science **142**:411–412.
4. Thompson, W. D., Jr. and L. W. Sontag. 1956. Behavioral effects in the offspring of rats subjected to audiogenic seizure during the gestational period. J. Comp. and Physiol. Psychol. **49**:454–456.
5. Richards, T. W. and V. L. Nelson. 1938. Studies in mental development: II. Analysis of abilities tested at the age of six months by the Gesell Schedule. J. Genet. Psychol. **52**:327–331.
6. Lacey, J. I. and B. C. Lacey. 1958. The relationship of resting autonomic activity to motor impulsivity. Res. Pub. Assoc. Res. Nerv. Ment. Dis. **36**:144–209.
7. Lacey, J. I., J. Kagan, B. C. Lacey and H. A. Moss. 1962. The visceral level: Situational determinants and behavioral correlates of autonomic response patterns. *In* Expression of the Emotions in Man. P. J. Knapp, Ed. International Univ. Press. New York, N.Y.

8.

The biology of behavior

ROGER J. WILLIAMS

Biological individuality is the focus of a stimulating article in which Professor Williams emphasizes the need for an interdisciplinary approach to understanding human development. He believes that psychology will make more progress in explaining behavior when its practitioners join forces with biologists in explaining the predispositions

Saturday Review, 54(No. 5):17–19, January 30, 1971. Copyright 1971 Saturday Review, Inc. Roger J. Williams, Professor of Chemistry, University of Texas at Austin.

the individual inherits and *that are developed prenatally. Even those born with identical genes have different potentials by the time they are born. And the biological individuality becomes more distinct when the genetic streams are different. Unique brain structures and peripheral nervous systems cause the infant and child to pick up different messages.*

Williams' article is particularly pertinent in this book because the editors have a predisposition to highlight what parents, teachers, and child health specialists can do to provide a salutary environment. Williams makes it clear that there are limits, but also that if psychologists would draw some of their data from biologists they would be on the way to discovering specific ways in which the individuality of predispositions might best be directed. Men are not born to be musicians, criminals, or scientists, but if the individuality of babies can be accurately assessed the lives of those babies can be directed more wisely.

This article provides a theoretical backdrop against which many other articles—by Hunt, Gordon, Harlow, Birren and Hess, etc.— might appear in sharper perspective.

THE PREVALENCE of student rebellions throughout the world makes one wonder just how effectively modern education relates to real human problems. To approach the problems of generic man from a biological standpoint may be far too superficial in this scientific age with its tremendous advances in technology; yet, could not the general weakness of human science be the basis for the comment by Robert Frost: "Poets like Shakespeare knew more about psychiatry than any $25-an-hour man"?

Biologically, each member of the human family possesses inborn differences based on his brain structure and on his vast mosaic of endocrine glands—in fact, on every aspect of his physical being. Each of us has a distinctive set of drives—for physical activity, for food, for sexual expression, for power. Each one has his own mind qualities: abilities, ways of thinking, and patterns of mental conditions. Each one has his own emotional setup and his leanings toward music and art in its various forms, including literature. All these leanings are subject to change and development, but there is certainly no mass movement toward uniformity. No one ever "recovers" from the fact that he was born an individual.

When a husband and wife disagree on the temperature of the soup or on the amount of bed coverings, or if their sleep patterns do not jibe, this is evidence of inborn differences in physiology. If one child loves to read or is interested in science and another has strong likings for sports or for art, this is probably due to inborn differences in makeup. If two people disagree about food or drink, they should not disregard the fact that taste and smell reactions often widely differ and are inherited. If we see a person wearing loud clothing without apparent taste, we need to remember, in line with the investigations of Pickford in England, that each individual has a color vision all his own; some may deviate markedly from the pack.

The inborn leanings of Mozart were evident by age three, and he began composing when he was four. Capablanca was already a good chess player—good enough to beat his father—when at age five he played his first game. For many centuries, Indian philosophers have recognized innate individuality, which they explain on the basis of experience in previous incarnations.

Biology has always recognized inborn individuality. If this inborn distinctiveness had not always been the rule in biology, evolution could never have happened. It is a commonplace fact in biology that every living organism needs a heredity and a suitable environment. Unfortunately, in the minds of most intellectuals biological considerations have been pushed aside.

Professor Jerry Hirsch, a psychologist at the University of Illinois, has protested in *Science* that "the opinion makers of two generations have literally excommunicated heredity from the behavioral sciences." This neglect of the study of heredity has effectively produced a wide gap between biology and psychology. Biology deals with living things, and psychology is logically an important phase of biology.

Bernard Rimland, director of the Institute for Child Behavior Research in San Diego, in reviewing my book *You Are Extraordinary* in *American Psychologist,* wrote: "Since between-group differences are commonly a small fraction of the enormous, important, and very interesting within-group (individual) difference, psychology's focus on average values for heterogenous groups represents, as Williams indicates, a chronic case of throwing out the babies with the bath water. 'Throwing out the babies' is bad enough, but we psychologists have the dubious distinction of making this error not only repeatedly but *on purpose."*

Social solidarity exists and social problems are pressing, but we cannot hope to deal with these successfully by considering only generic man, that is, average values for heterogenous groups. We need a better understanding of *men.*

THE basic problem of generic man is how to achieve "life, liberty, and the pursuit of happiness." The writers of our Declaration of Independence were on solid ground, biologically speaking, when they took the position that each human being has inalienable rights and that no one has, by virtue of his imagined "royal blood," the right to rule over another. In their emphasis on mankind as individuals, Jefferson and his co-authors were closer to biological reality than are those of our time who divorce psychology from biology and center their attention on that statistical artifact, the average man.

Because each of us is distinctive, we lean in different directions in achieving life, liberty, and the pursuit of happiness. Happiness may come to individual people in vastly different ways, and so the human problem of achieving life and the pursuit of happiness resolves itself, more than it is comfortable to admit, into a series of highly individual human problems. We need to take this consideration into account in attempting to build an advanced society.

In understanding the scope of human desires, it is worthwhile to consider briefly the problems that real—as opposed to theoretical—people face. These may be grouped under four headings: 1) making a livelihood; 2) maintaining health; 3) getting along with others; and 4) getting along with one's self. These four categories, singly or in combination, cover most of the familiar human problems—marriage and divorce, crime, disease, war, housing, air and water pollution, urban congestion, race relations, poverty, the population explosion, the all-pervading problem of education, and the building of an abundant life.

The importance of approaching the problem of making a livelihood from the individual's standpoint lies in the fact that in our complex society a multitude of ways exist—an estimated 23,000—in which people can make a living. People are not by any means interchangeable parts in society. While some might function well in any one of a large number of capacities, many others might be highly restricted in their capabilities and yet be extremely valuable members of society. The idea that it is all a matter of education and training cannot possibly be squared with the hard biological facts of inborn individuality. This perversion of education perpetuates the banishment of heredity—an ever present biological fact—from our thinking. Fitting together people and jobs is just as real and compelling as fitting shoes to people. People sometimes suffer from ill-fitting shoes; they suffer more often from ill-fitting jobs.

The maintenance of health—both physical and mental—involves individual problems to such a degree that it is difficult to exaggerate their role. Ever since the days of Hippocrates it has been known in a vague way that "different sorts of people have different maladies," but we are only beginning to learn how to sort people on the basis of their inborn individual characteristics. When we have become expert in this area, vast progress will result, particularly in the prevention of metabolic and psychosomatic diseases, i.e., those not resulting from infection. As long as we dodge the biological fact of inborn individuality, we remain relatively impotent in the handling of diseases that arise from within individual constitutions.

The problem of getting along with others is a very broad one, in which individual problems are basic. If husbands and wives and members of the same family always get along well together, we would have some reason to be surprised when squabbles break out within business, religious, or political groups. If all these kinds of squabbles were non-existent, we would have a basis for being surprised at the phenomenon of war.

While self-interest and differences in training are vital factors in these common conflicts, another factor should not be overlooked: the inborn individuality of the participants. There is a mass of evidence to support the thesis that every individual, by virtue of his or her unique brain structure and peripheral nervous system, is psychologically conditionable in a distinctive manner. Thus, a person's unique nervous system picks up distinctive sets of impulses, and because his interpretive apparatus is also unique he learns different things and interprets the world in a distinctive manner. Even if two individuals were to have exactly the same learning opportunities, each would think differently and not quite like anyone else. This is the basis for the observation by Santayana: "Friendship is almost always the union of a part of one mind with another; people are friends in spots." In spite of our attempts to do so, individual minds cannot be compared on a quantitative basis. The minds of Shakespeare and Einstein cannot be weighed one against the other; there were many facets to the minds of each. At birth the two minds were equally blank, but as they matured, each saw, perceived, and paid attention to different aspects of the world around it. Each was conditionable in a unique way.

The recognition of the uniqueness of human minds is essential to human understanding. By developing expertness in this area, psychology will eventually become far more valuable. In an advanced society with a growing population and closer associations, it is obviously essential that we learn better how to get along with each other. When we are unaware of the innate differences that reside within each of us, it becomes very easy to think of one who disagrees with us as a "nitwit" or a "jerk," or perhaps as belonging to the "lunatic fringe." When we appreciate the existence of innate differences, we are far more likely to be understanding and charitable. Strife will not be automatically eliminated, but tensions can be decreased immeasurably.

Individual problems are at the root of the problem of crime. Many years ago, James Devon placed his finger on the crucial point. "There is only one principle in penology that is worth any consideration: It is to find out why a man does wrong and make it not worth his while." The question "Why does a particular man commit crime?" is a cogent one; the question "Why does man turn to crime?" is relatively nonsensical.

Since all human beings are individual by nature, they do not tick in a uniform way nor for the same reasons. Broadly speaking, however, many doubtless turn to crime because society has not provided other outlets for their energies. If we could find a suitable job for every individual, the problem of crime would largely vanish. The problem of crime is thoroughly permeated with individual problems; it cannot be blamed solely on social conditions, because as the studies of Sheldon and Eleanor Glueck have shown, highly respected citizens may come from areas where these conditions are the worst.

Racial relations would ease tremendously if we faced squarely the biological facts of individuality. If we were all educated to *know* that all whites are not the same, that all Negroes do not fit in the same pattern, that all Latins are not identical, that all American Indians are individuals, and that all Jews do not fit a stereotype, it would help us to treat every member of the human race as an individual.

It is no denial of the existence of racial problems to assert that individual problems need to be stressed more than they are. For individual Negroes and individual whites, the pursuit of happiness is by no means a uniform pursuit. Doubtlessly, although there are whites and Negroes who would think they had reached Utopia if they had a decent shelter and were assured three meals a day, this would not satisfy millions of others for whom striving and a sense of accomplishment are paramount. "The Negro problem" or "the white problem"—depending on one's point of view—is shot through with a host of individual problems.

Learning to live with one's self is certainly an individual problem, and will be greatly eased by recognition of inborn individuality. Much unhappiness and many suicides can be traced to misguided desire to be something other than one's self. Each of us as an individual has the problem of finding his way through life as best he can. Knowing one's self as a distinctive individual should be an important goal of education; it will help pave the road each of us travels in his pursuit of happiness.

Why have these facts of individuality not been generally accepted as a backdrop in every consideration of human problems? For one thing, many people, including scholars, like being grandiose and self-inflationary. To make sweeping pronouncements about "man" sounds more impressive than to express more limited concerns. Simplicity, too, has an attractiveness; if life could be made to fit a simple formula, this might be regarded as a happy outcome.

One excuse for excommunicating inheritance from the behavioral sciences for two generations has been the fact that inheritance in mammals is recognized by careful students as being exceedingly complex and difficult to interpret. It is true that some few characteristics may be inherited through the operation of single genes or a few recognizable ones. But other characteristics—those that differ in quantity—are considered to be inherited in obscure and indefinable ways commonly ascribed to multiple genes of indefinite number and character. These multiple-gene characteristics include, to quote the geneticists Snyder and David, "the more deep-seated characters of a race, such as form, yield, intelligence, speed, fertility, strength, development of parts, and so on." To say that a particular characteristic is inherited through the mediation of multiple genes is to admit that we are largely ignorant of how this inheritance comes about.

Recently, some light has been thrown on this problem by experiments carried out in our laboratories. These experiments involved armadillos, which are unusual mammals in that they commonly produce litters of four monozygous ("identical") quadruplets that are necessarily all males or all females.

By making measurements and studying sixteen sets of these animals at birth, it became evident that although they develop from identical genes, they are not identical at all. Organ weights may differ by as much as twofold, the free amino acids in the brain may vary fivefold, and certain hormone levels may vary as much as seven-, sixteen-, or even thirty-twofold. These findings clearly suggest that inheritance comes not by genes alone but by cytoplasmic factors that help govern the size of organs (including endocrine glands) and the cellular makeup of the central nervous system. "Identical" twins are not identical except with respect to the genes in the nucleus of the egg cell from which they developed.

One of the most interesting suggestions arising out of this study is the probability that individual brain structures, which have been known to have "enormous" differences since the investigations of Lashley more than twenty years ago, are made distinctive by the same mechanisms that make for differences in organ weights. The size, number, and distributions of neurons in normal brains vary greatly; this is biologically in line with the uniqueness of human minds. The further elucidation of this type of inheritance should help to focus more attention on heredity.

If this line of thought is valid it makes even more ridiculous the invitation issued by the Ford Foundation to the biological sciences to stay out of the precinct of human behavior. The expression "behavioral science" came into being many years ago as a result of the formulation of the Ford Foundation-supported programs. Biochemistry and genetics, for example, were kept apart from the "scientific activities designed to increase knowledge of factors which influence or determine human conduct."

What can be done to bridge the gap between psychology and biology? More importantly, how can we develop expertise in dealing with the human problems that plague us but at present go unsolved?

A broad, long-range, and practical strategy for learning how to deal more effectively with human problems is to explore, problem by problem, the inborn human characteristics that are pertinent to each one. Differential psychology, for example, needs to be intensified and greatly expanded; this can probably be done most effectively in connection with a series of problem-centered explorations.

Some of the specific problem-areas that require study from the standpoint of how inborn characteristics come into play are: delinquency and crime, alcoholism, drug addiction, unemployability, accident proneness, cancer, heart disease, arthritic disease, mental disease, and, broadest of all, education. Each of these problems could be vastly better understood as the result of interdisciplinary study of the influences of inborn characteristics. Such study would include differential psychology when applicable, combined with extensive and intensive biochemical and physiological examinations, for example, of blood, saliva, urine, and biopsy materials. To expedite these investigations, automated equipment and computer techniques would be used extensively to help interpret the complex data.

It is not likely that these explorations will find that some individuals are born criminals, others alcoholics, etc. Once we recognize the unique leanings that are a part of each of us, we will see how, by adjusting the environment, these leanings can be turned toward ends that are socially constructive. Every inherited factor can be influenced by an appropriate adjustment of the environment. All this should not be made to sound too easy; it may be more difficult than going to the moon, but it will be far more worthwhile.

One of these specific problems—alcoholism—has been of special interest to me. After about twenty-five years of study, I am convinced that inborn biochemical characteristics are basic to this disease, but that expert application of knowledge about cellular nutrition (which is not far off) will make it scientifically possible to prevent the disease completely and to correct the condition if the application of corrective measures is not too long delayed.

Inborn inherited characteristics have a direct bearing on the current revolt against the Establishment. If biology had not been banished from behavioral science, and if students and other intellectuals were well aware of the biological roots of their existence, it would be taken for granted that conformity is not a rule of life.

If all that we human beings inherit is our humanity, then we all should be reaching for the same uniform goal: becoming a thoroughly representative and respectable specimen of Homo sapiens. There is rebellion against this idea. Revolters want to do "their thing." The revolt takes on many forms because many unique individuals are involved.

If non-conformity had a better status in the eyes of the Establishment (and it would have if our thinking were more biologically oriented), exhibitionism would be diminished and the desire of each individual to live his own life could be fostered in a natural way.

Human beings are not carbon copies of one another. Students and others who are in revolt have found this out. Perhaps without fully recognizing it, they are pleading for a recognition of inborn individuality. This is essentially a legitimate plea, but it can take the form of disastrous anarchy. A peaceful means of helping resolve the ideological mess we are in is to recognize heredity by having a happy marriage of biology and behavioral science.

9.

Early malnutrition and human development

Delbert H. Dayton

Research in many disciplines is contributing to the acceleration of knowledge about human development. None of the encouraging discoveries is more stimulating to the editors than research findings regarding that most distinctive feature of man—his brain. Although Dayton's article reports the relationship of mental deficiency and malnutrition, the obverse is that we are simultaneously defining the nutritional needs for optimal development and functioning of the brain.

This article also indicates what the preceding one by Williams pleads for, i.e., the necessity for an interdisciplinary approach to the study of human development. For instance, Dayton implies the need for cultural anthropology, political science, economics, and demography in addition to medical science and biological studies.

The fact that two-thirds of the children in the developing areas of the world are not getting enough to eat, plus the fact that even more are not getting sufficient protein for adequate brain development, causes us to suggest jumping ahead and reading the article by Professor Asimov (selection 60).

THE EFFECTS of malnutrition on human physical growth and mental development are of great concern today not only in less affluent countries of the world but also in the United States. However, while many studies on malnutrition have been carried out in various parts of the world, there is still a great lack of knowledge regarding the importance of proper nutrition to specific aspects of growth and development.

Investigators continue to search for knowledge of the critical developmental periods during which malnutrition produces organic change. If such change *is* produced by nutritional deficits, however, there are still the questions of whether it is reversible or permanent and of whether or not it alters the affected child's functional capacity. Studies are needed not only to answer such questions about nutritional effects but also to answer questions about the physical, biological, and sociocultural factors that also influence growth and development and are intimately related to nutrition.

One study that promises to produce important information is currently being carried out in Guatemala among matched groups of children from

Children, 16(No.6):210–217, November–December, 1969. Delbert H. Dayton, Research Associate, Growth and Development Branch, National Institute of Child Health and Human Development.

three rural villages where extreme malnutrition is prevalent. These children will be studied closely from birth until they are 7 years old. In each village, newborns will be assigned to one of the two groups. The children in one group will live on the customary diet of the people in the area; the children in the other group, matched with the first on many important variables, are being provided a nutritious supplement. The comparison of the two groups of children as they grow older will provide important data not available from cross-sectional studies. Multifocused and interdisciplinary, the Guatemalan study involves the behavioral as well as the biologic sciences.

In the United States, two nutrition surveys are being supported by the Department of Health, Education, and Welfare (HEW), one through the Public Health Service under the direction of Arnold Schaefer, chief of HEW's nutrition program, and the other through a Children's Bureau research grant under the direction of George M. Owen, associate professor of pediatrics at Ohio State University. Although neither of these studies has been completed, their preliminary data indicate that malnutrition among certain groups of children also exists in the United States. The problem in the United States differs in cause and degree from that in less affluent countries and so requires different methods for solution, but the basic questions needing to be answered about the effects of malnutrition on growth and development of children are the same. New or improved nutrition programs will need to be organized wherever malnutrition exists, but these will be most useful if they are designed not only to serve the needs of malnourished people, but also to establish a baseline of information from which their success or failure can be measured. Evaluative methods built into such programs could help answer many remaining questions about the specific effects of malnutrition.

For many years there has been controversy among biomedical scientists regarding the effects of a woman's nutritional status on the product of conception. Until the Second World War, it was generally believed that the health status and nutritional status of women during pregnancy were of minor importance to fetal development. The fetus was considered to be a parasite that could obtain all it needed from even a nutritionally deficient mother. However, this assumption began to be questioned after the war when analyses were made of the records of malnourished women in Holland[1] and other parts of Europe[2, 3] who gave birth during periods of extreme wartime starvation. In Holland, the median birth weight of the babies born in these periods was 240 grams less than the birth weight of prewar babies, and birth length was also less, but the decline in birth length between the prewar and wartime periods was much less than in birth weight. Others studies have shown varying decreases in birth weights between the prewar and postwar periods, but the weights remained within the normal range for full-term newborns.

Further information on the effects of maternal nutrition on fetal development is needed to determine whether a small difference in birth weight makes a difference in the child's prenatal and postnatal development and functioning. Studies in this area are especially important since maternal malnutrition is known to be associated with increased rates of morbidity during pregnancy and of premature delivery. However, a cause-and-effect relationship between maternal malnutrition and either morbidity or prematurity has not been established. Many other factors that might also be contributing to these phenomena exist in areas where malnutrition is endemic.

In studies of maternal malnutrition, it is important to distinguish between an acute, sudden onset of malnutrition of a specific duration in a population—as in a war—and the type of chronic malnutrition that exists in developing countries. Evidence is increasing that the nutritional experiences of the potential mother before conception may also be extremely important to subsequent intrauterine growth. This means that where malnutrition occurs in critical periods of development, such as adolescence, future generations may be affected.

Various studies have shown differences in birth weights according to socioeconomic status within the same ethnic group. Their results are complicated by sample bias caused by the inclusion of hospital patients or the inclusion or exclusion of premature infants. However, in most studies of Europeans and North Americans, mean birth weights are about 3,300 grams, whereas mean birth weights in other populations are nearer 3,000 grams.[4] Because of the wide variation in normal birth weights within any one group, such differences are difficult to assess. Better knowledge of body composition and stores of nutrients within the bodies of the children in these two groups would be helpful.

Some studies have shown that breast-fed infants from areas in various parts of the world have patterns of growth during the first 6 months of life very similar to well-nourished infants in North America.[5] Many studies in developing countries also suggest that growth progresses satisfactorily during the first 4 to 6 months of life while the child is breast feeding and the mother's milk supply is adequate. But growth normally progresses rapidly in infants, and after 6 months, or even sooner, breast milk alone may become inadequate to sustain a child even when the mother's milk production is maintained. Where the mother's milk is not supplemented with other foods, the growth patterns of breast-fed children begin to diverge from the North American standards. Studies have shown that even though growth velocity normally slows down at a later age, the child may never be able to catch up to the original growth curve.

Small size per se is not what matters to the health of the child, but what may go with it—possible changes in metabolic pathways, body composition, and ultimate functional ability. If such changes do occur, research is needed to determine the most critical periods for growth failure and whether changes that occur in these periods are reversible. In many developing countries, it is not uncommon for breast feeding to continue throughout the first 18 to 24 months of life and supplementation of the diet with solid foods to be inadequate and begun late. If the supply of maternal milk is insufficient or if the mother is unable to nurse, the life of the infant is greatly jeopardized, for inadequate substitution of other food may result in serious protein malnutrition and poor hygienic conditions may result in fatal infection from contaminated, prepared formulas. This underscores the great importance of a good supply of breast milk for such infants—a supply which seems to be related to the nutritional status in the mother. In the United States where formulas are extremely popular, insufficient breast milk supplies and unsanitary feeding conditions are not such a great problem. But mothers need to be made fully aware of infants' nutritional needs during the early months when growth and development proceed rapidly. Children in certain poverty-stricken groups of the United States appear to have the same nutritional problems at the age of weaning as children in developing countries.

A composite picture of the growth patterns in some 400 male children from 1 month to 78 months of age in rural Guatemala is shown in the [accompanying] graph. A similar pattern has also been found in a sample

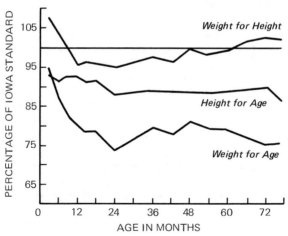

IOWA HEIGHT AND WEIGHT STANDARDS
400 RURAL GUATEMALAN MALE
PRESCHOOL CHILDREN—1967

of female children of the same age and background. The diets of these children were significantly deficient in calories, protein, riboflavin, and vitamin A.[6] The straight horizontal line at 100 percent in the graph represents the mean weight for age, height for age, and weight for height of children studied in Iowa, known among nutritionists as the Iowa growth standards.[7] Birth weights are not available from the Guatemala study. The graph shows that both weight and height for age in Guatemala fall below the Iowa standards throughout all ages, but the deficit is very small in the first few months of life. But when the child's weight is considered in relation to his height, regardless of the standard for his age, the Guatemalan children follow the Iowa standards more closely. However, the Guatemalan children are very short, which may be a result of malnutrition. Therefore, when their weight is considered even in relation to such a substandard height, they still show a weight deficit from the latter part of their first year until they are about 42 months old.

This graph brings out the marked importance of the second year of life in demonstrating growth deficits. At this age, the child is still dependent upon others to supply his nutrients and cannot fend for himself. He is affected by food taboos and cultural patterns that dictate what his family considers to be proper food for him. He is constantly exposed to infectious agents, especially when he lives under poor hygienic conditions. And if a second child comes along at this time, he loses the maternal milk supply that may be acting as the sole source of protein in a meager diet. This is the age when the classic picture of severe protein malnutrition (kwashiorkor) frequently becomes evident.

MENTAL DEVELOPMENT

There is a great deal of concern today over the possible effects of malnutrition on mental development. This can readily be understood in view of the great numbers of children in the world who are malnourished and who, therefore, may not only fail to achieve optimal physical growth, but may be unable to realize their full potential for mental maturation.

Studies of animals have shown that the effects of malnutrition on the nervous system and total body growth are dependent upon the time, duration, and the severity of the nutritional deficit.[8] Throughout the life cycle there is an orderly development of body tissues. Certain tissues seem to have a higher priority for development at particular times of life during which they are more vulnerable to the insult of malnutrition. The level of functioning of the endocrine system may also affect growth patterns modified by malnutrition.

Today tissue growth can be measured indirectly by determining the number of cells within a given organ. Since the amount of desoxyribonucleic acid (DNA) within the nucleus of a cell is constant for any given species,[9] the total number of cells can be calculated by measuring the total amount of DNA within an organ.

Studies of animals have indicated that growth in all organs occurs in three phases: (1) hyperplasia, during which the number of cells increases; (2) hyperplasia and hypertrophy, during which the number of cells continues to increase and the size of the individual cells also increases; and (3) hypertrophy, where growth occurs only by increase in cell size.[10] These studies suggest that during the phase of hyperplasia, malnutrition can interfere with cell division, resulting in fewer cells in the brain, which seems to be a permanent effect, whereas malnutrition during the phase of hypertrophy results in a smaller than normal cell size, which can be corrected by providing adequate nutrition.[11] Therefore, the nutritional status during the phase of hyperplasia, in the early periods of nervous system development, would seem to be exceedingly critical.

In humans the greatest growth spurt for the brain occurs during the fetal period. By the end of the first year of life, the brain has assumed approximately 70 percent of its adult weight, and by the end of the second year its growth is almost complete. Studies of the human brain have shown a very rapid increase in DNA content toward the end of the period of gestation; the increase slows down after birth but continues until the child is 5 or 6 months of age.[12] These findings suggest that cell division in the brain normally occurs during gestation and the early part of the first year of life. Markedly fewer cells (less DNA) were found in the brains of a small sample of children who died of malnutrition during the first year of life than in the brains of a sample of well-nourished children who died in accidents.[12] It is not known whether this represents irreversible change or how severe the nutritional deprivation must be to show these effects. But, the studies demonstrate the importance of gestation and early infancy in nervous system development.

VALIDATION NEEDED

These results must be validated in larger studies. Furthermore, such biochemical studies of malnourished children need to be coupled with detailed information about the mothers' pregnancies, the severity and duration of the malnutrition and the periods of gestation and early life in which it occurred, and the health and nutritional status of the mother. Such studies also need to be related to the level of the child's later mental functioning. Past studies of intellectual development in malnourished children have shown significant differences on mental tests between malnourished children and better nourished children in control groups.

For example, Stoch and Smythe,[13, 14] in Capetown, South Africa, compared a group of children so severely malnourished as to be marasmic with a control group matched for age and sex. Both groups represented children from the lower socioeconomic level. After an 11-year followup during which the diets of the experimental group were improved, the group that had been severely malnourished continued to show significantly lower results than the control group on physical measurements (height, weight, and head circumference) and on various intelligence tests.

Differences were especially significant in visual-motor ability and pattern perception, when measured by the new South African Individual Scale. Because of inadequate dietary information during the later part of the study, these deficits cannot be explained on the basis of early malnutrition alone. Moreover, differences in the social environment of the two groups were variables that could also be responsible for part of the difference found on mental tests. However, the smaller head circumference in the malnourished group, suggests that a stunting of brain growth may have resulted from malnutrition during the period when brain growth is normally rapid.

In Guatemala, Klein[15] compared a rehabilitated group of severely malnourished children with a similar group of children who had never manifested overt signs of severe malnutrition. He demonstrated differences between these groups on a battery of psychological tests in items involving short-term memory.

Cravioto,[16] using Gesell's methods, studied a group of 20 Guatemalan infants and preschool children who had recuperated from severe protein malnutrition, following some of them 6½ months. These children scored lower than a control group of children, matched for age and ethnic background, who had never manifested signs of severe malnutrition. As the children grew older, the differences between the two groups became less marked in the areas of adaptive, motor, language, and personal-social behavior, except for those who suffered malnutrition very early in life. Infants who had recovered from severe malnutrition before they were 6 months old continued to show deficits throughout the study. These studies also suggest that early malnutrition during the period of rapid brain growth might produce permanent mental deficits.

In a later study of rural Guatemalan children from 6 to 11 years of age, Cravioto correlated stature with neuro-integrative function.[17] Ranking the children by height for age, he selected one group from the quartile including the shortest for age and another from the quartile including the tallest for age. All the children were from the same rural village and of the same ethnic background. The children from the lower quartile for height produced a greater number of errors on intersensory testing, but these differences diminished with increasing age. However, these studies do not provide evidence that malnutrition alone was responsible for the differences in intersensory testing since social impoverishment may also have been a factor. A similar study of a group of upper class urban children, also in Guatemala, did not demonstrate such differences associated with stature.

Further studies of mental development in malnourished children as measured by psychological tests are needed. At present, almost all available information comes from cross-sectional studies of children and very little from longitudinal studies that follow the same children over an extended period of time. Without information from longitudinal studies, it is difficult to prove a cause-and-effect relationship between nutrition and mental development. Many factors other than nutritional status can affect a child's mental functioning—parent-child relationships, parental expectations, intellectual stimulation, infectious diseases, parental intelligence, sociocultural patterns, and other genetic and environmental factors. The longitudinal approach to research is also necessary to determine the periods of life when mental development is most vulnerable to malnutrition, the degree and duration of malnutrition required to produce functional change, and whether or not such change is reversible.

NUTRITIONAL ASSESSMENT

Growth retardation and various clinical syndromes resulting from malnutrition in animals and man have been described in the professional literature for many years. In 1931, Cicely Williams first described the syndrome now called kwashiorkor when she was working in the part of Africa then called the Gold Coast (now Ghana). Although kwashiorkor involves multiple nutritional deficiencies, the major cause is an extremely inadequate intake of protein foods. Dr. Williams not only described the main clinical features of kwashiorkor, a condition that if unchecked leads to marasmus and eventual death, but she also produced cures by feeding milk to children suffering from it, thereby showing that this was a disease of malnutrition.

Surveys to determine the prevalence of protein-calorie malnutrition followed in Africa,[18] Central America,[19] Brazil,[20] and other parts of the world. Their findings suggest that perhaps two-thirds of the children in developing areas of the world are not obtaining enough to eat. This does not mean that these children are all suffering from kwashiorkor. On the contrary, probably only 5 to 10 percent at any given point in time can be shown to exhibit this severe form of malnutrition. But it would not be unrealistic to state that at least 50 to 75 percent of the children in the developing countries have a degree of malnutrition that has caused physical growth failure as evaluated by height and weight data and assessment of bone development. Nutritional problems in the United States, though less extensive, do exist.

An assessment of the nutritional status of a population, including identification of deficiencies, is essential for sound social and economic planning. As a first step in such an assessment, it is important to find out what kind of food is available to the population, how food is distributed between different socioeconomic groups, and how and what the patterns of consumption are in these groups. A review of morbidity and mortality data will identify the groups within the population that are at high risk of malnutrition. Dietary surveys of individuals or families in a selected sample of these groups can provide much pertinent information. Clinical nutritional examinations, anthropometric studies, and bone X-rays can provide information on deficits in health and in physical development, while biochemical studies can aid in evaluating nutritional status and in determining recent nutrient intake.

In studies of bone maturation, radiographs taken of the hand, to determine the cortical thickness of the second metacarpal bone, and of the wrist, to identify the order and timing of appearance of ossification centers, have shown significant differences between well-nourished populations and poorly nourished populations.

Biochemical determinations in population surveys permit assessment of inadequate protein intake for the total population. At present, however, these biochemical tools are incapable of identifying protein deficiency in an individual child until shortly before the onset of overt kwashiorkor. This is because there is a wide range of normal values among individuals and also because the homeostatic mechanisms of the body compensate for nutritional deficits until the point at which the internal equilibrium is overwhelmed and biochemical disease results.[21] Therefore, still more sensitive tests are needed for the evaluation of individual nutritional status.

At present, in assessing the nutritional status of an individual child, the guide most frequently used is evaluation of height and weight over a period of time and comparison of this pattern of growth with previously established growth standards based on a well-nourished sample. Any marked variation from an established growth pattern over a period of time suggests the need to evaluate the child further to determine the cause, including in the evaluation an assessment of nutritional intake, biochemical determinations, and general health status.

Although clinical signs of malnutrition have been used to assess nutritional status, it has been found in Guatemala that these signs do not occur in the preschool child with sufficient frequency to be of great value.[22] They are of greatest evidence in the very severe cases where no doubt about the existence of malnutrition is any longer possible. In the less severe stages of malnutrition, they are not as frequently found. Moreover, some of the early signs of malnutrition are not specific to malnutrition alone and interpretation of these signs must always be made with the aid of biochemical, anthropometric, and dietary information.

The effect of infectious disease on the malnourished child is also an important consideration in an overall assessment of nutritional status. Full-blown kwashiorkor is frequently triggered by an infectious episode in a child who is living in a state of precarious nutritional balance. When this precarious balance is upset by the added insult of an infectious process, the child can no longer compensate for the chronic nutritional deficits. Moreover, in children with such a precarious nutritional balance, the common childhood diseases like measles and chickenpox bring markedly increased mortality and morbidity. Thus, the synergism, or interplay, between nutrition and infection[23] complicates any prediction regarding the development of the child caught in a complex net of nutritional deficits, poor hygienic conditions, inadequate medical care, and sociocultural patterns that tend to perpetuate such problems.

SOME SOLUTIONS

The most obvious solution to the problem of malnutrition would seem to be to provide food. But this is a markedly oversimplified solution for such a complex problem. There is, of course, real reason to be concerned about food shortages in many parts of the world. Attempts have been made in the past to provide surplus food from the more prosperous countries to feed the hungry in less prosperous areas. However, such surpluses are dwindling and are not presently adequate to feed all the hungry people in the world. In addition, there is the problem of high costs of transporting such foodstuffs for great distances, losses due to spoilage, and destruction by pests and rodents in transit and in storage. At best, supplying food from other countries is a temporary solution to an increasingly serious problem. Ultimately, it becomes essential for supplemental food supplies to be produced in the areas in which they are consumed. But this measure, of course, does not solve the problem of malnutrition in prosperous countries like our own where nutritious foods are abundant.

In the prosperous industrial nations, foods containing protein of high biological value come primarily from animal sources. Since abundant animal protein products are not available in developing countries, mixtures of plant proteins are being investigated as possible substitutes. Various mixtures of plant proteins of high biological value have already been utilized in some parts of the world. Seafood products are also being investigated as a source of needed protein. It will take time to evaluate the adequacy of such dietary supplements for inducing acceptable growth and development in infants and young children.

It has long been known that if a food supplement is to be successful in nourishing a malnourished population, it must be acceptable to the people for whom it is intended. Changing food fads and habits even in malnourished populations is extremely difficult. Therefore, nutrition education is of the utmost importance to any nutrition program, whether in the United States or in other countries. Economic problems also have to be reckoned with as high cost food supplements could not be purchased by low-income families, the greatest victims of malnutrition.

Malnutrition is now recognized as a major factor in childhood morbidity and mortality, as well as growth failure, wherever poverty exists. However, any attack on this problem to be successful must also include an attack on related sociocultural problems, especially the problem of psychosocial deprivation in early life. Dynamic nutritional programs are certainly needed both in our own country and in other countries. But the search for more knowledge about malnutrition and its effects must go on if malnutrition is to be prevented and corrected. Information gained from investigations in developing countries, as in the Guatemalan studies, have implications for the improvement of nutritional status as important for children in the United States as for children elsewhere.

REFERENCES

1. Smith, C. A.: Effects of maternal undernutrition upon the newborn infant in Holland (1944–45). *Journal of Pediatrics,* March 1947.
2. Antonov, A. N.: Children born during the seige of Leningrad in 1942. *Journal of Pediatrics,* March 1947.
3. McCance, R. A.; Widdowson, E. M.; Dean, R. F. A.: Studies of undernutrition, Wuppertal, 1946–49. Special Report Series No. 275. Medical Research Council, London, England. 1951.
4. World Health Organization: Nutrition in pregnancy and lactation: report of a WHO expert committee. Technical Report Series No. 302. Geneva, Switzerland. 1965.
5. Jackson, R. L.: Effects of malnutrition on growth of the preschool child. National Academy of Sciences, National Research Council, Washington, D.C. 1966.
6. Canosa, Cipriano A.: Nutrition, physical growth and mental development. Advisory Committee on Medical Research, Pan American Health Organization, Washington, D.C. 1968.
7. Nelson, W. E. (ed.): Textbook of pediatrics. W. B. Saunders & Co., Philadelphia, Pa. 1964.
8. Widdowson, E. M.; McCance, R. A.: The effect of finite periods of undernutrition at different ages on the composition and subsequent development of the rat. *Proceedings of the Royal Society of London, B.* Vol. 158, 1963.
9. Enesco, M.; LeBlond, C. P.: Increase in cell number as a factor in the growth of the organs and tissues of the young male rat. *Journal of Embryology and Experimental Morphology,* December 1962.
10. Winick, M.; Noble, A.: Quantitative changes in DNA, RNA, and protein during prenatal and postnatal growth in the rat. *Developmental Biology,* December 1965.
11. ———: Cellular response in rats during malnutrition at various ages. *Journal of Nutrition,* July 1966.
12. Winick, M.: Changes in nucleic acid and protein content of the human brain during growth. *Pediatric Research,* September 1968.
13. Stoch, M. B.; Smythe, P. M.: Does undernutrition during infancy inhibit brain growth and subsequent intellectual development? *Archives of Disease in Childhood,* December 1963.
14. ———: Undernutrition during infancy and subsequent brain growth and intellectual development. *In* Malnutrition, learning and behavior. (N. S. Scrimshaw and J. E. Gordon, eds.) M.I.T. Press, Cambridge, Mass. 1968.
15. Klein, R. E.; Gilbert, O.: Malnutrition and intellectual development. Paper presented at the XI Inter-American Congress of Psychology, Mexico City, Mexico. 1967. (Unpublished.)
16. Cravioto, J.; Robles, B.: Evolution of adaptive and motor behavior during

rehabilitation from kwashiorkor. *American Journal of Orthopsychiatry,* April 1965.

17. Cravioto, J.; DeLicarie, E. R.; Birth, H. G.: Nutrition, growth, and neurointegrative development: an experimental and ecologic study. Supplement to *Pediatrics,* Vol. 38, 1966 (No. 2, pt. II).

18. Brock, J. F.; Autret, M.: Kwashiorkor in Africa. World Health Organization, Geneva, Switzerland. WHO Monograph Series No. 8. 1952.

19. Autret, M.; Behar, M.: Sindrome pluricarencial infantil (kwashiorkor) and its prevention in Central America. Food and Agriculture Organization of the United Nations, Rome, Italy. FAO Nutritional Series No. 13. 1954.

20. Waterlow, J. C.; Vergara, A.: Protein malnutrition in Brazil. Food and Agriculture Organization of the United Nations, Rome, Italy. FAO Nutritional Studies No. 14. 1956.

21. Arroyave, G.: Biochemical evaluation of nutritional status in man. *Federation Proceedings* (Supplement No. 7), March 1961, pt. III.

22. Dayton, Delbert: Unpublished data.

23. Scrimshaw, N. S.; Guzman, M. A.; Gordon, J. E.: Nutrition and infection field study in Guatemalan villages, 1959–64. *Archives of Environmental Health,* May 1967.

section iii

Principles of development

10.

Educational relevance and Jensen's conclusions

Nicholas Anastasiow

Psychologists were shaken, in 1969, by Arthur R. Jensen's carefully summarizing the results of thorough, mediocre, and superficial studies of the relative contribution of heredity and environment to intellectual development. He concluded that heredity was preponderant. A few experts agreed, but . . . many were vehemently opposed to the findings and their implications—especially those implications which had to do with the intellectual potential of blacks and those which were related to early childhood education. The psychological disturbance began with Jensen's article in the 1969 winter issue of Harvard Educational Review. *It has continued there but has spread to other journals, to conventions, and to class discussions.*

Jensen's article is the longest (123 pages) ever presented in the Harvard Educational Review, *so we sought an article that would fairly represent the author and also present some of the points of dissension. We believe that the article by Anastasiow does precisely that.*

We endorse, enthusiastically, Anastasiow's assertion that the real issue is not heredity versus environment but how environment can be used to maximize the potential which heredity provides. Jensen, in a footnote, states that while IQ may not change much because of early education, more positive statements can be made about self-confidence, motivation, and attitudes toward school. And with this, the reader might again examine Otto's article (selection 4) on how little of our potential is used.

Probably nothing on today's educational scene has created more attention and controversy than Arthur R. Jensen's *Harvard Educational Review* article of last winter and the discussions by Jerome Kagan, J. McV. Hunt, J. F. Crow, Carl Bereiter, David Elkind, Lee Cronbach, and W. F. Brazziel published in the spring issue. National news media gave the original article wide coverage, with focus on specific sections, stimulating a wide variety of

Phi Delta Kappan, 51:32–35, September, 1969. Nicholas Anastasiow, Director, Institute for Child Study, Indiana University.

continuing reaction. Diverse though the responses may be, remarkably similar issues keep cropping up. I shall review these recurrent themes.

It is generally agreed that Jensen's article exhibits breadth of scholarship, that it makes a contribution to scholarly dialogue, and that there is a genetic factor in intelligence. There has been general disagreement about two of Jensen's conclusions, those two which have been most widely quoted:

1. "That genetic factors are strongly implicated in the average Negrowhite intelligence difference. The preponderance of evidence is, in my [Jensen's] opinion, less consistent with a strictly environmental hypothesis than with a genetic hypothesis, which, of course, does not exclude the influence of environment or its interrelation with genetic factors."[1]

2. [That] compensatory education has been tried and it apparently has failed."[2]

Several of the *Review* discussants have also raised questions as to conclusions Jensen draws from the data of his research and that of other research he reports, and there has been criticism of his failure to include consideration of the findings of other pertinent studies, particularly in the area of socialization and early child growth and development.

In the main, Jensen discusses intelligence, how it is measured, its correlates, and its hereditability. He reviews a wide range of research studies in genetics, intelligence testing, and psychology, and draws the conclusion that attempts to raise intelligence are fruitless. He concludes not only that there are genetic differences between individuals but that there are genetic differences in intelligence between whites and Negroes. Further, he says that specific aptitudes should be identified and school curriculum and techniques should be designed to teach to these aptitudes.

Jensen argues that the "environmentalists" have misled us in regard to how much environment can modify intelligence. He bases his argument on a series of earlier research studies in which he and his students worked extensively with white, Negro, and Mexican-American students. These studies appear to be well executed and controlled. They suggest that, while there are social class differences in children's performances of complex tasks, there do not seem to be the same kinds of differences among social classes on associative learning tasks.

In general, the discussants in the spring issue of the *Review* agree with the need to recognize special abilities and aptitudes, and consider Jensen's scholarship of high caliber. However, they do not all agree when Jensen attributes the difference in intellectual functions of the lower-class child (particularly the Negro) not to the psycho-socio-cultural deprivation hypothesis so ably prepared by Hunt[3] but to basic genetic factors. Jensen suggests that about 80 percent of intelligence can be accounted for by genetics alone. Crow appears to agree. Cronbach[4] raises some question about this figure. And there are newer conceptions of genetics not discussed by Jensen which would set this limit nearer 50–60 percent.

What is troubling about Jensen's hypothesis of racial differences in I.Q. is that he appears to seek truth and make known his findings, yet seems to close off alternative hypotheses to explain the data. At the same time, he asks us to consider the tenability of an older hypothesis of racial differences in I.Q. which his data, to this reviewer, fail to support. Equally ironic is the fact that some of his severest critics in the news media appear to be closed to the hypothesis he suggests. Rather than analyze data and offer alternative interpretations, they condemn Jensen. Neither approach will serve science and education.

To support his hypothesis of racial differences in I.Q., Jensen draws upon data from several areas, one of which consists of studies of genetic influence on height and weight. To Jensen, these suggest racial and genetic limitations. As Cronbach indicates in his discussion, Jensen is on weak ground here. Height and weight can be modified and are not under purely genetic control, as an earlier study by Greulich[5] of Japanese-Americans and their Japanese cousins strongly documents.

Greulich's studies controlled for genetic factors and found marked differences in height, weight, and chest expansion in favor of the California subjects who came from the same gene pool as the comparison group, but whose dietetic, climatic, and other environmental conditions were more conducive to optimum development. Thus supposed racial traits proved modifiable by environmental conditions.

Jensen dismisses the environmental-influence-on-intelligence point of view rather lightly, although he does mention some studies. He questions it by stating that "disadvantaged children are not reared in anything like the degree of sensory and motor deprivation that characterizes, say, the children of the Skeels study."[6] *However,* the breadth of studies by Spitz, Bowlby, Anna Freud, Skodak and Skeels, and Skeels and Heinicke[7] on the effects of deprivation, separation, and adoption have well demonstrated the effects of physical, emotional, perceptual, and environmental conditions on intellectual functioning and adult academic attainments.

Perhaps, in working with 5-year-olds in California, Jensen has not seen the effects of lack of stimulation on the 2–5-month-old infant. There is, however, ample evidence reported by reputable research psychologists to support the fact that there are marked conditions of economic and social and psychological lacks among the poor of this nation.

The issue of environment versus heredity was ably handled by Anastasi and Foley[8] years ago as an interaction phenomenon. As Piaget and Inhelder[9] suggest, mental development is influenced by maturation or organic growth, the role of exercise and acquired experience, social interaction and transmission, and an internal mechanism of equilibration. Knowledge, to Piaget and Inhelder, is derived from action; thus the culture, the socialization processes and techniques used to train the child, greatly influence what we measure on an I.Q. test. If Jensen's otherwise excellent article has a major weakness, it is in its naive conception of growth and development and the critical area of the socialization process on the intellectual functioning of the child. For example, both physical and language development appear globally undifferentiated in the young child and are progressively differentiated through learning and experience. As Elkind[10] states in his review, the Piagetian view is that intelligence develops through experience.

The paradox of Jensen's article is that it contains one of the clearest descriptions of what is required for school success as schools now exist, then states a faulty assumption with respect to the way children acquire skills that lead to school success. Let's look at Jensen's excellent paragraph:

> Our thinking almost always takes as granted such features as beginning formal instruction at the same age for all children (universally between ages five and six), instruction of children in groups, keeping the same groups together in lock-step fashion through the first several years of schooling, and an active-passive, showing-seeing, telling-listening relationship between teacher and pupils. Satisfactory learning occurs under these conditions only when children come to school with certain prerequisite abilities and skills: an attention span long enough to encompass the teacher's utterances and demonstrations, the ability to comprehend verbal utterances and to grasp relationships between things and their symbolic representations, the ability to inhibit large-muscle activity and engage in covert "mental" activity, to repeat instruction to oneself, to persist in a task until a self-determined standard is attained—in short, the ability to engage in what might be called self-instructional activities, without which group instruction alone remains ineffectual.[11]

Children of middle-class homes have been prepared to meet these conditions and are carefully trained to be able to function within the school situation, as shown by Sears, Maccoby and Levin, Loevinger, and Schaeffer.[12] In the majority of cases, children of lower-class homes have not received such training (see Hess and Shipman[13]). When the lower-class child begins school, he is usually required to act as if he has already mastered the necessary prerequisites for verbally oriented group instruction, though in fact he has not because the socialization process—particularly of the Negro—has not so prepared him. Hess and Shipman, Anastasi, Hertzig, Birch, Thomas and Mendez,[14] and others have shown in comparisons of lower-class mothers with middle-class mothers marked differences in what is taught and how it is taught. What is taught by the lower-class mother appears to be nonverbal cognitive systems which may reflect intellectual functionings that our typical intelligence tests do not measure. However, as McNeill[15] states, in our schools verbal facility is usually measured by the most peripheral aspects of language; phonology and morphology are taken as signs of intelligence. Kagan[16] also suggests that the deprived or poverty child has not had the necessary early stimulation which with the middle-class child begins as early as 3–6 months.

The issue of Negro-white intellectual differences is often argued without taking into account those very early child trainings which Piaget[17] and Hunt[18] regard as crucial. Isolated from the main stream of America, many poverty mothers have not been provided with the necessary techniques to maximize their children's intellectual potential.

The Negro is frequently compared disparagingly, as Jensen infers, with European immigrants who have been assimilated into the culture and are functioning successfully within it, acquiring power and prestige positions. The analogy is a gross fallacy, because it fails to take account of two relevant facts: 1) European immigrants were usually motivated toward the same kind of success as white Americans and brought with them a predominantly verbally oriented culture. 2) The immigrant's child, once he mastered the outward manifestations of middle-class acceptability in speech and dress, could not be stigmatized as to ethnic origin and had access to the middle- and upper-class prestige positions. No matter how accurate a Negro's speech, how skillfully he masters the formalities of middle-class attitudinal and value systems, he is still unable to melt into the culture because of his color. Unfortunately, teaching to individual differences will not assure adult success until we cast aside the Neanderthal notion that skin color is related to intelligence. Guskin's[19] recent work is a case in point. Teachers listening to tape recordings of speech by Negro children purportedly reading their own compositions rated them lower than white children who read the same passages.

Jensen does, however, present some very reasonable suggestions for beginning instruction with poverty children. He reviews his own research and that of Lesser, Fifer, and Clark[20] to demonstrate different patterns of ability among ethnic groups which may not be related to social class. If the deprived child uses different modes of thought, we should teach to those modes, Jensen suggests. There is a difference, however, between Jensen's position that there is a limited number of skills that can be taught to poverty children and conclusions that can be drawn from research with lower-class children. Jensen feels that most school skills can be taught and acquired by associative learning, which he calls Level I learning. He appears to imply that racial lower-class groups are so different from others as to preclude their developing abstract reasoning and conceptual thinking (Level II learning). Apparently, he believes that the lower-class minority has failed with these tasks and cannot be expected to master them. Other learning theorists postulate that styles or modes of thought do not preclude problem solving. Rather, they believe that how a child is taught abstract reasoning and problem-solving skills should vary, depending upon the child's strengths or skill profiles. Jensen seems to want to close the door that it has taken a decade of special educators and modern curriculum personnel in the Dewey,[21] Taba[22] tradition to open. That is, the major question is not why a child can't function now but how we can provide him with an educational program so that he can. Therefore, although Jensen agrees that early education programs have not focused on the relevant tasks, his conclusion that they have failed and will fail does not logically follow from his discussion. Both Hunt[23] and Kagan[24] point out that early education programs have not been developed adequately for assessment to be valid at this time.

Many compensatory education programs have been based upon what has been successful with the "task-oriented" middle-class child. We are only beginning to find out what are appropriate interventions for the deprived child. In addition, the compensatory programs have been built too often upon the weakest of the middle-class preschool models, which deal largely with drill and practice techniques and total group activities rather than individual child opportunities to explore, manipulate, and deal with the environment. Maturation of functions demands different modes of transaction with the child, and learning requires reward, reinforcement, and tasks near the child's current level of functioning.[25] Our teaching procedures must come to match the competencies and the level of development the child brings with the requirements of the task to be learned. To do this takes time and careful analysis of the learning task and the stage of the child's development. As Tyler[26] long ago pointed out, it often takes teachers three years to be able to perform the teaching procedures that an innovative program intends to implement.

If there are weaknesses in these programs (and there undoubtedly are), they may well reside in our techniques of training teachers to meet marked individual and subcultural differences and our lack of stronger in-service training programs. Until we are more successful in preparing teachers, we will not identify those components of instruction that enable the child to develop the multiplicity of intellectual competencies available at birth regardless of what the ultimate capacity may be.

Jensen could have assisted us greatly by establishing what the real issue for educators is. It is *not* one of heredity versus environment; it is concerned with discovering what kind of environmental stimulations are necessary to reach the potential of what is inherited. We must adopt a more dynamic approach to intelligence and mental development than that presented by Jensen.

Piaget and Inhelder[27] state it beautifully: "It may even seem that effective dynamic factors provide the key to all mental development and that in the last analysis it is the need to grow, to assert oneself, to look, to be admired that constitutes the motive force of intelligence, as well as behavior in its totality and its increasing complexity."

REFERENCES

1. Arthur R. Jensen, "How Much Can We Boost I.Q. and Scholastic Achievement?," *Harvard Educational Review*, Winter, 1969, p. 82.

2. *Ibid.,* p. 2.
3. J. McVicker Hunt, *Intelligence and Experience.* New York: Ronald Press, 1961.
4. Lee Cronbach, "Heredity, Environment, and Educational Policy," *Harvard Educational Review,* Spring, 1969, pp. 338–47.
5. William W. Greulich, "A Comparison of the Physical Growth and Development of American-born and Native Japanese Children," *American Journal of Physical Anthropology,* December, 1957, pp. 489–516.
6. Jensen, *op. cit.,* p. 61.
7. ᵃ Rene Spitz, "Hospitalism: An Inquiry into the Genesis of Psychiatric Conditions in Early Childhood," *Psychoanalytic Studies of the Child.* New York: International Universities Press, 1945, p. 53–74.
   ᵇ John Bowlby, Mary Arnsworth, Mary Boston, and Dina Rosenbluth, "The Effects of Mother-Child Separation," *British Journal of Medical Psychology,* Part 4, 1956, pp. 211–47.
   ᶜ Anna Freud, *Infants Without Families.* New York: International Universities Press, 1944.
   ᵈ Marie Skodak and Harold M. Skeels, "A Final Follow-up Study of One Hundred Adopted Children," *Journal of Genetic Psychology,* September, 1949, pp. 85–125.
   ᵉ Harold M. Skeels, *Adult Status of Children with Contrasting Early Life Experiences: A Follow-up Study,* Monograph of the Society for Research in Child Development, Serial No. 105, 1966.
   ᶠ Christoph M. Heinicke, "Some Effects of Separating Two-Year-Old Children from Their Parents," *Human Relations,* May, 1956, pp. 106–76.
8. Anne Anastasi, and John Foley, "Proposed Reorientation in the Heredity-Environment Controversy," *Psychological Review,* May, 1948, pp. 239–49.
9. Jean Piaget and Barbel Inhelder, *The Psychology of the Child.* New York: Basic Books, 1969.
10. David Elkind, "Piagetian and Psychometric Conceptions of Intelligence," *Harvard Educational Review,* Spring, 1969, pp. 319–37.
11. Jensen, *op. cit.,* p. 10.
12. ᵃ Robert R. Sears, Eleanor E. Maccoby, and Harry Levin, *Patterns of Child Rearing.* Evanston, Ill.: Row, Peterson, 1957.
   ᵇ Jane Loevinger, "On the Proportional Contributions of Differences in Nature and Nurture to Differences in Intelligence," *Psychological Bulletin,* December, 1943, pp. 725–56.
   ᶜ Earl S. Schaeffer, "A Circumplex Model for Maternal Behavior," *Journal of Abnormal Social Psychology,* Volume 59, 1959, pp. 226–36.
13. Robert D. Hess and Virginia C. Shipman, "Early Experiences and the Socialization of Cognitive Modes in Children," *Child Development,* December, 1965, pp. 869–86.
14. ᵃ *Ibid.*
   ᵇ Anne Anastasi, *Differential Psychology,* 3rd ed. New York: Macmillan, 1958.
   ᶜ Margaret E. Hertzig, Herbert Birch, Alexander Thomas, and Olga Aran Mendez, *Class and Ethnic Differences in the Responsiveness of Preschool Children to Cognitive Demands,* Monograph of the Society for Research in Child Development, Serial No. 117, 1968.
15. David McNeill, "The Development of Language," ERIC, Document No. ED021218, 1968.
16. Jerome Kagan, "Inadequate Evidence and Illogical Conclusions," *Harvard Educational Review,* Spring, 1969, pp. 224–77.

17. Jean Piaget, *The Origins of Intelligence in Children* (trans. by Margaret Cook). New York: International Universities Press, 1952.
18. Hunt, *op. cit.*
19. Judith Guskin, "Current Approaches to the Study of Language Behavior and Some Recent Research on Mental Retardation," mimeographed, 1968.
20. Gerald Lesser, Gordon Fifer, and Donald Clark, *Mental Abilities of Children from Different Social-class and Cultural Groups,* Monograph of the Society for Research in Child Development, Serial No. 102, 1965.
21. John Dewey, *How We Think,* rev. ed. Boston: Heath, 1933.
22. Hilda Taba, *Teaching Strategies and Cognitive Functioning in Elementary School Children,* Cooperative Research Project No. 2404. San Francisco: San Francisco State College, 1966.
23. J. McVicker Hunt, "Has Compensatory Education Failed? Has It Been Attempted?," *Harvard Educational Review,* Spring, 1969, pp. 278–300.
24. Kagan, *op. cit.*
25. Robert M. Gagné. "The Acquisition of Knowledge," *Psychological Review,* July, 1962, pp. 355–65.
26. Ralph Tyler, *Appraising and Recording Students' Progress.* New York: Harper & Brothers, 1942.
27. Piaget and Inhelder, *op. cit.*

11.

The developmental point of view with special reference to the principle of reciprocal neuromotor interweaving

LOUISE BATES AMES
FRANCES L. ILG

This article by Ames and Ilg is one of those whose wealth of relevant content merits reading and re-reading. The editors were helped in their perusal and comprehension by some understanding of the principle of developmental tasks formulated by Havighurst.* Such tasks are identified with a certain period of life. Successful achievement of each as it comes leads to happiness and to success with later tasks. That is, one must learn to talk before he can learn to get along with age mates and to do this before he can learn an appropriate sex role. Tasks and stages of development are sequential.

The Journal of Genetic Psychology, 105:195–209, 1964. Louise Bates Ames and Frances L. Ilg, Gesell Institute of Child Development, Yale University.
* Robert J. Havighurst, 1952, *Developmental Tasks and Education,* New York:Longmans, Green and Co., Inc.

As Ames and Ilg point out, neural development happens in a cephalocaudal (head to foot) and central-peripheral (inside to outside) progression. If something interferes it is often necessary to begin over again and to retrain in proper sequence. Body management and physical therapy exercises are conducted in accord with this principle.

It is important to realize that because of individual differences, the age level and behavior correlates described may not occur precisely as indicated even though they can be expected to happen in the anticipated sequence. It would be unwise, for one example among many, to generalize and to state unequivocally that all three-year-olds should be conforming and cooperative and to feel that one's child was not normal if he were still rigid, domineering, and demanding at thirty-six months.

A. INTRODUCTION

Behavior, like physical structure, has shape and pattern, and also like physical structure it grows through a series of patterned, predictable changes. The developmental point of view in child psychology has concerned itself with the study of those growth patterns that appear to characterize the growing human organism from the time of conception at least through adolescence. It holds, as Gesell has commented (2, p. 313), that "environmental factors support, inflect, and specify but they do not engender the basic forms and sequences of ontogenesis."

Investigators who work within the developmental frame of reference are concerned with three main aspects of behavior, and in this order: (*a*) common and characteristic age changes in behavior that appear to be shared by most growing human organisms; (*b*) individuality characteristics that uniquely and consistently characterize each individual human organism; and (*c*) environmental factors and the ways in which they can affect the organism, with reference to its age and individuality characteristics. The present paper discusses some of the basic principles that appear to lie behind the patterned changes in behavior that occur in infancy and childhood.

The chief principle that underlies the developmental point of view is the one named above: that behavior in virtually any field of human activity proceeds in a patterned lawful manner through stages that, though they may differ in their manner of expression and in their timing, are consistent in basic structure and sequence from one organism to another.

More specifically, we may name two principles: the *principle of developmental direction* and the *principle of reciprocal neuromotor interweaving.*

1. Developmental Direction

The principle of developmental direction recognizes that the action system of the infant does not increase symmetrically like an expanding balloon, but is subject to the far-reaching consequences of the biological factor of anterior-posterior differentiation. That is, the development of behavior abilities in the human organism proceeds in a cephalocaudad direction—from the head end to the foot end of the body. Thus the human infant in the first year of life gains reasonably adequate control of eyes, head, upper trunk, and arms long before he can effectively control his lower trunk and his legs.

Furthermore, just as neuromotor organization proceeds from head to foot in the direction of the longitudinal axis; so it tends to proceed from the central to peripheral segments. There is progressive advance of motor control from the larger fundamental muscles to the smaller muscles that execute the more refined movements. Thus during the earlier periods of development the arms and also the legs tend to react as wholes, the impulses arising mainly from the shoulder and from the pelvic girdles. With advancing maturity, mobility asserts itself at the elbow and wrist joints and at the knee and ankle joints. Forearm, foreleg, hand, and foot show specific segmental activity. Because the proximo-distal trends overlap with the cephalocaudal trends, independent activity of the distal segments becomes apparent in the upper extremities before it is evident in the lower extremities.

In the development of prehension there is not only a proximo-distal but also an ulnar-radial shift. The ulnar side of the hand is used effectively in grasping long before the radial side is used. This fact means that poking with the index finger and precise pincer prehension do not occur in the average infant until somewhere around 40 weeks of age, even though he may have been able to grasp objects crudely with the outer side of his hand long before this.

All of these laws of development as applied to human behavior have been recognized for a relatively long time and are described fully by Gesell and others in various publications (2, 3, 5, 6, 9, 10). Less familiar is the *principle of reciprocal neuromotor interweaving* (1) with which the present paper is concerned.

2. Reciprocal Neuromotor Interweaving

The principle of reciprocal interweaving, when applied at a simple motor level, implies neurologically an intricate cross-stitching or involuted interlacing that organizes opposing muscle systems into reciprocal and increasingly mature relationships. Functionally, such a process results in a progressive spiral kind of reincorporation of sequential forms of behavior. Flexion and extension are the most fundamental components of muscular movement. The inhibition of one set of muscles while the opposing muscles are in excitation is a condition for effective movement. Reciprocal innervation is a mode of coordination, a physiological mechanism.

In the ontogenesis of the neuromotor system a complicated integration must likewise be achieved between antagonistic muscles. Appropriate structures for subserving inhibition must be progressively provided. There is a mode of growth that asserts itself in a developmental fluctuation of dominance in flexors *versus* extensors and also in unilateral and cross-lateral *versus* bilateral muscle groups.

More simply stated, it seems possible to identify (in any growing behavior) paired but opposed types of response that occur alternately, now one and now the other in repeated alternation, until the behavior has reached its final or complete stage. In practical everyday life, one of these two opposed types of response is likely to be thought of as immature or less desirable; the other, as mature and more desirable. When patterns of human behavior were first being identified and described, it was believed by some that behavior in the human infant and child developed in a straightline manner, being first immature and then gradually more mature. Careful observation, however, indicated that development was far more complex. Instead of the immature type of response dropping out completely once and for all and, with increasing age, being replaced by the more mature, it appeared that type of response alternated between less and more mature.

However, this was not simply a matter of an infant going back to exactly the same earlier type of immature behavior, but rather it was as though the path of development spiralled upward from left to right (but always upward) stressing now the less mature and now the more mature side of the spiral.

a. Prone Progression. This principle of development is perhaps most clearly expressed in the first year of life, as the infant develops the ability to crawl, to creep, to stand, and to walk. We have identified 22 stages which the normal infant customarily goes through as he lies prone (6). We note that, first, arms and legs are flexed; at a later stage they are extended; at a still later stage they are again flexed; still later they are extended; and so on repeatedly until finally the infant stands and walks erect.

The most conspicuous alternations in creeping behavior are the alternations of predominant flexion and predominant extension of the arms and of the legs. (See Figure 1.) However, we may note also, as the patterns of prone progression unfold, an alternation of abduction and adduction of both arm and leg movements, and also of bilateral and unilateral movements.

Because the adult as a rule places no special value judgment on either flexor or extensor posturings, it is relatively easy for him to observe the patterned alternation of flexor and extensor stages objectively. For the most part, people do not believe that the child assumes these postures because of something that somebody has done or in response to other environmental stimuli. As the child grows older—and the kinds of behavior that characterize the succeeding age levels may be (and usually are) considered as good or bad by the culture—it becomes, for many, less easy to see the child's behavior as coming from within and occurring in response to internal-growth stimuli and more easy to consider that somebody has caused it. We cannot always prove that the behavior of concern is not externally caused, though we favor internal growth stimuli as the source.

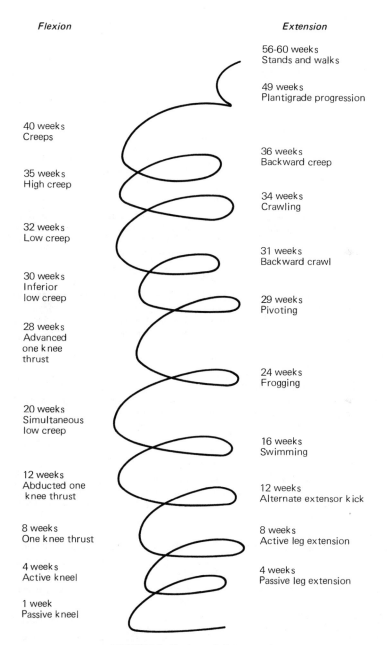

FIGURE 1. Reciprocal interweaving

TABLE 1. COMPARISON OF SPONTANEOUS SUPINE AND PRONE LEG POSTURES OF
THE HUMAN INFANT*

Supine	Prone
1 Week	
Bilateral flexion in external rotation. Legs passive.	Bilateral flexion, nearly under trunk. Legs passive.
4 Weeks	
Bilateral flexion, less passive. One leg flexes and extends.	Bilateral flexion, less passive. One leg flexes and extends.
8 Weeks	
Like 4 weeks but less active. More bilateral extension in slight outward rotation.	Like 4 weeks but less active. More bilateral extension in slight outward rotation, feet raised slightly from supporting surface.
12 Weeks	
Bilateral flexion with outward rotation and some extension at hips, feet invert. Legs flex, feet in step position, bilateral.	Legs extend in outward rotation with extension at hips. Bilateral. Move in a unilateral backward-upward kick or unilateral knee thrust.
16 Weeks	
Bilateral extension, back arches. Bilateral flexion in abduction, outward rotation at hips. Bilateral flexion, knees together, soles on platform; or unilateral posture, one foot on opposite knee.	Bilateral upward extension, back arches. Bilateral flexion in abduction, outward rotation. Unilateral forward knee thrust.
20 Weeks	
Legs flex up toward trunk, knees together. Jerky flexion and extension of one or both legs.	Legs flex up toward (under) trunk, knees together. Jerky flexion and extension of one or both legs.
24 Weeks	
Bilateral frogging, external rotation.	Bilateral frogging, external rotation.
28 Weeks	
Foot to knee, or both legs flexed upward in external rotation, or both extend upward at right angles to trunk.	One knee thrust, or both legs extend.

* The mean—normative—age for independent standing is 56 weeks; for independent walking, it is about 62 weeks.

TABLE 1—*Continued*

Supine	Prone

32 Weeks

Like 28 weeks, but predominantly in bilateral extension in line with trunk. A transition age.	Pivoting. Inferior low creep position. Some bilateral extension, slightly frogged. Legs extend bilaterally. A transition age.

36 Weeks

Legs extend bilaterally, rather close together, feet straight. Legs flex up bilaterally. Legs flex, feet in step position.	Legs extend bilaterally, or maintain bilateral flexion when child is in creep position.

40 Weeks

50 per cent of infants have legs predominantly in bilateral extension. Others have legs flexed, feet straight, in step position.	Both legs flex as child maintains creep position or creeps. Feet straight.

44 Weeks

Legs extend in line with trunk, wider apart. Feet evert. Foot to knee. Legs flex, feet in step position; or one leg extends, one flexes.	Creeps one step with one leg flexed and one extended, one knee and one foot contacting supporting surface, or may creep with both legs flexed.

48 Weeks

Legs extend, feet evert, legs wide apart. Legs frog loosely (i.e., maintain external rotation), feet evert.	All fours, both legs extended, feet everted, weight on hands and feet. Legs at right angles to trunk.

52 Weeks

Legs extend, feet straight, legs wide apart; or legs extend, one foot straight, one everted.	Upright posture; legs extend in line with trunk, wide apart, feet straight.

We should like to demonstrate that the successive stages of prone behavior (at least) do not occur primarily in response to environmental stimuli —that is, the child does not assume various postures because, as he lies prone, he is trying to reach some desired stimulus object. Our evidence comes—by means of cinemanalysis (7)—from a careful comparison of typical postures in prone and supine positions. As the child lies on his back, with no stimulus object or goal or reasonable likelihood of progressing, he has been observed to assume posturings that correspond almost identically (with respect to timing of flexion, extension, unilaterality, bilaterality and the like) with the postures assumed by the prone infant. Table 1 compares characteristic prone and supine postures at succeeding age levels.

The alternating stages of flexion and extension that we see in prone progression do not as a rule concern the parent and, for the most part, knowledge of them is largely of theoretical importance.

b. Handedness. For handedness, the preceding statement is not true. There has been much discussion in the past (in both the scientific and in the popular literature) as to whether the adults should try to change a child's handedness, especially in instances when the child seems to prefer his left hand. Current opinion is that it is probably best not to interfere drastically in the matter, but rather to allow the child to use his preferred hand, especially when the preference is marked. Our own findings support this policy of nonintervention.

Careful observation of children who, as they grow older, showed marked and consistent preference for their right hands, has revealed the fact that establishment of handedness seems to be one of the many areas for which we can identify a principle of reciprocal interweaving at work.

Thus, as Figure 2 and the material below illustrate, even a child who (for all intents and purposes) is strongly and completely right handed does, in infancy at least and often for some months or years beyond, alternate in hand preference. In a typically right-handed child [see (8)] we have observed alternations as follows:

Around 16 to 20 Weeks

When first hand contact with objects occurs, this contact may be with the left hand, possibly because a right-handed infant may still be showing remnants of a typically right-tonic-neck reflex, which extends the right arm and brings the fisted left hand (because of left-arm flexion) closest to an object which is presented to the child.

24 Weeks

After the tonic-neck reflex wanes, around 24 weeks, most right-handed children seem to go through a brief bilateral stage.

28 to 32 Weeks

A period of transfer of objects. Infants use hands alternately. However one hand is used at a time, the right most, though left hand has its turn.

32 to 36 Weeks

A second period of bilaterality.

40 to 44 Weeks

A strong unilateral, right-handed period.

48 Weeks

Unilateral and in many a left-handed period.

52 to 56 Weeks

Right handedness prevails.

18 Months

In many, a period of unilateral use of the nondominant (left) hand.

2 Years

Right handedness in most, and in some it appears to be established at this age. (In others, further periods of bilaterality and left handedness continue to alternate with right handedness.)

2½ Years

Bilateral behavior in many.

3 Years

Unilateral right handedness.

If nature is working out something so complex, it seems obvious that, in all probability, best results will be obtained if parents do not interfere with the child's natural expression of handedness other than, perhaps, to present objects nearest to his right hand. And, if the path that leads toward eventual dominance of the right hand is so complex and intricate (even in potentially fully right-handed children), obviously it is even more complex and intricate in children who seem more naturally endowed with ambidexterity.

Though many parents exhibit a strong tendency to influence and to determine handedness in their children, some are able to remain fairly objective and noninterfering and are able to observe the interweaving of the various types of handedness response (right, left and ambidextrous) with some degree of neutrality, realizing that the tendency to respond in one or the other of these ways does come largely from within.

c. Ages of Equilibrium and Disequilibrium. When the two strands of behavior that are interweaving are tendencies to equilibrium and disequilibrium of response, it is difficult for most parents to remain objective and it is natural for them to seek an "environmental" explanation of behavior. The "good" child is suddenly "bad." Something, parents say to themselves, must have caused the bad behavior.

Nevertheless, the marked similarity in behavior changes with age that are observed in many children has led us to believe that forces of reciprocal interweaving may play a vital part even in an area as global as the total way a child responds to the world about him.

We have earlier observed (9) that a child's behavior at any given age seems to consist of more than the sum of the things he is able to do. Behavior at any given age seems almost to have an individuality of its own, reflecting the stage of growth that the child has reached. There are some ages that, in the majority of children, seem to be characterized by a general equilibrium, an easy adaptation to environmental factors and the demands of daily living.

Other ages are just the opposite and seem characterized by a general

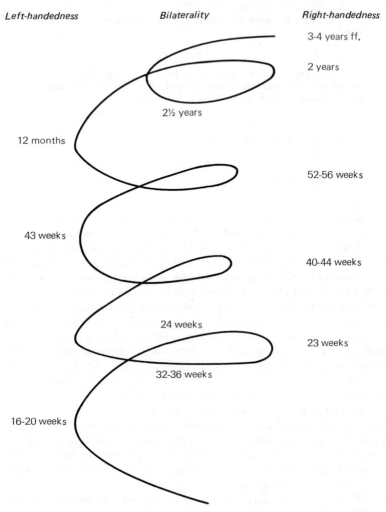

FIGURE 2. *Typical age changes in handedness in a right-handed child*

disequilibrium. At such ages all areas of living may be affected and the child may have trouble with eating, sleeping, response to other people, and to life in general.

Though such alternations or interweavings of ages of equilibrium and disequilibrium may be observed even in infancy, we have not as yet worked out their course in final detail. However, from 18 months through 5½ to 6 years (a period when understanding of what is going on within the child is

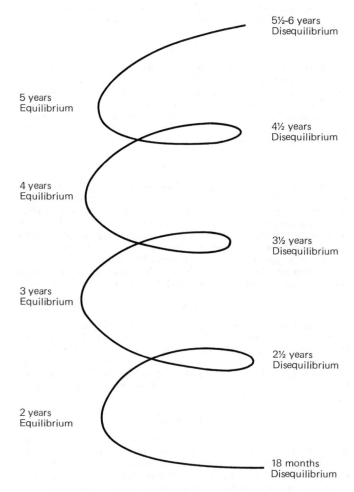

5½-6 years
Disequilibrium

5 years
Equilibrium

4½ years
Disequilibrium

4 years
Equilibrium

3½ years
Disequilibrium

3 years
Equilibrium

2½ years
Disequilibrium

2 years
Equilibrium

18 months
Disequilibrium

FIGURE 3. Ages of equilibrium and disequilibrium

most important for parent and specialist), we can chart these alternations clearly, as Figure 3 shows. Briefly described, age expectations in general (and any child of course may be ahead of or behind this timetable) are as follows:

18 Months

The 18-month-old child walks down a one-way street, and this street more often than not leads in a direction exactly opposite to that which the adult has in mind. It is difficult for the child to mind when spoken to, to respond to commands, to keep within reasonable bounds. And he is extremely strong-willed. His immaturities in motor, adaptive, language, and emotional fields may lead to tantrums. This is a marked stage of disequilibrium in many children.

2 Years

Things are much smoother in nearly every field of behavior. Added maturity and a calm willingness to do what he can do and to not try too hard to do things he cannot manage result in rather good equilibrium. The child is now surer of himself both motorwise and languagewise. Emotionally, too, he finds life easier (as his demands are not so strong as earlier), and he has developed an ability to wait and to suffer slight or temporary frustration if need be.

2½ Years

This is an age of marked disequilibrium. The child of this age tends to be rigid and inflexible—he wants exactly what he wants when he wants it. Everything has to be in what he considers its proper place, everything done exactly so. He sets up rigid routines which he expects everyone to follow. Furthermore, he is domineering and demanding. *He* must make the decisions. His emotions are violent. And, most of all, this is an age of opposite extremes. The child has no ability to choose between alternatives; so he shuttles back and forth endlessly between any two extremes: "I want—I don't want"; "I will—I won't."

3 Years

Things quiet down briefly at 3 for most children. Whereas the 2½-year-old loved to resist, Three loves to conform. The child now likes to give as well as take. He likes to cooperate. He wants to please. He seems to be in good equilibrium not only with those about him but within himself. People are important to him and he likes to make friends. His increased language ability allows him to enjoy language and to respond well to language cues.

3½ Years

In many, there is even more marked disequilibrium than at two-and-a-half. The child at this age exhibits an extremely strong will, and any sort of compliance is hard to obtain. He may resist any and every routine. He insists on having his own way and seems to resist for the sheer pleasure of resisting. Though quite unwilling to please, he is emotionally very vulnerable and is quick to question "Do you love me?" He cannot stand to be ignored; but too much attention, also, disquiets him: "Don't laugh!" he commands.

4 Years

This is an expansive, out-of-bounds age. Motorwise the child may hit, kick, throw stones, break things, run away. Emotionally he exhibits loud silly laughter or fits of rage. Verbally he is extremely out-of-bounds; he lies, swears, boasts, resists. He loves to defy parental commands and seems to thrive on punishment. A terrible toughness comes over many: they swagger, swear, boast, defy. And yet within himself the child of this age does not seem to be in any great trouble, and he can be quite delightful and enjoyable in spite of his out-of-bounds qualities.

4½ Years

Half way between Out-of-Bounds Four and Calm Five, the child of this age often doesn't seem to know where he is functioning and, as a result, his behavior can be extremely variable and unpredictable. It is this extreme variability and unpredictability that makes life difficult for the child himself and for those around him.

5 Years

A period of extreme and delightful equilibrium. The child of this age tends to be calm, stable, reliable, well adjusted. He is friendly and undemanding with others. He loves to please. His mother seems to be the center of his world and he likes to be with her, to do what she asks, to please her. "Today I'm going to do all of the good things and none of the bad things," a 5-year-old will say. Five likes to be instructed and to get permission and then to obey. He likes to help. Briefly he is a delightful social being.

5½ to 6 Years

Equable Five is followed by Tumultuous Six, the breakup starting around 5½. Behavior resembles that seen at 2½ in that the child is violently emotional and tends to function at opposite extremes: "I love—I hate." He himself is now the center of his own world and he wants to be loved most, to be first, to have everything. When anything is wrong he blames his mother and takes things out on her. He cannot stand to lose, to take his turn, to share. He has to be right, needs to win, demands praise. If things go well he is warm, enthusiastic, eager, ready for anything. If they go badly, he resorts to tears and tantrums.

d. Cycles of Behavior. Though it does seem possible, at least during the first six years of life, to characterize alternating stages of behavior as equilibrated or disequilibrated; other forces appear to be at work. The most conspicuous of these is a tendency, at successive stages, for behavior to be either expansive or pulled in. Both of these sets of factors must be considered if we are to attain a long-range view of the kinds of behavior that may be expected as the child matures.

Not only do equilibrium and disequilibrium and "inwardizing" and "outwardizing" factors seem to alternate at successive and adjacent age stages, but a rather complex cycle of behavior-stages that we have identified as occurring between 2 and 5 years seems to repeat itself twice more in the years from 5 through 16.

The ages of 2, 5, and 10 constitute focal points at which behavior seems to be in good equilibrium, the child having relatively little difficulty within himself or with the world about him. Each of these relatively smooth and untroubled ages is followed by a brief period when behavior appears to be very much broken up, disturbed, and troubled, and when the child shows himself to be in marked disequilibrium. Thus the smoothness of 2-year-old behavior characteristically breaks up at 2½, 5-year-old behavior breaks up at 5½ to 6, and 10 breaks up at eleven—the 11-year-old child characteristically showing himself to be at definite odds with his environment and with himself.

Each of these ages is followed, once more, by a period of relative equilibrium at 3, 6½, and 12 years, respectively, when life's forces seem to be in good balance. The child is happy both within himself and in his environment.

These are followed by ages when there is a very pronounced "inwardizing" or drawing in of outer impressions and experiences to be mulled over, thought about, and digested. These ages are 3½, 7, and 13 years. At 3½ this inner process often has disturbing side effects: general emotional instability, a variety of fears, poor spatial orientation, hand tremor, a whining and highly tremulous voice, stuttering, and stumbling. Seven and 13 are more stable ages and better ready to stand the strain of this "inwardizing" period of growth. The side effects at these latter ages are more apt to be expressed in marked sensitivity and touchiness, in excessive withdrawal and moroseness, and in a minor and pessimistic attitude toward life in general.

Each of the three ages just mentioned (3½, 7, and 13) is followed by a period of extreme expansiveness. Four, 8, and 14 are times at which the child's behavior is markedly outgoing in most major respects. He is even in danger of expanding too much. He wanders from home and gets lost at 4, he demands to ride his bicycle in the street at 8 and may get hit, and he gets all tangled in his multiple and conflicting social plans at 14.

The next three ages (4½ years, 9, and 15) are ages about which we perhaps know the least, but we do know enough to recognize certain similarities about the three periods. In each, behavior is less outgoing than at the age that directly preceded it. In each it is in less good equilibrium. Child specialists have frequently described each of these as "neurotic," though each may represent a perfectly normal stage of growth, and when behavior takes a positive turn at any of these ages it can be unusually positive and productive.

Then, once more in each instance, we come to an age of stability and of relatively good equilibrium: 5, 10, and 16.

TABLE 2

Ages			Behavior
2	5	10	Smooth, consolidated.
2½	5½–6	11	Breaking up.
3	6½	12	Rounded—balanced.
3½	7	13	Inwardized.
4	8	14	Vigorous, expansive.
4½	9	15	Inwardized-outwardized, troubled, "neurotic."
5	10	16	Smooth, consolidated.

A brief and schematic tabular presentation of the age changes from 2 years on, as described above, is given in Table 2.

B. SUMMARY

According to the developmental point of view, behavior in the human infant and child develops in a patterned, orderly manner, through stages that are largely predictable and similar from child to child as to their content and timing. Two of the outstanding laws or rules of development are (*a*) the principle of cephalocaudad development and (*b*) the principle of reciprocal interweaving. According to the first, we find that behavior in the human organism develops chiefly in a head-to-foot direction. According to the second, in any growing behavior (or area of behavior) it is possible to identify paired-but-opposed types of response that occur in repeated alternation until the behavior has reached its final or complete stage, spiralling upward as it progresses.

Thus behavior does not simply develop in a straightline direction, the immature gradually and without lapse giving way to the mature; but, rather, if one of these opposites can be identified as immature and the other as mature (as is usually the case), we must anticipate repeated recurrences of the more immature behavior alternating with the more mature as the child grows older.

In such an area as prone progression, where the chief alternating behaviors are flexion and extension, the adult as a rule can view these alternations objectively. In such an area as handedness (where the responses alternating may be right handedness, left handedness, and bilaterality), the adult is more likely to be inclined to step in, too soon, to try to influence behavior.

In such an emotionally toned area as the child's response to his mother or his total response to life situations in general, where the two factors that alternate and interweave are a basic disequilibrium and a basic equilibrium, it is more difficult for the adult to remain objective. Knowledge of approximately when to expect recurring stages of disequilibrium, and an appreciation of the fact that a total disequilibrium of response may be expected to characterize certain age levels (regardless of the excellence of environmental conditions or of parental handling) can be useful to the parent in guiding the child, and to the pediatrician in guiding the parent.

REFERENCES

1. Gesell, A. Reciprocal interweaving in neuro-motor development. A principle of spiral organization shown in the patterning of infant behavior. *J. Comp. Neurol.*, 1939, **70** (2), 161–180.

2. ———. The ontogenesis of infant behavior. In L. Carmichael (Ed.), *Manual of Child Psychology*. New York: Wiley, 1946. Pp. 295–331.
3. Gesell, A., *et al.* First Five Years of Life. New York: Harper, 1940.
4. ———., *et al.* Embryology of Behavior. 16 mm. film. Chicago: Internat. Film Bureau.
5. Gesell, A., & Amatruda, C. S. Developmental Diagnosis (2nd ed.) New York: Hoeber, 1947.
6. Gesell, A., & Ames, L. B. The ontogenetic organization of prone behavior in human infant. *J. Genet. Psychol.,* 1940, **56**, 247–263.
7. ———. Ontogenetic correspondences in the supine and prone postures of the human infant. *Yale J. Biol. & Med.,* 1943, **15** (4), 565–573.
8. ———. The development of handedness. *J. Genet. Psychol.,* 1947, **70**, 155–175.
9. Gesell, A., & Ilg, F. L. Infant and Child in the Culture of Today. New York: Harper, 1943.
10. Ilg, F. L., & Ames, L. B. Child Behavior. New York: Harper, 1955.

12.

The theory of stages in cognitive development

JEAN PIAGET

As we look at the intriguing and complex creature called man and as we try to explain his behavior and his development, the ideas of some individuals often must be recognized as aiding more in the interpretive process and as helping us to reach more tenable explanations than those of others. Jean Piaget, a well-known Swiss psychologist, is such a person. His thinking in the area of intellectual development has gained such recognition and acceptance among behavioral scientists in the past several years that it is almost a badge of professional competence to be able to converse knowledgeably about his ideas.

It appears that there is much to be learned from Piaget about psychological-research methodology. We read between the lines and we realize that what he has to say can only have resulted from meticulous observation of human behavior. We confess a bias that rats in mazes can never be as productive an avenue for understanding people as Piaget's direct observation of human behavior.

This selection, one of his most recent pronouncements, can provide only a brief introduction to Piaget's thinking. It will acquaint the reader with the broad stages of intellectual development as Piaget sees them, and its perusal will provide some insight into cognitive-behavior capabilities or structures that can be expected to develop in

From Green, *Measurement and Piaget* (New York: McGraw-Hill, 1971); as taken from Piaget, *The Theory of Stages in Cognitive Development* (Monterey, Calif.: California Test Bureau/McGraw-Hill), copyright 1969 by McGraw-Hill, Inc. Used by permission of the publisher. Jean Piaget, Professor of Psychology, University of Geneva, Switzerland.

each stage. An understanding of these stages operates to keep expecta-
tions for learning and psychological growth realistic.

LADIES AND GENTLEMEN: I should first like to thank the organizers of this small conference on the role of ordinal scales in the problem of development for having invited both my collaborator and friend, Bärbel Inhelder, and me to participate in your meeting. To be quite honest, I am not an expert in ordinal scales. Since you do me the honor of inviting me to address you, however, I feel that the problem of stages is one that should serve as an introduction to the discussions to be held on ordinal scales.

There are two reasons for this. First, a theoretical one. If ordinal scales do indeed have some basis in reality, then a succession of stages must exist in some form or another. And second, as you all know full well, no general agreement has as yet been reached about the existence of these stages. Our own hypotheses about the existence and the necessary sequence of these stages are not accepted by everybody. Consequently, I feel that it might be useful for Bärbel Inhelder and me if I were to discuss the question of stages with you and thus come to know your criticisms, objections, and the problems involved. Generally speaking, however, I feel that it is this working group, whose objective is to study ordinal scales, that will eventually solve the problem of stages. Today, therefore, I shall merely outline the problem and make a few brief comments.

Each time that a specific problem is studied, as for instance that of causality which is currently receiving our attention, the analysis of the responses and reactions of children of different ages seems to point to the existence of relatively well-defined stages in this limited area. The important point, however, is to discover whether there are any general overall stages in development, and whether the different stages found in these more limited and specific areas contain any elements in common. In other words, is it possible to detect broad periods in development with characteristics that can be applied in a general manner to all the events of these periods? This is the hypothesis that we are trying to investigate.

We postulate four major periods in development. First of all there is a sensorimotor period which occurs before the advent of language. This period is characterized by what we call sensorimotor intelligence, which is a type of intelligence resulting in a certain number of performances, such as the organization of spatial relationships, the organization of objects and a notion of their permanence, the organization of causal relationships, etc. After the sensorimotor period, at around the age of two years, comes another period which starts with the symbolic or semiotic function. This is called the period of preoperational thought since the child is now capable of having representational thought by means of the symbolic function. At this stage, though, the child cannot perform operations in the way that I define this term. In my terminology, operations are internalized actions which are reversible; that is, they can be performed in opposite directions. Finally, they are coordinated into overall structures, and these structures give rise to a feeling of intrinsic necessity.

The third major period starts at around the age of seven or eight years and is characterized by the inception of operations. Initially these operations are concrete; that is, they are used directly on objects in order to manipulate these objects. For instance, the child can classify concrete objects, or order them, or establish correspondences between them, or use numerical operations on them, or measure them from a spatial point of view. The operations remain concrete until the child is about eleven or twelve years of age. Then, at approximately this age, the fourth major period begins. This period can be characterized by formal or propositional operations. This means that the operations are no longer applied solely to the manipulation of concrete objects, but now cover hypotheses and propositions that the child can use as abstract hypotheses and from which he can reach deductions by formal or logical means.

If these four major periods do indeed exist, then we should be able to characterize them in a precise manner. What we have tried to do in the past, and what we are still trying to do, is to describe the characteristics of these stages in terms of general overall structures which become integrated. With development, the more elementary structures become incorporated into higher level structures, and these in turn are incorporated into structures of an even higher level.

Not everyone believes that it is necessary to characterize stages in terms of overall structures. For example, Freud's stages of emotional development are characterized by their dominant traits. There is the oral stage, or the anal stage, or the narcissistic or primary stage, and so forth. The different characteristics exist at all the stages, but at any particular moment one of the characteristics predominates. Freud's stages can therefore be described in terms of dominant characteristics.

Such a characterization is not, I believe, adequate for the cognitive functions. In this area we should attempt to go beyond this. If we were to remain satisfied with the notion of dominant characteristics for the cognitive functions, it would always be somewhat arbitrary as to what exactly is dominant and what is not. This is why we are trying to discover the overall structures in cognition rather than specify the dominant characteristics. This means that we are looking for total structures or systems with their own laws, for systems which incorporate all their elements and whose laws cover the entire set of elements in the system. It would be these structures which become integrated with development. I shall stop here. But before ending I should like to repeat that this is an important problem, because there is no consensus as to the existence of such structures. I shall therefore try to support my views in the remainder of my address.

The existence of these overall structures raises a problem: do they in fact really exist in the mind of the subject being studied, or are they merely an invention of the psychologist who studies children or adults? The notion of overall structures presents two difficulties. First, the subject is not conscious of the existence of his cognitive structures. For example, he does not know what a seriation is, or a classification, or a relationship of correspondence. He himself has never given a thought to the nature of these overall structures. He acts, he operates, he behaves. And from this behavior we, the psychologists, detect the structures; but the structures are unconscious. They are expressed in regular forms of responses that we believe we are discovering in the subject's behavior. We also feel that if the underlying structures did not exist, we would not be able to explain such behavior. But the subject himself is not aware of these structures. He is neither a professor of psychology, nor a professor of logic. He does not reflect upon the structures that he uses. He simply uses them. This, then, is the first difficulty: do the structures really exist in the subject's mind, or have we perhaps invented them?

The second difficulty is this: if we are to be convinced of the existence of these structures, we should be able to formalize them in logical terms. We then try to adapt this formalization to what we are able to observe in the child. But we can never be sure whether we have invented the formalization or whether it really is an expression of what is to be found in the mind of the child. So you see I am very much aware of the various problems involved in the notion of overall structures. Let me, however, deal with some of them by means of a simple example.

I refer here to the example of seriation. Seriation consists of the ordering of a series of sticks from the smallest one to the tallest. Bärbel Inhelder, Mimi Sinclair, and I have once again returned to this problem of seriation in our recent studies on memory, and our findings confirm the stages discovered in our earlier work. For instance, we found that during the initial stage the youngest subjects maintain that all the sticks are of equal length. During the next stage, which we may call stage "B," the subjects divide the sticks into two categories: large and small, with no ordering of the elements. At stage "C," the children talk of the large ones, the middle-sized ones, and the small ones. At level "D," the child constructs a series in an empirical fashion, by trial and error, but he is not able to produce immediately a faultless construction. And finally, at the last level, the child discovers a method: he chooses the largest of all the sticks and he sets this on the table. Then he takes the largest of all the remaining sticks and places this beside the first stick, and then the largest of the remaining ones, until he has placed all of the sticks on the table. At this level, he constructs a correct ordering without any hesitation, and this construction presupposes a reversible relation. That is to say, an element a is both smaller than the ones which have gone before it and larger than the ones to follow. This is a good example of what I mean by a structure.

But let us see what the logicians have to say about this problem. What is a seriation from the formal point of view? And can we discover any relationship between the logician's formalization of a seriation and the child's structure of the same notion? For the logician, a seriation is a chaining of asymmetrical, connex, and transitive relations. As far as asymmetry is concerned, this seems obvious in the present example. This means that one element is larger than another. As for connectivity, this means that all the elements are different and that there are no two alike. And lastly, there is the transitivity relationship. This means that if A is larger than B, and B larger than C, then A is automatically larger than C. In the above-mentioned seriation problem, we did not see any evidence of transitivity. Is it part of the structure? Does it exist? Here we can do some separate experiments on the problem by taking three sticks of unequal length. We compare the first with the second, and then hide the first under the table. Then we compare the second with the third, and we say to the child, "You saw beforehand that the first was larger than the second, and now you can see that the second is larger than the third. What is the one under the table like compared to the third one? Is it larger, smaller, or just the same?" Experience has shown that very young children are not able to use the deductive method and are thus unable to solve the problem of transitivity. They reply, "I don't know. I haven't seen them next to each other. I need to see all three together at the same time before I can answer your question."

For the older children, however, who use the deductive method, transitivity is evident. Not only is it evident, but it also is necessary. And here we touch upon the real problem of overall structures: the problem of the appearance at a particular point in development of the feeling of necessity. Until this point, a certain occurrence was either absent or simply probable; now it becomes necessary. How can one explain the apparition of necessity from the psychological point of view? This, I feel, is the real problem of overall structures. How is it that a phenomenon which had, until then, been merely noted empirically, or else had been felt to be simply probable, now becomes logically necessary from the subject's point of view?

One first reply could be to say that it is an illusion. Hume, as you know, in his studies on the notion of causality, maintained that the necessary cause-effect relationship was in fact not necessary at all, but simply due to our associations of ideas or to our habits. So one could say that this feeling of necessity is simply a habit. However, the striking thing here is that the child reaches this feeling of necessity as soon as he has understood the phenomenon in question. One can sometimes witness the precise moment when he discovers this necessity. At the beginning of his reasoning, he is not at all sure of what he is stating. Then suddenly he says, "But it's obvious." In another experiment where Bärbel Inhelder was questioning a child on a problem which is not that of seriation but of recurrent reasoning, but which also involves the feeling of necessity, the child was at first very uncertain. Then suddenly he said, "Once one knows, one knows forever and ever." In other words, at one point the child automatically acquires this feeling of necessity. Where does this necessity come from?

My personal feeling is that there is only one acceptable psychological explanation: this feeling of necessity comes from the closure or completion of a structure. One could, of course, also maintain that necessity is simply an awareness of an idea which was predetermined in the mind, an innate or *a priori* idea. But this is not a true psychological solution for it defies verification. Also, if this were indeed true, the feeling of necessity would appear much earlier than it actually does.

This is why I believe that the feeling of necessity is neither a subjective illusion nor an innate or *a priori* idea. It is an idea which is constructed at the same time as the overall structures. As soon as a structure is sufficiently complete for closure to occur, or, in other words, once the internal compositions of the structure become interdependent and independent of external elements and are sufficiently numerous to allow for all types of arrangements, then the feeling of necessity manifests itself. I believe that it is this feeling of necessity which constitutes evidence of the existence of the overall structures which characterize our stages.

I do not want to describe here all the overall structures that can be found. They naturally vary according to the four major periods mentioned earlier. At the sensorimotor level we find composite actions which are performed in a step-by-step or contiguous manner, since the child is not capable of representation which would allow for more complex relationships. His compositions are simply actions which are chained to one another, but which nevertheless still form some kind of structure. We find, for instance, in the organization of space, an organization of movements and of positions which mathematicians call the group of displacements. This is one example of a structure, with its characteristic of necessity. That is to say it is possible to return to the point of departure, and this is a necessary return. Also it is possible to reach one point by a variety of different routes, and those are called detour behaviors. So already in these two types of behavior, return and detour, we see the characteristic of necessity and the existence of overall structures.

At the level of preoperational thought we find other overall structures. These are not yet operational structures in the sense that I described earlier; that is, they are not yet reversible, but they are nonetheless structures with their own laws. Take for example the notion of a function. As an example, we have a piece of string which can be pulled over a spring. If you tie a weight to the segment called A, the segment A′ will become shorter. When A becomes shorter, A′ becomes longer; when A′ becomes shorter, A becomes longer. So the lengthening of A is a function of the shortening of A′. At this point of development the child has not yet acquired conservation. If we were to ask the child if the whole string (B) were equal to the sum of the two parts (A and A′), i.e., $B = A + A'$, in both cases, that is when the string has been pulled down with the weight or not, the child would not give the correct answer because he cannot conserve. This is an example of a function but without reversibility.

In other experiments we also find functions, as for instance in the many-to-one relationship, but this is not accompanied by the reverse relationship of one-to-many. In the one-to-many relationship, or the many-to-one, the child reaches only a partial logic; he has not yet acquired the other half of logic which would be reversibility. Other examples of structures at this level are those of qualitative identity. For example, if one pours liquid from one glass to another as in the well-known experiments on conservation, the child at this stage does not accept the conservation of quantity, but he already admits to the qualitative identity. He will say that it is the same water in both cases, but not the same quantity. Qualitative identity is far easier to achieve. All the child needs to do is to isolate the qualities, whereas for conservation the child must construct the quantities, and this is another matter.

I do not need to remind you that at the level of the concrete operations we find a great many overall structures which are much richer than those of the preoperational level and which we have called groupings. Examples are the notion of seriation mentioned previously, classification, one-to-one correspondence, and many-to-one or one-to-many correspondences. At this level quantification becomes possible as a result of the overall structures, and consequently so too do the notions of conservation which were lacking at the preoperational level. Even identity changes and becomes operational and additive. For example, in the conservation problem, the child will say, "It's the same quantity, because you haven't added anything or taken anything away." Nothing has been added and nothing taken away; this is an additive identity and therefore a quantitative one, and no longer simply qualitative identity as when the child says, "It's the same water. It's the same color," etc.

There is no need for me to remind you that at the level of formal or propositional operations we also find even richer structures which are a synthesis of the previous ones. For instance, we have the group of four transformations which combine into a single system the structures of inversion $(A - A = 0)$ and the structures of reciprocity $(A = B$ therefore $B = A)$. These formal structures incorporate the preceding ones and constitute the termination of the construction of overall structures which has been going on throughout the entire period of childhood. The stages are therefore characterized by successive structures which do not replace each other, but which are integrated into one another. The simplest ones become incorporated into later more complex ones. For example, the preoperational functions, or identities, are integrated into the concrete operations; then later, these concrete operational structures become incorporated into the formal operational structures.

At this point of our study I should like to note that these two notions of stages and overall structures, which I believe are necessarily closely bound together, have a meaning which is not only a logical and formal one. Despite their formalization, these structures have essentially a biological meaning, in the sense that the order of the stages is constant and sequential.

Each stage is necessary for the following one. If this were not the case, one would be in no position to talk of stages. Naturally, the ages at which different children reach the stages may vary. In some social environments the stages are accelerated, whereas in others they are more or less systematically retarded. This differential development shows that stages are not purely a question of the maturation of the nervous system but are dependent upon interaction with the social environment and with experience in general. The order, however, remains constant.

Furthermore, the accelerations or retardations raise one problem which has not yet been studied sufficiently but which will have to be considered in the future. This is the problem of the optimal speed of development. What advantages are to be gained from speeding up the stages? I am often asked the following question in this country: Can one accelerate the stages indefinitely? My reply is to ask: Is there any advantage to be derived from such acceleration? Take experiments like those of Gruber where he finds that kittens acquire the requisite reactions towards the permanent object by the age of four months; that is, they search for objects hidden under a screen. It takes the human baby nine months to reach this self-same point of development. One can consequently ask whether it would be advantageous for the human baby to reach this point at four instead of nine months? I do not think so, because the kitten does not go very much further. Once it reaches a certain level, it scarcely progresses beyond this point. The human baby, on the other hand, develops more slowly, but in the long run he goes much further. One must remember that the higher the zoological species the longer is its period of infancy. There is a reason for this, and it may be that there is an optimal speed of development for each species. So we return to biology.

Our stages are very similar to those described by Waddington when he speaks of necessary courses which lead to a certain result. He calls these necessary courses or channels "creodes." He also describes certain forms of equilibrium which occur when there is a deviation from the creode due to unforeseen circumstances. In this case some force acts to bring the development back to its normal course. Waddington calls this "homeorhesis." It is a dynamic equilibrium, as opposed to homeostasis which is static. And finally, Waddington stresses what he calls the time-tally. This particular notion of a time-tally raises the problem of the optimal speed of the stages of development. One last point is that the stages in embryology have a sequential ordering, with each stage being necessary for the following one. It is not possible to miss a stage in development.

If this were true of psychology, then there would be a relationship or a very close analogy with embryological development. I repeat that this does not mean that everything is genetically or internally determined within a hereditary program, since accelerations or retardations can occur in mental development which appear to be of an even greater magnitude than in embryology.

The present basic problem in the question of stages is that of the passage from one stage to the next. What mechanisms are responsible for this passage? Bärbel Inhelder and her collaborators have been dealing with this specific problem in their study of the possibility of certain forms of learning. These are not the types of learning that take place as a result of repetition or of the external reinforcements as in habit learning. Rather, she has been studying the type of learning which consists of isolating the factors which we believe are active in normal development in order to show how variations in these factors can produce accelerations in certain areas of development, and, more particularly, can result in certain correlations between the various learning experiences.

But I do not wish to discuss this problem here since it is currently in the process of investigation and the results will shortly be published in a book by Inhelder and her collaborators. What I would like to do, and this will lead to my conclusion, is to raise the general problem of the passage from one stage to the next. I should like to approach this problem in the following manner. Three models can be used to describe this passage from one stage to the next. First, one could maintain that the successive acquisitions which characterize the stages mentioned earlier are acquisitions which are purely and simply due to environmental pressures, to experience, or to more or less random encounters with certain aspects of the daily social and physical environment. In this case, the succession of the stages would no longer be necessary. It might be a regular succession, with some regularities being more or less emphasized or attenuated depending upon the environment, but there would be no necessary succession.

The second possibility would be that the stages are internally determined; that is, they are predetermined. The succession of stages would be somehow preformed in the hereditary equipment of each individual. This approach is a return to the conception of innate ideas, and as you know, this notion which was not very popular some years ago, has now become fashionable again. I refer in particular to the work being carried out in psycholinguistics by Chomsky, and to work done by certain psychologists who maintain that they are able to find notions of conservation very early in life, and that these notions then deteriorate, I am not quite sure how, only to reappear eventually at a later stage in development. I would classify this second solution as one of predetermination.

And then there is a third approach which is the one to which we subscribe. This solution is difficult to prove. It is even difficult to express or to explain. But once one has understood it, it seems that it is a compelling one, although it still remains to be proved. This third solution is that the stages result in a certain number of overall structures which become necessary with development, but are not so at the beginning of life. For example, the formal structures become necessary once the child possesses the concrete operations. As soon as he can perform the concrete operations, sooner or later he will begin to coordinate reversibility by inversion with reversibility by reciprocity and hence construct the group of four transformations. Similarly, once he is able to manipulate the classifications, sooner or later he will construct a classification of all the classifications, and thus he will end up by producing the combinatorial, which is a necessary form of formal thought.

Thus stages are characterized by overall structures which become necessary but which are not so initially. Formal structures become necessary when the concrete structures are complete; concrete structures become necessary when the structures of identity, of functions, etc., are complete; and these in turn become necessary when the sensorimotor functions are complete. But nothing is given in an *a priori* or innate fashion; nothing is preformed or predetermined in the activity of the baby. For instance, we could search far and wide in the behavior of the baby without finding even the rudiments of the group of four transformations, or of the combinatorial. These are all constructed and the construction—this I find to be the great mystery of the stages—becomes more and more necessary with time. The necessity is at the end of development, not at the point of departure. This, then, is the model upon which we are trying to base our work and our experiments.

There are still two more remarks that I should like to add before closing. First, that the stages which I have just discussed are those of intelligence, of the development of intelligence, and more particularly of the development of the logico-mathematical operations. They refer to those operations of which the subject is, in a way, the master or the director and which he can apply at will, in such a manner as he deems suitable, to a particular group of objects. When we study other cognitive functions, things naturally become more complex and the stages may be far less evident. In the field of perception, for example, we find hardly any stages as far as the primary or field effects are concerned. We do find some semi-stages in the perceptual activities, but these are not nearly as well defined as the stages of intelligence.

With mental imagery, we find essentially two periods. There is one preceding the concrete operations when mental images are mainly reproductory and static. During this period children have great difficulty in representing or imagining transformations or movements. The anticipatory images which are necessary for the representation of transformations only make their appearance at the level of the concrete operations. So here we find the beginnings of a stage, but again far less evident than in the field of intelligence.

In our recent research into memory, we find three distinctions. These are: recognitive memory, which is by far the earliest type of memory to appear and which is found right at the beginning of the sensorimotor level; evocative memory, which only appears with the semiotic function from the age of two or three years onwards; and then, between the two, there is a level of reconstructive memory which is still bound up with movement, with action, but which is more than simple recognition. These are very elementary distinctions which don't go very far in the differentiation of stages.

Even in the area of intelligence, as I mentioned before, the stages which I have just described are those of the logico-mathematical operations. Because here the subject does what he wants, in a manner of speaking. For the notion of causality, on the other hand, which we are studying at present, knowledge is physical and no longer logico-mathematical, and so the resistances of the object present all sorts of new problems. Consequently the stages are far less clear. At first, we had the impression that there were very few stages in the development of the notion of causality. Now we are slowly finding some. However, we are not yet at the point of being able to describe these stages in terms of the characteristics of overall structures such as described earlier. This is the first of my two concluding remarks.

Finally, a fairly important problem for the theory of stages is that of time lags. At certain ages the child is able to solve problems in quite specific areas. But if one changes to another material or to another situation, even with a problem which seems to be closely related, lags of several months are noted, and in some cases even of one or two years. Let us take one example: the problem of inclusion. The child is given a bunch of flowers, some of which are primroses, whilst others are tulips, daisies, or any other flowers. If you were to ask the child, "Are all the primroses flowers?" he will reply, "Of course." If you then ask, "Are there more flowers or more primroses in this bunch?" the child, instead of comparing the primroses with all the flowers, will compare them with all the flowers which are not primroses. And he will answer, "There are more," or, "There are less," or, "There are the same number," depending upon the result of this comparison, as if he were not able to include the part in the whole. This is the problem of class inclusion.

This problem is solved at approximately the age of eight years for the flowers. But Bärbel Inhelder and I have noted that if one uses animals, for example, the problem becomes more complicated. If one asks the child, "Are all sea gulls birds?" he will reply, "Of course." If you ask, "Are all the birds sea gulls?" he will reply, "Of course not. There are also blackbirds, sparrows, etc." Then if you ask, "If you look out of the window, can you tell me whether there are more sea gulls or more birds in Geneva?" the child finds this more difficult to answer than for the flowers. Why is this? Is it because one cannot make a bunch with the sea gulls as with the flowers? I do not know. But this is one example of the problem. It is possibly a poorly chosen one, but there are any number of these problems of time lags between the solution of a problem with a certain material and the solution of the same problem with another material.

I have often been reproached for not having produced a sufficiently precise theory of these time lags in the same way as one can try to produce a theory of the overall structures or of the positive characteristics of stages. But time lags are a negative characteristic which form an obstacle to the construction of the overall structures. My reply to such a reproach is merely the following. Time lags are always due to an interaction between the person's structures on the one hand, and the resistances of the object on the other. The object may be flowers, which offer little resistance; one places them on the table, and one makes a bunch of them. But there are other objects which offer more resistance, as for instance the birds. One cannot put them on the table. Some resistances of objects are unpredictable. When one encounters them, one can explain them, but always after the event. It is not possible to have a general theory of these resistances.

And so, in concluding, I should like to find some sort of an excuse for this failure by a comparison with physics. Physics is a much more advanced science than psychology, a more exact science which permits mathematical theories in almost all areas. But there is one area where physicists have not yet managed to produce a general theory. This is the problem of friction. Friction is the resistance of an object when you make it move along a surface. Physicists explain the role of friction in such and such a situation, but they have not yet come up with a general theory for this phenomenon. Time lags are somewhat analogous; they are comparable to all the concrete situations where friction is involved. Some areas are manipulated with ease; others offer all sorts of resistances. This problem still remains to be solved.

As you see, I have tried to be honest in my address by pointing out the various problems and difficulties which still remain. But I repeat, I am counting especially on the work that you are going to do here in your meeting on ordinal scales to shed some light on the difficult question of stages.

Thank you for your attention.

section **iv**

Teaching-learning relationships

13.

Theories of learning

Morris L. Bigge

Living and learning are part of the same process and, unfortunately, too little is known about the dynamics of either. This is not because efforts to understand and explain have been lacking. The various theories presented by the author of this article attest to this. His assertion that each theory as it developed seldom displaced its predecessors but merely competed with them, substantiates the statement that there is too little really verifiable information concerning the learning process in man.

Here the reader may find it profitable to speculate concerning his own ideas of how people learn and how he himself learns. He may wish to think back to see whether he can identify the theories of learning that were held by some of his teachers and under which he was educated. Hopefully, he may be able to review what already has been said about the limitations and applications of research methodology and to understand why it has proved to be so difficult to design experiments that give conclusive answers to problems of human development.

SINCE ANCIENT times, most civilized societies have developed and, to some degree, tested theories about how man learns. As each new theory has gained support, it has seldom displaced its predecessors but merely competed with them. For this reason, the educational philosophies and practices of many teachers may include ideas from a variety of learning theories, some of which are basically contradictory in nature.

Each theory of learning is linked to a conception of the basic nature of man: In basic moral inclination, is he innately good, is he evil, or is he neutral? Then, in relation to his environment, is he active, passive, or interactive? Each of the different conceptions has its adherents, and each has its own approach to learning.

The accompanying chart outlines the concepts involved in ten major

N.E.A. Journal, 55(No. 3):15–17, March, 1966. Morris L. Bigge, Chairman, Department of Advanced Studies, School of Education, Fresno (California) State College.

REPRESENTATIVE THEORIES OF LEARNING AND THEIR IMPLICATIONS FOR EDUCATION

	I Theory of Learning	II Psychological System or Outlook	III Assumption Concerning the Basic Moral and Psychological Nature of Man	IV Basis for Transfer of Learning	V Main Emphasis in Teaching	VI Key Persons	VII Contemporary Exponents
MIND SUBSTANCE FAMILY	1. Theistic mental discipline	faculty psychology	bad-active mind substance continues active until curbed	exercised faculties, automatic transfer	exercise of faculties—the "muscles" of the mind	St. Augustine, John Calvin, J. Edwards	many Hebraic-Christian fundamentalists
	2. Humanistic mental discipline	classicism	neutral-active mind substance to be developed through exercise	cultivated mind or intellect	training of intrinsic mental power	Plato, Aristotle	M. J. Adler, St. John's College
	3. Natural unfoldment	romantic naturalism	good-active natural personality to unfold	recapitulation of racial history, no transfer needed	negative or permissive education	J. J. Rousseau, F. Froebel	extreme progressivists
	4. Apperception or Herbartionism	structuralism	neutral-passive mind composed of active mental states or ideas	growing apperceptive mass	addition of new mental states or ideas to a store of old ones in subconscious mind	J. F. Herbart, E. B. Titchener	many teachers and administrators
	5. S-R bond	connectionism	neutral-passive or reactive organism with many potential S-R connections	identical elements	promotion of acquisition of desired S-R connections	E. L. Thorndike	J. M. Stephens, A. I. Gates

130

Family	Theory	School	Nature of person	What is learned	Educational aim	Proponents	
CONDITIONING THEORIES OF STIMULUS-RESPONSE (S-R) FAMILY	6. Conditioning (with no reinforcement)	behaviorism	neutral-passive or reactive organism with innate reflexive drives and emotions	conditioned responses or reflexes	promotion of adhesion of desired responses to appropriate stimuli	J. B. Watson	E. R. Guthrie
ASSOCIATIONISTIC FAMILY	7. Reinforcement and conditioning	reinforcement	neutral-passive organism with innate reflexes and needs with their drive stimuli	reinforced or conditioned responses	successive, systematic changes in organisms' environment to increase the probability of desired responses (operants)	C. L. Hull	B. F. Skinner, K. W. Spence
	8. Insight	Gestalt psychology	naturally active being whose activity follows psychological laws of organization	transposition of insights	promotion of insightful learning	M. Wertheimer, K. Koffka	W. Köhler
COGNITIVE THEORIES OF GESTALT-FIELD FAMILY	9. Goal insight	configurationism	neutral-interactive purposive individual in sequential relationships with environment	tested insights	aid students in trial-and-error, goal-directed learning	B. H. Bode, R. H. Wheeler	E. E. Bayles
	10. Cognitive-field	field psychology or relativism	neutral-interactive purposive person in simultaneous mutual interaction with environment, including other persons	continuity of life spaces, experience, or insights	help students restructure their life spaces—gain new insights into their contemporaneous situations	Kurt Lewin, E. C. Tolman, J. S. Bruner	R. G. Barker, A. W. Combs, H. F. Wright, M. L. Bigge

learning theories (Column I) either prevalent in today's schools or advocated by leading psychologists. Reinforcement and conditioning (No. 7),
especially as represented by B. F. Skinner's "operant conditioning" and the
cognitive-field theory (No. 10), first advanced by Kurt Lewin but refined
by contemporary psychologists, are two leading contenders in the present
scene.

Teachers may find this chart useful in thinking through and noting
possible inconsistencies in their own educational outlook and how their
outlook agrees or disagrees with that of their school administration. Although some of the theories have roots that go back to antiquity, they all
still exert influence in present-day schools.

Each theory has its unique approach to education. However, some of
them have enough in common to justify grouping them in families. Thus,
in a more general sense, there are only five basic outlooks in regard to
learning—the three families plus thories 3 and 4.

14.

Some new views of learning and instruction

ROBERT M. GAGNÉ

*Here is a recognition that research in the area of human learning and
behaving is in a time of great ferment and change. This author looks
at some of these changes. He makes it clear that he is not developing
new theory but simply speculating on the direction in which learning
theory appears to be heading.*

*The editors are impressed by, and ask the reader to note, the
citing of relevant sources and research in questioning the older, and
in describing the more recent, concepts of learning. The author discusses the implications that the newer ideas have for learning. We
suggest that the reader do a little pragmatic validation experiment on
his own in this respect—apply the four implications described in a
conscientious, consistent manner over a substantial length of time to
your own study. Determine for yourself whether or not they really
work. That is, do you really remember better? Do the answers come
more easily and are you getting empirical evidence in the form of
higher grades?*

DURING RECENT years there has been an increased recognition of, and even
emphasis on, the importance of principles of learning in the design of in-

Phi Delta Kappan, 51(9):468–472, May, 1970. Robert M. Gagné, Professor of Educational
Psychology, Florida State University, Tallahassee.

struction for the schools. This recognition of the central role of learning in school-centered education seems to be accorded whether one thinks of the instruction as being designed by a teacher, by a textbook writer, or by a group of scholars developing a curriculum.

When the findings of research studies of learning are taken into account, one usually finds questions about instruction to be concerned with such matters as these:

1. For student learning to be most effective, how should the learning task be presented? That is, how should it be communicated to the student?

2. When the student undertakes a learning task, what kinds of activity on his part should be required or encouraged?

3. What provisions must be made to insure that what is learned is remembered and is usable in further learning and problem solving?

Questions such as these are persistent in education. The answers given today are not exactly the same as those given yesterday, and they are likely to be altered again tomorrow. The major reason for these changes is our continually deepening knowledge of human behavior and of the factors which determine it. One should not, I believe, shun such changes nor adopt a point of view which makes difficult the application of new knowledge to the design of novel procedures for instruction. The opportunities for improvement seem great and the risks small.

STATUS OF LEARNING RESEARCH

As a field of endeavor, research on how human beings learn and remember is in a state of great ferment today. Many changes have taken place, and are still taking place, in the conception of what human learning is and how it occurs. Perhaps the most general description that can be made of these changes is that investigators are shifting from what may be called a *connectionist* view of learning to an *information processing* view. From an older view which held that learning is a matter of establishing *connections* between stimuli and responses, we are moving rapidly to acceptance of a view that stimuli are *processed* in quite a number of different ways by the human central nervous system, and that understanding learning is a matter of figuring out how these various processes operate. Connecting one neural event with another may still be the most basic component of these processes, but their varied nature makes connection itself too simple a model for learning and remembering.

My purpose here is to outline some of these changes in the conception of human learning and memory, and to show what implications they may have for the design and practice of instruction. I emphasize that I am not proposing a new theory; I am simply speculating on what seems to me to be the direction in which learning theory is heading.

THE OLDER CONCEPTION

The older conception of learning was that it was always basically the same process, whether the learner was learning to say a new word, to tie a shoelace, to multiply fractions, to recount the facts of history, or to solve a problem concerning rotary motion. Edward L. Thorndike held essentially this view. He stated that he had observed people performing learning tasks of varied degrees of complexity and had concluded that learning was invariably subject to the same influences and the same laws.[1] What was this model of learning that was considered to have such broad generalizability?

One prototype is the conditioned response, in which there is a pairing of stimuli, repeated over a series of trials. The two stimuli must be presented together, or nearly together, in time. They are typically associated with an "emotional" response of the human being, such as an eyeblink or a change in the amount of electrical resistance of the skin (the galvanic skin reflex). The size of the conditioned response begins at a low base-line level, and progressively increases as more and more repetitions of the two stimuli are given. Such results have been taken to indicate that repetition brings about an increasingly "strong" learned connection—with an increase in strength that is rapid at first and then more slow.

Learning curves with similar characteristics have been obtained from various other kinds of learned activities, such as simple motor skills like dart-throwing and memorization of lists of words or sets of word-pairs.

Remembering. What about the remembering of such learned activities? Is learning retained better as a result of repetition? Is something that is repeated over and over at the time of learning better recalled after the passage of several weeks or months? The curve which describes forgetting is perhaps equally familiar. Forgetting of such things as lists of nonsense syllables is quite rapid in the beginning, and after several weeks descends to a point at which only about 20 percent is remembered. A motor task is usually retained a great deal better, and after the same amount of time its retention may be as much as 80 percent.

These are the basic facts about remembering. But how is it affected by repetition? Is retention better if the original learning situation has been repeated many times? Evidence is often cited that this is so. Increasing the number of trials of repetition during original learning has the effect of slowing down the "curve of forgetting," i.e., of improving the amount of retention measured at any particular time. Underwood,[2] for example, has stated that "degree of learning" of the task to be recalled is one of the two major factors which influence forgetting in a substantial manner. The second factor is interfering associations, whose strength is also determined by their degree of learning. It should be pointed out that when Underwood uses the phrase "degree of learning" he refers to amount of practice—in other words, to amount of repetition.

At this point, let me summarize what I believe are the important implications for instruction of what I call the "older" conceptions of learning and memory. The designer of instruction, or the teacher, had to do two major things: First, he had to arrange external conditions of presentation so that the stimulus and response had the proper timing—in other words, so that there was *contiguity* between the presentation of the stimulus and the occurrence of the response. Second, he had to insure that sufficient *repetition* occurred. Such repetition was necessary for two reasons: It would increase the strength of the learned connections; the more the repetition, within limits, the better the learning. Also, repetition was needed to insure remembering—the greater the number of repetitions, the better the retention. Presumably, whole generations of instructional materials and teacher procedures have been influenced in a variety of ways by application of these conceptions of learning to the process of instruction.

QUESTIONING OLDER CONCEPTIONS

During recent years, a number of significant experimental studies of learning and memory have been carried out which call into question some of these older conceptions. (Of course there have always been a certain number of individuals—voices in the wilderness—who doubted that these principles had the general applicability claimed for them.) I shall describe only a few of the actual new studies here, to illustrate the perennial questions and their possible answers.

Does learning require repetition? A most provocative study on this question was carried out by Rock[3] as long ago as 1957. It has stimulated many other studies since that time, some pointing out its methodological defects, others supporting its conclusions.[4] The finding of interest is that in learning sets of verbal paired associates, practice does not increase the strength of each learned item; each one is either learned or not learned. To be sure, some are learned on the first practice trial, some on the second, some on the third, and so on; but an item once learned is fully learned.

So far as school subjects are concerned, a number of studies have failed to find evidence of the effectiveness of repetition for learning and remembering. This was true in an investigation by Gagné, Mayor, Garstens, and Paradise,[5] in which seventh-graders were learning about the addition of integers. One group of children was given four or five times as many practice problems on each of 10 subordinate skills as were given to another group, and no difference appeared in their final performance. A further test of this question was made in a study by Jeanne Gibson,[6] who set out to teach third- and fourth-graders to read decimals from a number line.

First, she made sure that subordinate skills (reading a number in decimal form, writing a number in decimal form, locating a decimal number on a number line) were learned thoroughly by each child. One group of students was then given a total of 10 practice examples for each subordinate skill, a second group 25 for each, and a third none at all. The study thus contrasted the effects of no repetition of learned skills, an intermediate amount of repetition, and a large amount of repetition. This variable was not found to have an effect on performance, both when tested immediately after learning and five weeks later. Those students who practiced repeated examples were not shown to do better, or to remember better, than those who practiced not at all.

Still another study of fairly recent origin is by Reynolds and Glaser,[7] who used an instructional program to teach 10 topics in biology. They inserted frames containing half as many repetitions, in one case, and one-and-a-half times as many repetitions, in another, as those in a standard program. The repetitions involved definitions of technical terms. When retention of these terms was measured after an interval of three weeks, the investigators were unable to find any difference in recall related to the amount of repetition.

I must insert a caveat here. All of the studies I have mentioned are concerned with the effects of repetition immediately after learning. They do not, however, test the effect of repetition in the form of *spaced reviews*. Other evidence suggests the importance of such reviews; in fact, this kind of treatment was found to exert a significant effect in the Reynolds and Glaser study. Note, though, that this result may have quite a different explanation than that of "strengthening learned connections."

MODERN CONCEPTIONS OF LEARNING

Many modern learning theorists seem to have come to the conclusion that conceiving learning as a matter of strengthening connections is entirely too simple. Modern conceptions of learning tend to be highly analytical about the events that take place in learning, both *outside* the learner and also *inside*. The modern point of view about learning tends to view it as a complex of processes taking place in the learner's nervous system. This view is often called an "information-processing" conception.

One example of an information processing theory is that of Atkinson and Shiffrin.[8] According to this theory, information is first registered by the senses and remains in an essentially unaltered form for a short period of time. It then enters what is called the short-term store, where it can be retained for 30 seconds or so. This short-term store has a limited capacity, so that new information coming into it simply pushes aside what may already be stored there. But an important process takes place in this short-term memory, according to Atkinson and Shiffrin. There is a kind of internal reviewing mechanism (a "rehearsal buffer") which organizes and rehearses the material even within this short period of time. Then it is ready to be transferred to long-term store. But when this happens it is first subjected to a process called *coding*. In other words, it is not transferred in raw form, but is transformed in some way which will make it easier to remember at a later time. Still another process is *retrieval*, which comes into play at the time the individual attempts to remember what he has learned.

It is easy to see that a much more sophisticated theory of learning and memory is implied here. It goes far beyond the notion of gradually increasing the strength of a single connection.

Prerequisites for Learning. If repetition or practice is not the major factor in learning, what is? The answer I am inclined to give is that the most dependable condition for the insurance of learning is the prior learning of prerequisite capabilities. Some people would call these "specific readinesses" for learning; others would call them "enabling conditions." If one wants to insure that a student can learn some specific new activity, the very best guarantee is to be sure he has previously learned the prerequisite capabilities. When this in fact has been accomplished, it seems to me quite likely that he will learn the new skill without repetition.

Let me illustrate this point by reference to a study carried out by Virginia Wiegand.[9] She attempted to identify all the prerequisite capabilities needed for sixth-grade students to learn to formulate a general expression relating the variables in an inclined plane. Without using the exact terminology of physics, let us note that the task was to formulate an expression relating the *height* of the plane, the *weight* of the body traversing downwards, and the *amount of push* imparted to an object at the end of the plane. (Wiegand was not trying to teach physics, but to see if the children could learn to formulate a physical relationship which was quite novel to them.) The expression aimed for was, "Distance pushed times a constant block weight equals height of plane times weight of cart."

Initially, what was wanted was explained carefully to the students; the plane and the cart were demonstrated. Thirty students (out of 31) were found who could not accomplish the task; that is, they did not know how to solve the problem. What was it they didn't know? According to the hypothesis being investigated, they didn't know some *prerequisite* things. Figure 1 shows what these missing intellectual skills were thought to be.

What Wiegand did was to find out which of these prerequisite skills were present in each student and which were not present. She did this by starting at the top of the hierarchy and working downwards, testing at each point whether the student could do the designated task or not. In some students, only two or three skills were missing; in others, seven or eight. When she had worked down to the point where these subordinate capabilities *were* present, Wiegand turned around and went the other way. She now made sure that all the prerequisite skills were present, right up to, but not including, the final inclined plane problem.

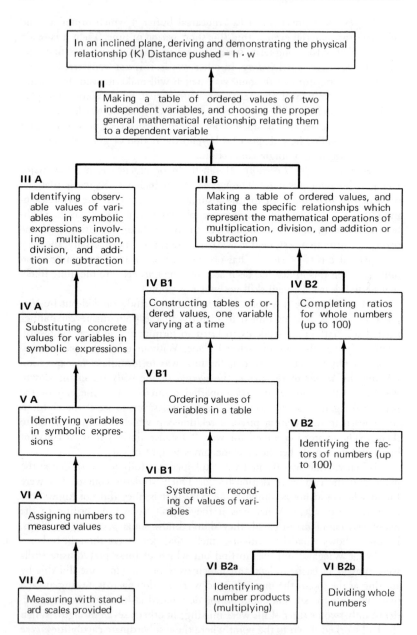

FIGURE 1. *A hierarchy of subordinate intellectual skills applicable to the problem of deriving a general expression relating variables in an inclined plane (Wiegand, 1969).*

The question being asked in this study was, If all the prerequisite skills are present, can the students now solve this physical problem which they were unable to solve previously? Wiegand's results are quite clear-cut. Having learned the prerequisites, nine out of 10 students were able to solve the problem which they were initially unable to solve. They now solved the problem without hesitation and with no practice on the problem itself. On the other hand, for students who did not have a chance to learn the prerequisites, only three of 10 solved the problem (and these were students who had no "missing" skills). This is the kind of evidence that makes me emphasize the critical importance of prerequisite intellectual skills. Any particular learning is not at all difficult if one is truly prepared for it.

Coding and Remembering. Quite a number of studies appear in the experimental literature pertaining to the effects of coding of information on its retention. I choose as an illustration a study by Bower and Clark.[10] These investigators studied the recall by college students of 12 lists of 10 nouns apiece. In learning each list, each student was encouraged to make up a story connecting the nouns. For each student there was a yoked control who was not encouraged to make up a story but who was permitted the same amount of time to learn each list of nouns.

Here is an example of a story which one of the subjects constructed for the words *vegetable, instrument, college, nail, fence, basin, merchant, queen, scale,* and *goat:* "A vegetable can be a useful instrument for a college student. A carrot can be a nail for your fence or basin. But a merchant of the queen would scale that fence and feed the carrot to a goat."

The subjects were asked to recall each list immediately after their study of it. They recalled 99 percent under both conditions. The subjects were later asked to recall all of the lists, after they had learned all 12. In this case there was an enormous difference: The recall of the narrative group averaged 93 percent, that of the non-narrative group only 13 percent. In other words, deliberate coding had increased recall by seven times.

Retrieval and Remembering. Suppose that learning has indeed occurred; what will insure that whatever has been learned will be remembered? There seems to be at least some absence of evidence that simply practicing or repeating things after they have been learned has the effect of improving retention. What the individual does when he is asked to remember something is to *retrieve* it; that is, he brings to bear a process of searching and finding, in his memory, something he is looking for. This process is probably very little understood at present, but there is increasing evidence that it does occur and that it plays a crucial role in remembering.

Some interesting work has been done on the subject of retrieval. In one experiment, Tulving and Pearlstone[11] had groups of high school students learn lists of words of various lengths: 12 words, 24 words, or 48 words. The words themselves were instances of categories, such as four-footed animals (cow, rat); weapons (bomb, cannon); forms of entertainment (radio, music); professions (lawyer, engineer), and so on. The words were presented one at a time in mixed-up order. Different lists also used one, two, or four words in each category.

Once the lists of words had been learned, recall was measured under two different conditions. In the first, the learners were simply told to write down all the words they could remember. In the second, the category names were used as cues to recall; that is, the learners were asked to write down all the words they remembered which were "forms of entertainment," all which were "four-footed animals," and so on. These extra cues worked wonders on recall. The effect was more marked the greater the number of words that had to be recalled. The differences among those learning 48 words was striking, amounting to a twofold increase.

These results show in a rather clear way how powerful is the effect of such extra cues on retrieval of information that has been learned. In this study, the words themselves can be said to have been "equally well learned" in all the groups. What was different between the groups was the aid they were given in retrieving what they had learned. This is only one of the ac-cumulating pieces of evidence that remembering is markedly affected by retrieval at the time of recall, more than it is, perhaps, by events taking place at the time of learning.

IMPLICATIONS FOR INSTRUCTION

The contrasts between older and newer conceptions of learning and memory seem to me quite remarkable. What implications do they have for instruction? If there are indeed newly discovered ways to affect learning and remembering, how might they be put to use in the classroom and in ma-terials of the curriculum?

First, there is the very fundamental point that each learner approaches each new learning task with a different collection of previously learned pre-requisite skills. To be effective, therefore, a learning program for each child must take fully into account what he knows how to do already, and what he doesn't know how to do already. One must find out what prerequisites he has already mastered—not in a general sense, but in a very precise sense for each learner. Does this mean one must do "diagnostic testing"? Yes, that's exactly what it means. To do so, of course, one must first develop the requisite diagnostic tests. By and large, we don't have them.

Second, the most important guide to the learning that needs to be ac-complished is the set of prerequisites that the student has not yet mastered. Remember here Wiegand's experiment. When she systematically saw to it that students climbed the hierarchy, skill by skill, this was what was spe-cifically needed to get them to engage in the problem solving they were originally unable to do.

Third, do students need additional practice to insure retention? If by this is meant, "Should they be given many additional examples so that what they have learned will be 'strengthened'?," I think the evidence says it probably won't work this way. Periodic and spaced reviews, however, are another matter, and it seems likely that these have an important role to play in retention. Notice that when a review is given the student has to exercise his strategies of retrieval.

This brings me to the final point, which concerns the processes of coding and retrieval. Probably what should be aimed for here is the learning by students of strategies of coding. These are by no means the same as what are called "mnemonic systems," although it is possible that such systems have a contribution to make in teaching us how coding might be done. For meaningful learning, it appears even more likely that notions like "advance organizers" and "anchoring ideas," as studied by Ausubel,[12] may be particularly powerful.

Similarly, retrieval strategies are also a class of objective that might be valued for instruction. From the evidence we have, I should say that retrieval strategies might very well consist in networks of superordinate categories into which newly learned specific information, or specific intellectual skills, can be placed. Having students learn to retrieve information by a process of search which first locates such superordinate networks may be a major way of providing them with the capability of good retention.

Even these two or three aspects of modern learning conceptions, it seems to me, lead to a very different view of what instruction is all about. In the most general sense, instruction becomes not primarily a matter of communicating something that is to be stored. Instead, it is a matter of stimulating the use of capabilities the learner already has at his disposal, and of making sure he has the requisite capabilities for the present learning task, as well as for many more to come.

REFERENCES

1. E. L. Thorndike, *Human Learning.* New York: Appleton-Century, 1931, p. 160.

2. B. J. Underwood, "Laboratory Studies of Verbal Learning," in E. R. Hilgard (ed.), *Theories of Learning and Instruction. Sixty-third Yearbook, Part I.* Chicago: National Society for the Study of Education, 1964, p. 148.

3. I. Rock, "The Role of Repetition in Associative Learning," *American Journal of Psychology,* June, 1957, pp. 186–93.

4. W. K. Estes, B. L. Hopkins, and E. J. Crothers, "All-or-None and Conservation Effects in the Learning and Retention of Paired Associates," *Journal of Experimental Psychology,* December, 1960, pp. 329–39.

5. R. M. Gagné, J. R. Mayor, H. L. Garstens, and N. E. Paradise, "Factors in Acquiring Knowledge of a Mathematical Task," *Psychological Monographs,* No. 7, 1962 (Whole No. 526).

6. J. R. Gibson, "Transfer Effects of Practice Variety in Principle Learning." Berkeley: University of California. Ph.D. Dissertation, 1964.

7. J. H. Reynolds and R. Glaser, "Effects of Repetition and Spaced Review upon Retention of a Complex Learning Task," *Journal of Educational Psychology,* October, 1964, pp. 297–308.

8. R. C. Atkinson and R. M. Shiffrin, "Human Memory: A Proposed System and Its Control Processes," in K. W. Spence and J. T. Spence (eds.), *The Psychology of Learning and Motivation: Advances in Research and Theory,* Vol. 2. New York: Academic Press, 1968, pp. 89–195.

9. V. K. Wiegand, "A Study of Subordinate Skills in Science Problem Solving." Berkeley: University of California. Ph.D. Dissertation, 1969.

10. G. H. Bower and M. C. Clark, "Narrative Stories as Mediators for Serial Learning," *Psychonomic Science,* April, 1969, pp. 181–82.

11. E. Tulving and Z. Pearlstone, "Availability versus Accessibility of Information in Memory for Words," *Journal of Verbal Learning and Verbal Behavior,* August, 1966, pp. 381–91.

12. D. P. Ausubel, *Educational Psychology: A Cognitive View.* New York: Holt, Rinehart and Winston, 1968.

15.

Suburbia: a wasteland of disadvantaged youth and negligent schools?

JAMES A. MEYER

Here is an article that may be considered as either irrelevant or long overdue, depending upon the reader's own attitude and convictions. Low income and ghetto living are not necessarily the only existing conditions that deprive young people of opportunity and justify their being labelled disadvantaged.

The editors are disposed to agree that there are many ways in which "advantaged" young people are socially short changed. We question the common assumption that dealing with culture deprivation automatically is the responsibility of the schools. The fact is that schools are agents of society and they function to preserve and to transmit the culture. From this point of view the schools are functioning pretty well. In addition, schools seem to be passing on the alienation, frustration, and doubt which characterize these times. We think it unfair and unrealistic to expect education to be, and to do, something vastly different from the supporting culture. To expect abrupt change is to make for disillusion and to bring pressure to bear where no real power exists.

Teachers and schools often are threatened to the point of inaction and a sort of neurotic immobility. Responsibility cannot accrue

Phi Delta Kappan, 50:575–578, 1969. James A. Meyer, Assistant Supervising Principal for Instruction, New Hartford (New York) Central Schools.

without power and any power the schools may have is conferred
rather than being indigenous. A basic problem is cultural apathy and
lack of support. This, in turn, hinges upon the noninvolvement of in-
dividuals. Perhaps the beginning should be involvement. The editors
believe that human relations programs mentioned by the author offer
promise. Does the reader agree? Should we begin with youngsters or
their parents? Or with ourselves and our own relationships?

THE TIME has come to include our suburbias in any comprehensive assessment of the strengths and weaknesses of American education. At least
among the vast middle classes, suburban life has long been thought of as
ideal and suburban educational systems as exemplary; but there is mount-
ing evidence that even by conventional standards such is not the case. One
need look no further than the suburban youth—products of our so-called
social utopias—to suspect that suburban societies and their educational institutions have been overrated and underproductive.

Indeed, suburban youth can no longer be taken for granted. How can
they be, considering today's frightening world of aimless youth? The average suburban teen-ager is often pictured as either consumed with self pity
or alienated into withdrawal from society. He is said to know it all, to be
intelligent and amoral, well-mannered yet merciless, cynical in a young-old
way, and oh so sophisticated. Some suburban youngsters are in flight from
their own lives; others are deeply worried about what the future holds for
them; and some are in revolt against their parents' suburban values.

At first glance most of our suburban youth share a common background of comfortable homes, loving parents, "good schools," high intelligence, excellent health, and almost unlimited opportunities for self-development. They have almost all the advantages that many of their mothers and
fathers growing up during the Great Depression and World War II were
denied. Yet many of today's middle-class suburban youngsters exhibit disturbing character qualities—sexual libertarianism, vehement rejection of
adult authority, and a widespread disposition to experiment with drugs.[1]

Is the older generation really at fault? Or is this rebelling suburban
generation the product of an overpermissive educational system? Are modern suburbia and its so-called cultural attributes a myth? Do the hypocrisy
and callousness of suburban living really distort the values of modern
youth? Unfortunately, it does seem that the tremendous reservoir of young,
creative talent located in suburbia is not being cultivated in a manner essential to effective growth of democratic ideals; and there are now some real
doubts emerging about the kinds of leadership suburban youth might someday contribute to our society.

SUBURBAN DEPRIVATION

Our nation's suburbias are evidently becoming so segregated that children can grow up without genuine contact with others of different racial,

religious, or social backgrounds. The result is a growing provincialism in spite of ease of travel and communication. Suburbia's children are living and learning in a land of distorted values and faulty perceptions. They have only the slightest notion of others; they judge them on the basis of suburban standards (such as "cleanliness" and "niceness"), generalize about groups on the basis of the few they might have known, and think in stereotypes. In short, they usually have little association with or knowledge of people who differ in appearance or attitudes.

Dan Dodson, director of the Center for Human Relations and Community Studies at New York University, addressing himself to the problems facing youngsters living in suburban societies, declared: "In the suburbs a significant hardship on youngsters is their essential uselessness. They are 'kept' people well into their teens and often longer. There is little a youth can do to contribute to his family's well-being except to make top grades. But this contribution can go to a limited number only."[2]

Dodson further claims that there is considerable evidence that life in the suburbs is harder on boys than on girls. One reason is that the fathers are away from home so much of the time that their sons have only a vaguely conceptualized father-figure with which to identify.

Similarly, the values, attitudes, and behavior of older generation suburbanites are often exposed by the mass media as superficial and empty. For example, youthful critics of the middle-class suburban society vividly illustrated their rejection of suburbanite values in their acceptance of *The Graduate,* a film which devastatingly portrays the affluent, banal, swimming pool-and-corner-bar suburban set as seen through the eyes of its youthful "hero." The chief reason this film became such a social phenomenon is, perhaps, the forlorn manner in which the protagonist copes with the phoniness of a materially comfortable contemporary society. It says something about the meaninglessness of affluent life which distorts youthful aims and ambitions. It dramatizes the generation gap, portraying a youth almost paralyzed by the rapacious hedonism of his suburbanite parents.

Some authorities suggest that this alienation of the suburban child from "others" is a recent phenomenon stemming from the unique structure of suburban life. Discussing this idea, Goldman[3] uses the words *sidewalk* and *station wagon* as keys to understanding:

> The sidewalk [once] symbolized the avenue of communication between one child and another. In many areas this has vanished. . . . Sidewalks are no longer built . . . in some suburban housing developments. The response to the disappearing sidewalk is the mother-driven station wagon. Instead of relying upon informal mingling of children, the image of the station wagon implies a planned, structured mingling of children: the Boy Scout meeting at 7:30, the Little League game at 4:00, the music lesson at 5:00, etc. What is gained by structuring common activities for children may be lost by some of the concomitant results—the loss of spontaneity when games and recreation must be carefully scheduled and supervised, the early creation of the

"organization man," etc. The increased number of nursery schools is part of the same response to the deprivation of young children.

Other critics of contemporary suburban life have asserted that parents in suburbia pamper and spoil their children to such an extent that the children grow up without any real parental supervision. Halleck has declared that "some parents in suburbia have, through painstaking efforts to avoid creating neuroses in their children, abdicated their responsibility to teach and discipline their children. In so doing they have reared a generation of spoiled, greedy youth who are unable to tolerate the slightest frustration without showing an angry or infantile response."[4]

On the other hand, many critics put the blame for youthful unrest in suburbia on the way the children are overprotected and parentally dominated. This goes beyond an overabundance of material things. Rather, it consists of parental hovering and a reluctance to let their youngsters assume self-responsibility and self-direction. Perhaps some suburban parents fear their children will make mistakes and embarrass them. In any case, from an early age many suburban children are given little opportunity to use their own resources and make appropriate decisions.

Obviously, both extremes are unhealthy and undoubtedly contribute greatly to the restlessness and antisocial behavior patterns of rebelling suburban youth.

Of one thing we are sure, and that is that parental influence over suburban youths has deteriorated markedly; and children are cheated and deprived of experiences essential for effective development of wholesome ideals and attitudes. Unless more authentic human values are developed within our suburbias, the suburban style of life will significantly contribute to the further deprivation of suburban youth. While little can be done about the attitudes and values inherited from parents, the schools still have the opportunity to reach these restless youth and redirect their energies. But first the challenge must be recognized.

SCHOOLS SHARE THE BLAME

"Suburban children are underprivileged. . . . There is little in their education, formal or otherwise, to familiarize them with the rich diversity of American life." This judgment by Alice Miel in *The Shortchanged Children of Suburbia*[5] grew out of a series of research studies designed to explore life in suburbia and to determine what is being taught about human differences in our schools. Her findings were alarming and resulted in a sharp indictment of the suburban school for failure to do something about preparing suburban children for a healthy, wholesome life in our society. The results of this study indicate that:

The typical suburban elementary school student's life is almost totally insulated and circumscribed.

Suburban youngsters learn, individually, to be bigoted and hypocritical about racial, religious, economic, and ethnic differences at an early age.

Group prejudices, too, take root early—and go deep.

Materialism, selfishness, misplaced aggression, fake values, and anxiety top the list of common characteristics.

Yet many educators today are neither adequately trained nor perceptive enough to cope with the problems experienced by adolescents growing up in our affluent suburbs, and these inadequacies of staff hamper efforts to provide compensatory treatment.

For example, on the basis of some recent career pattern studies, it is now estimated that about 85 out of every 100 secondary school teachers in our suburban schools are from family backgrounds that differ markedly from those of the majority of the students in their classrooms. These teachers are said to undergo an emotional trauma when teaching suburban pupils. Problems of adaptation and adjustment are many. Faced with an "affluence" and "sophistication" (as doubtful as it may be) that they themselves might never have experienced, teachers in suburbia often expect and accept different standards of behavior. It stands to reason that by condoning these unique standards of behavior, teachers must bear some responsibility for the distorted values and attitudes as well as the antisocial behavior patterns often displayed by suburban youth.

Not only are some suburban educators not emotionally equipped to teach suburban youth—they may not be intellectually equipped either. "Many secondary school teachers have lower I.Q.'s than those of the suburban children they teach." This is what S. Alan Cohen of Yeshiva University said about suburban educators when he suggested that:

> These teachers are unable to challenge their better students because they are afraid to. Many teachers are terrorized by the intellectual precocity of middle-class children. As a result, they cling tenaciously to rigid, lock-step pedagogies and mediocre materials to hold down the natural flow of intellectual curiosity.[6]

In asserting that suburban middle-class schools are not providing as good an education as they should, critic Cohen cites the growing evidence of educational inadequacy—the irrelevancy of curriculum content and the poor pedagogy—and concludes that superior test performances of children from "Scarsdales" tend to reflect the enriched verbal home environments rather than the school's educational program. "As a result," says Cohen, "the weak content and pedagogy in the middle-class schools are good enough, or perhaps more accurately, not bad enough to ruin these children."

Disappointingly enough, there are reports that school guidance counselors also experience difficulties when counseling in suburban schools. College counseling, for example, is theoretically only part of the total guidance function in secondary education. But in suburbia, college counseling becomes a major item of responsibility, and the counselor must become a master at it. Indeed, in the wealthy suburbs, where the citizenry have the money and desperately want to send their children to "good" colleges, they generally perceive counseling in "college" terms. Irvin Faust,[7] a suburban counselor, has written that:

> The trouble with most college-oriented communities and the coun-
> selors they hire is that college placement rather than welfare of stu-
> dents proves the guidance program; it becomes the total force rather
> than the natural result of a developmental counseling experience. . . .
> Whatever else arises is subordinate. He's awash in the suburban syn-
> drome that says it's worse not to get into college than to flunk out.
> And it's worse not to get into a particular college, or colleges, for
> collecting acceptances is part of the game.

Suburban youths themselves have become progressively more sensitive to the lack of substance and meaning in the curriculum of their schools and are voicing strong concerns over the lack of relevancy. Many suburban youngsters, for example, are now said to be articulate, irreverent, humorless, and relentless in their contempt for what they honestly view as the mean-inglessness of suburban education. They turn to one another when shaping beliefs or seeking advice, for they have learned to distrust both their parents and their teachers.

For some time now, the attentions and interests of most educators have been directed toward the educational problems relative to urban conditions of life. Recently, however, some concern has been given to shortcomings in rural education. But only little concern has been shown toward the possible needs of suburban youth, and the thought of any possible weakness in the education of suburbia's children has been virtually nonexistent. But the cultural circumstances of the suburbs are alive with challenges to the schools. Without compensatory approaches in the educational program, the suburban schools will fall far short of achieving the high purposes they are expected to achieve.

COMPENSATORY PROGRAMS

Occasionally school officials and boards of education in affluent sub-urban communities are perceptive enough to grasp the defects of contem-porary suburban life and commit themselves to some form of action. There have been some noteworthy attempts to revitalize the suburban curriculum and bring meaning and substance to instruction. One major illustration of this is the growing tendency among suburban schools to emphasize a human relations approach to instruction in the classroom.

Indeed, human relations programs hold promise for the future of sub-urban youngsters. Without instruction relative to the human environment in the suburban schools, many suburban youngsters will grow up with little chance for wholesome personal development. But setbacks do occur. In one well-known Buffalo suburban community—Williamsville, New York—the board of education backed away from a regional Title III project which would have sent a corps of teachers into its schools to improve instruction in human relations. The reason? A band of more than 100 citizens opposed the program, claiming "it would interfere with parents' lessons in human relations."[8] A sad day for Williamsville.

There are other programs suburban educators might seriously consider introducing in their schools if they would wish to see their students overcome the restrictive aspects of suburban life. Examples include:

Instruction about different groups and cultures which could help eliminate prejudices and misconceptions about others. Personal experience with children of other groups can show a disadvantaged suburban youth directly, immediately, and concretely that not all members of a different group are "stupid, dirty, or dishonest." Suburban youths need supplementary reality experiences to make it possible for them to "see" society as it really is so that they may develop the empathy and compassion essential for the development of wholesome values and attitudes.

More social, interscholastic, and subject-matter club activities in order to involve students in meaningful intergroup situations. Service clubs and school-community organizations serve as a very useful vehicle in relating the schooling process to community needs while restoring a sense of personal worth for our troubled suburban youth.

Suburban schools should actively assist in fostering a return of the "family unit" by encouraging child-parent attendance at school functions. Rather than tolerate parental isolation, the suburban schools must assist in creating a climate conducive to close family ties through school-centered activities, attempting primarily to entice fathers to share in these school events with their children.

The schools of suburbia must expand the counseling staff at both the secondary and elementary levels. Individual and group counseling is imperative—especially in the elementary grades when attitudes are still malleable. After-school counseling with parents also seems essential, in view of the alarming increase in family conflicts occurring within the suburban communities.

A major factor—perhaps the most important one—in providing suburban youth with direction and eliminating youthful prejudices is that of teacher attitudes.[9] Suburban educators must teach suburban youth with warmth, respect, and understanding. This, however, can only follow self-examination and insightful knowledge of the problems and pressures experienced by suburban youth. The attitudes of teachers about themselves and their relationships with and responsibilities to the suburban disadvantaged must first be clarified through in-service programs. Suburban teachers must develop a more comprehensive understanding of the nature of suburban life and its inherent defects.

The schools should involve students more deeply in the task of teaching and curriculum construction, thereby serving two purposes: 1) determining just what aspects of the curriculum are indeed relevant from the student's point of view, and 2) improving the sense of worth of the student through responsible participation in the educational process. Why not have students contribute their views through the previewing of audio or visual materials; through examination of textbooks, library books, and other resource materials; through assisting in the instruction of slower or retarded children; through assuming leadership responsibilities in discussion groups and seminars? Why not delegate to the students more responsibility in designing school codes of conduct; supervision of study, library, or lunch areas; and enforcement of school discipline? Much could be gained—both by the schools and the students.

THE defects of suburban society and the misconceptions brought by suburban students to the schools remain serious obstacles in the path of social progress. If the people of the suburbs—including suburbia's educators—would have their children grow up to respect all men and to seek for others the same scope of opportunity available to themselves, it is imperative that the suburban schools help develop the understandings and attitudes essential for constructive citizenship. Otherwise, the American Dream becomes the American Tragedy, and alienation and isolation become even more a way of life for youth trapped in their suburban environment.

NOTES AND REFERENCES

1. Yet Kenneth Keniston in *Notes On Committed Youth* (New York: Harcourt, Brace and World, 1968) asserts that these young radicals are unusually "healthy" youth who have solved their psychological problems to a higher degree than most and have achieved "an unusual degree of psychological integration." With respect to drug use, read "Scarsdale Seeks To Curb Use of Drugs," *New York Times,* January 27, 1969, and "Cause Shown," *American School Board Journal,* February, 1969, p. 5.

2. Dan Dodson, "Are We Segregating Our Children?" *Parents Magazine,* September, 1963.

3. Louis Goldman, "Varieties of Alienation and Educational Responses." *Teachers College Record,* January, 1968, pp. 331–44; Charles H. Harrison, "In the Suburbs," *Education News,* September, 1968, pp. 15, 19.

4. S. L. Halleck, "Hypotheses of Student Unrest," *Phi Delta Kappan,* September, 1968, pp. 2–9.

5. Alice Miel and Edwin Kieste, *The Shortchanged Children of Suburbia.* New York: Institute of Human Relations Press, American Jewish Committee, 1967. It is interesting to contrast Miel's publication with the University of Chicago's recent study, *The Quality of Inequality: Urban and Suburban Pub-*

lic Schools (Chicago: The University of Chicago Center for Public Study, 1968), the authors of which seem to feel that suburban schools are successful by any measure and provide the efforts necessary to offset deficiencies of environment. In all fairness, however, this title is misleading, for the book primarily examines the problems of urban education and only indirectly addresses itself to the defects of suburban schooling.

6. S. Alan Cohen, "Local Control and the Cultural Deprivation Fallacy," *Phi Delta Kappa,* January, 1969, pp. 255–59.

7. Irvin Faust, "Guidance Counseling in Suburbia," *Teachers College Record,* February, 1968, pp. 449–58.

8. "Suspect Negroes of Being Human," *Education News,* September 9, 1968.

9. See *Report of the National Advisory Council on the Education of Disadvantaged Children.* Washington, D.C.: Government Printing Office, January 31, 1967.

16.

Conditions productive of superior children

ROBERT J. HAVIGHURST

Havighurst describes and cites examples of desirable environmental conditions and their effect upon human achievement. On the face of it, it would appear that anything which can be so described also could be created. Further, it would appear that following the engineering of such conditions, superior humans could be expected as a result. But it is not so simple. If it were, we should have provided for the development of superior people long ago. We are much less adept at engineering humans than we are at engineering things. Perhaps our success with the latter operates to curb our ability to deal effectively with people, for we continually fail to get the results we wish. A nonemotional impersonalism is essential for the one—it adds to problems for the other.

The editors think it is significant that interactions between people in one form or another are recognized by this author as being the factor which determines or inhibits achievement in able students. Unfortunately, we know least well how to conduct and to teach human relations. We have wars, divorces, broken homes, and riots because so little is known about how people get along with and affect each other. When and if we find out, we shall know not only the conditions which produce superior people but also how to contrive situations that promote development of unused potential in all of us.

Teachers College Record, 62:524–531, April, 1961. Robert J. Havighurst, Professor of Education and Human Development, The University of Chicago.

CHILDREN BECOME mentally superior through a combination of being born with superior potential and being raised in a superior environment. Nobody knows the relative importance of these two factors. Certainly, biological intelligence is too low in some children to permit them to develop even average mental ability. Probably a severe environmental handicap can prevent the potentially most able child from showing more than average mental ability.

It seems probable that our society actually discovers and develops no more than perhaps half its potential intellectual talent. Some evidence for this statement lies in the fact that former immigrant groups, which at one time did the heavy labor of America, at first produced very few mentally superior children; but after a sojourn in this country of two or three generations, they have produced large numbers of mentally superior people. They did this through bettering the environment in which they reared their children. The same process is now going on in the underprivileged groups of today—the Negroes, the Puerto Ricans, the rural southern whites—as they secure better economic conditions and then create a more favorable environment for the mental development of their children.

There is some validity to a view of the production of mentally superior people as a *processing* of human material. Some of this material is of better biological quality than other parts of it, but it all depends heavily on social processing for the quality of the final product.

In this paper we shall deliberately ignore the biological element in the production of mentally superior children and consider only the cultivation of mental superiority through the family, the school, and the community. We shall try to answer the question: What kind of social environment produces mentally superior children most efficiently, and how can we expand this environment and make it more effective?

SOCIAL CLASS AND CITIES

Mentally superior children come in relatively high proportions from upper and upper-middle class families and in relatively lower proportions from lower working class families. This fact has been affirmed in dozens of studies of the relations between IQ and socio-economic status.

Some idea of the relative efficiencies of the various social classes in processing their children for mental ability is given in Table 1, which comes from a study of all the children in the sixth grade of the public schools of a medium-sized mid-western city. The upper and upper-middle classes, combined, produced 1.8 times as many children in the upper quarter of the IQ distribution as they would if all social classes had been equally efficient at this, and only .4 times as many children in the lowest quarter. The lower working class showed a reversal of these efficiency ratios.

If all four socio-economic groups had been as efficient as the upper and

TABLE 1. Efficiencies of the Various Social Classes in Producing Children in the Top and Bottom Quarters of IQ Distribution (Sixth Grade in River City)

Social Class	Percentage Distribution of Children	Efficiency Ratio[1] in Producing Children in	
		Top Quarter	Bottom Quarter
Upper and Upper Middle	10	1.8	.4
Lower Middle	27	1.5	.6
Upper Lower	39	.8	1.1
Lower Lower	24	.4	1.6

1. These ratios indicate the relative efficiencies of the various social classes. If all classes were equally efficient in producing children of a given quartile in IQ, the ratios would all be 1.

upper-middle class groups in providing children with IQ's in the top quarter (above about 110), there would have been 180 children with IQ's over 110 in this community for every 100 such children today. In other words, the numbers of mentally superior children would have been almost doubled, and the intelligence level of the child population would have been lifted enormously.

Similar conclusions arise from a study of high school seniors in a city of 500,000. Roughly 5 per cent of the seniors were selected by a systematic screening program as being "academically superior." As can be seen in Table 2, the various high schools contributed to this total in rough proportion to the socio-economic status of the parents. The school with highest socio-economic status contributed 19 per cent of its seniors to the select group. Within this group, 92 per cent of the fathers were high school graduates; 65 per cent were college graduates. The three schools with lowest socio-economic status contributed 1.5 per cent of their seniors to the select group. Less than 40 per cent of the fathers of the superior students in these three schools were high school graduates. If all schools had contributed as efficiently as School A to the production of superior students, there would have been 532 instead of 194, or almost three times as many. Probably the reason this proportion is higher than the proportion reported in Table 1 is that Table 1 refers to sixth graders, Table 2 to twelfth graders. The cultural advantages of the higher status children probably cumulated between the sixth and twelfth grades to give them even greater superiority over their less privileged agemates.

Granted the assumption we are making in this paper—that mental superiority is largely a product of social environment—the mental level of the population would be raised very greatly if we could give all children

TABLE 2. Efficiencies of Schools of Various Socio-Economic Levels in Producing Academically Superior High School Seniors (Data from an American City of 500,000 Population)

| | High School | | | | | | |
	A	B	C	D	E	FGH	Total
No. of graduates	412	392	325	71	400	1,203	2,803
No. of superior students in graduating class	77	45	30	5	17	20	194
Per cent of superior students	19	12	9	7	4	1.5	5.1
Rank in Socio-economic status	1	2	3	4	5	7	
No. of superior students if A ratio prevailed	77	74	62	14	76	229	532

the kinds of social environment which upper middle class children have today.

Mentally superior children also tend to come from urban and suburban communities, rather than from rural communities. This is not as pronounced an effect as the social class effect, but it seems to indicate that the urban-suburban environment is more stimulating mentally than the rural environment.

Within the families lower on the socio-economic scale, there is enough production of mentally superior youth to indicate that socio-economic status alone is not what makes the difference between a good and poor environment for mental growth. It is probably certain cultural and motivational deprivations that often go with low socio-economic status that reduce the efficiency of lower status families. Whenever a very bright boy or girl is discovered in a family of low economic status, it turns out that this family has unusual characteristics which give the youth an advantage. These characteristics may consist of thrift and ambition or of an interest on the part of the mother or father in literature, art, or science.

Summing up the argument thus far, it seems that boys and girls who are mentally superior have become so because of (1) a home and school environment which stimulated them to learn and to enjoy learning, (2) parents and other significant persons who set examples of interest and attainment in education which the children unconsciously imitated, and (3) early family training which produced a desire for achievement in the child. When these influences act upon a child with average or better biological equipment for learning, the child will become mentally superior. They are sometimes found in unexpected places.

For instance, Paul is a very good student in high school. His mother has worked as a waitress for years, since her husband deserted her, to support herself and Paul. She placed Paul in a boys' home sponsored by a church, and he has lived there from the age of 8 until his present age of 18. He says, "My father and mother never went to college. I thought I'd like to do better in life than they did." At the boys' home, the superintendent and the teachers were demanding but warm. Under them, Paul performed well in the elementary school until time for senior high, when he went to the local public school. Here he had some difficulty at first. He says, "English was about my worst subject. The teacher helped me though, and I improved a lot. I consider her an important person in my life." A careers unit in civics helped him to decide on engineering or mathematics, and he will go to college with scholarship help. Two of his closest friends have college plans. The superintendent of the home has urged him to go. "He told me to go to college. He said I was a good student, and I ought to go to college."

DIVERGENT THINKERS

Among the mentally superior part of the population some people are creative and some are not. Much attention has been paid recently to the quality or qualities of creativity on the assumptions that our society needs not only intellectually facile people but, more especially, creative people, and that a high IQ does not guarantee creativity.

Guilford and others have made a distinction between "convergent thinking" and "divergent thinking." The person with "convergent" intellectual ability is retentive and docile. He tends to seek the single, predetermined "correct" answer to an intellectual problem. On the other hand, the "divergent" thinker is constructive and creative. He tends to seek the novel, experimental, and multiple answer to an intellectual problem.

Guilford has devised a number of tests of creative intelligence which have only a low positive correlation with the usual intelligence tests. Getzels and Jackson,[3] using these tests, picked out a group of high school pupils who were high in IQ (average 150) but not especially high in creative thinking for comparison with a group high in creative thinking but lower in IQ (average 127). The two groups did equally well in achievement tests, but the high intelligence, non-creative group were preferred by their teachers as the kind of students they liked to have in their classes. The high creative group, in freely-written stories, showed more humor, more unexpected endings, more incongruities, and generally a freer play of fantasy. Similarly, Cattell and Drevdahl[2] compared outstanding research scientists with outstanding teachers and administrators in the same fields on the 16 P.F. Personality Inventory. They found the researchers to be more self-sufficient and schizothymic (introverted), to have a greater drive for mastery, and to entertain more radical ideas.

We know relatively little, as yet, about creative people and even less about what makes them creative. If it proves to be true that some or all of the qualities of creativity can be taught, this will become another goal in the society's processing of mentally superior children.

THE UNDERACHIEVERS

In the study of intellectually superior children, attention has been called to a substantial group whose educational performance falls below what might reasonably be expected from their performance on intelligence tests. These mentally superior underachievers are people with biological or environmental superiority who have not put their superiority to use in school. They may be regarded as products of an inadequate processing in the home, community, or the school. This conclusion emerges from a number of recent studies of bright underachievers.

Thus, Terman and Oden, in their study of adults whom they had followed from childhood as gifted children,[8] compared the 150 men in their sample who had been most successful in their occupations with the 150 least successful men. As children, these men had all had IQ's of 135 or higher. The more successful group had had an average IQ of 155 in 1922, while the less successful had had an average of 150. However, there were considerable differences in other respects between the two groups. Ninety per cent of the more successful had been graduated from college, compared with 37 per cent of the less successful. Fifty per cent of the fathers of the more successful group were college graduates, compared with only 16 per cent of the fathers of the less successful. In occupation, 38 per cent of the fathers of the more successful were professional men, compared with 19 per cent of the fathers of the less successful.

Terman concludes, "Where all are so intelligent, it follows necessarily that differences in success must be due largely to non-intellectual factors"; and "Everything considered, there is nothing in which the (more successful and less successful) groups present a greater contrast than in drive to achieve and in all-round social adjustment. . . . At any rate, we have seen that intellect and achievement are far from perfectly correlated."

Most of the studies of underachievement have been made on boys rather than girls, because bright boys are underachievers in school much more frequently than girls are. The many studies have produced substantially similar results and point to underachievement as a form of personal and social maladjustment. In one or another of these studies, the following characteristics of underachieving able students appear:

1. They see themselves as inadequate persons.
2. They have lower aspirations than achievers.
3. They do not like school as well as achievers do.

4. They do not enjoy learning from books.
5. They have lower popularity and leadership status in the eyes of their age-mates.
6. They tend to come from homes that are broken or emotionally inadequate in other ways.
7. They tend to come from homes of low socio-economic status.
8. Their vocational goals are not as clearly defined as those of achievers.
9. Their study habits are not as good as those of achievers.
10. They have narrower interests than those of achievers.
11. They have poorer personal adjustment than that of achievers.

Haggard,[6] comparing high with low achieving high IQ children, found that the high achievers had better mental health. In particular, the high achievers in arithmetic, "had by far the best-developed and healthiest egos, both in relation to their own emotions and mental processes and in their greater maturity in dealing with the outside world of people and things." Haggard concluded, "Our findings indicate that the best way to produce clear thinking is to help children develop into anxiety-free, emotionally healthy individuals who are also trained to master a variety of intellectual tasks."

Much the same conclusion is expressed by Gowan[4] after reviewing a number of studies of underachievement. He says, "To summarize, achievement is an indication that the individual has successfully transferred a large enough portion of his basic libidinal drives to areas of cultural accomplishment so that he derives a significant portion of his gratification from them."

Although the general proposition seems justified that high IQ under-achievers are people with inadequate socialization and poor personal-social adjustment, there are two major exceptions to this generalization. One exception refers to a group of high IQ boys with a limited horizon. They are well-adjusted within a small world which does not require more than average school achievement and does not require a college education. Take Kenny, for example. With an IQ of 145, Kenny found school work easy and more or less coasted through his studies, doing enough work to get fairly good grades, but falling down somewhat in high school, where he graduated at about the middle of his class. Kenny's parents were earnest people, good church members, with little formal education. They did not read very much and had no intellectual interests. They were satisfied with Kenny's report cards and pleased that he was going further in school than they had gone. They were especially pleased with Kenny's interest in earning money. He always had several jobs waiting for him and showed great enterprise as a salesman. During his later years in high school, he worked in a shoe store where his employer was so pleased with his work that he offered Kenny a full-time job and a chance to buy into his business when he was graduated from high school. This seemed good to Kenny, and he is now getting along well as junior partner in the store.

The other exception refers to a rather large group of girls with high intelligence who achieve very well up to the end of high school, when their grades fall off and they show little or no interest in going to college. These girls either get married as soon as they finish high school or they take a job in an office or a shop for a few years until they marry. Girls do not generally show as underachievers because their school grades are pretty well maintained until the end of high school. But they would be called underachievers if underachievement were defined as failure to go as far in education as one's abilities would justify.

With this broad definition of underachievement, one can say that the gifted underachievers have not been effectively processed by the society for maximal or optimal educational achievement for one or more of the following reasons:

Inadequate home environment leaves them personally maladjusted and unable to use their intellectual ability.

Inadequate home environment limits their horizon and fails to stimulate them to use education for vocational achievement, although they are personally well adjusted.

Inadequate home environment fails to instill in them a deep drive or need for achievement.

School and home together fail to instill in them an intrinsic love of learning.

The social role of wife and mother is seen by some girls as more important than that of student; and the home, school, and community have caused them to see a conflict between marriage and a home, on the one hand, and continued educational achievement on the other.

INCREASING THE SUPPLY

Holding to our tentative assumption that production of mentally superior people is more a matter of social engineering than of discovery and exploitation of a rare natural resource, we may essay an answer to the question of how to increase the supply of mentally superior children who are well motivated to achieve in school and college.

First, it must be remembered that our culturally deprived families, both in the big cities and in isolated rural areas, have always in the past improved themselves as producers of superior children when they had economic opportunity. The same process of improvement is evident today among working class Negroes, Puerto Ricans, and white emigrants from the rural South. It is to these groups that we may look for an increased supply of able youngsters, and the rate of increase is likely to be considerably facilitated by increasing their degree of economic opportunity and enriching their cultural environment. This point is a central one for those social policies related to our long-range needs for manpower and for school programs aimed at the underprivileged and academically impoverished. Within the schools, there is a grave need for greater attention to rewards for achievement within these groups, for a keener recognition of developing intellectual effort, and for a greater responsiveness to embryonic academic motives.

Second, counseling and guidance services could usefully focus on increasing educational motivation among superior pupils. The well adjusted child with limited horizons, like Kenny, represents a kind of national loss. If education is concerned with the actualizing of individual potentialities, then special attention to youngsters of this kind is more than warranted. A sound argument can be made for the school counselor's devoting more of his time to this sort of developmental enterprise than to the remediation of "problem cases" and to the support of the pathological, the delinquent, and the dull. Both kinds of service are desirable and necessary, of course; but we may have overemphasized the guidance worker's obligation to the educationally handicapped to the serious neglect, both in training and in on-the-job functionings, of his potentialities for working productively with the superior child with low academic motivation.

Third, studies of the unconscious drive for achievement, like those by McClelland[7] and Rosen,[8] indicate that the early training of boys in the home has a great deal to do with their motivation to use their mental ability for school achievement. Closer collaboration between school and home, especially with lower class parent groups, can be helpful here. Even more, an explicit and articulate concern with the development of intellectual motivations in the earliest school years could possibly harvest a more widespread drive for academic achievement and a deeper channeling of intellectual capacities into school work and the kinds of goals that our schools and colleges represent. It is not so much that boys lack a need to achieve, but they often find little reward in harnessing their motives to the activities of the conventional classroom or school.

Fourth, the demonstration that intellectually superior and "creative" abilities are not the same thing suggests that we could profitably expand our search for the gifted to include the "divergent thinker." More clarity and precision in our methods of identifying creative youngsters with above-average but not extremely high IQ's, and more imagination and effort in our attention to such children might yield a happy increment in the numbers of those able to think inventively about important problems. This approach requires, of course, that we reward the innovator, the person with new and deviant ways of dealing with the world; and while this requirement is one to which we all pay lip service, it is one that is likely to entail trouble and inconvenience if it is realistically met. That the trouble and inconvenience will be worth the result is highly probable, but the result hardly alters, although it may more than justify, the cost.

Finally, the most potent means of increasing the numbers of mentally superior children that lies at hand for teachers is to teach so that learning is made more attractive to children. This alone will cause children to increase their own mental abilities. For example, the experiment in Manhattanville Junior High School and the George Washington Senior High School in New York City is having this effect.[1] Boys and girls from culturally deprived families are getting an enriched program, combined with guidance and attempts to improve the home environment. This program has kept pupils in school longer, and there has been a measurable increase in IQ points for these children as they have progressed from the sixth to the ninth grades.

REFERENCES

1. Board of Education of the City of New York. Demonstration guidance project: Junior High School 43 Manhattan and George Washington High School. *Third Annu. Progr. Rep.*, 1958–59.

2. Cattell, R. B., & Drevdahl, J. E. A comparison of the Personality Profile (16 P.F.) of eminent researchers with that of eminent teachers and administrators, and of the general population. *British J. Psychol.*, 1955, *46*, 248–261.

3. Getzels, J. W., & Jackson, P. W. The highly creative and the highly intelligent adolescent. In *Third University of Utah Research Conference on the Identification of Creative Scientific Talent*. Univer. of Utah Press, 1959. Pp. 46–57.

4. Gowan, J. C. Factors of achievement in high school and college. *J. counsel. Psychol.*, 1960, *7*, 91–95.

5. Guilford, J. P. The structure of intellect. *Psychol. Bull.*, 1956. *53*, 267–293.

6. Haggard, F. A. Socialization, personality, and academic achievement in gifted children. *School Rev.*, 1957, *65*, 388–414.

7. McClelland, D. C., Atkinson, J., Clark, R., & Lowell, E. *The achievement motive*. New York: Appleton-Century-Crofts, 1953.

8. Rosen, B. C., & D'Andrade, R. The psychosocial origins of achievement motivation, *Sociometry*, 1959, *22*, 185–218.

9. Terman, L. M., & Oden, Melita. *The gifted child grows up*. Stanford, Calif.: Stanford Univer. Press, 1947.

section **V**

Intellectual development

17.

Psychoneurobiochemeducation

DAVID KRECH

What may happen when and if people learn how to combine their penchant for pills with their urge to find things out? The author of this selection furnishes speculations which are both stimulating and frightening. He hints at the development of greatly increased mental power through combining educational techniques with the heightened brain receptivity and retention that can be brought about by the use of chemicals. Then he asks the disturbing question: "Who will direct this process; who will control the brain controllers?" (See selection 1.)

More than ever in the past few years, men have been faced with the question of how to manage the power they have unleashed. Power is dangerous; when it cannot be controlled or when it may be controlled improperly, it can be terrifying. But until now, this power has been mostly physical in nature. Men have not had to deal with substantial increases in mental and psychological power. Understandably, both threat and pressure are involved. While power may mean an opportunity for exploitation to those who are unscrupulous, its possession may serve more to increase the pressure of responsibility for those who are not. The editors are inclined to believe (to hope) with the author that the necessary capacity to manage will be (must be) inherent in the increased intelligence.

Another question: What about the concept of "species specific experience"? Would you believe that ". . . the study of how language is acquired may provide insight into the very basis of mental life"? Could you design research to test such a hypothesis?

I AM a rat-brain psychologist with a weakness for speculation. Now time was when rat research was a fairly harmless activity, pursued by underpaid, dedicated, well-meaning characters. The world took little note and cared even less about our researches on how rats learned to thread their way

Phi Delta Kappan, 50:370–375, 1969. David Krech, Professor of Psychology, University of California, Berkeley.

through mazes. Oh, occasionally a misguided educator would take us seriously and try to fashion an educational psychology out of our rats-in-a maze studies. But the classroom teachers—once removed from the school of education—would quickly see through such nonsense, and, forsaking all rats, would turn to the serious and difficult task of teaching children—unencumbered and unaided by our research and theory.

But time no longer is. Our psychology—especially when combined with educational practice and theory—must now be listed among the Powerful and, even perhaps, the Dangerous sciences. I refer specifically to the recent research developments in brain biochemistry and behavior—to some of which research I now turn.

The research I will discuss really concerns itself with the venerable mind-body problem beloved of philosophers and theologians. For brain biochemistry and behavior research seeks to find the *physical* basis for memory. In essence it asks the following question: In what corporal forms do we retain the remembrance of things past? What are the chemical or neurological or anatomical substrates of the evocative ghosts we call "memories"? Over the centuries of thought and decades of scientific research we have gained but very little on this question. Today, however, there is a feeling abroad that we are on the verge of great discoveries. Indeed, some researchers believe that we already know, in the rough, the form the final answer will take to the question I have raised. And it is this: The physical basis of any memory, whatever else it may be, involves either the production of new proteins, the release of differentiated molecules of ribonucleic acids (RNA's) or the induction of higher enzymatic activity levels in the brain. In a word, for every separate memory in the mind we will eventually find a differentiated chemical in the brain—"chemical memory pellets," as it were.

What warrant do we have for such a prophecy? To begin with, we have reason to believe that the storage of memory in the brain is a many-splendored, multi-phased, actively changing affair. That is, any single memory is not merely "deposited" in a completed form in the brain. Rather, it goes through a complex developmental history in the brain in which it changes from a short-term into a long-term memory. And each stage in this consolidation process seems to be dependent upon different although interrelated chemical mechanisms. Let me indicate to you one set (of quite a number which are now available) of speculative hypotheses concerning this developmental transformation of memories.

First we can assume that immediately after every experience, a relatively short-lived reverberatory process is set up within the brain. This process continues for a time after the stimulus disappears and permits us to remember events which occurred moments or minutes ago. But this reverberatory process fairly quickly decays and disappears—and as it does, so does the related memory. However, under certain conditions, the short-term reverberatory process, before it disappears completely from the scene, triggers off a second and quite different series of events in the brain. This second series of events involves the release of new RNA's or the production of new proteins and other macromolecules. And these chemical changes are relatively long-lasting and serve as the physical bases of our long-term memories.

Now it can be supposed that if we increased the robustness or the survival time of the initial reverberatory process we might increase the probability of converting the short-term memory into a long-term memory. There are several ways one could do that. Through the repetition of the same stimulus one could presumably prolong or continually reinstate the reverberatory process and thus, perhaps, make it more effective in inducing permanent chemical changes in the brain. The old-fashioned term for this procedure is "drill" or "practice," and drill and practice are indeed effective techniques for helping the conversion of short-term memories into long-term ones.

But James McGaugh, at the University of California at Irvine, got the bright idea that he could achieve much the same results chemically. His argument—very much simplified—went something like this: A drug which would increase neural and chemical activity within the brain might either increase the vigor of the reverberatory process, or the ease with which the long-term chemical processes would "take off," and thus facilitate the conversion of short-term memories into long-term ones. Apparently his idea was a sound one, for with the use of chemical compounds like strychnine and metrazol, which are central nervous system stimulants, McGaugh has been eminently successful in raising the intellectual level of hundreds of southern California mice.

In one of his experiments which is most pregnant with social implications and promises and forebodings for the future, McGaugh tested the maze-learning ability of two quite different strains of mice. One of the strains was, by heredity, particularly adept at maze learning; the other, particularly stupid at that task. Some animals from each strain were injected with different doses of metrazol after each daily learning trial to see whether there would be an improvement in their ability to retain what they had learned on that trial—and some were not. The findings pleased everyone—presumably even the mice. With the optimal dosage of metrazol, the chemically treated mice were 40 percent better in remembering their daily lessons than were their untreated brothers. Indeed, under metrazol treatment the hereditarily stupid mice were able to turn in better performances than their hereditarily superior but untreated colleagues. Here we have a "chemical memory pill" which not only improves memory and learning but can serve to make all mice equal whom God—or genetics—hath created unequal. May I suggest that some place in the back of your mind, you might begin to speculate on what it can mean—socially, educationally, politically—if and when we find drugs which will be similarly effective for human beings.

But let me continue with my story. What chemistry can give, it can also take away—as Agranoff and his now notorious goldfish at the University of Michigan have shown. Agranoff argued that if we could prevent the brain from manufacturing the chemicals involved in the long-term memory process, then we would create an animal which might have normal short-term memories, but would be incapable of establishing enduring memories. Agranoff trained his fish to swim from one side of an aquarium to another, whenever a signal light was turned on, in order to avoid an electric shock. Goldfish can learn this task within a 40-minute period, and once it is learned, they remember it over many days. Now Agranoff varied his experiments. Immediately before, and in some experiments immediately after, training, Agranoff injected puromycin or actinomycin-D (two antibiotics which prevent the formation of new proteins or nuclear RNA) into the brains of a new group of goldfish. His findings were most encouraging (to Agranoff, that is, not necessarily to the goldfish). The injected goldfish were not impaired in their *learning* of the shock-avoidance task since, presumably, the short-term reverberatory process which enables a fish to remember its lesson from one trial to another—a matter of a few seconds— does not involve the synthesis of new proteins or nuclear RNA. But when tested a day or two later the fish showed almost no retention for the task they had known so well the day before—indicating that the long-term process *is* dependent upon the synthesis of these compounds in the brain. Here, then, we find not only support for our general theory but we have a suggestion that there exist in antimetabolites whole families of chemical memory preventatives which seem not to interfere with the individual's immediate capacity to obey immediate orders, but which do prevent him from building up a permanent body of experiences, expectations, and skills. Conjure up, if you are of that mind, what evils such weapons can wreak in the hands of the Orwellian authorities of 1984—but I must hurry on to our next set of experiments.

A number of years ago, James McConnell at the University of Michigan threw all the brain researchers into a tizzy by reporting that he had succeeded in teaching planaria—a fairly primitive type of flatworm—to make a simple response to a light signal, that he then ground up his educated flatworms, fed the pieces to untrained fellow worms—and lo and behold, the uneducated flatworms wound up with the *memories* of the worms which they had just eaten, and, without any training, could perform the response of the late-lamented and digested "donor" worms!

But then all hell broke loose when other workers in other laboratories and in other countries reported that they could train a *rat,* make an extract from its brain, inject this extract into an untrained rat, and by so doing cause the recipient rat to acquire the memories of the now-dead donor rat. It is one thing to claim this for the primitive planaria, which, after all, do not have very much in the way of a structurally differentiated and organized brain. It is a very different thing to claim it for the rat, which *is* a serious mammal, with a highly developed brain, not too different in complexity, in differentiation, and in organization from our own.

The dust raised by these reports has not yet settled. Indeed, most scientists are definitely on the side of the nonbelievers—but the work goes on, and we cannot predict the final outcome of these experiments, many of which have given negative results. However, as a result of this work, a number of brain researchers have been moved, over the last two or three years, from the position of stiff-necked disbelief to the position of "well, maybe—I don't believe it, but well, maybe." And this is where *I* stand at the moment—fearless and foursquare proclaiming "well, maybe. . . ." Now, if it should come to pass that McConnell and his fellow believers are right, then we will indeed have made a huge jump forward. For we would then have a most effective behavioral assay method which should enable us to zero in on this marvelous brain-goulash which can transfer information from one brain to another, and isolate and identify in detail all the "memory" proteins, enzymes, RNA's, or other macromolecules. After that—the world of the mind is ours! But that day is not here yet. Let me leave these brave new world experimenters and go on with another question and another set of experiments.

DOES the research I have reviewed mean that if and when we will have developed get-smart pills (*a la* McGaugh), or chemical erasures of wrong mental habits (*a la* Agranoff), or specific knowledge pills (*a la* McConnell), we will be able to do without Head Start programs, educational enrichment programs, school supervisors, educational research, and, indeed, without most of our educational paraphernalia? The answer to this question, gentlemen, is a most reassuring "NO." I might even say, *"Au contraire."* Precisely because of the advances in brain biochemistry, the significance of the educator will be greatly increased—*and just as greatly changed.* Let me tell you why I think so by describing to you the results of some of our own work in the Berkeley laboratories.

Some time ago we set ourselves the following problem: If the laying down of memories involves the synthesis of chemical products in the brain, then one should find that an animal which has lived a life replete with opportunities for learning and memorizing would end with a brain chemically and morphologically different from an animal which has lived out an intellectually impoverished life. For almost two decades, now, E. L. Bennett, Marion Diamond, M. R. Rosenzweig, and I, together with technical assistants, graduate students, and thousands of rats, have labored—and some of us have even sacrificed our lives—to find such evidence. Let me tell you some of what we found.

At weaning time we divide our experimental rats into two groups, half of the rats being placed in an "intellectually enriched" environment, the other half—their brothers—in the deprived environment. While both groups receive identical food and water, their psychological environments differ greatly. The animals in the first group live together in one large cage, are provided with many rat toys (tunnels to explore, ladders to climb, levers to press), and they are assigned to graduate students who are admonished to give these rats loving care and kindness, teach them to run mazes, and in general to provide them with the best and most expensive supervised higher education available to any young rat at the University of California. While these rats are thus being encouraged to store up many and varied memories, their brother rats, in the deprived group, live in isolated, barren cages, devoid of stimulation by either their environmental appurtenances, fellow rats, or graduate students. After about 80 days of this differential treatment, all the animals are sacrificed, their brains dissected out, and various chemical and histological analyses performed. The results are convincing. The brain from a rat from the enriched environment—and presumably, therefore, with many more stored memories—has a heavier and thicker cortex, a better blood supply, larger brain cells, more glia cells, and increased activity of two brain enzymes, acetylcholinesterase and cholinesterase, than does the brain from an animal whose life has been less memorable.

We can draw several morals from these experiments. First, the growing animal's psychological environment is of crucial importance for the development of its brain. By manipulating the environment of the young, one can truly create a "lame brain"—with lighter cortex, shrunken brain cells, fewer glia cells, smaller blood vessels, and lower enzymatic activity levels—or one can create a more robust, a healthier, a more metabolically active brain. If it should turn out that what is true for the rat brain is also true for the human brain, and that by careful manipulation of this or that group's early environment we can develop among them bigger and better brains or smaller and meaner ones, the wondrous promises of a glorious future or the monstrous horrors of a Huxlian brave new world are fairly self-evident.

The second conclusion I draw from our experiments is this: Since the effect of any chemical upon an organ is, in part, a function of the beginning chemical status of that organ, and since—as we have just seen—the chemical and anatomical status of the individual's brain is determined by his educational experience, then the effectiveness of the biochemist's "get smart pill" will depend upon how the educator has prepared the brain in the first instance. Indeed, a review of all the data indicates that manipulating the educational and psychological environment is a more effective way of inducing long-lasting brain changes than direct administration of drugs. Educators probably change brain structure and chemistry to a greater degree than any biochemist in the business. Another way of saying this is: The educator *can potentiate or undo the work of the brain biochemist.*

But there is still more to report, and more lessons to draw. Consider the experimental problem we faced when we tried to create a psychologically enriched environment for our Berkeley rats. We did not really know how, so we threw everything into the environment, including almost the kitchen sink, and called it "a psychologically enriched environment." The cages were kept in brightly lighted, sound-filled rooms; the rats were given playmates to relate to, games to manipulate, maze problems to solve, new areas to explore. They were fondled and tamed and chucked under the chin at the drop of a site-visitor. In other words, we provided our happy rats with almost every kind of stimulation we could think of—or afford. And it seems to have worked. But of course it is quite possible that in our "kitchen-sink design," many of the things we did were not at all necessary—indeed, some may have had an adverse effect. And so we undertook a series of experiments to discover which elements of our environment were effective and which were not. I shall not bore you with the details of the many experiments already run and the many more which are now being run in the Berkeley laboratory. Let me list, however, some of the tentative conclusions which one can already make:

First: Sheer exercise or physical-activity alone is not at all effective in developing the brain. A physical training director seems not to be an adequate substitute for a teacher.

Second: Varied visual stimulation, or indeed any kind of visual stimulation, is neither necessary nor sufficient to develop the brain, as we were able to demonstrate by using rats blinded at weaning age.

Third: Handling, or taming, or petting is also without effect in developing the growing rat's brain. Love is Not Enough.

Fourth: The presence of a brother rat in our intellectually deprived rat's cage helps him not a whit. *Bruderschaft* is not enough.

Fifth: Teaching the rat to press levers for food—that and only that seems to help somewhat, but only minimally. Not every problem-set will do, either.

The only experience we have thus far found really effective is freedom to roam around in a large object-filled space. From a recent experiment in Diamond's laboratory there are some suggestions that if the young rat is given continuous and varied maze-problems to solve—that and little else— the rat will develop a number of the same brain changes (at least the morphological ones) which we had observed in our randomly "enriched" environment.

It is clear, then, that not *every* experience or variation in stimulation contributes equally to the development of the brain. But of even greater interest is the suggestion in the above data that the most effective way to develop the brain is through what I will call *species-specific enrichment experiences.*

Here is what I mean: The ability of a rat to learn its way through tunnels and dark passages, to localize points in a three-dimensional space full of objects to be climbed upon, burrowed under, and crawled through is, we can assume, of particular survival value for the rat as he is now constituted. Presumably, through the selective evolutionary process, the rat has developed a brain which is peculiarly fitted to support and enhance these skills. The "effective rat brain," therefore, is one which is a good "space-brain"— not a lever-pressing brain or an arithmetic-reasoning brain. The effective stimulating environment, correspondingly, would be one which makes *spatial learning* demands on that brain—which "pushes" that particular kind of brain in that particular way. To generalize this hypothesis, I would suggest that *for each species there exists a set of species-specific experiences which are maximally enriching and which are maximally efficient in developing its brain.*

If there be any validity to my hypothesis, then the challenge to the human educator is clear. For the educator, too, you may have noticed, has been using the kitchen-sink approach when he seeks to design a psychologically or educationally enriched environment for the child. Some educators would bombard the child—practically from infancy on—with every kind of stimulus change imaginable. His crib is festooned with jumping beads and dangling colored bits and pieces of wood (all sold very expensively to his affluent parents); he is given squishy, squeaking, squawking toys to play with, to fondle, to be frightened by, to choke on. He is jounced and bounced and picked up and put down. And when he goes to school—he finds the same blooming, buzzing confusion. He is stimulated with play activities, with opportunities for social interaction, with rhythmic movements, with music, with visual displays, with contact sports, with tactual experiences, and with anything and everything which the school system can think of—or afford. But it may be that a "stimulating environment" and an "enriched environment" are not one and the same thing. It is not true that a brain is a brain is a brain. The rat is a rat and he hath a rat's brain; the child is a child and he hath a child's brain—and each, according to my hypothesis, requires its own educational nutrient. What, then, are the species-specific enrichments for the human child?

Of course I do not know the answer to this question, but let me share with you my present enthusiastic guess that in the language arts will you find part of the answer.

I can start with no better text than a quotation from my teacher, Edward Chace Tolman, who was a completely devoted rat psychologist. "Speech," he wrote, ". . . is in any really developed and characteristic sense, the sole prerogative of the human being. . . . It is speech which first and foremost distinguishes man from the great apes." (1932)[1] In my opinion, it is in the study of language, above anything else, that the psychologist will discover the psychology of man, and that the educator will discover how to educate man.

In the first place, and we must be clear about this, human language, with its complex and *abstract structure,* has *nothing* in common with animal communication. Language is probably the clearest instance of a pure species-specific behavior. This is true whether you study language as a neurologist, or as a psychologist. Let us look at some brain research first.

Recently Robinson, at the National Institute of Mental Health (1967), attempted to discover which areas of the monkey's brain controlled its vocalizations.[2] Now the monkey most certainly uses vocalization for communication, but principally for communications with emotional tone such as threat, fear, pain, and pleasure. In Robinson's study 15 unanesthetized animals, with brains exposed by surgery, were used. Some 5,880 different loci or spots in the brain were stimulated by electrodes to see whether such stimulation could bring forth vocalization. The loci explored included neocortical areas as well as areas in the limbic system, that older part of the mammalian brain which is most intimately involved with motivational and emotional responses.

Robinson's results were clear-cut: First, despite his exploration of several hundred different neocortical sites he was unable to raise a single sound from his animals by stimulating their *neocortex.* Second, stimulation of the limbic system brought forth regular, consistent, and identifiable vocalizations.

These results differ sharply from those found with the human brain. While there is some evidence that human cries and exclamations—uttered in moments of excitement—are also controlled by the limbic system, *speech and language clearly depend upon neocortical areas*—areas for which there simply are no analogues in the brain of any other animal. These areas are, of course, the well-known Broca and Wernicke areas in the left hemisphere of the human brain. It seems clear, as Robinson puts it, that "human speech did not develop 'out of' primate vocalization, but arose from *new tissue* [italics my own] which permitted it the necessary detachment from immediate, emotional situations." Man's brain, *and man's brain alone,* is a language-supporting brain.

Corresponding to the neurological picture is the psycholinguist's view of language. Almost every psycholinguist is impressed not only with the unique nature of language itself but with its unique mode of achievement by the child. Whatever value so-called reinforcement or stimulus-response theories of learning may have for describing acquisition of motor skills by people, maze-learning by rats, and bar-pressing by pigeons—these theories are assessed as completely trivial and utterly irrelevant when it comes to understanding that "stunning intellectual achievement" (McNeill, 1966),[3] the acquisition of language by the child. Indeed, in reading the psycholinguist's work one is left with the impression that we will have to develop a species-specific learning theory for this species-specific behavior of language. I must confess that I agree with them. And if we ever achieve an understanding of language development, and if we learn how to push the *human* brain with this *human* experience, then will we indeed be on our way.

I know that other people have proposed other ways with which to enrich the child's education. Some plug for what are referred to as "cognitive" experience or "productive thinking" experiences, etc. Let me hasten to record that I quite agree with them. As a matter of fact, I am not at all certain that I am saying anything other than what my cognitive friends propose. For I hold with McNeill's judgment that ". . . the study of how language is acquired may provide insight into the very basis of mental life." And, I would go on, being human *means* having an effective mental, cognitive life.

It is for these and many, many other reasons that I would urge the educator to turn to the psycholinguist—as well as to Piaget and Crutchfield and Bruner—for his major guides in designing a rational educational enrichment program.

Whether my guess merits this enthusiasm or not will perhaps eventually be determined by research. But here is the challenge and here is the promise for the educator. Drop your kitchen-sink approach, and specify and define for us the species-specific psychologically enriching experiences for the child—and we will be off and running!

Where will we run? Let me speculate out loud. It is perfectly reasonable to suppose that we will be able to find specific biochemical boosters and biochemical inhibitors for different kinds of memories and imagery, or for different kinds of abilities, or for different kinds of personality or temperament traits. With such chemical agents in hand, and with appropriate educational and training procedures, we may use them as supplementary therapy for those failing in this or that trait and thus will we be able to rectify and heal some of the mentally retarded and the senile. Of course we may use these agents for evil—to create docile, intellectually limited, but efficient human beasts of burden without memories beyond the order of the day (remember Agranoff's fish?).

But above all, there will be great changes made in the first and foremost and continuing business of society: the education and training of the young. The development of the mind of the child will come to rest in the knowledge and skills of the biochemist, and pharmacologist, and neurologist, and psychologist, and educator. And there will be a new expert abroad in the land—the psychoneurobiochemeducator. This multi-hybrid expert will have recourse—as I have suggested elsewhere—to protein memory consolidators, antimetabolite memory inhibitors, enzymatic learning stimulants, and many other potions and elixers of the mind from our new psychoneurobiochemopharmacopia.

THERE is a grievous problem here, however. Experts, whatever else they may be, are notorious order-takers. *Who* will direct our psychoneurobiochemeducator where to work his expertise, and *what* shall we tell him to do? Here we are talking about goals, values, and aims. Shall our expert raise or lower docility, aggressiveness, musical ability, engineering ability, artistic sensitivity, effective intellectual functioning? Shall different ethnic or racial or national or social groups receive different treatments? In past centuries, and even today, this differential group treatment is precisely what our relatively primitive but quite effective medical and educational experts have been ordered by us to carry out. And lo, they have done so! On one side of the town they have created enclaves of the sickly, the weak, the ignorant, the unskilled—in a word, the brutalized social vanquished. On the other side of the town they have created the social victors—the healthy, the strong, the knowledgeable, the skilled. Will we continue to do this in the future with our much more sophisticated and effective psychoneurobiochemeducators? Who, in other words, will control the brain controllers—and to what ends?

I have thought and worried about these questions, and I must confess to you that I cannot avoid a dread feeling of unease about the future.

At the same time I keep whistling the following tune in an attempt to cheer myself up: If there be any validity at all to my speculations this afternoon, they add up to this: The biochemist, neurologist, psychologist, and educator will eventually add to the intellectual stature of man. With this in mind, and clinging to a life-long faith in the virtues of knowledge and the intellect (for certainly, at this stage I can do no less), I find myself believing that man who by taking thought will have added cubits to his intellectual stature, will also acquire the added bit of wisdom and humaneness that will save us all. Let me stop on this note—before I scrutinize this faith and this hope too carefully.

REFERENCES

1. Edward Chace Tolman, *Purposive Behavior in Animals and Men.* New York: The Century Company, 1932.
2. B. W. Robinson, "Vocalization Evoked from Forebrain in *Macaca Mulatta*," *Physiology and Behavior,* 1967, No. 2, pp. 345–54.
3. D. McNeill, "The Creation of Language," *Discovery,* 1966, No. 27, pp. 34–38.

18.

Three processes in the child's acquisition of syntax

Roger Brown
Ursula Bellugi

*In the previous article, Krech suggests that language provides nutri-
tion for the brain; he quotes Tolman as stating that language will remain the focus of questions about how humans learn. The following
article by Brown and Bellugi seems to provide verification for the
centrality of language in understanding human development.*

*A child's learning language is not merely imitative—it is creative
and interpretive. He does not hear his parents say "push car" or
"Mommy eggnog," yet he gets and gives the message. This creative
aspect of language development shows some of the paucity of learning
theories (see selection 1). It might be noted, too, that the method used
by Brown has some similarity to the approaches used by Piaget (see
selection 12).*

*When Adam said, "I digged a hole," he may have been antici-
pating something he will say thirty or so years later when, as a life
scientist, he attempts to formulate a simple statement of how one
learns to speak, think, and establish goals.*

Some time in the second six months of life most children say a first intelligible word. A few months later most children are saying many words and
some children go about the house all day long naming things (*table, doggie,
ball,* etc.) and actions (*play, see, drop,* etc.) and an occasional quality (*blue,
broke, bad,* etc.). At about eighteen months children are likely to begin
constructing two-word utterances; such a one, for instance, as *Push car.*

A construction such as *Push car* is not just two single-word utterances
spoken in a certain order. As single word utterances (they are sometimes
called holophrases) both *push* and *car* would have primary stresses and
terminal intonation contours. When they are two words programmed as a
single utterance the primary stress would fall on *car* and so would the highest level of pitch. *Push* would be subordinated to *car* by a lesser stress and
a lower pitch; the unity of the whole would appear in the absence of a
terminal contour between words and the presence of such a contour at the
end of the full sequence.

Harvard Educational Review, 34(No. 2):133–151, 1964. Copyright 1964 by Harvard
Educational Review. Roger Brown, Professor of Social Psychology; Ursula Bellugi, Department of Social Relations, Harvard University.

This investigation was supported in whole by Public Health Service Research Grant
MH7088 from the National Institute of Mental Health.

By the age of thirty-six months some children are so advanced in the construction process as to produce all of the major varieties of English simple sentences up to a length of ten or eleven words. For several years we have been studying the development of English syntax, of the sentence-constructing process, in children between eighteen and thirty-six months of age. Most recently we have made a longitudinal study of a boy and girl whom we shall call Adam and Eve. We began work with Adam and Eve in October of 1962 when Adam was twenty-seven months old and Eve eighteen months old. The two children were selected from some thirty whom we considered. They were selected primarily because their speech was exceptionally intelligible and because they talked a lot. We wanted to make it as easy as possible to transcribe accurately large quantities of child speech. Adam and Eve are the children of highly-educated parents, the fathers were graduate students at Harvard and the mothers are both college graduates. Both Adam and Eve were single children when we began the study. These facts must be remembered in generalizing the outcomes of the research.

While Adam is nine months older than Eve, his speech was only a little more advanced in October of 1962. The best single index of the level of speech development is the average length of utterance and in October, 1962, Adam's average was 1.84 morphemes and Eve's was 1.40 morphemes. The two children stayed fairly close together in the year that followed; in the records for the thirty-eighth week Adam's average was 3.55 and Eve's, 3.27. The processes we shall describe appeared in both children.

Every second week we visited each child for at least two hours and made a tape recording of everything said by the child as well as of everything said to the child. The mother was always present and most of the speech to the child is hers. Both mother and child became very accustomed to our presence and learned to continue their usual routine with us as the observers.

One of us always made a written transcription, on the scene, of the speech of mother and child with notes about important actions and objects of attention. From this transcription and the tape a final transcription was made and these transcriptions constitute the primary data of the study. For many purposes we require a "distributional analysis" of the speech of the child. To this end the child's utterances in a given transcription were cross classified and relisted under such headings as: "*A* + noun"; "Noun + verb"; "Verbs in the past"; "Utterances containing the pronoun *it*," etc. The categorized utterances expose the syntactic regularities of the child's speech.

Each week we met as a research seminar, with students of the psychology of language,[1] to discuss the state of the construction process in one of the two children as of that date. In these discussions small experiments were often suggested, experiments that had to be done within a few days if they were to be informative. At one time, for instance, we were uncertain whether Adam understood the semantic difference between putting a noun in subject position and putting it in object position. Consequently one of us paid an extra visit to Adam equipped with some toys. "Adam," we said, "show us the duck pushing the boat." And, when he had done so: "Now show us the boat pushing the duck."

Another week we noticed that Adam would sometimes pluralize nouns when they should have been pluralized and sometimes would not. We wondered if he could make grammatical judgments about the plural, if he could distinguish a correct form from an incorrect form. "Adam," we asked, "which is right, 'two shoes' or 'two shoe'?" His answer on that occasion, produced with explosive enthusiasm, was "Pop goes the weasel!" The two-year-old child does not make a perfectly docile experimental subject.

The dialogue between mother and child does not read like a transcribed dialogue between two adults. Table 1 offers a sample section from

---

TABLE 1. A Section from Adam's First Record

Adam	Mother
See truck, Mommy.	
See truck.	
	Did you see the truck?
No I see truck.	
	No, you didn't see it?
	There goes one.
There go one.	
	Yes, there goes one.
See a truck.	
See truck, Mommy.	
See truck.	
Truck.	
Put truck, Mommy.	
	Put the truck where?
Put truck window.	
	I think that one's too large to go in the window.

---

an early transcribed record. It has some interesting properties. The conversation is, in the first place, very much in the here and now. From the child there is no speech of the sort that Bloomfield called "displaced," speech about other times and other places. Adam's utterances in the early months were largely a coding of contemporaneous events and impulses. The mother's speech differs from the speech that adults use to one another in many ways. Her sentences are short and simple; for the most part they are the kinds of sentences that Adam will produce a year later.

Perhaps because they are short, the sentences of the mother are perfectly grammatical. The sentences adults use to one another, perhaps because they are longer and more complex, are very often not grammatical, not well formed. Here for instance is a rather representative example produced at a conference of psychologists and linguists: "As far as I know, no one yet has done the in a way obvious now and interesting problem of doing a in a sense a structural frequency study of the alternative syntactical in a given language, say, like English, the alternative possible structures, and how what their hierarchical probability of occurrence structure is."[2] It seems unlikely that a child could learn the patterns of English syntax from such speech. His introduction to English ordinarily comes in the form of a simplified, repetitive, and idealized dialect. It may be that such an introduction is necessary for the acquisition of syntax to be possible but we do not know that.

In the course of the brief interchange of Table 1 Adam imitates his mother in saying: "There go one" immediately after she says "There goes one." The imitation is not perfect; Adam omits the inflection on the verb. His imitation is a reduction in that it omits something from the original. This kind of imitation with reduction is extremely common in the records of Adam and Eve and it is the first process we shall discuss.

IMITATION AND REDUCTION

Table 2 presents some model sentences spoken by the mothers and the imitations produced by Adam and Eve. These were selected from hundreds in the records in order to illustrate some general propositions. The first thing to notice is that the imitations preserve the word order of the model

TABLE 2. Some Imitations Produced by Adam and Eve

Model Utterance	Child's Imitation
Tank car	*Tank car*
Wait a minute	*Wait a minute*
Daddy's brief case	*Daddy brief case*
Fraser will be unhappy	*Fraser unhappy*
He's going out	*He go out*
That's an old time train	*Old time train*
It's not the same dog as Pepper	*Dog Pepper*
No, you can't write on Mr. Cromer's shoe	*Write Cromer shoe*

sentences. To be sure, words in the model are often missing from the imitation but the words preserved are in the order of the original. This is a fact that is so familiar and somehow reasonable that we did not at once recognize it as an empirical outcome rather than as a natural necessity. But of course it is not a necessity, the outcome could have been otherwise. For example, words could have been said back in the reverse of their original order, the most recent first. The preservation of order suggests that the model sentence is processed by the child as a total construction rather than as a list of words.

In English the order of words in a sentence is an important grammatical signal. Order is used to distinguish among subject, direct object, and indirect object and it is one of the marks of imperative and interrogative constructions. The fact that the child's first sentences preserve the word order of their models partially accounts for the ability of an adult to "understand" these sentences and so to feel that he is in communication with the child. It is conceivable that the child "intends" the meanings coded by his word orders and that, when he preserves the order of an adult sentence, he does so because he wants to say what the order says. It is also possible that he preserves word order just because his brain works that way and that he has no comprehension of the semantic contrasts involved. In some languages word order is not an important grammatical signal. In Latin, for instance, "Agricola amat puellam" has the same meaning as "Puellam amat agricola" and subject-object relations are signalled by case endings. We would be interested to know whether children who are exposed to languages that do not utilize word order as a major syntactic signal, preserve order as reliably as do children exposed to English.

The second thing to notice in Table 2 is the fact that when the models increase in length there is not a corresponding increase in the imitation. The imitations stay in the range of two to four morphemes which was the range characteristic of the children at this time. The children were operating under some constraint of length or span. This is not a limitation of vocabulary; the children knew hundreds of words. Neither is it a constraint of immediate memory. We infer this from the fact that the average length of utterances produced spontaneously, where immediate memory is not involved, is about the same as the average length of utterances produced as immediate imitations. The constraint is a limitation on the length of utterance the children are able to program or plan.[3] This kind of narrow span limitation in children is characteristic of most or all of their intellectual operations. The limitation grows less restrictive with age as a consequence, probably, of both neurological growth and of practice, but of course it is never lifted altogether.

A constraint on length compels the imitating child to omit some words or morphemes from the mother's longer sentences. Which forms are retained and which omitted? The selection is not random but highly systematic. Forms retained in the examples of Table 2 include: *Daddy, Fraser,*

Pepper, and *Cromer; tank car, minute, briefcase, train, dog,* and *shoe; wait, go,* and *write; unhappy* and *old time.* For the most part they are nouns, verbs, and adjectives, though there are exceptions, as witness the initial pronoun *He* and the preposition *out* and the indefinite article *a.* Forms omitted in the samples of Table 2 include: the possessive inflection *–s,* the modal auxiliary *will,* the contraction of the auxiliary verb *is,* the progressive inflection *–ing,* the preposition *on,* the articles *the* and *an,* and the modal auxiliary *can.* It is possible to make a general characterization of the forms likely to be retained that distinguishes them as a total class from the forms likely to be omitted.

Forms likely to be retained are nouns and verbs and, less often, adjectives, and these are the three large and "open" parts-of-speech in English. The number of forms in any one of these parts-of-speech is extremely large and always growing. Words belonging to these classes are sometimes called "contentives" because they have semantic content. Forms likely to be omitted are inflections, auxiliary verbs, articles, prepositions, and conjunctions. These forms belong to syntactic classes that are small and closed. Any one class has few members and new members are not readily added. The omitted forms are the ones that linguists sometimes call "functors," their grammatical *functions* being more obvious than their semantic content.

Why should young children omit functors and retain contentives? There is more than one plausible answer. Nouns, verbs, and adjectives are words that make reference. One can conceive of teaching the meanings of these words by speaking them, one at a time, and pointing at things or actions or qualities. And of course parents do exactly that. These are the kinds of words that children have been encouraged to practice speaking one at a time. The child arrives at the age of sentence construction with a stock of well-practiced nouns, verbs, and adjectives. Is it not likely then that this prior practice causes him to retain the contentives from model sentences too long to be reproduced in full, that the child imitates those forms in the speech he hears which are already well developed in him as individual habits? There is probably some truth in this explanation but it is not the only determinant since children will often select for retention contentives that are relatively unfamiliar to them.

We adults sometimes operate under a constraint on length and the curious fact is that the English we produce in these circumstances bears a formal resemblance to the English produced by two-year-old children. When words cost money there is a premium on brevity or to put it otherwise, a constraint on length. The result is "telegraphic" English and telegraphic English is an English of nouns, verbs, and adjectives. One does not send a cable reading: "My car has broken down and I have lost my wallet; send money to me at the American Express in Paris" but rather "Car broken down; wallet lost; send money American Express Paris." The telegram omits: *my, has, and, I, have, my, to, me, at, the, in.* All of these are functors. We make the same kind of telegraphic reduction when time or fatigue constrain us to be brief, as witness any set of notes taken at a fast-moving lecture.

A telegraphic transformation of English generally communicates very well. It does so because it retains the high-information words and drops the low-information words. We are here using "information" in the sense of the mathematical theory of communication. The information carried by a word is inversely related to the chances of guessing it from context. From a given string of content words, missing functors can often be guessed but the message "my has and I have my to me at the in" will not serve to get money to Paris. Perhaps children are able to make a communication analysis of adult speech and so adapt in an optimal way to their limitation of span. There is, however, another way in which the adaptive outcome might be achieved.

If you say aloud the model sentences of Table 2 you will find that you place the heavier stresses, the primary and secondary stresses in the sentences, on contentives rather than on functors. In fact the heavier stresses fall, for the most part, on the words the child retains. We first realized that this was the case when we found that in transcribing tapes, the words of the mother that we could hear most clearly were usually the words that the child reproduced. We had trouble hearing the weakly stressed functors and, of course, the child usually failed to reproduce them. Differential stress may then be the cause of the child's differential retention. The outcome is a maximally informative reduction but the cause of this outcome need not be the making of an information analysis. The outcome may be an incidental consequence of the fact that English is a well-designed language that places its heavier stresses where they are needed, on contentives that cannot easily be guessed from context.

We are fairly sure that differential stress is one of the determinants of the child's telegraphic productions. For one thing, stress will also account for the way in which children reproduce polysyllabic words when the total is too much for them. Adam, for instance, gave us *'pression* for *expression* and Eve gave us *'raff* for *giraffe;* the more heavily-stressed syllables were the ones retained. In addition we have tried the effect of placing heavy stresses on functors which do not ordinarily receive such stresses. To Adam we said: "You say what I say" and then, speaking in a normal way at first: "The doggie will bite." Adam gave back: "Doggie bite." Then we stressed the auxiliary: "The doggie *will* bite" and, after a few trials, Adam made attempts at reproducing that auxiliary. A science fiction experiment comes to mind. If there were parents who stressed functors rather than contentives would they have children whose speech was a kind of "reciprocal telegraphic" made up of articles, prepositions, conjunctions, auxiliaries, and the like? Such children would be out of touch with the community as real children are not.

It may be that all the factors we have mentioned play some part in determining the child's selective imitations; the reference-making function of contentives, the fact that they are practiced as single words, the fact that they cannot be guessed from context, and the heavy stresses they receive. There are also other possible factors: for example, the left-to-right, earlier-to-later position of words in a sentence, but these make too long a story to tell here.[4] Whatever the causes, the first utterances produced as imitations of adult sentences are highly systematic reductions of their models. Furthermore, the telegraphic properties of these imitations appear also in the child's spontaneously produced utterances. When his speech is not modeled on an immediately prior adult sentence, it observes the same limitation on length and the same predilection for contentives as when it is modeled on an immediately prior sentence.

IMITATION WITH EXPANSION

In the course of the brief conversation set down in Table 1, Adam's mother at one point imitates Adam. The boy says: "There go one" and mother responds: "Yes, there goes one." She does not exactly reproduce the model sentence of the child but instead adds something to it or expands it. What she adds is a functor, the inflection for third-person on the verb, the very form that Adam had omitted when he imitated his mother.

One of the first things we noticed when we began to study child speech several years ago was the frequency with which adults imitated children. Indeed they seemed to imitate more often than did the children themselves. We later came to realize that adult imitations are seldom exact reproductions; they are usually expansions. The mothers of Adam and Eve responded to the speech of their children with expansions about thirty per cent of the time. We did it ourselves when we talked with the children. Indeed we found it very difficult to withhold expansions. A reduced or incomplete English sentence seems to constrain the English-speaking adult to expand it into the nearest properly formed complete sentence. Table 3 lists a few sample expansions from the hundreds in the records.

TABLE 3. EXPANSIONS OF CHILD SPEECH PRODUCED BY MOTHERS

Child	Mother
Baby highchair	*Baby is in the highchair*
Mommy eggnog	*Mommy had her eggnog*
Eve lunch	*Eve is having lunch*
Mommy sandwich	*Mommy'll have a sandwich*
Sat wall	*He sat on the wall*
Throw Daddy	*Throw it to Daddy*
Pick glove	*Pick the glove up*

The first thing worthy of attention in the expansions of Table 3 is the fact that the words spoken by the mother preserve the order of the words in the child's sentences. To be sure, words and inflections are added but they are fitted in—before, and after and between the words the child used; they are not generally permitted to disturb the order of the child's words. It is as if these latter were taken as constants by the mother, constants to which some sentence had to be fitted. She acts as if she were assuming that the child means everything he says, all the words and also their order, but as if he might also mean more than he says. From the mother's point of view an expansion is a kind of communication check; it says in effect: "Is this what you mean?"

The second thing to notice about Table 3 is the character of the forms added to the child's utterances. They include the auxiliaries *is* and *will;* the prepositions *in, on, to,* and *up;* the verb forms *is, have, had,* and *having;* the articles *a* and *the;* the pronouns *her, he,* and *it.* For the most part, the words added are functors and functors are of course the words that the child omits in his reductions.

The interaction between mother and child is, much of the time, a cycle of reductions and expansions. There are two transformations involved. The reduction transformation has an almost completely specifiable and so mechanical character. One could program a machine to do it with the following instructions: "Retain contentives (or stressed forms) in the order given up to some limit of length." The expansion accomplished by Adam's mother when she added the third-person inflection to the verb and said "There goes one" is also a completely specifiable transformation. The instructions would read: "Retain the forms given in the order given and supply obligatory grammatical forms." To be sure this mother-machine would have to be supplied with the obligatory rules of English grammar but that could be done. However, the sentence "There goes one" is atypical in that it only adds a compulsory and redundant inflection. The expansions of Table 3 all add forms that are not grammatically compulsory or redundant and these expansions cannot be mechanically generated by grammatical rules alone.

In Table 3 the topmost four utterances produced by the child are all of the same grammatical type; all four consist of a proper noun followed by a common noun. However, the four are expanded in quite different ways. In particular the form of the verb changes: it is in the first case in the simple present tense; in the second case the simple past; in the third case the present progressive; in the last case the simple future. All of these are perfectly grammatical but they are different. The second set of child utterances is formally uniform in that each one consists of a verb followed by a noun. The expansions are again all grammatical but quite unlike, especially with regard to the preposition supplied. In general, then, there are radical changes in the mother's expansions when there are no changes in the formal character of the utterances expanded. It follows that the expansions cannot be produced simply by making grammatically compulsory additions to the child's utterances.

How does a mother decide on the correct expansion of one of her child's utterances? Consider the utterance "Eve lunch." So far as grammar is concerned this utterance could be appropriately expanded in any of a number of ways: "Eve is having lunch"; "Eve had lunch"; "Eve will have lunch"; "Eve's lunch," etc. On the occasion when Eve produced the utterance, however, one expansion seemed more appropriate than any other. It was then the noon hour, Eve was sitting at the table with a plate of food before her, and her spoon and fingers were busy. In these circumstances "Eve lunch" had to mean "Eve is having lunch." A little later when the plate had been stacked in the sink and Eve was getting down from her chair the utterance "Eve lunch" would have suggested the expansion "Eve has had her lunch." Most expansions are not only responsive to the child's words but also to the circumstances attending their utterance.

What kind of instructions will generate the mother's expansions? The following are approximately correct: "Retain the words given in the order given and add those functors that will result in a well-formed simple sentence that is appropriate to the circumstances." These are not instructions that any machine could follow. A machine could act on the instructions only if it were provided with detailed specifications for judging appropriateness and no such specifications can, at present, be written. They exist, however, in implicit form in the brains of mothers and in the brains of all English-speaking adults and so judgments of appropriateness can be made by such adults.

The expansion encodes aspects of reality that are not coded by the child's telegraphic utterance. Functors have meaning but it is meaning that accrues to them in context rather than in isolation. The meanings that are added by functors seem to be nothing less than the basic terms in which we construe reality: the time of an action, whether it is ongoing or completed, whether it is presently relevant or not; the concept of possession and such relational concepts as are coded by *in, on, up, down,* and the like; the difference between a particular instance of a class ("Has anybody seen *the* paper?") and any instance of a class ("Has anybody seen *a* paper?"); the difference between extended substances given shape and size by an "accidental" container (*sand, water, syrup,* etc.) and countable "things" having a characteristic fixed shape and size (*a cup, a man, a tree,* etc.). It seems to us that a mother in expanding speech may be teaching more than grammar; she may be teaching something like a world-view.

As yet it has not been demonstrated that expansions are *necessary* for learning either grammar or a construction of reality. It has not even been demonstrated that expansions contribute to such learning. All we know is that some parents do expand and their children do learn. It is perfectly possible, however, that children can and do learn simply from hearing their parents or others make well-formed sentences in connection with various nonverbal circumstances. It may not be necessary or even helpful for these sentences to be expansions of utterances of the child. Only experiments contrasting expansion training with simple exposure to English will settle the matter. We hope to do such experiments.

There are, of course, reasons for expecting the expansion transformation to be an effective tutorial technique. By adding something to the words the child has just produced one confirms his response insofar as it is appropriate. In addition one takes him somewhat beyond that response but not greatly beyond it. One encodes additional meanings at a moment when he is most likely to be attending to the cues that can teach that meaning.

INDUCTION OF THE LATENT STRUCTURE

Adam, in the course of the conversation with his mother set down in Table 1, produced one utterance for which no adult is likely ever to have provided an exact model: "No I see truck." His mother elects to expand it as "No, you didn't see it" and this expansion suggests that the child might have created the utterance by reducing an adult model containing the form *didn't*. However, the mother's expansion in this case does some violence to Adam's original version. He did not say *no* as his mother said it, with primary stress and final contour; Adam's *no* had secondary stress and no final contour. It is not easy to imagine an adult model for this utterance. It seems more likely that the utterance was created by Adam as part of a continuing effort to discover the general rules for constructing English negatives.

In Table 4 we have listed some utterances produced by Adam or Eve

TABLE 4. Utterances Not Likely to be Imitations

My Cromer suitcase	*You naughty are*
Two foot	*Why it can't turn off?*
A bags	*Put on it*
A scissor	*Cowboy did fighting me*
A this truck	*Put a gas in*

for which it is difficult to imagine any adult model. It is unlikely that any adult said any of these to Adam or Eve since they are very simple utterances and yet definitely ungrammatical. In addition it is difficult, by adding functors alone, to build any of them up to simple grammatical sentences. Consequently it does not seem likely that these utterances are reductions of adult originals. It is more likely that they are mistakes which externalize the child's search for the regularities of English syntax.

We have long realized that the occurrence of certain kinds of errors on the level of morphology (or word construction) reveals the child's effort to induce regularities from speech. So long as a child speaks correctly, or at any rate so long as he speaks as correctly as the adults he hears, there is no way to tell whether he is simply repeating what he has heard or whether he is actually constructing. However, when he says something like "I digged a hole" we can often be sure that he is constructing. We can be sure because it is unlikely that he would have heard *digged* from anyone and because we can see how, in processing words he has heard, he might have come by *digged*. It looks like an overgeneralization of the regular past inflection. The inductive operations of the child's mind are externalized in such a creation. Overgeneralizations on the level of syntax (or sentence construction) are more difficult to identify because there are so many ways of adding functors so as to build up conceivable models. But this is difficult to do for the examples of Table 4 and for several hundred other utterances in our records.

The processes of imitation and expansion are not sufficient to account for the degree of linguistic competence that children regularly acquire. These processes alone cannot teach more than the sum total of sentences that speakers of English have either modeled for a child to imitate or built up from a child's reductions. However, a child's linguistic competence extends far beyond this sum total of sentences. All children are able to understand and construct sentences they have never heard but which are nevertheless well-formed, well-formed in terms of general rules that are implicit in the sentences the child has heard. Somehow, then, every child processes the speech to which he is exposed so as to induce from it a latent structure. This latent rule structure is so general that a child can spin out its implications all his life long. It is both semantic and syntactic. The discovery of latent structure is the greatest of the processes involved in language acquisition and the most difficult to understand. We will provide an example of how the analysis can proceed by discussing the evolution in child speech of noun phrases.

A noun phrase in adult English includes a noun but also more than a noun. One variety consists of a noun with assorted modifiers: *The girl; The pretty girl; That pretty girl; My girl, etc.* All of these are constructions which have the same syntactic privileges as do nouns alone. One can use a noun phrase in isolation to name or request something; one can use it in sentences, in subject position or in object position or in predicate nominative position. All of these are slots that nouns alone can also fill. A larger construction having the same syntactic privileges as its "head" word is called in linguistics an "endocentric" construction and noun phrases are endocentric constructions.

For both Adam and Eve, in the early records, noun phrases usually occur as total independent utterances rather than as components of sentences. Table 5 presents an assortment of such utterances at Time 1. They consist in each case of some sort of modifier, just one, preceding a noun. The modifiers, or as they are sometimes called the "pivot" words, are a much smaller class than the noun class. Three students of child speech have independently discovered that this kind of construction is extremely common when children first begin to combine words.[5,6,7]

It is possible to generalize the cases of Table 5 into a simple implicit rule. The rule symbolized in Table 5 reads: "In order to form a noun

---

TABLE 5. NOUN PHRASES IN ISOLATION AND RULE FOR GENERATING NOUN PHRASES AT TIME 1

A coat	*More coffee*
*A celery**	*More nut**
*A Becky**	*Two sock**
*A hands**	*Two shoes*
The top	*two tinker-toy**
My Mommy	*Big boot*
That Adam	*Poor man*
My stool	*Little top*
That knee	*Dirty knee*

$$NP \rightarrow M + N$$

$M \rightarrow$ *a, big, dirty, little, more, my, poor, that, the, two.*

$N \rightarrow$ *Adam, Becky, boot, coat, coffee, knee, man, Mommy, nut, sock, stool, tinker-toy, top,* and very many others.

* Ungrammatical for an adult

---

phrase of this type, select first one word from the small class of modifiers and select, second, one word from the large class of nouns." This is a "generative" rule by which we mean it is a program that would actually serve to build constructions of the type in question. It is offered as a model of the mental mechanism by which Adam and Eve generated such utterances. Furthermore, judging from our work with other children and from the reports of Braine and of Miller and Ervin, the model describes a mechanism present in many children when their average utterance is approximately two morphemes long.

We have found that even in our earliest records the M + N construction is sometimes used as a component of larger constructions. For instance, Eve said: "Fix a Lassie" and "Turn the page" and "A horsie stuck" and Adam even said: "Adam wear a shirt." There are, at first, only a handful of these larger constructions but there are very many constructions in which single nouns occur in subject or in object position.

Let us look again at the utterances of Table 5 and the rule generalizing them. The class M does not correspond with any syntactic class of adult English. In the class M are articles, a possessive pronoun, a cardinal number, a demonstrative adjective or pronoun, a quantifier, and some descriptive adjectives—a mixed bag indeed. For adult English these words cannot belong to the same syntactic class because they have very different privileges of occurrence in sentences. For the children the words do seem to function as one class having the common privilege of occurrence before nouns.

If the initial words of the utterances in Table 5 are treated as one class M then many utterances are generated which an adult speaker would judge to be ungrammatical. Consider the indefinite article *a*. Adults use it only to modify common count nouns in the singular such as *coat, dog, cup,* etc. We would not say *a celery,* or *a cereal,* or *a dirt; celery, cereal,* and *dirt* are mass nouns. We would not say *a Becky* or *a Jimmy; Becky* and *Jimmy* are proper nouns. We would not say *a hands* or *a shoes; hands* and *shoes* are plural nouns. Adam and Eve, at first, did form ungrammatical combinations such as these.

The numeral *two* we use only with count nouns in the plural. We would not say *two sock* since *sock* is singular, nor *two water* since *water* is a mass noun. The word *more* we use before count nouns in the plural (*more nuts*) or mass nouns in the singular (*more coffee*). Adam and Eve made a number of combinations involving *two* or *more* that we would not make.

Given the initial very undiscriminating use of words in the class M it follows that one dimension of development must be a progressive differentiation of privileges, which means the division of M into smaller classes. There must also be subdivision of the noun class (N) for the reason that the privileges of occurrence of various kinds of modifiers must be described in terms of such sub-varieties of N as the common noun and proper noun, the count noun and mass noun. There must eventually emerge a distinction between nouns singular and nouns plural since this distinction figures in the privileges of occurrence of the several sorts of modifiers.

Sixteen weeks after our first records from Adam and Eve (Time 2), the differentiation process had begun. By this time there were distributional reasons for separating our articles (*a, the*) from demonstrative pronouns (*this, that*) and both of these from the residual class of modifiers. Some of the evidence for this conclusion appears in Table 6. In general one syntactic class is distinguished from another when the members of one class have combinational privileges not enjoyed by the members of the other. Consider, for example, the reasons for distinguishing articles (Art) from modifiers in general (M). Both articles and modifiers appeared in front of nouns in two-word utterances. However, in three-word utterances that were made up from the total pool of words and that had a noun in final position, the privileges of *a* and *the* were different from the privileges of all other modifiers. The articles occurred in initial position followed by a member of class M other than an article. No other modifier occurred in this first position; notice the "Not obtained" examples of Table 6A. If the children had produced utterances like those (for example, *blue a flower, your a car*)

TABLE 6. SUBDIVISION OF THE MODIFIER CLASS

A) PRIVILEGES PECULIAR TO ARTICLES

Obtained	Not Obtained
A blue flower	*Blue a flower*
A nice nap	*Nice a nap*
A your car	*Your a car*
A my pencil	*My a pencil*

B) PRIVILEGES PECULIAR TO DEMONSTRATIVE PRONOUNS

Obtained	Not Obtained
That my cup	*My that cup*
That a horse	*A that horse*
That a blue flower	*A that blue flower*
	Blue a that flower

there would have been no difference in the privileges of occurrence of articles and modifiers and therefore no reason to separate out articles.

The record of Adam is especially instructive. He created such notably ungrammatical combinations as "a your car" and "a my pencil." It is very unlikely that adults provided models for these. They argue strongly that Adam regarded all the words in the residual M class as syntactic equivalents and so generated these very odd utterances in which possessive pronouns appear where descriptive adjectives would be more acceptable.

Table 6 also presents some of the evidence for distinguishing demonstrative pronouns (Dem) from articles and modifiers. (Table 6B). The pronouns occurred first and ahead of articles in three-and-four-word utterances —a position that neither articles nor modifiers ever filled. The sentences with demonstrative pronouns are recognizable as reductions which omit the copular verb *is*. Such sentences are not noun phrases in adult English and ultimately they will not function as noun phrases in the speech of the children, but for the present they are not distinguishable distributionally from noun phrases.

Recall now the generative formula of Table 5 which constructs noun phrases by simply placing a modifier (M) before a noun (N). The differentiation of privileges illustrated in Table 6, and the syntactic classes this evidence motivates us to create, complicate the formula for generating noun phrases. In Table 7 we have written a single general formula for producing all noun phrases at Time 2 [NP → (Dem) + (Art) + (M) + N] and also the numerous more specific rules which are summarized by the general formula.

By the time of the thirteenth transcription, twenty-six weeks after we

TABLE 7. RULES FOR GENERATING NOUN PHRASES AT TIME 2

$NP_1 \rightarrow Dem + Art + M + N$	$NP \rightarrow (Dem) + (Art) + (M) + N$
$NP_2 \rightarrow Art + M + N$	
$NP_3 \rightarrow Dem + M + N$	
$NP_4 \rightarrow Art + N$	( ) means class within
$NP_5 \rightarrow M + N$	parentheses is optional
$NP_6 \rightarrow Dem + N$	
$NP_7 \rightarrow Dem + Art + N$	

began our study, privileges of occurrence were much more finely differentiated and syntactic classes were consequently more numerous. From the distributional evidence we judged that Adam had made five classes of his original class M: articles, descriptive adjectives, possessive pronouns, demonstrative pronouns, and a residual class of modifiers. The generative rules of Table 7 had become inadequate; there were no longer, for instance, any combinations like "A your car." Eve had the same set except that she used two residual classes of modifiers. In addition nouns had begun to subdivide for both children. The usage of proper nouns had become clearly distinct from the usage of count nouns. For Eve the evidence justified separating count nouns from mass nouns, but for Adam it still did not. Both children by this time were frequently pluralizing nouns but as yet their syntactic control of the singular-plural distinction was imperfect.

In summary, one major aspect of the development of general structure in child speech is a progressive differentiation in the usage of words and therefore a progressive differentiation of syntactic classes. At the same time, however, there is an integrative process at work. From the first, an occasional noun phrase occurred as a component of some larger construction. At first these noun phrases were just two words long and the range of positions in which they could occur was small. With time the noun phrases grew longer, were more frequently used, and were used in a greater range of positions. The noun phrase structure as a whole, in all the permissible combinations of modifiers and nouns, was assuming the combinational privileges enjoyed by nouns in isolation.

In Table 8 we have set down some of the sentence positions in which both nouns and noun phrases occurred in the speech of Adam and Eve. It is the close match between the positions of nouns alone and of nouns with modifiers in the speech of Adam and Eve that justifies us in calling the longer constructions noun phrases. These longer constructions are, as they should be, endocentric; the head word alone has the same syntactic privileges as the head word with its modifiers. The continuing failure to find in noun phrase positions whole constructions of the type "That a blue flower" signals the fact that these constructions are telegraphic versions of

TABLE 8. SOME PRIVILEGES OF THE NOUN PHRASE

Noun Positions	Noun Phrase Positions
That (flower)	*That (a blue flower)*
Where (ball) go?	*Where (the puzzle) go?*
Adam write (penguin)	*Doggie eat (the breakfast)*
(Horsie) stop	*(A horsie) crying*
Put (hat) on	*Put (the red hat) on*

predicate nominative sentences omitting the verb form *is*. Examples of the kind of construction not obtained are: "That (that a blue flower)"; "Where (that a blue flower)?"

For adults the noun phrase is a subwhole of the sentence, what linguists call an "immediate constituent." The noun phrase has a kind of psychological unity. There are signs that the noun phrase was also an immediate constituent for Adam and Eve. Consider the sentence using the separable verb *put on*. The noun phrase in "Put the red hat on" is, as a whole, fitted in between the verb and the particle even as is the noun alone in "Put hat on." What is more, however, the location of pauses in the longer sentence, on several occasions, suggested the psychological organization: "Put . . . the red hat . . . on" rather than "Put the red . . . hat on" or "Put the . . . red hat on." In addition to this evidence the use of pronouns suggests that the noun phrase is a psychological unit.

The unity of noun phrases in adult English is evidenced, in the first place, by the syntactic equivalence between such phrases and nouns alone. It is evidenced, in the second place, by the fact that pronouns are able to substitute for total noun phrases. In our immediately preceding sentence the pronoun "It" stands for the rather involved construction from the first sentence of this paragraph: "The unity of noun phrases in adult English." The words called "pronouns" in English would more aptly be called "pronoun-phrases" since it is the phrase rather than the noun which they usually replace. One does not replace "unity" with "it" and say "The *it* of noun phrases in adult English." In the speech of Adam and Eve, too, the pronoun came to function as a replacement for the noun phrase. Some of the clearer cases appear in Table 9.

Adam characteristically externalizes more of his learning than does Eve and his record is especially instructive in connection with the learning of pronouns. In his first eight records, the first sixteen weeks of the study, Adam quite often produced sentences containing both the pronoun and the noun or noun phrase that the pronoun should have replaced. One can here see the equivalence in the process of establishment. First the substitute is produced and then, as if in explication, the form or forms that will eventually be replaced by the substitute. Adam spoke out his pronoun

TABLE 9. Pronouns Replacing Nouns or Noun Phrases and Pronouns Produced Together with Nouns or Noun Phrases

Noun Phrases Replaced by Pronouns	Pronouns and Noun Phrases in Same Utterances
Hit ball	*Mommy get it ladder*
Get it	*Mommy get it my ladder*
Ball go?	*Saw it ball*
Go get it	*Miss it garage*
Made it	*I miss it cowboy boot*
Made a ship	*I Adam drive that*
Fix a tricycle	*I Adam drive*
Fix it	*I Adam don't*

antecedents as chronological consequents. This is additional evidence of the unity of the noun phrase since the noun phrases *my ladder* and *cowboy boot* are linked with *it* in Adam's speech in just the same way as the nouns *ladder* and *ball*.

We have described three processes involved in the child's acquisition of syntax. It is clear that the last of these, the induction of latent structure, is by far the most complex. It looks as if this last process will put a serious strain on any learning theory thus far conceived by psychology. The very intricate simultaneous differentiation and integration that constitutes the evolution of the noun phrase is more reminiscent of the biological development of an embryo than it is of the acquisition of a conditional reflex.

NOTES AND REFERENCES

1. We are grateful for intellectual stimulation and lighthearted companionship to Dr. Jean Berko Gleason, Mr. Samuel Anderson, Mr. Colin Fraser, Dr. David McNeill, and Dr. Daniel Slobin.

2. H. Maclay and C. E. Osgood, "Hesitation phenomena in spontaneous English speech," *Word,* XV (1959), 19–44.

3. Additional evidence of the constraint on sentence length may be found in R. Brown and C. Fraser, "The acquisition of syntax," C. N. Cofer and Barbara Musgrave, eds., *Verbal Behavior and Learning* (New York: McGraw-Hill, 1963).

4. Brown and Fraser, *ibid.*

5. M. D. S. Braine, "The ontogeny of English phrase structure: the first phrase," *Language,* XXXIX (1963), 1–13.

6. W. Miller and Susan Ervin, "The development of grammar in child language," Ursula Bellugi and R. Brown, eds., *The Acquisition of Language, Child Developm. Monogr.* (1964).

7. Brown and Fraser, *op. cit.*

19.

The uncommitted cortex, the child's changing brain

Wilder Penfield

Can certain areas of a child's brain be "staked out" in much the same manner as a mining claim? The author of this selection believes that this not only can, but should, be done. The article emphasizes several points. The first is that development, both physical and mental, proceeds in a sequential manner in accord with a sort of built-in biological clock. For maximal learning to occur, it must take place when the organism is "ready." There is a certain best time to master most of the skills necessary for effective living. A second point to be emphasized is the tremendous importance of speech in human development (see selections 4, 17, and 23). Such essential components of successful living as one's ability to communicate with others and his image of self are dependent upon his ability to verbalize—"The most precious and indispensable portion of the adult's cortex is the major speech area." A third point is that it is essential for mental development that certain sets or predispositions to learn be established and that others be avoided. It may be that a negative attitude toward reading and mathematics can be as handicapping for a learner as the failure to establish, before the age of ten or twelve, the proper neural connections for learning secondary languages.

This selection provides an explanation of why early learning is of such great importance. The mental competence of a child of four has been said to have an approximate correlation of .50 with his eventual adult competence. At age twelve the correlation increases to approximately .80. This helps us to understand why young people are flexible and adaptable to change and why it is difficult to "teach an old dog new tricks."

UNLESS THERE is action in the brain, a man has no thoughts and no consciousness, no awareness. This is a surmise of science, and there is as yet no good scientific reason to doubt it. Action, when it takes place within the brain, spinal cord, and nerves, is electrical. During effective brain action, electric potentials or impulses travel in everchanging patterns along the integrating circuits within the brain. It is then that the mind is alert. But we are only just beginning to be able to match the patterns of electric movement through the brain with the varying nature of thoughts or sensations or memories.

Atlantic, 214 (No. 1):77–81, July, 1964. Copyright 1964, by The Atlantic Monthly Company, Boston, Mass. Reprinted with permission. Wilder Penfield, Director, Montreal Neurological Institute of McGill University.

William James, the Harvard philosopher, observed that consciousness is a river, forever flowing, forever changing. He meant to indicate that the content of consciousness is never the same from moment to moment. If that is the case, we must assume that the electric potentials passing along the central system of connections within the brain never follow a pattern that is quite the same as the previous pattern. The flowing of the river seems to stop during sleep and in coma and in death. The traveling of the electric potentials slows down or stops also. When I refer to the river of the mind, it is only honest to say "seems to stop," for although science can detect and measure the passage of electric potentials, it can neither define nor measure consciousness and thought. It can only measure the results of thinking as soon as they are expressed through body activity.

Some philosophers adopt the hypothesis that thought and brain action are one, but the physiologist, who works with the brain, cannot take this as proven, for it is the very thing he has set out, with an open mind, to prove or to disprove. Meanwhile, he can only use the language of dualism, referring to brain and mind as related phenomena. Since he is a workman, he can see that a "creative thought" may precede brain action. He can see that brain action may accompany or may be followed by thought. That is as far as his evidence goes.

Take as an example a man, A, who is talking to a second man, B. The thinking of A must either precede or accompany or follow the action of his brain. In any case, his brain activity causes him to speak. The sound vibrations reach the ears of B, and corresponding potentials pass along B's auditory nerves into his brain, creating there a pattern of traveling electric impulses similar to that of A moments before. The result is that B thinks A's thoughts with certain inevitable modifications of his own drawn from his memory and the conditioning of his own past experience. B's thinking has been evoked, and it is either simultaneous with the action of his brain or immediately subsequent to it.

Sir Charles Sherrington, the great physiologist and student of the integrative action of the nervous system, has this to say: "That our being should consist of two separate elements offers, I suppose, no greater inherent improbability than that it should rest on one only." I would add that if the basic element is unitary, it still remains for us to explain its dual manifestation.

The human brain is a living, growing, changing organ. It can even carry out its own repairs to some extent. But it is bound by the inexorable evolution of its functional aptitudes, and no one can alter this, not even an educator or psychiatrist. One can draw up a functional timetable for the brain of a child. One might well say there is a built-in biological clock that tells the passing time of educational opportunity.

In India in 1957, while visiting some of the universities, I received a surprising request from the Department of Education to give a series of two broadcasts over the All-India Radio on the teaching of secondary languages. Following that came a plan to print 10,000 copies of the broadcasts and send them out to teachers in the schools of India. Some educator, I reflected, must indeed be desperate, to ask advice from a brain surgeon! I knew quite well that the teaching of secondary languages was in some ways the most urgent problem of modern education in India, with its many local dialects and its plan to teach all the people two secondary languages, English and Hindustani.

I am not a language teacher. My own studies of three secondary languages were truly remarkable, but only because so much toil, after the age of sixteen, resulted in such a pitiful harvest. My wife tried to reassure me by pointing out that our own children had gained a reasonable command of two extra languages because we had arranged to have them hear German and French well spoken in their early childhood. Was it, after all, as simple as that?

From a scientific point of view, the problem of speech was not new to me. For ten years I had been working on the manuscript of a book on the subject with the help of an associate, Dr. Lamar Roberts. It was self-evident that the beginning of mastery of at least one language is the prerequisite to formal teaching. Speaking and reading and writing are the basic skills of education.

During most of my years of medical practice I had had the advantage of living in a bilingual society in Montreal, where my patients spoke French as often as English. All the while, the problem had grown more challenging, the findings more exciting. I had seen children under the age of ten or twelve lose the power of speech when the speech convolutions in the left hemisphere of the brain had been destroyed by a head injury or a brain tumor. I had seen them recover after a year of dumbness and aphasia. In time they spoke as well as ever, because the child's brain is functionally flexible for the start of a language. They began all over again and established a speech center located on the other side of the brain in what is called the nondominant hemisphere. (In a right-handed person, the left hemisphere is normally dominant for speech—that is, it contains the specialized speech centers.)

When the major speech center is severely injured in adult life, the adult cannot do what the child does. He may improve, but he is using the remaining uninjured cortex on the side of injury. He cannot establish a complete new center on the nondominant side, not because he is senile, but because he has by that time taken over the initially uncommitted convolutions of his brain for other uses. This uncommitted cortex is the part of the human brain that makes man teachable and thus lifts him above all other species.

Gray matter is made up of many millions of living nerve cells that are capable of receiving and sending electric impulses. The cerebral cortex, which is the thick layer of gray matter covering the outer surface of the brain, has been called "new" since it is found to be more and more voluminous as one ascends the phylogenetic scale from fish to man. It covers the convolutions and dips down into the fissures between the convolutions. The white matter beneath is made up of the branching connections of the nerve cells, which are capable of transmitting electric potentials like insulated wires. Some of the connections pass inward into the "old" gray matter of the brain stem (the old brain); some pass through it to the eyes and ears; some pass down the spinal cord and along the nerves to the muscles and the skin.

Certain parts of the cerebral cortex, the so-called "sensory cortex" and "motor cortex," can be used only for sensory and motor purposes because these parts have fixed functional connections from birth onward.

But there is a large area of cortex underneath the temples and covering a given part of each of the two temporal lobes that is uncommitted at birth. This uncommitted cortex will in time be used for language and for perception. It will make possible the memory and use of words, as well as the memory and interpretation of experience. As the child begins to understand, electric currents must pass in corresponding patterns through this cortex. After each time of passage, it is easier for the later currents to follow the same trail. This tendency toward facilitation of electric passage results in man's amazingly permanent records of the auditory and visual stream of his conscious life.

Now, if the posterior half of the left uncommitted cortex is used by the child for speech, as it usually is, it becomes the major speech cortex. Then the remaining three quarters is used for interpretation of experience (interpretive cortex). Functional connections are gradually established by the child, and the general uses of the uncommitted areas are fixed for life.

Much of this information about mechanisms of speech and perception has come to us during long operations on conscious, alert patients who were kept from pain by local novocaine injection into the scalp while a trapdoor opening was made in the skull. In the attempt to relieve each patient of his attacks of focal epilepsy, a preliminary survey of the brain was made after it was exposed. A gentle electrical stimulus was applied by touching the cortex here and there with an electrode. This served to map the sensory cortex by causing sensation (visual, auditory, or bodily, according to which of the different areas was touched) and the motor cortex by producing crude movement of the face or limb. When an abnormal area of brain was suspected of being the cause of fits, the electrode might produce, by stimulation there, the characteristic beginning of the attack from which the patient sought relief. Excision of areas of bad cortex is the method of treatment.

The most precious and indispensable portion of the adult's cortex is the major speech area. It might be worthwhile to forfeit other areas and so lose other functions in order to gain a cure, but never speech. Thus, the need of a method to map the exact territory devoted to speech was urgent.

When the electrode was applied to the speech cortex, it did not cause a man to speak. It seemed to have no effect. But if the patient tried to speak while the electrode was in place, he discovered that he could not find his words. If shown a pencil, he knew what it was and could make appropriate movements with the hand, but he had lost the power of speaking. He was aphasic. The gentle electric current was blocking the action of the speech cortex and its underlying connection without disturbing the function of the adjacent areas. When the patient was shown an object and was asked to name it, he perceived its nature, and he must have dispatched electric potentials along the brain's integrating circuits to the speech mechanism. But, to his surprise, he drew a blank.

Normally, when the appropriately patterned potentials reach the speech mechanism, the word is instantly available to consciousness—its sound, how to write it, how to speak it, and how to recognize the written word. As long as the electrode paralyzed the action of the speech unit, none of these was possible. But as the electrode was lifted, the patient, not knowing what was done, would exclaim, "Now I can speak! That was a pencil."

So we had a new method of mapping out the major speech area exactly, and the minor ones as well. And we could remove less useful cortex right up to it without fear of losing the precious jewel of the brain, speech function. We mapped out the cortical area thus in hundreds of cases and acquired precise scientific information to take the place of anatomical conjecture.

But what about the similar area in the nondominant hemisphere and the uncommitted temporal cortex farther forward on both sides? So far, neurologists had found no function for these areas. Stimulation in them never produced aphasia. What were they used for? One day I stumbled on a clue. I applied the electrode to the right temporal cortex (nondominant). The patient, a woman of middle age, exclaimed suddenly, "I seem to be the way I was when I was giving birth to my baby girl." I did not recognize this as a clue. I could not help feeling that the suddenness of her exclamation was strange, and so I made a note of it.

Several years later during a similar operation, the electrode caused a young girl to describe, with considerable emotion, a specific experience she had had when running through a meadow. There is no sensation in the cortex, and she could not know when I had touched the electrode to her right temporal lobe, but each time I did so she described the experience again and stopped when the electrode was removed. Since that day we have been on the alert and have gathered more and more cases which could be studied critically.

Our conclusion is as follows: There is within the adult human brain a remarkable record of the stream of each individual's awareness, his consciousness. It is as though the electrode cuts in, at random, on the record of that stream. The patient sees and hears what he saw and heard in some earlier strip of time, and he feels the same accompanying emotions.

The stream of consciousness flows again exactly as before, stopping instantly on removal of the electrode. He is aware of those things to which he paid attention in this earlier period, even twenty years ago. He is not aware of the things that were ignored. The experience evidently moves forward at the original pace. This is demonstrated by the fact that when the music of an orchestra or song or piano is heard and the patient is asked to hum in accompaniment, the tempo of his humming is what one would expect. He is still aware of being in the operating room, but he can describe this other run of consciousness at the same time.

The patient recognizes the experience as having been his own, although usually he could not have recalled it if he had tried. This complete record of his auditory and visual experience is not subject to conscious recall, but it is evidently used in the subconscious brain transaction that results in perception. By means of it, a man in normal life compares each succeeding experience with his own past experience. He knows at once whether it is familiar or not. If it is familiar, he interprets the present stream of consciousness in the light of the past. Careful comparison of all the brain maps we have made shows no overlap of the boundaries that separate speech cortex, which endows a man with memory of words, and the interpretive cortex, which gives him access to the memory of past similar experience and thus enables him to understand the present.

Before the child begins to speak and to perceive, the uncommitted cortex is a blank slate on which nothing has been written. In the ensuing years much is written, and the writing is never erased. After the age of ten or twelve, the general functional connections have been established and fixed for the speech cortex. After that, the speech center cannot be transferred to the cortex of the lesser side, which is then fully occupied with the business of perception.

The brain of the twelve-year-old, you may say, is prepared for rapid expansion of the vocabulary of the mother tongue and of the other languages he may have heard in the formative period. If he has heard these other languages, he has developed also a remarkable switch mechanism that enables him to turn from one language to another without confusion, without translation, without a mother-tongue accent.

In my broadcast to the teachers of India, I could only reason as follows: Do not turn without question to the West for your model of teaching secondary languages. Consider first the changing functional capacities of the child's brain. Most of our schools in the West begin the teaching of foreign languages by the dead-language technique. It was designed for adults learning Greek and Latin by means of word lists and grammar. Your hope that the people of India will speak English and Hindustani as living languages is doomed to failure if you follow this technique. It has its place, no doubt, but it should not be used in the years when the child is a genius at language initiation, the time when the uncommitted cortex can still be conditioned to foreign tongues.

But there is another method of beginning a language—the direct method that mothers use. It was used to teach foreign languages as well as the mother tongue in the families of ancient Ur and during the Roman Empire. It is used by some parents in the West and in the East today. Even a nursemaid or inexperienced tutor can use the mother's method for a second language. The mother does her teaching when the child's brain is ready for it. In three or four years she may give the child only a few hundred words, but he gets the set, acquires the units, creates the functional connections of the speech cortex. In unilingual countries the mother conducts the first stage of language learning by the direct method and the school carries on easily with the second stage, vocabulary expansion. If a nation is to be bilingual or trilingual or multilingual, the schools adopt the mother's direct method for the first stage of foreign-language teaching.

I ventured the opinion that India's problem was not at all insuperable. Use the mother's method at the beginning. Do not use translation at that stage. Conduct the kindergarten and the earliest grades in English for a year or two and in Hindustani for the same length of time. Better yet, make the elementary schools bilingual, teaching in English in the morning and in Hindustani in the afternoon. After two years of bilingual kindergarten and one in the first grade, the children will have started reading and writing. They are ready to carry on in either language smoothly and without accent or confusion. If desired they could start in still a third language. You must employ teachers who have begun the language they speak by the mother's direct method, and they must teach school in the language, not making language a subject in itself. To find such teachers is your primary problem, whatever your method may be.

The child is the genius in our society when it comes to acquiring the early set or the units of a language. The enlargement of vocabulary is another story. The ten-year-old or the twenty-year-old expands vocabulary, as he expands knowledge, far faster than the young child.

Many questions have been raised by those who are charged with the task of planning the curriculum of school and college: Does multilingualism decrease the eventual excellence of intellectual performance in any one culture? Does it increase the embarrassment of the child who already has a reading problem or a writing problem? Does a second language, started too soon, confuse the child? The answer that I would give to these questions, based on observations and physiological study, is no. Double learning may well confuse the scientist who seeks to discover how it is done, but not the child.

The secret of the child's success lies in the action of the switch mechanism, a conditioned reflex that works in his brain automatically. When the English child (or adult) hears a French word or meets a French person or enters a French school, he unconsciously switches on his French network with its vocabulary, however meager it may be. What he proceeds to learn is then added to the French network. In the brain, French, English, and Chinese, if learned, utilize the same area of speech cortex without demonstrable separation into different areas. Every adult who speaks second languages is aware of this subconscious reflex which brings the word bleistift to his mind, instead of pencil, as he turns to a German companion, or crayon as he enters the class conducted in French.

It is preferable, in my opinion, that in the early stages a bilingual adult should not switch back and forth from one language to another in conversation with a young child. But it works well to do what a bilingual mother of my acquaintance has done—establish upstairs in the home as a French-speaking area and downstairs for English. Her little children accepted it as no problem at all. Language to them is only a way of getting what is wanted or expressing ideas. Imitation of words comes only after months of hearing them in the earliest years. According to W. F. Leopold's careful study, there is a lag of two to seven months after the child hears a word in the second year of life before he uses it in a meaningful manner. Baby talk shows that the set of the brain for language is not established immediately. It takes time, and the baby's accent and the formal phrasing and organization of sentences alter gradually to those of the adult without the need of lectures on grammar.

In our own home the children heard German in the nursery from a governess who could speak nothing else. When she took them to French nursery school they switched to French as they entered the door and switched back again when they found her waiting outside at the close of school.

At the bilingual school conducted by the Sisters of Notre Dame de Sion in Montreal, the two years of kindergarten and the first year of school are conducted in French in the morning and, by a different set of teachers, in English in the afternoon (or vice versa). The children may be French-speaking or English-speaking at home, or even speak Italian or Polish. If so, they should be learning all the while in the mother's tongue at home and in the church—learning the folk songs and nursery rhymes, and also, one hopes, religion and moral values.

A unilingual adult who begins the learning of a second language late speaks it with a mother-tongue accent and tends to learn by translation. However, the adult who has previously learned some other second language in childhood is likely to learn a later third and fourth language faster and better than a unilingual adult. This greater facility of the bilingual adult may be due to the well-developed switch mechanism which he acquired in childhood. He is able to switch off the mother tongue easily, and thus to learn directly.

It follows that in a school district where the only foreign native-born teachers available are Swedish or Spanish, for example, it would be the part of wisdom to have beginning years taught in Swedish, or on a bilingual basis—Swedish in the mornings and Spanish in the afternoon. Those children who continue their schooling in English and eventually go on to college and into professional schools will be better prepared to learn the Russian and Chinese which intelligent English-speaking adults of the future will want to understand. English pronunciation and literature can be taught after the age of eight or ten. The bilingual child prepared for formal education by mother and nursemaid, or mother and a second-language kindergarten, has undoubted advantage over other children, whatever the second languages may have been and whatever the eventual work of the individual may prove to be.

In a study supported by the Carnegie Foundation and conducted under W. E. Lambert, professor of psychology at McGill University, it was concluded recently that bilingual children at the ten-year level in Montreal showed greater intelligence than unilingual children of the same age. Perhaps the key to success is to be sought in the elementary school.

The uncommitted cortex must be conditioned for speech in the first decade. This is the miracle that makes man's education possible. Time was, not so long ago, when all well-educated people had had basic training in the classics. But men no longer turn to the cultures of Greece and Rome. We are close to many contemporary races from whom we have much to learn and with whom we must be friends. In these changing times, educators, like other specialists, are turning to science for new horizons, chiefly seeking technical aids. While questioning traditions and classical methods, they might well examine the findings of human neuro-physiology. By definition, well-educated people are multilingual.

Educators must consider the mind as well as the brain, two sides perhaps of the same golden coin. On the one side they deal with behavior, morals, hopes, fears, school spirit. But on the other side they deal with the basic problems of education, the training of the brain. What the brain is allowed to record, how and when it is conditioned—these things prepare it for great achievement, or limit it to mediocrity. Boy and man are capable of so much more than is demanded of them! Adjust the time and the manner of learning; then you may double your demands and your expectations.

20.

Creativity: yesterday, today, and tomorrow

J. P. GUILFORD

*The type of intelligence that merely reproduces established informa-
tion or reconstructs already-known procedures has been termed
convergent. It tends to maintain what already is known and to perpetuate existing procedures and conditions. In contrast are those intellectual processes characterized as "divergent." These processes
function to recombine and to revise conventional ideas and operations
into new concepts and into different ways of doing things. This is the
kind of thinking and intelligence which promotes change, innovation, and creativity. Unfortunately, it is not the type of mental
functioning that is recognized and developed by authoritarian, infor-
mation-oriented teaching and by conventional measures of intelligence.
On the contrary, there is reason to believe that the divergent and creative thinker is disturbing to, and is not favored by, teachers and other
school personnel. The most widely used tests of intellectual competence
are based upon the conventional and conforming rather than the
imaginative answer.*

*If the early years of development function as strongly in estab-
lishing perceptual sets and behaviors as previous selections suggest,
then divergent and creative thinking must be rewarded and established as a major objective in one's early schooling and family experiences. To overlook or to postpone this may be to forfeit the
opportunity. Worse still, it may result in denying children the opportunity for maximum intellectual and personal development. Descriptions of self-actualizing people are so similar to those for creative
individuals that the conditions are much the same.*

THE LAUNCHING of a new journal devoted to the subject of creativity is an
appropriate occasion for considering how the study of creativity has
evolved, how matters in that subject stand, and what its future may be.
The trail of the past is largely on the record, and also some aspects of the
present status. The promise for the future can only be inferred from
present trends found outside the field of creativity as well as within its
borders. Interpretations and predictions are demanding mental exercises,
and must inevitably reflect subjective impressions and judgments. And no
one who undertakes these exercises is omniscient.

Journal of Creative Behavior, 1:3–14, 1967. J. P. Guilford, Director, Aptitudes Research
Center, University of Southern California.

FROM GALTON TO 1950

Although geniuses in various fields of human affairs have always been recognized and usually highly valued, it was not until Galton's studies of men of genius (1869) that the eyes of natural science were turned upon them. Galton did not seriously attempt to understand the mental operations by which distinguished leaders produce their novel ideas, but rather he tried to understand the hereditary determination of creative performances. His study became a classic, but he failed to reach uncontestable conclusions.

Reaching an understanding of exceptionally creative people and of the mental operations by which creative productions are achieved should have been the responsibility of psychologists. But early scientific psychologists were having such difficulty with more simple mental events such as sensation, perception, and memory that they had neither the time nor the courage to tackle problems of creativity. If anything at all related to the subject was mentioned in the textbooks, it was under the mysterious label of "imagination" or "creative imagination." Usually only passing mention was made of the concept. Then behaviorism swept the field of psychology—in the USA at least—and such mentalistic concepts were commonly forced off the pages of psychological writing. Only two writers (Schoen, 1930; Guilford, 1939, 1952), each devoting a chapter to the subject, have had much to say about creativity to the beginning student of psychology.

Psychometric Interests in Creativity

One kind of psychologist could not avoid the problem of creativity completely, for he dealt with the many characteristics in which one person differs from another. Among these characteristics are those that prepare some individuals for higher levels of performance, including invention and innovation. The first successful tests of intelligence, from Binet to Terman and others, were aimed at prediction of academic achievement at the elementary level, where almost no attention was given to self-initiated ideas when it came time to evaluate achievement. The selection of abilities to be measured in the first Stanford revision of the Binet scale omitted those especially relevant to the assessment of creative potential, due to an incidental result in a faulty experiment. Terman (1906) had administered to two extreme groups (of seven each, out of 500 subjects who had been ranked for brightness *versus* dullness by their teachers) a set of experimental tests, one of which he recognized as a test of ingenuity. The ingenuity test failed to discriminate the extreme groups, but all the other tests were successful in doing so. Thus, over the years, tests of creative qualities have been almost nonexistent in intelligence scales.

The lack of correlation between tests recognized as belonging in the creative category and tests common to intelligence scales has been noted in isolated studies over the years. Even before Terman's experience with an ingenuity test, Dearborn (1898) had found this relative independence to be true for his tests involving "productive imagination." Over the years, replications of such findings have been reported by Chassell (1916), Andrews (1930), and Welch (1946). Terman could have used Dearborn's finding as evidence supporting his own conclusion that inventive qualities were outside the realm of intelligence, where the latter pertains only to basic academic potential. Or he could have reached the more recently demonstrated conclusion that intelligence, broadly conceived, embraces several components, some of which, at least, do not correlate very much with others. But the prevailing notion was that intelligence was a monolithic ability, all-relevant and unanalyzable.

Anecdotal Studies of Creative Performance

While psychologists were doing very little to attempt to understand creative people and creative production, others, not willing to wait for enlightenment from that source, proceeded to do something about the matter. They recorded instances of discoveries in science, literary productions, and other examples of output from recognized creative geniuses. Samples of this kind of investigation may be seen in the books by Wallas (1926, 1945), Hadamard (1945), and Ghiselin (1952). Rossman (1931) made a more systematic study of inventors, utilizing a questionnaire approach.

The weaknesses of anecdotal methods for the purposes of extracting generalizations are well known. Still, such information can be fruitful by suggesting hypotheses that can be explored further by means of more rigorous scientific procedures. The most fruitful outcome of the study of creative episodes was a list of the stages of thinking that a creator typically exhibits in the total process, beginning with the realized need for creative effort to the "wrapping up" of the final product. Both Wallas and Rossman proposed steps that take place in the course of the total creative event— Rossman for inventors, specifically, and Wallas for creative production in general.

Experimental Studies of Creation

A few, but very few, investigators took seriously the creative steps proposed by Wallas—preparation, incubation, illumination, and elaboration. One of them was the psychologist Patrick (1935, 1937, 1938, 1941), who attempted to determine by experiments, mostly within the psychological laboratory, whether the Wallas processes could be identified, whether they run their courses in the given order, and what roles each of them play in a complete creative event. She found the process concepts relevant, but that the steps show many departures from the 1–2–3–4 order given by Wallas. The latter conclusion has been supported by similar findings of Eindhoven and Vinacke (1952).

Creative Production in Relation to Age

A more lively and more extensive area of investigation regarding creativity was that pertaining to the ages of life at which the highest quality of creative performances is most likely to occur, and to quantity of creative production as related to age. Studies by Lehman culminated in a book (Lehman, 1953). This kind of study has also been conducted by Dennis (1956).

This thumbnail sketch of the fate of the subject of creativity to midcentury has emphasized only a few points. The subject was almost entirely ignored by psychologists. Psychometric psychologists ruled creative potential out of intelligence, and behaviorism adopted a general viewpoint from which creativity could not be seen. Non-psychologists made a few attempts to fill the gap, utilizing an anecdotal approach. One beneficial consequence was the suggestion of stages in creative production, which implied hypotheses that could be and were investigated experimentally in a preliminary way. Genetic studies, utilizing biographical information, gave attention to the ages at which different degrees of quality and quantity of creative production occur. Almost nothing was learned about the nature of creative thinking itself, except that studies of such rare topics as insight have been shown to be relevant (Guilford, 1967).

CREATIVITY SINCE 1950

Although the year 1950 is generally regarded as the turning point with respect to interest in creativity, and sometimes the writer's APA address (Guilford, 1950) is cited as a stimulus, there were indications of other trends in our *Zeitgeist* that converged upon the same effects. The number of publications on the subject had shown some positive acceleration in the 30's and 40's, consistent with the explosive rate of activity of this sort since 1950.

A number of forces were undoubtedly at work. The second World War had called forth great efforts toward innovation in research and development, culminating in the atomic bomb. The coming of peace that was no peace left us in the cold war, which called for ever-accelerating efforts in a contest of intellects. Inventive brains were at a premium, and there were never enough. We were on the eve of the space age, and rockets were already taking trial flights, stirring our imaginations of things to come.

The stage was well set, then, ready for the psychologist to play his proper role in trying to fathom the creative person and his creative processes.

As more tangible evidence of the stirrings of interest in creativity, Alex F. Osborn had written his book on *Applied Imagination,* which was ready for publication in 1953. The book was immediately popular, and has gone through numerous printings. The fact that it has been translated into a number of languages indicates that the new attention to the subject has become world wide. Osborn also founded the *Creative Education Foundation* and the annual *Institute for Creative Problem Solving,* which has been held for twelve years at what is now the State University of New York at Buffalo. The Creative Education Foundation has initiated and is sponsoring this journal [*The Journal of Creative Behavior*].

New Investigations of Creativity

The lively research activity since 1950 has been variously motivated and has used several different approaches. There has been much theoretical interest, which leads to asking the questions of what, how, and why. There have been efforts to solve certain practical problems, some of them utilizing information derived from basic studies and some not.

Basic Information on the Nature of Creativity. New research in an area where there has been little precedent is likely to be exploratory, involving little or no hypothesis testing. Such is the case with a number of investigations of the characteristics of people of recognized creative performance, as the study of outstanding scientists by Ann Roe (1952) and the studies of recognized creative writers, architects, and mathematicians, by MacKinnon and Barron, and their associates in the Institute for Personality Assessment and Research at The University of California in Berkeley (MacKinnon, 1960). With a psychoanalytic theoretical bias, these studies emphasized motivational and temperamental characteristics. Some of the salient findings were that highly creative persons, at least in the groups examined, are inclined to be strongly interested in esthetic and theoretical matters and that they tend to be highly intuitive and introverted. As to intellectual status, most of the individuals were in the upper ranges of IQs, and within this range there was practically no correlation between IQ and level of creative performance.

Another major approach, which has emphasized the intellectual qualities that might contribute to creative thinking and creative performance, has been made through application of multivariate methods of factor analysis. The locale of this research has been the Aptitude Research Project at the University of Southern California, under the writer's direction. Rejecting the prevailing doctrine that intelligence is a single, monolithic ability, and also the view that creative talents are something outside the realm of intelligence, the studies began with the assumption that there are several, perhaps many, distinguishable abilities involved. It was also assumed that creative talents are not confined to a favored few individuals, but are probably widely distributed to different degrees throughout the population. Creative talents could therefore be investigated without being restricted to observation of the gifted few.

The initial factor analysis started with a prior hypothesis as to what distinctions were to be expected among abilities that should be relevant to creative performance. Most of the hypothesized abilities were demonstrated by a factor analysis (Wilson, *et al.,* 1954).

Within a setting of exploration of other hypothesized intellectual abilities, a general theory of intelligence and its components known as the "structure of intellect" was developed. This theory forecast many distinguishable abilities yet to be demonstrated, many of which could be especially relevant for creative performance. Subsequent factor analyses have supported all the hypothesized abilities that have been investigated. The outcomes of all these studies are summarized, and their implications will be treated in the writer's forthcoming volume on *The Nature of Human Intelligence* (Guilford, 1967).

Briefly, the abilities believed to be most relevant for creative thinking are in two categories. One category is "divergent-production" (DP) abilities. DP abilities pertain to generation of ideas, as in solving a problem, where variety is important. Some DP abilities have been characterized as kinds of fluency, some as kinds of flexibility, and others as elaboration abilities. The varieties of abilities within the DP category depend upon the kind of information with which the person is dealing. This circumstance strongly suggests that creative talents depend upon the media in which the person is working—for example, whether he deals with lines and colors, sounds, or words, as in the various arts.

The other potential source of creative talents is in the category of "transformation" abilities, which pertain to revising what one experiences or knows, thereby producing new forms and patterns. Readiness to be flexible is a general characteristic of this group of talents, where flexibility leads to reinterpretations and reorganizations. Again, the variety of transformation abilities depends upon the kind of information or media with which creators deal.

An important advantage of analyzing creative disposition in terms of abilities is that kinds of abilities also imply kinds of mental functions. Having taken this logical step, we are ready to talk about the process of creative thinking, as such. Discovery of the intellectual factors or abilities answers the question what; applying these answers to operations that the individual performs answers questions of how. Thus, the study of how a creative thinker operates is opened to us, for we have the concepts that we need—the handles that we can grasp in further research efforts.

Some Conditions of Creative Performance. Other traditional research approaches have been used for the problems of creative development and its promotion. Using tests of the kind developed through factor analysis, Torrance (1962) has examined the question of how creative potential changes as a function of age in children and adolescents. He has found that development does not occur at a uniform rate; the most significant departure is the "fourth-grade slump" at about the age of nine. Although the same tests show a leveling-off of averages in the late teens, other tests have shown further development even to the age of 30 (Trembly, 1964). The latter result supports the findings of Lehman, that quality of production commonly reaches its maximum in the early thirties. It is likely, however, that growth curves will be found to differ, depending upon which of the factorial abilities is being measured.

In line with the general optimism about improving abilities through favorable environmental conditions, some studies have been designed to assess improvement in creative activity as a result of various kinds of practice. From the factorial-theory view point, we may regard the relevant abilities as being intellectual skills with some degree of generality. This means that exercises of appropriate kinds should yield improved performance in the abilities concerned. Most of the studies have shown that changes in performance can be assessed and that improvements with some degree of durability do occur. Many of these studies have been conducted by Sidney Parnes and his associates at SUNY Buffalo, and by Irving Maltzman and his associates at UC Los Angeles.

Other experiments have concerned the nature of creative thinking and problem solving, which extensively overlap, to say the least, and with the conditions affecting those phenomena. For example, Torrance and his associates have examined the effects of criticism and other conditions of motivation upon creative performances of school children (Torrance, 1965). Other experimental studies have examined conditions affecting insight or intuition.

As stated earlier, the relation of creative potential and creative production to the traditional IQ has been found close to zero where groups of superior IQ are concerned. This finding has been verified by a number of investigations (e.g., Getzels and Jackson, 1961). But in the lower ranges of IQ there is a substantial correlation. When the whole range of IQ is included, say from 62 to 150, there is a characteristic scatter plot. This plot shows that when the IQ is low, scores on tests of creative potential can only be low. When the IQ is high, there can be a wide range in performance on creative tasks.

Assuming that IQ tests are very much confined to cognitive abilities (and this means essentially to amount of basic information possessed), IQ appears to set an upper limit on creative potential. The relationship described suggests that we have numerous creative underachievers but very few overachievers. A question of utmost educational import is whether ways can be found to bring creative underachievers up to cognitive potential, and whether the latter can also be raised by educational procedures. This is the great educational challenge of the immediate future.

Some Technological Problems

The pressing needs for more creative personnel, especially in the research and development arena, naturally directed considerable effort to finding more creative scientists and engineers, and to conditions in their working milieu that affect performance. The most outstanding example of this kind of effort has been the series of conferences on "The Identification of Creative Scientific Talent," sponsored by the University of Utah, under the leadership of Calvin W. Taylor. Six of these conferences have been held, culminating thus far in the publication of three books of proceedings (Taylor and Barron, 1963; Taylor, 1964; Taylor, 1966). The conferences included reports of basic research as well as technological matters. In pursuit of the main goal of these conferences, Taylor and his associates have tried to develop criteria for evaluating creative-research performance and to design a biographical-data scale for predicting research performance. McPherson and others have given much attention to the circumstances under which research scientists do their work, including problems of supervision.

Torrance and others have studied problems of creative teaching and procedures for developing creative behavior in the classroom. Getzels and Jackson (1961) and others have looked into the relation between scores on creative-thinking tests and measures of achievement in education. The problems of creativity in the educational setting are endless, and the scope of research in this area is rapidly spreading. It is quite appropriate that this new journal should have a strong interest in problems of creative education, and education for creativity.

CREATIVITY'S FUTURE

There seems little doubt that considerable momentum has been generated in investigations of creativity and consequent implementations in education and elsewhere. So many new avenues of theory and of ways of investigation have been opened that there should be little loss of momentum; there should, instead, be some continuation of the acceleration that has already been evident. Let us consider next some of the remaining problems, especially in the basic-research setting.

Needs for More Basic Research

Basic future investigations will probably take two major directions: toward a more detailed and complete understanding of the processes of creative thinking, and toward a survey of the conditions that influence creative thinking, positively or negatively.

The Nature of Creative Thinking. It is desirable to conceptualize the roles of fluency, flexibility, and elaboration in the operations of creative production and problem solving in general, in ways that suggest investigative operations. Fluency, for example, is largely a matter of retrieval of information from one's memory store, and comes under the historical concept of recall of learned information. Psychologists have studied the storing of information intensively; they have given relatively little attention to the *uses* of stored information. What little effort has been evident treats only what this writer (Guilford, 1967) has called "replicative recall." Not much has been done with the much more important "transfer recall." How does one get at one's stored information and use it in new connections and in novel ways?

As a deduction from structure-of-intellect theory regarding mental functions, one kind of flexibility is a matter of transformations of information. How are transformations brought about? How is information reinterpreted or redefined so as to adapt it resourcefully to new uses? Another type of flexibility concerns reclassifications. No doubt the classification of items of learned information has much to do with their efficient retrieval. Class ideas determine the areas of search. Each item of information has its "address" or "addresses," to use computer terminology, which help to locate it. Failure to recall may be due to persistence in the use of wrong addresses, a persistence within wrong or too limited classes.

What are the processes of elaboration, and how may they be facilitated? Structure-of-intellect theory conceives of elaboration as a matter of producing implications. What are the various kinds of connections by which one item of information comes to imply another, and produces chain-like thinking, each link bringing into view the next? This is really the old problem of association in new dress, envisaged in a way that should be more fruitful in accounting for thinking.

Transformations offer an important key to the understanding of insights or intuitions. The latter are often recognized as sudden changes, and changes are transformations. What are the principles or laws of transformation?

And what of the phenomenon of incubation, on which only one intentional study can be cited? Note that it is classed as a phenomenon rather than a process. It involves a period of relaxation of effort in the total event of solving a problem or producing a creative product. There is no doubt that the phenomenon exists and that some creators use it effectively. Why do some individuals keep a problem open, and keep coming back to it, when others regard early attempts as closed events? What kinds of mental processes occur during incubation? To say that unconscious thinking is going on tells us practically nothing. We have to infer what thinking events took place from the observed behavior of the individual before, during, and after the period of incubation.

Conditions Affecting Creative Thinking. Some of the questions just raised imply that there are determining conditions that affect creative-thinking processes, by way of facilitation or inhibition. Effects of evaluation, critical or otherwise, were touched upon earlier. Absence of self-evaluation while generating ideas has been known as "suspended judgment." There is still much to be learned about when and where evaluation should be applied, for evaluation of some kind there must be, if the end product is to be satisfying in certain respects.

A general source of determination of creative events lies in the area of motivation. In general, what motivates individuals to creative production? To make the question somewhat more specific, which needs, interests, and attitudes help the individual to be productive creatively and which put blocks in his way? How do certain attitudes and emotions affect various steps in the entire creative event? What are their influences upon recall, insight, and elaboration? The answers to all such questions provide bases for increased control over creative events.

Social Consequences

The consequences on the future of mankind of present and future efforts to gain understanding and control of creative performances are incalculable. It is apparent that the solutions to numerous human problems are dependent upon education of the world's population, both extensively and intensively. An informed people, with skills in using its information, is a creative, problem-solving people. In a real sense, mankind is involved in a race between expanding education on the one hand, and threatened disaster, perhaps oblivion, on the other.

To live is to have problems, and to solve problems is to grow intellectually. It is probably safe to say that at no time has a larger number of informed and otherwise intellectually able individuals lived on this planet, yet the problems to be solved seem almost overwhelming—how to keep the peace, how to feed and clothe an expanding population, how to keep the population from expanding too rapidly, and how to educate it. Education in the more enlightened countries has been rather successful in transmitting to younger generations the accomplishments of older generations. But as Torrance (1962) has pointed out, teaching has been much too authoritative. It has not given the younger generation instruction in how to use information in creative ways, or even the opportunity to do so in many cases. Creative education, on the other hand, aims at a self-starting, resourceful, and confident person, ready to face personal, interpersonal and other kinds of problems. Because he is confident, he is also tolerant where there should be tolerance. A world of tolerant people would be peaceful and cooperative people. Thus creativity is the key to education in its fullest sense and to the solution of mankind's most serious problems.

REFERENCES

Andrews, E. G. The development of imagination in the preschool child. *Univ. Iowa Stud. Character,* 1930, *3* (4).

Chassell, L. M. Tests for originality. *J. educ. Psychol.,* 1916, *7,* 317–329.

Dennis, W. Age and productivity among scientists. *Science,* 1956, *123,* 724–725.

Eindhoven, J. E., & Vinacke, W. E. Creative process in painting. *J. gen. Psychol.,* 1952, *47,* 139–164.

Galton, F. *Hereditary genius: An inquiry into its laws and consequences.* New York: Appleton, 1869.

Getzels, J. W., & Jackson, P. W. *Creativity and intelligence.* New York: Wiley, 1961.

Ghiselin, B. *The creative process.* Berkeley: Univ. of California Press, 1952; New York: Mentor, 1955.

Guilford, J. P. Creativity. *Amer. Psychol.,* 1950, *5,* 444–454.

Guilford, J. P. *General psychology.* Princeton, N.J.: D. Van Nostrand, 1939, 1952.

Guilford, J. P. *The nature of human intelligence.* New York: McGraw-Hill, 1967.

Hadamard, J. S. *An essay on the psychology of invention in the mathematical field.* Princeton, N.J.: Princeton Univ. Press, 1945.

Lehman, H. C. *Age and achievement.* Princeton, N.J.: Princeton Univ. Press, 1953.

MacKinnon, D. W. The highly effective individual. *Teachers Coll. Rec.,* 1960, *61,* 367–378.

McPherson, J. H. Environment and training for creativity; in C. W. Taylor (Ed.). *Creativity: Progress and potential.* New York: McGraw-Hill, 1964, 130–153.

Osborn, A. F. *Applied imagination.* Rev. ed. New York: Scribners, 1963.

Patrick, C. Creative thought in poets. *Archives Psychol.,* N.Y., 1935, *26,* 1–74.

Patrick, C. Creative thought in artists. *J. of Psychol.,* 1937, *4,* 35–73.

Patrick, C. Scientific thought. *J. of Psychol.,* 1938, *5,* 55–83.

Patrick, C. Whole and part relationship in creative thought. *Amer. J. Psychol.,* 1941, *54,* 128–131.

Roe, Anne. *The making of a scientist.* New York: Dodd, Mead, 1952.

Rossman, J. *The psychology of the inventor.* Washington, D.C.: Inventors Publishing Co., 1931.

Schoen, M. *Human nature. A first book in psychology.* New York: Harper, 1930.

Taylor, C. W. (ed.). *Instructional media and creativity.* New York: Wiley, 1966.

Taylor, C. W. *Widening horizons in creativity.* New York: Wiley, 1964.

Taylor, C. W., & Barron, F. *Scientific creativity: Its recognition and development.* New York: Wiley, 1963.

Terman, L. M. Genius and stupidity: A study of some of the intellectual processes of seven "bright" and seven "stupid" boys. *Ped. Sem.,* 1906, *13,* 307–373.

Torrance, E. P. *Guiding creative talent.* Englewood Cliffs, N.J.: Prentice-Hall, 1962.

Torrance, E. P. *Rewarding creative behavior.* Englewood Cliffs, N.J.: Prentice-Hall, 1965.

Trembly, D. Age and sex differences in creative thinking potential. *Amer. Psychol.* 1964, *19,* 516. (Abstract)

Wallas, G. *The art of thought.* London: C. A. Watts, 1945.

Welch, L. Recombination of ideas in creative thinking. *J. appl. Psychol.,* 1946, *30,* 638–643.

Wilson, R. C., Guilford, J. P., Christensen, P. R., & Lewis, D. J. A factor-analytic study of creative-thinking abilities. *Psychometrika,* 1954, *19,* 297–311.

part two

PHASES OF DEVELOPMENT

M AN, WITH his intellectual capacity to think abstractly and to join events from both the past and the future, is strongly tempted to categorize and classify. Human beings do not, because of wide ranges of potential, developed capacities, varied values, and different experiences, lend themselves to such sorting. If, however, the student of human development will bear in mind the limitations of categorizations, he can use the stages or phases of human development to reduce the range of considerations with which, at any one time, he needs to deal. Hence, in this part, articles are grouped around phases of development: infancy, early childhood, middle childhood, preadolescence, adolescence, and youth. The editors realize that growth is continuous and gradual rather than proceeding by spurts and bounds, although the words "phases" or "stages" may lead to a false impression of discreteness. We also realize that some young persons of a given age more accurately may be classified, in a developmental sense, in the category preceding or following than in the one typical for that age. We realize that one person's progression on uneven fronts—his advances and regressions—makes his inclusion in any category rather equivocal. The implication is: parents, teachers, nurses, social workers should not be alarmed if a given age child does not easily fit a category. In western culture we profess, even if we sometimes fail to implement, an appreciation and a valuing of human differences.

The kind of nourishment—physical, emotional, social, and intellectual—the infant receives during the period prior to his walking and talking has profound impact on subsequent development. However, we must avoid the temptation to think that diet, in whatever form, or heredity, however parsimonious or plentiful, provides all the necessary clues to infant development. As the authors of the articles (selections 22, 23, and 24) in this section indicate, there is also the matter of response. Kessen (selection 21) indicates that the question of maturation versus learning does not suffice. Neither is heredity versus environment sufficient to explain the phenomena of development and individual differences. One addition to such duality is response; how does the individual—infant, boy, youth, or man—respond to the environment

211

with the equipment he has. Differential responses begin early and trends are noted in infancy.

One hardly can avoid being impressed by both the potential and the abilities of infants. They look so helpless and unaware as they stare at you with unblinking blue eyes. If experience does not impress the reader that infants are tough, resilient, comprehending, perceptive, and responsive, then the readings should. Classical conditioning has been the theoretical explanation for most of the infant's learning; however, recent discoveries show that instrumental conditioning is also significant. Feedback, including much more than verbal response, suggests that communication affects infant behavior long before words become very meaningful.

Learning proceeds most rapidly in the early years of life, and the rapid change characteristic of infancy continues with only slight abatement during the early childhood years—from about age two to the time the child enters the first grade. There is a growing consensus, derived from the study of the culturally "disadvantaged" or culturally different child, that attempts at compensatory education are most successful if they concentrate on the early childhood years. From such studies it is postulated that there is much to be learned about the conditions which are most conducive to learning and intellectual development during these years. A typical assertion is that more research is needed.

We—the editors—have taken the position that the philosophical questions of "What is the nature of man?" and "what learnings are of most importance in the development of that nature?" should be basic to the gathering of research data if these are to be relevant and meaningful. We think that research is most justified when it bears upon the above questions and when its purpose is to improve the human condition. Research is not like beauty. It is not its own excuse for being.

The articles in the section on early childhood (selections 25, 26, and 27) reflect the bias that we admit having—and against which the reader is warned. We believe that one learns, to a remarkable extent, to become human. Attention, communication, and warm mothering are required for the young person to become fully human. Of more importance than "learning" to be intelligent and learning the tools for the continuous acquisition of knowledge is learning one's own worth. The proposition is advanced that the young person needs to learn that he is safe, that he is loved, that he merits the time of others and that he is capable, before he really is free to learn to use his intellectual potential to the best advantage. Curiosity, creativity, confidence in self are more important than elevated IQ's and skills of learning for effective living. Fortunately, there is much evidence that the matters of ego concept and knowledge acquisition are not polar opposites. There is considerable evidence in both early childhood and those years which follow that sturdy ego concepts enhance creativity, originality, requisite conformity, and other kinds of learning.

Middle childhood—roughly that period following the preschool years and preceding junior high school—sees the child facing only a *somewhat* distinct series of developmental tasks. The phrase "somewhat distinct" is used to suggest that certain of the tasks are only intensifications of learning which were earlier merely incipient. Other tasks continue after middle childhood in somewhat modified form. For example, peer relations begin early with one's siblings and playmates but during middle childhood they assume major status and consume considerably more time. For example, the urge for independence becomes more insistent under normal middle childhood conditions. Developing the fundamental skills of reading, writing, and calculating also requires considerably greater attention. The task of achieving a masculine or feminine role is intensified, but does not gain full momentum until subsequent developmental phases. The articles by Staffieri (selection 30) and Moss and Kagan (selection 31) should help to throw light upon some of the determining factors and to furnish needed emphasis concerning the long-term effects of behaviors developed during this stage.

Because learning is a central concern in middle childhood, we believe that to the article by Hess and Shipman (28) on blocks to learning should be added that by Penfield (19), which was included earlier in the section on intellectual development. Re-reading may prove profitable here.

Preadolescence is a phase of development that has been, and still is, rather neglected in study and research. Recent interest in the creation of the "middle school" has not yet provided any substantial answers. In fact, it has not yet been decided just what the middle school is or should be. The selections on preadolescence consider some of the related issues. Before the matter of sex behavior, in the biological sense, becomes a pressing problem, the matter of sex identity does become a concern. Bronfenbrenner (32) deals competently with some of the issues. Maw and Maw (33) deal more specifically with identity and self-concepts in relation to preadolescent boys. And Havighurst (34) considers some of the issues relating to preadolescence on a broader basis, i.e., developmental tasks. Altogether this trio of authors should reduce at least a little of the lack of knowledge that has been characteristic of the study of preadolescence.

It has been said that anything one says about adolescents is true— about some adolescents. In brief, generalizations about adolescents are hazardous because of the wide range of behavior and because of the element of truth that is contained in generalizations—which for the majority often are grossly inaccurate. In addition, there are varied viewpoints from which adolescence may be perceived. The spectacular view, that played up in the press to increase circulation, concentrates on the flamboyant deviation—delinquents, dropouts, hippies, chronic drug users, and the alienated. It seems possible that this viewpoint provides the adult who is less than well adjusted himself, some covert feeling of satisfaction and assurance. The stress and strain point of view emphasizes the difficulty of adjusting to changing body and changing demands. It overlooks those many adolescents who are really having a great time. The statistical view sees the fact that if five per cent of adolescents are delinquent, then ninety-five per cent are leading acceptable, if not always exemplary, lives. If ten per cent are dropouts, then ninety per cent are still trying to make use of developmental opportunities.

A viewpoint endorsed by the editors might be called the optimistic one. Young people have been "going to the dogs" since the time of Plato; yet somehow, as adults, they have managed to live acceptably and effectively. This justifies the optimistic orientation. The statistical view complements the optimistic one, and we believe that faith in today's adolescents has a sound basis. Many of their protests are quite relevant. Many of their accomplishments are astonishing. Even their following the crowd, if at times unwise, is an indication of a social orientation, of an attempt to achieve independence in spite of many obstacles. Moreover, the tendency for the self-fulfilling prophecy to influence behavior makes it wise to view clearly the assets and contributions of adolescents instead of focussing so uniformly on the trends that are admittedly dangerous. The articles in the section on adolescence provide what seems to us to be a balanced perspective.

The period of adolescence is conventionally labelled as one of stress and strain. The fact is that all phases of development have such features. If it were necessary to identify a most difficult phase of life, we would not vote for adolescence. Adolescents have the protection and guidance of parents and teachers to assist with difficulties—even though there is a quite commendable urge for independence which makes them resist such aid. In our opinion, a more difficult period would be the period of youth. In this period one must do more than anticipate adulthood; he is in the process of dealing with the challenges—and neither parents nor teachers are readily available. Decisions and early struggles with such important continuing issues as marriage, vocational adaptation, functional citizenship, assumption of responsibility, and final choices of values are difficult ones.

There is much in current literature regarding a youth culture. Some authorities minimize the distinctiveness of such a culture by citing the regularity with which young people come around to accept adult values and orientations. Others see the goals and aspirations as being so distinctly different from those of the adult society that the problem of bridging the generation gap is nearly impossible. The challenges to closing the gap are effectively presented by the authors of the articles in the section on youth.

The essence of all the articles is that there is a generation gap of considerable concern because change is so rapid that the parental and filial generations do live in quite different worlds. The approach to understanding is usually for the younger generation to see the value of mature ways; and the young see such action as "selling out." The task of understanding is difficult but probably not impossible. Youth have not experienced the world conditions that preceded the now. On the other hand, adults have experienced both worlds but because learning proceeds more slowly in later life, the comprehension of elders of the now is tardy. It all adds up to the conclusion that adults will have to make an effort to understand rather than to convince. In a sense, traditional teaching patterns are being, or at least should be, partially reversed. As the present and the future become less and less interpretable in terms of the past, youth's quicker comprehension and relative lack of sets to perceive enable them to function more realistically than their elders. This fresh and comparatively unclouded point of view well may be essential for human survival. Adults have much to learn from young people. The editors expect the necessity to learn from the young, the enlightenment possible, to increase with the acceleration of change.

Adults will have to learn to do more listening and less telling. Youth are not so much intractable and intransigent as they are aware and desirous of being a cause—to be recognized as persons. Adults take a step toward communicating across the gap as soon as they accept the fact that *youth were not there* yesterday and scoff at the "when I was young" lecture. It is largely up to adults to realize that conditions are markedly different from those prior to the computer, moon rockets, social security, the GI Bill, etc. After all, adults have been present at both scenes.

Development during infancy

21.

Research in the psychological
development of infants:
an overview

WILLIAM KESSEN

*The infant's world as viewed by the modern student of human be-
havior is no longer the "big, buzzing, blooming confusion" pictured by
early twentieth-century psychologists. Even the neonate exhibits active-
seeking as opposed to reactive behaviors. His relationship with his
social environment is reciprocal. This means that environmental effects
may have both earlier and greater impact than previously was supposed. It underlines the importance of early sensory stimulation if
development is to proceed properly. As soon as the infant discovers
that a certain cry gets certain results, a part of his behavior becomes
purposeful. He begins to act by reason rather than by accident and
starts to exert an active influence upon his own development.*

*The author of this selection discusses how hypotheses, method-
ology, and the results of research in the area of infantile learning and
behavior have changed and are changing. The editors would like to
endorse the emphasis he gives to the importance of studying the activities and learning behavior of the very young. In the past several
years the amount of difference made in the beginning phases of
development toward the limitation or expansion of adult effectiveness
increasingly has been recognized. Once the opportunity is lost and once
the best time for learning has passed, the occasion may never again be
so fitting. Compensatory education can never fill the gap completely.
Economic disadvantage is far easier to overcome than social disadvantage. The assumption should not be made that coping with the
former will eliminate the latter.*

THE INFANT has not always been treated kindly by American psychologists.
Although almost all theories—whether in the tradition of Watson, Freud,
or Koffka—celebrate the importance of infant behavior, and claim that the

Merrill-Palmer Quarterly, 9:83–94, April, 1963. William Kessen, Department of Psychology, Yale University.

baby is striking proof of the validity of their views, systematic empirical study of the child in his crucial first year has been an on-again, off-again affair. And for a number of reasons, not the least of which is the difficulty of seeing young children in the large numbers that we have at our command in studying the pre-school child or the adolescent. Once a child leaves the hospital after the lying-in period, he is not again easily available for research until he appears in nursery school. It may also be that the infant is so clearly one of us—in that he is human, and so clearly and incomprehensibly different, in that he is a baby—that we have, on occasion, escaped our frustration by constructing theoretical babies instead of observing real ones.

Happily, these disabilities no longer block research. There is evidence, and not only in the United States, that psychologists are studying the infant more closely than ever before. Merely to call the names of investigators and refer to some of their findings would consume many pages. This is not to say, by the way, that the theoretical or constructed child has disappeared. Far from it! Behind each empirical investigation, there is a model, and this model colors and sometimes dominates the interpretation that is given the empirical protocols.

I would like to be able to present a neat, clear (even if artificial) dichotomy or trichotomy of theoretical positions concerning infancy—I recall with some nostalgia our antique friend "maturation *versus* learning" —but the current situation in the psychological study of infancy does not accept such simple classification. It is only a modest exaggeration to say that a recitation of theoretical subtleties would approach the complexity of a recitation of research findings. In the face of this kind of variety, I cannot hope to lay out a complete or even a fair summary of current research and thought about the behavior of the infant. Rather, I will present for your comment, review, and evaluation, a short set of propositions about babies and studies of babies; under each of these loose-jointed statements, we can examine a part of the research and speculation that has appeared over the last several years.

The first proposition or summary statement that I will propose is that *a comparative psychology of infancy can be anticipated.* Harlow's well-known work [selection 46] on affectional systems in the monkey, though incomplete, is as stimulating a body of research as has been done on animal development over the last decade. Less widely known, but of at least equal theoretical impact, are T. C. Schneirla's (1959) speculations about approach and avoidance and their relation to stimulus intensity. Hess (1959), among others, has presented data and commentary on the phenomena of imprinting. Seymour Levine (1957) has contributed a number of papers on the effect of infantile stress on later behavior. These names only begin a list of the researchers who are working on developmental problems with infrahuman animals.

Two general comments are warranted here. The animal work which is now going on in developmental psychology is not "dry-as-dust" laboratory demonstration. Moreover, little of this work leads to procedures routinely applicable to children, in the way that some current studies of reinforcement are; nor is the current animal work aimed at elaboration of the obvious. The psychologists studying animal development are in advance of their colleagues in human developmental studies, not only in regard to novel empirical techniques, but more important, in their willingness to take an intellectual chance or risk a speculation. The second note to be appended to the work with animals is the classical one, namely, the possibility of experimental manipulation of more than a trivial sort. We have only seen the beginning of work with animals, and particularly with primates, that will permit us to examine experimentally propositions that would otherwise remain available only to limited observational examination. Studies of the relation of infant to parent, for example, can be investigated along all relevant dimensions only by the use of animals. That is not to say that once we have found the rhesus we can abandon the human being, but the thoughtfulness and energy of investigators currently working in animal research will have no small impact on current research in the psychology of development.

But let me put aside the allure of precision and control possible with animal work and confine the rest of my general propositions to those about human behavior.

The first proposition about children to be considered, and perhaps the most obvious, is that *infants are various*—young children are different from one another. I may see a straw man when I speak against the notion that human infants at birth, like well-made cigarettes, cannot be distinguished from one another; but there is still abroad in psychology—at least in the academical variety—the feeling that children at birth are, by and large, pretty much undifferentiated protoplasm or no more than merely randomly varying beings. Whatever the present state is of the pure, undifferentiated position in the sociology of knowledge, evidence is accumulating that parents and nurses were right all along—stable differences in behavior can be detected in the first days of life. Hammond (1957) has shown the stability of physical growth patterns. Richmond and his colleagues at Syracuse (1955) have reported psychophysical stabilities in the newborn. Thomas, Chess, Birch, and Hertzig (1960), although they have published only preliminary reports, have stated that on nine variables—among them, reactivity and irritability—they have found stability in children followed longitudinally over a period of two years. There are some suggestions in Bell's work (1960), and there are some findings in our work on newborns at Yale (1961), which tend to support a strong generalization that stable individual differences in a large number of behaviors—sucking, general movement, reactivity—exist very early in life. Yet, impressive as it is, the work on the assessment of individual differences among human infants has not, like some of the animal work, been "built out" from novel observations and speculations. Rather, it has come largely from the essential and tedious work of constructing adequate response measures. These advances in technology or method are clear and welcome, but they leave open two larger questions about individual differences.

First, what is the long-range stability or relevance of these differences? It is good to know that the newborn shows stable differences in activity level from his colleague in the next crib, but the importance of this observation is markedly reduced if the difference does not show up in some form later. Among the investigators, other than the Birch group, who have done some interesting speculative work on this score, is the French psychologist Stambak (1956). She has segregated two groups of infants—hypertonic and hypotonic—and has discussed the relation of this tendency to be active or quiet to such important developmental changes as onset of walking. In addition, the Czech group (Papousek, 1961) is investigating the stability of the infant's behavior during conditioning over the first six months of life. Such studies are provocative curtain-raisers on the intricate question of behavioral stability in infancy.

There is a second question about which we have very little evidence. How are these early behavioral variations related to variations in the environment? How do different combinations of infant and caretaker mesh together? We can tag babies as active or quiet; we can make this discrimination in the first five or ten days of life. We can suspect, too, that some mothers like active babies and some mothers like quiet babies. What do you get when you combine an active baby with a mother who wanted a quiet one or a quiet baby with a mother who wanted an active one? We have very little to go on here, not only because of the obvious technical difficulties of longitudinal studies of this kind, and not only because of the fluidity of our ideas about what is important in the home, but also because, until recently, we have not had reliable ways of describing the young child's environment. The technical advances in the methods of describing newborn behavior have not been matched by methods for describing the home. But here, again, there is promise. Schaefer, Bell, and Bayley (1959) have proposed a parent attitude scale. The important interview work of Sears *et al.* (1957) provides a framework for the description of parents' behavior. Rheingold (1960) has recently specified some of the dimensions of variation between home and institution. These papers point the way toward the time when a genuine analysis can be made of the interaction between mother and child. The word "genuine" reflects the hope that this analysis will not be a contaminated one; that we can make assessments of the status of the newborn, independent of observing the mother, and make assessment of the mother, independent of observing the child.

The next summary proposition that I want to suggest warrants detailed examination. I submit that *the young infant is not incompetent* or, by André-Thomas' (1954) catching phrase, "the neonate is not a neophyte."

We have passed the time, not so very long ago, when the newborn was considered to be sensorily bereft (e.g., Preyer's contention that children are born deaf), but the notion of newborn incompetence persists. It has perhaps its strongest statement in the work of the psychoanalysts, especially Spitz (1959), who maintains the existence of a non-differentiated phase in early life, where the newborn does not code inputs at all. In this view of the infant, by no means limited to psychoanalysts, both the baby's sensory capacities and his response capacities are held to be severely limited. The trend of recent research is clearly against this conception of the child. Research on newborn behavior over the last five years has invariably added to the newborn's list of abilities. Peiper (1956) in his encyclopedic treatment, André-Thomas (1954) and his colleagues in Paris, Madame Ste. Anne-Desgassies, and Prechtl (1958) are among the workers who have discussed the extended sensory and response range of the newborn in some detail. Gorman and his associates (1959) have recently found in a study of acuity that the newborn has visual resolving powers which are not markedly inferior to those of the older child. From the research available on the competence of the newborn, let me present three studies in some detail as illustrative and somewhat representative of this newer view of the newborn.

The first study, by Blauvelt (1960), deals with the precision of at least one response the newborn makes. Following up earlier work of Prechtl on head-turning, Blauvelt has studied the baby's response to a very simple stimulation, in which the experimenter moves her finger from the tragus of the baby's ear—the baby lying on its back in the crib—toward the baby's mouth and then away in a flat eliptical course. It turns out that the baby tracks this movement by turning his head at a speed and to a position that will reduce the distance between his mouth and the stimulating finger. He tracks this movement without special tuition; it is, if you like, built-in. The infant can pick up approaching stimulation and reduce the distance to it very quickly; he can "find" the approaching breast or bottle. What is impressive about this response is the precision of it. This is not the response of a wild newborn, flailing around uselessly and without direction; this is an organism making a precise and exact tracking response. It is a limited skill, to be sure, and certainly not widely generalizable to other activities, but it illustrates the responding precision of some newborn.

The second study illustrative of newborn competence may be one of the most important empirical research products of the last decade in infancy work. Bronshtein, Antonova, Kamenetskaya, Luppova, and Sytova (1958) have described a technique for assessing the limits of sensory differentiation in the infant that promises a precision in psychophysical description that has heretofore been possible only for the much older child. Briefly, the procedure is this. You permit or induce the child to suck, and record his rhythmic response. If, during sucking, you sound a brief tone, say of 512 cycles/sec., the baby stops sucking. When the tone stops, the baby begins to suck again. To a second stimulation of the same tone, he will stop sucking. This sequence can be repeated four or five times for sounds and then when you sound your 512-cycle tone he goes on sucking without interruption. He has adapted to that sound. If, however, you now present a different tone, say one of 1,024 cycles, he will stop sucking. If he continues to suck on the application of the second stimulus, this is presumptive evidence that he cannot discriminate the two stimuli. If he does stop sucking on the second stimulus, if it "undoes the adaptation," then there is evidence that he can discriminate these two stimuli. If this technique is as sensitive as the Russians suggest, we will be able to find out more about the sensory capacities of the young infant than we can find out about the sensory capacities of young five or six-year-olds. Bronshtein presents data to indicate that the infant makes clearly differential responses to variations in pitch, light intensity, and other stimulus changes. Lipsitt, at Brown, has adapted this technique to a study of olfactory stimulation and has found that not only is sucking inhibited and adapted in this fashion but so also is movement. Just as the Blauvelt study illustrates the possible response flexibility of the newborn, so the Bronshtein and Lipsitt studies indicate the remarkable amount of stimulus coding the newborn is capable of. The world of the infant is not a vast confusing "blob."

Consider yet a third study. In our work at Yale (1963), we have found that if you put a nipple in a baby's mouth, he will stop general movement at once, and when you take it out he will start moving again. This effect appears in the absence of nutrient; the nipple does not supply food—it only provides an opportunity to suck. And, this inhibition of movement takes place in the fourth or third or second, or even first day of life. The child is able to deal with a complex and vitally important input—namely, nipple or sucking—by a very regular response. Nor, apparently, does he have to learn either how to suck or how to quiet. There is of course the argument that he learned the responses *in utero,* but we have hardly advanced beyond Hippocrates' statement of that argument 2,500 years ago.

These studies suggest that the newborn has far greater capacities for sensory discrimination than could have been guessed a decade ago, and though less impressive, the evidence is beginning to indicate that he has surprising response competencies as well. But the evidence for newborn resourcefulness poses a peculiar paradox. To put the question very bluntly, if the human newborn is so capable, why does he not learn more? If he is so capable, why is he so stupid? These questions form the bridge to my next general proposition, one which seems so insecure that I have phrased it in the form of yet another question.

There is early adaptation, but is there early learning? The conflict represented in this question can be expressed simply enough. On the one hand the behavior of baby seems to change over the first few days of life. There are many examples; let me cite just one.

Peiper maintains that there are three techniques of infantile sucking. One of them is the response that most mammals use to get milk out of a breast; it is a lapping response that involves pressing the nipple against the roof of the mouth with the tongue and squeezing milk out of it. Another one is to reduce pressure inside the mouth so as to pull the milk in by a discrepancy in pressure. This is the way most babies suck from bottles. And the third, fairly infrequent technique—confined to bottle-fed babies for obvious reasons—is to bite hard at the back of the nipple and squirt milk into the mouth. This variation is interesting because babies apparently come to use one of these different patterns very quickly. They learn, if "learn" is appropriate, the kind of sucking to use.

The difficulty with calling this kind of change "learning" arises from our failure to demonstrate early learning in a controlled setting. If the newborn is capable of this natural learning it should be possible for a psychologist to teach him something in a systematic learning study. And yet the evidence, controlled evidence for newborn learning, hardly exists. There is research by Marquis (1931), recently replicated in the USSR, showing that the baby adapts to a feeding rhythm, but the evidence does not support the conclusion that learning according to the usual theoretical models takes place in the period of early infancy. The Russians, with their strong demand for environmental control of behavior, have tried a large number of times to condition young infants. Sometimes they are successful; oftentimes they are not. Russian studies do not report conditioning in children under eight or nine days of age, and most conditioning studies indicate that it may take weeks or even months to condition an infant child in the Pavlovian mode (Dashkovskaya, 1953). How do we interpret this curious discrepancy between the fact that the human baby seems to adapt his sucking style to his feeding routines on the one hand, and the difficulty that all investigators have had in demonstrating newborn learning on the other?[1]

The following three options seem available to us: First, in spite of my statements about newborn competence, there may be genuine neurological incapacity in the newborn. There is no such thing as early learning, in the usual sense, because the child is not complete. A case for this position can be made. There are data on myelinization, on changes in pattern of EEG, on developments of vision and prehension, on the appearance of smiling—to take the most obvious case—all of which can be used to bolster the view that the young infant is a neurologically deficient organism. Under this reading, how do we account for the changes in behavior that do take place? Perhaps by maintaining that the caretaker becomes more competent. This would be a case of training the parent to adapt more effectively to the child rather than teaching the child to adapt to his environment. And to the data from Bronshtein and Lipsitt on the ability of the young infant to make sensory discriminations, we would have to say, "True infants can make sensory discriminations, but there is no associative coding; there is a deficiency in the hooking of links together."

The second answer, and the one I think that would be given by the learning analysts (Gewirtz, 1961), is that nobody has tackled the problem of early learning. In particular, holders of this position would maintain that the procedures of classical conditioning as used by the Russians are the wrong tactics. What we should do if we want to demonstrate early learning is to use instrumental techniques; that is, to make some effective reinforcement contingent on the occurrence of some response of the infant. For example, let the baby turn his head and then give him something to suck on. This is a testable proposition and it is being tested.

I would like to suggest a third possibility—an unpopular one. In brief, there may be experimental effects that are not learning. To put it another way, not all adaptation of the infant represents either classical conditioning or instrumental learning. I think it is inappropriate to maintain that all changes in behavior that can be related to the child's contact with the environment are the result of reinforcement contingencies. Of course, the instrumental learning position can be made to fit them, but it seems to me that such a forced fit results in theoretical vagueness and a weakening of the instrumental position.

Perhaps in pulling apart the problem of behavioral change in early infancy to exaggerate the variation among options, I have only shown that the resolution of the problem will require revisions in method, new knowledge of infantile neurophysiology, and a reworking of contemporary learning theory.

But consider now another interesting problem which illuminates some theoretical disagreements among students of infancy. Two theoretical positions have occupied this field: the psychoanalytic and the learning theoretical. Justice can be done to neither in a summary presentation. Rapaport (1959) and Wolff (1960) present the psychoanalytic presuppositions in detail and with force; Gewirtz (1961) has prepared a closely reasoned argument for a learning analysis.[2] Now, there is a new entrant into the field of theories of mother attachment. John Bowlby in a series of recent papers (1958) has borrowed from the investigators of instinct in animals, a notion that sounds very much like imprinting and has suggested that the child's responses of suckling, clinging, and following lead to mother attachment. Just sucking, and just clinging, and just following on the part of the child, without obvious reinforcement or redistribution of cathexis, will result in a union between child and mother; much as the chick will imprint on a blinking light. Not only does Bowlby discuss what ties the child to his mother—namely, these three responses—but he also discusses what links the mother to the child. Not only does the child become attached to the mother because of sucking, clinging, and following, but the mother is drawn or attached—Bowlby does not use the word "imprinting"—to the child by the child's smiling and crying. Smiling and crying are held to be congenital or innate releases of material behavior.

It is difficult to evaluate this position and I am hard pressed to invent a satisfactory test for it. Perhaps we must call on animal research to work out the implications of Bowlby's assertions. But the main value of this new view will probably be the value of all theories of development—that they jog thinking, they make people run a study just to see what happens.

Certainly Bowlby's ideas have had that effect. His own research with Robertson on separation (1952), the work done by Schaffer (1959) on hospitalization of young children, and an unpublished study by Ainsworth (1961) have demonstrated the provocative effect of these speculations. One of the achievements of the work done by Ainsworth, in Uganda, is that, instead of discussing mother attachment as a unitary notion, she has, in these longitudinal field observations of the child between four weeks of age and fourteen months, described some ten or twelve indexes of the child's attachment to the mother, and in this way has made possible a more subtle analysis of the relation than we have had heretofore.

It is interesting to note, as an adjunct to the problem of mother attachment, that something very curious indeed seems to happen to children near the middle of the first year. Ambrose's (1961) results on smiling indicate that at 17–25 weeks, general social smiling begins to decay and the child begins to smile only at its caretakers. Schaffer's work indicates that children who are hospitalized before they are 28 weeks old, accept hospital routines and separation easily; children hospitalized after 28 weeks-of-age show striking symptom patterns of distress and refusal to accept normal hospital care. Ainsworth finds that almost all of her criteria of mother attachment begin to show transition in the period from 17 to 30 weeks, with much of the change occurring in the narrow band between 25 and 28 weeks. Somewhere in the middle of the first year, the child appears to shift from being attached to human beings at large to being attached to one, or two, or three human beings.

The Ainsworth study is comparable in its impact to Rheingold's (1956) study of caretaking in institutionalized infants—both of these studies represent the payoff for the theoretical positions underlying them. The psychology of infancy undoubtedly profits from being in a state of theoretical disequilibrium, and the diversity of ideas about the nature of the child's attachment to his mother will almost certainly be productive of important empirical advances.

Consider one last generalization about infancy. It is one where contention, compromise, and reciprocation among theoretical positions has already resulted in general agreement. *The infant is active, and the relation of infant and caretaker is reciprocal.*

It is on this issue that the psychologist's view of the child has changed most dramatically in recent years. The model of the child which was drawn from Pavlov through Watson, and supported by the development of learning psychology in the United States, was of a recipient organism—a reactive one. Behavior at any particular time is the function of the current stimulating environment. This remains technically a sound view, but the effect of it on the psychology of the infant was to diminish our appreciation of how complicated and subtle is the child.

Not only can the child be usefully seen as active, rather than merely as reactive, but it may also be useful to think of even the infant as a problem-solver. Certainly the child, like the adult, can be seen as encountering problems in his environment. At least from the age of six months, the child's behavior can be discussed in terms of discrepancy, goal-seeking, means to an end, and so on. One student of children has not deviated from this view of the active searching child. Piaget and his students have seen the child, especially the infant, as being in a constant exchange with the environment, meeting its demands, and what American investigators somehow forgot, making its own demands on that environment.

The shift in point-of-view—to set the antithesis sharply—has been from the child who is a passive receptacle, into which learning and maturation pour knowledge and skills and affects until he is full, to the child as a complex, competent organism who, by acting on the environment and being acted on in turn, develops more elaborated and balanced ways of dealing with discrepancy, conflict, and dis-equilibrium. This shift, I believe, is of incalculable implication and seems to have been accepted to some degree by almost all students of children. Bowlby emphasizes the control by the child in crying and smiling; psychoanalytic theory makes more space for autonomous ego functions; child psychologists dedicated to a learning analysis speak of the child as active; and I suspect Piaget thinks of how he knew it all the time. But this shift only sets the problem for the psychology of the infant; questions abound. What is a "problem" for the infant? What is an environmental discrepancy for the newborn, for the six-month old, for a walker? Do Piaget's speculations about assimilation, accommodation, and equilibration have more than a metaphorical value? Can child psychologists follow the lead of psychologists of cognition in adults, who use computer analogies? Can we build a theory of cognitive development without the use of terms like reinforcement, drive, or dissonance resolution?

Only one thing seems certain. We are better equipped, with attitude and technique, to make a systematic and meaningful analysis of infant behavior than ever before. The current psychology of infant behavior, by and large, is managing to steer skillfully between the Scylla of "Oh, Oh, look what the baby did!" and the Charybdis of "But the theory says thus and so." We are engaging in hot, theoretical debate, but more and more the debate refers back to the child—back to the theory illuminated facts.

REFERENCES

Ainsworth, M. D. The development of infant-child interaction among the Ganda. Paper read at Tavistock Study Group on Mother-Infant Interaction, London, 1961.

Ambrose, J. A. The development of smiling response in early infancy. In Foss, B. M. (Ed.), *Determinants of infant behavior.* New York: Wiley, 1961.

André-Thomas Ontogénèse de la vie psychoaffective et de la douleur. *Encéphale*, 1954, *43*, 289–311.

Bell, R. Q. Relations between behavior manifestations in the human neonate. *Child Develpm.*, 1960, *31*, 463–477.

Blauvelt, H., & McKenna, J. Capacity of the human newborn for mother-infant interaction. II. The temporal dimensions of a neonate response. *Psychiat. Res. Rep.*, 1960, *13*, 128–147.

Bowlby, J. The nature of the child's tie to his mother. *Int. J. Psychoanal.*, 1958, *39*, 1–24.

Bronshtein, A. I., Antonova, T. G., Kamenetskaya, A. G., Luppova, N. N., & Sytova, V. A. On the development of the functions of analyzers in infants and some animals at the early stage of ontogenesis. In *Problems of evolution of physiological functions*. OTS Report No. 50–61066. Translation obtainable from U.S. Dept. of Commerce. Moscow: Acad. Sci., 1958.

Dashkovskaya, V. S. First conditioned reactions in newly born children in normal state and in certain pathological states. *Zh. vyssh. nervn. Deiatel.*, 1953, *3*(2), 247–259.

Gewirtz, J. L. A learning analysis of the effects of normal stimulation, privation, and deprivation on the acquisition of social motivation and attachment. In Foss, B. M. (Ed.), *Determinants of infant behavior*. New York: Wiley, 1961.

Gorman, J. J., Cogan, D. G. & Gellis, S. S. A device for testing visual acuity in infants. *Sight-Saving Rev.*, 1959, *29*, 80–84.

Hammond, W. H. The constancy of physical types as determined by factorial analysis. *Hum. Biol.*, 1957, *29*, 40–61.

Harlow, H. F. The nature of love. *Amer. Psychologist*, 1958, *13*, 673–685.

Hess, E. H. Imprinting. *Science*, 1959, *130*, 133–141.

Kessen, W., Williams, E. J. & Williams, J. P. Selection and test of response measures in the study of the human newborn. *Child Develpm.*, 1961, *32*, 7–24.

Levine, S. Infantile experience and resistance to psychological stress. *Science*, 1957, *126*, 405.

Marquis, D. P. Can conditioned responses be established in the newborn infant? *J. genet. Psychol.*, 1931, *39*, 479–492.

Papoušek, H. A. A physiological view of early ontogenesis of so-called voluntary movements. In P. Sobotka (Ed.), *Functional and metabolic development of the central nervous system*. Prague: State Pedagogic Publ., 1961.

Peiper, A. *Die Eigenart der Kindlichen Hirntatigkeit* (2nd Ed.) Leipzig: Thieme, 1956.

Prechtl, H. F. R. The directed head turning response and allied movements of the human baby. *Behaviour*, 1958, *13*, 212–242.

Rapaport, D. The structure of psychoanalytic theory: A systematizing attempt. In Koch, S. (Ed.), *Psychology: a study of a science, vol. 3*. New York: McGraw-Hill, 1959.

Rheingold, H. L. The modification of social responsiveness in institutional babies. *Monogr. Soc. Res. Child Develpm.*, 1956, *21*(2).

Rheingold, H. L. The measurement of maternal care. *Child Develpm.*, 1960, *31*, 565–575.

Richmond, J. B. & Lustman, S. L. Autonomic function in the neonate: I. Implications for psychosomatic theory. *Psychosom. Med.*, 1955, *17*, 269–275.

Robertson, J. & Bowlby, J. Responses of young children to separation from their mothers. *Courrier de la Centre Internationale de l'Enfance*, 1952, *2*, 131–142.

Schaefer, E. S., Bell, R. Q. & Bayley, N. Development of a maternal behavior research instrument. *J. genet. Psychol.,* 1959, *95,* 83–104.

Schaffer, H. R. & Callender, W. M. Psychologic effects of hospitalization in infancy. *Pediatrics,* 1959, *24,* 528–539.

Schneirla, T. R. An evolutionary and developmental theory of biphasic processes underlying approach and withdrawal. In M. R. Jones (Ed.), *Nebraska symposium on motivation: 1959,* Lincoln: Univer. of Nebraska Press, 1959.

Sears, R. R., Maccoby, E. E. & Levin, H. *Patterns of child rearing.* Evanston, Ill.: Row Peterson, 1957.

Spitz, R. A. *A genetic field theory of ego formation: its implications for pathology.* New York: Internat. Univer. Press, 1959.

Stambak, M. Contribution à l'étude du developpement moteur chez le nourrisson. *Enfance,* 1956, *9*(4), 49–59.

Thomas, A., Chess, S., Birch, H. & Hertzig, M. E. A longitudinal study of primary reaction patterns in children. *Comprehensive Psychiat.,* 1960, *1,* 103–112.

Wolff, P. H. *The developmental psychologies of Jean Piaget and psychoanalysis.* New York: Internat. Univer. Press, 1960.

NOTES

1. The argument for early adaptation by the infant can probably be made much more forcefully, but a natural history of the first months of life remains to be written.

2. It should be noted in passing that a learning analysis is both stronger and in a better position for compromise with other views by virtue of a retreat from the drive-reduction interpretation of reinforcement and by recent animal studies which show stable secondary reinforcement effects.

22.

Consistency of maternal attitudes and personality from pregnancy to eight months following childbirth

ANTHONY DAVIDS
RAYMOND H. HOLDEN

The following brief article on mothers' attitudes and personality raises a great many more questions than it answers. If, however, one takes the position that sound education opens the way to continued learning, then the article is highly useful—for discussion, opening areas for investigation, or posing postulations for one's own behavior as a father or mother.

Typically it is admitted that mothers' attitudes and personality influence their babies' behavior and personality. The authors emphasize the counter-proposition that babies influence mothers' personalities. Crying, fretful babies can induce negative emotional responses from their mothers. Cheerful, calm, cute babies might have the power to convert a mother who initially disliked her baby or who was disgusted with her pregnancy. But questions might go beyond the highly valid proposition that babies affect mothers. Is it possible that a cross, wakeful baby who demands frequent feedings and regurgitates sour food might bring out the best in a mother? Maybe the mother needs to be needed—like the woman who finally separated from an alcoholic husband only to marry another man who is equally miserable.

Perhaps there should be psychology courses for mothers which would study mother-baby interaction and help mothers to analyze their own reactions. Such study could assist them to develop an enactive (planned and purposeful) psychology rather than to be reactive (unplanned and spontaneous).

FOR MANY years the general view of mother-child relations was similar to looking down a one-way street. The psychological literature (e.g., Hoffman & Hoffman, 1964) provides abundant support for the impression that maternal attitudes and child-rearing practices have pronounced effects on chil-

Developmental Psychology, 2:364–366, 1970. Anthony Davids, Walter S. Hunter Laboratory of Psychology, Brown University; Raymond H. Holden, Rhode Island College.

This study was made possible by Grant BP-2356 from the National Institute of Neurological Diseases and Blindness awarded to the Brown University Institute for the Health Sciences. This research was facilitated by the Child Development Study staff at the Providence Lying-In Hospital and the Carriage House in Providence.

dren's intellectual and emotional development. However, relatively little research attention has focused on this picture from the viewpoint of the child's effects on the mother (e.g., Caldwell, 1964). It seems likely that the most significant future contributions will come from investigations that view this situation as one of interaction (e.g., Thomas, Birch, Chess, Hertzig, & Korn, 1963), recognizing that enduring characteristics and changing features on the part of both participants play fundamental roles in their interactive behaviors.

In order eventually to understand the mutual effects of mothers and children upon one another, it seems important to gather systematic information about the stability of maternal characteristics revealed before childbirth and at some time after living with the child. This article describes a preliminary study, and presents some initial findings relevant to these issues.

METHOD

The present research was conducted in the context of the National Collaborative Project on perinatal factors in child development. The psychological test battery administered during pregnancy, and the assessment of mother and child 8 months after delivery have been described in previous publications (Davids & DeVault, 1962; Davids, DeVault, & Talmadge, 1961; Davids, Holden, & Gray, 1963).

Included in the pregnancy assessment was the Parental Attitude Research Instrument (PARI), originally described by Schaefer and Bell (1958). The adaption of the PARI used in the present study consists of the following six subscales: Marital Conflict, Irritability, Rejection of Homemaking, Ascendancy, Intrusiveness, and Deification. Each subscale is represented by 5 items, making a total of 30 items, with responses being indicated in terms of degree of agreement or disagreement with each statement on the questionnaire. Factor analyses have shown the subscales to form two main factors, one termed Hostility (consisting of Marital Conflict, Irritability, and Rejection of Homemaking) and the other termed Control (consisting of Ascendancy, Intrusiveness, and Deification). An objective score is obtained for each of these two main factors, and a total negative attitude score is derived by adding the scores for Hostility and Control.

Eight months following childbirth, the infant's mental and motor functioning were assessed. At this time, the mother was again administered the PARI. Upon completion of this 8-month assessment, on the basis of observations of the mother and mother-child interactions, the examining psychologist rated the mother on several personality characteristics. The ratings were made on 7-point scales, yielding scores for individual traits such as anxiety and depression, and also providing an overall maternal personality rating. The higher this total rating, the more favorable is the examiner's clinical examination of the mother's personality and the mother-child interaction. It should be emphasized that these personality evaluations were made completely independently of knowledge of the mother's responses to either administration of the PARI.

The subjects were 42 women in the third trimester of pregnancy at the time of psychological assessment. Of the 42 subjects, 35 were white and 7 were Negro; of these patients 25 were Catholic, 10 were Protestant, 1 was Jewish, and for the remaining 6, their religion is unknown. The number of children for these women was as follows: first pregnancy, 7; second, 16; third, 5; fourth, 4; fifth, 3; sixth, 4; seventh, 2; and ninth, 1. They were selected at random from a larger random sample of pregnant women participating in the National Collaborative Project and were representative of diverse socioeconomic and educational backgrounds. Their mean age was 25 years, and ranged from 17 to 37 years. The mean IQ, measured by the Wechsler-Bellevue Intelligence Scale, was 103, and ranged from 59 to 127. None of these women who were initially studied during pregnancy refused to participate in the follow-up assessment of mother and child. However, due to a modification of the 8-month assessment battery on the national level during the period of data collection, maternal personality ratings were available for only 27 of the original group of 42 women. The data were examined statistically to reveal (a) association between PARI scores obtained during pregnancy and 8 months postdelivery, and (b) association between PARI scores during pregnancy and maternal personality ratings received approximately 1 year later.

RESULTS AND DISCUSSION

The PARI scores obtained by the 42 women on the two administrations of this instrument were highly associated. Product-moment correlations were .54 for the Hostility factor, .80 for the Control factor, and .72 for total negative attitudes. All of these coefficients are significant beyond the .01 level. PARI scores during pregnancy were also associated with personality ratings received by 27 of the women at time of the 8-month assessment. The women whose PARI responses during pregnancy resulted in high standing on the Hostility factor were judged to be high on anxiety (.40, $p = .05$) and depression (.53, $p = .01$). Moreover, high scores on Hostility in family attitudes revealed during pregnancy were negatively associated ($-.36$, $p = .05$) with favorableness of overall personality evaluations at time of the follow-up assessment. A similar pattern of associations was found for the Control factor, although these coefficients were lower (.21 with anxiety, and $-.18$ with overall favorableness rating) and statistically significant only for the depression rating (.33, $p = .05$).

Correlations between total PARI scores during pregnancy and the follow-up personality ratings reveal a statistically significant pattern of socially undesirable family and child-rearing attitudes during pregnancy being positively associated with anxiety (.44, $p = .05$) and depression (.55, $p = .01$), and negatively associated ($-.33$, $p = .05$) with favorable ratings of mother-child interactions. Thus, this study provides statistical evidence of consistency in family and child-rearing attitudes avowed before childbirth and after living with the child for several months, as well as association between these prenatal maternal attitudes and independent clinical evaluation of the mother's personality characteristics and interactions with the child during the first year of their relationship.

While statistically significant association has been found between attitudes toward family and children revealed before the child is born and those avowed a year later, it must be recognized that the magnitude of the correlations leaves a large portion of unexplained variance. In other words, the sample contains some individuals who obtain very different PARI scores on the two occasions and, in these cases, the attitudes avowed prior to childbirth would *not* be predictive of those avowed a year later nor would they relate to clinical evaluation of the favorableness of the early mother-child relationship. These are the cases which must be better understood in future researches.

For example, why is it that a woman who avows highly positive maternal attitudes prior to childbirth shows highly negative ones a year later? Or, why is it that a woman who expresses socially undesirable maternal attitudes during pregnancy is judged clinically to be emotionally well adjusted and to evidence highly favorable social relations with her 8-month-old child?

Such changes in maternal characteristics might well be a function of the infant's physical and/or temperamental attributes. That is, whether the infant is healthy or sickly, unusually attractive or obviously handicapped, usually calm and contented or generally fussy and irritable, especially responsive to maternal contacts or somewhat rejecting of her—these are the kinds of infant variables that could well play a prominent role in modifying the mother's attitudes and personality during the first few months after childbirth. Then again, it might be that the infant's physical or emotional makeup has little to do with the mother's changed outlook or behavior. Rather, in certain cases, it might be that changes in the mother's physical condition, or changes in the husband-wife relationship (in either a positive or negative direction), or changes in the family's socioeconomic situation (for better or worse) are responsible for differences in maternal characteristics found during pregnancy and several months after childbirth.

Obviously, a host of other factors could account for consistencies and changes occurring within a family during pregnancy and throughout the child's earliest formative years. At present, however, attempts to account for stability and change in attitudes avowed before and after childbirth, as well as inconsistencies between these expressed attitudes and actual parental behaviors, are largely speculative and with little empirical foundation. Definitive answers to these interesting, and still baffling, questions must await considerable further investigation and will require use of more complex research designs (e.g., Davids, 1968) than those customarily employed to date.

REFERENCES

Caldwell, B. M. The effects of infant care. In M. L. Hoffman &. L. W. Hoffman (Eds.), *Review of child development research.* Vol. 1. New York: Russell Sage Foundation, 1964.

Davids, A. A research design for studying maternal emotionality before childbirth and after social interaction with the child. *Merrill-Palmer Quarterly,* 1968, **14,** 345–354.

Davids, A., & DeVault, S. Maternal anxiety during pregnancy and childbirth abnormalities. *Psychosomatic Medicine,* 1962, **24,** 464–470.

Davids, A., DeVault, S., & Talmadge, M. Psychological study of emotional factors in pregnancy: A preliminary report. *Psychosomatic Medicine,* 1961, **23,** 93–103.

Davids, A., Holden, R. H., & Gray, G. B. Maternal anxiety during pregnancy and adequacy of mother and child adjustment eight months following childbirth. *Child Development,* 1963, **34,** 993–1003.

Hoffman, M. L., & Hoffman, L. W. (Eds.) *Review of child development research.* Vol. 1. New York: Russell Sage Foundation, 1964.

Schaefer, E. S., & Bell, R. Q. Development of a Parental Attitude Research Instrument. *Child Development,* 1958, **29,** 339–361.

Thomas, A., Birch, H. G., Chess, S., Hertzig, M. E., & Korn, S. *Behavioral individuality in early childhood.* New York: New York University Press, 1963.

23.

Where education begins

J. McVicker Hunt
Interviewed by Patricia Pine

> *A set of hypotheses or assumptions usually is categorized as mere opinion; but sometimes, the reputation and experience of the holder may cause such a set to be described and accepted more as a shrewd guess or an educated hunch. When agreement between those of accepted reputation is manifest, we have what was termed earlier as "consensual validation."*

American Education, 4(No. 9):15–19, October, 1968. J. McVicker Hunt, Professor of Psychology, University of Illinois.

> *The editors believe that such a consensus exists among several of the authors, presented herein, concerning the great importance of sensory stimulation during early development. For example: we find the assertion made by Krech (selection 17) that the brains of rats from enriched environments have a heavier, thicker cortex, a better blood supply, and increased enzyme activity to furnish some validation for Hunt's statement that IQ's may be increased from 30 to 50 points by a judicious management of sensory stimulation in very early childhood. Kessen (selection 21) seems to corroborate Hunt.*
>
> *The amount and quality of present learning or intellectual growth are limited by the extent and calibre of previous learning. In much the same manner that money is required in order to make money, so the amount one is capable of learning depends in some measure upon what he already knows. The more he can interpret and make sensible, the more associations and applications are possible. Also, the more he is able to see need for greater learning, the greater his awareness of questions unanswered. So it is that the effects of learning are cumulative and accelerating.*

THERE'S A STRANGE, new figure peering over baby's crib these days: the educational researcher. From Moscow to Manhattan prominent psychologists, psychiatrists, and educators no longer think it beneath their dignity to arrange mobiles over infants' cribs and listen to mothers' reports of the coos, smiles, and gurgles that show the investigators' efforts are appreciated.

What lures these researchers to the nursery? It's a growing belief among some behavioral scientists that if more were understood about how babies learn during their first few months and years, it might be possible to speed infant development dramatically. As a result nurseries have been bedecked with colorful mobiles, tassels, noisemakers, and other devices that make life more interesting for baby—and that just might entice him to make that first blink, that first reach, a few days sooner.

One psychologist who has spent a great deal of his time lately investigating what fosters development in infants is J. McVicker Hunt, director of the Psychological Development Laboratory at the University of Illinois and former head of the National Laboratory on Early Childhood Education headquartered at Urbana. Only seven years ago Hunt was predicting that it might be possible to raise infant IQs 30 points by stimulation in very early childhood. Now with several years of experimentation behind him Hunt believes that the environment which infants encounter may vary their IQs by as much as 50 to 70 points. "This means," he says, "that infants with potential from a culturally deprived background might be elevated from the upper levels of mental retardation to do college work someday."

Hunt's beliefs are founded on results of experiments aimed at enriching an infant's circumstances during his first two years of life. In one such experiment Burton White of Harvard University and Richard Held of Massachusetts Institute of Technology attempted to liven up the dull, white surroundings of orphanage infants at Tewksbury State Hospital in Massachusetts. White and Held strung brightly colored stabiles over the cribs of infants a few weeks old. The infants were also treated to extra handling and were turned on their stomachs part of the time so they could watch what was going on around them. Under the traditional regime of child-caring at Tewksbury infants achieved a landmark stage in eye-hand co-ordination—swiping at objects with a closed fist—at a median of 72 days and began mature reaching at 145 days. With environmental enrichment infants began fisted-swiping nearly two weeks earlier; the time for top-level reaching dropped to about 87 days, a 58-day reduction. "In familiar terms of IQ," Hunt points out, "this 58-day difference accounts for an increase of 67 points for that item."

Hunt's own experiments at Urbana indicate that when mobiles with colorful tassels are hung over cribs of babies at home, the infants start blink-ing at about seven weeks—three weeks earlier than usual and an IQ in-crease of 50 points for blinking. "It's not that eye-hand coordination or blinking has any special significance in itself," Hunt explains, "but these findings illustrate that the rate of early development in infants is highly plastic. Not long ago it was thought to be something predetermined, some-thing fixed by heredity."

Does a child's early blinking indicate that he will be a whiz in the first grade, a successful college student? Although Hunt believes these abili-ties will turn out to be cumulative he feels that no one can say for certain. Most of the infants who have had the benefit of early stimulation are just now turning three or four. What he does say, emphatically, is that unless infants are provided with some sort of stimulating environment at home, they are likely to grow apathetic and develop a lack of motivation that could plague them for the rest of their lives. "We've actually seen cases where children who have literally been left alone showed evidence of cultural re-tardation as early as seven months," Hunt says with feeling. "Among chil-dren raised in less-than-desirable circumstances these symptoms are quite common by the time they're a year old."

To Hunt the education of infants is no longer an academic matter. In the face of the collision between cultural deprivation and the high level of skills society now demands, cultural retardation must be warded off early. "The time to prevent cultural retardation is infancy," he asserts. "Programs that start as late as age four are probably already remedial education."

According to the infant stimulation theorists, whether a child pro-gresses or slips backward during those first years depends largely on just how stimulating his surroundings happen to be. "If a child is born in an atmosphere where people play with him and talk with him while he's be-ing fed and bathed and where he has interesting things to look at and do," Hunt explains, "then he'll probably develop all right. But at these early stages you can dampen and almost kill a child's interest permanently. You can dampen it by letting him encounter the same situation over and over without any change. You can also do it by punishing the little pseudopods of interest that come along, by saying 'Hush' or 'Don't ask silly questions.' Sometimes children are sent to school with orders to 'be good,' 'be quiet,' and 'do like the teacher says.' Being 'good' is defined as being still and doing nothing—not exploring, not trying to deal with things.

"It's extremely important for children to have language models at home too," Hunt continues. "Often in the homes of the culturally deprived, nobody talks with the children. On the other hand, if a youngster is used to a lot of loud voice sounds that don't mean anything to him, he becomes habituated to them; they soon won't influence him. This often results from overcrowding, from having too many people in the same small area. If the child becomes habituated to loud voices then it's hard to make voice sounds serve as cues in learning."

Some experts are beginning to say that a child may be doomed from the cradle by poor nutrition, that lack of protein may create brain damage which can't be corrected at a later date. Hunt is reluctant to endorse this point of view fully without further study to compare the relative damage done by poor diet and poor environment. "I'm always dubious about anything that is said to be irreversible until every alternative has been explored," he cautions.

Those who believe in educating infants are going against a long-estab-lished tradition which insists that childhood should be preserved for chil-dren. "The traditionalists," says Hunt, "think you should depend on what comes naturally as a basis for fostering children's development. Out of this comes the notion that if you allow children to play and do what comes naturally, they'll develop at their own rates and in their own ways. The traditionalists also tend to believe, however, that the child's rate of de-velopment is predetermined at birth and that educators have no business meddling with it."

HUNT himself deserted the traditionalists not long ago: "In the early 1930's when I was in graduate school I was completely geared to the ideas of predetermined ability and fixed intelligence," he recalls. "I was working summers at the Nebraska Home for Dependent Children. If I wanted to place a child in a middle-class home I looked for developmental advance. For a lower-class home I'd look for less advance. I took seriously the idea that the age when each child would walk and talk was predetermined. If children failed to do this at typical ages it was because they weren't 'ready.' It was good for too-ambitious mothers," Hunt recalls, "but it kept us from even trying to push slow youngsters along."

The predetermined development theory did have its place in the growth of thought about child development: It helped break down earlier ideas that if you spared the rod you spoiled the child. "Some of our earliest thought on the subject goes back to Luther and Calvin," says Hunt. "They taught the child to read the Bible to save his soul. If he wouldn't learn to read, it was because Original Sin was at work in the background, and the only thing to do was to beat it out of him. It is to Arnold Gesell's credit that he advanced a biological argument against this kind of punishment, saying that such a child simply had not yet developed to the point where he could read."

Hunt's book, *Intelligence and Experience,* published in 1961, was one of the first well-documented, systematic attacks on the notions of predetermined development and fixed intelligence. Since 1966 Hunt has been testing out his theories, devising exciting new environments to stimulate infants at an orphanage in Teheran, Iran. A survey of these orphans in 1960 found that two-thirds of them could not sit alone at two years and that 84 percent did not walk at four. Now he and his associates are giving these infants something interesting to do.

It would not be hard to find some of Hunt's devices—mobiles that dance over the Teheran orphans' cribs—in many modern-day nurseries. But for babies accustomed to dull monotony a little variation in what they see may make quite a difference. Hunt's cribs are also equipped with tape recorders that entertain their occupants with a variety of noises, including human voice sounds. Before long the infants discover that by wiggling their bodies, they can make the mobile wave back and forth and bring different sounds from the tape recorder. With determined wiggling they can even turn on a vibrator that gives them a feeling that is a little like being rocked on someone's knee.

"Some of our home-reared infants learn to shake the mobile before they're two months old," Hunt reports. "They're learning that they can make interesting things happen, and we're betting we can avoid or even prevent some of the retardation and apathy that is so characteristic of orphanage-reared children."

The point of all this, according to Hunt, is that learning is fun—it's something children intrinsically want to do. "Insofar as you arrange situations that are interesting and attractive and that respond to an infant's own efforts," he says, "you're not only stimulating the child, but you're increasing his general interest in life and living." All mother—or teacher—has to do is find the thing that will whet baby's interest at the moment. "If you supply a child with a toy or object that is old hat you can't keep him interested," Hunt explains. "If you push him beyond his capacity then he'll be frustrated and get mad. Your cues of being somewhere near right lie in the evidences of his interest and positive concern with the situation."

WHAT are these cues? Just watch the child's responses, his interest, his surprise, the smiles and gurgles that indicate satisfaction. "Take baby talk for instance," says Hunt. "You can pick up a baby four or five months old and say, 'My, you're a pretty little baby!' Maybe he'll stare at you, and that's all. But if you ask his mother what kind of coos or grunts he's making or listen to him yourself, and make these noises back at him, what a difference! His eyes widen, his pupils enlarge, and he smiles! Because you've struck something familiar, something he can grasp. Then you can get a sort of conversation going—one without semantics or syntax but nevertheless a conversation. It's the kind of thing that's very exciting to a child and, incidentally, the beginning of learning about verbal communication."

Later on infants grow more interested in novelty. The change comes about partly through boredom. "But it's more than that. As babies learn to recognize a fair number of things," Hunt says firmly, "the idea grows up that things *ought* to be recognizable. If you don't recognize something you look at it hard, not just because it's pleasurable, but because you know it ought to make sense."

To many traditionalists in child development Hunt and his adherents seem to be hard, cold intellectuals, willing to sacrifice a child's emotional well-being for a few extra IQ points. As a father of two, Hunt, who likes to spend summers with his family in the Colorado Rockies, doesn't think the charge holds much water. "Stimulation takes such a small part of the baby's time," he argues. "Besides, I think a good many children who are moving at what is generally accepted as normal are living up to only half their potential. They're probably bored a good deal of the time, and life isn't as much fun as it might be."

Is there a danger of overstimulating a child?—the terror of traditional child development specialists. Hunt unhesitatingly says "Yes," and points to one experiment where researchers designed a large, complicated mobile that took in most of a child's viewing area. "The children couldn't escape from it," he explains. "It was just too much for them, and they cried a lot. Not only that, the amount of visual attention these children paid to things around them was actually well below average after several weeks of lying under this mobile." If a mother can find new tricks to increase her child's joy and foster his development, Hunt thinks this is fine. "If the circumstances are a source of exciting interest and joy for the baby, I don't think you ever hurt him. But you can do too much and overwhelm him. I've been distressed by some of the things mothers say after they've heard me speak. They'll come up and ask what they're supposed to do to speed up their babies' development. They're very concerned and anxious, but they're chiefly interested in making their children brilliant. If this is the upshot of the work I'm doing, then I'm worried."

But for children whose home environments are something less than stimulating, infant education already has something to offer. Its greatest promise lies in indications that if educational efforts begin early enough, it's much simpler than giving remedial education later on.

Just how much stimulation it takes to speed a child's development is still a moot point, since results of infant stimulation studies are just trickling in. However, Hunt can point to one study (by Wayne Dennis of

Brooklyn College in New York) which indicated that if infants in an orphanage were given interesting toys for an hour a day for four weeks, this could make up for about four months of missed development.

Good results have also come from intervention studies with other infants. Under the direction of Earl Schaefer of the National Institute of Mental Health, tutors were sent into the homes of 30 Washington, D.C., infants from disadvantaged families. The tutors, most of whom had no previous teaching experience, spent much of the time just talking with their charges. They also brought puzzles and picture books to help children learn to discern shapes and get used to the idea that books are important. The special program started when the infants were 15 months old; at age three their IQs were averaging about 17 points ahead of a control group of babies with no special stimulation, yet the tutors spent only one hour a day, five days a week in the homes.

If the researchers' attempts at stimulating infants' development are proving so successful, does this mean that education in the future—even for babies—should be left largely in the hands of the experts?

Hunt thinks it all depends on the circumstances. "There's a strong movement right now to start formal education as early as four and perhaps even at three. I'm not sure this is wise. If the child is doing all right at home then that may be the best place for him. If he lacks opportunities there then some other method may be the answer.

"I don't think that taking the child from the mother part of the day—even from an extremely good mother—is necessarily bad. One of the main advantages of nursery schools has been that they relieve the mother of continuous attention and let her follow her own interests for a while." But he admits that bringing children into a laboratory or other special facility for stimulation is an expensive business. Most of his own successful experiments at Urbana have been carried out in the infants' homes.

One fruitful new approach to infant education begins with the mother, teaching her to give her child good care and stimulation. This method has been used successfully by Susan Gray and James O. Miller at Peabody College in Nashville, Tenn., and by Ira Gordon of the Institute for the Development of Human Resources at the University of Florida. Gordon has designed "games" that mothers can use with their babies. Many involve commonplace things: To help baby learn to follow an object with his eyes mother dangles clinking keys over his head, moving them in an arc. A more complicated game resembles hide and seek. Mother hides a favorite toy behind a screen and then pulls it out. This helps baby understand a very important infant lesson: An object does not stop existing just because he can't see it.

Day care centers may also be part of the answer for infant education, at least where working mothers are concerned. In the U.S.S.R. day care centers have been commonplace for years, and the specialists who staff them have practiced early childhood stimulation techniques quite seriously.

"They've been able to train 18-month-olds to carry trays from the cafeteria to their tables," Hunt notes. "There's a great deal of emphasis on pride in group achievement, but independence and individual creativity are not especially encouraged."

In the United States there are just not enough day care centers to go around. There are about 475,000 children under licensed day care today. This leaves many, many more in "makeshift" arrangements.

Makeshift arrangements aren't necessarily bad, according to Hunt. Neither is the number of infants crucial. "One woman may 'care' for four babies by putting them in four cribs and just leaving them there alone. Another person may manage six or eight children and still furnish both warmth and interesting circumstances for all of them." The problem of how many children one adult can care for is still unsettled in child development circles. Although few try to duplicate the almost one-to-one ratio of mother and child many experts feel that things become impossible when there are more than four children per adult.

"I simply don't believe that," Hunt retorts, while admitting that more research on the subject would be helpful. "I can see the use of tape recorders and mobiles in day care centers, much as we're doing in Teheran. This would cut down personnel needs. Furthermore I think the director of a center could be assisted by neighborhood mothers and by older children taught to function as nonprofessional aides. These aides might be eight-to-twelve-year-olds or teenagers who play games with infants like those designed by Gordon or walk toddlers around and talk with them. They could also be learning about childrearing for their own future families."

Hunt also feels that day care centers might serve as a laboratory where mothers could pick up childrearing techniques to use at home. "In most cases," he says, "group counseling has not been effective for getting mothers to modify childraising practices. It's much better if you can actually give the mothers a model to imitate and illustrate what you're trying to say." He hopes that before long a wide system of public day care facilities will be set up that employ the latest techniques in infant education. "There is a real danger here," he warns, "that private nurseries, which serve mostly middle-class children, will pick up infant stimulation methods while the poor will still have to make do with child care arrangements which are far from adequate. Then we'll just spread individual and class differences even further."

One of the greatest problems with massive day care programs will be lack of personnel. Curriculum is also missing; Hunt predicts it may be a decade before solid curricula can be designed for infants and toddlers. He believes many current preschool programs fail to give disadvantaged children the things they need—language, motivation, pride of achievement. "You can push curriculum development so far," Hunt insists, "but no farther without more fundamental scientific research on why some things are working and others are not. This takes time."

Hunt hopes that one result of the National Laboratory on Early Childhood Education will be a union between research and curriculum development. Supported largely by the U.S. Office of Education the laboratory consists of centers at six universities and colleges which are doing pioneer research and development work in early childhood education. While Hunt concedes that there is plenty of room for study left in infant education, he believes that educators have enough to start going immediately. "If a thing is shown to be effective," he asserts, "and we don't have anything else, then for goodness' sake, use it, even though we are not yet clear on why it works."

Right now, the infant educators can provide several techniques, most of which are geared to early basic skills and language development. The most immediate benefits are likely to go to disadvantaged children as a means of overcoming retardation which occurred during infancy. But in the future there is a promising chance of uplifting the intellectual and cultural level of humanity in general. Whatever the eventual outcome one thing seems certain: The researchers in the nursery are not wasting their time.

24.

Malnutrition and learning

MERRILL S. READ

The article by Read on the effects of malnutrition is, we believe, especially important because of the long-standing erroneous belief that the fetus is well protected from stress and injury. The indications from recent studies are that pollution, malnutrition, drugs, and psychic trauma do affect the developmental patterns of fetus and neonate. The effects of malnutrition seem to be much like the effects of disease— slow mental response, lethargy, above average irritability in the face of obstacles. And the effects are not just temporary. It is highly probable that malnutrition results in fewer and smaller brain cells. The primary sufferers from the various grades of malnutrition are those who have certain colors of skin—black and red, especially.

The article is of added interest because, it seems, malnutrition may also be social as well as physiological; and each of the two types may be either a cause or a result of the other.

American Education, 5(No. 10):11–14, December, 1969. Merrill S. Read, Program Director, Growth and Development Branch, National Institute of Child Health and Human Development.

INCREASING KNOWLEDGE of the effects of malnutrition, combined with the social consciousness of the 1960's, has turned national attention to the nutritional status of Americans. Growing evidence that nutrition may affect intellectual and behavioral as well as physical growth has stimulated efforts to determine the extent of malnutrition in the United States and to assess its long-term impact.

Experts disagree about the extent of malnutrition in America partly because of a confusion of terms. Malnutrition is not synonymous with hunger but, of course, may result from long periods of insufficient food. Hunger can be easily and immediately relieved with food; malnutrition requires prolonged rehabilitation and may leave lasting effects.

Here malnutrition is defined as a state in which an individual lacks one or more nutrients to the extent that specific symptoms and conditions appear (such as anemia, goiter, rickets, or vitamin deficiencies) or retardation in physical development occurs. Severe malnutrition refers to two types of diseases resulting from prolonged protein and/or calorie insufficiency in early childhood: Marasmus results from severe restriction of food intake—particularly of calories—from birth or shortly after and is manifest in wasting of the tissues and severe growth retardation. Kwashiorkor, a result of inadequate protein intake, occurs most often when the child changes from breast or bottle milk to foods high in starch but low in protein. It produces extreme stunting of growth, water retention, skin sores, and discoloration of the hair to red or blond. Both diseases cause death if untreated.

Malnutrition is most often associated with poverty. Yet, determining its effects on a given individual is extremely difficult since many other factors influence human growth and behavioral development, including an individual's innate potential, his health status, the conditions in which he lives, and his relationships with his family and the rest of society.

The National Nutrition Survey, begun in 1968 and being carried out by the Department of Health, Education, and Welfare, is the first comprehensive effort to assess the nutritional status of the U.S. population. Preliminary results have been reported on the study of 12,000 people of all ages, randomly selected in poverty pockets in two States and several smaller areas; ultimately the sample will include pockets in 10 or more States. Because of the poverty orientation of these studies, the majority of people examined were Negroes, although other ethnic groups were included.

The survey found an unexpectedly high prevalence of symptoms associated with malnutrition. Four to five percent of the people examined exhibited symptoms sometimes associated with severe malnutrition, although very few cases of marasmus or kwashiorkor were found. One-third of the children under six years old and 15 percent of the total sample population were found to have low blood hemoglobin levels diagnosed as anemia or iron deficiency.

About 17 percent—nearly 2,000 of those examined—showed abnormally low protein levels in their blood. Vitamin D, necessary for the absorption of calcium and the normal development of bones, was found to be lower than normal in the blood of 58 children under six years of age, and 18 cases of rickets were diagnosed. Deficiencies in vitamins A and C and in iodine were also found in a significant number of persons examined.

OTHER surveys carried out in the United States generally confirm the existence among the poor of the nutritional problems found in the National Survey. One study compared 558 preschool children from several economic levels in 20 counties in Mississippi. The 210 children from poor families were found to eat fewer calories and to take in significantly less protein, calcium, and vitamin C than the other groups; they also were considerably smaller and lighter physically.

Surveys have shown that the average North American Indian family of five persons, living on a reservation, attempts to survive on an annual income below $2,000. A study of 195 Apache children between one and six years old disclosed that one-third of them had anemia and deficiencies in vitamins A and C. Virtually all 165 children examined in one clinic had dental disease; half the cases were described as severe. In another group of 126 families, marked growth retardation was seen in children through age five years. Cases of severe malnutrition in children have also been found on Navajo reservations in the Southwest.

The results of these surveys are preliminary and in many cases cannot be directly compared. However, in the absence of complete national statistics, these studies suggest that multiple deficiencies of specific nutrients occur in varying degrees and in higher-than-expected proportions among poor people. A major factor contributing to the poor nourishment of infants is the decline of breast feeding, combined with inadequate information about food substitutes and poor sanitary conditions in the use of alternate foods.

The consequences of malnutrition depend on the time in the life of the individual when nutritional deficits occur, as well as on their severity and duration. The brain may be damaged by various influences during the period of fastest growth, which in human beings occurs from about five months before to about 10 months after birth. At the end of the first year the brain has achieved approximately 70 percent of its adult weight, and by the end of the second year, it has practically completed its growth.

The brain grows both by increase in the number of cells and by increase in the size of each cell. Experiments with rats, made by Myron Winick of the Cornell University Medical College in New York, show that severe malnutrition during the period of cell division permanently reduces the total number of cells despite subsequent nutritional rehabilitation. Severe food restriction later during the growth period may reduce cell size during the period of starvation, but the cells retain the ability to enlarge with increased feeding.

Obviously, similar studies cannot be done with human infants. However, the brains of infants who died of marasmus in Chile were found by

Dr. Winick to have only 40 percent of the expected number of cells when compared with the brains of infants who died from accidents. Severe malnutrition in a pregnant woman probably affects the unborn child by reducing the nutrients available to it for normal cell growth. Also, severe malnutrition during the first six months of the infant's life further reduces the number of brain cells the baby will develop. The timing of nutritional deprivation, therefore, is crucial.

Although information from experiments with animals cannot be applied directly to humans, who are infinitely more complicated, it can point the way to possible consequences for man. Rats and pigs fed severely restricted diets during periods of fastest brain growth and then later fed good diets have shown changes in behavior as well as in the size and composition of their brains. The animals cannot learn as fast as their normal littermates, cannot unlearn a task they have finally mastered, and tend to overreact in an agitated and irritable way when exposed to unpleasant situations.

In a pioneer study begun in 1955 in South Africa, investigators compared a group of 20 severely malnourished Negro infants, mostly aged 10 months to two years, with a second group of better nourished babies matched for race, age, sex, and low socioeconomic class. Eleven years later the severely malnourished children displayed significantly smaller head sizes and much lower intellectual achievement on various test measures than did the second group. Although their greater emotional and social deprivation may have affected the first group's test performance, the implications of long-lasting effects of malnutrition on mental development could not be ignored.

ANOTHER important early study was done by Joaquin Cravioto, currently head of the department of nutrition, Hospital Infantil de Mexico, on 20 Guatemalan preschool children who had been hospitalized for severe malnutrition in earlier childhood and had recuperated. Here Dr. Cravioto found that intellectual development was related to the age of the child at the time of affliction and to the duration of the malnutrition: Events during the first six months of life appeared most critical for later normal development. For the first three years of their lives these children showed slower rates of mental and motor development than children matched in all ways except for the malnutrition. With time, some of the differences narrowed between the groups, except in cases in which the malnutrition occurred very early in life.

Recently Ernesto Pollitt, assistant professor of psychology at Yale, critically reviewed eight investigations—made in underdeveloped countries and completed in the last six years—in which children hospitalized with severe protein-calorie malnutrition were observed after recovery. Overall, the results suggested that kwashiorkor was not necessarily associated with permanent intellectual damage, at least if the child was older than 12 months when the condition began. Dr. Pollitt concluded that a child who suffers from kwashiorkor after an otherwise healthy early development seems to have a fair chance of recovering his full intellectual potential.

Children suffering from marasmus, on the other hand, were found to be more likely to have intellectual damage, probably because the brain grows faster during the early months of life when marasmus strikes. Marasmus might develop gradually from birth, increasingly debilitate the infant, and limit his responsiveness to his surroundings, especially his mother. As the child's responsiveness decreases, the mother may become disheartened and transfer her attention to other healthier children in the family. Thus, the marasmic child seems more likely to be permanently impaired because of his longer exposure to poor diet and multiple adverse environmental factors.

In Chile, Fernando B. Monckeberg, head of pediatrics at the University of Chile Medical School in Santiago, studied three groups of urban preschool children: a middle-class well-nourished group, a lower-class group participating in a nutritional supplementation program, and a group of lower-class malnourished children. He found the last group performed significantly poorer on tests of intellectual ability, even though their environment was similar to that of the second group. The first two groups performed essentially alike, despite their environmental differences. In this study, poor nutrition appeared to be associated with poor test performance.

Studying an impoverished area more closely, Dr. Monckeberg examined 150 preschool children and their mothers. From tests, he found poor intellectual performance to be highly associated with smaller head size and low protein diets of the children. After evaluating the mothers' intellectual abilities, he could also relate the low maternal performance with the children's poor nutritional conditions and poor intellectual performance. Thus, the interrelation between inheritance, social deprivation, and intellectual ability remained unresolved.

Although kwashiorkor and marasmus occur infrequently in the United States, cases are now being seen in hospitals that serve large lower-income populations. Peter Chase and colleagues at the University of Colorado Medical Center in Denver have reported a long-term follow-up study of 19 infants admitted to a hospital over a two-year period for treatment of marasmus or kwashiorkor. They compared these infants with another group which, so far as possible, were distinguished from them only by their state of nutrition. The investigators found that although all the children in the study showed an adequate growth rate three and one-half years after treatment, the malnourished children failed to catch up to the second group mentally or physically.

The researchers concluded that the duration of malnutrition in the first year of life of these infants correlated with their physical and mental development at the age of about four and one-half years when the children were studied. Examination of the family records showed that the mothers of the malnourished infants were under particular emotional and economic stress at the time of their infants' malnutrition, and that home conditions were especially bad. Furthermore, a primary cause of the poor nutritional condition of these infants was family disorganization, probably influenced by poverty and lack of education. In one case, an infant was left in the hands of her five-year-old sister. Since these social problems also may influence intellectual development, the effects of malnutrition alone are somewhat clouded in this study.

There are other conditions that tend to decrease learning experiences and possibly affect subsequent intellectual development. Children hospitalized with protein-calorie malnutrition may have experienced a form of social isolation in the period immediately preceding hospitalization. On top of this, opportunities for social contact frequently are reduced in the hospital rehabilitation ward. The child's fear of the new hospital environment also may inhibit his response to learning opportunities. Pertinent recent studies have shown that social isolation may reduce the size and number of cells in rat brain much the same as malnutrition.

The evidence strongly supports the conclusion that early severe malnutrition is associated with intellectual impairment. However, carefully planned studies are needed to determine whether any effects are due solely to malnutrition or to the unique constellation of environmental factors surrounding the malnourished hospitalized child who has most often been the subject for these studies.

Another major question concerns the effects of mild to moderate malnutrition on intellectual growth. These levels of undernutrition do not necessarily imperil survival, and hospitalization is not normally required, but they may cause growth retardation. Here there are few studies upon which to base a judgment, but the effects, if any, would certainly be expected to be less than for protein-calorie malnutrition. Furthermore, the interplay between social, medical, genetic, and nutritional variables might be expected to play a more prominent role.

In an eight-year study of Mexican children, investigators found that intellectual performance at the time of entry into school appeared to be related to the child's history of malnutrition. After the children spent four to five years in school, however, this relationship disappeared, and differences in performance appeared to be related more closely to socioeconomic conditions and regularity of school attendance.

Hence, iron deficiency anemia is the most frequently observed nutritional problem among infants, preschool, and young children. Its effects upon learning and behavior have not been systematically investigated. One study of 28 children under the age of three who were admitted to an American hospital with iron deficiency has been reported. The subjects were matched with a group not having anemia. A year after discharge from the hospital, the children who had had anemia were found to have more illnesses, more feeding difficulties, and more behavioral problems than those in the other group. The investigators attributed the behavioral deficits to parental failure and family disintegration rather than to nutritional insufficiency.

A key problem in determining whether malnutrition, disease, or the social environmental factors of poverty have the greatest effect on mental development hinges on the timing of the testing. Intellectual and behavioral measurements are best made in middle childhood, whereas the nutritional insult, if it has an effect, probably occurs in infancy. Long term studies monitoring nutritional intake and behavior development are essential.

A study that may provide some answers is now being done in Guatemala where many people still live in small, isolated villages, subsist on an inadequate diet, and till the overworked fields of their ancestors. Without adequate medical care many babies die before their first birthday, and those who survive are short and underdeveloped. In the villages under study, all participants receive heretofore unavailable medical care with special attention given to pregnant women, infants, and young children. The villages are studied in pairs so that they are as much alike as possible on socioeconomic, public health, cultural, and other bases. Each village in a pair receives added stimulation through a carefully planned visitation and examination program. One village in each pair also receives a specially designed nutritional supplement. Thus the investigators hope to define the effects of better nutrition as they follow the growth and development of the children over the first seven years of life.

Up to now it has been generally assumed that intellectual deficits would be proportional to the degree of malnutrition imposed. On the other hand, it is also possible that there may be a level of malnutrition in infancy below which neurological structures are so altered that retarded intellectual development is irreversible. Above this threshold, however, undernutrition would have no serious consequences for neurological development itself. Genetic endowment and sociological factors surrounding malnutrition would then be expected to exert increasingly significant effects on intellectual ability.

Those who have worked with undernourished or hungry children know that they exhibit behavioral alterations. These include apathy, lethargy, inability to pay attention, and perhaps, overconcern about food to such a degree that responses to classroom stimuli do not occur. A child in such condition no longer meets the expectations of his family or teachers. He begins to live in a world of his own and may seek recognition or gain attention by ways that disrupt learning experiences.

LEARNING is increasingly recognized as progressing in stages, each stage becoming a foundation for the next. By not responding to early stimulation, the child gradually becomes unable to benefit from "normal" experiences at a later period. He fails to learn, not because the genetic potential or neurological structures are absent, but because he lacks the experiential foundation. Improved nutrition alone will not correct this deficit. Neither will improved educational opportunities by themselves. Both must be provided in a coordinated program to develop the child's potential.

Foremost among the problems requiring resolution is the development of a battery of tests that can measure the behavioral and social variables involved and that are applicable to varied social groups. These tests need to be addressed to the changes that we now suspect are related to malnutrition. It is hoped that they will detect those low levels of change that might be expected under less severe nutritional conditions.

Before firm conclusions can be drawn that malnutrition per se is the cause of mental subnormality, carefully designed studies will be required to clarify the role of parents and of the social and environmental factors that accompany malnutrition. Because research cannot at this time give an unequivocal or complete answer to the question of what effect malnutrition has on intellectual development is no reason to delay programs for improving the nutritional status and eating practices of mothers and infants. Information demonstrating the benefits of good nutrition in improved health and physical growth already justify such efforts.

section **vii**

Early childhood years

25.

The child: his struggle for identity

JEROME KAGAN

In this selection one of this country's foremost authorities on child behavior emphasizes the importance of interpersonal transactions for the adequate development of humans. He begins by discussing the effects of the mother-child relationship and from there moves to consider the influence of parents. Later, he speaks of the impact of peer interaction and he concludes with comments concerning the manner in which children are affected by teachers. Throughout the article, a necessity is recognized for adequate adult models with whom a child may identify.

Particularly, the author stresses the need for early verbal stimulation. In contrast with other authorities who also recognize the importance of verbal ability for intellectual development, Kagan believes culturally disadvantaged infants do not suffer so much from a lack of stimulation as they do from a lack of stimulation that he describes as maximally distinctive. Other stimuli should not impinge and compete if important verbal learning is to progress satisfactorily.

The editors believe that this principle may have important implications for learning. Certainly it is one that a society which places masses of humanity in close proximity and which generates sound in crescendo proportions should contemplate.

THE NEWBORN CHILD is a remarkably capable organism from the moment he begins to breathe. He can see, hear, and smell, and is sensitive to pain, touch, and change in position. The only one of the five senses that may not be functioning immediately at birth is taste.

The newborn's behavioral equipment is also remarkably well developed. When only two hours old, he will follow a rapidly moving light with his eyes; his pupils will dilate in darkness and constrict in light; he will suck a finger or nipple inserted into his mouth; he will turn in the direction in which his cheek or the corner of his mouth is touched. He can cry,

Saturday Review, 51(No. 49):80–82+, December 7, 1968. Copyright 1968 Saturday Review, Inc. Jerome Kagan, Professor of Psychology, Harvard University.

cough, turn away, vomit, lift his chin from a prone position, and grasp an object placed in his palm. His body will react to a loud sound. He can flex and extend his limbs, smack his lips, and chew his fingers.

It is fortunate that the infant is so competent at birth because his new environment outside his mother's body subjects him suddenly to such unfamiliar stresses as hunger, heat, cold, and pain. During the first weeks of life, most of his behavior is in direct response to the unexpected interferences with his equilibrium. If he is hungry, he cries. If he is excited, he babbles. If he is in pain, he cries to the accompaniment of thrashing arms and legs.

These innate reactions alter his environment significantly by bringing another person to tend him. When this happens, the child—who instructed his mother more than she instructed him during his period in the womb— enters the active influence of the society to which he belongs. Thenceforth, according to the talents of those who serve him, certain of the infant's behaviors will be selectively strengthened and certain others will be selectively weakened.

The relation between infant and mother is a ballet, in which each partner responds to the steps of the other. If, when the infant cries, the mother bestows care and affection, the infant will be likely to cry on the next occasion when he is distressed. Thus the mother's actions are molding the infant's behavior. But the frequency and regularity with which the mother acts toward the child are also being affected by the infant. The mother is more likely to leave the living room and go to the infant's room if the infant cries than if the infant is quiet. As a result, irritable babies, who are more often boys than girls, typically share their mother's company more often than do placid, quiet babies. If a mother's attempts to soothe her infant are successful, she is more likely to come to the infant when he calls. The infant who smiles will elicit more smiling from the mother than a non-smiling baby. The infant girl who babbles provokes more imitative babbling from the mother than the infant who is quiet. In this sense, the infant is clearly shaping the mother's behavior as much as the mother influences the infant.

Another major determinant of the mother's actions, in addition to the child's moment-to-moment behavior, is her set of goals for the child. Most American middle-class mothers want their boys to be independent and self-reliant because contemporary American society rewards independence and competitiveness. Most Japanese middle-class mothers, by contrast, want their sons to be interdependent with the family and less self-reliant. The mothers' actions flow from these idealized models. Each mother loves her child equally and thinks she is doing the best for him.

Each set of parents has the difficult task of deciding what kind of child they wish to create. The decision can become excruciatingly difficult in times of great flux, like those through which we are now passing. The increasing population density in our cities, coupled with growing alienation of citizens from a sense of community, is causing many Americans to question whether individualism, carried to present-day extremes, is healthy. How does a particular set of parents react to this question? Depending on the strength of their commitment to traditions of competitive individualism versus their eagerness to participate in evolution of new cultural designs, their values may conflict with the values of their neighborhood. And if the characteristics of the child do not adapt him to whatever values are accepted by the parents, there is conflict within conflict.

THE child whose personality traits do not match the values of his society is not likely to be well adjusted. Such a child might be much happier in a society governed by a quite different set of values. The parental decision regarding the child is an overwhelmingly moral one, not to be decided on scientific evidence alone. Parents should appreciate that there is no ideal set of personality characteristics for a child nor any ideal set of parental practices. Each is relative to its own time and cultural context.

The child's perception of whether he is loved or rejected is also relative. If the child knows that the parents are poor, and it is a sacrifice for them to buy him a toy worth $5 for Christmas, he will interpret receipt of that toy as an act of love and affection; for he recognizes that the parents have given him something that required a personal sacrifice. The child of an affluent family who receives the same toy is not likely to view it as reflecting any special affection. For this boy, perhaps, a long walk in the forest, which is a sacrifice for a busy executive father, is the gift that is symbolic of love. Love or rejection is not contained in any specific set of behaviors by a mother or a father. Love or rejection is relative to the child's perceptions; for love, like beauty, is in the mind of the beholder.

The same reasoning holds for punishments. There is no specific effect of a verbal chastisement, a spanking, or a banishment from the company of parents or siblings. The effect of each of these punishments on the child is always dependent on the child's interpretation of that punishment. Each parent will be better able to socialize his child if he has access to the "tote board" of values the child holds. It is not an easy accomplishment, but its attainment is worth great effort.

The first year of life is marked by rapid development of perceptual structures in the child. Although we now know that the newborn child is far from being an amorphous bundle of insensitive flesh and bone, our contemporary understanding of cognitive growth resembles the state of chemical theory in the seventeenth century, when a scientist could relate either natural or purposive causes to obvious changes in the color, weight, smell, or texture of substances but could not explain what happened to bring the changes about.

Long before anything at all was known about the human brain, prescientific philosophers taught that the heart was the seat of human personality. Therefore, it is interesting that modern scientific research with children should demonstrate—as it has—that the heartbeat is a dependable signal of the child's attention. Experiments in our own and other laboratories during the last decade have tracked the processes of the infant mind by noting the occasions when the child's heartbeat suddenly slows. The resting heart rate of infants ranges from 120 to 180 beats per minute, with an average of about 145 beats. Experience has confirmed that decelerations greater than six or seven beats are most often associated with an attentive posture, and facial or motor responses indicating surprise. By measuring the child's heart rate and the duration of his gaze at various events, one can easily see that the earliest determinant of the infant's attention is high rate of change in the physical parameters of a stimulus. Lights that blink on and off are more likely to capture his attention than is a steady light source. Intermittent tones of sound are more attention getting than continuous ones. Visual events with high black-white contour contrast possess more power to recruit sustained attention than stimuli with minimal contour contrast. These conditions produce distinctiveness naturally. They elicit attention without prior learning. These factors dominate the attention during the first twelve weeks.

After that time, the infant's reactions show increasing signs of being controlled by experience. In other words, the child is beginning to think about what he sees. Attention is focused more and more in relation to the degree to which the elements of an event are a distortion or discrepancy from an established schema.

A schema is a representation of an external event. Like a caricature, it is defined by a set of distinctive elements. If the distinctive elements change, the schema changes. The four-month-old child's schema of a human face probably consists of an oval outline and two symmetrically placed eyes. When an infant of that age is shown a sketch of a face with asymmetric eyes or a face with no eyes, the child smiles markedly less than he smiles at a face with symmetrically placed eyes, with or without the presence of nose and mouth. The smile seems to be his "Aha" reaction—his way of saying the stimulus is familiar to him.

A child pays maximal attention to an event that is a slight deviation from the distinctive elements of his schema. The four-month-old baby will look longer at a photograph of a face—regular or moderately disfigured—than he would at a randomly generated nonsense figure with a high degree of black-white contrast. Furthermore, his cardiac deceleration will be greater to it than to the black-white nonsense figures. Since each child develops his own schema at his own rate, it follows that information intended to command his attention must be tailored to fit his schema.

Let us consider some economic class differences in cognitive functioning in light of the above. Our Harvard laboratory has studied more than 160 first-born Caucasian infants from lower-middle-class, middle-class, and upper-middle-class families. Lower-class infants come from families where one or both parents did not complete high school and where the fathers were in unskilled occupations. Upper-middle-class infants came from families where both parents were college graduates.

Each infant was exposed to two visual episodes in the laboratory at four months of age. In the first episode, each child was shown each of four different achromatic depictions of human faces. The four stimuli were a photograph of a male face, a schematic outline of a regular male face, a collage of the photograph of the face, and a collage of the schematic regular face. After a short recess, each child was shown a series of three-dimensional sculptured faces painted flesh color, and four presentations each of four different faces: a regular male face; a collage of that face with eyes, nose, and mouth rearranged; a regular face with no eyes; and a completely blank face with neither eyes, nose, nor mouth.

THE children from the lowest economic level displayed the smallest cardiac decelerations to all the stimuli. How are we to interpret this?

The lower-middle-class infants look as long at the faces as the upper-class babies do, but do not decelerate their heartbeats because the faces are not close enough to their schema for the faces of their parents. The favorite explanation for this difference in response is that the mother's face is a more distinctive stimulus for the upper-middle-class child than for the less privileged child. We believe that well educated mothers are more likely to engage in frequent, distinctive, face-to-face contact with their children, more likely to create conditions that will make the parent's countenance distinctive.

THE most dramatic differences between lower- and middle-class children of pre-school or school age involve language skills. Documentation for this conclusion is everywhere. A fast and often glib interpretation of it rests on the belief that lower-class parents talk less often to their children. This may be too simple an interpretation. We certainly do not wish to reject the idea totally but we prefer to balance it with the possibility that lower-class children are not so much deprived of parental vocalization as they are deprived of distinctive vocalization. The lower-class child does not receive distinctive verbal stimulation from adults and, as a result, is less likely to attend to human speech.

Some of the lower and middle-class children mentioned above were observed with their mothers in their homes for a day when the infants were four months old. A selected set of mother and child variables was recorded every five seconds. The observer wore in her ear a small, inconspicuous battery-powered device which produced a brief auditory signal every five seconds, and the observer recorded, in five-second units, variables that belonged to a prearranged code. Some of the variables included: mother vocalize to infant, mother touch infant, mother vigorously manipulate infant, mother pick up infant, child vocalize, child extend limbs, and child thrash.

Computation of the percentage of time the mother vocalized to the infant, regardless of what else she was doing, or where she was in the home, disclosed only a slight and nonsignificant tendency for the upper-middle-class mothers to vocalize more often than lower- or middle-class mothers to their daughters. There were even less striking differences for sons. However, when we examined the distinctiveness of the mothers' vocalization—vocalization that occurred when mother was face-to-face with her infant and doing nothing else but talking to her—more dramatic differences appeared.

Let us describe a hypothetical experience of an upper-middle-class girl and a lower-class girl.

The middle-class child is lying in her crib in her bedroom on the second floor of a suburban home. She wakes, the room is quiet, her mother is downstairs baking. The infant studies the crib and her fingers. Suddenly the quiet is broken as the mother enters, looks down at her baby, and speaks. This auditory intrusion is maximally distinctive and likely to orient the infant to her mother and to the vocalization. If the child responds vocally, the mother is apt to continue the dialogue.

An infant girl in a ghetto is lying on a couch in a two-room apartment with the television going and siblings peering into her face. The child lies in a sea of sound; like the sea, the sound is homogeneous. The mother approaches the child and says something. This communication is minimally distinctive from background noise and, as such, is not likely to recruit the infant's attention. Many of the infant's vocalizations during the day are not likely to be responded to by anyone nor are they likely to elicit a special response.

This research generates implications for preschool enrichment programs for lower-class children. There is a zealous attempt to bombard the lower-class child with pictures, crayons, books, speech, and typewriters, as if an intellectual deficit was akin to hunger and the proper therapy required filling of his cerebral gulleys with stuff.

I would like to argue for a more paced strategy, a self-conscious attempt to intervene when the intrusion is likely to be maximally distinctive. For example, teaching reading or vocabulary should be individual or in very small groups, and background contexts should be simple so that the material to be learned has maximal distinctiveness. Instructional speech should be paced so that each communication holds the attentional stage solo and does not share the child's limited attentional capacities with other attractions. We must initiate explicit attempts to diagnose the content and articulateness of the child's existing schema and to plan interventions that are moderate discrepancies from his schema.

Distinctiveness of events recruits the child's attention and can maintain it for five, ten, or even twenty seconds. But sustained attention for minutes requires more than discrepancy; it requires the possession of structures or chains of cognitive units that are specifically activated by the event.

When one sees a three-year-old devote a half hour to exploration of an old telephone, there is a temptation to smile and mumble something about the child's natural curiosity. However, long periods of sustained involvement are neither inherent in the event nor part of the child's natural equipment. It can be taken for granted that this particular child has either watched a telephone being used, or spoken into a telephone mouthpiece himself, or heard his parents explain what a telephone is for. Sustained involvement of any child is dependent on that child's previous acquisition of a set of hypotheses and reactions appropriate to the object. Without such prior learning, a potential thirty-minute exploration can be reduced to less than thirty seconds.

I recall a teacher who brought to class a dozen packs of Cape Cod seaweed stuffed with attractive samples of shells of diverse species. She gave each pair of six-year-old children one of these attractive toys and withdrew, expecting the pupils to display natural curiosity. Each child devoted less than ten seconds to the material before returning to his previous game. The teacher had failed to explain to the children that the shells were once inhabited by different kinds of animals, and that by looking carefully at a shell one could tell not only what kind of animal had lived there but how old the animal was when it left the shell.

A second anecdote is equally forceful. One of our graduate students raised an infant rhesus monkey from birth. The animal became an interesting sight around William James Hall on the Harvard campus. My daughter, twelve years old, begged to see the monkey. We arranged to have the student and monkey come to dinner. My daughter excitedly informed the neighborhood of the event. A few minutes after the student and monkey were seated in our living room, six children, from seven to eleven years of age, rang the doorbell. They ran to the monkey, looked and poked for about two minutes, and then casually walked off one by one to more interesting activities. We hadn't prepared the children to ask themselves logical questions about the monkey—what makes him afraid, what makes him run, what makes him smack his lips?

In short, curiosity may be only a romantic name for that phenomenon that occurs when a child tries out a set of acquired hypotheses on some new object that captures the child's attention.

In addition to the distinctive elements of new material, the child's motivation is another factor that controls the intensity of attention the child will devote to a task. The child's desire to be proud of his parents and similar to them in word and deed is one strong motivational force.

Lower-class parents may exhort their children to work hard for good grades in school, but the children do not perceive their parents as persons who publicly engage in or express a value in intellectual mastery themselves. As a result, the children cannot view mastery of intellectual skills as a way of being similar to their parents, or of gaining the adult resources of power and competence that the child perceives his parents to possess.

THE peer group is not unimportant in the development of standards and motives surrounding intellectual mastery. The child selects models from among his classmates once he begins school. As with the lower-class family, the lower-class peer group is biased against school achievement in favor of those behaviors that the boys and girls themselves define as masculine or feminine. This situation has serious consequences for school performance. The child of six years wants to maximize his similarity to whatever standards his schoolmates set for his sex. The child has learned that he or she is called a boy or a girl and rushes to elaborate this operational definition.

How does the child decide what events, objects, or actions are masculine or feminine? He works by a reliable formula. He implicitly computes the ratio of males to females associated with an event or action. If the ratio is lopsided in one direction, that activity is assigned the sex role of the majority party. Fishing is masculine, sewing is feminine. Any five-year-old will tell you this. School is usually classified as feminine by six-year-olds because in over 90 per cent of the primary grades in this nation, the activity of the classroom is monitored by a woman.

ONE implication of these data argues for the wisdom of segregating the sexes, especially in the primary grades of school. In a sex-segregated class, each child might learn to maximize in the school experience the sex role appropriate to himself. The presence of a man in the classroom would obviously have the strongest impact on a boy. But even changing the content of the reading curriculum should have some benefit.

Aside from the importance of modeling, the peers mediate other mechanisms that engage the motive to master academic tasks. Most children, especially boys, have a strong motive for power, a desire to play the dominant role in an interpersonal dyad. The uncorrupted sign of power for all children is strength. Strength is the only legitimate currency of power which cannot be corrupted, and children recognize this principle. The culture, in its wisdom, preaches substitute signs for power. Prowess at athletics, skill at adult activities, signs of intelligence can function as badges of potency if the group accepts that currency. The middle-class child is likely to find himself in a peer group where the right to dominate is given to the child with good grades, to the child with a quick answer, to the child with a catalogue of facts. Lower-class peer cultures rarely adopt this translation of power. Thus the lower-class child, already unable to find models for intellectual striving in his parents, is further deprived of a primary motive to master intellectual skills.

The two themes in this brief essay stress the dramatic psychological growth that occurs in the opening years and the importance of the parent-child relationship for that growth. It is believed that a large share of the child's desire to adopt the values and skills of society, including the wish to master the tasks of the school, derive from a close parent-child relationship in the first few years of life. The child comes to value the parent and is, therefore, receptive to adopting the parent's motivations for him. There is growing interest in establishing day care centers for economically under-privileged mothers who wish to work and need a place where they can leave their infant for most of the day. We believe this plan has potential dangers for the child's growth, for it could produce a child who has a seriously diluted tie to his parents. It will also weaken the emotional in-volvement of the mother with her own child. It would perhaps be wise to consider paying the mothers to stay with the children and beginning strong educational programs for parents, to educate them into the nature of the child and the nature of his psychological growth.

However, implementation of this suggestion will not by itself amelio-rate the awesome educational deficiencies of many economically deprived children. The poor progress of these children in school is probably the re-sult of many factors, including low income, residence in a slum neighbor-hood, an unstable family organization, absence of a father, a peer group that does not value school success, and, in some cases, inadequate nutrition of the individual child. It is not possible to state with confidence which of these factors produces the child's problems in school. Cures are most effec-tive when diagnoses are accurate. We must therefore be cautious about simple plans or devices that promise to solve "the problem" when we are still unclear about the fundamental nature of the problem.

26.

The beginnings of self: the problem of the nurturing environment

IRA J. GORDON

Part of the lively interest the editors have in this article lies with a point that does not appear to be of primary concern to the author. Reference is made to the fact that various schools, or viewpoints, in psychology are made to appear contradictory or mutually exclusive in many publications. Gordon, in tracing the development of self, shows how behavioristic psychology, Freudian concepts, and the emerging humanistic psychologies may play sequential and supplementary roles. For instance, the child does learn about self from the way he is treated by his mother (Freudian interpretations); he is conditioned

Phi Delta Kappan, 50:375–378, 1969. Ira J. Gordon, Professor of Education and Director, Institute for Development of Human Resources, University of Florida.

by his successes and failures (behaviorism); and ". . . the role of the
infant himself as an active, striving, curious, learning organism who
makes his impact on his family, this is no "tabula rasa child" (humanistic or proactive psychology). This view of the relationship of
psychological theories is the bonus; the main dividend consists of
practical suggestions for helping children develop healthy ego concepts.

THE CONCEPT of the self is an old one in religion and philosophy and has
been discussed endlessly as a part of man's search for identity, as he sought
to answer the question, "Who am I?" For Descartes the answer was, "Co-
gito ergo sum"—I think, therefore I am. This statement marked a sharp
break with medieval thought, and contributed to the age of reason. For
Descartes, cognition or reason was superior to emotion. Knowing was the
self's primary function. The self was active, aware, free; the senses and
emotions were passive, or confused influences upon the mind. From the
early seventeenth until the late nineteenth century, this view reigned.

Freud broke with this tradition by centering upon the emotions, by
denying free will, and by focusing upon the influence of the child's experiences in the earliest years. Since Freud, the Descartian answer is insufficient. We now seek to define ourselves in ways which include our feelings
as well as our thoughts, and look for the origins of our personality in the
first dim moments of life long before cognition seemed possible. Because
of Freud, our notion of self-definition has required that its origins be in
early childhood and that it be developed from the experiences we have had
in that most intimate of circles—our family. For modern man, this is a
truism; but it also leaves unanswered a myriad of questions concerning how
we got that way.

The first step in self-awareness is both affective and cognitive: the discovery of one's own body as distinct and pleasurable. When the infant puts
thumb in mouth, he experiences sensation in both his thumb and his mouth
and learns that the thumb is part of him. When the numerous other objects
that the infant places in his mouth do not yield the double sensation, he
separates self from other. This process, labeled "self-sentience" by Sullivan,[1]
provides the infant with his first anchorage point, his first awareness of
separateness. To paraphrase Descartes, if the infant could speak, he might
say, "I experience me, therefore I am."

The second marking point is the awareness of "other." The separation
of "I" or "me" from "not me" requires the introduction of people and objects from outside the child. The child needs enough of them, with enough
frequency and consistency, that they can be differentiated. The infant at
three months engages in social smiles,[2] but much has gone on before this
time to enable the child to reach this major social event. It is not purely the
"maturation" of an inadequate organism toward social behavior. William
James, at the turn of the century, defined the world of the infant as a
blooming, buzzing confusion, but current research in learning indicates

that infants are able to make much more elaborate differentiations of their physical environment in terms of sight and sound and sense than James would have thought possible.

For example, Lipsitt's research at Brown[3] indicates the ways in which both operant and classical conditioning can occur in infancy. Although its approach is not psychoanalytic, current research in infant learning substantiates the psychoanalyst's view of the infant's ability to learn and thus supports the notion of the importance of this early period. But what is it the child learns, in addition to such behaviors as feeding or cooing responses, smiles, and cries? The period of infancy has been seen as the time the child learns basic trust.[4] The nature of the inputs—that is, the way he is handled and fondled, dealt with and responded to, and how his body reacts to these events—teaches the child whether or not the world is a safe or terrifying place, and whether he can trust it or not.

Since the separation of self and world is incomplete, the self-concept, the "I," is part of the world. It is both cognitive and affective, active and passive. "I" is not only in the brain but also in the viscera. It is both Cartesian and Freudian.

Specifically, what are some of the inputs in the very early years which influence the initial picture of the self? Robert Sears and his colleagues,[5,6] in a series of studies which applied learning theory rigor to psychoanalytic concepts, indicated that parental attitudes and behavior (disciplinary techniques, permissiveness, severity, temperamental qualities, and aspirations) exhibited in the areas of hunger, elimination, dependency, sex, and aggression were important factors in development and in sex-role identification, a major dimension of the self-concept. But these external inputs emphasize the affective side of life. They do not adequately consider either the cognitive dimension or the role of the child himself.

Current thought emphasizes the competence of the infant and brings together both the cognitive and affective elements of the child into one system. It emphasizes the importance of not only the characteristic child-rearing patterns described by Sears, and the family drama so dear to the psychoanalyst, but also the role of the infant himself as an active, striving, curious, learning organism who makes his impact on his family. This is no *tabula rasa* child. And the child's view of himself is not simply a mirror image of the external events which surround him early in life. From the very beginning it includes his own organism as it senses, feels, learns, and assigns meaning to these external stimuli. The child learns who he is from what happens to him, from the language that surrounds him, from the people who are dear to him, from the opportunities to deal with the objects and events in his immediate world, and from his own responses to the welter of stimuli. His self-esteem represents his unique organization of his own biological makeup, the evaluations made of him by significant adults, and his own learning from trial and manipulation and feedback from his world. Cognitive development is inseparable from personality development.

The child obviously cannot define "self" as distinct from "other" before he has a permanent frame of reference. One measure of this frame is Piaget's "object permanence," manifested by the individual's recognition that an object continues to exist even though it is no longer visible to him. He arrives at this point somewhere in the second year of life. It is a growth marker because now he can relate affectively to other individuals in some consistent fashion, and cognitively he has achieved a level where he can actively engage in searching his environment. Gaining this ability is a giant step forward and gives the child a sense of competence in relating to his world.

We can make an intuitive leap from object permanence to Erikson's basic trust. Both mean that the child has now organized at least a portion of his world so that it is orderly and predictable—and therefore manageable. With this he can structure a positive self-concept. Without a sense of object permanence, he is powerless. Psychological inputs are important here, because only on the basis of broad experience can the child discover that both people and things have external reality. With the establishment of "other," the child's own behavior can now include role-taking and role-playing.[7] This process enables him to shift from Piaget's "egocentric" stage toward "decentration." That is, he develops from seeing others as just like him toward a recognition of the fact that what one sees and believes depends upon where he stands and what he already knows. Parents not only influence opportunities for such role-playing, but also provide the basic models for imitation. Through the ways in which they teach or deny opportunities for dramatic play, they influence both the cognitive and affective dimensions of the self-concept. Smilansky[8] has described the way parents affect this phase of learning.

Piaget's theoretical exposition of cognitive development returns us to the epistemological position of Descartes, but with added knowledge from Freud and the behavioral scientists. Décarie,[9] for example, was able to investigate both Piagetian and psychoanalytic views about the process, timing, and meaning of arrival at object permanence. Generally, she found empirical support for both, and concluded that parents are the most effective agents in presenting both cognitive and affective experience to the young child. Piaget wrote in 1954:

> The other person is of course an emotional object to the highest degree but at the same time is the most interesting cognitive object, the most alive, the most unexpected. . . . The other person is an object which implies a multitude of exchanges in which cognitive as well as affective factors play a role, and if this object is of paramount importance in one of these respects, it is, I think, equally important in the other.[10]

How important are these early years? Gardner Murphy has indicated that the self-picture is fairly well integrated by the third year of life. Once it has developed, it becomes the evaluator, selector, judger, and organizer of future experience, and the child's behavior may be seen as organized to enhance and maintain his view. Such a picture sounds harsh and deterministic if we did not understand that possibilities for change are always present. Life is not over at age three, but the general view toward the world and toward one's self is already present.

The longitudinal data which support the importance of early childhood are fairly consistent. Bloom indicated on the basis of reviews of longitudinal research[11] that half of what accounts for the variance in adults in aggressiveness in males and dependence in females seems to be present by age four. Not only Bloom's summary but also the classical longitudinal studies conducted in California[12] and the longitudinal studies of the Fels Institute at Yellow Springs, Ohio,[13] demonstrated the effects of parental behavior in the child's first six years on his behavior and attitudes in subsequent years.

One of Bayley's findings is that the mother's affectional behavior toward her son in the first three years of his life was related to his friendship, cooperation, and attentiveness when he became a school child and an adolescent. These behaviors may be inferred to be reflections of feelings of security, a fundamental dimension of self-concept.

One of Freud's contributions is the concept of identification, and, more specifically, sex-role identification. We noted earlier that Sears adopted this concept and applied general behavior methodology to its investigation. It is central also to Kagan and Moss. For them, the notion of sex-role identification is a core concept in influencing stability of behavior from childhood through adulthood. Events early in life lead not only to the child's sex-role identification but also determine his general social expectancy for all behavior. Boys are expected to behave more aggressively, more competently, and in more task-oriented fashions; girls are to be more nurturant, more person-oriented. Parent behavior in the first six years of life influences the child's identity and the standards he will set for typical sex-related behavior. Kagan and Moss conclude that the individual's own desire to make his behavior agree with the culture's definition of sex is a major factor determining the stability of his behavior over time.

Longitudinal studies indicate how very important it is to analyze data about children by sex as well as by age. They indicate the differential effects of parental behavior on boys and girls. This should not surprise us, but it often gets overlooked. In both the cognitive and affective aspects of the self, boys and girls view themselves differently, tend to use different learning styles, tend to evaluate different aspects of self and world as important. The origins lie both in biology and in differential treatment.

Unfortunately, most of the children studied in longitudinal research have been middle-class, from somewhat stable families, where conditions might generally foster the mix of intellectual and emotional inputs that lead to positive views of the self. They fit Lois Murphy's observation that

"Each experience of mastery and triumph sets the stage for better efforts in the next experience. Confidence, hope, and a sense of self-worth are increased along with the increase in cognitive and motor skills, which can contribute to better use of the resources."[14] Their world provides them with both intellectual challenge and emotional support. Both the cognitive and affective "matches"—the connection between the child's motives and cognitive level on the one hand and the experiences being offered to him on the other[15,16]—are in phase. His positive self-image receives verification from his competence in dealing with the world.

Unfortunately, not all children have the sense of triumph described by Lois Murphy, nor do their selves match the world's demands. Yarrow's studies[17] of maternal deprivation indicate the difficulties encountered by children who lack a mother figure to provide them with some stable anchorage points. In the social domain, Clark,[18] Deutsch,[19] Smilansky,[20] Marans,[21] and Wortis,[22] among others, point out the devastating effects of social deprivation on building positive self-esteem. Although the child's view of himself does not mirror and is not an exact replica of his world's picture of him, for many youngsters it comes quite close. If the larger society conceives of the child as not worthwhile and demonstrates consistently to him that it so judges him, it is difficult for the child to value himself. Children in the ghetto, children classified as slow learners, children who for a variety of reasons are told even in these early years that they are not quite good enough or smart enough or handsome enough tend to devalue themselves and thus to set the stage for continuously poorer levels of performance than might otherwise be their lot. These images are already set before entry into school.[23] Children growing up in psychologically disorganized homes suffer similar fates, as Pavenstedt[24] has indicated about South Boston children.

"As the twig is bent . . ." has long been part of Western folklore. Scientific data now support this view. The origins of the self lie in the early years. How the child will see himself is influenced by the way he is treated, the opportunities provided for him, how he is evaluated as he copes with these opportunities, and how he perceives these evaluations.

If these early years are crucial in determining school performance through the mechanism of the self-concept, then society cannot shrug off its responsibility. For very young children, negative self-views may be as damaging as physical illness or actual physical handicap. We are rapidly making provision for medical help. We need to create nurturing environments early in life so that children's concepts of themselves may possibly emerge as positive. Whether the school systems as now constructed are the appropriate agencies to reach down to the younger years is open to debate. The example of Head Start programs and the present Parent and Child Center movement indicate that new social agencies consisting of and requiring the participation of those for whom the service is intended may provide effective vehicles for change. What is needed is education so designed that parents can provide children not only with an *affective* climate which tells them they are loved and worthy but also with a *cognitive* climate that allows the child to be competent as well as feel loved. Adequate self-esteem requires this combination.

A characteristic of the American society is its own self-concept that it is capable of solving the problems which afflict it, once the problems are pointed out. The issue is clear. What is required now are social engineering skills. Intervention is essential. We have some ideas of what it should be and who should render it. Now we need to develop the types of programs which provide for all children the psychological inputs which lead to positive self-esteem.

REFERENCES

1. H. S. Sullivan, *The Interpersonal Theory of Psychiatry*. New York: W. W. Norton, 1953.

2. René Spitz, *The First Year of Life*. New York: International Universities Press, 1965.

3. L. Lipsitt, "Learning in the Human Infant," in H. W. Stevenson, E. H. Hess, and H. L. Rheingold (eds.), *Early Behavior: Comparative and Developmental Approaches*. New York: Wiley, 1967, pp. 225–48.

4. E. Erikson, *Childhood and Society*. New York: Norton, 1951.

5. R. Sears, E. Maccoby, and H. Levin, *Patterns of Child Rearing*. Evanston, Ill.: Row Peterson, 1957.

6. R. Sears, *et al., Identification and Child Rearing*. Stanford, Calif.: Stanford University Press, 1965.

7. G. H. Mead, *Mind, Self and Society*. Chicago: University of Chicago, 1940.

8. S. Smilansky, *The Effects of Sociodramatic Play on Disadvantaged Pre-school Children*. New York: Wiley, 1968.

9. T. Décarie, *Intelligence and Affectivity in Early Childhood*. New York: International Universities Press, 1965. (Translated by Elisabeth and Lewis Brandt)

10. J. Piaget, *Les Relations Entre l'Affectivité et l'Intelligence Dans la Développement Mental de l'Enfant*. Paris: Centre de Documentation Universitaire, 1954.

11. B. Bloom, *Stability and Change in Human Characteristics*. New York: Wiley, 1964.

12. N. Bayley, "Consistency of Maternal and Child Behaviors in the Berkeley Growth Study," *Vita Humana*, 1964, pp. 73–95.

13. J. Kagan and H. Moss, *Birth to Maturity*. New York: Wiley, 1962.

14. L. Murphy and associates, *The Widening World of Childhood*. New York: Basic Books, 1962.

15. J. McV. Hunt, *Intelligence and Experience*. New York: The Ronald Press, 1961.

16. Ira J. Gordon, *Studying the Child in School*. New York: Wiley, 1966.

17. L. Yarrow, "Separation from Parents During Early Childhood," in Martin L. Hoffman and Lois W. Hoffman (eds.), *Review of Child Development Research*, Vol. 1. New York: Russell Sage, 1964, pp. 89–136.

18. K. Clark, *Dark Ghetto*. New York: Harper & Row, 1965.

19. M. Deutsch and associates, *The Disadvantaged Child*. New York: Basic Books, 1967.

20. Smilansky, *op. cit.*

21. A. Marans, D. Meers, and D. Huntington, "The Children's Hospital in Washington, D.C.," in Laura L. Dittmann (ed.), *Early Child Care, the New Perspective*. New York: Atherton, 1968, pp. 287–301.

22. H. Wortis, *et al.*, "Child-rearing Practices in a Low Socio-economic Group," *Pediatrics*, 1933, pp. 298–307.

23. B. Long and E. Henderson, "Social Schemata of School Beginners: Some Demographic Correlates," in *Proceedings*, 75th Annual Convention, American Psychological Association, 1967, pp. 329–30.

24. E. Pavenstedt (ed.), *The Drifters*. Boston: Little, Brown, 1967.

27.

Early childhood education: for what goals?

MILTON J. E. SENN

As Alexander Pope warned, "A little knowledge is a dangerous thing." The author of this selection views with alarm the tendency to emphasize the transmission of information as the "be all and end all" of education. He is concerned that the emotional and human relation aspects of living may be ignored when teaching is oriented toward rote memorization and answer giving. This, he says, is the difference between educating for intelligence and teaching for intellect.

The editors tend to agree with the contention that contact with human beings is more important than stimulation from impersonal objects. We also would agree that the work of teachers who construe their function as one of information transmission might better be done by teaching machines and computers. Stimuli of a factual and skill nature and the necessary reinforcements can be more consistently and patiently presented mechanically. Further, the learner is not negatively valued or minimized as a person. In our opinion, effectiveness in teaching facts is one of the reasons for the current entrancement with mechanical models of learning. It is easier to

Children, 16(No. 1):8–13, 1969. Milton J. E. Senn, Sterling Professor of Pediatrics and Psychiatry, Yale University.

turn the job of instruction over to the ubiquitous machine than to look carefully at the interpersonal relationship between teacher and student and its effects upon learning. We think machines only can teach a learner to function in a mechanical manner. If pupils are to learn to interact as human beings, effective human models are necessary. What is your assessment of teachers and teaching machines?

THERE IS today a cleavage between educators of young children who favor educational practices based on concepts of the child in relation to his *whole* emotional-cognitive development and those who favor practices aimed only at developing certain measurable skills defined as "intelligence."

In my opinion the sane perspectives on the hierarchy of values have been turned on end. We are now urged to believe that highly structured, mechanical, and rigid practices in teaching are superior to those that are flexible, child-experience oriented, and focused on human relationships. We are being led to expect both immediate and lasting results from programs aimed at speeding up the learning in the youngest minds. Emphasis on the intelligence quotient as the measure of achievement continues despite strong evidence that questions the validity of this practice.

Obviously the changing nature of societies forces a reconsideration of how to educate a new generation. The Russian launching of Sputnik in 1956 triggered a near phobia about making American minds equal, if not superior, to those of our cold war competitors. More recently the civil rights movement has moved us as never before to take stock of our human resources. Now there is a readiness to accept the long-held premise of persons in the field of child development that the beginnings of waste start in the early years, and research in the education of young children is proliferating.

We have had few great educational theorists in the United States other than G. Stanley Hall, John Dewey, and William James to lead the way. For the most part we have looked to foreign countries for basic theories about the nature of man, his attributes, and his needs and for concepts of how these are to be dealt with educationally—to such geniuses as Jean Jacques Rousseau, John Locke, Henry Pestalozzi, Friedrich Wilhelm Froebel, Maria Montessori, and of course Sigmund Freud. To this list has recently been added the contemporary Swiss epistemologist, Jean Piaget, who has had a profound influence on American psychologists and researchers in child development since the early 1950's.

PIAGET'S INFLUENCE

Piaget and his colleagues in Geneva are primarily recognized for the work they have done in the field of cognition, although Piaget has been mostly concerned with the nature of knowledge and with the structures and processes by which it is acquired. His discoveries that experiences in the first 5 years of life are vital and long lasting and that infantile sensory-motor coordinations are forerunners of the form and content of adult thought substantiate the theories of Freud. While Piaget is informed about Freudian theories and has long realized the importance of emotional processes in learning, he has said that time has limited his considerations to study of *intellectual development* and that he would leave to others the consideration of *feeling states* and their relationship to learning. However, few of his disciples in the field of experimental psychology have been inclined to integrate their research on cognition with research on personality development.

Piaget views the growth of the structures of knowing as proceeding over time, beginning in early infancy and ending in adolescence.[1] Not only is there a distinct beginning and ending in the schema he presents, but there are also certain *critical periods* along the way. Human intelligence (or knowing) begins with the phase of sensory-motor responsiveness. The infant is equipped by heredity and constitution with reflex patterns for reacting to touch, vision, sound, and kinesthesis; his behavior is shaped by external demands imposed by the environment; response to these demands goads his mental growth.

As he assimilates his experiences, the baby learns strategies for coping with both external and internal demands, and with time he organizes the information he has acquired into systems. By the end of his first year the child is able to construct a theory of the world that transcends direct sensory experience, as when he appreciates the existence of an object he cannot see and develops skill in searching for the unseen. By the time he develops language, which is dependent on his sensory-motor functions, he is more manipulatable in thought and more susceptible to social correction. We say he is able to "internalize his actions," to use his mind and proceed from perception and manipulation to reflection.

The phases of intellectual development follow each other, not in strictly chronological fashion, but in a sequential and orderly manner from early infancy into early adolescence. Piaget believes that these phases may be accelerated to some extent by manipulating the environment but that such manipulation will only be effective up to a certain point. The environment *is* important but only as a child is able to pay attention to it, and this ability depends on the degree of assimilation which has taken place. However, the greater the *variety* of experiences a child copes with, the greater becomes his ability to cope.

Piaget never points to any practical implications of his work. Aware of what some of his followers are doing in the application of his studies to the education of young children, he has issued a timely warning by inquiring, "What is learning for—to know a certain *number* of things, or to be capable of creating or inventing new things?"

There continues to be much unclarity in the minds of many of Piaget's adherents about the meaning of the term "cognition." Piaget himself, pointing out that his theories are unfinished, continues to change his emphasis, concepts, and terminology.

Cognitive psychologists interested in infant behavior and learning have also found encouragement in the research of other scientists who have studied babies reared in different environments. René Spitz and others, for example, have reported harmful effects of impersonal care and under-stimulation suffered by babies reared in foundling hospitals.[2] Although the emphasis in such research was at first on affect deprivation, later investigators have reported damage to cognitive functions as well.[3]

EARLY STIMULATION

For the past several years there has been a burgeoning of investigation into the physiological, psycho-social, and intellectual deficiencies resulting from understimulation and of efforts to prevent and ameliorate deficiencies by sensory stimulation. Studies of sense organ stimulation in newborn infants have had special appeal to investigators. Often this research has resembled the experiments conducted in Russia for over a decade, in Moscow under A. S. Louria and in Leningrad under the Pavlovian-trained pediatrician Nicholas Krasnagorski. The American investigators, like the Russian, have found that a baby not only changes his physiological reflex responses after sensory stimulation, but that he learns to change his behavior if he feels rewarded by the process of stimulation. For example, newborn babies learn how to change their rate of sucking and how to move a mobile with their toes when pleasurably stimulated by sight and sound. The inference from such findings is that babies can learn more than we realize if they are taught by techniques that stimulate the nervous system.

The Russians believe that through conditioning they can overcome the ill effects of prematurity very early in infancy. While this theory has never been validated elsewhere, many American cognitive psychologists believe that through early stimulation of the central nervous system of normal babies, they may speed up their intellectual development so that by the time the children are 4 years old they will be greatly beyond the normally expected level. Since it is commonly believed that by age 4 a child has attained half of his final intellectual capability, the race seems to be on not only to have American children attain their full intellectual potential before adolescence, but to keep it increasing to a higher degree than is normally attained.

Some cognitive psychologists believe that future generations can reach 30 IQ points ahead of the present generation through better management of their early environment, beginning in infancy. Yet the definition of intelligence remains unclear. Moreover, there is no agreement on the details of *how* and *when* to manipulate the environment.

In reviews of the research on stimulation of infants, one rarely finds words of warning or descriptions of any harmful effects of early stimulation. But the research of Burton L. White of Harvard points in that direction.[4] In studying institutionalized infants, he found what Spitz and others had described: delays in motor response due to lack of visual stimulation. In attempts to find ways of preventing such deficiencies, White studied a group of 6-day-old normal babies in a hospital. He saw that they got more physical handling, more opportunity to look around, and more bright objects to see than is usual. He found that this special stimulation upset the babies; they cried a lot and paid less attention to their surroundings. However, when he provided similar ministrations to babies $2\frac{1}{2}$ months old, favorable responses resulted; these babies smiled at objects, vocalized, and seemed happier than unstimulated controls. Thus, the timing and amount of external stimulation are important.

The Russians report that although a newborn baby may be helped to mature more rapidly by conditioning, all newborns do not respond favorably to such treatment. This is because there is a basic difference in equipment in each individual, which makes the *timing* of the conditioning important. As one would surmise, the more mature babies respond more favorably than the less mature. Nevertheless, in Russia all normal newborns in hospital nurseries are stimulated visually and aurally; "teachers" sing to them at prescribed times each day, dangle colored rings before their eyes, and shake a tambourine next to their ears.

John L. Fuller, senior staff scientist at the Jackson Laboratory in Bar Harbor, Me., has also substantiated the theory that timing and quality of stimulation are important. Experimenting with dogs, he discovered that animals that had been isolated and deprived of sensory stimulation from birth could be helped to overcome their deficits only if the changes in their environment were made gradually and in a way that permitted their sensory-motor capacities to adapt slowly. When the transition from the depriving to the stimulating environment was made too rapidly, the adaptive mechanisms were overstrained and the dogs became especially fearful.[5]

Fuller described another important aspect of appropriate stimulation when he reported that only when the stimulated animals' stress was reduced by stroking and handling were they able to make any contact with other objects, whether toys or humans, without irrational fear. These observations tend to verify the conviction of many teachers that contact with humans is more important than stimulation from impersonal objects and that human relationships are the primary factors in helping children to learn.

Other psychologists have found that children who have been deprived and are abruptly exposed to new stimulating experiences do not learn readily, because they become excited and have less control over their impulses than usual.

Another researcher speaks to the question of appropriate quality of stimulation when he describes his longitudinal studies on infants from 4 months to 4 years of age. Measuring how much babies in the first year of life perceive and understand of their environment, Jerome Kagan of Harvard University observed differences between babies from different socioeconomic backgrounds. The *distinctiveness* of the stimulation, more than the *amount* of stimulation, marked the difference between children from middle and lower socioeconomic groups. Kagan has concluded that learning should be fostered in infancy through a *distinctive* (not yet clearly defined) stimulation provided by parents and that all parents need education about this process. He also believes that the classroom environment for children must be designed to fit the child's needs, and that these needs vary according to the child's early rearing.[6] Thus, inappropriate stimulation, as well as overstimulation, may be as disastrous for children as understimulation.

PRESCHOOL PROGRAMS

Awareness of the great difference in learning between slum children and those reared in more affluent circumstances led to the founding of Project Headstart in 1965. Unfortunately, it was begun as a crash program, without sufficient time to recruit well-trained, experienced teachers. Many of those who accepted teaching and administrative roles received only short periods of training before they began to work. Often they did not know the characteristics of children aged 3 to 5 years of any racial or socioeconomic background, nor how to fashion appropriate learning opportunities, and they were unprepared for the upsurge of their own feelings in dealing with the children brought to them. Therefore, many of the Headstart classes have failed to give children enough of the kinds of experience they most needed.

This is not to say that gains have not resulted from Headstart. Although the greatest gains may come from the early recognition of disease and the correction of physical defects in children who otherwise would not have received any medical care, children may also have gained educationally by becoming better informed about themselves, their neighborhoods, and the world around them. Too frequently, however, Headstart programs have failed to teach children what they were ready for, such as a better use of language for communication. On the other hand, in a few sophisticated urban communities, the Headstart program has become a pawn in the struggle between advocates of differing methods of early childhood education.

Some critics of the standard, play-oriented nursery school approach have recommended more structured and didactic methods of teaching, not only for Headstart but for all early childhood education. A program originated by Siegfried Engelmann and Carl Bereiter at the University of Illinois concentrates on teaching children certain special *items* which these experimenters believe every child must know when he enters first grade. The program has three distinctive characteristics: (1) a high ratio of teachers to students, (2) reliance on drill, and (3) learning by rote. Children are made to repeat after the teacher the names of objects, numbers, and descriptions of various items held in front of them. No deviation of response is permitted; there is always only one right answer. The children are asked to answer in unison as well as individually. There is little tolerance or time for an original idea or an association spontaneously expressed. The conditions are conducive neither to curiosity nor to learning the connections between the things recited and things experienced.

This method of teaching will be remembered by many older persons as the kind they experienced in school. However, it differs in one respect in that the young pupils are not expected to sit impassively with hands folded. The children are encouraged to recite as a group with simultaneous loud clapping of hands and other rhythmic movements.

In watching any of these classes, one is impressed with the seriousness of the work at hand. The emphasis in learning is on work, not play, and on making everything count as if time needed to be conserved. Disapproval of mistakes is expressed not only in strong words but occasionally by slapping a child's hands, as if to emphasize that a person must feel guilty when he makes mistakes and that errors are similar to misbehavior in being punishable.

It is not easy to determine the effects of this kind of teaching on children. Engelmann and Bereiter have been pleased that their children learned to speak in sentences, progressed in arithmetic, reading, and spelling, and in general increased their IQ levels.[7] There are reports that the children have made gains in psycholinguistic ability. There are also reports that the children are very often tense and frightened and respond automatically. Some child development specialists doubt whether the results of rote learning will carry over into the later years of schooling and suggest that the children may even develop a fear of and distaste for school.

The question arises as to whether children taught by these methods have really learned to think, to reason, and to conceptualize, or merely to parrot unquestioningly whatever they are told by authoritarian teachers.

In an experiment at the University of Florida, mothers of very young babies are being taught in well-baby clinics how to use toys so that their children will learn concepts of size, relationships, and color. This program is similar to one in Russia wherein mothers are taught how to play with their children and to use toys recommended by the poly-clinic staff. The Florida experimenters, like the Russian, emphasize attention to small muscle movements, exercises, and body massage as ways of producing kinesthetic stimulation and fostering mental development. Here again, the emphasis seems to be on how to get the children to learn *more* and to develop various *skills* without any attempt to foster their creativity or individuality.

Teaching the use of toys in such a didactic manner resembles the methods of Montessori. This Italian physician-educationist worked with slum children 3 to 7 years of age in a day-care center in Rome in the early part of this century. She invented educational toys and used them in didactic teaching to help children develop their intelligence. She also sought to inculcate discipline and good habits of study. But in contrast to some present-day American educators, she was also concerned with the cultivation of independence and curiosity as well as persistence in learning.

The Montessori system never really got started in the United States until about 10 years ago, when it suddenly spread across the country. However, there have been so much unorthodoxy and deviation from the original methods that it is rare to find two Montessori nursery schools in which the methods are applied alike. The revisionists have tended to favor modification in the use of the equipment, flexibility in programing, and more free play.

What the long-term effects of these various techniques will be remains unclear. Those researchers who are providing more stimulation to children have not demonstrated that sensory stimulation enhances the use and understanding of symbols, which are necessary for the development of a sense of meaning. Those who use teaching machines acknowledge that unless wisely used such products of educational technology could destroy initiative and individuality, "making all men alike and not necessarily alike in nice ways."

Barbara Biber of the Bank Street College of Education has pointed out that "the method, through its effects on attitude and therefore on motivation, becomes a secondary determinant of how far the original learning goal will be realized."[8]

DEFINING GOALS

Program planners today in discussing appropriate goals for early childhood education show little understanding of *the difference between intelligence and intellect* and to which of these qualities educational efforts should be directed.

The historian, Richard Hofstadter of Columbia University, however, has given much thought to the differences between intelligence and intellect. "Intelligence," he says, "is an excellence of mind that is employed in a fairly narrow, immediate, and predictable range. Intellect on the other hand is the critical, creative, and contemplative side of mind. Whereas *intelligence* seeks to grasp, manipulate, reorder, adjust, *intellect* evaluates and looks for the meanings of situations as a whole. It implies a special sense of the ultimate value and the act of comprehension. Socrates struck its essence when he said that the unexamined life is not worth living."[9]

In assessing the effects of programs, emphasis too often has been on measuring cognitive development or other learning on the basis of changes in IQ scores. Many of the new teaching techniques do seem to bring about significant increases in IQ scores. Others, however, do not effect gains as measured by tests, yet do help disadvantaged children develop skills they would not otherwise have. This discrepancy between test results and achievement has led clinical psychologists to reappraise the standard tests of intelligence, and to attempt to design substitutes that take into consideration the tested child's cultural heritage and areas of deprivation and that can detect gains in ability to learn as well as changes in IQ.

Martin Deutsch of the Institute of Developmental Studies, New York City, in discussing the relevance of intelligence testing to work with socially deprived children, warns that the current faith in test results tends to overshadow another worthwhile source of evaluation—reports of individual teachers. He points out that teachers stimulate *curiosity* and *initiative* in children, two characteristics that the usual testing in schools does not measure.

In early childhood education, as in all child care and rearing, we should be concerned with the "whole child," the total self, not just the development of certain mental characteristics or the learning of skills. The conception of the whole child need not be as generalized, vague, or overflowing with inspirational platitudes as some people have made it. The "whole child" represents a composite organism, the physical, emotional, and social self that learns through a variety of processes, cognitive learning being only one important component and one which also involves feelings and emotions.

When I say I believe in helping children experience joy and happiness in learning, I do not mean protecting them artificially against the crises of life or from all experiences of fear, anxiety, and unhappiness. When I say I want children to feel free to ask questions, to explore, to experiment, to be spontaneous, I am not advocating license in a classroom that is unsupervised or led by a teacher who is incompetent or irresponsible. I expect teachers to be informed about appropriate curricular materials, but also to know how to incite the deep interest of children through their teaching skill and their relationship with pupils, without resorting to pedagogical tricks. I expect educational programs to help children find themselves as individuals—learners, thinkers, doers, persons with feelings, increasing clarity as to their identities, and appropriate roles in life. Such programs can be based on sound experimental studies of learning and teaching and the results evaluated by rigorous methods that go beyond the measurement of changes in IQ.

Herbert J. Muller puts it this way: "What is needed, under any name, is the view of the biological whole man, a view in which we can make out the full value of the rational, but also the necessity of the nonrational—feeling, sentiment, desire. The activities of the higher motor centers, known as the exercise of reason, are the most advanced point in man's development, the finest means of adaptation; but they do *not by themselves* actually run man. They belong to a nervous system, which, in turn, is subordinate to the system of needs and purposes that is the whole organism."[10]

It seems to me that, at the very least, our goal should be the enhancement of all those factors that inevitably interact and foster the appropriate development of all parts of a child as he moves from infancy to childhood, then to adolescence and to adulthood. This will include the environmental, emotional, social, psychological influences as well as the cognitive and all other elements involved in learning. Above all we should avoid the myopia of fragmentation wherein understanding of the whole organism is obscured by focus on a part.

Children do need to learn how to adapt to a rapidly changing world, but a speedup in their learning, in skill proficiency, does not guarantee ability to cope with life at any tempo. Too frequently today the emphasis is on speed, on hastening learning. Children are denied time to reflect, to cogitate, to dream. I believe this denial hinders the development of the intellect as distinguished from development of intelligence.

By concentrating on intelligence and discouraging intellect, current educational methods may lead to the unexamined life deplored by Socrates. Yet without the ability to examine life, the individual is impoverished and society is deprived; it could be that without the ability and the will to examine life we may stop living.

What goals are we striving for in education and child rearing? My personal hope is that our passion for mass education will be founded primarily on belief in the desirability of developing the mind, and on a pride in learning and culture for their own sakes, rather than on political or economic benefits; and having set that goal, that we will implement it by doing whatever is necessary, so that we may finally realize the kind of education we have idealized in words for over 200 years.

REFERENCES

1. Piaget, J.: Six psychological studies. Random House, New York. 1967.
2. Spitz, R. A.: Hospitalism: an inquiry into the genesis of psychiatric conditions in early childhood. *In* The psychoanalytic study of the child. Vol. I. International Universities Press, New York. 1945.
3. Goldfarb, W.: Emotional and intellectual consequences of psychologic deprivation in infancy: a re-evaluation. *In* Psychopathology of childhood. Grune & Stratton, New York. 1955.
4. White, B. L.; Held, R.: Plasticity of sensory-motor development in the

young infant. *In* The causes of behavior: readings in child development and educational psychology. Allyn & Bacon, Boston. 1966.

5. Fuller, J. L.: Experimental deprivation and later behavior. *Science,* December 29, 1967.

6. Kagan, J.; Lewis, M.: Studies of attention in the human infant. *Merrill-Palmer Quarterly,* April 1965.

7. Bereiter, C.; Engelmann, S.: Teaching disadvantaged children in the preschool. Prentice-Hall, Englewood Cliffs, N.J. 1966.

8. Biber, B.: A learning-teaching paradigm integrating intellectual and affective processes. *In* Behavioral science frontiers in education. John Wiley & Sons, New York. 1967.

9. Hofstadter, R.: Anti-intellectualism in American life. Vintage Books, New York. 1966.

10. Muller, H. J.: Science and criticism. Yale University Press, New Haven, Conn. 1964.

Middle childhood

28.

Early blocks to children's learning

ROBERT D. HESS
VIRGINIA SHIPMAN

This selection fits well with the emphasis these readings have placed upon learning experiences. It focuses upon one of mankind's most important relationships: that which exists between mother and child. And it relates this to one of mankind's most important skills: verbal communication. Further, the concept is developed that a lack of opportunity to master this essential skill underlies the social condition we have come to call disadvantaged.

The ability to verbalize is so important to human development that anthropologists sometimes are tempted to engage in a sort of chicken-egg speculation. Has man's remarkable brain evolved because of his ability to speak or has his verbal ability come about because of his mental capacity? (See selections 17 and 18.) However that may be, the two appear both concomitant and inseparable. The developers of the most widely used measures of intelligence recognize vocabulary subtests as possessing high reliability and validity. And there is speculation and some agreement that an individual's concept of self is directly affected by his ability to use verbal symbols.

Human interaction is essentially a process of communication and communication is largely a matter of verbalization. Most emotional upset occurs because of ineffective communication or interpersonal-transaction ability and because of concepts of self which are inadequate and difficult to live with. The editors are convinced that the effective individual learns to apply verbal symbols and techniques to his psycho-personal as well as his physical-environment problems. Like the authors, we think this process can be taught.

Children, 12:189–194, 1965. Robert D. Hess, Chairman, Committee on Human Development, The University of Chicago; Virginia Shipman, Research Associate and Assistant Professor, The University of Chicago.

Based on a paper presented at the National Conference on Day Care Services. The research described is supported by the Children's Bureau, the Ford Foundation, and The University of Chicago.

IN THE context of today's urgent need for preschool education, the central question is: Can we successfully intervene on a massive scale in the cycle of generation-to-generation transmission of poverty and semi-illiteracy? Any answer given at the present time would be based more on optimism than on experience and results. It would be naive, misleading, and irresponsible to make promises of easy success and instant results from large scale programs intended to raise the educational level of children and families of low socioeconomic groups. There is some reason to be hopeful, but, at the present time, little basis for unrestrained enthusiasm.

Research now under way at the Urban Child Center of the University of Chicago is attempting to reach a greater understanding of two related questions: (1) When we strip away personal concern and sympathy for human tragedy, and after we discard the political slogans, what *is* cultural deprivation and how does it act to shape and depress the resources of the human mind? (2) How does cultural disadvantage affect the mind of the young child?

Our hypotheses are these: first, that the behavior which leads to social, educational, and economic poverty is socialized in early childhood, that is, it is learned; and, second, that the central factor involved in the effects of cultural deprivation is a lack of cognitive meaning in the mother-child communication system.

We proceed on the assumptions (1) that the structure of the social system and the structure of the family shape communication and language; and (2) that language shapes thought and cognitive styles of problem-solving. In the deprived-family context, this means that the nature of the control system which relates parent to child restricts the number and kind of alternatives for action and thought that are opened to the child. Such constriction precludes a tendency for the child to reflect, to consider and choose among alternatives for speech and action, and develops modes for dealing with stimuli and with problems which are impulsive rather than reflective, which deal with the immediate rather than the future, and which are disconnected rather than sequential.

This position draws from the work of Basil Bernstein of the University of London. In his view, language conditions what the child learns, and how he learns, thus setting limits to his future learning.[1] He identifies two forms of communication codes or styles of verbal behavior: *restricted* and *elaborate*.

Restricted codes are stereotyped, limited, and condensed, lacking in specificity and in the exactness needed for precise conceptualization and differentiation. Sentences are short, simple, often unfinished; there is little use of subordinate clauses for elaborating the content of sentences: it is a language of implicit meaning, easily understood and commonly shared. It is the language often used in impersonal situations when the intent is to promote solidarity or reduce tension. Restricted codes are nonspecific cliches, statements, or observations about events, made in general terms that will be readily understood. By its nature, this mode limits the range and detail of concept and information involved.

Elaborate codes are those in which communication is individualized. The resultant message is specific to a particular situation, topic, and person: it is more particular, more differentiated, and more precise; and it permits expression of a wider and more complex range of thought, tending toward discrimination among cognitive and affective content.

Such early experiences affect not only the communication modes and cognitive structure; they also establish potential patterns of relationship with the external world. One of the dynamic features of Bernstein's work is his view of language as social behavior. As such, language is used by participants of a social network to elaborate and express interpersonal relationships and thus shape and determine these relationships. An understanding of the integral association between language and social structure is of critical importance for an understanding of the effects of poverty upon children. Within the individual family, this association emerges in terms of the principles which govern the decision-making activities, which, themselves, help regulate the nature and amount of social exchange.

TWO FAMILY TYPES

The interlacing of social interaction and language is illustrated by the distinction Bernstein makes between two types of families—those oriented toward control by *status* appeal, or ascribed role norms, and those oriented toward *persons*.[2]

In status-oriented families, behavior tends to be regulated in terms of role expectations. There is little opportunity in these families for the unique characteristics of the child to influence the decision-making process or the interaction between parent and child, the internal or personal needs of the children not being influential as a basis for decision. Norms of behavior are stressed with such imperatives as "You must do this because I say so," "Girls don't act like that," or other statements which rely, for justification, on the status of the participants or a behavior norm.

In the person-oriented family, the unique characteristics of the child modify status demands and are taken into account in interaction. The decisions of this type of family are individualized and less frequently related to status or role ascriptions. Behavior is justified in terms of feelings, preference, personal and unique reactions, and subjective states. This philosophy not only permits, but demands, an elaborated linguistic code and a wide range of linguistic and behavior alternatives in interpersonal interaction. Status-oriented families may be regulated by less individuated commands, messages, and responses than person-oriented families. (Indeed, by its nature, the status-oriented family relies more heavily on a restricted code; the verbal exchange is inherent in the structure, regulates it and is regulated by it.)

These distinctions may be clarified by two examples of mother-child communication, using these two types of codes.

Assume that the emotional climate of two homes is approximately the same, the significant difference between them being in the style of communication employed. A child is playing noisily in the kitchen with an assortment of pots and pans when the telephone rings. In one home, the mother says, "Be quiet," "Shut up," or gives some other short, peremptory command, and answers the phone while the child sits still on the floor. In the other home, the mother asks: "Would you keep quiet while I answer the phone?"

The questions our study poses are these: What inner response is elicited in the child in each of these two situations, and what is the effect upon his developing cognitive network of concepts and meaning?

In one instance, the child is asked for a simple mental response. He is asked to attend to an uncomplicated message and to make a conditioned response (to comply); he is not called upon to reflect or make mental discriminations. In the other example, the child is required to follow two or three ideas; he is asked to relate his behavior to a time dimension; he must think of this behavior in relation to its effect upon another person; he must perform a complicated task in following the communication of his mother, in that his relationship to her is mediated in part through concepts and shared ideas; and his mind is stimulated or exercised (in an elementary fashion) by a more elaborate and complex verbal communication initiated by the mother.

As objects of these two divergent styles of communication, repeated in various ways, in similar situations and circumstances during the preschool years, these two imaginary children would be expected to develop significantly different verbal facility and cognitive equipment by the time they entered the public school system.

In our project, we view the child as an organism which receives a great deal of information of many kinds, much more than he can accommodate. What he responds to, how he interprets stimuli, and how he reacts to it, the child learns in interaction with the environment. In other words, he is taught what to attend to, how to interpret messages, and how to respond. These patterns of cognitive activity, socialized in early experience in the home, become the basis upon which the child's further cognitive development proceeds.

An analysis of language and social structure is necessarily concerned with the consequences of linguistic codes and their accompanying patterns of social interaction upon the developing cognitive faculties of the child. It is our argument that person-oriented families tend to justify behavior and emphasize its consequences; and that status-oriented families ask for rote learning and acceptance of the *status quo*—that is, they use a more rigid learning and teaching model, in which compliance, rather than rationale, is stressed.

THE PROJECT

For our research, 160 Negro mothers and their 4 year old children were selected from four different socioeconomic levels: Group A came from college-educated professional, executive, and managerial occupational levels; Group B from skilled blue-collar occupational levels, with not more than high school education; Group C from unskilled or semi-skilled occupational levels, with predominantly elementary school education; and Group D from unskilled or semiskilled occupational levels, with fathers absent and family supported by public assistance.

These mothers were interviewed twice in their homes and brought to the university for testing in an interaction session between mother and child in which the mother was taught three simple tasks by the staff member, then asked to teach these tasks to the child.

One of these tasks was to sort or group a number of plastic toys by color and by function. The second was to sort eight blocks by two characteristics simultaneously. The third required mother and child to work together to copy five designs on a toy called "Etch-a-Sketch."

The objective of the project is to relate the behavior and performance of individual mothers to the cognitive and scholastic behavior of their own children. We expect to follow the children of the study through the first 4 years of school, to obtain data on a more complete range of behavior. At our present, relatively early, stage of analysis, data are being examined in terms of social class differences among the four socioeconomic groups of the study—professional (middle), skilled workers (upper lower), unskilled (lower lower), and public assistance (AFDC). At this point in the project, our data about the cognitive behavior and language skills of the children are limited.

The wide range of individual differences in linguistic and interactional styles of these mothers may be illustrated by excerpts from recordings of one of the structured teaching situations, the task of the mothers being to teach the child how to group, or sort, a small number of toys.

The first mother outlines the task for the child, giving sufficient help and explanation to permit the child to proceed on his own. She says:

> "All right, this board is the place where we put the little toys. First of all, you're supposed to learn how to place them according to color. Can you do that? The things that are all the same color you put in one section; in the second section you put another group of colors and in the third section you put the last group of colors. Can you do that? Or would you like to see me do it first?"
>
> *Child:* "I want to do it."

This mother has given explicit information about the task and what is expected of the child; she has offered support and help of various kinds; and she has made it clear that she impelled the child to perform.

The style of a second mother is not quite so easily grasped by the child. She says, in introducing the same task:

"Now I'll take them off the board; now you put them all back on the board. What are these?"
Child: "A truck."
"All right, just put them right here; put the other one right here; all right the other one there."

This mother relies more on physical signs and nonverbal communication in her commands; she does not define the task for the child; the child is not provided with ideas or information that he can grasp in attempting to solve the problem; neither is he told what to expect or, even in general terms, what the task is.

A third mother is even less explicit. She introduces the task as follows:

"I've got some chairs and cars. Do you want to play the game?"
The child does not respond.
The mother continues: "O.K. What's this?"
Child: "A wagon?"
Mother: "This is not a wagon. What's this?"

The conversation continues with this sort of exchange. Here again, the child is not provided with the essential information he needs to solve or to understand the problem. There is clearly some coercion, on the part of the mother, for the child to perform; but the child has not been told what he is to do.

Each teaching session was concluded with an assessment by a staff member of the extent to which the child had learned the concepts taught by the mother. His achievement was scored in two ways: first, the ability to place or sort the objects correctly; and second, the ability to verbalize the principle on which the sorting or grouping was made.

SOCIAL CLASS DIFFERENCES

There were marked social class differences in the ability of the children to learn from their mothers in the teaching sessions. Children from middle-class homes ranked above children from the lower socio-economic levels in performance on these sorting tasks, particularly in offering verbal explanations as to the basis for sorting. Over 60 percent of middle-class children placed the objects correctly on all tasks. The performance of children from the other groups ranged as low as 33 percent correct. Approximately 40 percent of the middle-class children who were successful were able to verbalize the sorting principle. Children from the lower socio-economic groups were, on the whole, less able to explain the sorting principle. These differences clearly paralleled the relative abilities and teaching skills of the mothers from the different groups.

The differences among the four socioeconomic levels were apparent not only in sorting and verbal skills, but also in the mother's ability to regulate her own behavior and her child's in performing tasks which require planning or care rather than verbal or conceptual skill.

These differences were revealed by the mother-child performance on the "Etch-a-Sketch" task.

An "Etch-a-Sketch" toy is a small, flat box with a screen on which lines can be drawn by a device within the box. The marker is controlled by two knobs: one for horizontal movement, the other for vertical. The mother is assigned one knob, the child the other. The mother is then shown several designs which are to be reproduced. Together, they attempt to copy the models. The products are scored by measuring deviations from the original designs. The mother decides when their product is a satisfactory copy of the original designs.

These sessions were recorded, and the nonverbal interaction was described by an observer. Some of the most relevant results were these: middle-class mothers and children performed better on the task (14.6 points) than mothers and children from the other groups (9.2; 8.3; 9.5). Mothers of the three lower socioeconomic groups were relatively persistent, rejecting more complete figures than the middle-class mothers; mothers from the middle class praised the child's efforts more than other mothers did, but gave just as much criticism; the child's cooperation, as rated by the observer, was as good or better in low socioeconomic groups as in middle-class pairs; and there was little difference between the groups in affect expressed to the child by the mother.

In these data, as in others, the mothers differed relatively little in the affective elements of their interaction with their children. The gross differences appeared in the verbal and cognitive environments which they presented. The significance of the maternal environment lies not only in the lack of verbal exchange but also in the kind of interaction that develops between learner and teacher. Mothers of blue-collar classes appear to be socializing passive learning styles on the part of the child, teaching him to be docile in such learning situations—in contrast to the more active, initiatory behavior of the child from a middle-class home.

ONE QUESTION, SEVERAL RESPONSES

The women in the study also varied in their perception of school. Applying Bernstein's concept of status-oriented and person-oriented families to our data, we analyzed maternal responses to the question: "Imagine your child is old enough to go to public school for the first time. How would you prepare him? What would you tell him?"

One mother, who was person-oriented and used elaborated verbal codes, replied as follows:

> "First of all, I would remind her that she was going to school to learn, that her teacher would take my place, and that she would be expected to follow instructions. Also that her time was to be spent mostly in the classroom with other children, and that she could consult with her teacher for assistance on any questions or problems that she might have."
> "Anything else?"
> "No. Anything else would probably be confusing for her at her age."

In terms of promoting educability, what did this mother do in her response? First, she was informative, presenting the school situation as comparable to one already familiar to the child; second, she offered reassurance and support to help the child deal with anxiety; third, she described the school situation as one which involves a personal relationship between the child and the teacher; and fourth, she presented the classroom situation as one in which the child was to learn.

A second mother responded as follows to the same question:

> "Well, John, it's time to go to school now. You must know how to behave. The first day at school you should be a good boy and should do just what the teacher tells you to do."

In contrast to the first mother, what did this mother do? First, she defined the role of the child as passive and compliant; second, the central issues she presented were those dealing with authority and the institution, rather than with learning; third, the relationship and roles she portrayed were sketched in terms of status and role expectations, rather than in personal terms; and fourth, her message was general, restricted, and vague, lacking information about how to deal with the problems of school, except by passive compliance.

These responses illustrated the tendency for status-oriented families and relationships to restrict the linguistic codes used in communication. The child who comes to school with a status orientation is prepared to engage in rote learning with passive acceptance of school authority in the learning situation. His initiative and participation in the learning possibilities of the school are meager. Not all such children accept the authority of the school in this unquestioning fashion, but they have few alternatives except to resist and rebel. The range of choice open to them is limited by the nature of the cognitive and interactional environment in which they have had experience.

A more detailed analysis of the mothers' responses to this question

grouped their statements as *imperative* or *instructive*. An imperative statement was defined as an unqualified injunction or command, such as:
"Mind the teacher and do what she tells you to do," or "The first thing
you have to do is be on time," or "Be nice and do not fight." An instructive
statement offers information or commands which carry a rationale or
justification for the rule to be observed. Examples: "If you are tardy, or if
you stay away from school, your marks will go down," or "I would tell him
about the importance of minding the teacher. The teacher needs his full
cooperation. She will have so many children that she won't be able to
pamper any youngster."

CULTURAL DEPRIVATION

Against this background let us return to the problem of the meaning,
or perhaps more correctly the lack of meaning in cultural deprivation.
One of the features of the behavior of mothers and children of lower socio-
economic class is a tendency to act without taking sufficient time for reflection and planning. In a sense, one might call this impulsive behavior,
not the acting out of unconscious or forbidden impulses, but a type of
activity in which a particular act seems to be unrelated to the act that preceded it, or to its consequences. In this sense, it lacks meaning; it is not
sufficiently related to the context in which it occurs, to the motivations of
the participants, or to the goals of the task.

This behavior may be verbal or motor and it shows itself in several
ways. On the "Etch-a-Sketch" task, for example, the mother may silently
watch a child make an error, and then punish him. Another mother will
anticipate the error and warn the child that he is about to reach a decision
point; she will prepare him by verbal and nonverbal cues to be careful,
to look ahead, and avoid the mistake. He is encouraged to reflect, to
anticipate the consequences of his action and in this way avoid error.

Recall the example of the mothers and the telephone calls: one child
was prompted to relate his actions to those of another person and to a
time dimension, to delay, to observe, and to consider the consequences; the
other was given a command that called for no reflection and did not require
him to relate his behavior to the context in which it occurred. This is a
model of a conditioned response, rather than a problem solving strategy. A
problem-solving approach requires reflection and the ability to weigh decisions, to choose among alternatives. The effect of restricted speech and of
status orientation is to foreclose the need for reflective weighing of alternatives and consequences. The use of an elaborated code, with its orientation
to persons and to consequences (including future), tends to produce
cognitive styles more easily adapted to problem-solving and reflection.

The objective of our study is to discover how teaching styles of the
mothers induce and shape learning styles and information-processing strat-

egies in the children. The picture that is beginning to emerge is that the meaning of deprivation is a deprivation of meaning—a cognitive environment in which behavior is controlled by status rules, rather than by attention to the individual characteristics of a specific situation, and one in which behavior is not mediated by verbal cues or by teaching which relates events to one another and the present to the future. This environment produces a child who relates to authority rather than to rationale; who, although often compliant, is not reflective in his behavior; and for whom the consequences of an act are largely considered in terms of immediate punishment or reward, rather than future effects and long-range goals.

PROGRAM IMPLICATIONS

If this picture is substantially correct, there are several implications for preschool programs.

For example, it would argue that enrichment for the sake of enrichment may miss the point—that it is not additional, or even more varied, stimulation that is needed, but experiences which give stimuli a pattern of sequential meaning. It argues that such programs must not merely teach the child new words, but must show the child how ideas and events are related to one another. And it argues that the transition that a child must make from a cognitive style of immediate reactivity to one of problem-solving must be made by experiences with authority, not with machines.

When the data are more complete, a more detailed analysis of the findings will enable us to examine the effect of maternal cognitive environments in terms of individual mother-child transactions, rather than in the gross categories of social class. This analysis will not only help us to understand how social class environment is mediated through the interaction between mother and child, but will also give more precise information about the effects of individual maternal environments on the cognitive growth of the young child.

REFERENCES

1. Bernstein, Basil: Social class and linguistic development: a theory of social learning. *In* Education, economy, and society. (A. H. Halsey, Jean Floud, and C. Arnold Anderson, eds.) Free Press of Glencoe, New York. 1961.

2. ———: Family role systems, communications, and socialization. Unpublished paper prepared for the Cross-National Conference on Research on Children and Adolescents, University of Chicago, Chicago, Ill. Feb. 20–28, 1964.

29.

Hemispheric dominance, handedness, mirror imaging, and auditory sequencing

ALEX D. BANNATYNE
PENNY WICHIARAJOTE

Mouthing the words "individual differences" is frequently not accompanied by an appreciation of what differences really may mean. The article by Bannatyne and Wichiarajote provides another clue to the meaning of individuality. In addition it illustrates (1) our cumulating knowledge about the intricate psychological makeup of humans and (2) the fact that discovering one more bit of information about development poses additional questions.

The editors were attracted by the article because of its implications for appreciating the concept of styles of learning. We believe that a gigantic stride will be made in learning efficiency when each child's learning style is analyzed and maximum use is made of his natural inclinations. (We must note that we do not infer that learning styles which do not come easily to a learner should be neglected. We suggest that parents and teachers should work from strengths to weaknesses, rather than hoping that weaknesses may be regimented into strengths.) This article shows that there is an organic, a physiological, basis for at least some of the uniqueness of learning style.

It is suggested that this article, in regard to the commitment of certain areas of the brain to certain activities, be studied in relation to Penfield's article (selection 19).

THE RELATIONSHIPS between learned and unlearned handedness, spelling ability, mirror imaging, motor functioning, balance, memory for designs, and auditory vocal sequencing were investigated in terms of hemispheric activity and "dominance" on a representative sample of 50 "normal" 8 year old third grade children from three schools (30 boys and 20 girls). Correlations, differences of means, and a varimax factor analysis were used to analyze the data from an extensive battery of tests. In terms of this exploratory research, the results indicated that at least three types of brain function may exist: (a) an efficient well balanced brain associated with unlearned

Exceptional Children, 36:27–36, September, 1969. Alex D. Bannatyne and Penny Wichiarajote, Children's Research Center, University of Illinois, Champaign.

The research reported herein was supported in part by Public Health Service Research Grant NB07346 from the National Institute of Mental Health.

handedness, balancing ability, and competent spelling; (b) a less efficient brain which seems to be given to mirror imaging, verbal incompetence, and left handedness; and (c) a brain which is visuospatially inept, even though it is not given to the drawing of mirror images. It is tentatively suggested that while the brain described in (b) above may be caused by a maturational lag, the brain described in (c) above (which is also associated with left handedness) may result from minimal central nervous system dysfunction. Unlearned left handedness (right hemisphere activity) was correlated with visuospatial competence and skill in three auditory sequencing tests. Learned left handedness (right hemisphere activity) was correlated with visuospatial competence and skill in three auditory sequencing tests. Learned left handedness was significantly associated with the choosing of mirror image designs on a motor free visuospatial memory test. Three separate mirror image tests had scores either negatively correlated with right handedness or positively correlated with left handedness. The overall tentative conclusions were that the findings supported the hypothesis of right hemisphere "dominance" of visuospatial brain function (Benton, 1966; Bannatyne, 1966), and that mirror imaging in writing and possibly reading is attributable to right hemisphere activity (Orton, 1937). Further support for these conclusions is also drawn from the relevant research literature. Spelling was selected as a key written verbal test as it is an excellent indicator of reading disability (Walker & Cole, 1965; Wolf, 1967).

The mean IQ (Stanford-Binet) for the 30 boys was 99.8 and for the 20 girls was 101.5, a negligible difference. The mean IQ (Stanford-Binet) for the 25 worst spellers was 100.2 and for the 25 best spellers was 100.8 (product moment correlation $r = +.059$), a result which suggests that, in this study at least, intelligence and spelling skills were unrelated. Therefore, in the reported results and discussion below any significant finding cannot be attributed to sex differences between the spelling ability groups.

RESEARCH DESIGN

The 50 children were given a battery of tests, the results of which were analyzed by means of product moment correlations. Other results were obtained by calculating t tests to discover if there were significant differences between the means for (a) boys versus girls and (b) good spellers versus poor spellers.

A varimax factor analysis was made of the total correlation matrix even though the battery of tests was not selected to cover evenly a wide area of psychophysical functioning. Six complex factors were extracted, all of which tended to support the interpretations of the correlations given in this article. For reasons of space and unnecessary discussion, the actual factors will not be discussed at length, but reference will be made mostly to the original correlations. Factor 4, which delineated spelling as a function, is to be found in another article (Bannatyne & Wichiarajote, 1969). The total number of variables taken from the tests for statistical analysis was 47, most of which would not be predicted to intercorrelate.

TEST BATTERY

The Bannatyne Visuo-Spatial Memory Test (BVSMT). This test was devised to assess a person's visuospatial memory for designs in a pure way without involving motor activity. Each of 15 separate stimulus designs is presented in turn for 4 seconds. After the presentation of each design, a blank page is turned, an operation which takes one second. The purpose of the blank page is to help eliminate afterimages. This reveals a page of eight designs, the subject being required to select one design (in a multiple choice situation) as the exact equivalent of the original stimulus design. The eight designs, which are randomized on the page, are all, except one, slight variants of the stimulus design. They include, in addition to the original design, a simplified version of it, a mirror image, a 90 degree rotation, a fragmentation, an out of proportion version of it, a complicated version, and a symmetrical version. The subject is told beforehand that one design is the same as the original design and he must select that particular one. On the above sample of 50 eight year old third grade school children, the distribution of correct answers and the scatter of item difficulty were near normally distributed.

ITPA. The Revised Illinois Test of Psycholinguistic Abilities (Kirk, McCarthy, & Kirk, 1968) cannot be described in detail here. Visual closure, auditory sequencing (digit span memory), visual sequencing memory for nonmeaningful geometrical designs, auditory closure, and sound blending subtests were used in this study.

Written Spelling (Encoding). A standardized, graded word spelling test (Schonell & Schonell, 1960) was used but it was not scored for motor (writing ability) variables.

Balance. The subject had to stand on one foot with his eyes open and arms folded. The score was the number of seconds this posture could be maintained without undue wobbling. A prior subtest using two feet with eyes closed was included, and the results of both subtests separately and combined were included in the analysis.

Simultaneous Writing. The mirror writing score was obtained from the simultaneous writing test in which the subject has to write the numbers 1 through 12 down the page as quickly as possible using both left and right hands simultaneously. The mirror writing score was obtained by counting up the number of mirrored numbers in the column written by (a) the dominant hand and (b) the nondominant hand. For the purposes of this test, hand dominance or laterality was decided on the basis of the learned handedness test described below.

Laterality of Handedness. The unlearned handedness test consisted of three items—folding arms, clasping hands together with meshed fingers, and touching the left ear with a particular hand. A very careful analysis was made of the results of these three subtests to insure that there was a generalized commonality of handedness across all three in terms of laterality. An ambidexterity score was obtained if an item was performed in an ambidextrous way (e.g., thumbs aligned) or if one item was performed with the right hand and another with the left hand. The latter preferences were still used to contribute to the right and left scores. When both measures of ambidexterity occurred, the results were combined.

The learned handedness test was composed of the following items: (a) which hand the child could better write with, (b) which hand could pile 10 cards more quickly, and (c) which hand was uppermost when the child clapped hands. It could be argued that the latter is untrained but it is the authors' opinion that it is reasonable to assume that most children are deliberately taught to clap hands in infancy by parents and siblings. Ambidexterity was calculated in the same manner as for the unlearned handedness test.

It should be noted that in a sample of 8 year old children there will be a higher proportion of less well lateralized subjects than would be the case with older children or adults since lateralization is a function of maturation (Hecaen & Ajuriaguerra, 1964).

MFD. All 15 designs from the Graham-Kendall Memory-for-Designs Test were used, the child being required to *draw* each from memory. By contrast, the BVSMT, to which the MFD is closely equivalent, involves no motor activity other than pointing. The MFD drawings were subsequently judged, rated, and scored in the same categories as the eight BVSMT design choices except that the correct drawings were split into two categories, "very accurate" and "less accurate."

Letter Span. The letter span memory test was devised to parallel the digit span test (ITPA) but used consonants instead of numbers. The correlation between the two tests was high, $r = +.66$.

PERC Auditory Discrimination. This test, which is very similar to Wepman's, requires the subject to discriminate whether pairs of similar sounding words are the same or different. The test was tape recorded for standard administration and 60 pairs of words were used.

Xylophone Melody Discrimination Test. Ten pairs of four note melodies were recorded on tape, four of the pairs being identical tunes within pairs. Each of the other six pairs were different within pairs either because the pitch of one was altered or because the sequence of two notes was reversed. The child was required to say after the presentation of each of the ten pairs if they were the same or not the same. The number of correct answers was noted.

DISCUSSION OF RESULTS

Correlations of Unlearned and Learned Handedness. The correlations between unlearned and learned handedness tests were not significant, a fact which should give pause to everyone concerned with the measurement of laterality. The correlations indicated that even within such a narrow field of study as handedness, a split half reliability check, so to speak, indicates that certain unlearned items may be measuring very different laterality functions (in terms of the brain) than those tasks which test learned laterality. It would seem to make an item analysis, in the interests of homogeneity, obligatory in the formation of all laterality tests. One thing is certain—we can no longer automatically assume that because a test item involves some form of laterality, it measures the same thing as the next item.

Unlearned Handedness. The results indicated that unlearned right handedness is correlated significantly ($r = +.30$) with a tendency to select rotated designs on the BVSMT. Traditionally, the rotation of designs is considered an indicator of brain damage but here it may be regarded simply as a particular type of visuospatial inefficiency. Unlearned right handedness is negatively correlated at a highly significant level ($r = -.44$) with the selection of accurate original designs on the BVSMT. The fact that a significant negative correlation ($r = -.31$) was also obtained with the revised ITPA visual closure subtest confirms that these results are not a test artifact. It is to be stressed that neither of these visuospatial tests involved manual dexterity of any kind. The implication is that unlearned right handedness is associated with poor visuospatial ability insofar as it is measured by these tests. It will be remembered that the right hand is largely controlled from the left hemisphere and that this hemisphere appears to be less concerned with the control of visuospatial functions (see further discussion below). In fact, most authorities are in little doubt that the vast majority of people process language functions predominantly in the left hemisphere, and they process visuospatial functions probably predominantly in the right hemisphere, the latter also involving the left hemisphere and even the right temporal lobe in specific ways (Benton, 1966; Hecaen & Ajuriaguerra, 1964; Luria, 1966; Milner, 1962; Penfield & Roberts, 1959; Sperry, 1962, 1964; Teuber, 1962; Weinstein, 1964; Zangwill, 1962).

Unlearned Left Handedness. This variable was highly correlated ($r = +.50$) with the selection of the accurate original designs on the BVSMT test. Unlearned left handedness was negatively correlated with the selection of BVSMT rotated designs ($r = -.42$) and fragmented design choices ($r = -.31$). This would help confirm the hypothesis that the right hemisphere has as one of its primary concerns visuospatial processing, particularly when these results are compared with those given above for the right hand (left hemisphere).

Handedness and Auditory Sequencing Memory. Another surprising result in terms of the overall hypothesis that language functions take place in the left hemisphere (for which there is already considerable evidence—see above references) was the significant positive correlation between unlearned left handedness (right hemisphere) and the revised ITPA auditory sequencing test score ($r = +.31$). This subtest is a digit span memory test and one explanation of the correlation may be that in a rote memory test such as this, the dictated numbers have little or no numerical value and are processed more on the level of musical notes than of words. Milner (1926) found that on the Seashore Tests of Musical Talent patients with right temporal lesions made more errors than did those with left lesions, the difference being most marked for tonal memory. On this hypothesis, digit span memory would take place at least partly in the primary auditory sensory areas and related secondary areas in the right temporal lobe. This is somewhat supported by the significant positive correlation ($r = +.40$) between auditory closure and the xylophone melody discrimination test even though this latter test was not itself correlated with auditory sequencing. The unlearned left handedness score was significantly correlated ($r = +.31$) with the xylophone melody discrimination test.

Some additional support for a partial right temporal lobe control of auditory sequencing memory comes from another research study. Spreen, Benton, and Fincham (1965) found that defective identification of meaningful sounds within the settings of adequate hearing for pure tones is also shown more frequently by patients with right hemisphere disease. In other words, some sounds appear to be processed in the right hemisphere—specifically discrimination and memory as measured by auditory discrimination, letter sequencing, and melody discrimination.

The Efficient Well Balanced Brain Hypothesis. Another explanation or hypothesis, not incompatible with the one just given, is that unlearned ambidexterity and/or unlearned left handedness is indicative of a brain with overall superior visuomotor-praxic neurological functioning—one which balances the body well and does not distort visuospatial material (as frequently occurs in a neurologically dysfunctioning brain, according to Abercrombie, Gardiner, Hansen, Jonckheere, Lindon, Solomon, & Tyson, 1964).

This efficient (unlearned ambidextrous or even left handed) brain in verbally competent subjects such as those in this sample would process various specific language functions reasonably efficiently in the left or right hemisphere, but mainly in the left. It would also process visuospatial material in both hemispheres but primarily in the right. Unlearned ambidexterity was well correlated with graded word spelling at a highly significant level ($r = +.42$). The correlations indicated that spelling, along with sound blending, has a visuospatial unit design element in it, as indicated by the correlation of spelling with MFD very accurate design score ($r = +.33$) and with BVSMT simplification design choice ($r = -.29$). This statement was also supported by the spontaneous occurrence of mirror imaged letters in the written spelling of some children. An implication of the above correlation of spelling with unlearned ambidexterity is that both sides of the brain may contribute visuospatially and visuomotorically to written spelling. The low but significant correlation of unlearned ambidexterity with balance ($r = +.28$) supported this view; it is perhaps not surprising, from a wider viewpoint, that skill with both hands correlates with the ability to balance, the neurological implication being that a fine motor/kinesthetic and visual field feedback control of equal quality in both hemispheres would seem necessary for the precise maintenance of a balancing posture.

Woodburne (1967) stated that balance requires the integration of visual, proprioceptive, vestibular (semicircular canals), and muscular information. The ability to balance on one leg with the eyes open is positively correlated with spelling achievement ($r = +.33$) which, though not a high correlation, suggests that overall coordinated motor control, eye motor coordination, etc. (probably involving the cerebellum) is necessary to good spelling. Even though the spelling test required a written response, it should be stressed here that the quality of the writing was ignored. Therefore, this correlation was not predisposed by a built in motor competency score. It is not suggested, of course, that balance itself or a training in balancing contributes to spelling ability. It is rather suggested that an efficient motor/kinesthetic/vocal/visual/vestibular system is very likely to effect (a) good balance, (b) high quality vocal-motor activity, and (c) manual dexterity, each as separate functions. It is also not suggested that efficiency in one function automatically guarantees or implies efficiency in any one or more of the others. Factor 4 in the factor analysis defined this as dual hemisphere fluent motor encoding functioning. A more detailed discussion of the specific research findings related to spelling, balance, and vocal motor sequencing is presented in another article (Bannatyne & Wichiarajote, 1969). It was found that reading and spelling problems may be helped by teaching sequencing skills (Bannatyne, 1969).

Learned Handedness. It was found that learned right handedness correlated negatively at a significant level with mirror writing with the dominant hand ($r = -.33$) and with MFD fragmented drawings ($r = -.32$). In other words, the more one has been trained to use one's right hand (if dominant) and the more firmly that this has been established, the less likely one is to exhibit mirror writing with that right hand on a simultaneous handwriting test. The implication is that dominant hand mirror writing occurs more in (learned) ambidextrous or left handed people, a statement supported by the trend of the correlations which, probably because they are divided between the two variables, were not quite significant (when they were combined, the correlations were significant). On Factor 5, mirror writing with the dominant hand and learned left handedness were strongly associated in terms of their positive loadings. Learned ambidexterity was significantly and negatively correlated with MFD accurate original drawings ($r = -.32$) and MFD mirror image drawings ($r = -.32$), and positively correlated with MFD out of proportion drawings ($r = +.29$). This confirms that learned ambidexterity (or an inability to learn a strong hand lateralization) is related to visuospatial incompetence and is unrelated to unlearned ambidexterity (actual correlation, $r = +.02$). Learned left handedness was significantly correlated with the choice of mirror image designs on the BVSMT and this also, in a sense, confirms the negative finding about mirror writing with the dominant hand.

Factor 2 suggested that right handedness forms a bipolar factor with ambidexterity, the latter being its opposite rather than left handedness. This finding is in agreement with Naidoo's (1961) very similar result (see below).

All the correlations concerned with handedness, visuospatial memory for designs, mirror writing, and balance supported the hypothesis that mirror writing and mirror imaging occurs less frequently in learned right handed children. The results also supported the hypothesis in the right hemisphere (wherever else it may also be processed) and that, additionally, some types of verbal material may also be processed there, at least in part. In this respect, it should be noted that auditory closure and sound blending were not significantly correlated with any handedness variables whereas the three tests of auditory sequencing were positively correlated with one handedness variable, unlearned left handedness.

Sex Differences. Sex correlated significantly with only two variables, the choice of rotated designs ($r = +.29$) and of complicated designs on the BVSMT ($r = -.28$). The results suggest that girls chose the rotated designs more frequently than did boys. The rotation of designs is traditionally considered indicative of brain dysfunction (Shapiro, 1953) but this is unlikely to be the cause in a sample of normally functioning third grade girls. On the other hand, the boys tended to complicate designs more often than did girls.

OTHER RELEVANT RESEARCH STUDIES

The extremely abundant research data on handedness is in contrast to the almost nonexistent research information on mirror imaging in writing.

Handedness. Most studies investigating heredity and handedness (as measured by conventional handedness tests) indicate that laterality is not proven to be innate. Rife, in three studies (1940, 1941, 1951), found no conclusive evidence for the inheritance of handedness in familial studies, twin studies, or sex differences research.

With respect to the relationship between laterality and reading, Tinker (1964) found that scores on laterality tests and letter reversal tests were uncorrelated in reading disability cases as well as in normal readers. It should be noted that in the present study none of the learned handed tests discriminated between poor and good spellers.

Naidoo (1961) gave a battery of tests to 418 children and found that the greatest difference in performance in all fields (motor skill, early speech, articulation, sound discrimination, WISC performance, and visual perception) lay between the right handed children and the ambiguously handed. On the whole, there was less difference between the dextrals and sinistrals. In almost all the verbal tests, considerable differences were noted between the ambiguously handed and the right handed. The ambiguously handed had more histories of birth complications and slow speech development.

If Naidoo's ambiguously handed group are equated with the learned ambidextrous group of the present research, the findings of the two studies are in approximate agreement. The present negative correlation between learned ambidexterity and MFD accurate original drawn and MFD mirror image drawn, and the positive correlation of it with the MFD out of proportion designs drawn, indicate an incompetency of performance which parallels Naidoo's results. By contrast, unlearned ambidexterity was positively correlated with balance and correct spelling, indicating considerable motor and verbal competency. On this evidence, then, it could be postulated that learned ambidexterity is actually an inability to learn successfully to lateralize handedness despite attempts at training, the implication being that something is inhibiting the training process.

Harris (1957) also found that mixed handedness was a characteristic of reading disability cases in 7 and 9 year old children. The latter group included some strong left lateralized children. On the other hand, Hillman (1956) found laterality unrelated to reading achievement, a result supported by the research of Coleman and Deutsch (1964).

In an investigation of the visual, haptic, and kinesthetic sense modalities in terms of geometric form reproduction, Birch and Lefford (1963) found that left handers had no significant differences in the performance levels between their two hands as did right handed children. They also noted that fewer errors were made with the preferred hand by the whole group except in judging identical forms. As the group were mostly right handed, the implication is that the left hand is at least (if not more) competent in this delicate praxic task.

In another study, Belmont and Birch (1963) found mixed handedness was more common in the 5 to 9 year old group than in the 9 to 13 year old group. Karlin (West, 1960) tabulated IQ against handedness (disregarding chronological age) in mentally defective children and the correlation between IQ and lateralized handedness appeared both positive and high. Koos (1964) also found that the influence of dominance variables varied with IQ level. Cohen and Glass (1968) reported that good first grade readers were more likely to have a dominant hand and poor readers were more likely to have mixed hand dominance, but this was not so in fourth grade children.

In the present study of third grade children, none of the various laterality variables were correlated with Stanford-Binet IQ. However, on

Factor 5, verbal IQ was negatively loaded against learned left handedness and mirroring activities. The correlation between unlearned ambidexterity and spelling was highly significant ($r = +.42$), but spelling and IQ were not correlated.

The implication of these research reports is that (a) learned handedness lateralization is a maturational factor in children of mental ages up to 5, 6, or 7 years of age, and (b) most often training before, during, and after school entry effects a ceiling threshold in or around second grade (for children of at least average intelligence who are functionally intact). Some few children may have a generalized incompetency which may be reflected in continued ambidexterity (or rather inadequately learned lateralization), poor reading, and poor visuospatial abilities (Naidoo, 1961; and the present study). These conclusions are quite separate from the correlates of unlearned ambidexterity which are reflected in good performances in balance tasks and spelling. This latter unlearned ambidexterity group may also be composed of two subgroups—the well lateralized and the competent ambidextrous.

Mirror Imaging. Only two studies in this area are relevant. From a sample of 586 children 5 to 9 years of age, Fabian (1945) found a maturational decrease in the number of figures rotated (Bender test). There were no sex differences and 80 percent of the rotations were mirror images. Wechsler and Hagin (1964) found significant relationships between design rotations (Lamb Chop Test) and reading readiness and reading achievement scores. The authors reported that left-right reversals appeared frequently in the study and through age 6 could "almost be regarded as normal." They became increasingly infrequent among older children. Other types of rotation which persist to age 6 were indicative of slow reading progress.

In the present study, simultaneous mirror writing with the dominant hand correlated significantly and negatively with verbal IQ ($r = -.33$) and positively with the choosing of BVSMT mirror image designs ($r = +.43$); it also correlated negatively with learned right handedness ($r = -.33$). Mirror image MFD drawing negatively correlated with BVSMT choice of mirror design ($r = -.28$), with rotated MFD drawings ($r = -.33$), with unlearned right handedness ($r = -.28$), and with learned ambidexterity ($r = -.32$). This suggests that MFD mirror image design drawing is qualitatively superior to both mirror writing with the dominant hand and to choosing mirror designs (BVSMT). BVSMT mirror design choice significantly correlated ($r = +.43$) with mirror writing with the dominant hand, with MFD simplified drawings ($r = +.33$), with learned left handedness ($r = +.31$), with MFD mirror drawings ($r = -.28$), and with MFD total number correctly drawn ($r = -.29$). These correlations suggest the operation of some form of visuospatial or visuomotor disability and auditory-verbal incompetence, possibly caused by a maturational lag. The maturational lag causation is also suggested by the above review of relevant research. Certainly mirror imaging in all three test forms (on the strength of three significant correlations) is either negatively correlated with right handedness or is positively correlated with left handedness or ambidexterity.

Factor 6 seemed to typify a syndrome of neurological dysfunction in the visuospatial and visuomotor areas, with particular reference to the disorganization (but not rotation) of design layout (loadings: MFD overlapping designs +.65, BVSMT out of proportion choice +.50, MFD fragmented designs +.48, MFD good distribution of designs −.74).

CONCLUSIONS

The following points emerged as tentative conclusions from this research:

1. Most existing laterality tests inadequately measure a complex set of heterogeneous variables which require a much more detailed examination in terms of functions.

2. Unlearned right handedness as measured in this study is indicative of poor visuospatial ability, a finding that supports those research studies which have found visuospatial activity to be primarily but not completely a right hemisphere function. This result is also supported by the positive significant correlation of unlearned left handedness with competent visuospatital memory.

3. Mirror writing with the dominant hand, mirror image design selection, and mirror image drawing are positively associated in a variety of combinations with left handedness and are negatively related in various ways to right handedness. This suggests mirror imaging is a result of right hemisphere activity.

4. Some automatic verbal and auditory memory processing (digit span, letter span, and melody discrimination) may also occur in the right hemisphere. Other research (Milner, 1962) also suggests auditory memory processing may operate in the right temporal area.

5. Unlearned ambidexterity, which correlated with competency in spelling and balance and which by implication was associated with unlearned left handedness (also indicative of competence both visuospatially and in auditory sequencing memory), is thought to be the outcome of a well organized, balanced brain which has superior visuomotor-praxic and auditory functioning. The strong research support for this hypothesis is somewhat at variance with the traditional viewpoint that the "mature" brain is decidedly left hemisphere dominant in almost all its functions. The neuropsychological situation would appear to be much more subtle and complex in the light of this research. The cerebellum may be a key factor in the automatized coordinated functioning of the efficient "well-balanced" brain.

6. In contrast to the efficient well balanced brain that appears to be associated with unlearned handedness, Factors 5 and 6 indicated two
separate types of inefficient brain functioning. One is described as an
immature and rather mixed factor characterized by mirror imaging
and poor verbal ability (maturational lag), while the second is strongly
loaded with visuospatial disorganization. Both factors are associated
with left handedness, the second suggestive of neurological dysfunction.
With respect to Factor 5 and immaturity, both Fabian (1945) and
Wechsler and Hagin (1964) found mirror imaging associated with
maturation.

7. Unlearned left handedness is significantly and positively correlated
with both visuospatial capability of a nonmotor kind (BVSMT) and
with competent auditory sequencing memory (on three separate sequencing tests). This conclusion supports the hypothesis that the right
hemisphere of the brain plays a major part in processing visuospatial
(and other) material (Bannatyne, 1966; Benton, 1966). It also supports
Milner's (1962) findings that auditory sequencing, at least in some
forms (see third conclusion above), takes place in the right temporal
lobe. This is not the case for sound blending and spelling, the sequencing
for which, on the basis of the results of this research, appears to be
determined by vocal/motor/kinesthetic encoding processes rather than
visual or auditory sequencing (see Bannatyne & Wichiarajote, 1969).

8. There are very tentative indications that third grade girls tend to select
rotated designs (BVSMT) more frequently than do boys, while the
boys tend to select complicated designs more. The sex difference trends
indicated in this research are in accord with the extensive relevant research reviews by Maccoby (1966) on sex differences.

The theory (Bannatyne, 1966; Orton, 1937) that mirror imaging in
writing (and possibly in reading, since the BVSMT is nonmotor) is the
result of right hemisphere activity in a brain which is *not* necessarily
neurologically dysfunctioning in any of the usual "damage" senses of the
term is supported by the present research. Children who mirror image or
mirror write in this way appear to be auditorially incompetent in certain
ways and to have a low verbal (Stanford-Binet) IQ. They also find it
difficult to remember correctly geometric designs, their tendency being
to mirror image designs or simplify them.

A quite separate syndrome is that in which geometric designs are
drawn or selected in a disorganized way. This characteristic is also separately associated with learned left handedness and unlearned right handedness. It is conjectured that this latter group suffers a visuospatial and
visuomotor neurological dysfunction probably very minimal in nature.

Whether or not the results reported above apply to groups of reading
and spelling disability children (Bannatyne, 1966) requires further re-

search on homogeneous samples of learning disability children. This research itself also needs to be validated on a wider sample in terms of both age and geographical location.

REFERENCES

Abercrombie, M. L. J., Gardiner, P. A. G., Hansen, E., Jonckheere, J., Lindon, R. L., Solomon, G., & Tyson, M. C. Visual, perceptual and visuomotor disorders in a school for physically handicapped children. In M. L. J. Abercrombie (Ed.), *Perceptual and visuo-motor disorders in cerebral palsy.* London: William Heinemann, 1964. Pp. 40–41.

Bannatyne, A. D. Verbal and spatial abilities and reading. Paper presented at First International Reading Association Congress, Paris, France, 1966.

Bannatyne, A. D. *Psycholinguistic color system: A reading, writing, spelling and language program.* Urbana, Ill.: Learning Systems Press (P.O. Box 64), 1969.

Bannatyne, A. D., & Wichiarajote, P. Relationships between written spelling, motor functioning and sequencing skills. *Journal of Learning Disabilities,* 1969, **2,** 6–18.

Belmont, L., & Birch, H. G. Lateral dominance and right-left awareness in normal children. *Child Development,* 1963, **34,** 257–270.

Benton, A. L. The problem of cerebral dominance. *Bulletin of the Orton Society,* 1966, **16,** 38–54.

Birch, H. G., & Lefford, A. Intersensory development in children. *Child Development Monograph 89,* **28** (5).

Cohen, A., & Glass, C. C. Lateral dominance and reading ability. *The Reading Teacher,* 1968, **2,** 343–348.

Coleman, R. I., & Deutsch, C. P. Lateral dominance and right/left discrimination. A comparison of normal and retarded readers. *Perceptual and Motor Skills,* 1964, **19,** 43–50.

Fabian, A. A. Vertical rotation in visual motor performance: Its relationship to reading reversals. *Journal of Educational Psychology,* 1945, **36,** 129–145.

Harris, A. Lateral dominance, directional confusion, and reading disability. *Journal of Psychology,* 1957, **44,** 283–294.

Hecaen, H., & deAjuriaguerra, J. *Left-handedness.* New York: Grune & Stratton, 1964.

Hillman, H. H. The effect of laterality on reading disability. *Durham Research Review,* 1956, **7,** 86–96.

Kirk, S. A., McCarthy, J., & Kirk, W. *The Illinois Test of Psycholinguistic Abilities.* (Rev. Ed.) Urbana, Ill.: Illinois University Press, 1968.

Koos, E. M. Manifestations of cerebral dominance and reading retardation in primary grade children. *Journal of Genetic Psychology,* 1964, **104,** 155–166.

Luria, A. R. *Higher cortical functions in man.* New York: Basic Books, 1966.

Maccoby, E. *The development of sex differences.* Stanford, Calif.: Stanford University Press, 1966.

Milner, B. Laterality effects in audition. In V. B. Mountcastle (Ed.), *Interhemispheric relations and cerebral dominance.* Baltimore: Johns Hopkins Press, 1962. Pp. 177–196.

Naidoo, S. An investigation into some aspects of ambiguous handedness. Unpublished masters thesis, University of London, 1961.

Orton, S. T. *Reading, writing, and speech problems in children.* New York: Norton, 1937.

Penfield, W., & Roberts, L. *Speech and brain mechanisms.* Princeton, N.J.: Princeton University Press, 1959.

Rife, D. C. Handedness with special reference to twins. *Genetics,* 1940, **25,** 178–186.

Rife, D. C. Heredity and handedness. *Science Monthly,* 1951, **73,** 188–191.

Schonell, F. J., & Schonell, F. E. *Diagnostic and attainment testing.* London: Oliver and Boyd, 1960.

Shapiro, M. B. Experimental studies of a perceptual anomaly. III. The testing of an explanatory theory. *Journal of Mental Science,* 1953, **99,** 394–409.

Sperry, R. W. Some general aspects of interhemispheric integration. In V. B. Mountcastle (Ed.), *Interhemispheric relations and cerebral dominance.* Baltimore: Johns Hopkins Press, 1962. Pp. 43–50.

Sperry, R. W. The great cerebral commissure. *Scientific American,* 1964 (January). Reprint No. 174.

Spreen, O., Benton, A. L., & Fincham, R. W. Auditory agnosia without aphasia. *Archives of Neurology,* 1965, **13,** 84–92.

Teuber, H. Discussion of session on laterality effects in audition by Brenda Milner. In V. B. Mountcastle (Ed.), *Interhemispheric relations and cerebral dominance.* Baltimore: Johns Hopkins Press, 1962. Pp. 203–207.

Tinker, K. J. The role of laterality in reading disability. In International Reading Association, *Reading and inquiry.* Newark, Del.: IRA, 1964.

Walker, L., & Cole, E. M. Familial patterns of expression of specific reading disability in a population sample. Part 1. Prevalence, distribution and persistence. *Bulletin of the Orton Society,* 1965, **15,** 12–24.

Wechsler, D., & Hagin, R. A. The problem of arial rotation in reading disability. *Perceptual and Motor Skills,* 1964, **19,** 319–326.

Weinstein, S. Deficits concomitant with aphasia and lesions of either cerebral hemisphere. *Cortex,* 1964, **1,** 154–169.

West, R. What we must learn about childhood aphasia. In R. West (Ed.), *Childhood aphasia.* San Francisco: California Society for Crippled Children and Adults (228 McAllister St.), 1960. Pp. 1–2.

Wolf, C. W. An experimental investigation of specific language disability (dyslexia). *Bulletin of the Orton Society,* 1967, **17,** 32–39.

Zangwill, O. L. Dyslexia in relation to cerebral dominance. In J. Money (Ed.), *Reading disability.* Baltimore: Johns Hopkins Press, 1962. Pp. 103–113.

30.

A study of social stereotype
of body image in children

J. ROBERT STAFFIERI

*The editors would like to digress for a moment before presenting this
selection, since the topic it deals with, the implications that have been
drawn, and the history of the research accomplished are both interesting and, from our point of view, somewhat unusual.*

*The relation between physique and personality has been termed
"constitutional psychology" and has been a matter of speculation for
a long time. Formal research in the area probably began with Kretschmer in the 1920's and the publication of his book* Physique and
Character. *He identified three body types—the pyknic or the fat person, the athletic or average, muscular person, and the asthenic or lean,
skinny person. Some twenty years later, William Sheldon developed
a similar classification using different terms. Instead of pyknic, he called
the fat person an endomorph; the athletic type was labelled mesomorph; and the asthenic, ectomorph. Both Kretschmer and Sheldon
found questionable correlations between body type, personality traits,
and dispositions toward psychological illness. The whole idea has been
questioned by other investigators. Kretschmer and Sheldon described
the fat man or endomorph as comfort-loving, jolly, extroverted, and
disposed to manic-depressive psychoses. The mesomorph or athletic
type was characterized as active, aggressive, and inclined toward para-
noia when and if psychotic. And the ectomorph or asthenic was pictured as shy, withdrawing, introverted, and tending to become schizoid
if disorganized.*

*The author of this article reports research with middle childhood
boys, indicating a clear preference for the mesomorphic physique and
a significant tendency to attribute desirable personality traits to individuals of this body type.*

*The reader is asked to note the correspondence of the research
design employed to Coffield's (selection 3) description of the R-R
approach and to look closely at the high statistical significance of the
results reported (see also Brittain, selection 56).*

*Do you think that the clear-cut perceptual sets and expectations
identified by this study will operate to influence behaviors in the in-*

Journal of Personality and Social Psychology, 7:101–104. J. Robert Staffieri, Indiana
University.

This article is based on a dissertation submitted in partial fulfillment of the requirements
for the degree of Doctor of Education at Indiana University. The author wishes to express his appreciation to Boyd R. McCandless, under whose direction the investigation was
conducted.

dicated directions for individuals with these body types? That is, will a mesomorph tend to be friendly because this is expected and an endomorph tend to be lazy because he is viewed in this manner? If so, the expectations that others have for us are powerful determinants for the type of personality we develop.

THE ROLE of an individual's body configuration in social interactions and the effects of these interactions on self-concept is an important part of the total process of personality development. It is not uncommon to be the initiator or recipient of such statements as "He certainly is a crafty, wiry little thing," or "He is all skin and bones—must worry a lot." It is reasonable to assume that the individual who is the recipient of statements which are based on another person's perception of his body is likely to incorporate these perceptions into his own body concept. As a direct result of an individual's body configuration, he typically receives rather consistent reactions from others. These reactions thus provide a framework for his body concept, which becomes a significant part of the total self-concept.

One implication from this process is central to the concerns of this investigation. Since body configuration is objectively definable (e.g., tallness versus shortness, fatness versus thinness), it is reasonable to hypothesize a definable range of consistent and stable reactions to a particular body configuration.

Evidence linking body build and personality is at best tenuous. Perhaps the etiology of such a relationship (if it exists) lies in the realm of social learning rather than physical constitution per se. McCandless (1960) stated that ". . . there are suggestions that if substantial and consistent personality-body type relations should be demonstrated, patterned types of social response may constitute the responsible factor as reasonably as genetics [p. 47]."

Evidence suggests that individuals will behave to some degree in a manner consistent with the expectations of others. If these expectations are consistent over people and time, it is reasonable to expect emitted behavior consistent with the expectations. Once the individual accepts an expectation as being true of himself, the literature suggests that he will act in a manner to fulfill the belief, thus providing added continuity to behavior which was originally emitted because of expectation (e.g., Payne & Farquhar, 1962).

Most investigations relating body build to social-personal behaviors suggest that, although the magnitude of the correlations is not high and the proportion of correlations is not much higher than would be expected by chance, some support exists for acceptance of the concept of body-built-personality interrelations (e.g., Hanley, 1951; Walker, 1962, 1963).

Previous research has provided some evidence to suggest that a body type is capable of eliciting rather common reactions from adults in the form of descriptions of personality/behavior traits. Is the role of body type as a stimulus in social situations limited to the adult population?

What is the relation of age to this process? Is there a relationship between body image stereotype and individual process of perceiving? What part does body type play in social interactions? The purpose of this study was to investigate the role of body-image stereotypes in children with general reference to three areas: development, interpersonal functions, and social functions.

METHOD

Subjects

The subjects for this study were 90 male children from 6 to 10 years of age in the elementary division of the University School, Indiana University. The sample population consisted of 18 subjects at each age level (6 to 10 years), who were grouped (according to their relative fatness, muscularity, and thinness) on the basis of the ponderal index $\left(\dfrac{\text{height in inches}}{\sqrt[3]{\text{weight in pounds}}} \right)$ and teacher rating of body type. Although these groups (six subjects in each group at each age level) are referred to in the study as endomorph, mesomorph, and ectomorph, these are meant as descriptive characteristics of typically fat, muscular, and thin boys, respectively, and do not stringently represent a particular method of body typing. In addition, there was a sample of 12 4-year-old and 12 5-year-old subjects included in a part of the study, but the results utilized from this group are considered as a tentative pilot investigation.

Measures

Three measures were obtained for each subject who participated in the study: (*a*) assignment of adjectives to silhouettes representing three variations of body type, (*b*) determination of body type preference of each subject, and (*c*) a sociometric measure of each class.

Adjectives. A list of 39 descriptions (primarily one-word adjectives) was developed, each of which could be applied to any of the silhouettes. The descriptions, hereinafter referred to as adjectives, were selected on the basis of (*a*) a prior pilot study, (*b*) apparent relatedness to behavior/ personality variables, and (*c*) the likelihood of their meaning being known. The adjectives were not designed to survey all possible descriptions which could be applied to individuals, but were intended to be a reasonable sample of a more extensive universe.

Silhouettes. The stimuli to which the above mentioned adjectives were applied were three full-body silhouettes (black on white). Each silhouette profile was approximately the same height (13 inches), head

TABLE 1. FREQUENCY OF ASSIGNMENT OF ADJECTIVES TO SILHOUETTES BY SUBJECTS 6 TO 10 YEARS OLD

Adjectives	Silhouettes			
	En	M	Ec	χ^2
Strong	15	74	1	100.067***
Best friend	9	67	14	68.867***
Quiet	21	10	59	44.067***
Fights	40	45	5	31.667***
Kind	24	35	31	2.067
Cheats	63	9	18	55.800***
Clean	3	54	33	43.800***
Worries	30	11	49	24.067***
Lots of friends	8	69	13	74.467***
Nervous	42	5	43	31.267***
Happy	19	54	17	28.867***
Helps others	17	55	18	31.267***
Polite	13	50	27	23.267***
Argues	58	17	15	39.267***
Remembers	10	26	26	26.400***
Gets teased	60	4	26	53.067***
Lonely	33	9	48	25.800***
Sick	41	7	42	26.467***
Forgets	51	14	25	24.067***
Lazy	67	5	18	71.267***
Healthy	4	77	9	110.867***
Lies	56	10	24	37.067***
Sneaky	25	24	41	6.067*
Honest	13	61	16	48.200***
Sloppy	72	9	9	88.200***
Brave	8	68	14	72.800***
Teases	35	30	25	1.667
Naughty	46	18	26	13.867***
Good looking	1	74	15	100.067***
Mean	54	19	17	28.867***
Afraid	27	7	56	40.667***
Ugly	77	4	9	110.867***
Sad	31	11	48	22.867***
Smart	5	67	18	71.267***
Dirty	60	16	14	45.067***
Tired	39	12	39	16.200***
Stupid	58	8	24	43.467***
Weak	21	0	69	83.400***
Neat	2	73	15	95.267***

Note.—En = Endomorph; M = Mesomorph; Ec = Ectomorph.
 * $p < .05$.
*** $p < .001$.

shape, and facial outline. The distinguishing features were those which are commonly associated with the three gross bodily characteristics of extreme endomorph, mesomorph, and ectomorph. Essentially, the body curvature represented fat, muscular, and thin body types. In this study, there were two sets of three silhouettes each. One set was designed to represent adult figures, the other to represent child figures. The silhouettes were counterbalanced for both order in body-types presentation and child-adult form. This was also done for assignment of adjectives and body-

TABLE 2. BODY TYPE PREFERENCE OF SUBJECTS BY AGE

| Age | Silhouettes | | | |
	Endomorph	Mesomorph	Ectomorph	χ^2
4–5	8	6	10	1.000
6	5	7	6	.333
7	6	12	0	12.000**
8	1	16	1	26.833**
9	4	11	3	6.333*
10	0	16	2	23.333**

* $p < .05$.
** $p < .01$.

TABLE 3. ACCURACY OF SELF PERCEPTION OF A SELECTED GROUP OF SUBJECTS

| Self ratings | Subjects | | | |
	1–2	3	4–5	ϵ
1–2	7	4	3	14
3	3	10	8	21
4–5	0	1	4	5
ϵ	10	15	15	40

Note.—$\chi^2 = 10.367$ ($<.05$), C $= .454$.

type preference. In each age level, half of the subjects (nine) responded to child forms and half to adult forms. With three silhouettes, there were six possible orders of presentation, so that each subject of a particular body type in each age group responded to a different order of silhouettes. All three silhouettes were hung on a white background card (30 × 20 inches). They were clearly discriminable.

Body-type Preference. In order to determine the body type preferred, each subject was presented with five variations of body-type silhouettes. In addition to the three used in the assignment of adjectives, two silhouettes were cut representing endo-mesomorph and ecto-mesomorph. These five silhouettes represented a range of body type and were also counterbalanced for order in presentation and child-adult form.

Sociometry. The sociometric measure used in this study was responded to by most boys and girls in all classes from Grades 1 through 5. It was administered to all classes separately. The children were asked to indicate (in writing) who, in that class, were their five best friends and who were the three children that they "did not like so well." The instructions were constant for all classes and the list was ordered from their "very best friend" (first choice) to their fifth best friend (fifth choice), and from the person whom they disliked most (first choice) to the person that they disliked, but did not dislike as much as the first or second choice (third choice). The sociometric data for 6, 7, and 8-year old children were collected (using the same procedure) about 5 months prior to this study, and were available to the investigator. This measure provided data from each child in the class which indicated the number of times each subject was chosen as first best friend, second best friend, and so on, and most disliked, second most disliked, and third most disliked.

RESULTS

The results of the study indicate that:

1. Boys from 6 to 10 years old demonstrated a common concept of behavior/personality traits which were associated with various body types. These stereotypes began to appear in children 4 and 5 years old, but the evidence is tentative (Table 1).

2. All the significant adjectives assigned to the mesomorph image were favorable (16); the adjectives assigned the endomorph were unfavorable (socially) and primarily socially aggressive; the adjectives assigned to the ectomorph were primarily unfavorable (personally) and of a generally socially submissive type.

3. The assignment of adjectives to the images was not related to the body type of the subject who assigned them.

4. Subjects showed a clear preference to look like the mesomorph image. This preference became apparent between 6 and 7 years (Table 2).

5. A selected group of subjects demonstrated reasonable accuracy in perception of their own body types (Table 3).

6. Mesomorph subjects received a consistently high number of ac-

ceptance choices and endomorph subjects received a consistently low number of acceptance choices (Table 4).

TABLE 4. Number of Acceptance Choices Received by Subjects

Order	Subjects			
	Ectomorph	Mesomorph	Endomorph	χ^2
1st	59	76	41	10.443**
2nd	76	101	58	11.906**

** $p < .01$.

DISCUSSION

The results of this study indicate a rather clear stereotype pattern for the three body images within age levels and across age levels. The mesomorph image is perceived as entirely favorable. The ectomorph image is basically unfavorable, but different from the unfavorable concept for endomorph.

It is clear that the mesomorph body type for both children and adults is representative of an ideal male physique. The favorable stereotype of the mesomorph is evident at 6 years of age. However, the preference to look like the mesomorph does not appear until 7 years and is not clearly established until 8 years. Although the data are not sufficiently clear to warrant a firm conclusion, this difference may tentatively be attributed to inaccurate self-perceptions by the subjects at 6 and 7 years. Data suggest reasonable accuracy of self-perception of body type from 40 subjects, mostly 7- and 10-year olds. The 10-year-old boys were more accurate in their self-perceptions than the 7-year-old boys. If the younger boys do not perceive themselves accurately, there may not be sufficient motivation for them to report a preference to look differently. Subjects 8 years and older appear to report self-perceptions quite accurately, and clearly prefer to look like the mesomorph image. The point at which accuracy of self-perception becomes apparent (probably 8 to 9 years of age) may also be the beginning of dissatisfaction with one's body, and the degree of dissatisfaction may well be proportional to the extent that one's body differs from the mesomorph image.

While the results of this investigation do not provide an answer to the problem of whether body type constitutionally determines personality, or that body type is a determinant of personality through the process of social learning, there are some implications which support the latter point of view. Most authors would agree that, at least minimally, an individual's physical constitution determines certain behaviors which can be emitted. Beyond this point, however, the results of this study suggest that personality correlates of body type may be reasonably explained on the basis of expected behavior. Thus social expectation could explain the low but rather consistently found correlations between body type and behavior/ personality traits.

If children behave in a manner consistent with expectations, even to a minimal degree, some reinforcement of the expectations occurs and gives continued support to the stereotype.

REFERENCES

Hanley, C. Physique and reputation of junior high school boys. *Child Development,* 1951, **22,** 247–260.

McCandless, B. R. Rate of development, body build, and personality. *Psychiatric Research Reports,* 1960, **13,** 42–57.

Payne, D. A., & Farquhar, W. W. The dimensions of an objective measure of academic self-concept. *Journal of Educational Psychology,* 1962, **53,** 187–192.

Walker, R. N. Body build and behavior in young children: I. Body build and nursery school teachers' ratings. *Monograph of Social Research in Child Development,* 1962, **27,** No. 84.

Walker, R. N. Body build and behavior in young children: II. Body build and parents' ratings. *Child Development,* 1963, **34,** 1–23.

31.

Stability of achievement and recognition seeking behaviors from early childhood through adulthood[1]

HOWARD A. MOSS
JEROME KAGAN

In reporting the results of an investigation concerning the stability of achievement and recognition seeking behaviors, the authors of this article touch on most of the developmental phases from early childhood to maturity. Hence, this selection would be appropriate for inclusion with the readings for any of the different phases. The editors chose to include it with middle-childhood because it appears that be-

Journal of Abnormal and Social Psychology, 62:504–513, 1961. Howard A. Moss, Child Research Branch, National Institute of Mental Health; Jerome Kagan, Professor of Psychology, Harvard University.

haviors in this age range are the first from which accurate predictions of adult actions can be derived.

The longitudinal aspect of the study reported is something of a rarity in research with human subjects. This plus the description of the manner in which results were achieved and the discussion and summary, renders this article worthy of study and perhaps emulation. Furthermore, it meets the suggestions for discriminating reading advanced in the introduction to Part One of these readings.

The editors emphasize that stability and consistency of behavior also are factors which permit its prediction. In addition, they would call the reader's attention to the necessity for identifying causal reasons for behavior before that behavior can be controlled. In short, the physical and social factors which encourage the development of effective ways of acting must be known before they can be replicated and before increasing the probability of that type of behavior occurring more frequently. If men are to design and engineer their future—and it seems to us there is no alternative—research of this nature is essential.

THE SUPPOSITION that selected adult response patterns are established at an early age is a primary assumption of developmental theory. Although literary documents and psychotherapy protocols have provided anecdotal support for this hypothesis, more objective validation has been difficult to obtain. The present paper is a second report that has emerged from a larger project on the stability of childhood behavior. The first paper indicated that dependent behavior in girls showed moderately high stability from the early school years through young adulthood (Kagan & Moss, in press). The present report is concerned with the developmental consistency of two related behaviors: the tendency to strive for (*a*) mastery of selected skills (achievement behavior), and (*b*) social recognition through acquisition of specific goals or behaviors (recognition behavior).

The achievement variable emphasizes mastery of intellectual, athletic, mechanical, and artistic skills as well as competence in specialized crafts. Social recognition is obtained through acquisition of most of the above behaviors. For intellectual competence, athletic ability, acquisition of money, and positions of power in social groups are the primary methods of obtaining social recognition in the cultural milieu of our middle class population. Thus, the overt behaviors involved in achievement and recognition strivings overlap to some degree.

In an attempt to differentiate between these two variables, the investigators evaluated the degree to which the individual's mastery behavior was directed at satisfaction of an internal standard of excellence in order to gain self-approval (achievement motivation), in contrast to seeking approval from the social environment (recognition motivation). This is a difficult differentiation to make. The data to be presented reveal a high, positive correlation between ratings of these two behavioral variables. This interdependence suggests that it may be impossible to measure the "desire to improve at a skill" independent of the individual's "desire for social recognition" for this improvement.

METHOD

Subjects and General Procedure

The subjects were 36 males and 35 females from the Fels Research Institute's longitudinal population. They were enrolled in the project at birth, during the years 1929–1939. At the time of a recent adult assessment (1957–1959) they were between 20 and 29 years of age. The subjects came from predominantly middle class backgrounds, over half of the group were married; 70% had college degrees or were enrolled in a college, and the majority were living within a 30-mile radius of the institute. The adult group included 55 Protestants, 15 Catholics, and 1 Jew.

The heart of this study consists of correlations between the childhood information on these subjects and their adult behavior. The childhood data included (*a*) longitudinal observations of the child's behavior during the first 14 years of life in a variety of settings, (*b*) observations of the mother-child interaction during these years, (*c*) TAT protocols obtained in adolescence, (*d*) annual Stanford-Binet intelligence test scores during the ages 5–11. Although the data collected during adulthood (age range 20–29) sampled a variety of techniques, this report utilizes only two sources of adult information, 5 hours of interview, and a TAT protocol.

Longitudinal Observations: Birth to Age 14

As a standard procedure of the Fels longitudinal program, psychologists or psychologically trained personnel summarized their observations of the child in the home, in the Fels nursery school and day camp, and in the subject's public school. The home reports were based on a visit to the home where mother and child were observed for half-day sessions. These home visits were generally made semiannually for the first 6 years of life and annually from 6 to 12. Most of the mothers were interviewed each year for the first 14 years of the child's life. The nursery school summaries were based on semiannual, free-play sessions from age 2.5 to 5. The sessions usually consisted of 15 consecutive half-day periods in groups of 10–12 children. Day camp typically consisted of an annual 2 week session of half-day periods during age 6–10 in which free and structured group activities were observed. Public school visits, made semiannually, consisted of a half-day observation of the child in his routine classroom activities. Finally, the subjects of age 6–14 were interviewed each year at the institute and a summary of the interview was prepared. All of the longitudinal reports for each subject were collated in chronological order and placed in the subject's individual file.[2]

Scoring of Longitudinal Variables. A comprehensive list of rating scale variables (seven-point scale) was defined for the purpose of evaluating the narrative material just outlined. The material for each subject was divided into four age periods: 0–3, 3–6, 6–10, and 10–14. The senior author, who had no knowledge of the adult psychological status of the subjects, first read all the information for each subject for age 0–3 and made those ratings for which he had adequate information. Following a period of interpolated work, he studied each subject's material for age 3–6 and again made his ratings. This procedure was repeated for ages 6–10 and 10–14. A period of approximately 6 months intervened between the evaluation of the data for any one subject for each age period. This paper deals only with the stability of achievement and recognition behaviors and abridged definitions of these variables follow.

Child Variables

Achievement Behavior: (*Rated for Ages 0–3, 3–6, and 6–10*). This variable assessed the degree to which the subject tended to persist with challenging tasks, games, and problems, and his involvement in activities in which a standard of excellence was applicable. For 0–3, emphasis was given to persistence with perceptual-motor activities (e.g., making block towers, stringing beads, drawing, and coloring). For ages 3–6 and 6–10 the greatest weight was given to interest in and persistence with intellectual, mechanical, athletic, and fine motor activities.

For age 10–14 the general achievement variable defined above was differentiated into three variables dealing with different achievement areas (intellectual, mechanical, and athletic).

Intellectual Achievement: (*Rated for Age 10–14*). This variable assessed the degree to which the subject attempted to master language and numerical skills and showed involvement in the acquisition of knowledge.

Mechanical Achievement: (*Rated for Age 10–14*). This variable assessed the degree to which the subject attempted to master mechanical skills and manifested involvement in activities such as carpentry, construction of model vehicles, engines and motors, and craft work.

Athletic Achievement: (*Rated for Age 10–14*). This variable assessed the degree to which the subject attempted to master and showed involvement in athletic activities. These behaviors included swimming, hiking, baseball, football, basketball, tennis, acrobatics, and track events.

Recognition Seeking Behavior: (*Rated for Ages 6–10 and 10–14*). This variable assessed the subject's striving to obtain goals that led to recognition from parents, teachers, and peers. The behaviors emphasized in the rating were (*a*) grades in school and school honors, (*b*) stated desire for status-laden vocations or ostentatious material goods, (*c*) striving for leadership in teams or clubs, (*d*) attempts to get recognition from farm activities (e.g., raise the best calf, the highest corn, etc.).

Maternal Variables

Maternal Acceleration of Developmental Skills in Child: (*Rated for Ages 0–3, 3–6, and 6–10*). The home visits and maternal interviews yielded information on the mother's behavior and attitudes toward her child. The maternal variable that is directly relevant to the subject's achievement behavior was called *maternal acceleration*. It was defined in terms of the degree to which the mother showed concern over the subject's cognitive and motor development, and the degree to which she exhibited desires for precocious achievement in her child. The rating reflected the degree to which the mother "pushed" the subject's development beyond his abilities and her concern with his general achievement level.

Adult Interview

The junior author, who had no knowledge of the subject's childhood information, interviewed each subject and rated him (seven-point scale) on a variety of variables. The definitions of the variables related to achievement and recognition seeking behaviors follow.

Achievement Behavior. This variable evaluated the subject's behavioral attempts to master tasks for which "self-satisfaction" rather than social recognition was the *salient* goal. In achievement behavior, the subject was striving to attain a *self-imposed* standard of excellence. The rating was based on the subject's emphasis and concern with task mastery in his job and avocational pursuits.

Recognition Seeking Behavior. This variable evaluated the subject's behavioral attempt to obtain symbols of status and social recognition. The rating was based on evidences of strivings for (*a*) vocational recognition, (*b*) academic awards and honors, (*c*) positions of leadership or recognition in community or vocational groups, (*d*) concern with conspicuous material display, (*e*) striving for upward mobility in social class position.

Concern with Intellectual Competence. This variable assessed the value the subject placed upon intelligence, knowledge, academic achievement, and intellectual superiority regardless of whether the goal was to satisfy inner standards or to obtain social recognition.

Reliability of Longitudinal and Adult Interview Ratings

A random sample of 32 tape recorded adult interviews were independently studied and rated by a second judge to assess the reliability of the junior author's adult ratings. The reliabilities of the longitudinal variables were also assessed through independent ratings, by a second judge, of samples of 50–60 cases at each of the four age periods. The reliabilities of the adult and child ratings were determined by product-moment correlation coefficients.[3] For the adult ratings of achievement behavior, recognition behavior, and intellectual concern the reliability coefficients were .84, .99, and .98, respectively. With the exception of one child behavior variable, the reliabilities of the longitudinal ratings ranged from .74 to .90 with a median coefficient of .81. The one low longitudinal reliability was for child's achievement for age 0–3 ($r = +.35$; $p < .01$; two-tailed).

TAT Achievement Fantasy: Adolescent and Adult Protocols

Early adolescent (median age of 14–16) protocols were available for 67 of the 71 subjects, and all 71 subjects were administered TAT stimuli following the adult interview. The adolescent protocol was based on seven cards from the Murray (1943) series (Cards 1, 5, 14, 17BM, 3BM, 6BM, and 3GF). The male adult protocol was based on 13 cards (4, 8BM, 7BM, 6BM, 12M, 17BM, 13MF, 14, 3BM, 5, 1, 3GF, and 18GF). The adult females were also administered 13 cards (4, 6GF, 12F, 2, 8GF, 17BM, 13MF, 14, 3BM, 5, 1, 3GF, and 18GF). For both the adolescent and adult protocols achievement themes were scored according to the scheme described by McClelland, Atkinson, Clark, and Lowell (1953). Since incidence of the subcategories of the McClelland scoring system were infrequent, only stories in which achievement behavior was the major aspect of the plot were considered. These are scored Ach Th in the McClelland scheme. For the adolescent protocol, there was a lack of comparability among the examiners with respect to the inquiry questions and only the spontaneous verbalization of the subject was scored. Agreement between two independent coders was 95%. The longitudinal and interview ratings of achievement and recognition behavior were made *without knowledge* of the subject's adolescent or adult TAT stories. Thus, the behavior and interview ratings were independent of each other and of the TAT thematic scores.

IQ Change

Each child was given the Stanford-Binet, Forms L and M alternately, annually from ages 5 through 11 by the same psychologist.[4] The mean IQ for the entire Fels population is about 120 (*SD* of 15). For each subject, a smoothed plot of his IQ scores was obtained by averaging his three IQ scores around each age. For example, a child's smoothed or average IQ at age 6 was the result of averaging his IQ scores at ages 5, 6, and 7; his smoothed IQ at age 10 was the average of his IQs at ages 9, 10, and 11. This procedure tends to remove the chance variation associated with any one IQ score and has been used in other studies (Kagan, Sontag, Baker,

& Nelson, 1958; Sontag, Baker, & Nelson, 1958). Each subject's smoothed IQ at age 6 was then subtracted from his smoothed IQ at age 10 and the resulting difference was used as a measure of IQ change. As with achievement themes, the child and adult achievement ratings were made without knowledge of the subject's IQ or his IQ change score.

In summary, four independent sources of data were analyzed: child and maternal behaviors for the first 14 years of life, adult behavior, adolescent and adult achievement themes, and childhood IQ change scores.

Statistical Analysis

Relationships among the following variables were evaluated: (*a*) childhood achievement and maternal acceleration ratings with the adult interview ratings, (*b*) adolescent achievement themes with adult achievement themes, (*c*) adolescent and adult achievement themes with the longitudinal and adult ratings, and (*d*) IQ change scores with the childhood and adult ratings. Product-moment correlations were used except when the TAT achievement score was involved. Since achievement themes were not normally distributed, contingency coefficients[5] were used for all tests of association using this variable. Mechanical achievement for age 10–14 was the only variable for which there was a significant sex difference; the boys having a higher mean rating than the girls ($p < .05$; two-tailed).

RESULTS

Stability of Achievement and Recognition Behaviors

Table 1 presents the relationships between the child and adult ratings of achievement and recognition behavior, as well as the relation between maternal acceleration and the adult achievement variables. There are several important results in this table. The rating of achievement behavior for age 6–10 showed a significant, positive association with all three adult variables for both sexes. The rating of achievement for age 3–6 was predictive of adult behavior for the females but not for the males, a finding that suggests the earlier emergence of stable achievement strivings in girls' development than in boys. Of the three achievement behaviors rated for age 10–14, only intellectual mastery was predictive of adult achievement for both sexes. Involvement in mechanical activities was predictive of adult achievement for boys but not for girls. Athletic achievement showed no relationship to the rating of general adult achievement, and was negatively associated with intellectual concern for adult males ($p < .02$).

TABLE 1. Relation between Longitudinal Ratings of Childhood Achievement and Early Maternal Acceleration with Adult Achievement Behavior (product-moment correlations)

Childhood Variables	Age	Adult Variables					
		Achievement		Recognition		Intellectual Concerns	
		Males	Females	Males	Females	Males	Females
Recognition	6–10	.47***	.40**	.42**	.48***	.37**	.55****
	10–14	.25	.20	.36*	.39**	.24	.40**
Achievement	0–3	−.12	−.02	.01	−.22	−.08	−.02
	3–6	−.03	.45**	−.11	.49***	.13	.44**
	6–10	.46***	.38**	.57****	.51***	.69****	.49***
Achievement							
Intellectual	10–14	.40**	.42**	.60****	.56***	.66****	.49***
Mechanical	10–14	.20	.20	.46**	.02	.47**	.27
Athletic	10–14	−.18	.01	−.17	−.09	−.47**	.02
Maternal Ac-	0–3	.22	.36*	.44*	.41*	.09	.36*
celeration	3–6	.31	.09	.24	.12	.42**	.12
	6–10	.14	.33*	.16	.23	.32*	.43**

  * $p < .05$; one-tailed.
 ** $p < .02$; one-tailed.
 *** $p < .01$; one-tailed.
**** $p < .001$; one-tailed.

Recognition seeking behavior for age 6–10 was also predictive of
adult achievement behavior. A few of the child variables were moderately intercorrelated and the three adult variables were highly intercorrelated (Tables 4, 5, and 6). This lack of independence makes some
of the stability correlations between childhood and adulthood somewhat redundant.

Maternal Acceleration and Adult Behavior

Maternal concern with the child's developmental progress during
the first 10 years of life showed low to moderate correlations with
adult achievement behavior. The maternal rating for age 6–10 was not
a better predictor of adult behavior than the maternal rating for the
first 3 years of life. Moreover, the age 0–3 rating was associated with
all three adult, achievement variables for girls, while it predicted only
recognition behavior for adult males.

Stability of TAT Achievement Fantasy

Although different sets of TAT pictures were used in obtaining
the adolescent and adult protocols, the three pictures that usually elic-

ited achievement stories were presented at both administrations. Cards 1, 14, and 17BM, which elicited 77% of all the achievement themes, were common to both protocols. The strong tendency for these particular cards to elicit achievement themes has been noted in another study (Kagan & Moss, 1959). A typical achievement theme to Card 1 concerned a boy who wanted to master the violin and/or become a famous violinist. A typical achievement story to Card 17BM involved a person who was in a rope climbing contest and wanted to do his best to win. A common achievement story to Card 14 concerned an artist or student who had been working hard and was looking forward to fame and success as a result of his accomplishments.

The stability of the TAT achievement score between the adolescent and adult protocols was determined through the use of contingency coefficients. The stability coefficients were .34, .36, and .31 for boys, girls, and total group ($p < .10$, $< .05$, $< .02$; one-tailed). Thus, achievement themes also showed some degree of stability over this 10-year period. These data extend the findings of an earlier investigation (Kagan & Moss, 1959), in which the authors reported a 3 year stability coefficient of .32 ($p < .01$) for achievement themes obtained at median ages of 8–9 and 11–6. The stability coefficients between the adolescent and adult protocols are of the same magnitude as those found for the earlier age period.

Validity of Achievement Themes: Relations with
Child and Adult Behavior

Contingency coefficients were computed relating the occurrence of adolescent and adult achievement themes with the longitudinal and adult achievement ratings. These results are presented in Table 2. The highest and most consistent relations were between the adult achievement themes and adult interview ratings. The only significant relation between adult themes and the childhood ratings held for mechanical achievement ($C = +.63$; $p < .001$ for boys, and $-.50$; $p < .02$ for girls).

The adolescent TAT was also more predictive of adult behavior than it was of the childhood ratings. Adolescent achievement themes predicted adult achievement behavior for women ($C = +.44$; $p < .01$) and intellectual concerns for men ($C = +.44$; $p < .01$). Adolescent achievement themes showed minimal association with the child's achievement behavior. The only significant positive association was the age 3–6 achievement for boys. Once again the rating of mechanical achievement for girls was negatively associated with achievement themes. This negative correlation may be due to the fact that this is the only variable for which markedly different behavioral referents were used in rating the two sexes. For boys, involvement in carpentry, engines, motors, and model airplanes was emphasized in the rating. These activities are sex-typed and girls showed no interest in them. Participation in craft work (making jewelry, leather ar-

TABLE 2. Relation between TAT Achievement Themes and Child and Adult Achievement Behavior (contingency coefficients)

Longitudinal Variable	Age	Adolescent TAT (Median age 14–6)		Adult TAT (Median age 25)	
		Males	Females	Males	Females
Recognition	6–10	.21	.17	.26	.22
	10–14	−.20	−.18	−.31	.39
Achievement	0–3	−.15	−.25	−.20	.16
	0–6	.42*	.19	.19	.36
	6–10	.24	.15	.13	.30
Achievement					
Intellectual	10–14	.30	−.25	.26	.16
Mechanical	10–14	.31	−.62***	.63****	−.50**
Athletic	10–14	−.20	.12	.12	.17
Maternal acceleration	0–3	.11	.51**	.25	−.08
	3–6	.37	.23	.27	.28
	6–10	.51***	.26	.24	.41*
Adult interview variables (median age 25)					
Recognition		.17	.25	.40**	.52****
Achievement		.19	.44***	.37*	.52****
Intellectual concerns		.44***	.25	.31	.59****

    * $p < .05$; one-tailed.
   ** $p < .02$; one-tailed.
  *** $p < .01$; one-tailed.
 **** $p < .001$; one-tailed.

ticles) and sewing was also used as evidence of involvement in mechanical activities and girls tended to choose these behaviors.

Maternal acceleration during the first 10 years of life showed suggestive relationships with the adolescent achievement themes. For example, maternal acceleration for age 0–3 predicted achievement themes at adolescence for girls (C = +.51; $p < .02$), but not for boys. Maternal acceleration for age 6–10 predicted adolescent achievement themes for boys (C = +.51); $p < .01$) and adult achievement themes for girls (C = +.41; $p < .05$).

In summary, the adult and adolescent TAT stories showed moderate correlations with adult achievement but minimal association with the childhood achievement ratings. Maternal acceleration was associated, to some degree, with adolescent achievement themes.

IQ Increase and Achievement Behavior

The difference between the child's smoothed IQ at age 6 and 10 was used as a measure of IQ change. Earlier studies (Kagan et al., 1958; Sontag et al., 1958) have demonstrated that the amount of increase in IQ correlated both with independent behavioral indices of achievement strivings for age 6–10, and with early adolescent (age 10–14) achievement stories. These latter relations remain significant when the influence of the child's IQ at age 6 is statistically controlled. The present data allowed for a partial validation of these results and an extension of the Sontag et al. findings for adolescence and adulthood.[6]

Table 3 presents the correlations between changes in IQ during age

TABLE 3. RELATION BETWEEN IQ CHANGE AND CHILDHOOD AND ADULT ACHIEVEMENT VARIABLES (product-moment correlations)

Longitudinal Variables	Age	Males	Females
Recognition	6–10	.24	.21
Recognition	10–14	.41**	.09
Achievement	0–3	.13	.04
Achievement	3–6	—.02	.24
Achievement	6–10	.39***	.47***
Achievement-intellectual	10–14	.37*	.41**
Achievement-mechanical	10–14	.15	.14
Achievement-athletic	10–14	—.16	—.46**
Maternal acceleration	0–3	—.06	.20
Maternal acceleration	3–6	—.03	—.12
Maternal acceleration	6–10	.10	.54***
Adult interview variables			
Recognition		.48***	.25
Achievement		.38***	.38**
Intellectual concern		.49***	.42***

* $p < .05$; one-tailed.
** $p < .02$; one-tailed.
*** $p < .01$; one-tailed.

6–10 and the longitudinal and adult behaviors. The amount of IQ increase was a fairly sensitive predictor of both intellectual achievement for age 10–14 ($r = .37$ and .41 for boys and girls; $p < .01$), and concern with intellectual competence in adulthood ($r = .49$ and .42; $p < .01$). These results support and extend the earlier studies and indicate that amount of IQ increase during the first 4 years of school is a moderately accurate index of the subject's motivation to master intellectual tasks during adolescence and early adulthood. It is important to note that IQ change showed no relation to mechanical or athletic strivings for boys, and was negatively associated with athletic achievement for girls ($r = -.46$; $p < .02$). Thus, IQ increase is not a general measure of achievement strivings for all areas of task mastery. The IQ change measure predicts all three adult achievement ratings because the three adult variables are heavily weighted with concern over intellectual competence. Finally, the maternal acceleration rating for age 6–10 showed a positive relation with IQ change for girls ($r = +.54$; $p < .01$) but not for boys.

Intercorrelations among the Measures

There were, as might be anticipated, positive correlations among the achievement and recognition ratings. Tables 4, 5, and 6 present the intercorrelations among the variables that were rated for ages 6–10, 10–14, and adulthood. The correlations for the males are above and to the right of the diagonal; the female data are to the left and below the diagonal.

For all three age periods there were high, positive correlations among the achievement and recognition variables. For age 10–14, recognition behavior was highly correlated with achievement strivings in the intellectual area, but only minimally related to mechanical or athletic achievement. This finding suggests that, for this middle class sample, mastery of intellectual skills is the primary method chosen to obtain social recognition. Perhaps for lower class samples this generalization might be less valid. The high correlations between recognition behavior and intellectual concern in adulthood, together with the fact that maternal acceleration predicted both variables, suggests that it is difficult to separate "recognition seeking behavior" from "attempts to improve intellectual competence."

DISCUSSION

Stability of Achievement Strivings

The results indicate that strivings for intellectual mastery are moderately stable from the school years through early adulthood. This behavioral disposition emerges as a stable phenomenon at ages 3–6 for girls and 6–10 for boys. The stability of the behavior ratings is paralleled by the moderate stability of TAT achievement stories over a shorter age span. Moreover, achievement stories in adolescence and adulthood also predicted the adult behavior ratings. This consistent cluster of correlations adds construct va-

TABLE 4. INTERCORRELATIONS AMONG VARIABLES RATED FOR AGE 6–10

	Recognition	Achievement	Maternal Acceleration
Recognition	—	.77***	.57***
Achievement	.60***	—	.59***
Maternal acceleration	.39*	.44***	—

Note.—Data for males are in upper right; for females, in lower left.
* $p < .05$; two-tailed.
*** $p < .01$; two-tailed.

TABLE 5. INTERCORRELATIONS AMONG VARIABLES RATED FOR AGE 10–14

	Recognition	Intellectual Achievement	Mechanical Achievement	Athletic Achievement
Recognition	—	.74***	.23	.04
Intellectual achievement	.60***	—	.53***	−.11
Mechanical achievement	.17	.32	—	−.23
Athletic achievement	.24	.12	.07	—

Note.—Data for males are in upper right; for females, in lower left.
*** $p < .01$; two-tailed.

TABLE 6. INTERCORRELATIONS AMONG ADULT INTERVIEW VARIABLES

	Achievement	Recognition	Intellectual
Achievement	—	.72***	.73***
Recognition	.79***	—	.72***
Intellectual	.77***	.84***	—

Note.—Data for males are in upper right; for females, in lower left.
*** $p < .01$; two-tailed.

lidity to the TAT achievement variable and support to the conclusion that this class of behaviors is stable over time.

Involvement in athletics for age 10–14 showed no strong, positive relation to either IQ increase or adult achievement behavior and, in a few instances, negative relationships occurred. This was not because the interviewer failed to assess adult involvement in this particular activity. Rather, many of the adults who had been involved in athletics as early adolescents were not overly concerned with task mastery as adults and they tended to avoid intellectual activities.

The majority of the sample regarded positions of responsibility, intellectual challenge, and knowledge of the environment as highly desirable goals. If a subject had strong achievement motives he tended to gratify them through intellectually oriented endeavors. It is suggested that the mass media and social environment differentially emphasize the importance of different skills in accordance with the sex and age role characteristics of the individual. For adults, there tends to be an emphasis on intellectual competence and a de-emphasis on active mastery of athletic skills. Moreover, intellectual mastery is less involved in potential sex role conflict than mechanical or athletic behaviors. To excel at sports is one of the defining characteristics of masculinity. Some boys become involved in athletics in order to maintain their sex role identity and avoid peer rejection. An athletic girl will be subject to peer rejection for excessive participation in athletics. Thus, athletic mastery is under the control of motives and conflicts related to sex role identification in addition to needs for task mastery.

This latter point raises the question of the appropriate definition of achievement behavior and motivation. It is suggested that the concept of a general achievement motive is too broad a term, and it may be useful to replace this construct with a series of variables that relate to more specific behaviors. It seems more reasonable to talk about "desire to improve intellectual skills," or "desire to improve athletic skills" than to use the more global concept of need achievement. Individuals strive to perfect skills in different areas, and the motivations for these strivings are multiple. Prediction and comprehension of these phenomena might be facilitated if there was some differentiation among the behaviors and motives that are involved in task mastery.

The lack of predictive power of age 0–3 mastery behavior might have been due to the greater difficulty in rating this variable (the interrater reliability was .35). On the other hand, the behavioral referents for this rating differed from those used to assess mastery for the older age periods. Since 2-year-olds do not initiate intellectual or athletic mastery behavior, persistence with simple, perceptual-motor tasks (stringing beads, building towers) was the basis for this early rating. A high rating for 0–3 reflected a high threshold for satiation with simple, sensorimotor activities. At the older ages, the achievement rating was based on involvement with problem solving behaviors that were more similar in form to adult achievement behavior. The age 0–3 rating is dynamically different from the symbolic behaviors that characterize achievement during the preschool and school years.[7] This statement is supported by the fact that achievement for age 0–3 was negatively correlated with achievement for age 3–6 ($r = -.20$) and age 6–10 ($r = -.03$), and showed no relationship to achievement themes or IQ change. Persistence with simple sensorimotor tasks during the first 2 or 3 years of life is not an index of future intellectual, achievement strivings. The 2-year-old who will sit for 20 minutes trying to put a peg in a hole is not necessarily the ambitious scholar of the fifth grade.

Maternal Acceleration and Achievement

The ratings of maternal concern with the child's developmental skills were heavily weighted with encouragement of intellectual progress. The most consistent correlates of maternal acceleration were found with the ratings of adult concern with intellectual competence. Maternal acceleration for age 0–3 was slightly more predictive of adult behavior for girls than for boys. Similarly, maternal acceleration for age 6–10 was more predictive of IQ increase for daughters than for sons. The sex difference between these latter two correlations was significant at the .05 level. It is suggested that since the girl was more likely than the boy to identify with the mother, maternal encouragement of intellectual mastery should have had a greater effect on the development of the girl than on the boy.[8]

TAT Achievement Stories

Achievement themes on the TAT were moderately stable and were correlated with adult achievement behavior. The fact that the correlations were as high for females as for males, although the three critical cards illustrated male heroes, raises some question concerning the validity of the hero hypothesis. Since Cards 1, 14, and 17BM all picture a male in a potential achievement situation, one might expect that achievement themes for women would not be highly correlated with their achievement behavior. The present results indicate that the production of achievement themes may be more influenced by the subject's conception of what behaviors are appropriate for the hero, than by the degree of identification of storyteller with hero. Perhaps high achievement girls conceptualize the male role as being more associated with task mastery than do low achievement girls.

Atkinson (1957) has suggested that achievement themes have differential validity depending on whether or not the criterion task engages the subject's motivation. The achievement variables used in this study (ratings of overt behavior, IQ increase scores) measured "real life" behaviors that would be expected to engage the subject's motivation. The positive correlations obtained indicate that achievement themes are valid indices of intellective mastery when the conditions under which the behavioral samples are obtained are motive arousing.

Limitations on Generalizability

Although the stability correlations for achievement behavior are fairly high, the nature of this particular sample favored stability. The social milieu of these subjects remain constant throughout the first 17 years of their lives, and the parents and peers of these subjects retained their same values. The degree of stability obtained with this sample might not hold for populations that were more mobile, for different ethnic or social class groups, or for children subjected to major developmental traumata.

Social Reinforcement and Stability

The stability of achievement behavior is congruent with general reinforcement theory. Each time achievement strivings are rewarded through social approval or internal feelings of satisfaction, the strength of this behavioral tendency should be increased. If achievement strivings lead to failure, these behaviors should extinguish. The child who attains scholastic honors through effort is rewarded by the social environment, and this experience frequently leads to an expectancy of future success for similar behavior. This rewarding experience, coupled with the strong cultural approval for intellectual competence, increases the probability that the child will continue to engage in intellectual tasks. On the other hand, persistent failures in intellectually challenging situations are likely to lead to an expectancy of failure, and these expectancies can result in avoidance and/or withdrawal from involvement in intellectual behavior.

SUMMARY

This paper summarized results from a larger investigation on the stability of behavior from childhood through adulthood. This investigation dealt specifically with the long term stability of achievement and recognition seeking behaviors in subjects who were part of the Fels Research Institute's longitudinal population.

The subjects were 36 males and 35 females for whom extensive longitudinal information was available from birth through 14 years of age. One psychologist, who had no knowledge of the adult behavior of these subjects, studied narrative reports based on observations of the child in a variety of settings, and rated each child on achievement and recognition seeking behaviors for four age periods: 0–3, 3–6, 6–10, and 10–14. In addition, ratings were made for maternal acceleration of developmental skills for the first three age periods. A second psychologist, who had no knowledge of the childhood information, interviewed each subject in adulthood (age range 20–29) and rated him on three variables related to achievement and recognition seeking behavior in adulthood.

In addition, the following information was available for most subjects: (*a*) a 7 card TAT protocol administered during early adolescence (median age 14–6) and a 13 card TAT protocol following the adult interview, and (*b*) annual Stanford-Binet IQ tests from ages 5 through 11 which furnished an IQ change score over the years 6–10.

The major results were as follows:

1. Both achievement and recognition striving behaviors for age 6–10 showed significant positive correlations with similar behaviors during adulthood, the correlations ranged from .38 to .68 and all were significant at the .05 level or better.

2. Involvement in intellectual activities for age 10–14 showed high positive correlations with achievement behavior in adulthood while involvement in athletics during these years showed no positive relationship with adult achievement behavior. Involvement in mechanical tasks for age 10–14 showed positive correlations with adult achievement behavior for boys but not for girls.

3. Maternal acceleration of the child's developmental skills during the first 3 years of life predicted adult achievement behavior for women but not for men. Maternal acceleration of developmental skills during age 6–10 showed moderate correlations with adult concern with intellectual competence in both sexes.

4. Achievement stories told during adolescence and adulthood showed high positive correlations with adult achievement behavior. Maternal acceleration of developmental skills showed suggestive correlations with the occurrence of achievement stories in both adolescence and adulthood.

5. The amount of increase in IQ score during the years 6–10 showed high positive correlations with the ratings of achievement behavior during adulthood. In addition, increase in IQ showed positive correlations with age 6–10 achievement behavior, and with strivings for intellectual competence during age 10–14. Amount of IQ increase showed negative correlations with athletic achievement for age 10–14.

The results suggested that achievement strivings during the first 4 years of school are a moderately good index of future achievement behavior during adolescence and adulthood. There were high correlations between strivings for social recognition and intellectual achievement and it was suggested that these variables are intimately related in a middle class population.

REFERENCES

Atkinson, J. W. Motivational determinants of risk taking behavior, *Psychol. Rev.*, 1957, **64**, 359–372.

Kagan, J., & Moss, H. A. The stability and validity of achievement fantasy. *J. abnorm. soc. Psychol.*, 1959, **58**, 357–364.

Kagan, J., & Moss, H. A. The stability of passive and dependent behavior from childhood through adulthood. *Child Develpm.*, in press.

Kagan, J., Sontag, L. W., Baker, C. T., & Nelson, Virginia L. Personality and IQ change. *J. abnorm. soc. Psychol.*, 1958, **26**, 261–266.

McClelland, D. C., Atkinson, J. W., Clark, R. A., & Lowell, E. L. *The achievement motive.* New York: Appleton-Century-Crofts, 1953.

Mood, A. M. *Introduction to the theory of statistics.* New York: McGraw-Hill, 1950.

Murray, H. A. *Thematic Apperception Test Manual.* Cambridge: Harvard Univer. Press, 1943.

Peters, C. C., & Van Voorhis, W. R. *Statistical procedures and their mathematical bases.* New York: McGraw-Hill, 1940.

Piaget, J. *The origins of intelligence in children.* New York: International Univer. Press, 1952.

Sontag, L. W., Baker, C. T., & Nelson, Virginia L. Mental growth and personality development. *Monogr. Soc. Res. Child Develpm.*, 1958, **23**, No. 68.

NOTES

1. This research was supported, in part, by Research Grant M-1260 from the National Institute of Mental Health, United States Public Health Service.

2. The staff of the institute during the 24 years of data collection included Alfred L. Baldwin, Thomas W. Richards, Horace Champney, Virginia L. Nelson, assisted by Leah Levinger, Helen Marshall, Mary Frances Hartson, Joan Kalhorn Lasko, Faye Breese, Margaret Slutz, Marjorie Powell, Frances Best, and a group of assistants to whom the authors are indebted. Their efforts made this project possible.

3. All correlations were corrected for restricted range of scores using a procedure described by Peters and Van Voorhis (1940, pp. 395–398).

4. Virginia L. Nelson administered all of the IQ tests.

5. The contingency coefficients were based on chi squares computed from Mood's likelihood ratio test for a 3×2 distribution (Mood, 1950, p. 257).

6. In the present sample of 71 subjects, 50% of the males and 20% of the females overlapped with the group of 70 subjects studied by Sontag, Baker, and Nelson (1958). However, their data only dealt with the period from 3 to 10 years of age. The present behavioral material covered adolescence and early adulthood.

7. The differences in the content of mastery behaviors for ages 0–3 and 3–6 are analogous to Piaget's (1952) description of intellectual development. Piaget suggests that during the first 2 years the child is in the sensorimotor stage of intelligence in which simple perceptual-motor activity is salient. During the subsequent preschool years the child's intellectual activity becomes more symbolic and more comparable to adult problem solving behavior.

8. Research in progress at the institute, under the direction of Vaughn J. Crandall and Walter Katkovsky is assessing the role of both mother and father in the adoption of achievement motives and behaviors.

Adolescence

32.

The changing American child—
a speculative analysis[1]

URIE BRONFENBRENNER

Because early learning is of paramount importance, parents make the most profound and lasting impact upon the child. As far as the development of effective people is concerned, there is no job more important than that of being a parent nor any for which the preparation furnished by the culture is less adequate. Self-defeating behavior models are more apt to be passed from generation to generation than to be corrected through education, counseling, therapy, or other means of social intervention.

This author presents a research-substantiated speculation concerning the effect of changing concepts of male and female parental roles upon children. He points to the tendency of mothers to take on more of the authoritative-disciplinary aspects of parenting and the counter-inclination of fathers to adopt more nurturant, affectionate roles. He believes that the effects of this, especially for boys, may be deleterious and that such family arrangements may produce dependent offspring who do not take initiative and who cannot be depended upon to fulfill obligations. In other words, there is reason to question the efficacy of the so-called democratic or equalitarian family.

The editors are constrained to ask: What is so good about the traditional male-female models? Would people be happier if these roles were changed? Perhaps the competitive, male-dominated society could give way to the more feminine traits of nurturance and affection with positive effects.

Approach this article with anticipation. It will furnish food for thought and raise questions for consideration.

A QUESTION OF MOMENT

IT IS now a matter of scientific record that patterns of child rearing in the United States have changed appreciably over the past twenty-five years

Journal of Social Issues, 17:6–18, 1961. Urie Bronfenbrenner, Professor, Child Development and Family Relations, Cornell University.

(Bronfenbrenner, 1958). Middle class parents especially have moved away from the more rigid and strict styles of care and discipline advocated in the early Twenties and Thirties toward modes of response involving greater tolerance of the child's impulses and desires, freer expression of affection, and increased reliance on "psychological" methods of discipline, such as reasoning and appeals to guilt, as distinguished from more direct techniques like physical punishment. At the same time, the gap between the social classes in their goals and methods of child rearing appears to be narrowing, with working class parents beginning to adopt both the values and techniques of the middle class. Finally, there is dramatic correspondence between these observed shifts in parental values and behavior and the changing character of the attitudes and practices advocated in successive editions of such widely read manuals as the Children's Bureau bulletin on *Infant Care* and Spock's *Baby and Child Care*. Such correspondence should not be taken to mean that the expert has now become the principal instigator and instrument of social change, since the ideas of scientists and professional workers themselves reflect in part the operation of deep-rooted cultural processes. Nevertheless, the fact remains that changes in values and practices advocated by prestigeful professional figures can be substantially accelerated by rapid and widespread dissemination through the press, mass media of communication, and public discussion.

Given these facts, it becomes especially important to gauge the effect of the changes that are advocated and adopted. Nowhere is this issue more significant, both scientifically and socially, than in the sphere of familial values and behavior. It is certainly no trivial matter to ask whether the changes that have occurred in the attitudes and actions of parents over the past twenty-five years have been such as to affect the personality development of their children, so that the boys and girls of today are somewhat different in character structure from those of a decade or more ago. Or, to put the question more succinctly: has the changing American parent produced a changing American child?

A STRATEGY OF INFERENCE

Do we have any basis for answering this intriguing question? To begin with, do we have any evidence of changes in the behavior of children in successive decades analogous to those we have already been able to find for parents? If so, we could take an important first step toward a solution of the problem. Unfortunately, in contrast to his gratifying experience in seeking and finding appropriate data on parents, the present writer has, to date, been unable to locate enough instances in which comparable methods of behavioral assessment have been employed with different groups of children of similar ages over an extended period of time. Although the absence of such material precludes any direct and unequivocal approach to the question at hand, it is nevertheless possible, through a series of inferences from facts already known, to arrive at some estimate of what the answer might be. Specifically, although as yet we have no comparable data on the relation between parental and child behavior for different families at successive points in time, we do have facts on the influence of parental treatment on child behavior at a given point in time; that is, we know that certain variations in parental behavior tend to be accompanied by systematic differences in the personality characteristics of children. If we are willing to assume that these same relationships obtained not only at a given moment but across different points in time, we are in a position to infer the possible effects on children of changing patterns of child rearing over the years. It is this strategy that we propose to follow.

THE CHANGING AMERICAN PARENT

We have already noted the major changes in parental behavior discerned in a recent analysis of data reported over a twenty-five year period. These secular trends may be summarized as follows:

1. Greater permissiveness toward the child's spontaneous desires
2. Freer expression of affection
3. Increased reliance on indirect "psychological" techniques of discipline (such as reasoning or appeals to guilt) vs. direct methods (like physical punishment, scolding, or threats)
4. In consequence of the above shifts in the direction of what are predominantly middle class values and techniques, a narrowing of the gap between social classes in their patterns of child rearing

Since the above analysis was published, a new study has documented an additional trend. Bronson, Katten, and Livson (1959) have compared patterns of paternal and maternal authority and affection in two generations of families from the California Guidance Study. Unfortunately, the time span surveyed overlaps only partially with the twenty-five year period covered in our own analysis, the first California generation having been raised in the early 1900's and the second in the late '20's and early '30's. Accordingly, if we are to consider the California results along with the others cited above, we must make the somewhat risky assumption that a trend discerned in the first three decades of the century has continued in the same direction through the early 1950's. With this important qualification, an examination of the data cited by Bronson et al. (1959) points to still another, secular trend—a shift over the years in the pattern of parental role differentiation within the family. Specifically:

5. In succeeding generations the relative position of the father vis-à-vis the mother is shifting with the former becoming increasingly more affectionate and less authoritarian, and the latter becoming relatively more important as the agent of discipline, especially for boys.

"PSYCHOLOGICAL" TECHNIQUES OF DISCIPLINE
AND THEIR EFFECTS

In pursuing our analytic strategy, we next seek evidence of the effects on the behavior of children of variations in parental treatment of the type noted in our inventory. We may begin by noting that the variables involved in the first three secular trends constitute a complex that has received considerable attention in recent research in parent-child relationships. Within the last three years, two sets of investigators, working independently, have called attention to the greater efficacy of "love-oriented" or "psychological" techniques in bringing about desired behavior in the child (Sears, Maccoby, and Levin, 1957; Miller and Swanson, 1958; 1960). The present writer, noting that such methods are especially favored by middle class parents, offered the following analysis of the nature of these techniques and the reasons for their effectiveness.

Such parents are, in the first place, more likely to overlook offenses, and when they do punish, they are less likely to ridicule or inflict physical pain. Instead, they reason with the youngster, isolate him, appeal to guilt, show disappointment—in short, convey in a variety of ways, on the one hand, the kind of behavior that is expected of the child; on the other, the realization that transgression means the interruption of a mutually valued relationship. . . .

These findings (of greater efficacy) mean that middle class parents, though in one sense more lenient in their discipline techniques, are using methods that are actually more compelling. Moreover, the compelling power of these practices is probably enhanced by the more permissive treatment accorded to middle class children in the early years of life. The successful use of withdrawal of love as a discipline technique implies the prior existence of a gratifying relationship; the more love present in the first instance, the greater the threat implied in its withdrawal (Bronfenbrenner, 1958).

It is now a well established fact that children from middle class families tend to excel those from lower class in many characteristics ordinarily regarded as desirable, such as self-control, achievement, responsibility, leadership, popularity, and adjustment in general.[2] If, as seems plausible, such differences in behavior are attributable at least in part to class-linked variations in parental treatment, the strategy of inference we have adopted would appear on first blush to lead to a rather optimistic conclusion. Since, over the years, increasing numbers of parents have been adopting the more effective socialization techniques typically employed by the middle class, does it not follow that successive generations of children should show gains in the development of effective behavior and desirable personality characteristics?

Unfortunately, this welcome conclusion, however logical, is premature, for it fails to take into account all of the available facts.

SEX, SOCIALIZATION, AND SOCIAL CLASS

To begin with, the parental behaviors we have been discussing are differentially distributed not only by socio-economic status but also by sex. As we have pointed out elsewhere (Bronfenbrenner, 1961), girls are exposed to more affection and less punishment than boys, but at the same time are more likely to be subjected to "love-oriented" discipline of the type which encourages the development of internalized controls. And consistent with our line of reasoning, girls are found repeatedly to be "more obedient, cooperative, and in general better socialized than boys at comparable age levels." But this is not the whole story.

. . . At the same time, the research results indicate that girls tend to be more anxious, timid, dependent, and sensitive to rejection. If these differences are a function of differential treatment by parents, then it would seem that the more "efficient" methods of child rearing employed with girls involve some risk of what might be called "over-socialization" (Bronfenbrenner, 1961).

One could argue, of course, that the contrasting behaviors of boys and girls have less to do with differential parental treatment than with genetically-based maturational influences. Nevertheless, two independent lines of evidence suggest that socialization techniques do contribute to individual differences, *within the same sex,* precisely in the types of personality characteristics noted above. In the first place, variations in child behavior and parental treatment strikingly similar to those we have cited for the two sexes are reported in a recent comprehensive study of differences between first and later born children (Schacter, 1959). Like girls, first children receive more attention, are more likely to be exposed to "psychological" discipline, and end up more anxious and dependent, whereas later children, like boys, are more aggressive and self-confident.

A second line of evidence comes from our own current research. We have been concerned with the role of parents in the development of such "constructive" personality characteristics as responsibility and leadership among adolescent boys and girls. Our findings reveal not only the usual differences in adolescents and parents' behaviors associated with the sex of the child, but also a striking contrast in the relationship between parental and child behaviors for the two sexes. To start on firm and familiar ground, girls are rated by their teachers as more responsible than boys, whereas the latter obtain higher scores on leadership. Expected differences similarly appear in the realm of parental behavior: girls receive more affection, praise, and companionship; boys are subjected to more physical punishment and achievement demands. Quite unanticipated, however, at least by us, was the finding that both parental affection and discipline appeared to facilitate effective psychological functioning in boys, but to impede the development of such constructive behavior in girls. Closer examination of our data indicated that both extremes of either affection or discipline were deleterious for all children, but that the process of socialization entailed somewhat different risks for the two sexes. Girls were especially susceptible to the detrimental influence of over-protection; boys to the ill effects of insufficient parental discipline and support. Or, to put it in more colloquial terms: boys suffered more often from too little taming, girls from too much.

In an attempt to account for this contrasting pattern of relationships, we proposed the notion of differential optimal levels of affection and authority for the two sexes.

The qualities of independence, initiative, and self-sufficiency, which are especially valued for boys in our culture, apparently require for their development a somewhat different balance of authority and affection than is found in the "love-oriented" strategy characteristically applied with girls. While an affectional context is important for the socialization of boys, it must evidently be accompanied by and be compatible with a strong component of parental discipline. Otherwise, the boy finds himself in the same situation as the girl, who, having received greater affection, is more sensitive to its withdrawal, with the result that a little discipline goes a long way and strong authority is constricting rather than constructive (Bronfenbrenner, 1960).

What is more, available data suggest that this very process may already be operating for boys from upper middle class homes. To begin with, differential treatment of the sexes is at a minimum for these families. Contrasting parental attitudes and behaviors toward boys and girls are pronounced only at lower class levels, and decrease as one moves up the socio-economic scale (Kohn, 1959; Bronfenbrenner, 1960). Thus our own results show that it is primarily at lower middle class levels that boys get more punishment than girls, and the latter receive greater warmth and attention. With an increase in the family's social position, direct discipline drops off, especially for boys, and indulgence and protectiveness decrease for girls. As a result, patterns of parental treatment for the two sexes begin to converge. In like manner, we find that the differential effects of parental behavior on the two sexes are marked only in the lower middle class. It is here that girls especially risk being overprotected and boys not receiving sufficient discipline and support. In upper middle class the picture changes. Girls are not as readily debilitated by parental affection and power; nor is parental discipline as effective in fostering the development of responsibility and leadership in boys.

All these trends point to the conclusion that the "risks" experienced by each sex during the process of socialization tend to be somewhat different at different social class levels. Thus the danger of overprotection for girls is especially great in lower class families, but lower in upper middle class because of the decreased likelihood of overprotection. Analogously, boys are in greater danger of suffering from inadequate discipline and support in lower middle than in upper middle class. But the upper middle class boy, unlike the girl, exchanges one hazard for another. Since at this upper level the more potent "psychological" techniques of discipline are likely to be employed with both sexes, the boy presumably now too runs the risk of being "oversocialized," of losing some of his capacity for independent aggressive accomplishment.

Accordingly, if our line of reasoning is correct, we should expect a changing pattern of sex differences at successive socio-economic levels. Specifically, aspects of effective psychological functioning favoring girls should be most pronounced in the upper middle class; those favoring boys in the lower middle. A recent analysis of some of our data bears out this expectation. Girls excel boys on such variables as *responsibility* and *social acceptance* primarily at the higher socio-economic levels. In contrast, boys surpass girls on such traits as *leadership, level of aspiration,* and *competitiveness* almost exclusively in lower middle class. Indeed, with a rise in a family's social position, the differences tend to reverse themselves with girls now excelling boys.[3]

TRENDS IN PERSONALITY DEVELOPMENT: A FIRST APPROXIMATION

The implications for our original line of inquiry are clear. We are suggesting that the "love-oriented" socialization techniques, which over the past twenty-five years have been employed in increasing degree by American middle class families, may have negative as well as constructive aspects. While fostering the internalization of adult standards and the development of socialized behavior, they may also have the effect of undermining capacities for initiative and independence, particularly in boys. Males exposed to this "modern" pattern of child rearing might be expected to differ from their counterparts of a quarter century ago in being somewhat more conforming and anxious, less enterprising and self-sufficient, and, in general, possessing more of the virtues and liabilities commonly associated with feminine character structure.[4]

At long last, then, our strategy of inference has led us to a first major conclusion. The term "major" is appropriate since the conclusion takes as its points of departure and return four of the secular trends which served as the impetus for our inquiry. Specifically, through a series of empirical links and theoretical extrapolations, we have arrived at an estimate of the effects on children of the tendency of successive generations of parents to become progressively more permissive, to express affection more freely, to utilize "psychological" techniques of discipline, and, by moving in these directions to narrow the gap between the social classes in their patterns of child rearing.

FAMILY STRUCTURE AND PERSONALITY DEVELOPMENT

But one other secular trend remains to be considered: what of the changing pattern of parental role differentiation during the first three decades of the century? If our extrapolation is correct, the balance of power within the family has continued to shift with fathers yielding parental authority to mothers and taking on some of the nurturant and affectional functions traditionally associated with the maternal role. Again we have no direct evidence of the effects of such secular changes on successive generations of children, and must look for leads to analogous data on contemporaneous relationships.

We may begin by considering the contribution of each parent to the socialization processes we have examined thus far. Our data indicate that it is primarily mothers who tend to employ "love-oriented" techniques of discipline and fathers who rely on more direct methods like physical punishment. The above statement must be qualified, however, by reference to the sex of the child, for it is only in relation to boys that fathers use direct punishment more than mothers. More generally, . . . the results reveal a tendency for each parent to be somewhat more active, firm, and demanding with a child of the same sex, more lenient and indulgent with a child of the opposite sex. . . . The reversal is most complete with respect to discipline, with fathers being stricter with boys, mothers with girls. In the spheres of affection and protectiveness, there is no actual shift in preference, but the tendency to be especially warm and solicitous with girls is much more pronounced among fathers than among mothers. In fact, generally speaking, it is the father who is more likely to treat children of the two sexes differently (Bronfenbrenner, 1960).

Consistent with this pattern of results, it is primarily the behavior of fathers that accounts for the differential effects of parental behavior on the two sexes and for the individual differences within each sex. In other words, it is paternal authority and affection that tend especially to be salutary for sons but detrimental for daughters. But as might be anticipated from what we already know, these trends are pronounced only in the lower middle class; with a rise in the family's social status, both parents tend to have similar effects on their children, both within and across sexes. Such a trend is entirely to be expected since parental role differentiation tends to decrease markedly as one ascends the socio-economic ladder. It is almost exclusively in lower middle class homes that fathers are more strict with boys and mothers with girls. To the extent that direct discipline is employed in upper middle class families, it tends to be exercised by both parents equally.

Here again we see a parallelism between shifts in parental behavior across time and social class in the direction of forms (in this instance of family structure) favored by the upper middle class group.

What kinds of children, then, can we expect to develop in families in which the father plays a predominantly affectionate role, and a relatively low level of discipline is exercised equally by both parents? A tentative answer to this question is supplied by a preliminary analysis of our data in which the relation between parental role structure and adolescent behavior was examined with controls for the family's social class position. The results of this analysis are summarized as follows: . . . Both responsibility and leadership are fostered by the relatively greater salience of the parent of the same sex. . . . Boys tend to be more responsible when the father rather than the mother is the principal disciplinarian; girls are more dependable when the mother is the major authority figure. . . . In short, boys thrive in a patriarchal context, girls in a matriarchal. . . . The most dependent and least dependable adolescents describe family arrangements that are neither patriarchal nor matriarchal, but equalitarian. To state the issue in more provocative form, our data suggest that the democratic family, which for so many years has been held up and aspired to as a model by professionals and enlightened laymen, tends to produce young people who "do not take initiative," "look to others for direction and decision," and "cannot be counted on to fulfill obligations" (Bronfenbrenner, 1960).

In the wake of so sweeping a conclusion, it is important to call attention to the tentative, if not tenuous character of our findings. The results were based on a single study employing crude questionnaire methods and rating scales. Also, our interpretation is limited by the somewhat "attenuated" character of most of the families classified as patriarchal or matriarchal in our sample. Extreme concentrations of power in one or another parent were comparatively rare. Had they been more frequent, we suspect the data would have shown that such extreme asymmetrical patterns of authority were detrimental rather than salutary for effective psychological development, perhaps even more disorganizing than equalitarian forms.

Nevertheless, our findings do find some peripheral support in the work of others. A number of investigations, for example, point to the special importance of the father in the socialization of boys (Bandura and Walters, 1959; Mussen and Distler, 1959). Further corroborative evidence appears in the growing series of studies of effects of paternal absence (Bach, 1946; Sears, Pintler and Sears, 1946; Lynn and Sawrey, 1959; Tiller, 1958). The absence of the father apparently not only affects the behavior of the child directly but also influences the mother in the direction of greater overprotectiveness. The effect of both these tendencies is especially critical for male children; boys from father-absent homes tend to be markedly more submissive and dependent. Studies dealing explicitly with the influence of parental role structure in intact families are few and far between. Papanek (1957), in an unpublished doctoral dissertation, reports greater sex-role differentiation among children from homes in which the parental roles were differentiated. And in a carefully controlled study, Kohn and Clausen (1956) find that "schizophrenic patients more frequently than normal persons report that their mothers played a very strong authority role and the father a very weak authority role." Finally, what might best be called complementary evidence for our inferences regarding trends in family structure and their effects comes from the work of Miller, Swanson, and their associates (1958; 1960) on the differing patterns of behavior exhibited by families from *bureaucratic* and *entrepreneurial* work settings. These investigators argue that the entrepreneurial-bureaucratic dichotomy represents a new cleavage in American social structure that cuts across and overrides social class influences and carries with it its own characteristic patterns of family structure and socialization. Thus one investigation (Gold and Slater, 1958) contrasts the exercise of power in families of husbands employed in two kinds of job situations: a) those working in large organizations with three or more levels of supervision; b) those self-employed or working in small organizations with few levels of supervision. With appropriate controls for social class, equalitarian families were found more frequently in the bureaucratic groups; patriarchal and, to a lesser extent, matriarchal in the entrepreneurial setting. Another study (Miller and Swanson, 1958) shows that, in line with Miller and Swanson's hypotheses, parents from these same two groups tend to favor rather different ends and means of socialization, with entrepreneurial families putting considerably more emphasis on the development of independence and mastery and on the use of "psychological" techniques of discipline. These differences appear at both upper and lower middle class levels but are less pronounced in higher socio-economic strata. It is Miller and Swanson's belief, however, that the trend is toward the bureaucratic way of life, with its less structured patterns of family organization and child rearing. The evidence we have cited on secular changes in family structure and the inferences we have drawn regarding their possible effects on personality development are on the whole consistent with their views.

LOOKING FORWARD

If Miller and Swanson are correct in the prediction that America is moving toward a bureaucratic society that emphasizes, to put it colloquially, "getting along" rather than "getting ahead," then presumably we can look forward to ever increasing numbers of equalitarian families who, in turn, will produce successive generations of ever more adaptable but unaggressive "organization men." But recent signs do not all point in this direction. In our review of secular trends in child rearing practices we detected in the data from the more recent studies a slowing up in the headlong rush toward greater permissiveness and toward reliance on indirect methods of discipline. We pointed out also that if the most recent editions of well-thumbed guidebooks on child care are as reliable harbingers of the future as they have been in the past, we can anticipate something of a return to the more explicit discipline techniques of an earlier era. Perhaps the most important forces, however, acting to redirect both the aims and methods of child rearing in America emanate from behind the Iron Curtain. With the firing of the first Sputnik, Achievement began to replace Adjustment as the highest goal of the American way of life. We have become concerned—perhaps even obsessed—with "education for excellence" and the maximal utilization of our intellectual resources. Already ability grouping, and the guidance counselor who is its prophet, have moved down from the junior high to the elementary school, and parents can be counted on to do their part in preparing their youngsters for survival in the new competitive world of applications and achievement tests.

But if a new trend in parental behavior is to develop, it must do so in the context of changes already under way. And if the focus of parental authority is shifting from husband to wife, then perhaps we should anticipate that pressures for achievement will be imposed primarily by mothers rather than fathers. Moreover, the mother's continuing strong emotional investment in the child should provide her with a powerful lever for evoking desired performance. It is noteworthy in this connection that recent studies of the familial origins of need-achievement point to the matriarchy as the optimal context for development of the motive to excel (Strodtbeck, 1958; Rosen and D'Andrade, 1959).

The prospect of a society in which socialization techniques are directed toward maximizing achievement drive is not altogether a pleasant one. As a number of investigators have shown (Baldwin, Kalhorn and Breese, 1945; Baldwin, 1948; Haggard, 1957; Winterbottom, 1958; Rosen and D'Andrade, 1959), high achievement motivation appears to flourish in a family atmosphere of "cold democracy" in which initial high levels of maternal involvement are followed by pressures for independence and accomplishment.[5] Nor does the product of this process give ground for reassurance. True, children from achievement-oriented homes excel in planfulness and performance, but they are also more aggressive, tense, domineering, and cruel (Baldwin, Kalhorn and Breese, 1945; Baldwin, 1948; Haggard, 1957). It would appear that education for excellence if pursued single-mindedly may entail some sobering social costs.

But by now we are in danger of having stretched our chain of inference beyond the strength of its weakest link. Our speculative analysis has become far more speculative than analytic and to pursue it further would bring us past the bounds of science into the realms of science fiction. In concluding our discussion, we would re-emphasize that speculations should, by their very nature, be held suspect. It is for good reason that, like "damn Yankees" they too carry their almost inseparable sobriquets: speculations are either "idle" or "wild." Given the scientific and social importance of the issues we have raised, we would dismiss the first of these labels out of hand, but the second cannot be disposed of so easily. Like the impetuous child, the "wild" speculation responds best to the sobering influence of friendly but firm discipline, in this instance from the hand of the behavioral scientist. As we look ahead to the next twenty-five years of human socialization, let us hope that the "optimal levels" of involvement and discipline can be achieved not only by the parent who is unavoidably engaged in the process, but also by the scientist who attempts to understand its working, and who—also unavoidably—contributes to shaping its course.

REFERENCES

Bach, G. R., "Father-Fantasies and Father-Typing in Father-Separated Children," *Child Development,* 1946, **17**, 63–79.

Baldwin, A. L., Kalhorn, J., and Breese, F. H., "The Appraisal of Parent Behavior," *Psychological Monographs,* 1945, 58 No. 3 (Whole No. 268).

Baldwin, A. L., "Socialization and the Parent-Child Relationship," *Child Development,* 1948, **19**, 127–136.

Bandura, A., and Walters, R. H., *Adolescent Aggression,* New York: Ronald Press, 1959.

Bronfenbrenner, U., "Socialization and Social Class Through Time and Space," in Maccoby, E., Newcomb, T. M., and Hartley, E. L., *Readings in Social Psychology.* New York: Holt, 1958, pp. 400–425.

Bronfenbrenner, U., "Some Familial Antecedents of Responsibility and Leadership in Adolescents," in Petrullo, L., and Bass, B. M., *Leadership and Interpersonal Behavior,* New York: Holt, Rinehart, and Winston, 1961.

Bronson, W. C., Katten, E. S., and Livson, N., "Patterns of Authority and Affection in Two Generations," *Journal of Abnormal and Social Psychology,* 1959, **58**, pp. 143–152.

Gold, M., and Slater, C., "Office, Factory, Store—and Family: A Study of Integration Setting," *American Sociological Review,* 1959, **23**, 64–74.

Haggard, E. A., "Socialization, Personality, and Academic Achievement in Gifted Children," *The School Review,* 1957, **65**, 388–414.

Kohn, M. L., and Clausen, J. A., "Parental Authority Behavior and Schizophrenia," *American Journal of Orthopsychiatry,* 1956, **26**, 297–313.

Kohn, M. L., "Social Class and Parental Values," *American Journal of Sociology,* 1959, **44**, 337–351.

Lynn, D. B., and Sawrey, W. L., "The Effects of Father-Absence on Norwegian Boys and Girls," *Journal of Abnormal and Social Psychology,* 1959, **59**, 258–262.

Miller, D. R., and Swanson, G. E., *The Changing American Parent.* New York, John Wiley, 1958.

Miller, D. R., and Swanson, G. E., *Inner Conflict and Defense.* New York: Holt, 1960.

Mussen, P., and Distler, L., "Masculinity, Identification, and Father-Son Relationships," *Journal of Abnormal and Social Psychology,* 1959, **59**, 350–356.

Papanek, M., *Authority and Interpersonal Relations in the Family*. Unpublished doctoral dissertation on file at the Radcliffe College Library, 1957.

Rosen, B. L., and D'Andrade, R., "The Psychosocial Origins of Achievement Motivation," *Sociometry*, 1959, **22**, 185–217.

Schachter, S., *The Psychology of Affiliation*. Stanford, California; Stanford University Press, 1959.

Sears, R. R., Pintler, M. H., and Sears, P. S., "Effects of Father-Separation on Preschool Children's Doll Play Aggression," *Child Development*, 1946, **17**, 219–243.

Sears, R. R., Maccoby, Eleanor, and Levin, M., *Patterns of Child Rearing*. Evanston, Illinois: Row, Peterson, 1957.

Strodtbeck, F. L., "Family Interaction, Values, and Achievement" in McClelland, D. C., Baldwin, A. L., Bronfenbrenner, U., and Strodtbeck, F. L., *Talent and Society*. Princeton, New Jersey: Van Nostrand, 1958, pp. 135–194.

Tiller, P. O., "Father-Absence and Personality Development of Children in Sailor Families," *Nordisk Psykologis Monograph Series*, 1958, 9.

Winterbottom, M. R., "The Relation of Need Achievement to Learning Experiences in Independence and Mastery," in Atkinson, J. W., *Motives in Fantasy, Action, and Society*. Princeton, New Jersey: Van Nostrand, 1958, pp. 453–494.

NOTES

1. This paper draws heavily on results from a program of research being conducted by the author in collaboration with Edward C. Devereux and George J. Suci. The contribution of these colleagues to facts and ideas presented in this paper is gratefully acknowledged. The research program is supported in part with grants from the National Science Foundation and the National Institutes of Health.

2. For a summary of findings on social class differences in children's behavior and personality characteristics, see Mussen, P. H., and Conger, J. J., *Child Development and Personality*, New York: Harper, 1956.

3. These shifts in sex difference with a rise in class status are significant at the 5% level of confidence (one-tailed test).

4. Strikingly similar conclusions were reached almost fifteen years ago in a provocative essay by Arnold Green ("The Middle Class Male Child and Neurosis," *American Sociological Review*, 1946, 11, 31–41). With little to go on beyond scattered clinical observations and impressions, Green was able to detect many of the same trends which we have begun to discern in more recent systematic empirical data.

5. Cold democracy under female administration appears to foster the development of achievement not only in the home but in the classroom as well. In a review of research on teaching effectiveness, Ackerman reports that teachers most successful in bringing about gains in achievement score for their pupils were judged "least considerate," while those thought friendly and congenial were least effective. (Ackerman, W. I., "Teacher Competence and Pupil Change," *Harvard Educational Review*, 1954, 24, 273–289.)

33.

Self-concepts of high- and low-curiosity boys

WALLACE H. MAW
ETHEL W. MAW

A couple of principles of development are illustrated by the article by Maw and Maw on curiosity. One is the misconception of compensation in development. There are popular beliefs that if one has a weakness in one area, he will have strength in another: e.g., strong back, weak mind; beautiful but dumb; put him in the shop, he's no scholar. Each of these beliefs is more likely than not to be just the reverse. The pre-adolescent boys in this study may be lacking in curiosity, but they are also poorer than their compatriots in social affiliation, academic achievement, and personal adjustment.

The other point, which has been emphasized here and there in this book, is that how one feels about himself determines to a remarkable extent what he is and does. The editors think that they see in their students, associates, and counseling clients the great and basic importance of the self-concept. Hence, just one minor—and it is minor—exception to the article: the sentence, third from the last, "If further studies indicate that this is the case, curriculum studies might well be undertaken." We think there is only one solution—build that ego. Parents should become supportive, teachers should find many ways to praise, accept, acknowledge the boy as a person. See to it that regardless of curriculum, course, or subject, the boys' evaluations are based on the small bits of progress (success) each one makes from where he was rather than in comparison with others. Egos are built or rebuilt in the same way—small bits at a time.

DURING THE past few years, there has been a growing interest in the curiosity of elementary school children. Some research has revealed that it is possible to identify groups of children who differ in their level of what may be defined as curiosity (Maw & Maw 1964).

Since such groups can be identified, it is reasonable to assume that they may differ also on variables other than curiosity. If this is so, the discovery of the nature of these other variables may give us insight into circumstances conducive or not conducive to the development of curiosity in elementary school children.

Child Development, 41:123–129, 1970. © 1970 by the Society for Research in Child Development, Inc. All rights reserved. Wallace H. Maw, University of Delaware; Ethel W. Maw, Bryn Mawr College.

This study was supported in part by research grant CRP-1511 from the U.S. Office of Education.

Among such variables may be the child's conception of himself as a person. Mahone (1960) found that a person who has a low estimate of himself is strongly motivated to avoid failure and tends to set goals so low that he does not need to prove himself. On the other hand, Mahone found that people high in self-acceptance are willing to prove themselves. White (1959), in a study of competence, concluded that competence was the common outcome of visual exploration, activity, and manipulation, all related to what has been called curiosity. He said that "all of these behaviors have a common biological significance—they all form part of the process whereby the . . . child learns to react effectively with his environment." Seeman (1959) considered these concepts under what he called "organismic integration." In his opinion, they represent an underlying interaction which is both adaptive and self-enhancing.

From these findings, it can be hypothesized that children high in curiosity are also those who have successfully interacted with their environments and, as a result, have good self-concepts. In this study, this hypothesis is limited to groups of boys differing in degree of curiosity.

PROCEDURE

From this investigation, two major steps with several substeps were carried out. First, groups of boys differing in curiosity were identified. Second, members of these groups were measured to determine levels of self-esteem.

Definition of Curiosity

In order to obtain groups of boys differing in curiosity level, it was necessary to define curiosity. Several studies reported elsewhere, describe how a definition was obtained (Maw & Maw 1964, pp. 25–31.) These included formal and informal interviews, reviews of literature, and an analysis of other definitions. On the basis of these studies, an elementary school child was said to demonstrate curiosity when he (*a*) reacts positively to new, strange, incongruous, or mysterious elements in his environment by moving toward them, exploring them, or manipulating them; (*b*) exhibits a need or a desire to know more about himself and/or his environment; (*c*) scans his surroundings seeking new experiences; and/or (*d*) persists in examining and/or exploring stimuli in order to know more about them.

Nature of Sample

On the basis of this definition, 224 boys were selected from several fifth grades in the public schools in New Castle County, Delaware. Fifth grade was selected to avoid, as far as possible, children with developmental reading problems and children whose interests had crystallized—as is often the case of junior and senior high school pupils.

The state of Delaware provides special classes for the educable and trainable. Therefore, there were no children in the study with IQs low enough to be admitted to such classes. The mean IQ of the 224 boys in this study was 110.12.

In general, the children composing the sample were from middle-class white suburban families. No children were from predominantly less-chance, deprived areas. The majority of the children from upper-class families were probably attending private schools, since this is traditional in the area, and there are many excellent private schools located nearby.

Determining Criterion Groups

In order to ascertain whether groups of boys high in curiosity differ from groups low in curiosity, it was necessary to identify criterion groups. The boys in each classroom were rated on degree of curiosity by their teachers and their classmates. Two types of rating instruments were developed to aid in making the evaluations. Each instrument or procedure was designed to include all aspects of the definition of curiosity as used in this study.

Each of the 19 classroom teachers was given the definition of curiosity described above together with an illustration of the type of behavior suggested for each part of it (Maw & Maw 1964, pp. 132–133). The teacher was told that all kinds of behavior included might not be observable in any one boy but that it was reasonable to suppose that the more of them a boy showed, the more curious he was. The teacher was also cautioned that the boy who showed the most curiosity might not be the one who was making the best classroom adjustment. After being given these directions, each teacher was asked to rate the boys in his class.

This procedure was not appropriate for the children to use to evaluate their peers. Therefore, an instrument called the Who-Should-Play-the-Part test was created (Maw & Maw 1964, pp. 134–135). The children were given the descriptions of eight roles—four of children whose behavior was an example of high curiosity and four of children whose behavior was an example of low curiosity. The raters were told to select children in their classroom who were generally most like the characters required for the play.

An earlier study (Maw 1967, p. 14) had indicated that there was a moderate relationship ($r = .36$) between the ratings made of children's curiosity and their intelligence. It seemed appropriate, therefore, to take intelligence into account when establishing groups of boys differing in curiosity.

In order to control for intelligence in establishing groups differing in curiosity, the following steps were taken:

1. Each boy was judged by his peers and his teacher on the basis of the definition of curiosity developed for this study.
2. The peer judgments were correlated with intelligence.
3. The procedure was repeated for teacher judgments.
4. The regression equations for peer judgment on intelligence and for teacher judgment on intelligence were calculated.
5. Groups of boys whose scores differed from the regression lines by at least one standard error on both teacher judgment and peer judgment were selected.

These groups included 15 high-curiosity boys and 14 low-curiosity boys. The mean IQ and the variance of the IQs for the high group were 116.20 and 283.17, respectively; for the low group, they were 108.78 and 225.10. These differences were not significant at the .05 level, using the t test and the F ratio test.

Nature of Tests

Tests which logically seemed to measure aspects of self-conceptualization were administered to both high- and low-curiosity groups. For example, the following parts of the California Test of Personality (Thorpe, Clarke, & Tiegs 1953) seemed appropriate: (*a*) self-reliance; (*b*) sense of personal worth; (*c*) sense of personal freedom; (*d*) feeling of belonging; (*e*) withdrawing tendencies; and (*f*) total personal adjustment.

The following parts of the Children's Personality Questionnaire (Porter & Cattell 1960) were used; (*a*) ego strength; (*b*) high ergic tension; and (*c*) strong self-sentiment.

In addition, several tests developed for research purposes by the present authors and others were administered. These included a social attitudes scale constructed by Harris (1957), a social distance scale originally designed by Bogardus (1926) and modified by Maw and Maw (1965, p. 76), and an anti-democratic attitude instrument developed by Muuss (1959). Such instruments were administered because they probably indicate a concomitant of a positive self-concept—the ability to accept others.

Finally, in order to determine if these boys saw in their own behavior those characteristics considered to indicate curiosity, they were asked to rate themselves on a scale designed to measure curiosity. The scale that was used is described in detail in an earlier publication (Maw & Maw 1968).

RESULTS OF STUDY

The findings of this study may be considered in two parts: those concerned directly with self-conceptualization; those concerned with attitudes which may be considered to reflect differences in self-conceptualization.

The results of the tests indicated differences between high- and low-curiosity boys in the hypothesized direction. As can be seen in tables 1 and 2, 12 of the possible 13 differences were significant, four at the .01 level and eight at the .05 level.

TABLE 1. Results of Tests of Significance of Differences between Means of Scores of 15 High- and 14 Low- Curiosity Boys on Variables Related to Self-Conceptualization

	High Curiosity		Low Curiosity			
Variable	Mean	Vari-ance	Mean	Vari-ance	F^a	t^a
Self-reliance	7.80	2.74	6.42	5.80	2.11	1.77*
Sense of personal worth	9.06	3.63	6.57	9.18	2.52	2.63**
Sense of personal freedom	9.06	4.92	6.42	10.26	2.08	2.56**
Feeling of belonging...	9.40	5.54	7.64	8.55	1.54	1.77*
Strong self-sentiment ..	3.13	1.55	2.28	0.98	1.56	2.03*
High ergic tension	1.80	1.17	2.42	2.10	1.80	−1.31
Lack of withdrawing tendencies	9.13	6.40	6.28	10.52	1.64	2.62**
Ego strength	3.66	0.38	2.85	1.36	3.57**	2.31**
Total personal adjustment	52.86	98.26	40.00	234.15	2.38	2.66**

[a] Variance ratio tests are two-tailed; *t* tests are one-tailed.
* $p < .05$.
** $p < .01$.

TABLE 2. Results of Tests of Significance of Differences between Means of Tests of Social Attitudes and Self-Rating of Curiosity of 15 High- and 14 Low-Curiosity Boys

	High Curiosity		Low Curiosity			
Variable	Mean	Variance	Mean	Variance	F^a	t^a
Social attitudes	38.93	53.78	32.14	67.97	1.26	2.33*
Social distance	393.80	8,770.88	343.00	4,072.76	2.15	1.17*
Anti-democratic attitudes	7.40	17.40	12.07	20.84	1.19	−2.87**
Self-rating of curiosity ..	59.46	55.69	49.78	165.10	2.96*	2.45*

[a] Variance ratio tests are two-tailed; *t* tests are one-tailed.
* $p < .05$.
** $p < .01$.

Table 2 shows that high-curiosity boys as a group show significantly better overall personal adjustment than low-curiosity boys. This difference is significant at the .01 level. The data of table 1 indicate that low-curiosity boys have a lower sense of personal worth than high-curiosity boys, that is, the low-curiosity boy does not feel he is well regarded by others; he believes that his ability is less than average; he feels that he is not attractive. The difference between high and low groups was significant at the .01 level.

Examination of table 1 further reveals that high-curiosity boys differ significantly from low-curiosity boys in self-reliance, sense of personal freedom, feeling of belonging, strong self-sentiment, withdrawing tendencies, and ego strength. The difference between the means for the test of ergic tension was not significant at the .05 level, although the observed difference was in the hypothesized direction. Porter and Cattell (1960) describe children scoring high on this factor as being "irrationally worried, tense, 'driven,' irritable, and turmoil . . . [feeling] frustrated [and being] aware of being criticized."

Table 2 indicates that low-curiosity boys are more prejudiced than high-curiosity boys, have lower feelings of social responsibility, and are more intolerant of others than high-curiosity boys. The difference between the means of the two groups for the anti-democratic scale was significant at the .01 level; the differences between the means for the tests of social attitudes and social distance were significant at the .05 level.

When asked to rate their own curiosity, high-curiosity boys more than low-curiosity boys tended to report that they participate in activities that indicate curiosity. This difference, as seen in table 2, was significant at the .05 level.

In 11 cases, low-curiosity groups were more variable than high-curiosity groups. In only two cases, however, were the differences in variability significant at the .05 level or less.

DISCUSSION

It may be that boys with low self-concepts will tend not to exhibit curiosity because they expect failure and therefore avoid situations where failure might occur. Or it may be that, lacking curiosity, low-curiosity boys fail to reach out successfully into their environments and gain those experiences that will help them develop high levels of self-esteem. Still another explanation might well be that the conditions in the development of low-curiosity boys which create low self-concepts are also the conditions which promote low curiosity.

Whatever the case may be, it is obvious that here is a group of boys who may develop problems in trying to meet the demands of the school. They should be studied further for they may be the low achievers, the behavior problems, and the dropouts. If further studies indicate that this is the case, curriculum studies might well be undertaken. It may be possible to find ways to increase a child's overall level of curiosity. On the other hand, similar results might be obtained if efforts were placed on the general improvement of the self-concepts of all children.

REFERENCES

Bogardus, E. S. *The new social research*. Los Angeles: Miller, 1926.

Harris, D. B. A scale for measuring attitudes of social responsibility. *Journal of Abnormal and Social Psychology*, 1957, **54**, 322–326.

Mahone, C. H. Fear of failure and unrealistic vocational aspirations. *Journal of Abnormal and Social Psychology*, 1960, **60**, 253–261.

Maw, W. H. *A definition of curiosity: a factor analysis study*. Cooperative Research Project S-109, University of Delaware, 1967.

Maw, W. H., & Maw, E. W. Establishing criteria for evaluating measures of curiosity. *Journal of Experimental Education*, 1961, **29**, 299–306.

Maw, W. H., & Maw, E. W. *An exploratory investigation into the measurement of curiosity in elementary school children*. Cooperative Research Project 801, University of Delaware, 1964.

Maw, W. H., & Maw, E. W. *Personal and social variables differentiating children with high and low curiosity*. Cooperative Research Project 1511, University of Delaware, 1965.

Maw, W. H., & Maw, E. W. Self-appraisal of curiosity. *Journal of Educational Research*, 1968, **61**, 462–466.

Muuss, R. E. A comparison of "high causally" and "low causally" oriented sixth-grade children on personality variables indicative of mental health. Paper read at the Iowa Academy of Science, Mount Pleasant, Iowa, April 1959.

Porter, R. B., & Cattell, R. B. *Children's personality questionnaire*. Champaign, Ill.: Institute for Personality and Ability Testing, 1960.

Seeman, J. Toward a concept of personality integration. *American Psychologist*, 1959, **14**, 633–637.

Thorpe, L. B.; Clark, W. W.; & Tiegs, E. W. *California test of personality, elementary form A-A, revised*. Los Angeles: California Test Bureau, 1953.

White, R. W. Motivation reconsidered: the concept of competence. *Psychological Review*, 1959, **66**, 297–333.

34.

The middle school child in contemporary society

ROBERT J. HAVIGHURST

The concept of developmental tasks—learning problems appropriate to certain age groups as dictated by cultural demands—can be used advantageously to promote understanding of human development. In this selection, Havighurst describes those behaviors or tasks which are best learned during the preadolescent period of development. Here, it is important to reemphasize that if these tasks are not fulfilled at this particular time and in this sequence in development, subsequent learnings which are dependent upon their mastery cannot be accomplished effectively.

Whether or not the middle school was developed to meet preadolescent needs, as the author infers, or whether it was an administrative expedient brought about by crowded elementary and secondary schools is a moot question. However that may be, the middle school does appear to allow teachers to become more concerned with the learning needs or developmental tasks of this age group.

BEFORE 1950, boys and girls from ten to fourteen years of age were treated as if they were children, but ever since this date, they have been treated more and more as adults. They are pushed harder in their school work and are increasingly exposed to sexual stimulation through literature, movies, and television.

Some people argue that young people are *actually older* now than their parents were at the same age because they have developed more rapidly mentally and biologically. There is evidence that this is true to a limited degree. The age of first menstruation for girls in this country is now about nine months earlier, on the average, than at the beginning of the century. Presumably, this is due to a diet richer in vitamins and calcium than that which boys and girls received in the 19th century. Also, boys mature about three-quarters of a year earlier than they did 70 years ago.

In awareness of these changing growth patterns, the middle school idea is based on the concept that the preadolescent in today's society is capable of more mature behavior than was thought possible 30 years ago.

More important, it is based on the fact that the social environment is

Theory Into Practice, 7:120–122, 1968. Robert J. Havighurst, Professor of Education and Human Development, The University of Chicago.

more complex and that to cope with this, the young person must approach both book knowledge and his own social experience in a more mature way.

COPING WITH THE KNOWLEDGE AVALANCHE

One primary reason for the middle school idea is to help the school and the student to cope with the knowledge avalanche. There is far too much knowledge about any one school subject to try to teach comprehensively. For this reason, the strategy of teaching has changed in the direction of helping children learn the principles or the *structure* of a subject, with the expectation that they will then be able to go ahead and learn on their own initiative with the skillful use of libraries, field observation, laboratories, and so on.

In other words, we no longer treat the child's mind as a *storehouse of knowledge* but rather as an *instrument for learning*. Consequently, the new approach to the teaching of such subjects as mathematics, science, history, and geography is to teach the child to "think like an expert." That is, to think like a mathematician, historian, etc.

This approach requires a teacher who has worked hard at developing teaching methods which accomplish this objective. The teacher can no longer sit and "hear the children recite" but must work out an active teaching and learning program which may require a good deal of preparation.

In this kind of school, it may be better for teachers to specialize after about the fifth grade, in just one or two subject areas, than to teach all of the school subjects. Thus, the middle school provides a better setting for this kind of teaching, since it permits a teacher to become a specialist— often taking the lead with other younger teachers assisting.

DEVELOPMENTAL TASKS OF PREADOLESCENCE

Another goal of the middle school is to enable the school to do a better job in helping children achieve the three major developmental tasks of preadolescence that are the special concern of school: (1) organizing one's knowledge of social and physical reality, (2) learning to work well in the peer group, and (3) becoming an independent person.

1. Organizing One's Knowledge of Social and Physical Reality. Preadolescence is a period when children develop an interest in ordering, organizing, and systematizing their knowledge. By this time, they have developed some interests in certain fields of knowledge and become somewhat selective about what they choose to learn. That is, one youngster may like geography; another, animals; and a third, music. But all may want to get their store of facts and concepts systematically ordered and organized. A middle school with a more highly organized curriculum, under-girded by people who are specialized in particular subjects, is better for this purpose than the less specialized, self-contained classroom with one teacher presiding over all the aspects of knowledge.

2. *Learning to Work Well in the Peer Group.* From the fifth grade on, boys and girls are very much concerned with their abilities to get along with their age-mates in the peer group. They form teams, committees, and clubs and are very much aware of the personalities of people of their own age. This is the time for the development of a democratic social relationship, gained by working out the rules of playing and living with one's equals.

The middle school is better for this than one in which the 10- and 11-year-olds are associating with younger children. A large middle school is also good for the development of democratic habits and social attitudes among youngsters from a variety of social, economic, and racial groups. For example, recently in Kansas City, children from an entire block were transported from overcrowded schools in a Negro area to underpopulated schools in an upper middle-class white area. At the receiving school, they were distributed from the first through the sixth grade, three to four to each classroom.

After the first month, the principal reported that the experiment was working better than expected—"We are already beginning to get some good results," she reported. She described an incident resulting from redistributing children in the fifth grade because there were enough pupils to add another class. In doing this, she picked children from each of the existing classes and put them into the new class. One little girl came to her crying—she was a white girl who was a native of that school—and complained, "You are separating me from Brenda." Brenda was a colored girl with whom she had become fast friends.

3. *Becoming an Independent Person.* Youngsters at the preadolescent age are expected to become physically independent—not emotionally, but physically independent. We expect them to be able to be away from home at night or at camp in the summer, etc., without getting terribly home-sick. A 7-year-old is expected to run home to mother when things are difficult, but not a 10-year-old. In this instance, too, the more complex structure of the middle school can better prepare for development of this kind of independence, for our society is increasingly taxing a person's ego strength. Modern society requires people to have tough personalities—tough in terms of being able to withstand a variety of pushes and attacks. The middle school would overcome the problem of overprotection that exists in the present self-contained classrooms in the junior high.

In connection with providing opportunities for independence, there are some real problems in the conduct of a middle school. One is the problem of controlling behavior. Not all youngsters of 10 or 12 years have enough self-control to get along in this more complex structure. For example, one characteristic of the middle school is that the classes change about every forty minutes. Instead of having one teacher for the whole day, the child has to pass from the math to the English teacher, for example, or he may have to move from a small group of only fifteen into a group of one hundred for a lecture and demonstration. This requires the ability to adapt one's behavior to a variety of situations.

Therefore, the kind of middle school which is no more than a departmentalized set of intermediate grades is likely to fail in the inner city slum area. This is the most severe test of the middle school idea. Just as the conventional elementary school does not succeed well with many inner city children, so a middle school would fail unless it could solve the problems of motivation and method.

CONCLUSION

The middle school is in a good position to strike a balance between the conventional instrumental goals of the school and the emerging expressive goals. Writers on the middle school curriculum are stressing the message that children can enjoy learning for its own sake, and it is in the middle grades that they can really begin to make something of themselves as independent learners, who enjoy this day in school for its own sake, as well as for its instrumental value in getting them into high school, college, and on into a successful career.

35.

Social change: impact on the adolescent

JAMES S. COLEMAN

A noted observer of human relationships discusses a major problem stage of development in this selection. This is the so-called awkward age when the individual is neither child nor adult—a time when identification with the peer group and a disaffiliation with parents and establishment are developmental tasks. Yet dependence, at least in an economic sense, is not an easy thing to overcome in a technical and automated culture. It is not as possible for young people to strike out on their own in their late teens as it once was. The protracted period

National Association of Secondary School Principals Bulletin, 49:11–14, 1965. James S. Coleman, Professor of Social Relations, The Johns Hopkins University.

*necessary for gaining the increasingly complex skills and knowledge
required for self-support and social and economic advancement keeps
many youngsters tied to parental apron strings until they complete
four years of college. Responsible adult functioning and adult identity
is denied them until age twenty-two or later. Further, as Coleman
points out, improved nutrition and changes in social stimulation cause
adolescence to begin as much as a year earlier than formerly. Hence,
whatever the effects may be, problems of identity now operate over a
longer period of time and perhaps with greater consequence than ever
before. Probably, changes that occur during this period of life, when
an individual is not sure about himself, cause questions of his function
and his place to impose greater stress and pressure than they do at
other stages of living. Some of these changes and their effects are
listed and considered here.*

Adults have a special reason today to shake their heads and mutter,
"the younger generation . . .," as adults are wont to do. For today's
adults and today's teenagers have special problems of communication that
make it more and more difficult for each to understand what the other
is up to. These communication problems arise not because teenagers are
in some strange new way different than ever before, but because of
changes in the structure of our society. These changes have produced a
number of special problems in education and in the whole process of
growing up, of which the communication gap is only one. I would like
to indicate what some of these structural changes are, and some of their
consequences for adolescents.

SOCIAL CHANGES AND FAMILY COHESION

A number of changes have combined to make the family a less cohesive, less effective agent within which to raise children than ever before.
One of these changes is the entry of large numbers of women into the
labor force. Prior to World War II, in March 1940, 16.7 per cent of
married women held jobs outside the home. By March 1961, this had
doubled to 34.0 per cent. (In 1890, it was 4.5 per cent.) This change
need not, of course, make a given family less tightly knit, nor give adolescent children a less rich "psychological home," but it tends to do so, and
the overall social impact must be in this direction.

Another change is the smaller and smaller number of families that
have relatives—aunts, uncles, grandparents—living in the household.
This means that the typical family of today in America is parents and
children, with nothing more. Thus the family's strength depends far more
on the parents than ever before. The relatives are not there to provide adults
for the children to model themselves after, or adults in whom they can
confide.

A third change, which reinforces the preceding one, is the greater geographic mobility of families, particularly since World War II. An urban or suburban family today does not have a homestead that passes from one generation to another; nor does it even have a stable place of residence for a single generation. More and more, the typical "life cycle" of a family begins with a newly-married couple living in an apartment in the city; then with the first child comes a move to a suburb of families with young children; then later, as income and family grow, to a suburb of larger houses and older children; then finally, after the children are gone, back to an apartment in the city.

Such moves mean that the adult neighborhood, which was once an extension of the household itself, is hardly so now. Children make neighborhood friends quickly, but their parents do not; and perhaps most important, the children have few contacts and even fewer stable relationships with other adults in the neighborhood.

Finally, a change that has been going on for a long time is the shift of the father's work from the home or the neighborhood (e.g., the farmer or merchant) to a distant office or factory. Thus, the son knows only abstractly what his father does; and he can never enter into the father's work.

CONSEQUENCES OF CHANGES

The effects of these changes on the adolescent are many. One of the most interesting indicators is the recent large increase in "going steady" among adolescents. This phenomenon, virtually unknown in Europe, can be explained only in terms of overall changes that have taken place in the teenager's life. Looking closely at the practice of going steady indicates that it is not (as some adults fear) principally a license for sexual freedom. Instead, its basis is more nearly in the kind of psychological security it provides, a psychological closeness that today's adolescents seem to need. When we ask why they need it, the answer is clear: the family no longer provides the closeness and security it once did. Because of the structural changes indicated above, the family fails to provide the kind of close, secure relationships that the adolescent had as a child and will once again have when he himself forms a family. His response comes by finding that close security in an attachment to another.

Going steady is only one of the consequences of these structural changes in society. Another is the greater and greater burden that falls on the school. The school was once a supplement to the activities of the family in making adults of its children. But the roles have reversed for today's adolescents: the home is more and more merely a supplement to the adolescent's life, which focuses more and more on the school. It may be, as some school administrators feel, that this places too great a responsibility on the school. Yet the condition exists, and many families, with their working parents, high mobility, and lack of other relatives in the household, are in no position to change the condition. The adolescents turn to one another, to the school, and to the entertainments of the larger society, for these are their only resources.

Another consequence of the family's weakness, one that stems from the same needs as does going steady, is the earlier age of dating and of interest in the opposite sex. The consequences of this for interest in schoolwork is particularly marked for girls. There is a sharp shift in early adolescence from high evaluation of the bright girl to a much lower evaluation —for the girl who appears especially bright does not fare well in dates with boys. Among schools I studied a few years ago, this shift started slightly later in the rural schools than in the urban and suburban ones. In the former, the shift occurred during the ninth grade; in the latter, the shift had largely taken place before the ninth grade. In both sets of schools, the devaluation of brightness and the emphasis on good looks and popularity with boys was at its peak in middle adolescence. In the rural schools, it had sharply declined by the senior year in high school, while in the urban and suburban ones, the decline had already begun in the junior year. It appears that the most intense focus of adolescent girls on problems of popularity and dating, and the greatest devaluation of schoolwork occurs when the rating and dating system is still unsettled, and the uncertainty of who will ask whom for a date is at its height. These years, among modern adolescents, are earlier than ever before—in junior high school and early high school. The consequence for schools may be a peculiar one: to make the junior high school years more difficult ones than in the past, for adolescents and for teachers and school administrators, and to make the senior high school years (in three-year high schools) less difficult.

The earlier age of interest in the opposite sex, and the consequent earlier shift of adolescent values in this direction derives only in part from weakened family ties. It derives in part from all of the changes in society that bring about early social sophistication among adolescents. Partly urban and suburban living, partly television and other mass media (for example, both popular music and movies have come to be more and more oriented to teenagers), partly the money they now have to spend, partly their better-educated parents, and partly the school itself, have made adolescents more wise in the ways of the world.

THE DESIRE FOR SOPHISTICATION

In the schools I studied recently, the sharpest difference I found in the adolescents of the most rural schools and those of the most middle-class urban and suburban ones, was in the sophistication of the latter. The rural 9th graders were still children, obedient to teachers, and the middle-class suburban pupils were already disdainful of the ways of childhood.

Such sophistication, and desire for sophistication, is a double-edged sword. It means that adolescents are more ready for new ideas, new experiences, quicker to grasp things. But it also makes them far less easy to teach, less willing to remain in the role of a learner, impatient with teachers, less likely to look at the teacher as a model or an authority. It need not make them more interested in school, but perhaps even less so. For the world whose sophistication they are taking on is one outside the school. Schoolwork, with its daily assignments and homework, they associate with childhood. Many of these children learn only years later, in college or after, that hard work and carrying out of assignments, attention to the demands of the teacher, become more important, rather than less, the farther they go in school.

Of all the recent changes in adolescents, this early desire for sophistication poses perhaps the greatest problem and the greatest challenge for secondary schools. Teenagers are less willing to respond to the teacher just because he is a teacher; less willing to "be taught." But they are more responsive if their imagination is captured, more able and willing to respond to a real challenge. It makes the school's task more difficult, for it cannot take the adolescent's interest for granted; it must find new ways of capturing this interest and energy. It has no other alternative but to accept these more sophisticated adolescents, and turn their sophistication to the advantage of education.

Altogether, recent changes in society have had a sharp impact on our adolescents. They present now, and they will present even more in the future, both difficulty and opportunity to the schools.

36.

A developmental approach to adolescence

LEON EISENBERG

There is general agreement in this culture that adolescence is a problem age. Parents, teachers, and other adults have come to expect teenagers to be difficult and the young people have come to expect difficulty. There is reason for believing that, at least in part, the attitude makes it happen. The idea that adolescence is a problem stage of development operates to some degree as a self-fulfilling prophecy. What-

Children, 12(No. 4):131–135, 1965. Leon Eisenberg, Professor of Child Psychiatry, The Johns Hopkins University School of Medicine.

ever the influence of expectation may be, we do know that in some cultures adolescence is a relatively simple concern. Children are passed into adulthood with social ceremonies and puberty rites. Doubts as to status, role, and responsibilities do not arise. There is little socio-developmental ambivalence to foment insecurity for the individual and for those who deal with him.

The author of this selection manages a surprisingly comprehensive treatment of the phenomena of adolescence within a few pages. He speaks of the tasks or need requirements of adolescents and of the obstructions within the culture that inhibit their realization. He finds grounds for hope in the very fluidity and flexibility of adolescent adjustments. And he sees adolescence more as a stage of development which has distinction to offer rather than as merely another transitional step on the way to adulthood. Perhaps if more of us could move toward this point of view the problem-age expectation placed upon young people would no longer operate to make it happen.

ADOLESCENCE MAY be defined as a critical period of human development manifested at the biological, psychological, and social levels of integration, of variable onset and duration but marking the end of childhood and setting the foundation for maturity. Biologically, its onset is signaled by the acceleration of physiological growth and the beginnings of secondary sexual development, its termination by the fusion of the epiphyses of the bones and the completion of sexual maturation. Psychologically, it is marked by an acceleration of cognitive growth and of personality formation, both of which continue to be subject to further evolution, though at a less marked rate, in subsequent stages of adulthood. Socially, it is a period of intensified preparation for the assumption of an adult role, and its termination is signaled when the individual is accorded full adult prerogatives, the timing and nature of which vary widely from society to society.

Adolescence is a "critical period" in development in being both a time of rapid and profound change in the organism and a time providing the necessary—but not sufficient—conditions for full maturation in adulthood. Optimal development in adolescence depends on successful accomplishment of the developmental tasks in infancy and childhood. Thus, clinical experience has indicated that adolescence is likely to be particularly stormy, prolonged, and sometimes poorly resolved if it follows a childhood marked by severe deficits.

Whether or not appropriate "experiential supplements" during adolescence can lead to successful negotiation of this period despite pathology in earlier life is not known. The heuristic hypothesis is to assume that repair can occur and that the task of the physician is to search for ways of encouraging optimal growth during the adolescence of a previously damaged child.

Although a rich, fulfilling adolescence provides the best groundwork for a successful adulthood, such an outcome is not automatic; it depends, in turn, on the provision of opportunities during adulthood for the creative exercise of the abilities achieved in adolescence.

The structural groundwork for adolescent development is laid by physical maturation. This developmental sequence is not preformed or automatic but depends upon an interaction between biological capacity and environmental stimulation. Just as growth requires adequate nutrition—being subject to delay or even cessation in the presence of starvation and to acceleration in the presence of optimal intake—so psychological maturation is dependent upon "psychological nutrition," that is, sequential opportunities for cognitive and social stimulation so timed that they promote further mental development.

INTERDEPENDENT DEVELOPMENTS

Thus, adolescence is simultaneously a biological, a social, and a psychological phenomenon. Development at each of these levels of integration proceeds not independently but with significant interaction, with events at any one level able to impede or to accelerate developments at each of the others.

For example, although the time at which the hypothalamic-pituitary axis initiates the biological sequence of adolescent growth is a function of individual heredity, it may, in a given individual, be delayed or advanced by environmental factors. Thus, the ultimate height attained by adolescents in economically developing countries has shown striking gains as nutrition has improved. Similarly, the time of menarche has shown a trend toward acceleration in countries in which increasingly better health of the children has been achieved. These physiological trends are the result of industrial and social organization.

Or again, biological maturation provides the increasing muscular strength and dexterity which permit the adolescent to participate successfully in the activities of his social group, thus acquiring a psychological sense of adequacy. At the same time, positive psychological motivation is a prerequisite for task perseverance and the search for variety of experience, which provide the conditions necessary for full muscular development through exercise.

Developments at the biological and psychological levels occur in a social framework, which may promote or retard them. Thus, scientific notions about diet prevalent in a specific culture may lead to inadequate nutritional intake, and social prejudices against minority group members may deprive them of experiences necessary for full development.

The importance of such reciprocal influences is underscored by the fact that each society is dependent upon its adolescents as its future adults. Failure to provide them with the conditions necessary for optimal development will severely handicap the growth potential of that society.

Biological adolescence has fairly precise signs of its onset and termination, such as growth acceleration, sexual development, and epiphyseal fusion, but there is remarkable variation in the timing of their appearance in different individuals. Onset in normal children may occur as early as age 7 or 8 or as late as 17 or 18; termination as early as 15 or 16 or as late as 24 or 25. The timing seems to be a function both of internal factors, such as sex and inheritance, and external factors, such as nutrition or illness. In other words, the biological factors set wide limits for the onset, termination, and achievements of adolescence, the potential limits being subject to modification by environmental influences, among which both psychological and social factors play a role.

SOCIAL PREPARATION

Adolescence as a social phenomenon, though restricted in range by biological considerations, is a function of cultural norms. In general, the more sophisticated the society is in its technology, the more prolonged is adolescence, since the complexity of the preparation required for the assumption of adult roles depends upon the demands the society sets. In the United States, for example, the long period of study required for specialized occupational roles delays the age of self-support, the opportunity for marriage, and the age of creative contribution to society—all attributes of the adult role.

In many cultures, the onset of adolescence is clearly signaled by puberty rites, usually in the form of tests of strength and courage, the completion of which entitles the individual to recognition as a young adult. In technologically advanced societies, such clear signification of the end of childhood is absent and the requirements for adulthood less clearly defined: the individual must, therefore, undergo a more prolonged and, at times, confused struggle to attain adult status.

Each culture provides experience specifically designated as part of the training of the adolescent, such as schooling and apprenticeship; other experiences, such as dating and courtship, which are for the most part limited to adolescence but are not formally organized; and other non-age-related opportunities for personal development which may be particularly meaningful for the adolescent, such as opportunities to participate in cultural and political life.

Deliberate social planning based on a scientific analysis of adolescents' needs has been relatively neglected, the forms and structures society provides having evolved empirically. Only within school systems has such planning been explicit, but even there with little careful research. Yet careful assessment of the needs of adolescents at all levels of developmental integration could lead to the design and provision of external conditions that would greatly accelerate the rate, and markedly increase the ultimate level, of the development of the human adolescent's full potentialities.

THE IDEALISM OF ADOLESCENCE

At a psychological level, the most striking attainment during adolescence is the ability to conceptualize at an abstract level. The further evolution of what Piaget calls the "concrete operations" of childhood[1] through interaction with increasingly more demanding intellectual tasks, provided both by formal schooling and informal social experience, leads to the ability to "think about thinking" and to analyze problems at a high level of generalization. It is here that the *Anlage* of scientific thought and creativity is to be found. This evolution of intellectual function requires appropriate environmental stimulation.

The adolescent's capacity for abstract thought accounts for his increasing concern with, on the one hand, national and international problems and, on the other, with the basic meanings and values of human existence. This "idealism" of adolescence is, of course, shaped by the cultural envelope which surrounds the individual, but its very existence leads to questioning, to examination of basic premises, and to dissatisfaction with the imperfections in the world adults have created. Its cultivation may be regarded as one of the most important tasks of society.

Fostering and strengthening this "suprapersonal" psychological trait in adolescents will lead to the creation of adults who will in turn enhance the society that bred them. The lack of adequate opportunity for its positive expression will warp the adolescent's normal development and lead to a generation of self-preoccupied adults who will fail to meet the challenge of history.

PERSONAL IDENTITY

A second and related psychological theme of adolescence is the search for a sense of personal identity, to employ the terminology of Erikson.[2] No longer a child and not yet an adult, the adolescent is busily engaged in determining who he is and what he is to become.

In this effort, he examines his parents from a more critical perspective and leans more to peer groups for his sense of belonging. If his relations with his parents have been soundly constructed during earlier years, and if they meet his doubts and criticisms with sympathetic understanding, this temporary unsettling of his prior role as a child leads to a resynthesis of his relations with them on a firm and lasting basis, one marked by reciprocal respect and by personal independence without abandonment of filial loyalty. Where the parent-child relationship has been one of excessive dependence or excessive hostility, the turmoil of adolescence may be prolonged and lead either to failure of emancipation or to rejection of family ties and a lasting sense of isolation.

SEXUAL ROLE

A third key developmental task consists of the further evolution of sexual identity and role-appropriate behavior. Learning the social role of one's sex is firmly rooted in childhood—in culturally differentiated role assignments, in emulation of the like-sexed parent, and in peer interactions. These experiences provide a constant feedback, both by comparison of the self with others and by praise or blame from them, which informs the child as to what sex he is and what kind of behavior expectations this entails. These preliminary psychological structures are challenged by the adolescent's consciousness of his development of adult sexual characteristics and his experience of a bewildering array of new physical sensations, both of which lead to an upsurge of interest in physical sex and a psychological sensitization to a new aspect of interpersonal relationships. The forces in the social field then determine the further steps in his sexual development.

Comparative studies indicate that, as the evolutionary scale is ascended, sexual behavior is less dependent upon hormones and more upon learning. In man, the role of hormones is limited to priming the organism for biological sexual maturation and to influencing—but not solely determining—the level of libido; the direction, nature, and adequacy of sexual performance are controlled by psychosocial factors. Thus, the many investigations of the biology of sex deviants have failed to identify chromosomal, hormonal, or gonadal aberrations; and conversely, individuals with such biological incongruencies usually exhibit a sex-role identity conforming to sex-role assignment.

The remarkable variation in sexual behavior between societies as well as between social classes within a single society emphasizes the cultural determination of sexual behavior, given adequate biological maturation.

The ambivalence of Western society toward sexuality—manifested by the conflicts between official attitudes and private behavior, and the pervasive emphasis on sex side by side with sanctions against its expression—accounts for the difficulty, so common in adolescence, of attaining the basis for a sense of competence, freedom, and pleasure as a sexually functioning adult. Persons concerned with the development of adolescents have an important obligation to give them a clear and full explanation of biological function with emphasis on its *ethical significance* based upon a mutually meaningful relationship between human beings. Adolescents need a comprehensive knowledge of the physical and physiological differences between the sexes, of the development of sexuality, and of the appropriate stages of sexual experience en route to full maturity.

Commonly expressed fears that giving adolescents such information will lead to premature experimentation run contrary to clinical experience which indicates that ignorance and impoverishment of human relationships account for most sexual misadventures. A sense of inadequacy in sexuality not only impairs sexual function but also leads to disabilities in other adult roles and is an important source of psychological malfunction.

ORIGINS OF DELINQUENCY

The search for identity is markedly influenced by peer groups. If these are constructive social groups which provide creative outlets for adolescent energy, the result is a sense of meaningful membership in the community and identification with its larger goals. If the peer group is a delinquent gang, with values antagonistic to those of the larger society, the result is likely to be antisocial personality organization—especially if the adolescent is a victim of discrimination for religious, ethnic, political, or economic reasons.

The experience of growing up as a member of a disadvantaged minority group, with attendant humiliation and denial of opportunity, makes it difficult for the adolescent to identify with the values of the society at large and favors, instead, hostility toward its norms and a disposition to anarchistic individualism. However, even under these circumstances, leadership and social forms which permit the disadvantaged adolescent to employ his energy in efforts to change unjust social patterns can foster his emergence into creative adulthood. If such opportunities for constructive social action are denied, the distortion of development leads to a frustrating and progressively more embittering "individual war against society" characterized by criminal activities.

Some theorists focus upon family pathology in explaining the evolution of delinquent behavior. Their thesis is based upon the finding that family psychopathology is frequent in the history of delinquents. The family is indeed an important agent in transmitting the behavior pattern and values expected of the adolescent by society. Consequently, distortions in family structure, whether idiosyncratic or socially induced, will inevitably have profound effects upon individual development. However, the family-centered viewpoint fails to recognize that family psychopathology is closely related to social structure and that the adolescent is also molded by social experiences outside the family.

The social consequences of economic disadvantage—poor health and reduced longevity, poor education, extralegal marital arrangements, inability to plan for future contingencies, necessity of exploiting children economically—themselves erode family structure and are likely to cause the victims of these social circumstances, the genesis of which they do not understand, to turn on each other in destructive ways. The unemployed, drifting father and the unmarried, deserted mother not only fail to provide their children with adequate nurture but also serve as poor identification models.

However, even though family structure be distorted, the adolescent may attain a degree of normal development *if* provided adequate education and constructive peer group experience. Unfortunately, the aggregation of disadvantaged families in decaying neighborhoods is all too likely to reinforce family psychopathology and, by exposing the adolescent to delinquent gangs and ineffective schooling, heighten his growing sense of bitterness.

HAZARDS AND SYMPTOMS

The sensitivity of the adolescent to the good opinion of his peers and the dependence of his sense of identity upon the attainment of competence in an adult role render him psychologically vulnerable to variation in physiological development, such as precocious or delayed growth, facial acne, obesity, enlarged mammary glands in the male, or inadequate or overabundant breast development in the female. These deviations from the expected pattern of maturation, though of no great medical significance, may, nonetheless, lead to major psychological trauma if not offset by sensitive guidance.

The adolescent with limited intellectual or physical capacity can develop a persisting and even irremedial feeling of inferiority if he is forced to compete in situations in which he experiences continual failure. The individualization of educational and vocational training for adolescents is essential, both to permit the talented individual to exploit his abilities, as well as to direct the youngster with specific limitations to activities which will develop what abilities he has.

Characteristic of adolescence is fluidity of psychological structure in the struggle to attain a new and more meaningful sense of identity. In consequence, the formation of transient symptoms, resembling many of the psychopathological syndromes of adulthood, is not uncommon during this period. The clinician must exercise great caution lest he attribute too great a significance to the turbulent but temporary maladaptive patterns manifested by the adolescent. Incorrect diagnostic formulations may lead to social consequences—for example, withdrawal from school or institutionalization—that will freeze into permanence an otherwise readily correctable deviation in the growth pattern.

It is, of course, important to recognize that schizophrenia often first appears in adolescence, as does manic-depressive psychosis. However, these are uncommon disorders and may be simulated by panic reactions in the youngster who is confronted by overwhelming internal and external stimulation. If the recent trend toward a specialty of adolescent psychiatry has any justification, it lies in the opportunity for psychiatrists to acquire particular competence in the differential diagnosis and special management of adolescents' adjustment reactions. Experience with the psychiatric problems of adolescents leads to respect for their extraordinary range of individual variability and their remarkable restorative capacity under corrective and supportive experience. The psychological basis for a sense of individual worth as an adult rests upon the acquisition of competence in a work role during adolescence. A sense of competence is not acquired on the basis of "reassurance," but rather upon the actual experience of succeeding in a socially important task. The challenge to the educator, therefore, is to stimulate abilities to the utmost without setting standards so high that they lead to an enduring sense of defeat.

The educational accomplishment must be matched by an opportunity for the individual to exercise his competence as a worker in the economic world. The sustained motivation necessary for mastering a difficult work role is only possible when there is a real likelihood of fulfilling that role in adult life and having it respected by others. The task of providing full employment in a world in which automation is revolutionizing traditional work roles provides a challenge to the abilities of leading thinkers in all societies.

THE WORLD'S HOPE

No society can hope to survive that does not succeed in harnessing the constructive, searching suprapersonal and supranational drives of the adolescent. In recent world history, adolescents in underdeveloped countries have participated heroically in overthrowing the dead hand of the past and attaining the beginnings of a meaningful nationhood. The picture in the relatively developed countries is less clear and less heartening. As affluence is attained, societies tend to become frozen into traditional molds, with resultant trends toward self-preoccupation and egocentric goals that afford less challenge to adolescents. There are, fortunately, notable and inspiring exceptions to this self-preoccupation, as youngsters dedicate their energies to social betterment in underdeveloped countries far from their shores.

The capacity for engagement in meaningful social activity is clearly present in young people in every country of the world. The challenge to the behavioral scientist is to help his own country develop the forms and means to enable the adolescent to take a leading role in the struggle for the attainment of a world in which peace, freedom, and economic opportunity are omnipresent. No task is more suited to the adolescent. No task has greater potentiality for permitting the full flowering of his capacities.

Thus, the provision of an optimal framework for adolescent development is inseparable from the struggle to create a better world by helping to mold the citizens who will build it.

REFERENCES

1. Flavell, J. H.: The developmental psychology of Jean Piaget. Van Nostrand, New York. 1963.
2. Erikson, E. H.: Identity and the life cycle. *In* Psychological issues, monograph 1. International Universities Press, New York. 1959.

37.

Social class and attitudes toward fathers

THOMAS EWIN SMITH

The complexity of behavior is again illustrated in Smith's study of adolescent boys' attitudes toward their fathers. The article also supports the contentions made by Kessen (selection 21) and Davids and Holden (selection 22) that the growing individual is not a passive receptor of external stimuli. In this article, adolescent boys are the active perceivers of what their fathers are and their (fathers') deserving to be emulated.

The article also reemphasizes what new and current knowledge does to beliefs; e.g., the wide generalization ("Lower class fathers are . . ." or "Middle class children are . . .") is likely to be erroneous in that it does not sufficiently account for variation, for exceptions. The article also demonstrates how new knowledge seems to make more necessary some information about subaspects of behavioral causation. The more we know, the more we realize that we need to know still more.

After such articles as this are studied, we might ask, "Will the perceptions of lower class boys change as the result of 'poor power' and 'revolt of the masses'?"

OVER THE YEARS, there have been hints of a positive relationship between family social class and the favorableness of adolescents' attitudes toward their parents. More than two decades ago, Margaret Mead[1] noted "a feeling of shame" for parents' lack of success, among many young people in the American lower classes. Some criminologists[2] have held the opinion that

Sociology and Social Research, 53:217–226, 1969. Thomas Ewin Smith, Assistant Professor of Sociology, Ball State University, Muncie, Indiana.

The author wishes to express gratitude for the advice and assistance given by Professor Reuben Hill, of the University of Minnesota, who served as thesis advisor on the project reported in this article.

lack of respect for lower-class parents and a consequent reluctance to follow their directives has been a factor in the disproportionately-high incidence of juvenile delinquency in the lower classes. In contrast to the negative attitudes toward parents, which these social scientists have noted in lower-class youth, there have been indications of more positive attitudes among young people in higher social classes. Kohn and Carroll,[3] for example, found that middle-class boys in their sample of children were more likely than working-class boys to "act like" their fathers. In a sample of high school students, Smith[4] found significant positive correlations between family social class and adolescents' desires to adopt parents' ideas about dating.

The present study tests the relationship between social class and late adolescents' attitudes toward adopting or rejecting their fathers' ideas and ways of thinking. The study also takes the next step in theory building, by supplying evidence bearing upon two plausible explanations of the relationship in question.

An Explanation in Terms of Subjective Evaluations. The first of our theoretical explanations suggests that adolescents subjectively evaluate others, in part, on the basis of social class and that their subjective evaluations influence their attitudes toward those evaluated. A social-class position may be regarded as symbolizing success or failure. Even if an individual's own effort or lack of effort has not been primarily responsible for his position in the social-class hierarchy, his access or lack of access to the valued goods, services, and honors of the society creates an aura of success or failure. It seems reasonable to assume that individuals who recognize social-class distinctions will tend to regard individuals with high social-class positions as "successes" and individuals with low positions as "failures." It also seems reasonable to assume that late adolescents—young people of 18, 19, and 20 years of age—recognize social-class distinctions. In fact, social scientists have long known that elementary-school children[5] and high-school students[6] are aware of such distinctions. With this fact in mind, it is assumed that the late adolescent will be more likely to regard his father as a "success" if the father is high in social class than if he is low.

The assumption does not apply to the case of the mother. Her social-class position, like that of the offspring, is derived, not from her own qualities, but from those of the husband-father. Thus, it seems unlikely that the late adolescent's view of his mother as a success or failure will be related to social class.

Thusfar, it has been indicated that the adolescent's view of his father as a success or failure is related to the father's social-class position. Next, a logical connection needs to be established between the adolescent's subjective view of his father as a success or failure and his attitude toward adopting his father's ideas and ways of thinking. This link in the theoretical explanation involves a well-established empirical generalization drawn from social psychology: namely, that individuals tend to choose "successful" rather than "failing" groups as reference groups (sources of mental perspectives). Small-group experiments[7] have indicated that "successful" groups have more influence upon their members than "failing" groups. Other experiments[8] have indicated that "successful" groups are more attractive to their members than are "failing" groups. In a field study of reference-group choices by new immigrants to Israel, Eisenstadt[9] has found that high-status groups are more frequently chosen than low-status groups and that they are chosen because of their high statuses.

Since a father is not a group, he cannot be called a reference group; but the research findings regarding reference-group choices may be pertinent to the establishment of certain attitudes toward fathers. A father may be a source of ideas and ways of thinking, just as a group may be; and the same mechanisms which influence an individual's choice of a reference group may influence an adolescent's attitude toward adopting his father's mental perspective. The father who is a source of the mental perspective of an offspring might be called "a referent" for that offspring. (Hereafter, the adolescent's attitude toward adopting or rejecting his father's ideas and ways of thinking will be called referent attitude toward the father.)

By extending the empirical generalization drawn from social psychology from the level of reference-group theory to the level of the individual referent, we are now in a position to make another prediction. We would expect the adolescent's referent attitude toward the father to be positively related to the adolescent's subjective view of the father's success. This prediction completes the groundwork for the present theoretical explanation.

The explanation which is offered for the relationship between social class and referent attitude toward the father holds that these two variables are connected through an intervening variable,[10] the adolescent's subjective view of the father's success. Subjective view of the father's success is positively related to the father's social class; the adolescent's referent attitude toward the father is positively related to his view of the father's success; that is why, according to this explanation, there is a positive relationship between social class and referent attitude. View of success—a subjective evaluation on the part of the adolescent—is regarded as the mechanism through which the two variables are connected. Since each of the three variables is expected to be positively related to both of the others, it is, of course, expected that the relationship between the father's social class and the adolescent's referent attitude toward the father will be reduced when subjective view of the father's success is taken into account in partial correlation.

The final prediction derived from our first theoretical explanation is that subjective view of the father's success will be more strongly related to referent attitude toward the father than will objective social class. This prediction rests on two ideas. First, the adolescent's view of the father's success is not an entirely accurate reflection of objective social class. The subjective variable may, for example, be influenced by the extent of the adolescent's exposure to social classes other than his own or by factors which are not associated with social class at all. Second, our theoretical explanation indicates that objective social class influences referent attitude indirectly (through the adolescent's subjective view of the father's success), while view of success influences referent attitude directly. Thus, if the explanation is correct, any divergence between adolescents' subjective views of their fathers' success and the fathers' objective social-class positions would weaken the relationship between social class and referent attitude toward the father but would not weaken the relationship between subjective view of the father's success and referent attitude.

The predictions which have been derived from the preceding theoretical explanation may now be stated as hypotheses.

Hypothesis One. Referent attitude toward the father will be positively related to social class.

Hypothesis Two. Subjective view of the father's success will be positively related to both social class and referent attitude toward the father, and the relationship between the latter two variables will be reduced in strength when partialed over view of success.

Hypothesis Three. Referent attitude toward the mother will not be positively related to social class.

Hypothesis Four. Referent attitude toward the father will be more strongly related to subjective view of the father's success than to social class.

An Explanation in Terms of Child-Rearing Practices. One alternative explanation for the relationship between social class and referent attitude toward the father involves paternal child-rearing practices. Research has indicated that child-rearing practices vary with social class, and it seems reasonable to assume that an adolescent's referent attitude toward his father might be influenced by the past treatment accorded him by the father. Thus, certain child-rearing practices must be investigated as possible intervening variables, connecting social class and referent attitude.

Bronfenbrenner,[11] in a review of research, found that parental display of affection was directly related to social class and that parental use of physical punishment was inversely related to social class. Since parental display of affection might be expected to create favorable attitudes toward parents and the use of physical punishment by parents might be expected to create unfavorable attitudes, these two child-rearing practices seem likely candidates for intervening variables. Either or both might be the conveyer of the social class influence upon referent attitude.

The following hypotheses are derived from our second explanation of the relationship between social class and referent attitude toward the father.

Hypothesis Five. The adolescent's memory of the father's affectionateness will be positively related to both social class and referent attitude toward the father, and the relationship between the latter two variables will be reduced in strength when partialed over memory of the father's affectionateness.

Hypothesis Six. The adolescent's memory of the father's physical punitiveness will be negatively related to both social class and referent attitude toward the father, and the relationship between the latter two variables will be reduced in strength when partialed over memory of the father's physical punitiveness.

METHOD

The data to test the research hypotheses were gathered by means of a questionnaire, which was administered to students in two sections of an introductory sociology course and two sections of an introductory psychology course at the University of Minnesota. But not all of the students who completed questionnaires in the four class sections were included as subjects of the study. To control certain variables, which were not relevant to the theory underlying the study but which might have influenced referent attitudes, it was decided to homogenize the sample. The actual sample included only students who (1) were freshmen or sophomores, between their eighteenth and twenty-first birthdays; (2) came from nonfarm families; (3) had parents of both sexes who were living together; (4) had not lived away from their parental homes for as long as two years; and (5) were single. This homogenized sample included 382 individuals, 249 males and 133 females.

In the data-gathering questionnaire, referent attitude was measured by a set of ten items of the Likert type, five positive and five negative in direction. For example, the statements in two of the positive items were, "My father's ideas are modern and up-to-date," and "My father's opinion of my behavior and ideas would mean more to me than the opinion of any of my friends." Two of the negative statements were, "For the most part, my ideas are different from those of my father," and "My father has had little, if any, influence on the way I think about things." The response alternatives for each item were *strongly disagree, disagree, uncertain, agree,* and *strongly agree.* The responses were scored, in order, from zero through four for positive items and from four through zero for negative items. All items were selected from a set of 20, which had been validated by an expert jury of social scientists and proven internally consistent by item analysis in a previous study.[12]

Actually, of course, the referent attitude scale appeared twice in the questionnaire. In one appearance, the statements referred to the father; in the other, they referred to the mother. Thus, referent attitude toward each parent was measured.

The Hollingshead[13] "Two-Factor Index" was used to measure social class. The "Two-Factor Index" consists of a seven-category scale of occupations and a seven-category scale of formal education, the former receiving a weight of seven, relative to a weight of four for the latter. The scales, of course, were applied to respondent's fathers, who determine family social class. In the statistical analysis, social class was treated as a continuous dimension, not divided into strata. While this approach does violence to the literal meaning of the word *class,* it is in keeping with a prevalent conception of social class as a prestige continuum.

A specific respondent's subjective view of the father's success was determined in a way which took account of that respondent's placement of his father on three success dimensions and the relative importance attached to the dimensions by the respondent. The respondent rated his father, relative to other fathers his age, on a seven point scale for each of three qualities: occupational prestige, level of education, and ability to provide physically for the family. Before rating his father on these qualities, however, the respondent ranked the three qualities as determinants of a man's prestige in the community. The ranking was used in computing a score on subjective view of the father's success. The rating of the father on the quality which the respondent ranked first was multiplied by three; the rating on the quality ranked second was multiplied by one. The sum of the three products was the score on subjective view of the father's success. This procedure was intended to take into account the specific respondent's impression of the components of success.

The child-rearing variables were measured by scales drawn from Bronfenbrenner's[14] "Family Life Inventory." Bronfenbrenner's "Affection" scale was used to measure memory of the father's affectionateness, and his "Physical Punishment and Threat" scale was used to measure memory of the father's physical punitiveness. Each of the scales consists of five items, each item requiring the respondent to indicate his impression of the frequency with which his father engaged in a specific kind of activity in rearing him. Two of the paternal activities dealt with in the "Affection" scale are hugging and kissing and the use of pet names. The "Physical Punishment and Threat" scale includes such behaviors as spanking and hitting with a fist, switch, stick, or belt.

The statistical technique which was used in testing for associations among the research variables was product moment correlation, r. Since the hypotheses predicted the directions of relationships, one-tailed tests of significance were employed. The critical level for the rejection of null hypotheses was set at .05.

FINDINGS AND DISCUSSION

The two tables of correlation coefficients show that hypotheses one through four (derived from the explanation in terms of subjective evaluations) are supported by the data for both males and females, while neither of the hypotheses derived from the alternative explanation is supported for either sex. Hypothesis one, that social class and referent attitude toward the father will be positively related, is supported by a statistically significant, though rather low, positive correlation of .19 for each sex. Hypothesis two, that subjective view of the father's success will be positively related to both social class and referent attitude and that the relationship between the latter two variables will be reduced in strength when partialed over view of success, is strongly supported. The correlations between subjective view of the father's success and the other two variables are so strong that the positive relationship between social class and referent attitude actually becomes a negative relationship in the partial correlation for each sex. Hypothesis three, that referent attitude toward the mother will not be positively related to social class, also receives support. In fact, the correlations between social class and referent attitude toward the mother are negative for males and for females. Hypothesis four, predicting that referent attitude toward the father will be more strongly related to subjective view of the father's success than to objective social class, is the only remaining hypothesis which is supported by the data. It is supported by the differences in strength between the correlations in question. The coefficients representing the correlations between referent attitude and subjective view of success have more than twice the magnitude of those representing the correlations between referent attitude and social class.

TABLE I. Zero-order Coefficients of Correlation

| | r | |
Variables Correlated	Males	Females
Social Class and Referent Attitude Toward the Father	.19**	.19*
Social Class and View of the Father's Success	.63**	.69**
Social Class and Memory of Physical Punitiveness	—.02	—.05
Social Class and Memory of the Father's Affectionateness	.02	.09
Social Class and Referent Attitude Toward the Mother	—.14	—.03
Subjective View of the Father's Success and Referent Attitude Toward the Father	.39**	.40**
Memory of the Father's Physical Punitiveness and Referent Attitude Toward the Father	—.22**	—.31**
Memory of the Father's Affectionateness and Referent Attitude Toward the Father	.37**	.43**

* p is less than .05
** p is less than .01

The data do not support either of the two hypotheses involving child-rearing practices. While both memory of the father's affectionateness and memory of the father's physical punitiveness are significantly correlated with referent attitude toward the father, neither of these memories of child-

TABLE II. COEFFICIENTS OF CORRELATION BETWEEN SOCIAL CLASS AND REFERENT ATTITUDE TOWARD THE FATHER (PARTIALED OVER INTERVENING VARIABLES)

Intervening Variable	Partial r Males	Females
Subjective View of the Father's Success	−.08	−.13
Memory of the Father's Physical Punitiveness	.19	.18
Memory of the Father's Affectionateness	.19	.16

rearing practices is correlated significantly with social class. The lack of relationship between the two child-rearing variables and social class, of course, prevents the partial correlations involving these two variables from making substantial reductions in the relationship between referent attitude and social class. If the widely-accepted relationships between social class and child-rearing practices exist in the general population, paternal affectionateness and punitiveness may convey a part of the social class influence upon attitudes toward fathers. But child-rearing practices do not appear to operate as intervening variables in the sample of individuals used in the present study.

The explanation of the relationship between social class and referent attitude toward the father in terms of subjective evaluations is not, of course, proven correct by the fact that the data support four hypotheses derived from that explanation and do not support the hypotheses derived from an alternative explanation. The explanation in terms of subjective evaluations (holding that the objective social class of the father influences the adolescent's subjective view of the father's success, which, in turn, influences referent attitude toward the father) includes statements of causality, which cannot be proven by the correlational analysis of the present study. The most that can be said is that the present research supplies evidence in support of one plausible explanation of the relationship between family social-class positions and attitudes toward adopting or rejecting fathers' ideas as ways of thinking and fails to find evidence supporting another plausible explanation.

NOTES

1. Margaret Mead, *And Keep Your Powder Dry* (New York: William Morrow and Co., 1942), 193–97.
2. Milton L. Barron, *Juvenile in Delinquent Society* (New York: Alfred A. Knopf, 1954), 128–49.
3. Melvin L. Kohn and Eleanor E. Carroll, "Social Class and the Allocation of Parental Responsibilities," *Sociometry,* 23 (December, 1960), 372–92.

4. Thomas E. Smith, "Socio-Economic Status and Adolescents' Desire to Adopt Their Parents as Dating Referents," Unpublished M.A. thesis (University of Alabama: Department of Sociology, 1961).

5. Celia Burns Stendler, *Children of Brasstown* (University of Illinois, Urbana: Bureau of Research and Service, College of Education, 1949).

6. August B. Hollingshead, *Elmtown's Youth* (New York: John Wiley and Sons, Inc., 1949).

7. The following research articles exemplify the experiments indicating a greater influence upon group members by "successful" than by "unsuccessful" groups: J. S. Kidd and Donald T. Campbell, "Conformity to Groups As a Function of Group Success," *Journal of Abnormal and Social Psychology,* 51 (November, 1955), 390–93. Harry P. Shelley, "Level of Aspiration Phenomena in Small Groups," *Journal of Social Psychology,* 11 (August, 1954), 149–64.

8. A sample of the research indicating that individuals are more attracted to "successful" than to "failing" groups may be found in the following articles: M. Deutsch, "Some Factors Effecting Membership Motivation and Achievement Motivation," *Human Relations,* 12 (February, 1959), 81–95. E. Stotlund, "Determinants of Attraction to Groups," *The Journal of Social Psychology,* 49 (February, 1959), 71–80. J. Thibaut, "An Experimental Study of the Cohesiveness of Underpriviledged Groups," *Human Relations,* 3 (August, 1950), 251–78.

9. M. Eisenstadt, "Reference Group Behavior and Social Integration, An Exploratory Study," *American Sociological Review,* 19 (April, 1954), 175–85.

10. It may be enlightening, with regard to the design of the present study, to consider two distinct points of view on the intervening variable which have been influential in the social sciences: Patricia L. Kendall and Paul F. Lazarsfeld, "Problems of Survey Analysis," in Robert K. Merton and Paul F. Lazarsfeld, eds., *Continuities in Social Research* (New York: The Free Press, a Division of The Macmillan Co., 1950), 157; and Kenneth MacCorquodale and Paul E. Meehl, "On a Distinction Between Hypothetical Constructs and Intervening Variables," *Psychological Review,* 55 (March, 1948), 95–107. The adolescent's view of the father's success does not meet MacCorquodale and Meehl's primary criterion for an intervening variable: its mathematical expression cannot be formed simply by an equation containing a suitable grouping of terms representing other variables, which are observable. View of success might be regarded as a hypothetical construct for which an empirical indicator is available, but MacCorquodale and Meehl reserve the term *hypothetical construct* for an unmeasured explanatory fiction. The adolescent's view of the father's success is measured through verbalized expression, in the usual manner of measuring subjective variables. In the original inception of the present study, the writer developed view of success as a hypothetical construct to explain the relationship between social class and referent attitude toward the father. Then, a measure was developed, and the possibility of measurement took view of the father's success outside of the scope of the MacCorquodale and Meehl distinction between hypothetical constructs and intervening variables. Yet, view of success is regarded theoretically as intervening between social class and referent attitude, since it is thought of as conveying the influence of social class upon referent attitude toward the father. Thus, it seems appropriate to designate the variable, view of the father's success, as an intervening variable in the theoretical-statistical sense of the term employed by Kendall and Lazarsfeld. For them, an intervening variable is one which conveys the causal effect of an antecedent variable upon

a consequent. Controlling the intervening variable (within this framework) is expected to reduce the strength of the relationship between the other two variables. In this article, the term, *intervening variable,* is used as Kendall and Lazarsfeld use it.

11. Urie Bronfenbrenner, "Socialization and Social Class Through Time and Space," in Eleanor Maccoby, Theodore M. Newcomb, and Eugene L. Hartley, eds., *Readings in Social Psychology* (New York: Henry Holt and Co., 1958), 400–24.

12. Thomas E. Smith, *op. cit.*

13. August B. Hollingshead, "A Two-Factor Index of Social Position." (Mimeographed material available from the author.)

14. Urie Bronfenbrenner, "Family Life Inventory." (Mimeographed material available from the author.)

38.

Crises in normal personality development

GORDON W. ALLPORT

One of the most respected psychologists of our time shares some penetrating insights concerning the nature of adolescent development. He believes that development during this period is of an episodic, crisis-oriented nature as contrasted with the relatively smooth and gradual growth pattern experienced prior to this time. Situations of considerable emotional and mental stress are apt to require significant changes of outlook within a short period of time. These are the crises of which the author speaks. At such times experiences and interpersonal transactions have great impact. Contacts with teachers, for example, are vividly recalled and exert a profound influence.

Allport also advances the opinion that the major problem, or developmental task, for adolescents is one of interiorizing motivation; of becoming self- or inner-directed rather than other- or exterior-directed. He recognizes that during this time, as individuals experience more freedom, assume new responsibilities, and make more decisions, the tendency often is manifest to use scapegoats and to rationalize ineffective behavior. At the risk of appearing to moralize, the editors would like to share an observation which they have found to be personally helpful. That is, to rationalize or to scapegoat constitutes an abdication of personal responsibility and power. It is tantamount to saying that someone else has determined what one should do and has made him do it. A person cannot claim to do his own thing and exert personal

Teachers College Record, 66:235–241, 1964. Gordon W. Allport, late Professor of Psychology, Harvard University.

control and continue to place the blame for his own actions on anyone else. Crises of development can be constructive and conducive to personal growth when approached from this point of view. They may be frustrating and personally demeaning otherwise.

THERE IS one trick every teacher knows: When trapped in a state of ignorance throw the question back to the class. Without suspecting the teacher's predicament, bright students will often rescue him.

This is the strategy I employed to learn something about crises in normal personality development. I passed along the assignment to my class of 100 captive undergraduates, and they obligingly provided me, through their own autobiographical writing, with the insights that I articulate now. Parenthetically, let me say that in my opinion no teacher or counselor has the right to require intimate autobiographical documents from students. Yet when given a completely free choice, the large majority will choose to write in the autobiographical vein. For the few who would find the experience too threatening, it should not be prescribed.

INFLUENCE OF TEACHERS

First I shall report a minor investigation related to our main topic. I asked the hundred students, mostly sophomores and juniors, four questions with the results reported here. My first question was "Approximately how many different teachers at school and college have you had up to the present stage of your education?" The 100 respondents mentioned a total of 4,632 teachers. The three remaining queries were concerned with varying degrees of influence exercised by the teachers on the development of these students. With the percentages indicated as having played formative roles in student lives, the questions and their answers were as follows:

> How many teachers had a very strong or powerful influence on your intellectual or personal development? (8.5 per cent) How many others would you say had a reasonably strong, well-remembered influence? (14.8 per cent)
>
> How many do you remember only vaguely, or who seem to have had no substantial influence on your development? (76.7 per cent)

We are immediately struck by the fact that more than three-quarters of the teachers are remembered only vaguely and are credited with no appreciable influence, whether intellectual or personal. As teachers, we all know the shock of discovering how little impact we have had. A former student of mine brightened my day by remarking, "Years ago I took a course with you, but all I can remember about it is that the textbook had a blue cover." He grinned pleasantly while I shuddered inwardly.

Only about eight per cent of teachers are reported as having a very strong influence, and about 15 per cent are credited with a less strong but well-remembered influence. Another way of stating this finding is to say that the average teacher (assuming all teachers are equally effective) "gets through" to less than a quarter of the class, and exerts a really strong influence on not more than one student in ten.

VARIETIES OF INFLUENCE

Asked to tell when and in what way they were influenced the students give us three facts of special interest. First, about half of all their examples deal with experiences of intellectual awakening. For example,

> She encouraged me to read poetry and drama beyond the class assignment.
>   In chemistry the instructor asked us why bubbles appeared overnight in a water glass. When we said we had never wondered about that, he told us that everyone must question even the most common and seemingly trivial things.

And about half of the examples deal with personal development:

> She made me see that others did not judge me as harshly as I was judging myself.
>   He had so much warmth and humanity that I wanted to be like him.
>   She seemed tough and disagreeable, but was so kind and helpful to me that I realized I must think twice before passing judgment on anyone.

A second insight, based on the large array of illustrative incidents, reveals the remarkably *casual* nature of the influence. In hardly any case could the teacher or counselor have known that what he was saying at a given moment would make a lasting impression upon the growing mind and character of the student. Elsewhere[1] I have argued that in teaching values and attitudes it is not the deliberately adopted curriculum that is effective; it is rather the *obiter dicta,* the parenthetical remark, the "little true things," and above all the example of the teacher that count. And what holds for teachers no doubt holds for the counselor, too.

Finally, and most relevant to my topic, is the finding that in elementary school there are few remembered influences of special strength. Apparently development is gradual at this time, and the teacher does not often bring a sudden and traumatic experience of "dawn" to the pupil. Only 12 per cent report any strong or even appreciable teacher influence in elementary school. Fully 88 per cent of the reports date the occurrences in high school (58 per cent) or in college (30 per cent, with the college years still incomplete).

So it is in middle and late adolescence where the role of the teacher is most vivid to the student. It is in this period, according to Erikson,[4] that the identity crisis is in the ascendance. The young person seems to be moving from past childhood into present adulthood in a jerky manner. Development is not continuous like a hill; rather, it is episodic like a flight of stairs. It is the episodic or crisis character of development that brings both challenge and opportunity to the guidance officer.

NATURE OF CRISIS

What precisely is a "crisis"? It is a situation of emotional and mental stress requiring significant alterations of outlook within a short period of time. These alterations of outlook frequently involve changes in the structure of personality. The resulting changes may be progressive in the life or they may be regressive. By definition, a person in crisis cannot stand still; that is to say, he cannot redact his present traumatic experience into familiar and routine categories or employ simple habitual modes of adjustment. He must either separate himself further from childhood and move toward adulthood, or else move backward to earlier levels of adjustment which may mean becoming disorganized, dropping out of school, escaping from the field, developing hostilities and defenses, and in general becoming a thorn in the flesh of the teacher, the parent, the counselor, the dean, and occasionally of the police. Sometimes, following a crisis, the adolescent will become stabilized anew after four or five weeks of severe disorganization; but in many cases the trauma retards development for a year or more, and may even leave a life-long scar.

Turning now to my data, drawn from college undergraduates, we ask first about the phenomenology of crisis. What does it "feel" like to the student? Common is a sense of numbness and apathy. Upon entering college, the youth finds fewer strict role-prescriptions than at home. He is no longer tied to his domestic filial role, to the highly structured routine of high school, to his siblings, to his church connections, to his teen-age sub-cultures. He has left his possessions behind—his stamp collection, his television, his girl friends, his boy friends. All his familiar roles are in suspension. As one student writes,

> The complete freedom of college is itself a crisis. For the first time
> I live in close contact with people who are not members of my family.
> They don't even resemble people I have known before. They have
> different opinions, different origins, and different emotions. I feel
> numbed by it all.

Interestingly enough, this sense of hollowness does not necessarily have its maximum effect during the freshman year. The excitement of new scenes and especially frequent correspondence with and visits back to the home town keep the silver cord intact. The student feels that he should prove to his parents, teachers, friends, that he can master the college environment and thus please them and win their approval as he has done in the past. The impending crisis has not yet overwhelmed him (or her—for what I am saying is as true for college girls as for boys).

It is the sophomore year that seems (from my data) to be the year of crisis *par excellence*. Suddenly it becomes no longer tolerable to live one's life for the edification of people "back home." The time has come for the child of the past to be separated once and for all from the adult of the present. Here are typical phenomenological statements of this stage of the crisis:

> I feel I have been dragged into something against my will.
> I feel like a rat in a maze.
> I want to be a law unto myself, but cannot.
> It seems suddenly that the decisions I make must be valid for the rest of my life.
> To shake off parental norms and values seems to me the most important thing I must do.

The life of the past and the life of the future seem suddenly to be at cross purposes. There is often an intolerable feeling of suspended animation. Recrystallization is not yet possible. The youth is waiting still to make a choice of careers, a suitable marriage, and to find an integrative philosophy of life which his diverse college courses are too discordant to supply.

APATHY AND ANXIETY

It is small wonder that apathy and a paralysis of will often occur. But apathy is only a mask for anxiety. The whole framework of life is disturbed. Whereas the majority of students contrive gradually to build a new framework in spite of, or perhaps because of, the goals of anxiety, yet a large minority cannot cope with the situation unaided.

From my data, I would estimate that three-quarters are able to take the progressive road in creating their new frame of existence. About one-quarter cannot immediately do so. Proof of this point is that the dropout rate during undergraduate years is surprisingly high—over 20 per cent at Harvard, about three-quarters of the cases representing voluntary withdrawals.[3] The dropouts present a special problem of guidance. Blaine and McArthur[3] write,

> The drop-outs as a group ultimately do quite well if properly handled. We attempt to establish a relationship, however brief or tenuous, with these students, not so much to prevent their leaving school, but rather in the hope of giving them some insight into the determinants of their difficulties so that their dropping out can be ultimately converted into a meaningful constructive experience instead of mere failure.

After a year or two of constructive work elsewhere, the majority of voluntary dropouts return to college and graduate. But they could not have met their crisis by remaining in the environment that was the context of their conflict.

The regressive road is surprisingly common. Among eventual drop-outs, but also among other students, we find such self-destroying behavior as quitting classes, a compulsion to do trivial things, playing bridge until four AM, drinking bouts, feelings of unreality, fugues, and general debauch-ery. The candid documents received startle me a bit by the extent of plain juvenile delinquency among my innocent-appearing students:

> One student finding himself unable to handle his conflicts over choice of career and over friction with his roommate, indulged in plagiarism on a term paper in such a way that he would be caught and forcibly separated from college. In this case a wise instructor, catching him in the transgression, turned the occasion into constructive counseling, forgave the deed, and put the lad onto the progressive rather than re-gressive road.

Here I venture a theoretical digression. The problem, as I see it, is one of interiorizing motivation. To put it in a student's words: "I am fed up with having everybody else cheer me on. I want to work to please myself rather than others, but I don't know how to do it." This plaintive statement points to a serious dilemma in our educational process. In school, the child is rewarded and punished by good grades and bad grades. Even in college, As and Bs are pats on the back, Ds and Fs are punishments. To gain love, the student must read books and toe the academic line. Finally, he obtains his degree (which is a symbol of academic love) and is freed from this ex-ternal form of motivation. What then happens?

We know that a shockingly high percentage of college graduates rarely or never read another book after receiving their bachelor's degree. Why should they? Their love now comes from their employer, their wife, their children, not from the approval of parents and teachers. For them, intellectual curiosity never became a motive in its own right. External re-wards are appropriate props in early childhood. But we educators, being limited by current inadequate theories of learning, do not know how to help the student free himself from the props of reward and develop a func-tionally autonomous zeal for learning. With our slavish dependence on reinforcement theory, I think it surprising that we arouse as much internal motivation as we do. In any event, we cannot be proud of the many educa-tional cripples who after graduation, lacking the routine incentive of col-lege, sink into intellectual apathy.

CRISIS AREAS

The counselor or teacher, of course, cannot wait for better theories of learning. He is confronted here and now with crises in the concrete. Four areas of conflict, judging from my data, are especially common.

Intellectual Crises. First, there are students whose problem is one of intellectual malplacement. Among my cases, a large number report that in primary and secondary school they were too bright for their class. The penalty is one of boredom lasting down into college work, which they still do not find challenging enough for their abilities. At the same time, double promotions in elementary and high school are not a solution. To be placed with older children often creates social difficulties far more serious than boredom. In fact, the evil consequences reported from double promotion are so numerous that we should challenge this particular solution of the bright child's dilemma.

The opposite type of intellectual crisis is also common. It is the deep disturbance that often results in college from intensified competition. It is statistically impossible for most students to maintain the same relative superiority in college that they enjoyed in high school. While this fact does not trouble the majority, it is a critical experience for those who depend on scholarship aid or who frame their self-image almost entirely in terms of scholarly pre-eminence. They are suffering a severe narcissistic wound.

Specific Inferiorities. A second area of crisis is the old, familiar "inferiority complex." Besides the sense of intellectual inferiority just described, we encounter deep disturbance due to physical handicaps or to plain physical appearance, with resulting shyness, loneliness, and misery. To be poor at athletics creates a crisis for males, probably more acute in high school than in college. To be a member of a minority group likewise creates an inevitable crisis somewhere along the line. Here again I suspect the major adjustments and defenses are prepared before the college age. Occasionally, the inferiority concerns guilt due to moral lapses. One student is still haunted by her dishonesty which enabled her to pass a certain course three years ago. She has felt miserable ever since about this critical experience and badly needs a means of expiation.

In this connection we may speak of religious crises. While they are uncommon in my sample, Havens[6] estimates that at any given time 12 per cent of college students have a critical concern, and sometimes acute crises, due to their religious conflicts. I suspect the concern is even more widespread, but since it pertains to one's whole ground of being, it is seldom configurated as a specific crisis at a given moment of time.

Another area, seldom mentioned but surely important, is the ideological crisis of modern society as a whole. Youth is inevitably worried, as are adults, by our uncertain future. Elsewhere I have discussed the withdrawal of American youth from their social and political context.[5] Both the earlier and present data show an almost exclusive concern among American youth with their own lives. Compared with autobiographies of youth in other cultures, the American documents are far more self-centered, more privatistic. They are too baffled to articulate their distress, and so take refuge in their private concerns.

SEX AND FAMILY

Sex Conflicts

Needless to say, our candid discussions of crises frequently, in fact usually, report acute sex conflicts. Extremely common are breakups in boy-girl relationships which are usually taken as a disaster only slightly less fatal than the end of the world. Such breakups are so recently experienced that college students do not realize that they will, in spite of their present feelings, eventually make a good recovery.

We should face the fact that at least in the early years of college life crises in the sexual sphere are for the most part frankly genital in their reference. The biological drive is so powerful that the youth is concerned with it almost by itself. Its integration into mature love, into marriage, into career plans, into an embracing philosophy of life, exceeds his present capacity. He is likely to think that genitality by itself is maturity. Sexual gratification is frankly the aim, often with devastating consequences. At this stage of development, the students have much to say about sex and little to say about mature love.

Family Conflicts

I have left until last the most pervasive area of conflict and crisis. I am referring, of course, to the situation that exists between every adolescent and his parents. It is not enough to say that adolescent rebellion against the parents is the rule. Of course it is; but my documents show that the whole history of the relationships from the time of earliest memories is important. Almost any irregularity in normal family life is felt bitterly and may trouble a student even into adulthood. A mother who is neglectful or self-centered, or perhaps overpossessive and neurotic, leaves traumatic traces in the child's life. A father who is ineffectual and weak, or cruel, or absent (if only for wartime service) leaves the child with a lasting feeling of protest.

One document of unusual maturity notes that many college students seem to need their parents as scapegoats. They find it comfortable to blame parents for their own shortcomings. Perceiving that their parents are not all-powerful, all-wise, and all-perfect, they can say, "Well, no wonder I am having a hard time growing up; they didn't raise me right." Thus, an adolescent, having no genuine ground for complaint, may yet soak himself in self pity, not being mature enough to relate his restricted image of his parents to the totality of human nature—not yet ready to appreciate the fact that his parents, considering human limitations, may have done a good job. Even if the job was not especially good, the adolescent seems not yet able to appreciate his parents' good intentions as an important value in their own right. From talking with many parents, I hazard the hypothesis that normally it is not until the age of 23 that a child encounters his parents on a mature, adult-to-adult basis.

This brief account of crises emanating from the parent-child relationship leads me to a final point. My students were required to discuss their crises from the point of view of personality theory. They were free to employ any of the theories they were studying in my course. Most of them took Freud. (I may add that the reason was not because Freud was their instructor's favorite author.)

THE CONDITIONS OF THEORY

Now my observation is this: Their Freudian interpretations seemed to fit well if and when the family situation in early life was disturbed. When the father was absent or ineffectual, when the mother was notably aggressive, when there was deliberate sex stimulation within the family—in such cases, it seems that the Oedipal formula provides a good fit, together with all its theoretical accoutrements of identification, superego conflict, defense mechanisms, castration threats, and all the rest.

When, on the other hand, the family life is reasonably normal and secure, a Freudian conceptualization seems forced and artificial. If we say, by way of rough estimate, that 60 per cent of the students try a Freudian conceptualization of their own cases, about 10 per cent turn out to be wholly convincing and theoretically appropriate. The remaining 50 per cent appear to be somehow contrived and badly strained.

I am wondering whether the same ratio might be applicable to cases that come to counselors. If a counselor or a therapist approaches every client or patient with the preconceived belief that his life must fit a Freudian frame of conceptualization, he may win in a minority of the cases, but lose in the majority.

Even where a Freudian approach is clearly justified, exclusive adherence to it may distract the counselor from many significant developments within the life—for example, from the present functional significance of religious and aesthetic values, from the competence and interests that extend beyond the neurotic core, from the client's conscious plans for the future, and from his "will to meaning" and existential concern with life as a whole.

Every person concerned with guidance, or for that matter with teaching, needs as background some general theory of the nature of human personality.[2] Our tendency, I fear, is to draw our theories from the realm of illness and deviance. It is somehow tempting to apply psychiatric rubrics to all personalities, for psychiatric rubrics are vivid, incisive, dramatic, and easy. Our conceptual banners bear such sloganized concepts as Oedipal complex, character disorder, identity diffusion, schizoid, acting out, and maybe an array of dimensions drawn from the Minnesota Multiphasic Personality Inventory. All such concepts, of course, have their proper place. But personality theory for guidance and teaching needs also to be woven of less lurid fabrics.

Youth, whatever neurotic threads may lie in his nature, is busy with his realistic perceptions, with his gradual learning and quiet coping, with the slow extension of selfhood, with noncritical failures and successes, with developing a generic conscience and a personal style of life. Even in the throes of crisis, he seeks in undramatic ways to consolidate his gains and continue on the path of becoming. A theory of personality adequate to undergird the art of guidance will keep such nondramatic facts in mind. Crises in normal personality development are important, but so too is the slow growth of each youth's unique style of life.

REFERENCES

1. Allport, G. W. Values and our youth. *Teach. Coll. Rec.*, 1961, *63*, 211–219.
2. Allport, G. W. Psychological models for guidance. *Harvard educ. Rev.*, 1962, *32*, 373–381.
3. Blaine, G. B., & McArthur, C. C. *Emotional problems of the student.* New York: Appleton-Century-Crofts, 1961.
4. Erikson, E. *Childhood and society.* New York: Norton, 1950.
5. Gillespie, J. M., & Allport, G. W. *Youth's outlook on the future.* New York: Doubleday, 1955.
6. Havens, J. A study of religious conflict in college students. *J. sci. Stud. Relig.*, 1963, *3*, 52–69.

The years of youth

39.

A memorandum on identity and Negro youth

Erik H. Erikson

In this article, an authority on the subject of identity shares some insights for understanding human development and behavior. But this understanding may not come easily. Because many ideas are advanced and because any number of associations and new perspectives may be generated, this selection may prove profitable to read, to consider, and to read again. Even though ostensibly written about black youth, what is said is applicable to the total of humanity and much of it is fraught with meaning. Passage after passage strikes a responsive chord. One of these is the observation that moralities sooner or later outlive themselves but that ethics never do. One must probe and think if he is to grasp the meaning here.

A second section that in our opinion merits quoting for emphasis and its pertinence to development and to youth is: ". . . in youth the tables of childhood dependence begin slowly to turn: it is no longer exclusively for the old to teach the young the meaning of life, whether individual or collective. It is the young who, by their responses and actions, tell the old whether life as represented by their elders and as presented to the young has meaning; and it is the young who carry in them the power to confirm those who confirm them and, joining the issues, to renew and to regenerate, or to reform and to rebel."

We have seen this happen in our own lives. We remember our own small youngsters trying to join and to identify with us and we find ourselves, now that they are older, gaining meaning and identity by associating with them—the process of gaining an identity cannot be divorced from the process of associating with others.

INTRODUCTION

A LACK OF familiarity with the problem of Negro youth and with the actions by which Negro youth hopes to solve these problems is a marked de-

Journal of Social Issues, 20:29–42, October, 1964. Erik H. Erikson, Professor of Human Development, Harvard University.

ficiency in my life and work which cannot be compensated for with theoretical speculation; and this least of all at a time when Negro writers are finding superb new ways of stating their and our predicament and when Negro youth finds itself involved in action which would have seemed unimaginable only a very few years ago. But since it is felt that some of my concepts might be helpful in further discussion, I will in the following recapitulate the pertinent ideas on identity contained in my writings.[1] This I do only in the hope that what is clear may prove helpful and what is not will become clearer in joint studies.

The fact that problems of Negro youth span the whole phenomenology of aggravated identity confusion and rapid new identity formation—cutting across phenomena judged antisocial and prosocial, violent and heroic, fanatic and ethically advanced—makes it advisable to include remarks concerning the origin of the concept of ego-identity in clinical observation in this review. However, the concept has come a long way since we first used it to define a syndrome in war—neurotics in World War II: I recently heard in India that Nehru had used the terms "identity" to describe a new quality which, he felt, Gandhi had given India after offering her the equivalent of a "psychoanalysis of her past."

1. CHILDHOOD AND IDENTITY

a. The growing child must derive a vitalizing sense of reality from the awareness that his individual way of mastering experience is a successful variant of a group identity and is in accord with its spacetime and life plan. Minute displays of emotion such as affection, pride, anger, guilt, anxiety, sexual arousal (rather than the words used, the meanings intended, or the philosophy implied), transmit to the human child the outlines of what really counts in his world, i.e., the variables of his group's space-time and the perspectives of its life plan.

Here is the first observation I made (a decade and a half ago) on Negro children. I will quote it to characterize the point-of-view with which I started. The babies of our colored countrymen, I said, often receive sensual satisfactions which provide them with enough oral and sensory surplus for a lifetime, as clearly betrayed in the way they move, laugh, talk, sing. Their forced symbiosis with the feudal South capitalized on this oral sensory treasure and helped to build a slave's identity: mild, submissive, dependent, somewhat querulous, but always ready to serve, with occasional empathy and childlike wisdom. But underneath a dangerous split occurred. The Negro's unavoidable identification with the dominant race, and the need of the master race to protect its own identity against the very sensual and oral temptations emanating from the race held to be inferior (whence came their mammies), established in both groups an association: light—clean—clever—white, and dark—dirty—dumb—nigger. The result, especially in those Negroes who left the poor haven of their Southern homes, was often a violently sudden and cruel cleanliness training, as attested to in the autobiographies of Negro writers. It is as if by cleansing, a whiter identity could be achieved. The attending disillusionment transmits itself to the phallic-locomotor stage, when restrictions as to what shade of girl one may dream of interfere with the free transfer of the original narcissistic sensuality to the genital sphere. Three identities are formed: (1) mammy's oral-sensual "honey-child"—tender, expressive, rhythmical; (2) the evil identity of the dirty, anal-sadistic, phallic-rapist "nigger"; and (3) the clean, anal-compulsive, restrained, friendly, but always sad "white man's Negro."

So-called opportunities offered the migrating Negro often only turn out to be a more subtly restricted prison which endangers his only historically "successful" identity (that of the slave) and fails to provide a reintegration of the other identity fragments mentioned. These fragments, then, become dominant in the form of racial caricatures which are underscored and stereotyped by the entertainment industry. Tired of his own caricature, the colored individual often retires into hypochondriac invalidism as a condition which represents an analogy to the dependence and the relative safety of defined restriction in the South: a neurotic regression to the ego identity of the slave.

Mixed-blood Sioux Indians in areas where they hardly ever see Negroes refer to their full-blood brothers as "niggers," thus indicating the power of the dominant national imagery which serves to counterpoint the ideal and the evil images in the inventory of available prototypes. No individual can escape this opposition of images, which is all-pervasive in the men and in the women, in the majorities and in the minorities, and in all the classes of a given national or cultural unit. Psychoanalysis shows that the unconscious evil identity (the composite of everything which arouses negative identification—i.e., the wish not to resemble it) consists of the images of the violated (castrated) body, the "marked" outgroup, and the exploited minority. Thus a pronounced he-man may, in his dreams and prejudices, prove to be mortally afraid of ever displaying a woman's sentiments, a Negro's submissiveness, or a Jew's intellectuality. For the ego, in the course of its synthesizing efforts, attempts to subsume the most powerful evil and ideal prototypes (the final contestants, as it were) and with them the whole existing imagery of superior and inferior, good and bad, masculine and feminine, free and slave, potent and impotent, beautiful and ugly, fast and slow, tall and small, in a simple alternative, in order to make one battle and one strategy out of a bewildering number of skirmishes.

I knew a colored boy who, like our boys, listened every night to Red Rider. Then he sat up in bed, imagining that he was Red Rider. But the moment came when he saw himself galloping after some masked offender and suddenly noticed that in his fancy Red Rider was a colored man. He stopped his fantasy. While a small child, this boy was extremely expressive, both in his pleasures and in his sorrows. Today he is calm and always smiles; his language is soft and blurred; nobody can hurry him or worry him—or please him. White people like him.

As such boys and girls look around now, what other ideal (and evil) images are at their disposal? And how do they connect with the past? (Does non-violence connect totalistically or holistically with traditional patience and tolerance of pain?)

b. When children enter the stage of the adolescent Identity Crisis, a factor enters which characterizes the real kind of *crisis,* namely, a moment of decision between strong contending forces. "A moment" means that here something can happen very rapidly; "decision," that divergence becomes permanent; "strong and contending," that these are intense matters.

Developmentally speaking the sense of ego identity is the accrued confidence that one's ability to maintain inner sameness and continuity (one's ego in the psychoanalytic sense) is matched by the sameness and continuity of one's meaning for others. The growing child must, at every step, derive a vitalizing sense of reality from the awareness that his individual way of mastering experience is a successful variant of the way other people around him master experience and recognize such mastery.

In this, children cannot be fooled by empty praise and condescending encouragement. They may have to accept artificial bolstering of their self-esteem in lieu of something better, but what I call their accruing ego identity gains real strength only from whole-hearted and consistent recognition of real accomplishment, that is, achievement that has meaning in their culture. On the other hand, should a child feel that the environment tries to deprive him too radically of all the forms of expression which permit him to develop and to integrate the next step in his ego identity, he will resist with the astonishing strength encountered in animals who are suddenly forced to defend their lives. Indeed, in the social jungle of human existence, there is no feeling of being alive without a sense of ego identity. Or else, there may be total self-abnegation (in more or less malignant forms) as illustrated in this observation. And here is an example of total denial of identity:

A four-year-old Negro girl in the Arsenal Nursery School in Pittsburgh used to stand in front of a mirror and scrub her skin with soap. When gently diverted from this she began to scrub the mirror. Finally, when induced to paint instead, she first angrily filled sheets of paper with the colors brown and black. But then she brought to the teacher what she called "a really good picture." The teacher first could see only a white sheet, until she looked closer and saw that the little girl had covered every inch of the white sheet with white paint. This playful episode of total self-eradication occurred and could only occur in a "desegregated" school: it illustrates the extent to which infantile drive control (cleanliness) and social self-esteem (color) are associated in childhood. But it also points to the extent of the crime which is perpetrated wherever, in the service of seemingly civilized values, groups of people are made to feel so inexorably "different" that legal desegregation can only be the beginning of a long and painful inner reidentification.

Such crises come when their parents and teachers, losing trust in themselves and using sudden correctives in order to approach the vague but pervasive Anglo-Saxon ideal, create violent discontinuities; or where, indeed, the children themselves learn to disavow their sensual and overprotective mothers as temptations and a hindrance to the formation of a more "American" personality.

If we, then, speak of the community's response to the young individual's need to be "recognized" by those around him, we mean something beyond a mere recognition of achievement; for it is of great relevance to the young individual's identity formation that he be responded to, and be given function and status as a person whose gradual growth and transformation make sense to those who begin to make sense to him. Identity formation goes beyond the process of *identifying oneself* with ideal others in a one-way fashion; it is a process based on a heightened cognitive and emotional capacity to *let oneself be identified* by concrete persons as a circumscribed individual in relation to a predictable universe which transcends the family. Identity thus is not the sum of childhood identifications, but rather a new combination of old and new identification fragments. For this very reason societies *confirm* an individual at this time in all kinds of ideological frameworks and assign roles and tasks to him in which he can *recognize himself and feel recognized*. Ritual confirmations, initiations, and indoctrinations only sharpen an indispensable process of self-verification by which healthy societies bestow and receive the distilled strength of generations. By this process, societies, in turn, are themselves historically verified.

The danger of this stage is *identity diffusion;* as Biff puts it in Arthur Miller's *Death of a Salesman,* "I just can't take hold, Mom, I can't take hold of some kind of a life." Where such a dilemma is based on a strong previous doubt of one's ethnic and sexual identity, delinquent and outright psychotic incidents are not uncommon. Youth after youth, bewildered by some assumed role, a role forced on him by the inexorable standardization of American adolescence, runs away in one form or another; leaving schools and jobs, staying out all night, or withdrawing into bizarre and inaccessible moods. Once "delinquent," his greatest need and often his only salvation, is the refusal on the part of older friends, advisers, and judiciary personnel to type him further by pat diagnoses and social judgments which ignore the special dynamic conditions of adolescence. For if diagnosed and treated correctly, seemingly psychotic and criminal incidents do not in adolescence have the same fatal significance which they have at other ages. Yet many a youth, finding the authorities expect him to be "a nigger," "a bum," or "a queer," perversely obliges by becoming just that.

To keep themselves together, individuals and groups treated in this fashion temporarily overidentify, to the point of apparent complete loss of individual identity, with the heroes of cliques and crowds. On the other hand, they become remarkably clannish, intolerant, and cruel in their exclusion of others who are "different," in skin color or cultural background, in tastes and gifts, and often in entirely petty aspects of dress and gesture arbitrarily selected as *the* signs of an in-grouper or out-grouper. It is important to understand (which does not mean condone or participate in) such tolerance as the necessary *defense against a sense of identity diffusion,* which is unavoidable at a time of life when the body changes its proportions radically, when genital maturity floods body and imagination with all manners of drives, when intimacy with the other sex offers intense complications, and when life lies before one with a variety of conflicting possibilities and choices. Adolescents help one another temporarily through such discomfort by forming cliques and by stereotyping themselves, their ideals, and their enemies.

In general, one may say that we are apt to view the social play of adolescents as we once judged the play of children. We alternately consider such behavior irrelevant, unnecessary, or irrational, and ascribe to it purely delinquent or neurotic meanings. As in the past the study of children's spontaneous games was neglected in favor of that of solitary play, so now the mutual "joinedness" of adolescent clique behavior fails to be properly assessed in our concern for the individual adolescent. Children and adolescents in their presocieties provide for one another a sanctioned moratorium and joint support for free experimentation with inner and outer dangers (including those emanating from the adult world). Whether or not a given adolescent's newly acquired capacities are drawn back into infantile conflict depends to a significant extent on the quality of the opportunities and rewards available to him in his peer clique, as well as on the more formal ways in which society at large invites a transition from social play to work experimentation, and from rituals of transit to final commitments: all of which must be based on an implicit mutual contract between the individual and society.

2. TOTALISM AND NEGATIVE IDENTITY

If such contact is deficient, youth may seek perverse restoration in a negative identity, "totalistically" enforced. Here we must reconsider the proposition that the need for identity is experienced as a need for a certain wholeness in the experience of oneself within the community (and community here is as wide as one's social vision); and that, where such wholeness is impossible, such need turns to "totalism."

To be a bit didactic: *Wholeness* connotes an assembly of parts, even quite diversified parts, that enter into fruitful association and organization. This concept is most strikingly expressed in such terms as wholeheartedness, wholemindedness, and wholesomeness. In human development as well as in history, then, wholeness emphasizes a progressive coherence of diversified functions and parts. *Totality,* on the contrary, evokes a Gestalt in which an absolute boundary is emphasized: given a certain arbitrary delineation, nothing that belongs inside must be left outside; nothing that must be outside should be tolerated inside. A totality must be as absolutely inclusive as it is absolutely exclusive. The word "utter" conveys the element of force, which overrides the question whether the category-to-be-made-absolute is an organic and a logical one, and whether the parts, so to speak, really have a natural affinity to one another.

To say it in one sentence: Where the human being despairs of an essential wholeness of experience, he restructures himself and the world by taking refuge in a totalistic world view. Thus there appears both in individuals and in groups a periodical need for a totality without further choice or alternation, even if it implies the abandonment of a much-needed wholeness. This can consist of a lone-wolf's negativism; of a delinquent group's seeming nihilism; or in the case of national or racial groups, in a defiant glorification of one's own caricature.

Thus, patients (and I think it is in this respect that patients can help us understand analogous group processes) choose a *negative identity,* i.e., an identity perversely based on all those identifications and roles which, at critical stages of development, had been presented to them as most undesirable or dangerous, and yet also as most real. For example, a mother having lost her first-born son may (because of complicated guilt feelings) be unable to attach to her later surviving children the same amount of religious devotion that she bestows on the memory of her dead child and may well arouse in one of her sons the conviction that to be sick or dead is a better assurance of being "recognized" than to be healthy and about. A mother who is filled with unconscious ambivalence toward a brother who disintegrated into alcoholism may again and again respond selectively only to those traits in her son which seem to point to a repetition of her brother's fate, in which case this "negative" identity may take on more reality for the son than all his natural attempts at being good: he may work hard on becoming a drunkard and, lacking the necessary ingredients, may end up in a state of stubborn paralysis of choice. The daughter of a man of brilliant showmanship may run away from college and be arrested as a prostitute in the Negro quarter of a Southern city; while the daughter of an influential Southern Negro preacher may be found among narcotic addicts in Chicago. In such cases it is of utmost importance to recognize the mockery and the vindictive pretense in such role playing; for the white girl may not have really prostituted herself, and the colored girl may not really become an addict—yet. Needless to say, however, each of them could have placed herself in a marginal social area, leaving it to law-enforcement officers and to psychiatric agencies to decide what stamp to put on such behavior. A corresponding case is that of a boy presented to a psychiatric clinic as "the village homosexual" of a small town. On investigation, it appeared that the boy had succeeded in assuming this fame without any actual acts of homosexuality, except that much earlier in his life he had been raped by some older boys.

Such vindictive choices of a negative identity represent, of course, a desperate attempt to regain some mastery in a situation in which the available positive identity elements cancel each other out. The history of such choice reveals a set of conditions in which it is easier to derive a sense of identity out of a *total* identification with that which one is *least* supposed to be than to struggle for a feeling of reality in acceptable roles which are unattainable with the patient's inner means.

There is a "lower lower" snobbism too, which is based on the pride of having achieved a semblance of nothingness. At any rate, many a late adolescent, if faced with continuing diffusion, would rather *be a total nobody, somebody totally bad, or indeed dead—and all of this by free choice—than be not-quite-somebody.*

Thus, individuals, when caught up in the necessity to regroup an old identity or to gain a new and inescapable one, are subject to influences which offer them a way to wholeness. Obviously, revolutions do the first to gain the second. At any rate, the problem of totalism vs. wholeness seems to be represented in its organized form in the Black Muslims who insist on a totally "black" solution reinforced by historical and religious mysticism on the one hand; and the movement of non-violent and legal insistence on civil rights, on the other. Once such a polarization is established, it seems imperative to investigate what powerful self-images (traditional, revolutionary, and, as it were, evolutionary) have entered the picture, in mutually exclusive or mutually inclusive form, and what the corresponding symptoms are, in individuals and in the masses.

3. "CONVERSION" AND MORE INCLUSIVE IDENTITY

In a little-known passage, Bernard Shaw relates the story of his "conversion": "I was *drawn* into the Socialist *revival of* the early eighties, among Englishmen *intensely serious* and *burning with indignation* at very *real* and very *fundamental evils* that affected *all the world."* The words here italicized convey to me the following implications. "Drawn into": an ideology has a compelling power. "Revival": it consists of a traditional force in a state of rejuvenation. "Intensely serious": it permits even the cynical to make an investment of sincerity. "Burning with indignation": it gives to the need for repudiation the sanction of righteousness. "Real": it projects a vague inner evil into a circumscribed horror in reality. "Fundamental": it promises participation in an effort at basic reconstruction of society. "All the world": it gives structure to a totally defined world image. Here, then, are the elements by which a group identity harnesses the young individual's aggressive and discriminative energies, and encompasses, as it completes it, the individual's identity in the service of its ideology. Thus, identity and ideology are two aspects of the same process. Both provide the necessary condition for further individual maturation and, with it, for the next higher form of identification, namely, *the solidarity linking common identities.* For the need to bind irrational self-hate and irrational repudiation makes young people, on occasion, mortally compulsive and conservative even where and when they seem most anarchic and radical; the same need makes them potentially "ideological," i.e., more or less explicitly in search of a world image held together by what Shaw called "a clear comprehension of life in the light of an intelligible theory."

What are, then, the available ideological ingredients of the new Negro and the new American identity? For (such is the nature of a revolutionary movement) the new Negro cannot afford any longer just to become "equal" to the old White. As he becomes something new, he also forces the white man as well as the advanced Negro to become newer than they are.

4. WEAKNESS AND STRENGTH

a. In my clinical writings I have suggested that delinquent joining stands in the same dynamic relationship to schizoid isolation, as (according to Freud) perversion does to neurosis: negative *group* identities (gangs, cliques, rings, mobs) "save" the individual from the symptoms of a negative identity neurosis, to wit: a disintegration of the sense of time; morbid identity consciousness; work paralysis; bisexual confusion; and authority diffusion.

Unnecessary to say, however, a *transitory* "negative identity" is often the necessary pre-condition for a truly positive and truly new one. In this respect, I would think that American Negro writers may turn out to be as important for American literature as Irish expatriates were in the Europe of an earlier period.

On the other hand, there are certain strengths in the Negro which have evolved out of or at least along with his very submission. Such a statement will, I trust, not be misunderstood as an argument for continued submission. What I have in mind are strengths which one would hope for the sake of all of us, could remain part of a future Negro identity. Here I have in mind such a traditional phenomenon as the power of the Negro mother. As pointed out, I must glean examples from experiences accessible to me; the following observation on Caribbean motherhood will, I hope, be put into its proper perspective by experts on the whole life-space of the Negro on the American continent.

b. Churchmen have had reason to deplore, and anthropologists to explore, the pattern of Caribbean family life, obviously an outgrowth of the slavery days of Plantation America, which extended from the Northeast Coast of Brazil in a half-circle into the Southeast of the United States.

Plantations, of course, were agricultural factories, owned and operated by gentlemen, whose cultural and economic identity had its roots in a supra-regional upper class. They were worked by slaves, that is, men who, being mere equipment put to use when and where necessary, had to relinquish all chance of being the masters of their families and communities. Thus, the women were left with the offspring of a variety of men who could give no protection as they could provide no identity, except that of a subordinate species. The family system which ensued can be described in scientific terms only by circumscriptions dignifying what is not there: the rendering of "sexual services" between persons who cannot be called anything more definite than "lovers"; "maximum instability" in the sexual lives of young girls, whose pattern it is to relinquish the care of their offspring to their mothers; and mothers and grandmothers who determine that "standardized mode of co-activity" which is the minimum requirement for calling a group of individuals a family. They are, then, mostly called "household groups"— single dwellings, occupied by people sharing a common food supply. These households are "matrifocal," a word understating the grandiose role of the all powerful mother-figure who will encourage her daughters to leave their infants with her, or, at any rate, to stay with her as long as they con-tinue to bear children. Motherhood thus becomes community life; and where churchmen could find little or no morality, and casual observers, little or no order at all, the mothers and grandmothers in fact also became father and grandfathers,[2] in the sense that they exerted that authoritative influence which resulted in an ever newly improvised set of rules for the economic obligations of the men who had fathered the children, and up-held the rules of incestuous avoidance. Above all, they provided the only superidentity which was left open after the enslavement of the men, namely, that of the mother who will nurture a human infant irrespective of his parentage. It is well known how many poor little rich and white gentlemen benefited from the extended fervor of the Negro women who nursed them as Southern mammies, as creole das, or as Brazilian babas. This cultural fact is, of course, being played down by the racists as mere servitude while the predominance of maternal warmth in Caribbean women is char-acterized as African sensualism, and vicariously enjoyed by refugees from "Continental" womanhood. One may, however, see at the root of this maternalism a grandiose gesture of human adaptation which has given the area of the Caribbean (now searching for a political and economic pattern to do justice to its cultural unity) both the promise of a positive (female) identity and the threat of a negative (male) one; for here, the fact that identity depended on the procreative worth of being born, has undoubtedly weakened the striving for becoming somebody by individual effort.

(This is an ancient pattern taking many forms in the modern Negro world. But—parenthetically speaking—it may give us one more access to a better understanding of the magnificently bearded group of men and boys who have taken over one of the islands and insist on proving that the Caribbean male can earn his worth in production as well as in procreation.)

My question is whether such maternal strength has survived not only in parts of our South but also in family patterns of Negro migrants; whether it is viewed as undesirable and treated as delinquent by Negroes as well as whites; and whether America can afford to lose it all at a time when women must help men more planfully not only to preserve the naked life of the human race but also some "inalienable" values.

c. This brings me, finally, to the issue of Fidelity, that virtue and quality of adolescent ego strength which belongs to man's evolutionary heritage, but which—like all the basic virtues—can arise only in the interplay of a stage of life with the social forces of a true community.

To be a *special kind,* has been an important element in the human need for personal and collective identities. They have found a transitory fulfillment in man's greatest moments of cultural identity and civilized perfection, and each such tradition of identity and perfection has highlighted what man could be, could he fulfil all his potentials at one time. The utopia of our own era predicts that man will be one species in one world, with a universal identity to replace the illusory super-identities which have divided him, and with an international ethic replacing all moral systems of superstition, repression, and suppression. Whatever the political arrangement that will further this utopia, we can only point to the human strengths which potentially emerge with the stages of life and indicate their dependence on communal life. In youth, ego strength emerges from the mutual confirmation of individual and community, in the sense that society recognizes the young individual as a bearer of fresh energy and that the individual so confirmed recognizes society as a living process which inspires loyalty as it receives it, maintains allegiance as it attracts it, honors confidence as it demands it. All this I subsume under the term Fidelity.

Diversity and fidelity are polarized: they make each other significant and keep each other alive. Fidelity without a sense of diversity can become an obsession and a bore; diversity without a sense of fidelity, an empty relativism.

But Fidelity also stands in a certain polarity to adolescent sexuality: both sexual fulfillment and "sublimation" depend on this polarity.

The various hindrances to a full consummation of adolescent genital maturation have many deep consequences for man which pose an important problem for future planning. Best studied is the regressive revival of that earlier stage of psychosexuality which preceded even the emotionally quiet first school years, that is, the infantile genital and locomotor stage, with its tendency toward auto-erotic manipulation, grandiose phantasy, and vigorous play. But in youth, auto-erotism, grandiosity, and playfulness are all immensely amplified by genital potency and locomotor maturation, and are vastly complicated by what we will presently describe as the youthful mind's historical perspective.

The most widespread expression of the discontented search of youth is the craving for locomotion, whether expressed in a general "being on the go," "tearing after something," or "running around"; or in locomotion proper, as in vigorous work, in absorbing sports, in rapt dancing, in shiftless *Wanderschaft,* and in the employment and misuse of speedy animals and machines. But it also finds expression through participation in the movements of the day (whether the riots of a local commotion or the parades and campaigns of major ideological forces); if they only appeal to the need for feeling "moved" and for feeling essential in moving something along toward an open future. It is clear that societies offer any number of ritual combinations of ideological perspective and vigorous movement (dance, sports, parades, demonstrations, riots) to harness youth in the service of their historical aims; and that where societies fail to do so, these patterns will seek their own combinations, in small groups occupied with serious games, good-natured foolishness, cruel prankishness, and delinquent warfare. In no other stage of the life cycle, then, are the promise of finding oneself and the threat of losing oneself so closely allied.

To summarize: Fidelity, when fully matured, is the strength of disciplined devotion. It is gained in the involvement of youth in such experiences as reveal the essence of the era they are to join—as the beneficiaries of its tradition, as the practitioners and innovators of its technology, as renewers of its ethical strength, as rebels bent on the destruction of the outlived, and as deviants with deviant commitments. This, at least, is the potential of youth in psychosocial evolution; and while this may sound like a rationalization endorsing any high sounding self-delusion in youth, any self-indulgence masquerading as devotion, or any righteous excuse for blind destruction, it makes intelligible the tremendous waste attending this as any other mechanism of human adaptation, especially if its excesses meet with more moral condemnation than ethical guidance. On the other hand, our understanding of these processes is not furthered by the "clinical" reduction of adolescent phenomena to their infantile antecedents and to an underlying dichotomy of drive and conscience. Adolescent development comprises a new set of identification processes, both with significant persons and with ideological forces, which give importance to individual life by relating it to a living community and to ongoing history, and by counterpointing the newly won individual identity with some communal solidarity.

In youth, then, the life history intersects with history: here individuals are confirmed in their identities, societies regenerated in their life style. This process also implies a fateful survival of adolescent modes of thinking in man's historical and ideological perspectives.

Historical processes, of course, have already entered the individual's core in childhood. Both ideal and evil images and the moral prototypes guiding parental administrations originate in the past struggles of contending cultural and national "species," which also color fairytale and family lore, superstition and gossip, and the simple lessons of early verbal training. Historians on the whole make little of this; they describe the visible emergence and the contest of autonomous historical ideas, unconcerned with the fact that these ideas reach down into the everyday lives of generations and re-emerge through the daily awakening and training of historical consciousness in young individuals.

It is youth which begins to develop that sense of historical irreversibility which can lead to what we may call acute historical estrangement. This lies behind the fervent quest for a sure meaning in individual life history and in collective history, and behind the questioning of the laws of relevancy which bind datum and principles, event and movement. But it is also, alas, behind the bland carelessness of that youth which denies its own vital need to develop and cultivate a historical consciousness—and conscience.

To enter history, each generation of young persons must find an identity consonant with its own childhood and consonant with an ideological promise in the perceptible historical process. But in youth the tables of childhood dependence begin slowly to turn: it is no longer exclusively for the old to teach the young the meaning of life, whether individual or collective. It is the young who, by their responses and actions, tell the old whether life as represented by their elders and as presented to the young has meaning; and it is the young who carry in them the power to confirm those who confirm them and, joining the issues, to renew and to regenerate, or to reform and to rebel.

I will not at this point review the institutions which participate in creating the retrospective and the prospective mythology offering historical orientation to youth. Obviously, the mythmakers of religion and politics, the arts and the sciences, the stage and fiction—all contribute to the historical logic presented to youth more or less consciously, more or less responsibly. And today we must add, at least in the United States, psychiatry; and all over the world, the press, which forces leaders to make history in the open and to accept reportorial distortion as a major historical factor.

Moralities sooner or later outlive themselves, ethics never: this is what the need for identity and for fidelity, reborn with each generation, seems to point to. Morality in the moralistic sense can be shown by modern means of inquiry to be predicated on superstitions and irrational inner mechanisms which ever again undermine the ethical fiber of generations; but morality is expendable only where ethics prevail. This is the wisdom that the words of many languages have tried to tell man. He has tenaciously clung to the words, even though he has understood them only vaguely, and in his actions has disregarded or perverted them completely. But there is much in ancient wisdom which can now become knowledge.

What then, are the sources of a new ethical orientation which may have roots in Negro tradition and yet also reach into the heroic striving for a new identity within the universal ethics emanating from world-wide technology and communication? This question may sound strenuously inspirational or academic; yet, I have in mind the study of concrete sources of morale and strength, lying within the vitality of bodily experience, the identity of individual experience, and the fidelity developed in methods of work and cooperation, methods of solidarity and political action, and methods permitting a simple and direct manifestation of human values such as having survived centuries of suppression. As a clinician, I am probably more competent to judge the conditions which continue to *suppress* and attempt to *crush* such strengths; and yet I have also found that diagnosis and anamnesis can turn out to be of little help where one ignores sources of recovery often found in surprising and surprisingly powerful constellations.

NOTES

1. See *"Childhood and Society,"* W. W. Norton and Co., Inc., New York, 1950; *"Wholeness and Totality,"* In *Totalitarianism,* Proceedings of a Conference held at the Am. Academy of Arts and Sciences, C. J. Friedrich, ed. Cambridge: Harvard University Press, 1954; "Identity and the Life Cycle," Monograph, *Psychological Issues,* Vol. I, No. 1, New York: Int'l Universities Press, 1959 with an intro. by D. Rapaport; "Youth: Fidelity and Diversity," *Daedalus,* 91:5–27, 1962.
2. See the title "My Mother Who Fathered Me."

40.

College students and children in developmental institutions

Kenneth Keniston

Author-psychiatrist, Keniston is noted for his analyses of education of the culturally different child and for his appreciation of the current dilemmas of youth. In this article he shows some rather surprising similarities between youth and "disadvantage." Those who think youth have too much freedom may be called upon to do some rethinking. Herein, Keniston reports his findings of a six-year study of alienated students at Harvard University. With the apparently still rising disaf-

Children, 14(No. 1):3–7, January–February, 1967. Kenneth Keniston, Associate Professor of Psychology, Department of Psychiatry, Yale University School of Medicine.

fection of so many young people, both in high school and in college, it appears to be important (as widely varied antidotes are suggested) that the causes of disorder, ailments, symptoms, or whatever be analyzed and, if possible, understood. This author, together with other authors in this section, may help to promote such understanding.

AT FIRST GLANCE, few groups seem more dissimilar than the talented, privileged students who attend residential liberal arts colleges and the unwanted or neglected children who live in group residential centers. Yet behind the real differences in age and social privilege that separate these two groups, there are profound similarities in their situations. Essentially the same issues arise in planning for what one college dean calls "the care and feeding of college students" as in planning for the group residential care of children.

As Erving Goffman has pointed out, there are a few institutions in modern society that may encompass practically all aspects of a person's life. He calls these "total institutions,"[1] for in them residential life, social life, and work life are combined—often within the same walls, certainly within the same institutional framework. As examples he cites merchant ships, military services, mental hospitals, prisons, monasteries, and residential treatment institutions. He might also have cited institutions for neglected and dependent children.

This concept of "total institution" becomes more useful if we distinguish between different kinds of total institutions. There are three types: (1) those institutions that could be called *instrumental* because they are trying to get a job done in the outside world—for instance, a merchant ship carrying a cargo across the sea; (2) those institutions whose purpose is at least nominally *therapeutic,* preventative, or corrective, such as a prison or mental hospital; and (3) a small group of institutions whose explicit purpose is *developmental,* such as a residential college, a boarding school, or a residential center for neglected and dependent children.

A residential college, of course, is less "total" than an army or a prison: Students are on the whole free to enter and leave at will. But for most college students, during the academic year at least, their lives are embodied and to some extent regulated within a single framework and a set of walls. And obviously group residential centers for children are total institutions in the full sense of the word.

Developmental institutions, whether colleges or children's "homes," have a number of common characteristics. For one, they at least nominally accept as their primary objective the promotion of the "normal" or optimal development of their charges, the residents. They therefore usually try to ally themselves with what they take to be the natural forces for growth and development in the individual. They see their task as somehow stimulating, supporting, and confirming the development of each resident. In this respect they differ sharply from an instrumental institution like an army or a merchant ship, which may ignore or even impede the individual's overall development. And they also differ from therapeutic institutions like good mental hospitals, which have as a primary task to intervene and correct faulty development. This does not mean that developmental institutions like colleges or institutions for children do not have ways of correcting faulty development. But, on the whole, their goals are not so much to correct failures as to promote normal healthy growth.

A second characteristic of developmental institutions is that they exercise quasi-familial functions. Ordinarily, such institutions arise in situations where families cannot or are thought not to be able to do an adequate job. A children's institution, for example, usually enters the picture when there is no family that can take care of the child, or when the child's actual family is exerting a destructive influence on his development. Boarding schools and residential colleges generally arise because individual families cannot provide the kind of "character-building," intellectual stimulation, or environmental enrichment provided by a residential school. This does not mean that developmental institutions should think of themselves as families, for they can never perform all the functions of a family.

Many of the same kinds of practical and theoretical problems arise in all developmental institutions, whether they are dealing with adolescents and young adults or with infants and young children. Some of these problems were underscored in two studies with which I have recently been involved. One of these was a study of "alienated" college students—a small group of students who were extreme in their rejection of what they took to be the dominant values and roles of institutions in American society. The second is an ongoing study of gifted students who drop out of college.

THE PSYCHOLOGY OF ALIENATION

For about 6 years, I was involved in the study of alienated undergraduates at Harvard University. The initial research consisted chiefly of objective tests—the systematic comparison of alienated and nonalienated students through the use of questionnaires. Almost 2,000 students were involved, but although these statistical studies yielded useful information, they did not take me very far toward the question I was trying to answer: Why is it that some students are alienated whereas others are not?

To try to answer this question I turned to a more intensive study of 12 students who had been selected because of the extreme degree of their alienation as measured by questionnaires. This group was contrasted with another group of the same size at the opposite pole—"extremely unalienated" —and with a third control group that was not extreme in either way. All three groups were studied over the last 3 years of their college careers.

Each student spent altogether about 200 hours participating in the research. Each was interviewed about his views of the world, his current behavior, and his life history, and each took part in a large number of psychological experiments.

A comparison of the data from the alienated group with that from the other two groups revealed a number of distinctive patterns of ideology, behavior, life history, and fantasy among the alienated students. In addition to being alienated from American culture, they were on the whole pessimistic, distrustful, resentful, and cynical about human nature. They saw themselves as outsiders whose isolation and aloneness was part of the human condition, not their own personal problem. To them, the universe seemed a formless and unstructured chaos lacking in meaning and purpose. And they rejected all cooperative group endeavors on the grounds that conformity means the destruction of individuality.

Most of these students came from a similar family constellation. Characteristically, they described their mothers as magnetic, emotional, passionate, and attractive women to whom they, the sons, were extremely, often excessively, close. At the same time they described their mothers as possessive, confining, restrictive, nagging, and intrusive.

About their fathers, these alienated students volunteered very little information. When pressed to discuss their fathers, they described them as disappointed, frustrated, detached, outwardly cold men. However, the alienated students usually imagined that their fathers had, at one point in their own youth, possessed considerable imagination, idealism, and fire, which had been lost in adulthood. So the father, as the son saw him, was a man deeply disappointed by his own failure to realize his youthful dreams.

Such a family constellation, we felt, had obvious relationships to the development of alienation. Seeing their fathers as men who had been broken by life or by their marriages and thus defeated by "the American way of life," these students were determined not to let what happened to their fathers happen to them. In rejecting their fathers, they also felt it necessary to reject the society that, as they saw it, had ruined their fathers. In other words, from their fathers these students had derived an image of conventional masculine adulthood that was repugnant to them, so they spurned conventional adulthood in American society.[2]

In further explaining the alienation of these students, I should point out that Harvard undergraduates tend to be somewhat more alienated as seniors than as freshmen, although rarely to the extreme that these students reached. In addition, these students were on the whole an unusually imaginative, artistically oriented, and talented group of young men who argued that American society was in general not particularly hospitable to talented, creative persons. They were clearly reacting to the wider society as well as to their parents and family experiences.

FOUR MAJOR ISSUES

When I discuss this material, I am often asked a number of related questions: Is alienation a kind of psychopathology? Why did the researchers not do more to cure these students of their alienation? Is it not a dreadful commentary on a college that its students become more alienated? Should the institution be doing something to change such students? Is alienation a good thing or a bad thing?

None of these questions can be answered simply. I mention them only because they point to crucial issues that arise whenever we begin thinking about the development of a person in an institution:

1. What is "normal" development?

This first issue could be called the normative question—that is, the question of what kind of development the institution is trying to promote. Is the goal of a college, for example, to produce well-trained adults who will be able to fit smoothly into their positions in society? Or is it to promote critical intelligence and detachment from the immediate pressures and values of society? If we think that a smooth fit with society is the objective, then obviously any college that "alienates" its students from the prevailing society is a bad college. But if we think that critical intelligence and capacity for detachment from society is a good thing, then we may very well applaud a college that to some extent increases alienation in its students.

The normative question almost inevitably arises when one begins thinking about or planning an institutional framework that will encourage the "normal development" of the individual. Indeed, the terms "normal development" and "the optimal development of each individual" can be dangerous phrases since they may obscure the underlying value questions involved. We know that individuals can be stimulated to develop in a great variety of very different ways. But certain pathways to development may be mutually exclusive. For example, if a college tries to promote what some alumni groups call "loyalty and guts," it may be difficult for it also to promote such a quality as the critical use of intellect. Or in the case of small children, major emphasis on the group, as in the Israeli kibbutzim, may make it very difficult for a child to develop the intense attachment to a single mothering person that is characteristic of good family life in most Western societies.

It is not enough, then, to talk merely about "normal development" as the goal of a developmental institution. We know that parents have unconscious, preconscious, and conscious objectives in child rearing. They try to prevent Johnny from becoming like his alcoholic Uncle Harry; or to encourage Gertrude to become like her mother; or to develop orderliness, neatness, and parsimony in one child, or grace, freedom, agility, and imagination in another. The enormous variation in personalities produced by ordinary "healthy" families suggests that it is almost impossible not to stimulate certain developmental potentials and to inhibit or retard others.

But in a developmental institution, in contrast to a family, the normative question—what is "normal" development?—has to be made far more explicit and conscious in planning, programing, and evaluation. In these processes ethical questions cannot be avoided, they can only be evaded; and when they are evaded—when they are not openly faced and rationally considered—the results may be disastrous. For example, one way of characterizing those hygienic institutions whose toll on children's development has been so well documented[3-5] is to note that they have answered the normative question with an unconscious decision to produce children who will be as little trouble as possible, a goal that can be reached only by sacrificing the child's individuality.

Some American colleges operate with a comparable unconscious goal— to keep their students out of trouble until they are old enough to enter the labor market. Fortunately, adolescents are more resilient and rebellious than infants and can sometimes overcome this kind of pressure. But the long-run consequences of having this goal may be only slightly less deplorable than the consequences of having the goal of keeping children out of trouble in an antiseptic nursery. In children's institutions and in colleges alike, it is crucial to examine, reflect upon, and make explicit the specific developmental and educational objectives of the institution.

2. For what kind of society?

The second crucial issue raised by the study of alienated students is closely related to the first. It has to do with the nature of the society into which the developing individual will eventually move, and the demands, characteristics, and needs of the wider society. If, for example, it were clear that we lived in the best of all possible worlds, then alienation from our present society would definitely be an irrational and deplorable response. We would prescribe therapy for the alienated students and abolition or reform for "alienating" institutions. Or if we felt that criticism of society was always destructive, we should similarly deplore any degree of alienation.

In other words, any judgment as to the kind of human development we should ideally promote must be closely related to our picture of the nature of the wider society, of the demands it makes, and of its long-range needs. A developmental institution is preparing individuals for a particular society with special characteristics, pressures, and opportunities. It may be, for example, that certain kinds of child rearing will produce the kind of character structure and personality organization that is well suited to a Polynesian village but profoundly unsuited to American society. Or again, the kibbutz system of child rearing may produce the kind of adult who contributes a great deal to a kibbutz but one who would be unhappy and unproductive in American society.

Thus, in planning for the program or staffing of a developmental institution, we must consider the kind of society in which the "products" of the institution will live and their capacity for fulfillment and productivity in such a society. This does not mean that our goals should be to develop people who will unreflectively "adjust" to society. Obviously society needs social critics, independent thinkers, and even alienated men and women. But social critics also have to function within society.

Another study I have been involved in raises two more questions that are relevant to program planning in a developmental institution. This is an exploratory study of talented college dropouts. Every year hundreds of thousands of talented well-prepared young Americans drop out of colleges before graduating. We are trying to find out why. What does this mean in relation to the student's development? For whom is dropping out a progressive step, and for whom is it a regressive step?

This research at Yale University is in midstream. We are not even sure of all the questions we will ask, much less of the answers. But we are beginning to believe with Anna Freud that dropouts are people for whom the 4 years of college come at the worst possible time from a developmental point of view.[6] They feel, consciously and unconsciously, that further psychological development is impossible as long as they remain within a collegiate setting; and in many or most cases, they are probably right. At least those who return (the majority) believe that their years away have enabled them to grow and mature, and the judgments of their friends and teachers usually confirm this belief.

In our exploratory clinical studies, we have found that dropouts often have difficult problems of identification with their parents, problems that seem to prevent that slow and gradual development of commitments and the consolidation of identity that usually take place in students of their age. And one reason why dropouts find these problems (which are, after all, universal) so difficult to resolve within a collegiate context has to do with their perceptions of the college environment.

Thus we find an almost universal but often unconscious tendency among these college dropouts to perceive the college as a whole as if it were a large-scale edition of their families. We have been repeatedly impressed with the striking parallel between dropouts' descriptions of the college and their descriptions of their parents. One sophomore, for example, was struggling with great problems of identification with a father who was overly sadistic and brutal but who at the same time manifested through alcoholism an underlying passivity and dependency. This student describes the college as being authoritarian, harsh, and repressive, yet lacking in any real strength, decisiveness, or moral purpose. Another student, in the throes of attempting to reconcile conflicting identifications with warring parents, perceived the college as containing two conflicting sets of pressures, clearly identifiable with his parents.

This kind of "institutional transference"—equating the institution with the family—seems to be particularly widespread among students who drop out of college. Students who persist in college seem considerably less prone to identify college with their parents. To be sure, they, too, tend to relate to the institution globally, almost as if it were a family. But for them the college is like a *new* family, a facilitating, liberating environment in which they can escape earlier family pressures and move forward in their development.

Another incidental finding of this study is how few colleges recognize the existence of dropouts. Of every 100 freshmen entering 4-year colleges in America, only 40 graduate from the same college 4 years later. Transfers and temporary or permanent interruptions of college are the rule rather than the exception. But most colleges keep few figures about "dropouts," ignore their existence, or with little factual basis treat them all as psychological "misfits" or academic "failures."

This study of dropouts underscores two further issues that arise in all developmental institutions:

3. What are the effects of the institution as a whole, of its climate, culture, or morale, on the individual?

In the end, we can no doubt analyze a student's perception of a college into a thousand component interpersonal relationships and experiences. But the student himself experiences the institution globally *as an entity,* and he tends to relate himself to it almost as if it were a single, crucial person in his life. This fact may help explain one of the puzzling results of many studies of college students. It has been shown again and again that probably the most potent factor in determining how colleges affect students' development is that intangible quality called "institution morale," "college climate" or "campus culture." The effectiveness of an institution in promoting development seems more closely related to the characteristics of the institution as a whole than to any of its constituent parts—students, faculty, facilities, programs, residential arrangements, or curriculum.

In many discussions of the relationship of the college to students' development, this quality of "climate" is neglected, perhaps because it is so difficult to define and measure precisely. We hear endless discussions of curriculum reform, promotion policies, admissions procedures, and residential facilities, but very few discussions of how to create or facilitate the right kind of "climate" or "morale." Yet even an unmotivated and unpromising student, if he is fortunate enough to enter a first-class college with very high institutional morale, may find himself caught up in a general tide of enthusiasm that pushes him to a height of personal and intellectual development that he never before dreamed of. On the other hand, even a highly motivated freshman, if he enters an institution with low morale, may stagnate or regress.

In young children the ability to relate to an institution as a whole is, of course, more limited than it is in adolescents. Nevertheless, in developmental institutions for young children, the climate of the institution as a whole may similarly be more important than any specific programs, staffing policies, or residential arrangements. It is conceivable, for example, that there may be institutions for children where the physical facilities are poor, where the staff philosophy is reactionary, and yet where—for reasons that we do not quite understand—children manage to flourish and grow. And it is also possible that there are institutions with advanced facilities and modern ideas about child development where for lack of a good "climate" somehow everything seems to go wrong, including the children's development.

In thinking about how to create institutions that encourage human growth, we must recognize that individuals experience and respond to institutions as a whole, not only to their parts. We therefore need to plan not merely for programs, schedules, living arrangements, and so on, but also for how all of these variables might interact to produce the kind of staff morale, institutional climate, and intangible culture that nourishes healthy development.

4. Can the institution deal realistically and supportively with individuals who are "deviant" or "atypical" in terms of its ideals and norms?

All institutions, and especially developmental institutions, tend to have an implicit or explicit image of the "average expectable individual," the "typical Yale man," or the "normal child." Procedures, programs, publicity, and even perceptions are organized around this image. At times in a college the image of "the typical student" is so powerful that it blinds administration and faculty to the fact that a majority of students in no way conform to this image.

Other developmental institutions also tend to develop systematic blind spots and irrational ways of responding to members who do not fit their definition of the "average expectable individual." Sometimes the existence of persons who do not fit the expected pattern of development is simply denied by a refusal to notice that they exist. Sometimes those whose development deviates from the expected are treated as misfits, failures, or malcontents. In either case, their lives are dominated by fear, shame, and a sense of their own inadequacy.

One of the marks of a superior developmental institution, whether a college or a residence for children, is its capacity both to recognize explicitly and support persons whose developmental needs and schedules deviate from the mythical or actual norm—without needing to relegate them to a limbo of abnormality, psychopathology, failure, or nonexistence. Those American colleges that clearly facilitate genuine intellectual and personal growth are noted for their emphasis on encouraging individuality and recognizing the special qualities of each student.

Such colleges tend to have flexible institutional programs, to apply their rules according to the individual's needs and his development, and to be highly tolerant of dissent and deviance, both on campus and off. These colleges, and I suspect those children's institutions that facilitate healthy personality growth, explicitly recognize that individual human beings have differing needs at different stages of development, that the rates and phases of normal human growth are highly variable, and that, in a sense, exceptional development is not the exception at all but the rule in human life.

IN SUMMARY

Thus, despite the real differences between children in institutions and students in college, similar issues arise with regard to both groups. Both groups live in "developmental institutions" and the effectiveness of the institutions in promoting their growth depends in good part on how well these questions are answered: What is "normal" development? For what kind of society? What is the right "climate"? Can deviance be accepted? Planning, maintaining, or improving developmental institutions, therefore, demands not only attention to sound programing, staffing, and financing, but also a rational and informed examination of the underlying goals for its residents in the context of what is known about human development.

REFERENCES

1. Goffman, Erving: On the characteristics of total institutions. *In* Asylums: essays on the social situation of mental patients and other inmates. Anchor Publishing Co., Garden City, N.Y. 1961.
2. Keniston, Kenneth: The uncommitted. Harcourt, Brace & World, Inc., New York. 1965.
3. Provence, Sally; Lipton, Rose C.: Infants in institutions. International Universities Press, New York. 1962.
4. Spitz, René A.: Hospitalism—an inquiry into the genesis of psychiatric condition in early childhood. *In* The psychoanalytic study of the child, vol. 1, 1945. International Universities Press, New York.
5. Bowlby, John: Maternal care and mental health. World Health Organization Technical Monograph Series No. 2. Geneva. 1951.
6. Group for the Advancement of Psychiatry: Sex and the college student. Atheneum Publishers, New York. 1966. P. 33.

41.

The generation gap in the eyes of youth

ELIZABETH HERZOG
CECELIA E. SUDIA

With so many analyses of the perplexities of youth made by adults it should be of considerable merit to hear some of the voices of youth themselves. To a remarkable extent what the young people seem to be saying is that the generation gap is a communication gap. Another thing that seems to be apparent is that some of the conflict, be it generational or communication, is incapable of being easily generalized. There is too wide a variation in attitudes, values, and behaviors for adults to permit themselves the fallacy of blocking communication by inclusive generalizations. Perhaps the editors are doing just that, generalizing too broadly, by suggesting that adults do a little more listening and less telling. This article provides an opportunity to exercise that option. Instead of offering counterarguments, it might be well to say, "Ummm . . ." and provide a time gap for evaluation of what youth are saying.

In my group of friends, the generation gap is the main topic of conversation; we just don't refer to it by that name, but it all boils down to the same thing.

To teenagers the problem is, "I just can't talk to my parents—they don't even try to understand." And to Mom and Dad it's "Billy just doesn't make sense. Some of the ideas he has are so radical!"

These remarks illustrate two major themes in the responses received by the Children's Bureau from high school students to the following questions:

We hear a lot these days about the generation gap. We'd like to know what your friends think about it, and whether they think about it at all. If so, what are the main things that adults do or say or fail to understand that bother teenagers so much?

What about the other side of the coin? Do your friends think that some of the problems come from the teenagers? If so, what are the main things young people do or don't do that make things worse?

Children, 17:53–58, March–April, 1970. Elizabeth Herzog and Cecelia E. Sudia, Division of Research, Children's Bureau, U.S. Department of Health, Education, and Welfare.

In the spring of 1969 these questions were mailed to a panel of 407 high school students randomly selected from students in college preparatory courses in metropolitan areas situated in the four regions of the United States—North, South, Midwest, West. Replies were received from 251 students in 53 schools in 12 cities. The purpose was to find the main patterning of opinions among such young people rather than to obtain an exact count.

The complete results are being published in detail by the Office of Child Development as the first in a series of *Youth Reports*.[1] Here we will present only an outline of the general patterns that emerged—along with some illustrative excerpts.

Experience with analogous studies gives ground for confidence that the opinion profile obtained in the Children's Bureau study validly reflects the views of urban high school students enrolled in college preparatory courses.

Teenagers are no more unanimous than their elders on most subjects. In their comments about the generation gap, for every complaint against parents and adults generally, there are conflicting or qualified responses. Some say that their complaint holds for some adults but not all, or for teenagers as well as adults. Often a single response covers a range of opinions, in an effort to say which kinds of teenagers are likely to hold the various views expressed, or to explain that the writer and his friends do not share a particular view. Nevertheless, the main lines of prevalent opinions are clear, and it is possible to differentiate between broad consensus, evenly divided opinions, and views voiced only by a few.

IS THERE A PROBLEM GAP?

A wide range of opinions emerges about the existence and nature of a generation gap. About half the correspondents report that it is viewed as a real problem, and a few add that it is worse than in former years. The other half divides rather evenly between those who say it is not viewed as a problem at all and those who say it is seen as a problem by some young people but not by others.

In some instances the correspondent reports that it is not a problem for "me personally," or for "me and my friends," but that many young people find it a problem. Occasionally the latter are characterized as young people whose relations with their parents are not close, who do not appreciate what they receive, or who have been "brought up wrong."

> We don't talk about the generation gap, as such, because we all recognize it and accept it. Thus, it isn't a topic, but an assumption behind conversation. For example, the remark, "I had a pretty good talk with my Dad last night," is taken to mean that there has been a rare occurrence.

The substantial minority of the young people who dismiss the generation gap as a problem do so on various grounds. Over half report the opinion that a generation gap is normal and no worse now than in the past. Almost as many say it is seen as a problem mainly because it is "blown up by the media."

> From the way my grandparents talk, I'm pretty sure that my parents weren't understood. Of course, I probably won't understand my kids either.

Some who downgrade the importance of the generation gap add that other problems are much more important—for instance, poor quality education, racism, poverty; that difficulties between people are a matter of individuals, not of generations. What we have, they say, is a "people gap" or a "love gap." And a few see the generation gap as an excuse made up by adults as "a blind" for avoiding the "real" problems.

> The generation gap is, according to many kids—who have good relationships with their parents—an overemphasized, over-generalized, over-coined phrase, used to describe a rebelliousness occurring during the adolescent years accompanied by friction in the home.

A few, but very few, have a good word to say for the generation gap. Without it, they hold, there would be no progress. It forces teenagers to think for themselves, reach their own conclusions "so we will be a very determined people."

The nature and causes of the generation gap are discussed by many of the young people. By far the majority see it as a gap in understanding or communication. The most common complaint is that "they don't understand" or "we just can't communicate," sometimes because "they" (parents, or adults generally) don't want to, sometimes because they can't. Four out of five refer to failures of communication or understanding, or both.

Often the point is made with intense resentment against the failure of adults to try to understand, communicate, and explain. At the same time, a substantial minority view the communication failure more philosophically, as natural, inevitable, and probably chronic. And a few display sympathetic indulgence. "They can't help it," "they have their own problems."

> Our parents are both reticent and communicative and they always seem to be one when it should be the other.
> They don't *listen*. If we try to talk to them about a problem, they are either so involved in giving advice that they don't hear us at all or they aren't listening in the first place.
> Most of the kids feel that it is just a lack of interest by both parties to talk to each other.

PARENTAL SINS

Lagging behind the failure to understand and communicate, but nevertheless bulking larger than other complaints, is a cluster of protests against the failure of parents to grant the teenager full status as a person entitled to respect and trust. Parents, the complaints go, do not respect the teenager's opinions, fail to recognize that his problems are important to him, and do not trust him.

On the one hand such shortcomings are associated with adults' failure to recognize that the teenager is partly grown up and worthy of certain responsibilities. On the other hand, adults are occasionally charged with not making allowances for the teenager's youth and expecting him to be more grown up than he is. Either way, the individual and his growth phase are felt to be belittled or ignored.

> I just wish that sometimes they would give us a chance to show them what we have learned.

A less salient part of the sins-of-omission cluster is failure to give teenagers attention and love. Attention, however, is clearly not to be confused with the widely resented "nosiness." "They're too busy," "they don't take time," "they're too wrapped up in their own problems and fights," "it takes time to be a good parent," "kids rebel in order to get attention," "they don't give enough love."

Objections to what parents do stand out almost as much as objections to what they do not do.

Leading all sins of commission is the dual charge of rigidity and strictness: parents are always sure they are right; they refuse to reconsider what they have said, once they have said it; they are given to arbitrary rules and punishments.

> The main thing adults do wrong is that they think things are either black or white, only positive or negative. No compromising. Having this attitude, just makes teens kind of "burn" inside, almost until they explode.

On the other hand, a few teenagers complain that many parents spoil children by being overindulgent and overpermissive. One or two associate such indulgence with an effort to "buy love," adding that this only breeds disrespect.

> Parents mean well when they try to give you all the things that they never had. They want your life to be better than theirs was. But they don't realize that they might be forcing something onto you, and when you "fail them" or "rebel," they immediately hit you with,

"we've given you everything you've ever wanted," or "where did we
go wrong?"

A number of parental sins of omission are seen as contributing to sins
of commission: lack of understanding, refusal to listen, lack of trust and
respect for the teenager as an individual, lead parents to become "nosy,"
suspicious, and inconsiderate.

A different kind of objection to parental behavior is reported by about
one correspondent in 10, but always with intense feeling. This concerns
parents who set a poor example for their children, who "say one thing and
do another." Such parents are described with biting scorn as being "hypocritical," "phoney," "setting a bad example." They drink, they smoke, they
tell half truths, they practice "loose morality," and at the same time urge
their children not to do these things.

A small, equally vehement number of respondents report complaints
of parents who nag, "yell at their kids," and embarrass them in front of
others.

For both boys and girls, lack of understanding and communication
leads all complaints by a wide margin. Girls put most emphasis on lack of
respect and trust, often perceived as prying and interfering with social
activities. Boys also put most emphasis on rigidity and strictness but without
specifying the context. Lack of attention and love ranks higher among
girls' complaints than among boys'.

CONFLICT IN VALUES

Over one-third of the teenage reporters explicitly refer to value clashes
between the generations, and many more discuss value-related points in
connection with other complaints. Often the references are general: "We
don't have the same values." "We have two opposing philosophies." But
more often the conflict is specified: "They" are accused of insufficient interest in the overriding problems of our day, including war, poverty, and
racism. "They" are accused of materialism—over-emphasis on money, possessions, economic security, status, individual achievement.

Corollary to both these accusations is the charge that "They" emphasize
trivia at the expense of really important things, insist on conformity in
matters of dress and grooming, and judge people by externals.

Disapproval of parents' emphasis on nonessentials is linked with indignant protests against adult objections to teenage preferences in hair
styles, dress, and grooming. Over one-fourth of the correspondents report
such objections. "Parents don't understand fashions are changing" or they
think teenagers are "not responsible" if they are not dressed conservatively.
Among both boys and girls the subject frequently concerns the hair styles
of boys.

A very few of the young people criticize long-haired boys. One goes so far as to agree with his parents that "long hair is disgusting." On the whole, however, the teenagers defend their right to self-determination in dress and grooming, even though the defenders themselves may not exercise that right in ways deplored by their elders.

The teenagers tend to condemn the adults' "over-concern with external appearance" on two grounds: as reflecting a distorted sense of values; and as a violation of individual autonomy. Because of this dual significance, the reporters imply, teenage costume and grooming have taken on the attributes of symbol, of language, of badge, and of weapon—thus acquiring for the young an importance which may seem somewhat at odds with their objections to emphasizing external appearance.

> For the first quarter of the school year I kept my hair short and very conservative—I made straight A's. Now that's what they wanted me to do and I did it (make the grades, not the hair). But, nevertheless, I did what they wanted me to, without any qualms, but I ask them to let me let my hair grow long and the answer is an emphatic "no!" I got the grades, either way (and that gives them satisfaction)— why not let me have my way?

Sometimes the correspondents try to explain the value differences they report. Some of these discussions are bitter, some dispassionate, a few indulgent. The chief excuse offered for their parents is that because they grew up during the depression they attach greater significance to economic security than their children.

> Today's young people do not have to worry like their parents did about money and making a living. They can be concerned with other things . . .

Such comments are made by less than one in 15, and certainly not by those who report the views of the nonaffluent.

Nearly half the correspondents explain the value conflicts with adults in such statements as: "The world is changing too fast for them." Often the statement is made without explicit criticism. But more often it accompanies criticism of adults as resistant to change. The adults, it is said, not only fail to understand change but they definitely do not want it, while the younger generation definitely does. Thus, in a sense, change itself becomes a value—positive for the young and negative for adults.

> They have carved their own little niche in society and are fearful lest change will destroy it. We understand such fear. We can foresee the same fear ourselves when the next generation wants change.

Most bitter of all is the reported resentment against parents who want to make their children "into a carbon copy of themselves." When I was your age" is a particularly detested phrase.

SOME PARENTS ARE O.K.

While the wording of our questions tended to invite criticism of adults, the responses do not picture parents and other adults in wholly negative terms. Some respondents—nearly one in 10—explicitly state that they share the values of their own parents. Very few of these correspondents describe themselves as "conservative." They more commonly describe their parents as progressive in their thinking, understanding of young people, and keeping up with the times.

Sometimes the correspondents contrast their own parents with the parents of friends or acquaintances—that is, they view their parents as nice but unusual.

> I am thought to be extremely lucky because I get along with my parents . . . I am the exception.

THE WORLD "MESS"

Nearly a third of the correspondents confine their responses to a general consideration of whether there is or is not a generation gap. The remainder divide rather evenly into three groups: those who refer only to intrafamily relations and issues; those who refer only to social problems and issues; and those who talk about both.

Those who do mention society or social problems blame adults for allowing the world to get into "this mess." The positive social goals attributed to youth are pictured with varying degrees of specificity: to end war, to cure poverty, to "stop evils," to promote "spiritual and mental welfare," to reform political processes, to further peace, love, and brotherhood, to engage in community service.

> We are very much concerned about many grave problems, which threaten to destroy the advantages that civilization has given us. We are concerned about overpopulation, racism, poverty, pollution, and most of all, oppression and the stifling of the individual in what is supposed to be a democratic society. The reactions that we have seen to these concerns are very frustrating. School desegregation guidelines are relaxed . . . ; poverty programs are stifled because they might hurt the taxpayer; industry successfully blocks pollution control; and those who wish to democratize America are labeled Communist and suppressed, often violently.

The inevitable counter-point is presented by a very few dissenters who say teenagers are not really so idealistic themselves, but are in fact materialistic and lack positive goals. However, not one correspondent reports that teenagers are content with society as it is.

The specific problems of society most frequently mentioned concern riots, protests and disorders, war, race, and poverty.

> . . . what really annoys many teenagers is the "accepting" view adults have. They accept war, poverty, hunger as unchangeable. The teenagers look at war for what it is—man killing man senselessly. They see race riots, starvation and campus trouble. No wonder they're disgusted.

Comments about forms of protest more frequently disapprove than approve violent and disruptive dissent. Nevertheless, those who are moved to discuss such matters are obviously in sympathy with the reasons for active efforts to bring about change. About one in 20 reports the view that "shock treatment" in the form of violence and disruption may be necessary in order to "awaken the sleeping generation." Almost twice as many, however, see a need to keep violent dissidents within bounds.

> Also, violent marches and occupation of college buildings seem to be carrying things too far. However, many of my friends feel that at times, a peaceful march can be important to make grievances known. The inability of peaceful marches to remain peaceful is a major problem . . .
> A college is a place to learn—if the students don't like it, they can go someplace else!

All comments concerning war in general and most of those concerning the Vietnam war are strongly negative.

> We have to fill out c.o. forms to explain to you why we shouldn't kill, but you're the ones who should have to fill out forms telling us why we should kill.

That these views are not necessarily unanimous is suggested by the fact that the majority of the correspondents make no mention of war at all.

Many correspondents make no mention of race problems, but all who do are emphatic about the need to eliminate prejudice, discrimination, and inequalities. Not one reports endorsement of a "go-slow" policy. Little regional difference in views is perceptible. Among the very few who refer to interracial dating, all defend the practice as quite acceptable to youth though not to parents.

> I, as a teenager, think that because the older generations have tolerated racism and other forms of human cruelty, their concepts are wrong and should be abandoned.

On the whole, the views of black teenagers resemble those of white teenagers with regard to the existence and nature of the generation gap, although the emphasis is clearly influenced by keen awareness of their special problems. The proportions of those affirming or denying a genera-

tion gap are comparable. However, those who belittle the problem do so
with special scorn, pointing out that the real gaps are between "Uncle
Toms" and all the others, regardless of age.

> The gap between aware blacks and unaware blacks is not neces-
> sarily one of age. In most cases it involves the extent to which one has
> been brainwashed by white America . . . Some people as young as
> junior high school age have proven to be more stubborn to the "de-
> brainwashing" process than some grandparents.

Some reports from black students include poignant discussions of
problems that dwarf such considerations as the generation gap.

> I am one of the twelve Negroes who attends a predominantly
> white school of about 3,000 or more . . . I'm just like a walking test
> at school. Now the Negro is on stage, performing before an all white
> audience, trying to sway and correct their opinion of blacks.

The subject of poverty is among the least frequently mentioned in
comments about specific social problems. To some extent, however, economic inequalities are implied in references to social problems generally
and to race problems.

TEENAGERS ON TEENAGERS

In response to the specific inquiry about "the other side of the coin,"
over half of the reporters find some readiness to concede that there is
fault on the part of both generations. About one-third did not respond to
the question.

A number of teenage "sins" are specified, some of them mirror-images
of those ascribed to the older generation. Teenagers, like adults, are accused of not listening and not communicating. About two out of five
acknowledge that the obligation to give understanding, trust, and respect to
their elders is often unfulfilled. About one in seven criticizes the young for
not realizing that after all "they are still kids" and can learn from adults—
although half as many report belief that teenagers really do know more
about today's world than their parents.

> Some kids think it's all the parents' fault, but I think it's half and
> half.

> I think both sides need to do less talking and more listening.

In frequency and vehemence, criticisms of the older generation far
outweigh criticisms of teenagers, and are less often qualified or restricted
to an unrepresentative few. The prevailing view is definitely that the teen-

agers are not chiefly to blame for the generation gap; about one in 10 exonerates them altogether.

> But I just happen to think that the older generations are far more mistake prone, and will not face the reality when they are wrong.

Among the most indignant protests reported are objections to prejudice against teenagers as a group, levied in some form by about one in three, against parents, adults generally, and the "mass media." Nearly a fourth of all the correspondents concede that "some teenagers are really bad," but they usually add that the great majority are O.K. and should not suffer for the misdeeds of the misguided few. They maintain that adults expect the worst and act in such a way as to invite it.

> It seems they feel if one girl goes around with every boy in town and doesn't care what she does, that their daughter will do the same. They don't have enough faith in their own child-raising.

The media, it is charged, aggravate such attitudes, by playing up only the bad and ignoring the good.

> There are just that small minority of "weirdos" that there has always been, but, with the more publicity, they seem to be a larger group.

Mention of drugs comes in only incidentally, as an occasional specific under broader issues. Use of marijuana receives little support, and heavier drugs none at all. While drug users are sometimes described as "really bad," some sympathetic reference is made to the pressures that drive some young people to drugs.

> These kids are looking for something better like maybe through drugs, boy you can't find it that way.

Hippies and Yippies are referred to by about one in 10 correspondents, chiefly in connection with the tendency of adults to blame all teenagers for the misguided deviance of only a few. Less than one in 20 reflects a neutral attitude toward or sympathy with hippie motives and aims although not necessarily with their behavior.

> A minority group such as hippies, militants, drug addicts, draft dodgers ruin the reputation of the majority of good teenagers and terrify responsible parents.

> Maybe that is why hippies dress as they do. They want to bring to their parents' attention that no matter how unkempt they are they can still love their fellow man.

AUTONOMY AND IDENTITY

In one form or another, the drive for autonomy is conspicuous throughout the responses. Boys especially report a generalized protest against interference with "doing their own thing."

Adults' effort to control teenagers' appearance is regarded, on the one hand, as a defect in values—overemphasizing the trivial, judging the outward appearance rather than the inner man—and, on the other hand, as undue interference with individual autonomy. There is a tendency to contrast adults' emphasis on trivia and externals with teenagers' interest in broad positive goals and essential individual worth.

> Parents are always looking after their teenagers like their parents looked after them. But times are changing and this brings more freedom and independence to the teenager. He wants to lead his own life and not the one that his parents try to force him into. Parents, WAKE UP!!! He has his own life to live.

Since the questions were focused on adults' behavior lapses, it is probably not surprising that direct or indirect references to teenage identity problems were rare in the responses. Nevertheless, there are occasional reminders that young people are changing and groping, that one aim of young people is to "find themselves."

> I still have 2 years of high school left, and I intend to keep struggling in that time to be able to live the life and learn the things I need to, as it is necessary if I wish to be the type of person I think I am.

A number of our correspondents are very explicit about their future opportunity to improve our society, and their determination to make the most of it. "We are the leaders of tomorrow," they declare, adding that they hope to improve on what their elders have done. They clearly believe in their own moral superiority.

> We all know what kind of shape the world is in today, after the older generation had charge of it. Today's teenagers want to try and fix it, their own way, and if we don't succeed, it will be through our own mistakes, not through the mistakes of our parents. And we'll be the ones to have the power of changing the world soon.

EAGERNESS TO HELP

The correspondents' wish for understanding and communication between the generations is underscored by the nature of their response to the invitation to communicate with their Government. The response rate (63 percent) in itself is remarkably high for mail interviews, which as a rule evoke less than a 33-percent response.

Not many comment directly on the request to contribute to *Youth Reports,* but among those who do only three comment negatively while 20 are strongly positive.

> This questionnaire is just the typical kind of ineffectual thing the "older generation" would do—pardon my criticism—perhaps you'll get the new communication.

> Thank you, great impersonal governmental edifice—for the first chance I've had to express myself.

> I don't think it is a problem that can ever be solved, but Good Luck anyway. Maybe the government is good for something, and you can at least ease the pressure.

REFERENCE

1. Herzog, E.; Sudia, C.; Rosengard, B.; Harwood, J.: Teenagers discuss the generation gap. U.S. Department of Health, Education, and Welfare, Office of Child Development, Children's Bureau. Youth Report No. 1. 1970.

42.

The generation gap

EDGAR Z. FRIEDENBERG

Friedenberg finds that there is much that is praiseworthy in youth's alienation from society. For instance, he indicates that our emphasis on socialization, in fact, a form of coercion and indoctrination, may be either intentionally or inadvertently an attempt to reduce the scope of personal autonomy. Emphasis is placed on some of the things that young people, particularly hippies, have identified as being aspects of the culture that they disdain and abhor. Adolescents are "things" when they are not allowed to cut their hair as they wish or dress as they choose but can be drafted to fight a war that they (and many others) regard as being immoral. They are "things" when adult society can

The Annals of the American Academy of Political and Social Science, 382:32–42, 1969.
Edgar Z. Friedenberg, Professor of Sociology and Social Foundations of Education, State University of New York, Buffalo.

use liquor and view nude art but can deny the use of pot and porno-
graphic pictures to youth.
*   The Friedenberg piece may be viewed pessimistically if one is*
sure that the present verbally expressed morality is right and correct.
It may be viewed optimistically if the reader can agree that there are
some unwholesome features of adult society and that certain adoles-
cents are forcing examination and restructure of those unwholesome
features.

THE IDEA that what separates us from the young is something so passive that it may justly be called a "generation gap" is, I believe, itself a misleading article of middle-aged liberal ideology, serving to allay anxiety rather than to clarify the bases of intergenerational conflict. It is true, to be sure, that the phrase is strong enough to describe the barrier that separates many young people from their elders, for a majority still accept our society as providing a viable pattern of life and expectations for the future. Liberalism dies hard, and most young people, like some Negroes even today, are still willing to attribute their difficulties with their elders and society to mutual misunderstanding.

    I believe, however, that this is a false position. Though most adults maintain a benevolent posture in expressing their public attitudes toward youth and—though, I think, steadily fewer—young people still accept this as what their elders intend in principle, both young and old seem trapped in a false view of what is actually a profound conflict of interest in our society. What appears to be a consequence of mere cultural lag in responding to a new social and political maturity in the young, with distressing but unintended repressive consequences, is rather the expression of what has become genuine class-conflict between a dominant and exploitive older generation and youth who are slowly becoming more aware of what is happening to them as demands on them are, in the language of the time, escalated.[1]

DISCONTINUITY IN AN OPEN SOCIETY

    In all societies, so far as I know, young people enter the social system in subordinate roles while older people run things. This is true even in technically primitive cultures where the crude physical strength of youth is still of real productive advantage. Is there always a generational conflict? And, if so, does it always reflect as profound a division, and as severe a conflict of interest, as generational conflict in America today?

    There is, I believe, indeed an inherent basis for such a conflict in the fact that the old dominate the young and the young wish to replace them, but it is not as severe in most societies as in ours. Here, it has become different in kind, as the brightest and most articulate of the young declare that they will not even accept, when their turn comes, the kinds of roles—

in the kind of society—which their parents have held. As Bruno Bettel-heim[2] pointed out in a classic paper some years ago, factors that have traditionally mitigated generational conflict have become feeble or in-operative even in this country. The family, for example, which is the con-text within which the strongest—albeit ambivalent—affectual ties between the generations are formed, plays a decreasing role in the lives of its mem-bers and, certainly, in the socialization of the young. It has less effect on their life-chances than it once had. If the Victorian father or the head of a traditional rural household was often a tyrant, and more or less accepted as such by his neighbors and his children, he was also a man who felt that he could transmit his wealth, his trade, and his position in the community, by inheritance. His relationship to his sons was not purely competitive but complementary as well: it was they who would have to carry on his work as his own powers failed, and on whom he was therefore ultimately de-pendent if his accomplishment in life was to lead to anything permanent. The proper attitude of father to son—both the authority and the underlying tenderness—took account of this mutual though unequal dependency. And while excessive and inconsiderate longevity in a father might make his son's position grotesque, as that of mad old George III did to the Prince Regent's position, the problems of succession were usually made less abra-sive by the recognition of mutual need.

Moreover, so long as society changed slowly, elders really knew more that was useful than the young did; they were wiser; their authority was based on real superiority in the subtle techniques of living. This was never a very strong bond between the generations in America, where the sons of immigrants have always been as likely to find their greenhorn parents a source of embarrassment as of enlightenment; and generational conflict has probably always been more severe here than in more stable cultures—or would have been had there not also been a continent to escape into and de-velop.

But, today, the older generation has become not merely an embarrass-ment, but often an obstructive irrelevance to the young. We cannot even defend our former functions with respect to youth; for the ethos of modern liberalism condemns as inequitable, and a violation of equal opportunity, the arrangements on which continuity between the generations has been based. Bourgeois emphasis on private property and the rights of inheritance gave to the family the function of providing this continuity, which, under feudal conditions, would have been shared among several institutions—apprenticeship, for example. But the development of an open, bureaucratic society has weakened the influence of the family, and has transferred the task of distributing status among claimants primarily to the schools, which profess to judge them, so far as possible, without regard to their ante-cedents.

Today, college admissions officers agree that the sons of alumni should not be favored over more gifted applicants who seek admission solely on the basis of their academic record and recommendations. But this amounts to redefining merit to mean the kind of performance and personality that high school teachers and, increasingly, counselors like. Counselors now virtually control many a high school student's future chances, by their decision whether to assign him to a college-preparatory course, and by monitoring his applications for admission. Whether this whole process makes the contest more open, or merely changes the criteria for preferment, is hard to say.[3]

The effect of the high school, and especially of the counselor, on continuity of status between the generations, and hence on the bond between the generations, is the subject of a fascinating study—still little known after five years—by Aaron V. Cicourel and John I. Kitsuse.[4] While the entire work bears on this issue, one particular interview-excerpt is worth quoting here because of the clarity with which it shows a high school student from an upper-status suburban home being punished for his lack of humility in school by restriction of his future chances. This young man had already been classed by his counselor as an "underachiever." Here are some of the counselor's comments to Cicourel and Kitsuse's interviewer:

> COUNSELOR: His mother says he's a pleasant outgoing boy. His teachers will say he's either a pleasant boy or that he's a pest. I think he's arrogant. He thinks he's handsome. He's nice-looking, but not handsome. He thinks he owns Lakeshore. He talks to his teachers as if they were stupid. He's a good student. He's in biology and algebra honors.
>
> INTERVIEWER: Is he going to college?
>
> COUNSELOR: He plans college. I think he said he plans to go East like MIT, Harvard, etc. He won't make it. He's a candidate for a midwestern school.[5]

This excerpt, of course, illustrates certain very positive reasons for conflict between youth and older people: the constraint imposed by the school and its basic disrespect for its young captive. But I have introduced it here specifically to call attention to the fact that the school is here destroying the basis for continuity in the home by making it a condition—for higher- as well as for lower-status students—that the student *unlearn* what the home has taught him about himself if he wishes to retain access to his family's present socioeconomic status. In this way, older middle- and upper-class life-patterns are made positively dysfunctional for the young, just as lower-class life-patterns are, in the equalizing process of the school. Unless the tendency of the home is toward docile acceptance of the common-man pattern of life and expectation, the school will run counter to its influence.

The influence of the school itself is, in a matter of this complexity, difficult to isolate and appraise. But it is clear—and, I think, significant—that disaffection in the young is heavily concentrated among both the bright middle-class and upper-middle-class youth, on the one hand, and the lower-class, especially Negro, youth, on the other. The working class, young and old, is, in contrast, much more likely to be hostile to dissent, and especially to demonstrations, and to regard the school as the pathway to opportunity; its children are more willing to put on a clean shirt and tie and await the pleasure of the draft board or the interviewer from industry. For them, the school and family have worked together, and adult role-models retain their quite possibly fatal appeal.

YOUTH AS A DISCRIMINATED-AGAINST CLASS

I have already asserted that conflict between the generations is less a consequence of the ways in which old and young perceive, or misperceive, each other than of structurally created, genuine conflicts of interest. In this, as in other relationships, ideology follows self-interest: we impute to other people and social groups characteristics that justify the use we plan to make of them and the control over them that use requires. The subordinate group, in turn, often develops these very characteristics in response to the conditions that were imposed on them. Slaves, slum-dwellers, "teen-agers," and enlisted men do, indeed, often display a defensive stupidity and irresponsibility, which quickly abates in situations which they feel to be free of officious interference, with which they can deal, by means of their own institutions, in their own way.

For American youth, these occasions are few, and have grown relatively fewer with the escalation of the war in Vietnam. The Dominican intervention, the scale and permanence of our military investment in Southeast Asia, and the hunch that our economic system requires the engagement of its youth at low pay, or none, in a vast military-academic complex, in order to avoid disastrously widespread unemployment—even under present circumstances far greater among youth than among older persons—suggest to thoughtful young people that their bondage may be fundamental to the American political system and incapable of solution within its terms.

That bondage is remarkably complete—and so gross, in comparison to the way in which other members of the society are treated, that I find it difficult to accept the good faith of most adults who declare their sympathy with "the problems of youth" while remaining content to operate within the limits of the coercive system that deals with them, in any official capacity. To search for explanations of the problems of youth in America in primarily psychological terms while suggesting ways of easing the tension between them and the rest of society is rather like approaching the problem of "the American turkey in late autumn" with the same benign attitude. Turkeys would have no problem, except for the use we make of them, though I can imagine clearly enough the arguments that a cadre of specialists in poultry-relations might advance in defense of Thanksgiving, all of them true enough as far as they went: that wild turkeys could not support themselves under the demanding conditions of modern life; that there are now more turkeys than ever before and their general health and nutritional status, if not their life-expectancy, is much more favorable than in the past; that a turkey ought to have a chance to fulfill its obligations and realize the meaning of its life as a responsible member of society; that, despite the sentimental outcries of reformers, most turkeys seem contented with their lot—those that are not content being best treated by individual clinical means and, if necessary, an accelerated program; and that the discontented are not the fattest, anyway, only the brightest.

Young men in America, like most Negroes, are excluded from any opportunity to hold the kind of job or to earn the kind of money without which members of this society committed to affluence are treated with gross contempt. In a sense, the plight of youth is more oppressive, for the means by which they are constrained are held to be lawful, while discrimination against Negroes is now proscribed by law and what remains, though very serious indeed, is the massive toxic residue of past practice rather than current public policy.

Students are not paid for attending school; they are held to be investing in their future—though if, in fact, they invested as capital the difference between the normal wage of an employed adult high school graduate for four to seven years and what little they may have received as stipends during their academic careers for the same length of time, the return accrued to them might easily exceed the increment a degree will bring. But, of course, they have not got it to invest, and are not permitted to get it to live on. The draft siphons off working-class youth, while middle-class youth are constrained to remain in college to avoid it. If there were no draft, their impact on the economy would probably be ruinous. Trade-union restrictions and child-labor laws, in any case, prevent their gaining the kind of experience, prior to the age of eighteen—even as part of a high school program—that would qualify them for employment as adults by the time they reach their legal majority, though young workers could be protected by laws relating to working conditions, hours, and wage-rates, if this protection were indeed the intent of restrictive legislation, without eliminating his opportunity for employment.

Even the concept of a legal majority is itself a social artifact, defining the time at which the social structure is ready to concede a measure of equality to those of its members whom youthfulness has kept powerless, without reference to their real qualifications which, where relevant, could be directly tested. Nature knows no such sharp break in competence associated with maturation, except in the sexual sphere; and comparatively little of our economic and political behavior is overtly sexual. Perhaps if more were, we would be more forthright and less spiteful. Nor is there any general maturational factor, gradual but portentous in its cumulative effect, which is relevant to society's demands.

Neither wisdom nor emotional stability is particularly characteristic of American adults, as compared to the young; and where, in this country, would the electoral process become less rational if children were permitted to vote: southern California? Washington, D.C.? If there should be any age limitation on voting, it ought to apply, surely, to those so old that they may reasonably expect to escape the consequences of their political decisions, rather than to those who will be burdened and perhaps destroyed by them. Certainly, the disfranchisement of youth is impossible to square, morally, with the Selective Service Act—though politically, there is no inconsistency: the second implies the first. But the draft is pure exploitation, in a classical Marxian sense. The question of the need for an army is not the issue. A volunteer army could be raised, according to the conservative economist Milton Friedman,[6] for from four to twenty billion dollars per year; and to argue that even the larger sum is more than the nation can afford is merely to insist that draftees support the nation by paying, in kind, a tax-rate several times greater than the average paid by civilian tax-payers in money, instead of being compensated for their loss in liberty and added risk. To argue that military service is a duty owed to one's country seems quite beside the point: it is not owed more by a young man than by the old or the middle-aged. And, at a time when a large proportion of enlisted military assignments are in clerical and technical specialties identical with those for which civilians are highly paid, the draft seems merely a form of involuntary servitude.

Without a doubt, the Selective Service Act has done more than any other factor not only to exacerbate the conflict between generations, but to make it clear that it is a real conflict of interest. The draft makes those subject to it formally second-class citizens in a way to which no race is subjected any longer. The arrogance and inaccessibility of Selective Service officials, who are neither elected nor appointed for fixed terms subject to review; the fact that it has been necessary to take court action even to make public the names of draft-board members in some communities; the fact that registrants are specifically denied representation by counsel during their dealings with the Selective Service System and can only appeal to the courts after risking prosecution for the felony of refusing induction—all this is without parallel in the American legal process.

But the laws of the land are, after all, what define youth as a discriminated-against class. In fact, it is their discrimination that gives the term "youth" the only operational meaning it has: that of a person who, by reason of age, becomes subject to special constraint and penalties visited upon no other member of the commonwealth—for whom, by reason of age, certain conduct, otherwise lawful, is defined as criminal and to whom special administrative procedures, applicable to no other member of the commonwealth, are applied. The special characteristics of "youth culture" are derived from these disabilities rather than from any inherent age-graded characteristics. "Youth culture" is composed of individuals whose time is pre-empted by compulsory school attendance or the threat of induction into the Armed Service, who, regardless of their skills, cannot get and hold jobs that will pay enough to permit them to marry and build homes, and who are subject to surveillance at home or in school dormitories if they are detected in any form of sexual activity whatever. Youth and prisoners are the only people in America for whom *all* forms of sexual behavior are defined as illicit. It is absurd to scrutinize people who are forced to live under such extraordinary disabilities for psychological explanations of their resistance or bizarre conduct, except insofar as their state of mind can be related to their real situation.[7]

LAW ENFORCEMENT AND LEGAL PROCESS APPLIED TO YOUTH

In their relationship to the legal structure, youth operate under peculiar disabilities. The educational codes of the several states provide for considerably more restraint even than the compulsory attendance provisions provide—and that provision would be regarded as confiscatory, and hence doubtless unconstitutional, if applied to any member of the commonwealth old enough to be respected as having the right to dispose of his own time. Soldiers are at least paid *something*. But the code does more than pre-empt the students' time. It is usually interpreted by school authorities as giving them power to set standards of dress and grooming—some of which, like those pertaining to hair length, of a kind that cannot be set aside while the student is not in school. It becomes the basis for indoctrination with the values of a petty, clerical social subclass. Regulations on dress, speech, and conduct in school are justified by this subclass as being necessary because school is supposed to be businesslike; it is where you learn to behave like a businessman. This leaves the young with the alternative of becoming little-league businessmen or juvenile delinquents, for refusal to obey school regulations leads to charges of delinquency—which seems a rather narrow choice among the possibilities of youthful life.

But I have written so much more elsewhere about education as a social sanction that it seems inappropriate to devote more space to the functioning of the school as such. I have introduced the topic here simply to point out that the educational code, from the viewpoint of those subject to it, constitutes the most pervasive *legal* constraint on the movements and behavior of youth. It is not, however, from the viewpoint of legal theory, the most fundamental. The juvenile code and the juvenile court system provide even more direct contradictions to the standard of due process afforded adults in American courts.

For the juvenile court is, ostensibly, not a criminal court. It is technically a court of chancery before which a respondent is brought as a presumptive ward—not as an adversary, but as a dependent. It is assumed—the language is preserved in the legal documentation used in preparing juvenile court cases—that the authorities intervene *on behalf of the minor,* and with the purpose of setting up, where necessary, a regime designed to correct his wayward tendencies. The court may restrict; it may, as a condition of probation, insist that a respondent submit to a public spanking; it may detain and incarcerate in a reformatory indistinguishable from a prison for a period of years—but it may not punish. It is authorized only to correct.

Because action in juvenile court is not, therefore, regarded as an adversary proceeding, the juvenile courts provide few of the legal safeguards of a criminal court. There is considerable public misunderstanding about this, because the effect of recent Supreme Court decisions on the juvenile court process has been widely exaggerated, both by people who endorse and by people who deplore what the Court has done. What it *has* done, in effect, is to require the juvenile court to provide the usual safeguards if its actions are ever to become part of an adversary proceeding in a regular criminal court. Since the state may at its discretion, try as adults rather than as juveniles youngsters over a certain minimum age who are accused of actions that violate the criminal code, and since the more serious offenses are usually committed by older adolescents, it may choose to provide these accused with the safeguards granted adults from the time of arrest rather than impair its chances for subsequent successful prosecution. It is, therefore, becoming usual, for example, to provide counsel for juveniles in serious cases; to exclude, in the event of a subsequent criminal prosecution, statements taken by probation officers or youth-squad members in a legally improper manner; and to permit juvenile respondents to summon and cross-examine witnesses—procedures which have not been part of juvenile court practice in the past.

These are improvements, but they leave untouched the much vaster potential for intergenerational conflict afforded by the summary treatment of casual offenders, and, particularly, of those youngsters of whose behavior the law could take no cognizance if they were older; for example, truants, loiterers, runaways, curfew-violators, and twenty-year-olds who buy beer in a tavern. For such as these, there is no question of compromising future prosecution in a formal court, and their treatment has been affected very little, if at all, by high-court decisions. The law still presumes that its intervention in their lives is beneficial *per se,* and they have few enforceable civil rights with respect to it. If young people are "troublemakers," they are punished for it—that is all. Step out of line, and the police "take you away," as the Buffalo Springfield described it—on the occasion of a Los Angeles police roundup of the youngsters strolling on the Sunset Strip in the autumn of 1968—in the song, "For What It's Worth," that gained them a national reputation among teen-agers.

It is quite clear that one's moral judgment of the legal position of youth in American society depends very largely on the degree to which one shares the fundamental assumption on which juvenile proceedings are based: that they are designed to help; that the adults who carry them out will, by and large, have the wisdom and the resources, and the intent to help rather than to punish. Legal authorities have caviled at this assumption for some time. Thus, Paul W. Alexander writes in a paper on "Constitutional Rights in Juvenile Court":

> In the area of the child's constitutional rights the last decade has seen a minor but interesting revolt on the part of some highly distinguished judges. So repellent were some of the juvenile court practices that the judges were moved to repudiate the widely held majority rule that a delinquency hearing in a juvenile court is a civil, not a criminal action. . . . This doctrine appeared so distasteful to a California appellate court that the following language appeared in the opinion: "While the juvenile court law provides that adjudication of a minor to be a ward of the court should not be deemed to be a conviction of crime, nevertheless, for all practical purposes, this is a legal fiction, presenting a challenge to credulity and doing violence to reason."[8]

YOUTH TODAY HAVE NO RESPECT FOR THE LAW

The kind of legal structure which youth face would appear to be, of itself, sufficient to explain why young people are often inclined to be skeptical rather than enthusiastic about law and order—and about those of their number who are enthusiasts for law, as student leaders and prominent athletes tend to be. Yet, the hostile relations that develop between youth and law-enforcement agencies are, even so, probably more attributable to the way in which police generally respond to young people than to the oppressive character of the legal system itself—though the two factors are, of course, causally related, because the fact that youth have few rights and many liabilities before the law also makes it possible for law-enforcement agencies to behave more oppressively.

With respect to youth, law-enforcement agencies assume the role of enforcers of morals and proper social attitudes, as well as of the law, and—having few rights—there is not much the young can do about it. Police forces, moreover, provide a manpower-pool by "moonlighting," while off duty, as members of private enforcement squads hired to keep young people from getting out of hand, a task which they often try to perform by making themselves as conspicuous as possible in order to keep the young people from starting anything—exactly what police would *not* do in monitoring a group of orderly adults in a public place.

My own observations at folk-rock concerts and dances, for example, which are among the best places for learning how young people express themselves and communicate with one another, confirm that surveillance on these occasions is characteristically officious and oppressive. It often expresses a real contempt for the customs of the youngsters, even when these are appropriate to the occasion. Police, clubs in hand, will rush onstage or into the pit at any sign that the performers are about to mingle with the dancers or audience—if a soloist jumps down from the stage, say, or if members of the audience attempt to mount it; or they will have the lights turned up to interrupt a jam session or freakout that has gone on too long, or with too great intensity, for their taste; or insist on ruining a carefully designed and well-equipped light-show by requiring that the house-lights be kept bright. All this is done smirkingly, as if the youngsters at the concert knew that they were "getting out of line" in behaving differently from a philharmonic audience. It should be borne in mind, considering the fiscal basis for rights in our culture, that tickets for the Beach Boys or Jefferson Airplane are now likely to cost more than tickets for a symphony concert, and the youngsters are poorer than symphony subscribers, but they rarely enjoy the same right to listen to their music in their own way, unmolested.

The music itself provides some of the best evidence of the response of the "further-out" youngsters to police action, which, indeed, sometimes inflicts on them more serious damage than the annoyance of having a concert ruined. In Watts, San Francisco, and Memphis, the civil disorders associated with each city in recent years were triggered by the slaying of a Negro youth by a police officer. "Pot busts" are directed primarily against young people, among whom the use of marijuana has become something of a moral principle evoked by the destructive hostility of the legal means used to suppress it: thirty students at the State University of New York at Stony Brook, for example, were handcuffed and herded from their dormitories before dawn last winter, before the lenses of television cameras manned by news agencies which the Suffolk County police had thoughtfully notified of the impending raid.[9] Rock artists, speaking to, and to some degree for, youth, respond to the social climate which such incidents, often repeated, have established. I have already cited the Buffalo Springfield's song "For What It's Worth." The Mothers of Invention are even more direct in their new album, *We're Only In It for the Money,* where they represent the typical parent as believing that police brutality is justified toward teen-agers who look "too weird" and make "some noise."[10]

BRINGING IT ALL BACK HOME

Finally, exacerbating the confrontations between youth and adults is the fact that the control of youth has largely been entrusted to lower-status elements of the society. Custodial and control functions usually are so entrusted, for those in subjection have even lower status themselves, and do not command the services of the higher grades of personnel that their society affords. Having low status, moreover, prevents their being taken seriously as moral human beings. Society tends to assume that the moral demands made on the criminal, the mad, and the young by their respective wardens are for their own good and to reinforce those demands while limiting the subjects' opportunities for redress to those situations in which the grossest violations of the most fundamental human rights have occurred. The reader's moral evaluation of the conflict that I have described will, therefore, depend very largely, I believe, on the degree to which he shares society's assumption.

As has surely been obvious, I do not share it. The process by which youth is brought into line in American society is almost wholly destructive of the dignity and creative potential of the young, and the condition of the middle-aged and the old in America seems to me, on the whole, to make this proposition quite plausible. Nevertheless, the violation of the young in the process of socialization fulfills an essential function in making our society cohesive. And curiously—and rather perversely—this function depends on the fact that custody and indoctrination—education is not, after all, a very precise term for it—are lower-status functions.

American democracy depends, I believe, on the systematic humiliation of potential elites to keep it going. There is, perhaps, no other way in which an increasingly educated middle class, whose technical services cannot be spared, can be induced to acquiesce in the political demands of a deracinated and invidious populace, reluctant to accept any measure of social improvement, however generally advantageous, which might bring any segment of the society slightly more benefits than would accrue to it. Teachers, police, and parents in America are jointly in the business of rearing the young to be frightened of the vast majority who have been too scarred and embittered by the losses and compromises which they have endured in the process of becoming respectable to be treated in a way that would enrage them. Anything generous—or perhaps merely civil, like welcoming a Negro family into a previously white community, or letting your neighbor "blow a little grass" in peace—does enrage them, and so severely as to threaten the fabric of society. A conference of recent American leaders associated with a greater measure of generosity toward the deprived—John and Robert Kennedy, Martin Luther King, Jr., and Malcolm X, for a start— might, perhaps, agree, if it could be convened.

Many of today's middle-class youth, however—having been spared, by the prevailing affluence, the deprivations that make intimidation more effective in later life—are talking back; and some are even finding support, rather than betrayal, in their elders—the spectacle of older folks helping their radical sons to adjust their identifying armbands during the spring protests at Columbia University is said to have been both moving and fairly common. The protest, in any case, continues and mounts. So does the rage against the young. If the confrontation between the generations does pose, as many portentous civic leaders and upper-case "Educators" fear, a lethal threat to the integrity of the American social system, that threat may perhaps be accepted with graceful irony. Is there, after all, so much to lose? The American social system has never been noted for its integrity. In fact, it would be rather like depriving the Swiss of their surfing.

NOTES AND REFERENCES

1. I am indebted to John and Margaret Rowntree, of York University and the University of Toronto, respectively, for demonstrating, in their paper "The Political Economy of Youth in the United States," the class-dynamics of generational conflict. This document, prepared for presentation at the First Annual Meeting of the Committee on Socialist Studies in Calgary, Alberta, in June 1968, was published in the Montreal quarterly journal *Our Generation,* Vol. 6, No. 1, 1968. Their radical analysis simplifies many apparent paradoxes in the relationship between the generations.

2. Bruno Bettelheim, "The Problem of Generations," *Daedalus,* Vol. 91, No. 1 (Winter 1962), pp. 68–96.

3. Christopher Jencks and David Riesman, in *The Academic Revolution* (Garden City, N.Y.: Doubleday, 1968), pp. 146–154, provide a thoughtful, if rather gingerly, discussion of this issue.

4. Aaron V. Cicourel and John I. Kitsuse, *The Educational Decision-Makers* (Indianapolis: Bobbs-Merrill, 1963).

5. *Ibid.,* p. 72.

6. Quoted in *Newsweek,* December 19, 1966, p. 100.

7. To be sure, as we become more sophisticated in our conception of mental illness, this becomes more and more clearly true of all forms of mental illness. All states of mind have their psychodynamics; but, regardless of the school of psychodynamic thought to which one adheres, the most basic possible definition of mental illness seems to be "a chronic or recurring mental or emotional state which disturbs other people more powerful than the victim." Sometimes, of course, as in the case of certain kinds of paranoid schizophrenics, with good reason.

   As a corollary to this, it seems to follow that the head of a modern, centralized, national state—unlike his poor, royal predecessors—can never go officially mad until his government is overthrown.

8. Included in Margaret K. Rosenheim (ed.), *Justice for the Child* (New York: Free Press of Glencoe, 1962), p. 83.

9. *The New York Times,* January 18, 1968.

10. Copyright by Frank Zappa Music Company, Inc., a subsidiary of Third Story Music, Inc. (BMI)

part three

DEVELOPMENTAL FORCES

THE ARTICLES in this book have been grouped into three major divisions. In the first part the bases for human development were considered, including congenital endowment, responsiveness, and culture, along with intellectual potential and teaching-learning phenomena. Next the course of development which utilizes the above basic factors was studied in terms of phases—infancy, childhood, adolescence, and youth. Part Three presents articles which focus around the concept that man-made institutions designed for welfare and development are subject to better control—control by groups as well as by individual choice and action. Hereditary limitations are recognized. But regardless of whether or not congenital factors control ten, fifty, or ninety per cent of human development, it is in the matter of *response* that mankind presently exerts critical control. "What are we going to do with what we have?" This is the important consideration.

Fact and fallacy appear to be thoroughly mixed in thinking about that critical factor in human development—the family. Such factors as age of marriage, number of children, socioeconomic status, and the child's order of birth have been examined to see how they influence growth and learning. The results are equivocal and inconsistent. It does seem that the success of the family depends largely upon the personality maturity of parents.

It may be that the family will be replaced by other arrangements for the rearing of children. Man's adaptability is such that it is not reasonable to rule out such an eventuality. However, such replacement does not appear to be probable. When marriages work—and the majority do—they not only provide a salutary environment for child development but also constitute a source of multiple satisfactions to the adult participants. The selection on family stability as related to school dropouts is challenging. It is wise to think also of the relationship of family milieu to success in vocations and competent citizenship. After all is said and done, marriage, family, satisfaction in life, and optimum child-rearing conditions are related to the matters of social awareness and love. The editors are pleased to include Harlow's article, which appears to be in the process of becoming a classic in psychological literature. The school, as well as the family, is threatened by change and instances of inadequacy. The entire study of human development points to the qualities of individuality and distinctiveness, which have not been sufficiently recognized in our schools. For a long time, in the course of the history of western civilization, schools have been at least satisfactorily effective. When our cultures could afford to serve, educationally, only those whose intellectual talents developed most rapidly and who came to school highly motivated to achieve academically, the school did an acceptable job. Changes have taken place with such thundering speed in the past five to ten years that conventional school approaches are sternly challenged.

Technological changes have made the unskilled working man obsolete. Society has no place for the young to go except school—regardless of aptitude, learning style, achievement motivation, or background preparation. It is incumbent upon the school to adapt to this different clientele. Knowledge change has become knowledge explosion, and the aim of education—without solicitation or consultation—has changed. School is no longer preparation for life, or occupation, or profession; the purpose of school is to prepare the learner *to learn more* and still more. The shift has been made from education as a product (the issue has existed for years as a topic for discussion) to education as a process. The aims of the school are not so much to teach facts as they are to teach students how to learn about their own self worth; to learn their own life style and uniqueness; to learn the tools of learning; and learn to enjoy the process of learning. In all these ways the objective is to develop the habit and predisposition of continuous and self-directed learning.

Selections included in the section on schools provide data on the fresh challenges which change has presented to educators. Reading about the problem does not mean learning. Not until change in behavior results can one properly claim to have learned.

The section includes a group of articles on schools for the disadvantaged or, more realistically, schools for the culturally different. This topic has assumed a place of primary importance, for it has come to be appreciated that (1) we have hitherto neglected the development of a large source of potential talent, (2) undeveloped human resources constitute a genuine threat to national welfare and safety, and (3) an orientation of humanism demands that all young people must have the right to come closer to the actualization of their potential.

The question of schools for culturally different children is an important consideration when dealt with as a distinct entity. The topic gains additional importance as it is realized that children, whether privileged or disadvantaged, have common needs. Whatever their socioeconomic class, children are more alike in terms of motivation, responsiveness, and needs than they are different. Hence, what are readily perceived as ways to approach education for the culturally different also provide cogent clues for the improved teaching of pupils who heretofore have been considered adequate in achievement motivation.

Schools in general and schools for the culturally different have much in common. (1) Recognition of the individuality and uniqueness of pupils pays dividends in the rate of learning and the predisposition to adopt the habit of continuous learning. Emphases on varied curriculum and individually tailored learning programs must extend from verbalization to implementation. (2) The essence of a good teaching-learning situation, for the privileged and the culturally different as well as for other youngsters, resides in the nature of the human transaction—teacher-pupil relationships. (3) Cultivation of a healthy concept of self must become a primary concern of all schools in the 1970's.

If the shift from a teaching to a learning emphasis is to be made, it will be necessary to recognize and put to use the group as a milieu for learning. This applies to teachers as well as to pupils. The group emphasis is reflected in a selection of articles which examine peer relations and their impact on learning and motivation. The group emphasis is recognized also in an article which pertains mainly to adult groups. That is, if schools (and families) are to change to meet new and insistent demands, then teachers and parents can profit from group experience. Both the home and the school can have increased effectiveness as they act in concert. One teacher or one set of parents can have only limited influence. Groups of families and groups of teachers can have a more noticeable impact on planned change. In short, the planning of change is superior to actions which are limited to a mere responsiveness to change.

Many of the articles cited earlier in this book dealt in some measure with the various handicaps and hazards to development. But it may be that a treatment which presents in more detail some of the specific hazards will further enhance the study of how human beings grow and mature. For example, behavior disorders resulting from individual responses to strain, pressure, and neglect or cruelty can be considered as one category. In this respect, it is helpfully informative to know that situations which may be a cause for psychological retreat, attack, or capitulation in one child may be a challenge or may be ignored by another.

Recently one of the editors was asked, "What causes young people to take drugs?" The answer was, "I really don't know. Even the specialists are baffled by the question." The person asking the question was quite displeased. "There must be a cause. Why can't experts find the answer?" If one is not determined to find *the* cause for a behavior, the article by Jenkins can be quite instructive. There are many contributing factors. Only an explanation which recognizes the principle of multiple causation will suffice to throw light on complex behavior.

As science has advanced and man's control over nature has increased, it has begun to be appreciated that man is his own worst enemy. Pollution, war, overpopulation, delinquency, greed—all are man-made phenomena; and they can be controlled by man-made approaches. The problems selected to illustrate the hazards of this nature are delinquency, overpopulation, and drug abuse, but dropouts, accident proneness, alienation, or racial conflict could have served as readily as illustrations. In the case of drugs there are many articles dealing with speculations concerning causes, and we suggest that the reader study some of the most recent publications. In the meantime, a treatment of what might be done about the use of drugs by young people may be a productive orientation. Even though the causes are variable, perhaps the antidotes will work anyway. At least for the present, we regard the question addressed to young people, "Why do you take drugs?" as being less useful than "What are you going to do about it?" Too often telling why one takes drugs leads to a recital of negative influences which seem to justify or rationalize the action. "What are you going to do about it?" emphasizes the facts of choice and responsibility.

The final section may seem redundant, since the entire volume has dealt with ways in which human development may be facilitated. However, it seems justifiable to emphasize and pinpoint the phenomenon of self-actualization. Ultimately there comes a time, in the life of the normal individual, when parents, teachers, nurses, social workers, and law officers no longer can be responsible. The individual must make choices and formulate aspirations. The challenge is to admit the role of heredity and environment and, at the same time, acknowledge the fact of choice and responsibility. People concerned about the evils of their city have said much the same thing. "The trouble with Podunk is us." Without completely repudiating the "foul clutch of circumstance," the self-actualized person must say, "I am the master of my fate; I am the captain of my soul."

Developmental influences of the family

43.

The idealized model of the American family

RAY L. BIRDWHISTELL

The reader may be in for some culture shock when he reads Bird-whistell's evaluation of the overloaded, overvalued, and nonviable ro-manticized family life toward which so many strive. His evaluation goes much further than that of many critics of the family, whose ob-jections frequently focus on sexual satisfaction—in fact, he does not even mention this matter. His emphasis is on the need for greater affiliation with many people instead of the limited husband-wife and parents-children relationships which are becoming increasingly char-acteristic.

While the editors do not believe that the family is necessarily pro-ductive of pathology, we do agree with Birdwhistell on several points. For instance, we are pleased to see the challenge to the notion that parents produce the child's personality (see selections 7, 22, and 32). We, too, believe that there is a need for broader affiliation than is provided even by a highly stable family. We, too, agree that the setting aside of old people deprives young and middle-agers of developmental opportunities.

This article, so different from most studies of the family, can provide the starting point for some productive discussions—and for some self-evaluations.

OUTSIDE OF *government,* perhaps no social form has been so broadly dis-cussed, so idealized, so reviled, and so little understood as is *the family* and, particularly *the American family.* Perhaps this is because it is so difficult to see in perspective a new form whose novelty is masked by the fact that its function is so ancient. Accumulating evidence indicates that social organisms from fish to man, in order to survive, have found it neces-sary to order certain aspects of their lives around courtship, mating, re-production, and care of the young. The locale of such functioning has been

Social Casework, 51:195–198, April, 1970. Ray L. Birdwhistell, Senior Research Scien-tist, Eastern Pennsylvania Psychiatric Institute, and Visiting Professor of Communications, University of Pennsylvania.

determined by, and has, in turn, conditioned the territorial organization of the group. Yet, notwithstanding this long and multivariant history, and however inventive man himself has been over the ages, in the past century we may have developed a new type of organization in the so-called American family. The self-centered husband-wife, parent-child unit, so idealized in Western European and American society today may be not only a novel way of organizing familial functioning, but it may also be a temporary and ultimately nonviable social form.

In another article, I discussed the fact that a unit restricted to a husband and a wife and their offspring was a useful form for a pioneering or exploration group before settlement.[1] There seems to be ample evidence that this limited unit functioned well to permit individuals quick social mobility (up and down), in that, in the absence of extended loyalties, it allowed the individuals to leave homelands and traditional values with minimal strain. However, this "segmental" family could seldom become a secure base for socialization, maturation, and long-term satisfactory social living if its strength depended upon the exclusion or the secularization of loyalties to individuals or groups outside the husband-wife, parent-child range. Obviously, such a tight and limited form of family organization permits great flexibility as new territories are opened up or as the loosening of class barriers within societies permits individual men and women and their spouses and children easier passage from one social class to another. If, however, in order to permit mobility, the unit is so organized as to resist all interpersonal relationships with other than immediate family members, such a unit (except perhaps in societies far simpler than any we have yet discovered) lacks lateral supports. It must derive all its support from the impersonal structures of the society, the formalized governmental, educational, economic, and religious institutions. In other words, if the only legitimate personal relationships must come from *within* the unit, and if the young, as they mature, must leave the unit to set up another such unit, such an organization is, by necessity, short-lived and self-destructive, the elderly are left lonely and isolated, and the maturing young are guilty of destroying the unit by the act of maturation.

Although this husband-wife, parent-child family type has been seen as *the* American family and as such has been idealized by the press and has been overvalued by both moralists and social scientists of the last half century, it is a relatively recent development as far as actual and extensive operation is concerned. Sometime following the Civil War, two social inventions, which seemed to be the result of the emergent awareness of man's capacity to learn and to influence and be influenced by other men, changed the direction of both marital arrangements and child care. For a variety of reasons—and these reasons range all the way from the development of machine manufacture, the wide distribution of population, the development of mobility through education, and the changing role and expectations of women with the consequent change (although not nearly so recognized) in the role of men—there emerged a new concept of the ideal relationship between marriage partners: romantic marriage and the romanticized conjugal unit increasingly became the American ideal.

ROMANTICIZED RELATIONSHIPS

Romantic love is a concept that idealizes the feelings between a male and a female. It is not particularly new; a number of societies across the world have idealized this relationship and, at least since the time of the Greeks, there have been periods of varied emphasis upon this ideal in Western society. Traditionally, romantic love has been seen, however, as a premarital or an extramarital situation apart from the everyday, sustaining aspects of social living. As sociologists viewed it during the first quarter of this century, the trouble with romantic love was that it had lost its romantic function whereby men and women could escape in fantasy from everyday life. Romantic love became vulgarized and regarded as the justification or the necessary precondition for marriage.

Toward the end of the last century and during the first quarter of this century, romantic love was domesticated and extended in scope. There emerged the ideal of the romantic marriage in which one male and one female meet and fall in love and that love should be sufficient to sustain their relationship "until death do them part." This was a new development in that not only did the mating involve exclusive sexual rights and duties but all emotional response became included and negotiated under the compact. In short, the ideal stated and still states that one man and one woman should marry one another and contract to satisfy *all* of the other's emotional and physical needs. Concepts of sexual infidelity were unconsciously extended to include all the personal feelings of the two individuals involving outsiders. Not only does this involve a secularization of all nonfamilial associations but it illegitimatizes all those associations outside the marriage which threaten to become personal. If all personal attachments, to be legitimate, must be intrafamilial, the outside must be depersonalized. This situation is not an optimal one for the development of mutual understanding and conventions of fidelity. Counter-infidelity operations preclude the growth of fidelity operations. Loyalty becomes little more than an antidote to disloyalty and there is an accelerating isolation both inside and outside the family.

The concept of romantic marriage idealized the closed, exclusive, and isolating dyad. As such it must be threatened by the appearance of outsiders, including the children born to it. To include "parenting" as the natural extension of being a husband or wife does not reduce the strain upon the pair, particularly if the couple is caught in a system of values in which their love is finally proved by the personalities of their maturing children. As if this romanticized and overdemanding ideal of the dyad were not enough to impose upon man, a second invention just before the turn of the century completed the nonsense. This was the invention of defining parents not only as legally, morally, religiously, and economically responsible for their children, but also as finally responsible for the personalities of their children. As personality became seen as a result of "proper" child care and child care as the final responsibility of the parents, the parents (particularly the mother) were regarded as the cause of "bad" personalities.

IDEALIZED MODEL OF FAMILY LIFE

It is difficult to know just what proportion of the American population lives in these exclusive, self-concerned, segmentalized, husband-wife, parent-child units. It is even more difficult to know how many Americans use the ideal as a way of measuring their marriages, their parenthood, or their relationships to their spouses or children. It is, however, perfectly obvious that this is the model presented to the public by science, in art, and by the mass communication facilities. More seriously, it is the model used by our legal, social, psychiatric, and clerical experts. When all agencies designed to assist men and women and children in trouble accept as ideal the condition which occasioned the difficulty, the very devices for ameliorating social pathology contribute to it instead.

It requires but little reflection to see that the American family, as idealized, is an overloaded institution. It is easy to see, too, that the goals set by the concept are unattainable and leave people failing both as spouses and as parents. This can have even more tragic results if the people who find it impossible to live in such a situation, because they are human and have human needs, seek help to escape and are directed back into the pathological situation. The counselor, the therapist, or the legal adviser who accepts the ideal becomes the reenforcer of the pathology.

The ideal has far-reaching results and breeds its own mythologies. We have described our culture as child-centered and we have felt the children to be unappreciative to the attention given them. I am not at all sure this is true. Perhaps it would be better to say that we have become a "marriage and parenting-centered" society, with the children not the center of the attention but rather a necessary component of it. The behavior of the child is given attention not because of himself but as a measurement of the marriage or of the parents as parents. At least this is the way it appears to many of the young. The child says, "You don't care about me; you are only thinking of yourself." This makes little sense to the anxious parent who is constantly concerned with whether he or she is "doing the right thing with the child." Neither does the parent who tells the child, "Everything we do is for you and we want you to make us proud," make much sense to the child. Such statements as these delight the "expert" who sees the parent-child difficulty as a consequence of the failure of parents and children to communicate. In my opinion, we miss the point when we focus upon the ploys, the recurrent tactics of action and reaction *within* the family. Such a view obscures the more salient fact that the institution itself is distorted and must be reorganized; these small events are but symptoms of the larger pathology. Unless the family unit can be expanded and its members supported in larger social relationships, we can give little more than first aid to its members.

DETRIMENTAL EFFECTS OF THE IDEALIZED MODEL

I cannot pretend to be objective about my personal dismay at the mischief occasioned by the acceptance of this American family ideal. One aspect of the present conflict in America is the so-called generation gap. This concept is useful for pointing out the recent extraordinary acceleration of social time and for directing our energies toward the revision of increasingly outmoded legal, economic, educational, and religious formulations and structures. Unfortunately, for many adhering to the romanticized American family concept, *generation* translates *parent* and *child,* and as the adult deals with or reads about the young, he does so as a guilty or insufficiently appreciated parent; as the young attempt to deal with the adult world, they tend to operate by the same logic. Necessary social changes become points of nonproductive, intergenerational conflict when the adversary method is reduced to an extended family squabble. Creative energies are easily dissipated when the angry child tries to engage with the guilty adult in a way directly related to the idealized family sphere. The child has been instructed by the parent that his (the child's) personality success or failure can be directly related to the acts of commission or omission on the part of the parents. When the child angrily accuses, the parent accepts the charge in submissive impotence or is resentful because the child is insufficiently grateful for what the parent has been able to do. The fact that all adults become the "establishment" makes negotiation outside the family difficult too. Social change becomes inhibited or distorted by temper tantrums, sullenness, or whining on the part of the child. Angry, reactive government officials can confirm the adolescent conception of the outside world (as well as acting out the exasperation of the guilty parent); the equally reactive adolescent rebel leader often fulfills in his actions the projections of the guilty parent. It is not surprising that both the self-designated representatives of the adult establishment and the self-selected spokesmen of the disappointed adolescents disdain education, social science, and psychiatry and scorn those moderates and liberals who see choices other than those of armed rebellion or armed suppression.

It is not difficult to be critical or horrified at the effects of this impossibly overloaded and guilt-creating social unit, the family. There seems no reason to be amazed that even as an ideal the family has occasioned anger,

hostility, disappointment, and guilt, all of which contribute to neurosis if
not to psychosis and social pathology. It is amazing that so many people
have withstood the force of such a patently pathogenic institution and have
achieved a reasonable adaptation to living with other people. The number
of reasonably well-adjusted human beings in American society is indeed a
testament to man's flexibility, his ability to withstand a destructive environment, and his capacity for resistance to impossible idealizations.

CONCLUSION

It would be naive to believe that the present turmoil in America and
throughout the world is a *result* of "bad families," "bad mental health," or
the failure of communication between the generations. Such reductionism
is obscure and exhausting at a time when we must direct our energies to
the solution of critical domestic and international problems. Constructive,
even revolutionary, energies are all too easily dissipated by pseudofamilial
hyperbole, temper tantrums, and pout. These confrontations are effective,
however, because many Americans are so miserable in their limited and
emotionally depriving domestic existence. The idealized family with its
concentration upon intrafamilial matters is an aspect—and perhaps a
critical one—both of the organized immature anger that precludes effective
negotiation and of the weary isolationism of many who constitute the so-
called silent majority and whose painful preoccupation with unsatisfactory
marriages and stressful parent-child relationships saps their few energies.

We would not have a healthy society simply if husbands and wives
understood each other better, or if parents and children could be directed
toward less destructive interaction. If, however, we could reduce the
pathology inherent in the present family ideal by unmasking its impossible
goals, we might have better access to the talent and energy now so waste-
fully employed by so many unhappy and dissatisfied people.

The problem is how to open up these closed families and how to permit the flow of energy and information to and from them. It is clear that
that problem cannot be solved as long as our lawmakers, clinicians, and
moralists accept impossible ideals and operate in terms of them.

REFERENCE

1. Ray L. Birdwhistell, The American Family: Some Perspectives, *Psychiatry,*
   29:203–12 (August 1966).

44.

Family background, primary relationships, and the high school dropout

LUCIUS F. CERVANTES

The author of this selection reports research that further substantiates the importance of effective interpersonal relationships for learning and success in school. He indicates that four out of five high school dropouts are products of a rejecting family environment and that in the majority of cases the nonaccepting family pattern and the potential dropout can be identified by age six. It would appear that behaviors and self-regarding attitudes learned up to this age play a determining part in what may be learned subsequently. Let us call attention to the fact that these were interpersonal-transaction learnings, not academic learnings. Let us further emphasize that improper learning in this area apparently tends to render ineffectual such factors as teaching efforts, curriculum planning, administrative reorganization, and most of the rest of what schools do to improve instruction. It is time, we think, that educators begin to recognize the learner's emotional and psychological needs as taking precedence over those of a cognitive-intellectual nature.

One may be rejected, alienated, and drop out socially as well as educationally. Furthermore, dropping out may be accomplished psychologically as well as physically. It is hard to say how often school classes are occupied by people there in body but elsewhere in mind and spirit. It is less difficult to assess social dropouts in terms of statistics on penal inmates, neurotic and psychotic breakdowns, chronic alcoholic and other types of addicts. School dropouts are just part of an immense problem in this culture. Counseling at public expense might be one of the wisest investments that could be made.

DURING THE next decade, an estimated 8,000,000 United States youths will terminate their education before completing high school. Most studies that deal with this vast personal and social wastage conclude that the family of the dropout is in some way deficient. What has not been specified, however, is in exactly what ways this family differs from that of the graduate. It is to this question of the specific differences between the family backgrounds of the dropout and the high school graduate that this article addresses itself.

School authorities in Boston, St. Louis, New Orleans, Omaha, Denver, and Los Angeles each cooperated in providing 25 "matched" pairs of white

Journal of Marriage and the Family, 27:218–223, 1965. Director, Family Research Center, and Professor of Sociology, St. Louis University.

youths. In all pairs, one had dropped out of school and the other was successfully completing the last semester of his high school education.[1] The
youths were matched on the variables of sex, age, I.Q., high school attended,
and general socio-economic background. The youth originated in lower-
class families (70 percent blue-collar; 30 percent lower white-collar); the
median income was slightly less than $5,000 per year. The 300 respondents,
with but 14 exceptions, were either 17 or 18 years of age.

The three instruments of research which were utilized in processing
the teen-age sample were a questionnaire, a taped interview of approximately 40 minutes, and a Thematic Apperception Test.

ASSUMPTIONS AND HYPOTHESIS

This article works within the framework of two assumptions:

(1) In our automated, industrial society, the completion of a high school education is a minimum requirement for civilizational adequacy.
(2) The enduring core of the "school personality" is primarily fashioned within
the home and to a great extent mirrors the domestic subculture existent
there.

The guiding hypothesis tested in this segment of the research was
that the family background of the dropout is less characterized by primary
relationships than is the family background of the high school graduate.

The Primary Group as a Conceptual Framework

Central to the theoretical field of this study is the concept of primary
group. Cooley originated this concept to refer to "the nursery of human
nature." The importance of primary relations is that they provide the
experiences which are basic to the formation of personality.[2] Broom and
Selznick present three testable characteristics of the primary group relationship: (1) it is *personal,* (2) it involves *a depth of intercommunication,* and
(3) it gives *personal satisfactions.*[3]

I. *Acceptance of a Total Person*

The first criterion of the primary group tested was whether the members accept each other as persons. "To feel understood and accepted," "to
be a real member of the team," "to feel that you belong" are ways of expressing the resulting psychic state, or, in the words of Cooley, "Perhaps
the simplest way of describing this wholeness is by saying that it is a 'we';
it involves the sort of sympathy and mutual identification for which 'we'
is the natural expression."[4]

Four questions were asked of each of the teen-age respondents concerning this mode of acceptance:

(1) "Would you say that your whole family both understands and accepts each other?" tapped the general milieu of family common understanding and acceptance.

(2) "Would you say that your family both understands and accepts *you?*" established whether the respondent felt that he personally was understood and accepted by his family.

(3) "And would you say that you both understand and accept them?" ascertained whether this pattern was reciprocal.

(4) "Did your family encourage and help you in your plans for a good job or in your school plans?" assayed the "we-ness" or solidarity-feeling of the family as seen by the teenager.

Case Histories. In response to the first question, "Would you say that your *whole* family both understands and accepts each other?" the following replies may be cited as typical.

Dropout Edward, I.Q. 93, of New Orleans:

Very little. Like before you all came. We was having a big argument. My sister keeps dogging me. When I come in she tells me to get out or go to work or something like that. She is stupid. She don't understand me. And my mother doesn't understand me. She just don't have time to understand me. She's got to be worried with my brothers and sisters and I can take care of myself. I can look after myself and make my own decisions and all. . . .

Graduate José, Spanish-American, I.Q. 111, of Denver.

Yes, my mother and father both go to work in the morning and my brother and sisters and I have our certain jobs to do in the morning to clean the house up.

The responses that the 300 youths gave to the question, "Would you say that your *whole* family both understands and accepts each other?" were scored by a panel of three social scientists on a five-point scale of "Intrafamily Understanding and Acceptance." The results, in percentage distributions, are presented in Table 1.[5]

TABLE 1. INTRAFAMILY UNDERSTANDING AND ACCEPTANCE (IN PERCENTAGES)

	Very Little	Little	Moderate	Much	Very Much
Dropouts	43	41	9	5	2
Graduates	3	15	20	24	38[a]

[a] N = 300 (150 dropouts, 150 graduates). Hypothesis: Families of dropouts manifest less intrafamily understanding and acceptance than families of high school graduates. D = .439; χ^2(2df) = 130.28, p < .001.

The first approach in ascertaining the depth of "primariness" in the families of the dropouts and the graduates was decisive in its results. Of the dropouts, four out of five (43% + 41%) perceive their families as understanding and accepting each other either "very little" or "little." Of the graduates, four out of five (20% + 24% + 38%) perceive their family's understanding and acceptance of each other as "moderate," "much," or "very much." The overwhelming majority of the dropouts see their families as failing to accept each other; the overwhelming majority of the graduates see their families as accepting each other as complete persons.

How Do You Fit into the Picture? The first question does not adequately test the linkage between the family's pattern of personal acceptance and the teen-ager himself. Is the youth, in replying about the emotional interrelationships that exist within his family, likewise describing the types of relationship that exist between him and his family? When he states that his family accepts each other very well, is he implying that they accept him too? It is quite possible to conceive of cases where all the other members of the family understand and accept one another but the teen-ager feels that he is completely misunderstood and rejected. For this reason, the next question was more specific: "How do you fit into the picture? Would you say that your family both understands and accepts *you?*"

The replies to the second question mirrored those to the first question. Four out of five (79%) of the dropouts replied in terms approximating those of Dropout Dan Y. of Denver (age 17, I.Q. 123), who confessed that he had never felt understood or accepted:

> I always felt left out. But really I think I need the time that the others got. . . . It's just that I felt left out. It seems when I was little I was always left out. I wasn't one of the family, really.

Far different were the reports of the graduates. Four out of five (84%) judged that they were both understood and accepted by their families.[6]

And Would You Say that You Both Understand and Accept Them? This next question unintentionally served as a jolt to the standard egocentric adolescent belief that it is always the teen-age self that is misunderstood and never misunderstanding.

The statistical summary of responses to this third question yielded results identical to the previous two: four out of five (79%) of the dropouts judged themselves as understanding and accepting their families "very little" or "little" while four out of five (82%) of the graduates judged themselves as understanding and accepting their families "moderately," "much," or "very much."[7]

Did Your Family Encourage and Help You in Your Plans for a Good Job or in Your School Plans? A person engaged in a social system characterized by the "we" feeling of integration and solidarity demanded by the ideal primary group will subordinate to some significant extent his own interests to those of the other members of the group and will in turn feel supported by their encouragement and assistance. Group integration has been defined in operational terms as "the degree to which units of a social system are oriented toward optimizing rewards for other units of the system."[8]

It was hypothesized that the dropouts would perceive themselves as receiving less encouragement from their families in their educational and occupational plans than the graduates would perceive. As indicated in Table 2, this hypothesis was validated, but there were some surprises. Four out of ten of the graduates (30% + 11%) felt that their families had given them "very little" or "little" encouragement in their educational plans. As they perceived the situation, their academic success was due all but completely to their own efforts and not to their family's assistance.

TABLE 2. Family Encouragement of Their Teen-agers' Educational and Occupational Plans (In Percentages)

	Very Little	Little	Moderate	Much	Very Much	Too Much
Dropouts	31	18	16	16	1	18
Graduates	30	11	14	43	1	2[a]

[a] N = 300 (150 dropouts, 150 graduates). Hypothesis: Dropouts perceive themselves as receiving less encouragement from their families in their educational and occupational plans than graduates perceive. D = .268; χ^2(2df) = 23.08; p < .001.

Less surprising was the finding that nine times as many dropouts as graduates (18% vs. 2%) felt that their parents pushed "too much" by pressuring and nagging them. When a teen-ager is doing poorly in his school work, both he and his parents become sensitized and vulnerable, and adjust to the situation by various defensive and offensive techniques that prove exacerbating to all parties involved.

The youths' responses to the four questions concerning the first criterion of a primary group—personal acceptance—lead to the conclusion that in four out of five cases, the climates of the families of dropouts and stay-ins are at opposite poles of the acceptance-rejection continuum.

II. *Depth of Intercommunication*

Questioning respondents concerning their families' verbal communication patterns within their homes proved to be a fruitful source of affect-laden responses that sharply discriminated the perceived milieu of the family of the dropout from that of the graduate.

Does Your Family Talk Things Over with Each Other Very Often? Dropout Carole H., I.Q. 102, of Denver, replied,

No. Never! We all go our own ways. It's a family but I can't sit down and talk to my father about what I should do. And my brother and I don't even speak. There is no real companionship.

Graduate John D., I.Q. 93, of New Orleans, said,

Yes. . . . Lately my father talks with me and tells me why he wants me to go to college—why he and my mother definitely want me to try. And explains how it was for him. He quit when he was young and he works for the city—sanitation department. He had a heart attack about three years ago and now he is a watchman for them and I believe he makes only about $65.00 a week. He says there is no advancement for him. He wants me to get a good job . . . and there is one boy I run around with and he wants to go to college with me, and my girl wants me to go to college too.

The differences of family background between the dropout and graduate in intrafamily communication can be seen from the percentage distribution on a five-point scale (Table 3).

TABLE 3. Communication within the Home (In Percentages)

	Very Infrequent	Infrequent	Moderate	Frequent	Very Frequent
Dropouts	43	38	11	6	2
Graduates	3	17	20	24	36[a]

[a] $N = 300$ (150 dropouts, 150 graduates). Hypothesis: There is less intrafamily communication in the families of dropouts than in the families of graduates. $D = .633$; $\chi^2(2df) = 87.48$, $p < .001$.

The results of Table 3 are decisive: 81 percent ($43\% + 38\%$) of the dropouts receive their life's basic orientation in a nuclear family of inadequate intercommunication, and 80 percent ($20\% + 24\% + 36\%$) of the graduates receive their life's basic orientation in a nuclear family of at least adequate intercommunication.

III. *Pleasurable Experiences*

Closely allied to the level of verbal intercommunication within a family is its level of shared recreational activities. Enjoyment of each other's company in a variety of circumstances is the third characteristic of the primary group. A family that chooses to spend its leisure hours in each other's company manifests that antagonism and tension are not a staple of their relationships but rather that harmony and mutual enjoyment are.

Family and Leisure. In asking respondents, "If your *whole* family had some free time, how would they usually spend it?" the interest was not primarily in the type of leisure-time activities in which they indulged. General research has already established such data. The interest was rather in the frequency of intrafamilial recreational activities presumably indicative of the pleasure that the family experienced in being with each other under a variety of circumstances. Here are two typical replies:

Vivian M., I.Q. 100, of Omaha:

> We were all never together at one time. . . . My parents left at six in the morning and didn't get home until four. I just played hookey. . . . When I finally told them, they were sick about it but I had already signed myself out.

Patricia S., I.Q. 98, of New Orleans:

> We would all have dinner together and then maybe we would all go for a ride in the afternoon and maybe we would all go to a show that night or visit some of the relatives.

The over-all statistical picture of the 300 replies is perfectly clear in Table Four.

TABLE 4. FAMILY JOINT LEISURE SCALE (IN PERCENTAGES)

	Very Infrequently	Infrequently	Occasionally	Frequently	Very Frequently
Dropouts	53	26	13	6	2
Graduates	8	17	25	25	25[a]

[a] N = 300 (150 dropouts, 150 graduates). Hypothesis: Dropouts manifest less family joint leisure activity than graduates. D = .540; χ^2(2df) = 87.48, p < .001.

According to the perceptions of the youths, four out of five (79%) of the dropouts' families participate in leisure activities together either "very infrequently" or "infrequently." Three out of four (75%) of the graduates' families reportedly are accustomed to participation in such family activities.

IV. *Happiness Within the Home*

As a résumé of the differences between the family backgrounds of the dropouts and the graduates, all interviews were reviewed, and each was scored on the one variable of life-long family "happiness" as reported by the respondent.

To continue one's education beyond the obligatory date, which in all large U.S. cities is one's sixteenth birthday, means to retain one's dependent role upon one's parents at the very time that the teen-ager is striving to establish his identity as an independent agent. A youth in a less than pleasant home will have a bias to discontinue his abrasive dependence upon his family which the student role requires of him. A lower-class youth who does not experience in the domestic milieu that "state of well-being and pleasurable satisfaction" (the dictionary definition of "happiness") is not as likely to continue in his subordinate role as a domestic dependent but will more likely seek to terminate the dependence by making himself economically independent. A youth who is not having his basic needs of personal recognition, friendly intercommunication, and various pleasurable experiences realized within the family system will have to seek the satisfaction of these needs outside the family system. This will usually mean that he turns to the peer group. To the extent that this occurs, his commitment

TABLE 5. Happiness within the Home (In Percentages)

	Very Unhappy	Unhappy	Indifferent	Happy	Very Happy
Dropouts	35	27	25	10	3
Graduates	17	5	14	16	48[a]

[a] N = 300 (150 dropouts, 150 graduates). Hypothesis: The dropouts report their homes as being less happy than do the graduates. D = 4.2; $\chi^2 = 59.9$, p < .001.

to the family is minimized and to the peer group is maximized. That the family system is, within American culture, more characteristically pro-academic while the independent peer group culture is more characteristically anti-academic seems probable. A youth who is having long-term interpersonal problems in his home quite probably mirrors his troubled home situation in a troubled school situation. A seriously unhappy youth is more probably unable to be an academic achiever. This was the thinking behind summarizing the primary relations material in terms of "happiness."

To measure happiness within the home throughout the total life history of the respondent, this study uses the criterion of an ideal primary group. If the family has accepted each other as "total persons," if there has been a depth of intercommunication, and if there has been continued pleasure accruing from being with each other under a variety of circumstances, this family, in accord with the criteria of modern formulations, is considered to be both an ideal primary group and characterized by "happiness." Table 5 has been obtained by the three-member panel's evaluation of each of the 300 interviews and the registering of these valuations on a standard five-point scale.

The typical home of the dropout (35% + 27%) is reported as having been characteristically unhappy; the typical home of the graduate (16% + 48%) is reported as having been characteristically happy.

The homes of the youths interviewed were either in similar or identical neighborhoods. Externally, the homes appeared identical. Internally, there were on an average the same number of children, and by matched pairs the respondents were of the same age, the same sex, the same native ability, and had attended the same high schools. Yet the different climate of happiness in the homes of the dropouts as contrasted with the graduates is startling. Unhappiness is the characteristic of the one group, happiness that of the other.

SUMMARY AND INTERPRETATION

Each of the interview questions that reflected the climate of primary relations in the home distinguished the dropout from the graduate at the highest level of significance (.001). In the semantics of statistical tests, this means that the difference found between the two groups could not have happened once in a thousand times by chance.

Previous studies have noted that the family backgrounds of dropouts generally differ from those of graduates. The present study reconfirms this common observation but has gone a step further by specifying exactly how the domestic environment of the lower-class academic achievers differs from that of the non-achievers. It remains to point out the link between socialization in a home where primary relationships are dominant and success in the school context.

Every successful student needs three prerequisites. First, he needs a strong self-image that is the product of being accepted as a worthwhile person and of various success experiences. This self-image of personal worth insures the child that he is wanted and induces a feeling that he can succeed in a task undertaken. Secondly, the successful pupil needs the intellectual alertness, the vocabulary, and the reading potentials that only extensive intercommunication with sympathetic confidants can readily supply. Third, the advantaged young scholar needs to derive pleasure from team work, competition, and the discipline inherent in orderly social interaction. The import of this study is that these academic prerequisites are more readily acquired by the child who has been brought up in a family that is a primary group.

Registration on the first day of school does not bring these school readiness patterns to the six-year-old. The Gluecks maintain that the potential delinquent can be spotted with a 90 percent predictive reliability when he is six years old by an analysis of his family's patterns of affection, discipline, and solidarity.[9] The present conclusion suggests that the same predictive reliability of school success or failure could be made of a child of average I.Q. on the first day of school by analysis of the prevalence or absence of primary relations in his family background.

Many variables in addition to family background are highly significant in their impact upon premature withdrawal from the school process. I.Q., income, class affiliation, peer pressures, school experiences, and occupational orientations are but a few that can be mentioned. But no matter what other variables are at work, the nuclear family is of critical import. A law of polarization is evidence in the teen-age world today. The dropout is generally the product of a family deficient in primary relations. This study of a matched lower-class population indicates that the family which nurtured the youth who did not continue his education is of a different caliber than that which produced the teen-ager who continued his education at least to high school graduation.

NOTES AND REFERENCES

1. The research was subsidized by the Warren Benevolent Fund of Boston and directed by the author. Grace Husted was co-author of the research design and with Daniel Frank assisted with the interviewing. Advice on sample design and statistical problems was obtained from the Director of the Bureau of Institutional Research of Saint Louis University, Oliver Anderhalter. Joseph B. Ford of San Fernando Valley State College and Carle C. Zimmerman of Harvard University generously participated in interviews with resource persons. The interviews with teen-agers were conducted from January to May 1961. Mary Ann Bruce provided editorial and rewrite assistance. A more comprehensive treatment of the dropout problem is found in the author's *The Dropout: Causes and Cures,* Ann Arbor: U. of Michigan Press, 1965.
2. *The Two Major Works of Charles H. Cooley,* Glencoe, Ill.: Free Press, 1956, p. 23.
3. Leonard Broom and Philip Selznick, *Sociology,* New York: Harper and Row, 3rd Ed., 1964, pp. 135–170.
4. Cooley, *op. cit.,* p. 23.
5. In testing the hypotheses of this report for statistical significance, the Kolmogorov-Smirnov two-sample, one-tailed test is used. Cf. Sidney Siegel, *Nonparametric Statistics,* New York: McGraw-Hill, 1956, p. 127 ff. Because of the inadequacies of the "matching" of dropouts and graduates on I.Q. and socio-economic backgrounds, the nonparametric test for nonrelated data was used rather than the parametric test for related data. The use by different school administrations of different types of I.Q. tests and the inability to ascertain accurately some items of socio-economic background counseled this procedure. The resulting conclusions are therefore more conservative than would have resulted from the use of a parametric of significance.
6. Hypothesis: Dropouts perceive themselves as less understood and accepted by their families than do graduates. $D = .633$; $\chi^2(2df) = 120.2$, $p < .001$.
7. $D = .614$; $\chi^2(2df) = 113.09$, $p < .001$.
8. Robert L. Hamblin, "Group Integration During a Crisis," *Human Relations,* XI (November 1958), pp. 67–76; cf. Everett M. Rogers and Hans Sebald, "A Distinction between Familism, Family Integration and Kinship Orientation," *Marriage and Family Living,* XXIV (February 1962), pp. 25–30.
9. Eleanor T. Glueck, "Spotting Juvenile Delinquents: Can It Be Done?" *Federal Probation,* XX (September 1956), pp. 7–13. Sheldon Glueck, "Defense of the Glueck Social Prediction Table," in *The Sociology of Punishment and Correction,* ed. by Norman Johnson, Leonard Savitz, and Marvin E. Wolfgang, New York: John Wiley, 1960, pp. 265–272.

45.

Career and family orientations of husbands and wives in relation to marital happiness[1]

LOTTE BAILYN

Traditionally it has been held that a woman's place is in the home and a mother's place is with her children. But the gadget-emancipated house-wife with two children cannot be considered in the same manner as her early century, rural counterpart who raised several youngsters, did the washing and dishes by hand, and still found time to tend the garden. Now almost one-third of all women are employed outside the home and a sizeable portion of the nation's work force is female. Many studies, quite justifiably, have been made on the effect on children of the mother's working. We think that Bailyn's study about husband-wife interaction is, if anything, more justifiable than studying children's be-havior in relation to women's working. But this contention is based on a thesis that all might not accept; i.e., husband-wife felicitousness is the most important factor in salutary parenthood.

The editors concur with the postulation that child behavior is not a straight cause-effect relationship of maternal attitude and action. It would be more precise to conclude that the mother's behavior was at least in part an outcome of the child's responses and behavioral style (see selection 22). Hence, in the study of marriage and the wife's work-ing outside the home, it seems consistent to recognize the contingent effect of the husband's attitudes and behavioral style. This is the pattern of interaction Bailyn has studied and upon which she reports in this article.

THE ROLE of the educated married woman has been the subject of much debate in the past few decades. People concerned with the economy and the professions have urged trained women with families to enter the labor market—and women have responded, though their participation in the highest job levels is still limited (Fogarty, Rapoport, & Rapoport, 1967; Rendel, 1968). Some family experts, on the other hand, have warned about the possible disintegration of the family that would result if women forsook their traditional roles, though research findings, on the whole, have not supported this fear (Goode, 1963; Nye & Hoffman, 1963).

Both research and ideological pronouncements, however, have dealt almost exclusively with the life situation of the woman: with the complica-

Human Relations, 23(No. 2):97–113, April, 1970. Lotte Bailyn, Research Associate, Education Research Center, Massachusetts Institute of Technology.

tions and rewards she faces in trying to combine family and work. And though the importance of the husband is always assumed, little systematic attention has been given to the interplay between the chosen life style of an educated woman and that of her husband. Only recently have some writers begun to analyze the process by which men achieve an integration of family and their own work, and there has virtually been no study relating to married women's work patterns that deals simultaneously with husbands and wives.[2]

The hypothesis under investigation in this paper is that an educated, married woman's resolution of the 'career-family' dilemma cannot be adequately evaluated without knowledge of her husband's resolution—of the way he fits his work and his family into his life. In particular, it deals with the patterns that result when husbands with varying orientations to their families and their careers are combined with wives who also differ on this dimension, and it evaluates the different combinations by the degree of marital happiness associated with each.[3] The investigation is based on data from some two hundred British women, all university graduates of the year 1960, and from their husbands.[4]

HUSBAND'S ORIENTATION

It is assumed in our society that every man will spend a major portion of his time and energy on his work; and, indeed, every husband in the sample does so.[5] Yet the degree of men's involvement with their occupation varies greatly. Moore (1969) distinguishes between two approaches to work: *conditioning* (implying a reluctant adjustment to a harsh reality) or *commitment* (enthusiastic acceptance of pleasurable duties' p. 868). Masih (1967) identifies career-saliency as a dimension along which people vary and defines it as consisting of three elements: 'a) the degree to which a person is career motivated, b) the degree to which an occupation is important as a source of satisfaction, and c) the degree of priority ascribed to occupation among other sources of satisfaction' (pp. 653–4). Similar distinctions exist in the extent to which a married man's satisfactions are determined by his family, and it is the relative weight of these two potential sources of satisfaction—career and family—that is used to differentiate the husbands in the sample.

The specific measure is based on the following questions:

(a) Which of the following gives you the most satisfaction in your life?

(b) Which gives you the next greatest satisfaction?

Your career or occupation

Family relationships

Leisure time recreational activities

Religious beliefs or activities

Participation as a citizen in affairs of your community

Participation in activities directed towards
  national or international betterment

Running a home

Other

Over half of the husbands (58 percent) indicated that they derived most satisfaction from their families; a little over one fourth (27 percent) said their careers were most satisfying; only 14 men, a mere 6 percent of the

TABLE 1. HUSBANDS' SOURCES OF SATISFACTION

Mentioned as source of satisfaction:		*No.*	%		
Only Family		51	23		Family-oriented
1st choice		40	18		
2nd choice		11	5		
	140				
Both Family and Career					
Family first		89	41		
Career first		50	23		Career-oriented
Only Career		20	9		
1st choice	70	11		5	
2nd choice		9		4	
Neither Career nor Family		7	3		
TOTAL		217[a]	99		

[a]—6 men who did not answer this question at all were eliminated from the analysis.

sample, checked the third most frequent choice—leisure time recreational activities. Further, over two thirds (69 percent) of those whose greatest satisfaction comes from their families gave career as the source of their next greatest satisfaction, and over four fifths (82 percent) of those listing career first chose family as second. All in all, as may be seen in *Table 1,* only seven men did not mention either career or family as a source of great satisfaction for them.[6]

The 210 men who did mention career or family or both as sources of satisfaction in their lives, may be divided according to their primary emphasis, as indicated in *Table 1.* The 140 whose family relationships are their sole or greatest source of satisfaction comprise the group that is family-oriented; the 70 whose satisfactions stem more from their careers are considered career-oriented, a ratio of 2:1 in favor of the family.

The group of husbands as a whole, then, has a strong family emphasis. All are married and 88 percent either had children or were expecting their first child at the time they filled in their questionnaires, and both marriage and children increase the likelihood of men listing family relationships as their main source of satisfaction in life [Fogarty, Rapoport, & Rapoport, 1970 (in press), ch. V]. Further, this group of men all became part of the sample by being willing to answer a 'spouse questionnaire' for a study in which their wives, as 1960 university graduates, were the primary targets. This means that their family relations were close enough for them to cooperate with their wives in a joint venture, which, in itself, probably preselects those who are more oriented to their families. Also, not all of these men are university graduates themselves; on the contrary, almost one fourth of these husbands of university graduates had themselves not graduated from university and these tend to emphasize family more than do their counterparts who did graduate from university and who show a greater commitment to occupation.[7]

Still, both orientations are present in the sample: there are those whose primary emphasis is on their careers and those who emphasize their families more. The distinction is embedded in many aspects of a man's life; it cannot be isolated from his other attitudes or life experiences. Masih (1967) found that one of the main differences between male students whose careers were very salient for them and those for whom this was not the case, was the former group's lesser interest in interaction with the opposite sex and greater desire for 'enduring' long periods of work. In relation to a job, the 'high-saliency' group showed less concern about the security of steady work than did the group whose careers were less salient. In the present sample, too, such distinctions exist. The man whose primary emphasis is on his family is more concerned with human contact in the realm of work; the career-oriented men, in contrast, emphasize intellectual fulfillment more.[8] The latter group is more ambitious: 63 percent of the men whose primary emphasis is on their careers, as opposed to 49 percent of those more oriented to their families, fall into the ambitious category.[9]

These, then, are some of the characteristics that differentiate career-oriented from family-oriented men. They are obviously relevant to what happens when these men marry wives who differ in the degree to which they incorporate work into their lives.

WIFE'S ORIENTATION

The diversity of educated women's lives makes it particularly difficult to find a meaningful way of describing their career orientation at an early stage in their family life.[10] For the men in the sample, all of whom are married and working and, presumably, expecting to continue this double pattern, the relative contribution of these two realms to their satisfactions in life is a meaningful way of assessing career-family orientation. But these conditions do not hold for the women.[11] As has already been indicated, 88 percent of the wives in the sample either had children or were expecting their first child. And, only eight years after their graduation, the children were young: 83 percent of the families with children had at least one child under three. Thus, the pull of the traditional expectation that mothers of small children stay home must have been quite strong for these women.

Nonetheless, at the time of filling in the questionnaire, 46 percent of the wives were engaged in work for which they were paid, though only 15 percent were working more than 30 hours per week, and most of these (73 percent) were recruited from the small group without children. But, by itself, the fact of working is not a good indicator of career orientation. At any given moment in their lives, some wives who are working are doing so only out of necessity, waiting perhaps for circumstances to arise that would allow them to stop, and, conversely, some who are not working wish they could. In our sample, 45 percent of the non-working wives are not satisfied with their 'unemployed' state; and, among the sub-sample who are engaged in gainful work, fully 40 percent say specifically that they are *not* in favor of married women engaged in a career—of having any long-range occupational commitments.[12]

And even anticipated future work patterns—though not subject to these forces of the immediate situation—are not as good a measure of career commitment as one might wish. In the present state of flux in women's roles, the difficulties involved in any chosen style—and all paths have their difficulties—may lead one to view an opposing style as un-realistically attractive.[13] There is evidence, for instance, for the existence of what might be called the 'traditional dream'—an expectation on the part of married women that having children will make family life all-fulfilling for them. That this anticipation is not always met in reality is attested to by the fact that over one third (36 percent) of the wives with children expect to be working more or less continuously, even when their youngest child is under three, as contrasted with only 19 percent of the married women who have not yet had their first child.

If, then, one is interested in a women's career commitment at an early stage in her family life, it is necessary to find a way of gauging it that is as little contaminated as possible by the specific circumstances she finds herself in at that time, or by unrealistic expectations of the future—whether these take the form of a traditional or of a 'pioneering' dream.

The measure chosen, which seems to meet these requirements, is based on two elements: whether or not a woman is generally—abstractly—in favor of married women having a career, and whether or not she herself gets personal satisfaction from her career or occupation. The first element is measured by a question that asked everyone in the sample to give his attitude 'to married women engaging in a career (i.e., in which there is a long-term occupational commitment).' Forty-five percent ($N = 101$) of the wives indicated they were 'in favor'; 29 percent (N = 64) were 'mixed or neutral'; and 26 percent (N = 58) were 'against' married women engaging in a career. The second element—the satisfaction a woman derives from pursuing such an activity—is based on the same question that was used to determine the men's career orientation. But because of the preponderance of family and other home-oriented responses among the women, the answers were categorized differently. All the women who mentioned career as either their first (only 15 did so) or next greatest source of satisfaction in life were considered career-satisfied: 30 percent of the sample (67 people) fell into this group.

TABLE 2. Wives' Career Orientations

| Sources of Major Satisfaction:[b] | Attitude to Married Women Having a Career:[a] | |
	In Favor	Not in Favor
Career Mentioned	Integrated N = 45	Mixed (work-oriented) N = 22
Career Not Mentioned	Mixed (ideologically committed) N = 56	Traditional N = 99

	N	%
Integrated	45	20
Mixed	78	35
Traditional	99	45
TOTAL	222	100

a—3 wives who did not answer this question are classified as 'not in favor.'
b—1 woman who did not answer this question is eliminated from the table.

The measure of career orientation among the wives is derived from the relation between these two elements, as indicated in *Table 2*. Those 45 women (20 percent of the sample), who are in favor of married women pursuing careers and who themselves get satisfaction from their own career activities, we have called *integrated,* to indicate a predisposition to integrate a career with their family life. Those 99 women, on the other hand—almost half of the sample—who are not in favor of married women engaging in occupations requiring a long-term commitment and whose satisfactions do not depend on work outside the family, comprise the *traditional* group, the group subscribing to the conventional pattern for women. In between is a mixed group, consisting mainly of wives who favor women having careers but for whom a career or occupation is not personally a major source of satisfaction, as well as a small group (10 percent of the sample) who do get satisfaction from work even though ideologically they are not in favor of married women pursuing careers.

Thus there is a similar tendency among the women to that of the men: the ratio of traditional to career-integrated wives is just about the same (2:1) as the ratio of family-oriented men to career-oriented men. It is important, however, not to equate traditional wives with family-oriented men. Rather, by the definition of our measures as well as by the forces working in society today, it is the wives who integrate a career with their family responsibilities, whose style of life is more analogous to that of family-oriented men, i.e., those men who add to their traditional concerns with a career, a primary emphasis on their families. Both career-integrated wives and family-oriented husbands have forsaken the expected concentration of their sex on only one of these two realms; both have added to their traditional concerns an emphasis on the realm most commonly associated with the other sex.

These analogies are based, of course, on the presumption that a woman's career orientation will bear some relation to the actual career pattern she will follow in her life. There is evidence that indicates this to be likely: nearly all (88 percent) of the wives in the career-integrated group were working at the time of the questionnaire; and, over three fifths (61 percent) were planning to work more or less continuously, even when their youngest child was under three (a plan held by only a quarter of the other wives in the sample). The career-integrated wives, thus, are recruited primarily from those who are now working and are satisfied with this work, who feel it is proper for married women to have a career, and who themselves plan to continue to include work as part of their life styles. And this work is an addition to, not a substitute for, a family. These wives are already married and only two do not plan to have any children (out of a total of five in the whole sample). But they do seem more likely to limit the size of their families: only 32 percent plan to have more than two children; more than half of the other wives have this plan (61 percent of the traditionally-oriented wives hope for three or more children).

COUPLES' PATTERNS

When, now, the orientations of husbands are combined with those of their wives, 209 couples emerge whose distribution among the various patterns is given in *Table 3*. As the table shows, there is hardly any relation between husbands' and wives' orientations: career-oriented men are no more likely to marry traditional wives than are those whose emphasis is more on their families; nor do women who hope to integrate a career with their family lives show any preference for either family or career orientation in the men they marry. Clearly, career-family orientation is not a salient dimension when marriage decisions are made. Though such a state of affairs may not be optimal from the point of view of the individual marriage (and it sometimes is not, as will be seen), from the point of view of this study it is very useful since it permits one to investigate the different combinations of career orientations without too much concern for the possible effect of other related factors.

As was mentioned at the start, this paper is concerned with the extent of marital happiness associated with these different patterns. The following

TABLE 3. DISTRIBUTION OF COUPLE PATTERNS (NUMBER OF PEOPLE IN EACH COMBINATION)

Wife's Career Orientation:	Husband's Career-Family Orientation	
	Emphasis on Family	Emphasis on Career
Traditional	60 [64]^a (29%)	35 [31] (17%)
Mixed	53 [48] (25%)	19 [24] (9%)
Integrated	27 [28] (13%)	15 [14] (7%)
	N = 209^b (100%)	

a—Numbers in brackets indicate the frequencies expected in each cell if the two orientations are independent of each other: $\chi^2 = 2.75$, P = .25.
b—This number represents the number of men who could be classified by their career-family orientation (210, see *Table 1*) minus the one wife whose orientation to her career is unknown.

question, which was asked of every person in the sample, is used as the basis for classifying couples according to marital happiness:[14]

Taking things together, how do you really feel about your marriage?

Very happy
Pretty happy
Sometimes happy, sometimes unhappy
Not very happy
Unhappy

Sixty-one percent of the wives and 61 percent of the husbands stated that they were 'very happy' with their marriages; 25 percent and 28 percent, respectively, indicated that their marriages were 'pretty happy'; no wife said that her marriage was less than 'sometimes happy, sometimes unhappy,' though four husbands did. Not all couples agreed on the degree of their marital satisfaction: 13 percent of the husbands indicated a greater degree of happiness than did their wives; 12 percent of the wives rated themselves happier. Since consensus is a better way of characterizing a couple than is one partner's perception alone, only marriages in which *both* partners said that they were 'very happy' are classified as happy.[15] Fifty-five percent of the couples fall into this category.

It is obvious from *Table 4*—which indicates the marital happiness associated with each of the various combinations of career orientation—that one pattern stands out from all the others: marriages of men whose exclusive or primary emphasis is on their careers to women who themselves place store on integrating a career with their family lives are not very happy. As a matter of fact, the number of couples in this group who describe their marriages as 'very happy' is so low that it is not possible, with

TABLE 4. Couple Patterns and Marital Happiness (% of Couples with Very Happy Marriages)

	Husband's Career-Family Orientation	
	Emphasis on Family	Emphasis on Career
Wife's Orientation:		
		Conventional Pattern
Traditional	62% (N = 60)	54% (N = 35)
Mixed	62% (N = 53)	53% (N = 19)
Integrated	56% (N = 27)	13% (N = 15)
	Co-ordinate Pattern	

the present sample, to investigate the conditions that contribute to or might ease the strains of this pattern. It should be mentioned, however, that neither of the two couples of this pattern whose marriages are very happy has children; it should also be said that both husbands are in favor of married women having a career,[16] and both are very satisfied with their own work. It seems, then, that under special conditions this pattern can be accompanied by a happy marriage, but the conditions are rare in this sample.

All the other combinations in *Table 4* seem to be associated with about the same degree of marital happiness: between one half and two thirds of the marriages in each group are very satisfactory to both partners. In discussing the conditions that facilitate these successes, we shall emphasize two patterns: the conventional pattern (upper right cell of *Table 4*) and the co-ordinate pattern (lower left). Traditional wives married to career-oriented husbands represent the pattern, here called conventional, in which family roles are probably most differentiated by sex, with the man primarily oriented to his career and his wife primarily to the home. In contrast, it seems likely that the least differentiation of roles along traditionally accepted sex-linked lines occurs in the marriages of career-integrated wives to men who, though involved in a career, place primary emphasis on their families—the couples of the co-ordinate pattern.[17]

Table 5, which gives the basic data for this discussion, also includes information on the upper left cell of *Table 4,* in which traditional wives are paired with family-oriented husbands. This combination has the wife's orientation in common with the conventional pattern and the husband's orientation in common with the co-ordinate one. It thus allows one to make inferences as to the relative influence of each partner's orientation on the success of the contrasting family styles.

Conventional Pattern

According to prevailing social expectations, the conventional pattern would not seem to require any particular justification. But when one considers the separation of interests it implies, with the husband primarily concerned with his work and the wife with the house and family, it becomes less obvious why such a pattern is assumed to be such a satisfactory one. It is not altogether surprising, therefore, that marital happiness is increased under conditions that minimize the built-in separation of interests of this pattern. A look at the first column of *Table 5*[18] shows that the more children conventional couples have, the less likely they are to have very happy marriages (item 1). More children, by increasing the care and time necessary to meet the needs of the family, would seem to exaggerate the differentiation of roles in a pattern in which the family is the more or less exclusive concern of one partner. Moreover, item 2 shows that the proportion of happy marriages declines the more satisfied the husband in this pattern is with his present work situation. Such an increase in satisfaction, by adding strong motivational support to the husband's primary concern with his work, would also seem to exaggerate the differentiation of roles implicit in the pattern. Finally, the conventional pattern is the only one in which marital satisfaction is greater when the fields of husband and wife overlap (item 3). Such a common interest seems particularly important for the success of a pattern based on rather strict differentiation of roles.

Table 5 also shows that the conventional pattern is the only one in which marital happiness is negatively associated with income—in which there is a larger percentage of happy marriages when income is low than when it is high (item 4). Further analysis shows this to be particularly true when the husband's ambition is low. Under this condition, only 17 percent of those with high incomes have very happy marriages, as compared with 71 percent of those whose incomes are low. In other words, marital happiness is very low indeed if the husband in a conventional couple combines low ambition with high income. In this situation he has, perhaps, the least justification for his primary emphasis on career, since it is based

TABLE 5. Factors Associated with Marital Happiness for Different Couple Patterns (% of Couples with Very Happy Marriages)

	Conventional		Co-ordinate
	COUPLE PATTERNS		
Husband's Primary Emphasis: *Wife's Career Orientation:*	*career* *traditional* (N = 35)	*family* *traditional* (N = 60)	*family* *integrated* (N = 27)
1. Number of Children:	%	%	%
none (N = 33)[a]	67 (N = 9)	[100 (N = 3)][b]	50 (N = 6)
one (N = 41)	63 (N = 8)	64 (N = 14)	[75 (N = 4)]
two (N = 101)	47 (N = 15)	52 (N = 29)	53 (N = 15)
three or more (N = 34)	[33 (N = 31)]	71 (N = 14)	[50 (N = 2)]
2. Husband's Feelings About his Present Work Situation:[c]			
extremely satis-fied (N = 51)	43 (N = 7)	78 (N = 18)	[100 (N = 4)]
somewhat satis-fied (N = 115)	55 (N = 22)	65 (N = 31)	53 (N = 15)
neutral or dissatis-fied (N = 39)	67 (N = 6)	22 (N = 9)	29 (N = 7)
3. Relation of Own Spouse's Field of Work:[d]			
overlapping (N = 97)	67 (N = 18)	53 (N = 30)	57 (N = 14)
distinct (N = 100)	41 (N = 17)	69 (N = 29)	58 (N = 12)
4. Husband's Income:			
high (>£2000/year) (N = 75)	36 (N = 14)	77 (N = 22)	70 (N = 10)
low (≤£2000/year) (N = 128)	67 (N = 21)	57 (N = 35)	44 (N = 16)
Mother's Work Status While Growing Up:			
5. wife's mother did not work (N = 93)	62 (N = 16)	71 (N = 31)	62 (N = 8)
wife's mother did work (N = 114)	47 (N = 19)	56 (N = 27)	53 (N = 19)
6. husband's mother did not work (N = 85)	33 (N = 12)	62 (N = 32)	83 (N = 6)
husband's mother did work (N = 124)	65 (N = 23)	61 (N = 28)	48 (N = 21)
7. Dominant Values of Social Circle:[e]			
intellectual, academic (N = 95)	71 (N = 14)	67 (N = 21)	58 (N = 19)
suburban (N = 110)	46 (N = 24)	65 (N = 40)	62 (N = 8)
8. Attitude of Social Circle to Women Working:[f]			
same opportunities as men (N = 46)	[25 (N = 4)]	58 (N = 12)	56 (N = 9)
women's work secondary to home and family			

Table 5—*Continued*

obligations (N = 111)	50 (N = 24)	70 (N = 30)	58 (N = 12)
very mixed feelings (N = 44)	83 (N = 6)	53 (N = 15)	50 (N = 6)
9. Division of Labor in Household (supervision and care of children; shopping for food):[g]			
only wife usually does it (N = 102)	61 (N = 18)	55 (N = 29)	43 (N = 14)
wife has some help (N = 104)	44 (N = 16)	67 (N = 30)	69 (N = 13)

a. Numbers in parentheses indicate the number in the given category in the sample. They do not always add up to 209 because No Answers have been eliminated.

b. Percentages in brackets are based on very small N's.

c. In general, how do you feel about your present work situation? (If you are not working, indicate your feelings about being unemployed.)

Extremely satisfied   Somewhat dissatisfied
Somewhat satisfied   Extremely dissatisfied
Neutral

The last 3 categories are combined.

d. Do you consider that your own field of work and your spouse's field of work outside the home are:

Very close and similar to one another
Overlapping to some extent, but with major areas of difference
Quite distinct from one another

The first 2 categories are combined. Couples are classified on the basis of information from the wife.

e. Looking at your social circle as a whole, how would you characterize their main values or interests?

a. Suburban (emphasis on home, garden, kids, community etc.)
b. Intellectual, academic
A dominant value or characteristic
A secondary characteristic
Not a characteristic

N's represent the number of people who said the given factor was 'a dominant value or characteristic.' Some may have given this response to both of the listed factors. Couples are classified on the basis of information from the wife.

f. Looking at your social circle as a whole, how would you describe their attitude to women working?

i. Most people feel that women ought to have same opportunity to pursue an important career as men
ii. Most feel that women ought to be able to work a bit but not so as to allow it to interfere with home and family obligations
iii. Women ought not to work ouside the home
Very mixed feelings (some feel like *i*, some feel like *ii*, some like *iii*)

Categories *ii* and *iii* have been combined. Couples are classified on the basis of information from the wife.

g. Who usually does each of these things in your household?

a. Supervision and care of children
b. Shopping for food
Husband
Wife
Both
Domestic help
No-one in household

Those who responded 'wife' to *both* of these areas are compared to all the rest. Couples are classified on the basis of information from the wife.

neither on his ambition nor on the need to make money.[19] Both of these—career ambition and need for family income—are traditionally accepted reasons for a husband's one-sided emphasis on his work; when neither is in force, the conventional pattern is not very successful.

That the conventional pattern is not automatically satisfactory but needs some justification is shown also by one other item in *Table 5*. Item 6 shows that a greater proportion of conventional marriages are happy if the husband's mother worked while he was growing up than if she did not work. That is, the pattern seems to be *less* satisfactory if it is 'conventional' as far as the husband's personal experience is concerned—if, that is, it is merely a continuation in his adult life of the traditional pattern in which he grew up; it is *more* satisfactory if it represents a new family style in the husband's experience and is not merely fulfilling a social and personal expectation.

Thus it seems that the conventional pattern, if it is to be associated with marital happiness, requires support from a number of directions: some common focus or justification seems to be necessary. Items 7 and 8 of *Table 5* show, further, that its success is also dependent on support from the social circle in which it functions. The proportion of happy, conventional marriages decreases when a dominant value of the couple's social circle is the suburban one with emphasis on home, garden, kids, community, etc. (item 7)—a value more in line with a family-centered pattern—and when 'most people [in the couple's social circle] feel that women ought to have the same opportunity to pursue an important career as men' (item 8)—an attitude more consistent with a less differentiated pattern of family life.

Co-ordinate Pattern

The kind of support necessary for the success of the co-ordinate pattern is quite different from that required by the conventional one. As items 7 and 8 of the last column in *Table 5* indicate, the attitudes and values of the couple's social circle are not associated with marital happiness in this case (though it is of interest that, compared to the sample as a whole, a large proportion of couples in this group describe their social circles as predominantly intellectual and as having an equalitarian attitude to women's careers). Nor does the community of interest represented by overlapping fields (item 3) relate to marital happiness of co-ordinate couples. Rather, the factors associated with happy co-ordinate marriages are more managerial ones, those that ease the physical burdens of integrating the realms of family and work. The proportion of happy marriages in this pattern is greater when the wife is not alone responsible for the care of the house and the children (item 9) and, perhaps not unrelated, when income is high (item 4).

It has previously been hypothesized that family-oriented men, like career-integrated women, are oriented to both work and family and seek satisfaction in both spheres, a similarity that should make the differentiation of roles in the co-ordinate pattern more dependent on the particular personal characteristics of the partners than on those prescribed by social expectations. It was suggested, in other words, that the co-ordinate pattern represents a true integration of the realms of family and work for both husband and wife and is in no way a mere reversal of traditional family roles. Evidence from *Table 5* supports this line of reasoning. In contrast to the conventional pattern, happiness of co-ordinate marriages increases as the husband's work satisfaction increases (item 2). Also, further analysis shows that the proportion of happy co-ordinate marriages is particularly great when high income is combined with high ambition of the husband: 83 percent of the couples have very happy marriages. Thus, the family-orientation of the husband whose co-ordinate marriage is successful is not a substitute for work; on the contrary, work is both important and satisfactory to such a man and his family emphasis is based on choice, not on default.[20]

In one respect, the conditions associated with marital happiness of the co-ordinate pattern are similar to those of the conventional one: in both cases, marital happiness is greater if the life style of the family is different from the one in which the husband grew up. Item 6 of *Table 5* shows that co-ordinate marriages are happier if the husband's mother did not work while he was growing up than if she did. Couple patterns that represent a personally new style for the husband are thus more likely to be happy, no matter what that style may be.

The fact that the wife's mother plays no such differentiating role[21] is a first indication, perhaps, of the relative importance of the husband's orientation as compared to that of his wife in determining the personal satisfaction associated with a particular family pattern. Further corroboration comes from a look at the second column of *Table 5*. Couples in this column, as was previously stated, share the wife's traditional orientation with conventional couples and the husband's family emphasis with co-ordinate ones. For almost every item in *Table 5*, the distribution of happy marriages in this middle column matches that of the third column—the co-ordinate pattern—more closely than it does the first one—the conventional pattern. It is the husband's orientation, therefore—which the middle and co-ordinate columns have in common—more than that of the wife, that is crucial for the effects we have discussed.

The data of this study thus corroborate the hypothesis, stated at the start, that a husband's mode of integrating family and work in his own life is crucial for the success—at least in terms of marital satisfaction—of any attempt of his wife to include a career in her life. There is evidence, as a matter of fact, that identifying the conditions under which men find it possible to give primary emphasis to their families while at the same time functioning satisfactorily in their own careers may be even more relevant to the problem of careers for married women than the continued emphasis on the difficulties women face in integrating family and work.

REFERENCES

Bailyn, L. (1965). Notes on the role of choice in the psychology of professional women. In: R. J. Lifton (ed.). *The woman in America.* Boston: Houghton Mifflin.

Blood, R. O., Jr. & Wolfe, D. M. (1960). *Husbands and wives: the dynamics of married living.* Glencoe, Ill.: Free Press.

Brim, O. (1968). Adult socialization. In: J. Clausen (ed.). *Socialization and society.* Boston: Little Brown.

Fogarty, M., Rapoport, R. & Rapoport, R. N., (1967). *Women and top jobs.* London: Political and Economic Planning (P.E.P.)

Fogarty, M., Rapoport, R. & Rapoport, R. N. (1970, in press). *Careers and families: sex roles and achievements.* London: Allen & Unwin.

Goode, W. J. (1963). *World revolution and family patterns.* Glencoe, Ill.: Free Press; London: Collier-Macmillan.

Masih, L. K. (1967). Career saliency and its relation to certain needs, interests, and job values. *Personnel & guidance j.* **45**, 653–8.

Moore, W. E. (1969). Occupational socialization. In: D. A. Goslin (ed.) *Handbook of socialization theory and research.* Chicago: Rand McNally.

Mulvey, M. C. (1963). Psychological and sociological factors in prediction of career patterns of women, *Genetic psych. mon.* **68**, 309–86.

Nye, F. I. & Hoffman, L. W. (1963). *The employed mother in America.* Chicago: Rand McNally.

Nye, F. I. & MacDougall, E. (1959). The dependent variable in marital research. *Pacific sociol. rev.* **2**, 67–70.

Orden, S. R. & Bradburn, N. M. (1968). Dimensions of marriage happiness. *Am. j. sociol.* **73**, 715–31.

Orden, S. R. & Bradburn, N. M. (1969). Working wives and marriage happiness. *Am. j. sociol.* **74**, 392–407.

Rapoport, R. N. & Rapoport, R. (1965). Work and family in contemporary society. *Am. sociol. rev.* **30**, 381–394.

Rapoport, R. & Rapoport, R. N. (1969). The dual-career family: a variant pattern and social change. *Hum. relat.* **22**, 3–30.

Rendel, M. *et al.* (1968). *Equality for women.* London: Fabian Society.

Rossi, A. S. (1965a). Equality between the sexes: an immodest proposal. In: R. J. Lifton (ed.). *The woman in America.* Boston: Houghton Mifflin.

Rossi, A. S. (1965b). Barriers to the career choice of engineering, medicine, or science among American women. In: J. A. Mattfield & C. G. Van Aken (eds.). *Women and the scientific professions: the M.I.T. Symposium on American women in science and engineering.* Cambridge, Mass.: M.I.T. Press.

Weil, M. W. (1961). An analysis of the factors influencing married women's actual or planned work participation. *Am. sociol. rev.* **26**, 91–6.

NOTES

1. This paper is part of a larger study of highly qualified women and their careers sponsored by The Leverhulme Trust in a grant to Political and Economic Planning (P.E.P.) under the direction of Michael Fogarty and Rhona Rapoport (P.E.P.) and Robert Rapoport (Tavistock Institute) London. The author worked with the Rapoports on their 'couples' data in 1969. The report on the overall study will appear in Fogarty, Rapoport & Rapoport (1970, in press). The data on which the present paper on couples is based come from a sample of British graduates questioned in 1968, eight years after finishing university. The sampling frame was provided by Professor R. Kelsall from a National Survey of 1960 Graduates directed by R. K. Kelsall, A. Poole and A. Moore. The data were collected by Research Services Ltd., and some of the analysis was done with the assistance of L. Hawkins of Survey Analysis Ltd., London, using his newly developed Conversational Mode Survey Analysis Program. Some of the items in the survey, upon which this paper is based, are drawn from a questionnaire designed by Alice Rossi in her study of university graduates (which was associated with James Davis' survey of graduates) conducted by The National Opinion Research Center, Chicago, Illinois. Thanks are due to all of the above mentioned, but the author is particularly grateful to the Rapoports for their help at all stages of the work for this paper.

2. For an analysis of the problems confronting the professional woman who tries to combine career and family see Bailyn (1965). Writers who have concerned themselves with the relation of family and work in men as well as women include Brim (1968), who feels that one focus in the study of adult socialization should be on 'the two-way process of influence between the world of work and the world of the family in their varying demands upon the adult' (p. 203); Alice Rossi (1965a), whose emphasis on 'the development of a more androgynous conception of sex role' (p. 130) underlies all her work in this field; and Rapoport & Rapoport (1965), who emphasize the integration of the two realms at various periods of transition in the life cycle, an emphasis that has guided much of their research, including the study on which this paper is based. Their investigation of the 'dual-career family' (Rapoport & Rapoport, 1969)—an arrangement 'in which both husband and wife pursue careers (i.e., jobs which are highly salient personally, have a developmental sequence and require a high degree of commitment) and at the same time establish a family life with at least one child' (p. 3)—is one of the few that analyzes the work and family roles of husbands and wives simultaneously. See also Blood & Wolfe (1960) for a discussion of the effects of the comparative work participation of husband and wife on various aspects of the husband-wife relationship, though, not untypically, this information comes from interviews with wives only.

3. Other terms of evaluation are also possible: in particular, one would want to know about the consequences of the various combinations for the character of work produced by the couple, whether by one or both partners. It is entirely possible that a combination that is fully satisfactory to the individual couple may not be the most creative in its contribution to society. An evaluation in terms of work would be related to such questions as the distribution of talent and the special needs of the most creative minds. In this paper, we limit the context of our evaluation to the family.

4. Full details of the total sample (which includes men and women graduates, both married and single) are available in Fogarty, Rapoport & Rapoport (1970, in press). Here it is only necessary to say that each of 449 married women in the sample who had agreed to cooperate with the survey received two lengthy identical questionnaires through the mail: one for themselves and one for their husbands. Of these 348 (78 percent) returned their own questionnaires; 223 (64 percent) of the husbands of this group of respondents also returned questionnaires. These 446 questionnaires (223 filled in by the women; 223 by their husbands) comprise the data on which this paper is based. The 223 married women whose husbands also responded, were compared on a number of items to those who only returned their own questionnaires. The only differences found were in the small group without children. In that group, the wives in the 'couples' sample show somewhat greater marital happiness, are somewhat more likely to be working at the present time, and also hope for somewhat fewer children. Thus the 'couples' wives—as compared to the total sample of married women—slightly over-represent the group of childless, working, happily married wives, who are not planning on large families. By far the larger proportion of the couples, however, already had children; and in this group the relevant distributions are very similar to the sample of married women as a whole. More differences, as will be seen below, exist between the spouses of these wives and the sample of married men university graduates.

5. The few characteristics of husbands that have been studied in relation to married women's careers include occupation and income, attitude to women's work, willingness to help with household tasks (e.g., Mulvey, 1963; Weil, 1961). But there has been no effort to explore the relevance of men's attitudes to their own work and the part played in their lives by career and family.

6. This response may reflect a transient family-work situation: four of these seven have no children, the husbands in these couples are generally not very satisfied with their present work situation, and a disproportionate number of wives in this group did not answer questions relating to their anticipated future work patterns.

7. 74 percent of the husbands who did not graduate from university are family-oriented as opposed to 64 percent of the university graduates. When compared to the married men in the target sample of university graduates, husbands in the 'couples' group are also somewhat more likely to have working wives and to approve of this arrangement.

8. Each person was asked to indicate which of a number of 'factors which contribute to their personal ideals for a career' he personally considered most important. Two of these related to people:

	% giving each response:	
	career-oriented (N = 70)	family-oriented (N = 140)
an opportunity to work with people rather than exclusively with things and ideas	13%	19%
an opportunity to be helpful to other people	4%	8%
Total People Responses	17%	27%

Three concerned intellectual fulfillment:

a chance to use intellectual problem solving abilities	24%	19%
an opportunity to show what I can accomplish	17%	7%
an opportunity to be creative	11%	8%
Total Intellectual Responses	52%	34%

9. Included in the ambitious category are those men who, when asked to 'characterize your level of ambition' at the present time, said they wanted 'to get to the top'; as well as those who wanted only 'to hold a high position' but who, on another question, rated themselves as 'very' or 'somewhat ambitious'; and, finally, five who did not answer the main question but who rated themselves as 'very ambitious.' It should be noted that this difference in ambition is limited to husbands whose incomes are rated low ($\leqslant £2000/$ year). The group that combines low income with low ambition—of which 74 percent are family-oriented—stands out in a number of ways: it contains more non-graduates than any other, and the men in this group who did graduate from university received less good degrees; they rated themselves as less assertive (based on self-ratings on three interrelated characteristics: 'competitive occupationally,' 'competitive socially,' and 'dominant') and were less satisfied with their intellectual abilities; they gave the fewest work-oriented responses when considering their ideal jobs and were least satisfied with their present work situations. Their family orientation is a part of this syndrome.

10. Obviously this is not true if one can study women at a stage of their lives late enough to allow classification according to the actual work patterns they have followed. The problem here is to get a measure that can be presumed to be a fairly good predictor of these patterns.

11. Masih (1967), for instance, found that judges had much more trouble classifying female students according to the degree of their career-saliency than they had with men.

12. Not all of these 40 percent, of course, actually dislike working. We shall see later that some wives are ideologically against married women having long-range career plans but actually get a great deal of satisfaction from their own work. Orden & Bradburn (1969), who asked their married women respondents whether they would work if they didn't need the money, found that only 23 percent of their college graduates answered negatively (*Table 3*, p. 398).

13. Alice Rossi (1965b) indicates the way experience tempers the expectations of the women college graduates she studied:

. . . the pioneers [women whose long-range goals are in heavily masculine fields such as natural sciences, medicine, economics] had romantic notions concerning careers and work which the reality of advanced study and employment temper, and the homemakers [women with no career goal other than being 'housewives'] had romantic notions concerning marriage and family roles which the reality of marriage and motherhood tempers (p. 81).

14. Obviously we are not suggesting that all the meaningful aspects of a marriage can be represented by a global question on professed marital happiness. Yet, there is evidence that such a question correlates sufficiently well with more refined ways of measuring success in marriage to make it a useful indi-

cator for our purposes. In the present questionnaire the global question followed two others concerning the marital relationship: how well the respondent felt he was doing as a husband or wife and whether he ever felt he had married the wrong kind of person. Andrew Bebbington developed an index of marital satisfaction based on all three questions as well as on a measure of conflict based on the number of disagreements the couples had on a variety of subjects. Of all the items involved, the question used here had the highest correlation with the resulting index. Similarly, in a study of married women, Nye & MacDougall (1959, as presented in Nye & Hoffman, 1963, pp. 270–1) found that a global question on marital happiness along with questions on arguments and quarrels and on actual or contemplated separation met the Guttman criteria of scalability, hence, presumably, they all reflect a single dimension of marital success. In a more refined analysis of marriage happiness, based on data from married men and women (though not on couples), Orden & Bradburn (1968) develop a two-dimensional model of marriage adjustment: one dimension is positive, relating to the satisfactions—both the sociability and the companionship that husbands and wives share—of marriage; the other is negative, and concerns the tensions in marriage. The two aspects are independent of each other, yet they relate in the expected direction to a person's self-ratings of marital happiness. In comparing their Marriage Adjustment Balance Scale, which is based on the difference of the scores on the two dimensions, to self-ratings of marital happiness, they conclude that there is little to choose between the two approaches if one's interest is in a summary measure of marital happiness, though the MABS has the advantage of allowing one to consider its components separately.

15. These distributions are very close to those of a number of other surveys which have asked for self-ratings on marital happiness, ratings which have been found to be very stable over time; further, other studies have found that the validity of self-ratings is increased when they are checked by those of the spouse (Orden & Bradburn, 1968).

16. It is of interest that this is the *only* pattern whose success is at all dependent on the husband's attitude toward careers for married women. Most of the studies that have shown this factor to be important were based on a woman's assessment of her husband's attitude (e.g. Weil, 1961). In our sample, where we know the wife's perception of her husband's attitude as well as his actual views, we find that 69 percent of the wives gauge their husbands accurately—match, on a three-point scale, his stated view. With a 30 percent error of assessment, it is possible that the correlations found in previous studies reflect a woman's rationalization and justification of her behavior as much as they do the actual influence of her husband's attitude.

17. Rapoport & Rapoport (1969) in their investigation of the 'dual-career family' chose couples in which both partners had a career—couples who, in our terms, could fit into either of the bottom two cells of *Table 4*. Yet, 'with the exception of one of the couples studied, family life in general and children in particular were highly salient' (p. 9). Thus, their couples seem to represent the pattern we have called co-ordinate. Other people have also investigated the marital adjustment of employed married women (see e.g. Orden & Bradburn, 1969). But the large difference between the degree of marital happiness associated with the bottom two cells of *Table 4* makes it difficult to compare their results with ours.

18. In this discussion, we shall only refer to factors that make at least a 25 percent difference in marital happiness. The proportion of happy marriages is

about .5 in the groups under consideration. Under this condition, the probability of getting as large a difference as .25 or more is approximately .05 for
equal samples of n = 30.

19. The direction of causality here is by no means clear. It is entirely possible
that such a person emphasizes his career as a response to an unhappy marriage. In general, we view the association between a person's career-family
orientation and his marital happiness as the result of a process of reciprocal
influence—a process that can, however, be affected by other aspects of the
person's temperament or experience at any point. We do not view marital
happiness, therefore, as a direct consequence of a given pattern of career-
family orientations, but see it, rather, as one of a number of factors that
seem to go together under certain conditions.

20. It should be noted, however, that such an integration can result in a serious
problem of physical and psychological overload (Rapoport & Rapoport,
1969) and is probably not compatible with the super-involvement with career that has been expected in some professions.

21. We are talking here about a differentiating role in relation to marital happiness. There is a slight tendency (as shown by the N's in parentheses) for
wives whose mothers worked to be somewhat more frequently in the integrated group than there is for those whose mothers did not work.

46.

The nature of love

HARRY F. HARLOW

*The research Harlow reports in this article is one of the reasons why
he is both well known and highly regarded in psychological circles.
Strangely, for a discipline that has been almost immobilized by efforts
to emulate the physical sciences, this research and this topic concern
an intangible. The author deals with the nature of love and its effect
upon the development of young monkeys.*

*In a sense, what Harlow has to say about the need for affection
and psychological security and its effect upon functioning is similar to
Cervantes' observations concerning the relationship between rejecting
family environments and school dropouts. Both show that the animal
or person who does not learn how to love at a certain stage of development may never become sufficiently adept at bestowing and eliciting
affection. The fullness and effectiveness of the rest of his living may
be seriously limited.*

The American Psychologist, 13:673–685, 1958. Copyright 1958 by the American Psychological Association, and reproduced by permission. Harry F. Harlow, Professor of
Psychology, University of Wisconsin. *Note:* The figures in this article consisting of
photographs have been omitted.

The tendency of psychologists to prefer research dealing mostly with the tangible, observable, and consensually verifiable appears to have resulted in their having relatively little to offer toward the human problems of loving, cooperating, and transacting. Even though such intangibles as love, affection, and courage appear indispensable if man's potential is to be realized, it may be that too much psychological research continues to be primarily concerned with the maze-learning abilities of rats. The editors believe that this selection furnishes an example of how such research can be accomplished with tact and pertinence. Many more studies of this nature are needed.

LOVE IS a wondrous state, deep, tender, and rewarding. Because of its intimate and personal nature it is regarded by some as an improper topic for experimental research. But, whatever our personal feelings may be, our assigned mission as psychologists is to analyze all facets of human and animal behavior into their component variables. So far as love or affection is concerned, psychologists have failed in this mission. The little we know about love does not transcend simple observation, and the little we write about it has been written better by poets and novelists. But of greater concern is the fact that psychologists tend to give progressively less attention to a motive which pervades our entire lives. Psychologists, at least psychologists who write textbooks, not only show no interest in the origin and development of love or affection, but they seem to be unaware of its very existence.

The apparent repression of love by modern psychologists stands in sharp contrast with the attitude taken by many famous and normal people. The word "love" has the highest reference frequency of any word cited in Bartlett's book of *Familiar Quotations*. It would appear that this emotion has long had a vast interest and fascination for human beings, regardless of the attitude taken by psychologists; but the quotations cited, even by famous and normal people, have a mundane redundancy. These authors and authorities have stolen love from the child and infant and made it the exclusive property of the adolescent and adult.

Thoughtful men, and probably all women, have speculated on the nature of love. From the developmental point of view, the general plan is quite clear: The initial love responses of the human being are those made by the infant to the mother or some mother surrogate. From this intimate attachment of the child to the mother, multiple learned and generalized affectional responses are formed.

Unfortunately, beyond these simple facts we know little about the fundamental variables underlying the formation of affectional responses and little about the mechanisms through which the love of the infant for the mother develops into the multifaceted response patterns characterizing love or affection in the adult. Because of the dearth of experimentation, theories about the fundamental nature of affection have evolved at the level of observation, intuition, and discerning guesswork, whether these have been proposed by psychologists, sociologists, anthropologists, physicians, or psychoanalysts.

The position commonly held by psychologists and sociologists is quite clear: The basic motives are, for the most part, the primary drives—particularly hunger, thirst, elimination, pain, and sex—and all other motives, including love or affection, are derived or secondary drives. The mother is associated with the reduction of the primary drives—particularly hunger, thirst, and pain—and through learning, affection or love is derived.

It is entirely reasonable to believe that the mother through association with food may become a secondary-reinforcing agent, but this is an inadequate mechanism to account for the persistence of the infant-maternal ties. There is a spate of researches on the formation of secondary reinforcers to hunger and thirst reduction. There can be no question that almost any external stimulus can become a secondary reinforcer if properly associated with tissue-need reduction, but the fact remains that this redundant literature demonstrates unequivocally that such derived drives suffer relatively rapid experimental extinction. Contrariwise, human affection does not extinguish when the mother ceases to have intimate association with the drives in question. Instead, the affectional ties to the mother show a lifelong, unrelenting persistence and, even more surprising, widely expanding generality.

Oddly enough, one of the few psychologists who took a position counter to modern psychological dogma was John B. Watson, who believed that love was an innate emotion elicited by cutaneous stimulation of the erogenous zones. But experimental psychologists, with their peculiar propensity to discover facts that are not true, brushed this theory aside by demonstrating that the human neonate had no differentiable emotions, and they established a fundamental psychological law that prophets are without honor in their own profession.

The psychoanalysts have concerned themselves with the problem of the nature of the development of love in the neonate and infant, using ill and aging human beings as subjects. They have discovered the overwhelming importance of the breast and related this to the oral erotic tendencies developed at an age preceding their subjects' memories. Their theories range from a belief that the infant has an innate need to achieve and suckle at the breast to beliefs not unlike commonly accepted psychological theories. There are exceptions, as seen in the recent writings of John Bowlby, who attributes importance not only to food and thirst satisfaction, but also to "primary object-clinging," a need for intimate physical contact, which is initially associated with the mother.

As far as I know, there exists no direct experimental analysis of the relative importance of the stimulus variables determining the affectional or love responses in the neonatal and infant primate. Unfortunately, the human neonate is a limited experimental subject for such researches because of his inadequate motor capabilities. By the time the human infant's motor responses can be precisely measured, the antecedent determining conditions cannot be defined, having been lost in a jumble and jungle of confounded variables.

Many of these difficulties can be resolved by the use of the neonatal and infant macaque monkey as the subject for the analysis of basic affectional variables. It is possible to make precise measurements in this primate beginning at two to ten days of age, depending upon the maturational status of the individual animal at birth. The macaque infant differs from the human infant in that the monkey is more mature at birth and grows more rapidly; but the basic responses relating to affection, including nursing, contact, clinging, and even visual and auditory exploration, exhibit no fundamental differences in the two species. Even the development of perception, fear, frustration, and learning capability follows very similar sequences in rhesus monkeys and human children.

Three years' experimentation before we started our studies on affection gave us experience with the neonatal monkey. We had separated more than 60 of these animals from their mothers 6 to 12 hours after birth and suckled them on tiny bottles. The infant mortality was only a small fraction of what would have obtained had we let the monkey mothers raise their infants. Our bottle-fed babies were healthier and heavier than monkey-mother-reared infants. We know that we are better monkey mothers than are real monkey mothers thanks to synthetic diets, vitamins, iron extracts, penicillin, chloromycetin, 5% glucose, and constant, tender, loving care.

During the course of these studies we noticed that the laboratory-raised babies showed strong attachment to the cloth pads (folded gauze diapers) which were used to cover the hardware-cloth floors of their cages. The infants clung to these pads and engaged in violent temper tantrums when the pads were removed and replaced for sanitary reasons. Such contact-need or responsiveness had been reported previously by Gertrude van Wagenen for the monkey and by Thomas McCulloch and George Haslerud for the chimpanzee and is reminiscent of the devotion often exhibited by human infants to their pillows, blankets, and soft, cuddly stuffed toys. The baby, human or monkey, if it is to survive, must clutch at more than a straw.

We had also discovered during some allied observational studies that a baby monkey raised on a bare wire-mesh cage floor survives with difficulty, if at all, during the first five days of life. If a wire-mesh cone is introduced, the baby does better; and, if the cone is covered with terry cloth, husky, healthy, happy babies evolve. It takes more than a baby and a box to make a normal monkey. We were impressed by the possibility that, above and beyond the bubbling fountain of breast or bottle, contact comfort might be a very important variable in the development of the infant's affection for the mother.

At this point we decided to study the development of affectional responses of neonatal and infant monkeys to an artificial, inanimate mother, and so we built a surrogate mother which we hoped and believed would be a good surrogate mother. In devising this surrogate mother we were dependent neither upon the capriciousness of evolutionary processes nor upon mutations produced by chance radioactive fallout. Instead, we designed the mother surrogate in terms of modern human-engineering principles. We produced a perfectly proportioned, streamlined body stripped of unnecessary bulges and appendices. Redundancy in the surrogate mother's system was avoided by reducing the number of breasts from two to one and placing this unibreast in an upper-thoracic, sagittal position, thus maximizing the natural and known perceptual-motor capabilities of the infant operator. The surrogate was made from a block of wood, covered with sponge rubber, and sheathed in tan cotton terry cloth. A light bulb behind her radiated heat. The result was a mother, soft, warm, and tender, a mother with infinite patience, a mother available twenty-four hours a day, a mother that never scolded her infant and never struck or bit her baby in anger. Furthermore, we designed a mother-machine with maximal maintenance efficiency since failure of any system or function could be resolved by the simple substitution of black boxes and new component parts. It is our opinion that we engineered a very superior monkey mother, although this position is not held universally by the monkey fathers.

Before beginning our initial experiment we also designed and constructed a second mother surrogate, a surrogate in which we deliberately built less than the maximal capability for contact comfort. This surrogate mother is made of wire-mesh, a substance entirely adequate to provide postural support and nursing capability, and she is warmed by radiant heat. Her body differs in no essential way from that of the cloth mother surrogate other than in the quality of the contact comfort which she can supply.

In our initial experiment, the dual mother-surrogate condition, a cloth mother and a wire mother were placed in different cubicles attached to the infant's living cage. For four newborn monkeys the cloth mother lactated and the wire mother did not; and, for the other four, this condition was reversed. In either condition the infant received all its milk through the mother surrogate as soon as it was able to maintain itself in this way, a capability achieved within two or three days except in the case of very immature infants. Supplementary feedings were given until the milk intake from the mother surrogate was adequate. Thus, the experiment was designed as a test of the relative importance of the variables of contact comfort and nursing comfort. During the first 14 days of life the monkey's cage floor was covered with a heating pad wrapped in a folded gauze diaper, and thereafter the cage floor was bare. The infants were always free to leave the heating pad or cage floor to contact either mother, and the time spent on the surrogate mothers was automatically recorded. Figure 5 shows the total time spent on the cloth and wire mothers under the two conditions of feeding. These data make it obvious that contact comfort is a variable of overwhelming importance in the development of affectional responses, whereas lactation is a variable of negligible importance. With age and opportunity to learn, subjects with the lactating wire mother showed decreasing responsiveness to her and increasing responsiveness to the nonlactating cloth mother, a finding completely contrary to any interpretation of derived drive in which the mother-form becomes conditioned to hunger-thirst reduction. The persistence of these differential responses throughout 165 consecutive days of testing is evident in Figure 6.

One control group of neonatal monkeys was raised on a single wire mother, and a second control group was raised on a single cloth mother. There were no differences between these two groups in amount of milk ingested or in weight gain. The only difference between the groups lay in the

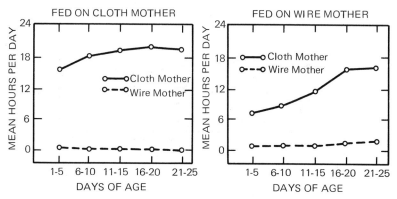

FIGURE 5. *Time spent on cloth and wire mother surrogates.*

composition of the feces, the softer stools of the wire-mother infants suggesting psychosomatic involvement. The wire mother is biologically adequate but psychologically inept.

We were not surprised to discover that contact comfort was an important basic affectional or love variable, but we did not expect it to overshadow so completely the variable of nursing; indeed, the disparity is so great as to suggest that the primary function of nursing as an affectional variable is that of insuring frequent and intimate body contact of the infant with the mother. Certainly, man cannot live by milk alone. Love is an emotion that does not need to be bottle- or spoon-fed, and we may be sure that there is nothing to be gained by giving lip service to love.

A charming lady once heard me describe these experiments; and, when I subsequently talked to her, her face brightened with sudden insight: "Now I know what's wrong with me," she said, "I'm just a wire mother." Perhaps she was lucky. She might have been a wire wife.

We believe that contact comfort has long served the animal kingdom as a motivating agent for affectional responses. Since at the present time we

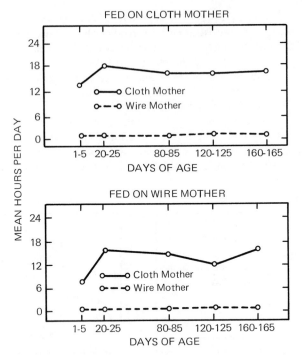

FIGURE 6. *Long-term contact time on cloth and wire mother surrogates.*

have no experimental data to substantiate this position, we supply information which must be accepted, if at all, on the basis of face validity:

The Hippopotamus

This is the skin some babies feel
Replete with hippo love appeal.
Each contact, cuddle, push, and shove
Elicits tons of baby love.

The Rhinocerus

The rhino's skin is thick and tough,
And yet this skin is soft enough
That baby rhinos always sense,
A love enormous and intense.

The Snake

To baby vipers, scaly skin
Engenders love 'twixt kith and kin.
Each animal by God is blessed
With kind of skin it loves the best.

The Elephant

Though mother may be short on arms,
Her skin is full of warmth and charms.
And mother's touch on baby's skin
Endears the heart that beats within.

The Crocodile

Here is the skin they love to touch.
It isn't soft and there isn't much,
But its contact comfort will beguile
Love from the infant crocodile.

One function of the real mother, human or sub-human, and presumably of a mother surrogate, is to provide a haven of safety for the infant in times

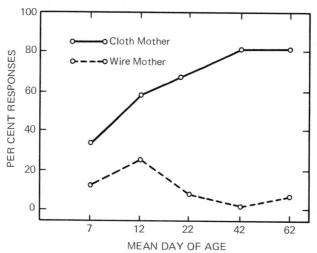

FIGURE 15. *Differential responsiveness in fear tests.*

of fear and danger. The frightened or ailing child clings to its mother, not its father; and this selective responsiveness in times of distress, disturbance, or danger may be used as a measure of the strength of affectional bonds. We have tested this kind of differential responsiveness by presenting to the infants in their cages, in the presence of the two mothers, various fear-producing stimuli such as the moving toy bear illustrated in Figure 13. A typical response to a fear stimulus is shown in Figure 14, and the data on differential responsiveness are presented in Figure 15. It is apparent that the cloth mother is highly preferred over the wire one, and this differential selectivity is enhanced by age and experience. In this situation, the variable of nursing appears to be of absolutely no importance: the infant consistently seeks the soft mother surrogate regardless of nursing condition.

Similarly, the mother or mother surrogate provides its young with a source of security, and this role or function is seen with special clarity when mother and child are in a strange situation. At the present time we have completed tests for this relationship on four of our eight baby monkeys assigned to the dual mother-surrogate condition by introducing them for three minutes into the strange environment of a room measuring six feet by six feet by six feet (also called the "open-field test") and containing multiple stimuli known to elicit curiosity-manipulatory responses in baby monkeys. The subjects were placed in this situation twice a week for eight

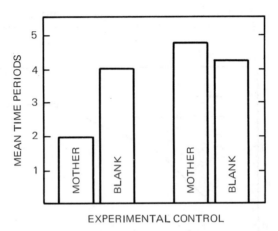

FIGURE 20. Emotionality index with and without the presence of the cloth mother.

weeks with no mother surrogate present during alternate sessions and the cloth mother present during the others. A cloth diaper was always available as one of the stimuli throughout all sessions. After one or two adaptation sessions, the infants always rushed to the mother surrogate when she was present and clutched her, rubbed their bodies against her, and frequently manipulated her body and face. After a few additional sessions, the infants began to use the mother surrogate as a source of security, a base of operations. They would explore and manipulate a stimulus and then return to the mother before adventuring again into the strange new world. The behavior of these infants was quite different when the mother was absent from the room. Frequently they would freeze in a crouched position. Emotionality indices such as vocalization, crouching, rocking, and sucking increased sharply, as shown in Figure 20. Total emotionality score was cut in half when the mother was present. In the absence of the mother some of the experimental monkeys would rush to the center of the room where the mother was customarily placed and then run rapidly from object to object, screaming and crying all the while. Continuous, frantic clutching of their bodies was very common, even when not in the crouching position. These monkeys frequently contacted and clutched the cloth diaper, but this action never pacified them. The same behavior occurred in the presence of the wire mother. No difference between the cloth-mother-fed and wire-mother-fed infants was demonstrated under either condition. Four control infants never raised with a mother surrogate showed the same emotionality scores when the mother was absent as the experimental infants showed in the absence of the mother, but the controls' scores were slightly larger in the presence of the mother surrogate than in her absence.

Some years ago Robert Butler demonstrated that mature monkeys enclosed in a dimly lighted box would open and reopen a door hour after hour and for no other reward than that of looking outside the box. We now have data indicating that neonatal monkeys show this same compulsive visual curiosity on their first test day in an adaptation of the Butler apparatus which we call the "love machine," an apparatus designed to measure love. Usually these tests are begun when the monkey is 10 days of age, but this same persistent visual exploration has been obtained in a three-day-old monkey during the first half-hour of testing. Butler also demonstrated that rhesus monkeys show selectivity in rate and frequency of door-opening to stimuli of differential attractiveness in the visual field outside the box. We have utilized this principle of response selectivity by the monkey to measure strength of affectional responsiveness in our infants in the baby version of the Butler box. The test sequence involves four repetitions of a test battery in which four stimuli—cloth mother, wire mother, infant monkey, and empty box—are presented for a 30-minute period on successive days. The first four subjects in the dual mother-surrogate group were given a single test sequence at 40 to 50 days of age, depending upon the availability of the apparatus, and only their data are presented. The second set of four subjects is being given repetitive tests to obtain information relating to the development of visual exploration. The apparatus is illustrated in Figure 21. The data obtained from the first four infants raised with the two mother surrogates are presented in the middle graph of Figure 22 and show approximately equal responding to the cloth mother and another infant monkey, and no greater responsiveness to the wire mother than to an empty box. Again, the results are independent of the kind of mother that lactated, cloth or wire. The same results are found for a control group raised, but not fed, on a single cloth mother; these data appear in the graph on the right. Contrariwise, the graph on the left shows no differential responsiveness to cloth and wire mothers by a second control group, which was not raised on any mother surrogate. We can be certain that not all love is blind.

The first four infant monkeys in the dual mother-surrogate group were separated from their mothers between 165 and 170 days of age and tested for retention during the following 9 days and then at 30-day intervals for

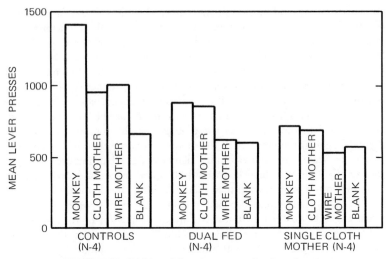

FIGURE 22. *Differential responses to visual exploration.*

six successive months. Affectional retention as measured by the modified Butler box is given in Figure 23. In keeping with the data obtained on adult monkeys by Butler, we find a high rate of responding to any stimulus, even the empty box. But throughout the entire 185-day retention period there is a consistent and significant difference in response frequency to the

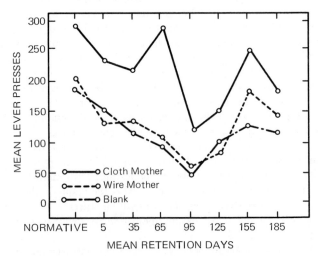

FIGURE 23. *Retention of differential visual-exploration responses.*

cloth mother contrasted with either the wire mother or the empty box, and no consistent difference between wire mother and empty box.

Affectional retention was also tested in the open field during the first 9 days after separation and then at 30-day intervals, and each test condition was run twice at each retention interval. The infant's behavior differed from that observed during the period preceding separation. When the cloth mother was present in the post-separation period, the babies rushed to her, climbed up, clung tightly to her, and rubbed their heads and faces against her body.' After this initial embrace and reunion, they played on the mother, including biting and tearing at her cloth cover; but they rarely made any attempt to leave her during the test period, nor did they manipulate or play with the objects in the room, in contrast with their behavior before maternal separation. The only exception was the occasional monkey that left the mother surrogate momentarily, grasped the folded piece of paper (one of the standard stimuli in the field), and brought it quickly back to the mother. It appeared that deprivation had enhanced the tie to the mother and rendered the contact-comfort need so prepotent that need for the mother overwhelmed the exploratory motives during the brief, three-minute test sessions. No change in these behaviors was observed throughout the 185-day period. When the mother was absent from the open field, the behavior of the infants was similar in the initial retention test to that during the preseparation tests; but they tended to show gradual adaptation to the open-field situation with repeated testing and, consequently, a reduction in their emotionality scores.

In the last five retention test periods, an additional test was introduced in which the surrogate mother was placed in the center of the room and covered with a clear Plexiglas box. The monkeys were initially disturbed and frustrated when their explorations and manipulations of the box failed to provide contact with the mother. However, all animals adapted to the situation rather rapidly. Soon they used the box as a place of orientation for exploratory and play behavior, made frequent contacts with the objects in the field, and very often brought these objects to the Plexiglas box. The emotionality index was slightly higher than in the condition of the available cloth mothers, but it in no way approached the emotionality level displayed when the cloth mother was absent. Obviously, the infant monkeys gained emotional security by the presence of the mother even though contact was denied.

Affectional retention has also been measured by tests in which the monkey must unfasten a three-device mechanical puzzle to obtain entrance into a compartment containing the mother surrogate. All the trials are initiated by allowing the infant to go through an unlocked door, and in half the trials it finds the mother present and in half, an empty compartment. The door is then locked and a ten-minute test conducted. In tests given prior to separation from the surrogate mothers, some of the infants had solved this puzzle and others had failed. The data of Figure 24 show

that on the last test before separation there were no differences in total
manipulation under mother-present and mother-absent conditions, but
striking differences exist between the two conditions throughout the post-
separation test periods. Again, there is no interaction with conditions of
feeding.

The over-all picture obtained from surveying the retention data is
unequivocal. There is little, if any, waning of responsiveness to the mother
throughout this five-month period as indicated by any measure. It becomes
perfectly obvious that this affectional bond is highly resistant to forgetting
and that it can be retained for very long periods of time by relatively in-

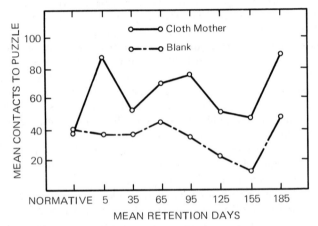

FIGURE 24. Retention of puzzle manipulation responsiveness.

frequent contact reinforcement. During the next year, retention tests will
be conducted at 90-day intervals, and further plans are dependent upon the
results obtained. It would appear that affectional responses may show as
much resistance to extinction as has been previously demonstrated for
learned fears and learned pain, and such data would be in keeping with
those of common human observation.

The infant's responses to the mother surrogate in the fear tests, the
open-field situation, and the baby Butler box and the responses on the retention tests cannot be described adequately with words. For supplementary
information we turn to the motion picture record. (At this point a 20-
minute film was presented illustrating and supplementing the behaviors
described thus far in the address.)

We have already described the group of four control infants that had
never lived in the presence of any mother surrogate and had demonstrated
no sign of affection or security in the presence of the cloth mothers in-

troduced in test sessions. When these infants reached the age of 250 days, cubicles containing both a cloth mother and a wire mother were attached to their cages. There was no lactation in these mothers, for the monkeys were on a solid-food diet. The initial reaction of the monkeys to the alterations was one of extreme disturbance. All the infants screamed violently and made repeated attempts to escape the cage whenever the door was opened. They

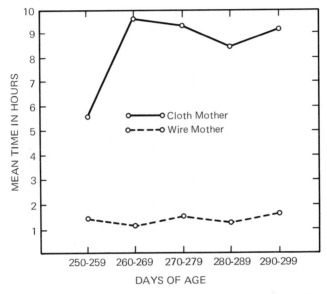

FIGURE 25. *Differential time spent on cloth and wire mother surrogates by monkeys started at 250 days of age.*

kept a maximum distance from the mother surrogates and exhibited a considerable amount of rocking and crouching behavior, indicative of emotionality. Our first thought was that the critical period for the development of maternally directed affection had passed and that these macaque children were doomed to live as affectional orphans. Fortunately, these behaviors continued for only 12 to 48 hours and then gradually ebbed, changing from indifference to active contact on, and exploration of, the surrogates. The home-cage behavior of these control monkeys slowly became progressively more vigorous to the point of actual mutilation, particularly during the morning after the cloth mother had been given her daily change of terry covering. The control subjects were now actively running to the cloth mother when frightened and had to be coaxed from her to be taken from the cage for formal testing.

Objective evidence of these changing behaviors is given in Figure 25, which plots the amount of time these infants spent on the mother surrogates. Within 10 days mean contact time is approximately nine hours, and this measure remains relatively constant throughout the next 30 days. Consistent with the results on the subjects reared from birth with dual mothers, these late-adopted infants spent less than one and one-half hours per day in contact with the wire mothers, and this activity level was relatively constant throughout the test sessions. Although the maximum time that the control monkeys spent on the cloth mother was only about half

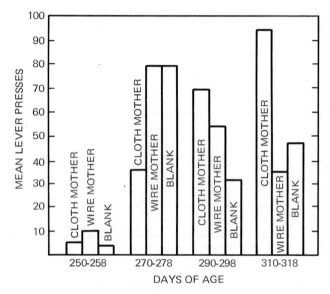

FIGURE 26. *Differential visual exploration of monkeys started at 250 days of age.*

that spent by the original dual mother-surrogate group, we cannot be sure that this discrepancy is a function of differential early experience. The control monkeys were about three months older when the mothers were attached to their cages than the experimental animals had been when their mothers were removed and the retention tests begun. Thus, we do not know what the amount of contact would be for a 250-day-old animal raised from birth with surrogate mothers. Nevertheless, the magnitude of the differences and the fact that the contact-time curves for the mothered-from-birth infants had remained constant for almost 150 days suggest that early experience with the mother is a variable of measurable importance.

The control group has also been tested for differential visual exploration after the introduction of the cloth and wire mothers; these behaviors are plotted in Figure 26. By the second test session a high level of exploratory behavior had developed, and the responsiveness to the wire mother and the empty box is significantly greater than that to the cloth mother. This is probably not an artifact since there is every reason to believe that the face of the cloth mother is a fear stimulus to most monkeys that have not had extensive experience with this object during the first 40 to 60 days of life. Within the third test session a sharp change in trend occurs, and the cloth mother is then more frequently viewed than the wire mother or the blank box; this trend continues during the fourth session, producing a significant preference for the cloth mother.

Before the introduction of the mother surrogate into the home-cage situation, only one of the four control monkeys had ever contacted the cloth mother in the open-field tests. In general, the surrogate mother not only gave the infants no security, but instead appeared to serve as a fear stimulus. The emotionality scores of these control subjects were slightly higher during the mother-present test sessions than during the mother-absent test sessions. These behaviors were changed radically by the fourth post-introduction test approximately 60 days later. In the absence of the cloth mothers the emotionality index in this fourth test remains near the earlier level, but the score is reduced by half when the mother is present, a result strikingly similar to that found for infants raised with the dual mother-surrogates from birth. The control infants now show increasing object exploration and play behavior, and they begin to use the mother as a base of operations, as did the infants raised from birth with the mother surrogates. However, there are still definite differences in the behavior of the two groups. The control infants do not rush directly to the mother and clutch her violently; but instead they go toward, and orient around, her, usually after an initial period during which they frequently show disturbed behavior, exploratory behavior, or both.

That the control monkeys develop affection or love for the cloth mother when she is introduced into the cage at 250 days of age cannot be questioned. There is every reason to believe, however, that this interval of delay depresses the intensity of the affectional response below that of the infant monkeys that were surrogate-mothered from birth onward. In interpreting these data it is well to remember that the control monkeys had had continuous opportunity to observe and hear other monkeys housed in adjacent cages and that they had had limited opportunity to view and contact surrogate mothers in the test situations, even though they did not exploit the opportunities.

During the last two years we have observed the behavior of two infants raised by their own mothers. Love for the real mother and love for the surrogate mother appear to be very similar. The baby macaque spends many hours a day clinging to its real mother. If away from the mother when frightened, it rushes to her and in her presence shows comfort and composure. As far as we can observe, the infant monkey's affection for the real mother is strong, but no stronger than that of the experimental monkey for the surrogate cloth mother, and the security that the infant gains from the presence of the real mother is no greater than the security it gains from a cloth surrogate. Next year we hope to put this problem to final, definitive, experimental test. But, whether the mother is real or a cloth surrogate, there does develop a deep and abiding bond between mother and child. In one case it may be the call of the wild and in the other the McCall of civilization, but in both cases there is "togetherness."

In spite of the importance of contact comfort, there is reason to believe that other variables of measurable importance will be discovered. Postural support may be such a variable, and it has been suggested that, when we build arms into the mother surrogate, 10 is the minimal number required to provide adequate child care. Rocking motion may be such a variable, and we are comparing rocking and stationary mother surrogates and inclined planes. The differential responsiveness to cloth mother and cloth-covered inclined plane suggests that clinging as well as contact is an affectional variable of importance. Sounds, particularly natural, maternal sounds, may operate as either unlearned or learned affectional variables. Visual responsiveness may be such a variable, and it is possible that some semblance of visual imprinting may develop in the neonatal monkey. There are indications that this becomes a variable of importance during the course of infancy through some maturational process.

John Bowlby has suggested that there is an affectional variable which he calls "primary object following," characterized by visual and oral search of the mother's face. Our surrogate-mother-raised baby monkeys are at first inattentive to her face, as are human neonates to human mother faces. But by 30 days of age ever-increasing responsiveness to the mother's face appears—whether through learning, maturation, or both—and we have reason to believe that the face becomes an object of special attention.

Our first surrogate-mother-raised baby had a mother whose head was just a ball of wood since the baby was a month early and we had not had time to design a more esthetic head and face. This baby had contact with the blank-faced mother for 180 days and was then placed with two cloth mothers, one motionless and one rocking, both being endowed with painted, ornamented faces. To our surprise the animal would compulsively rotate both faces 180 degrees so that it viewed only a round, smooth face and never the painted, ornamented face. Furthermore, it would do this as long as the patience of the experimenter in reorienting the faces persisted. The monkey showed no sign of fear or anxiety, but it showed unlimited persistence. Subsequently it improved its technique, compulsively removing the heads and rolling them into its cage as fast as they were returned. We are intrigued by this observation, and we plan to examine systematically the role of the mother face in the development of infant-monkey affections. Indeed, these observations suggest the need for a series of ethological-type researches on the two-faced female.

Although we have made no attempts thus far to study the generalization of infant-macaque affection or love, the techniques which we have developed offer promise in this uncharted field. Beyond this, there are few if any technical difficulties in studying the affection of the actual, living mother for the child, and the techniques developed can be utilized and expanded for the analysis and developmental study of father-infant and infant-infant affection.

Since we can measure neonatal and infant affectional responses to mother surrogates, and since we know they are strong and persisting, we are in a position to assess the effects of feeding and contactual schedules; consistency and inconsistency in the mother surrogates; and early, intermediate, and late maternal deprivation. Again, we have here a family of problems of fundamental interest and theoretical importance.

If the researches completed and proposed make a contribution, I shall be grateful; but I have also given full thought to possible practical applications. The socioeconomic demands of the present and the threatened socioeconomic demands of the future have led the American woman to displace, or threaten to displace, the American man in science and industry. If this process continues, the problem of proper child-rearing practices faces us with startling clarity. It is cheering in view of this trend to realize that the American male is physically endowed with all the really essential equipment to compete with the American female on equal terms in one essential activity: the rearing of infants. We now know that women in the working classes are not needed in the home because of their primary mammalian capabilities; and it is possible that in the foreseeable future neonatal nursing will not be regarded as a necessity, but as a luxury—to use Veblen's term—a form of conspicuous consumption limited perhaps to the upper classes. But whatever course history may take, it is comforting to know that we are now in contact with the nature of love.

The role of the school

47.

Cultivating new talents: a way to reach the educationally deprived

CALVIN W. TAYLOR

It is the belief of the editors that Taylor is far too humble in the selection of a title. In this article, he is suggesting a very practical approach to more effective education for all pupils—not just the educationally deprived. Education has been much too concerned with bringing the low-ranking child on various tests "up to average"—a self-defeating goal because if "successful," it serves to raise the average. Tests and interpersonal comparisons have stimulated the remedial concept in education. Taylor suggests an avenue of escape from these dubious concepts and practices: uncover new talents and cultivate them. Instead of relying on restricted tests which probe a narrow range of talents, let's use more tests to identify more talents.

We have the hope and faith that if more emphasis were placed on the strengths of a pupil—if that were the primary aim—that the less-developed talents would be improved because of an attendant strengthening of the pupil's ego concept. Again, this is not just a new way to reach the deprived; it is a way to lend excitement to the quest for knowledge on the part of all pupils.

FROM MOUNTAINSIDE TO VALLEY FLOOR

In a mining region near Salt Lake City, large and efficient mills have been built in order to process raw materials from which valuable metals can be extracted. Rocks and boulders from the mountainside are ground in successive steps until, with the addition of water, they are turned into a stream of fine silt. Next, the stream is processed to yield copper, the metal initially sought.

The Journal of Creative Behavior, 2(No. 2): 83–90, Spring, 1968. Calvin W. Taylor, Professor of Psychology, University of Utah.

The ideas developed herein are emphasized at the University of Utah Creativity Workshops which the author directs each June.

At that point, the procedure used to end. But now, modern mining engineers are alert to any discoveries through basic research of the existence of new and sometimes rare and precious metals. The mining specialists immediately try to identify each newly discovered metal in the residual stream that was once poured off as a mere waste product. If a new metal is present, they try to find ways of adding other processes in order to develop this additional metal out of the total potential in the stream—continuing at the same time, of course, to extract copper.

As they look backward over the years, the Utah miners realize that they have dumped onto the valley floor waste products that may contain metals of a larger total value than the ones already extracted.

MULTIPLE TALENTS

Is our educational system "dumping" valuable human resources? Is it as efficient as it could be in identifying and developing known talents? Is it alert to discover new talents, new resources?

The term "gifted" is one traditionally used to describe high scorers on an intelligence test (or the closely related academically talented). For the students so identified, educators have set up special classes for which the curricula and the teaching methods have been designed specifically to nurture this general type of talent. And yet, the term "gifted" is in fact an adjective that can be used to cover eight to ten other broad or general high level talents that may be equally important, such as creative talents, planning talents, wisdom or decision-making talents, forecasting talent, communication talents of several types, etc. Consequently, there are eight or ten types of giftedness that can be identified through testing (Taylor, 1966). Each of these general types is in turn composed of a particular sub-set of specific high-level talents. For example, Guilford has summarized and greatly augmented the work of Thurstone and his students who discovered about 20 specific talents initially called primary mental abilities. In Guilford's current version of his periodic table of the mind (called The Structure of Intellect), there are 120 possible specific high-level talents, with over 80 discovered to date (Guilford, 1964, 1967). Typical intelligence tests cover only a sub-set of about 8 specific talents or about 1/10th of those known—intelligence tests therefore do *not* cover the other 9/10ths known to date.

THEORY AND EVIDENCE

As a general rule, not all gifted persons excel in the same talents. If we conceive of each talent group as arranged on a ladder, we will find that those persons at the top of one ladder are essentially different ones than those at the top of another ladder. Furthermore, some of those at the top of one talent ladder may well be toward the bottom of another. If we begin to search for and develop a third talent, that ladder will show a composition of members quite different from the other two. Those at the bottom of a previous talent ladder may rise as a subgroup to be almost average as far as the new type of talent is concerned. A fraction of them (a third or more) are likely to be above average in the new talent area.

Some Calculations

Let us turn to mathematics for a clearer picture of what happens on the talent ladders.

If there were merely one type of talent, only 50% of the students would be talented above the average (median). If there were two unrelated talents with 50% above average on each, 25% would be above average on both talents and 75% would be above average on at least one talent. For three uncorrelated talents, 87.5% would be above average on at least one talent.

Number of Unrelated Talents	Percent Above Average in at Least One Talent
1	50.0%
2	75.0
3	87.5
4	93.8
5	96.9
6	98.4
7	99.2
8	99.6

Since high-level talents are not absolutely unrelated but tend to be lowly related in the positive direction, evidence indicates that the actual trends upward toward 100% do not climb as rapidly as in the theoretical picture above (based upon the extreme case of zero intercorrelations). In other words, there would be some slippage downward due to overlapping talents. In the case of two somewhat correlated talents, the expectation for the percentage above average would be in the high 60's (instead of 75%); for three talents it would be in the 70's (instead of 87.5%); for four talents in the 70's or possibly in the low 80's (instead of 93.8%), etc. The estimated downward slippage will depend upon the level of correlation found to be present—the more intercorrelation, the greater the slippage.

The same type of theoretical approach could be applied to the top end of the talent ladder. For example, considering the top 10% as highly gifted and looking across several types of talents or giftedness yields a similar important trend. If one type of talent is cultivated, only 10% will be "highly gifted." If talents are independent and two types are cultivated, 19% will be highly gifted. (One percent will be highly gifted in both types of talents and a total of 19% will be highly gifted in at least one.) This percent will likewise increase to 27 with three talents, to 35 with four talents, and will continue upward at a diminishing rate as each new type of talent is added; assuming that talents are completely unrelated.

However, in the usual case of talents being somewhat related, this percentage will not rise as rapidly. For example, if creativity is added as a second type of talent, the evidence suggests that a new 7% will be found to be in the top 10% of the highly talented in creativity along with 3% from the previous talent area who will have a high profile across both types of talent. Thus a total of 17% will be highly gifted in at least one of the two talent areas. By further taking into account the low interrelationships among different types of giftedness, approximately 22 to 23% will be found to be in the top 10% of at least one of three types of giftedness. This trend will continue so that if one cultivates at least six different types of giftedness in the classroom, about 30% of the students could be found to be highly gifted (in the top 10%) in at least one of the six high-level talent areas. Thus, the percent doubled with three talents and tripled with about six.

A SUNRISE FOR EDUCATION

These calculations yield a beautiful phenomenon and a most promising picture for educators: Not only do new star performers emerge from almost all levels of the previous talent ladder, but those who had not been flourishing in the old talent areas will rise toward the middle of their class in each new talent area in turn. Moreover, nearly all students will have the rewarding experience of being above average in one or another talent area if we cultivate enough different talents in the classroom. In addition, about a third of the students will be found to be highly gifted in at least one major talent area.

This is a very heartening outlook in terms of motivation of students and the potential in our human resources. The subgroup heretofore classified as educationally deprived will almost approach an average group in a new gifted area, and individually they will spread widely up and down this new type of gifted ladder—certainly not highly concentrated at the bottom. A third or more of them will tend to be above average, and a somewhat different third of them will be above average in each new area of giftedness focused upon.

The implications of this phenomenon are exciting because, if a variety of talents are tested and trained for, a student can learn a great deal about himself and his abilities and consequently become self-directed. He can steer himself throughout his life into activities that call for his best talents—a course that can well lead to optimum self-actualization and productivity.

If we are to do well in preparing students for change, for keeping on the "right side of change," and even for bringing about needed changes in knowledge and practices, our talent searches should occur right in the classroom where we can, with no extra time required, develop the talents of students in the regular curriculum while they are simultaneously acquiring knowledge. Since the various talents tend to be unrelated or not highly related, a different classroom approach to each one will result in much greater variety in education. It will also provide the best hope of reaching each and every person in the classroom, because almost everyone will be above average in one or more of these high-level talents.[1] At one time or another, then, we would be reaching almost all of those children who, under less felicitous circumstances, would be considered educationally deprived, drawing them off the bottom more toward the average.

HUTCHINSON'S DEMONSTRATIONS

Using this new talent approach in the classroom presents no basic difficulties as far as course content is concerned. Students grow in subject matter knowledge at least as fast, if not faster, when they utilize and develop new talents while acquiring subject matter. Hutchinson (1963, 1967), for one, found this to be true. Using matched sets of classes of junior high students, he worked with two different teaching methods. First he had four teachers use their typical method, and then with a comparable set of students they used a productive thinking method in which the students were conceived to be "thinkers" and not merely "learners." He held the content dimension constant by having all students deal with the same two-week unit of social studies subject matter. He varied the teaching methods and observed the thinking and learning processes in the students.

The students in the productive thinking classrooms appeared to enjoy school more and learned at least as much or more subject matter. And a new group of students (independent of "IQ" type of talent) emerged as the star performers in this second type of classroom. To be specific, IQ scores correlated only −.04 with the amount of subject matter learned (post-test minus pre-test achievement scores). Thus, in the traditional classes, the IQ type of giftedness was being utilized while subject matter was being learned and in the second type of classes an almost entirely different (productive thinking) type of giftedness was being used while the same content was being learned. And the poorest students in the first classroom were not the same type as those who were the poorest in the second classroom.

Recently Hutchinson decided to give a demonstration of his teaching methods to a set of teachers working in a poverty educational program. He again worked at the junior high level but he changed the subject matter to language arts. New groups of students continued to emerge as star performers when productive thinking processes were used in acquiring course content—and some of these star performers were below average students in the typical classroom.

PROGRAM FOR CREATIVE TALENTS

With the current emphasis on knowledge acquisition, a relatively narrow band of talents is probably being cultivated. In sharp contrast, if a multiple talent approach is used in the classroom, the band of talents would be deliberately widened, and, as an automatic by-product, the scope and type of knowledge acquired might also widen. In the cultivation of certain components of curiosity and creativity, for example, the student is required to expand his experience by working at and beyond the fringe of knowledge. To accomplish this particular expansion both of knowledge and of talents, an educator no longer needs to restrict himself solely to the academic talents but can break away initially to creative talents by experimenting with several approaches:

(1) Develop creative thinking and creative problem-solving characteristics.

(2) Develop creative personality and motivational characteristics.

(3) Overcome emotional hindrances and blocks to the creative processes.

(4) Develop an awareness of what is not yet known, encourage curiosity about it, and elicit ideas for launching creative ventures therein.

(5) Develop questioning abilities in teachers so that they learn to formulate thought-provoking questions about known subject matter and also about the unknowns, thereby giving students experience in dealing with contradictions and with knowledge of differing degrees of substantiation.

(6) Develop the ability of teachers to make direct statements that likewise provoke creative thought.

(7) Combine knowledge and creativity, or information and creativity, drawing upon cybernetics and information theory, including attempts to increase the creativeness of the input (receptional) processes and the output (expressional) processes.

(8) Elicit creative processes in classroom programs. (The creativeness of the internal central processes of students is a most challenging area.)

(9) Focus upon the creativeness of the students' products.

(10) Utilize related technology (such as inquiry training; discovery methods used in the arts and mathematics; programs in art education, dance, and writing for fostering creativity; and various training programs in industry designed to develop creativity).

(11) Develop programmed instruction for creativity.

(12) Modify existing creativity testing materials to make them suitable for situational training and other classroom instructional uses.

(13) Develop other special instructional media for creativity.

(14) Identify those teachers who are most masterful in fostering creative processes and creative behaviors in students; analyze and then duplicate their approaches.

SUMMARY

Basic research has indicated that there are at least eighty specific talents that can be identified and tested. If one formulates meaningful subgroups of these many talents, a larger category called "giftedness" can be identified. There are at least eight or ten types of giftedness for which students can be tested and trained.

All evidence and demonstrations to date show strongly that a largely new group will be found to be most gifted as we either test or train in the classroom for each new type of giftedness. Classroom searches and development of talent also show that those who are seen as academically deprived will move upward as each type of giftedness becomes the focus of attention in classroom activities. In turn a different subgroup of people slip downward to the bottom of the talent ladder for that particular type of giftedness.

The challenge, then, is to devise and initiate various educational programs focused on developing creative and other new talents, for the sake of both the educationally deprived and the unrecognized, underdeveloped gifted persons.

This entire approach is a very healthy one indeed and should make our school systems much more efficient in identifying and developing the nation's important human resources for the overall benefit of the individuals, the communities, the nation, and the world. And, as we discover, identify, and process new human resources, we may, like the mining specialists, wonder how long we had previously been pouring such resources untouched through the mills and out on the world, unnoticed, undeveloped, unused.

REFERENCES

Guilford, J. P. Progress in the discovery of intellectual factors. In C. W. Taylor (Ed.), *Widening horizons in creativity*. New York: Wiley, 1964, pp. 282–297.

Guilford, J. P. *The nature of human intelligence*. New York: McGraw-Hill, 1967.

Hutchinson, W. L. Creative and productive thinking in the classroom. Unpub. Doctoral dissertation, University of Utah, June 1963.

Hutchinson, W. L. Creative and productive thinking in the classroom. *J. of Crea. Behav.*, 1967, 1 (4), 419–427.

Taylor, C. W. Questioning and creating: a model for curriculum reform. *J. of Crea. Behav.*, 1967, 1 (1), 22–33.

ADDITIONAL READINGS

Taylor, C. W. Clues to creative teaching. A series of ten articles in *The Instructor* appearing from Sept. 1963—June 1964.

Taylor, C. W. (Ed.). *Creativity: progress and potential.* New York: McGraw-Hill, 1964.

Taylor, C. W. (Ed.). *Widening horizons in creativity.* New York: Wiley, 1964.

Taylor, C. W. (Ed.). *Creativity across education.* Selected papers from five annual creativity workshops held at the University of Utah. University of Utah Press, 1968.

Taylor, C. W., & Barron, F. (Eds.). *Scientific creativity: its recognition and development.* New York: Wiley, 1963.

Taylor, C. W., & Williams, F. (Eds.). *Instructional media and creativity.* New York: Wiley, 1966.

Taylor, C. W., Ghiselin, B., & Wolfer, J. A. Bridging the gap between basic research and educational practice. *NEA J., 1962, 51,* 23–25.

Taylor, C. W., Ghiselin, B., Wolfer, J. A., Loy, L., & Bourne, L. E., Jr. Development of a theory of education from psychological and other basic research findings. U.S. Office of Education Cooperative Research Project No. 621, August 1964. (Mimeo)

NOTES

1. It is also realistic to recognize that, contrarily, almost everyone is below average in at least one talent.

48.

Youth as advisers to adults and vice versa

HERBERT S. STREAN

Student protests seem to be a popular pastime for at least a minority of students. A tested procedure for dealing with this phenomenon is offered by Dr. Strean. His analysis suggests that deep down, young people do not want autonomy so much as they want to be heard, to have a voice in their own destinies. Most readers are acquainted with Abraham Maslow's theory of motivation dealing with the hierarchy of needs. Young people, at least in some degree, need the safety of rules, regulations, and adult counseling. There is a thrust for growth and independence, but it is an ambivalent, forward-and-back development. This concept is implicit in Strean's interpretation. His apprehension lies more in the possibility that adults might throw up their hands and abdicate parental and instructional responsibilities.

Children, 17:59–62, March–April, 1970. Herbert S. Strean, Associate Professor, Graduate School of Social Work, Rutgers University.

The appropriateness of this article in the section on the role of the school would seem to be dependent upon whether we perceive the school as an agent for developing the whole person or, as many people do, an agent for the transmission of knowledge and the development of academic skills. What position does the reader take?

THE PRESENT era is often described as an age of turmoil and drastic change. Young people everywhere are challenging the "establishment" of every type—papal authority, the military, governmental bureaucracies, university administrators, teachers, and parents. College presidents have been resigning in large numbers, and deans, school superintendents, principals, and leaders of youth-serving organizations are being pressured "to prove" themselves to maintain their prestige and status.

Those of us who teach, counsel, and live with children and young people are feeling a strong obligation to examine our transactions with them. "Now that students are voting members of the curriculum committee, what is our role with them?" teachers in colleges or high schools ask. Parents wonder about how much sexual freedom they can allow their offspring without abdicating their responsibilities; and even therapeutic counselors sometimes question whether they are imposing too much "professionalism" on their young clients.

Like many others who live and work with young people, in recent years I have gradually become plagued by many self-doubts as I have reflected on my activities with the young, as a social caseworker, a social worker educator, and a father. At times I have wondered whether I have been acting too benignly and so as "too much of an equal"; at other times I have berated myself for being too dogmatic and insufficiently related to the young person's needs. I have read many articles in professional journals and held long discussions with colleagues, members of my family, and friends in efforts to clarify my uncertainties.

This article is an attempt to report the partial *modus operandi* and *vivendi* that has evolved after a rather long period of self-examination. While buttressed by a theoretical rationale, the formulations to be discussed have arisen largely through personal and interpersonal struggles.

THEORETICAL RATIONALE

One of the most obvious modifications that has taken place in the last two decades in our society's child-rearing practices, educational efforts, and therapeutic interventions is that we have become more and more "child centered." Instead of feeding an infant on a predetermined schedule, we try to ascertain when he is expressing hunger pangs and then we give him something to eat. We await the maturation of his musculature before we train him to use the toilet. And instead of heaping a child with large doses of sexual information on his 14th birthday, we begin his sex education much earlier by answering his questions whenever he asserts his sexual curiosity.

In education, we speak of "reading readiness"; in psychotherapy and casework we "begin where the client is." As guidance counselors, we accept a youngster's resistance to accepting counsel, and as parents we frequently consult with our children in making family decisions.

Our theories of child development have paralleled these changes in our perspective. Psychosocial development is now regarded as more than the unfolding of instincts: the relatively new ego psychology emphasizes the "average expectable environment" and takes into account the ways the social network is transmitted to the child and transmitted by him.

The research of ego psychologists like Erikson[1] and Hartmann[2] has emphasized the need for the adult, whether teacher, parent, or therapist, to tune in to the child's spontaneous assertion of developmental needs and then to meet these needs. Consequently, the child who has "school phobia" for example, is now regarded as a youngster who is suffering not only from separation anxiety, but also from a dysfunctional social system in which the school, neighborhood, and home are not enacting roles entirely appropriate for meeting the maturational needs of the developing child.

"The corrective emotional experience" in psychotherapy,[3] the saliency of "object relationships" in dynamic psychology,[4] and the "opportunity structure"[5] in sociology are only a few of the theoretical constructs implying that helping agents and the social network must be constantly vigilant to the child's spontaneous expression of developmental needs. The appropriate parental, educational, or therapeutic stance, it is now alleged, should be dictated by the child's preverbal, verbal, or nonverbal expressions of need rather than by the adult's preconceived notions.

The classical experiment of Davis, in which infants managed on their own to eat nutritional foods without adult pressure, supports the theory that children are excellent judges of their own needs. The adult, however, must be there to listen and provide.[6] Lewin in his experiments with various types of adult leadership, demonstrated that adolescents are very knowledgeable about the amount and quality of limits, structure, and direction that they need.[7]

In social psychology much emphasis has been placed on mutual role expectations. Several writers have demonstrated that for a relationship to be harmonious and to be experienced as meaningful, role partners must be sensitive to each other's wishes. Studies of therapeutic and educational relationships within the framework of role theory particularly support this thesis.[8, 9]

The following examples are drawn from my social casework practice, teaching experience, and activities with my own children. They suggest that children and young people can offer helpful guidance to the adult when he attempts to counsel, teach, and live with them—in short, that they make eminently qualified consultants.

A CASEWORK EXAMPLE

Alfred, a 17-year-old high school dropout, who was a poor reader, was referred to me for social casework help. He was withdrawn from peers and adults, dressed poorly, ate irregularly, and seemed very depressed.

Inasmuch as Alfred had already defeated several guidance counselors and social workers, early in my first interview with him I said I guessed he did not "feel much like coming here." Alfred said I was right. He went on to say that he did not need help, that he knew what was best for himself, and that he hated anyone who told him what to do. He knew "the score." I asked Alfred what *was* best for him and he responded tersely, "Just leave me alone."

A 10-minute silence ensued and Alfred asked, "Can I go now?"

When I assured him that he *could* go, Alfred said, "At first I was sure you'd give me a long pep talk and tell me what to do. That was why I was ready to hate you, but now I'm thinking of coming back."

I told Alfred I would be glad to see him again if that was what he wanted.

In subsequent interviews, Alfred tried to test my sincerity and to ascertain whether I would professionalize the interview and explore his problems or let him set his own pace. He avoided a discussion of personal problems. Instead he discussed baseball, movies, checkers, and cops, and I joined in the discussion of these subjects when he asked my opinion. In the fifth interview Alfred suggested that maybe we could go to a baseball game together some day. I agreed that we might.

Subsequently, Alfred seemed to grow frightened of his positive feelings toward me. In his seventh session he said he would like to withdraw from treatment and not return for any more interviews. Referring to me as "baldy," he mildly ridiculed me for "smoking a stupid pipe," and "laughing peculiarly." When I asked him whether I should stop smoking and laughing, he commented, "You really think I know what's best! Don't you?"

I responded with the question, *"Don't you know what's best?"*

"Not always!" Alfred said.

Alfred went on to describe how he "cops out" when he "feels funny." He said that I knew about the reasons for his withdrawal and suggested that I tell him. I wondered out loud whether when he began to feel close to someone he became scared and withdrew, as perhaps he was doing "right now!"

In the next few sessions Alfred described several episodes in his life that corroborated my theory. In his 15th session, he told me that he expected other people to withdraw from him when he started to like them so he decided "to beat them to the punch."

Soon after gaining this bit of insight, Alfred returned to school and began a program in remedial reading and tutoring in several subjects. In his sessions with me, he went into a constructive discussion of his fears of being rejected.

My experience with Alfred demonstrates that when a young person's autonomy, negativism, and resistance to an adult are fully respected and not challenged, he tends to feel less vulnerable. From Alfred and other adolescents I have learned that young people are so ambivalent about wanting advice that when they are permitted to be in the "driver's seat" themselves —that is, to take the role of adviser—they move much closer to the adult. Apparently, when the negative part of their mixed feelings is not questioned, the more positive elements emerge.

Because many adults believe that their own knowledge, expertise, and experience places them in a position of "knowing more" than the young, they are often reluctant to abdicate the role of advice giver. However, a crucial factor for an adult in relating to the young person—particularly the teenager—seems to be recognition that if the teenager is allowed to stay in the "driver's seat" long enough, he will turn to an adult when he realizes that he needs direction.

STUDENT POWER

In these days of student unrest, young people and the adults in their lives are frequently engaged in a fracas over the issue of "power." Consequently, the more important issues of sound curriculum, morale, and educational objectives get sidetracked. It is easy for the adult to feel that his own power is being taken away, because to wrest it away is frequently the young person's initial goal. Arguments and counterarguments, demands and counterdemands about student and faculty prerogatives emerge, and the power struggle often does not abate until someone is psychologically or even physically hurt.

Use of the students as consultants on the concrete issues that they bring to their discussions with adult authorities can sometimes avert these struggles. The following example is from my experience as chairman of a casework sequence in a school of social work.

Early in the academic year I was approached by a delegation of students who demanded very belligerently that the casework curriculum be drastically revised. Their tone and manner seemed to invite a defensive argument. When I asked, "In what areas?" the students looked surprised. There was a silence of at least a full minute before a student answered, "It isn't sufficiently related to practice!"

"How could it be related more to practice?" I asked.

Another silence of about 30 seconds.

"The classes in school are too theoretical—they should be more specific!" bellowed another student.

Feeling a little irritated by now, but trying to maintain my "cool," I asked, "How can we be more specific?"

Another silence. Finally, one student said, "We have to learn more about psychodynamics."

When I asked the students what they would like, they decided to get together with their colleagues to prepare their demands in writing to present to me at another meeting because they had "just identified the problem in this meeting."

At the next meeting, a week later, my behavior at the previous meeting was characterized as being "on the defensive and not giving enough," and I was warned, "Don't tell us we're projecting!" Conceding that perhaps their charges were valid, I asked the students what we could give them.

"We want the 'dynamics' that we're supposed to get but aren't getting!"

The conversation then shifted to an examination of the casework curriculum and its relationship to the offerings of other departments. The students maintained that the faculty members were all "too sociologically oriented" and that the students needed more information on clinical syndromes. They said that they did not write anything up for this meeting "because this is your specialty."

I told the students what I thought they meant by clinical syndromes and they agreed that "this was the stuff." I also informed them that this type of material was supposed to be covered in another department. Then, at the students' suggestion, I arranged for consultations between the students, faculty members of several departments, and the dean. In these consultations, the students made concrete suggestions as to what could be added to their usual classes. Their suggested changes, which were adopted by the school, turned out to be rather easy to include in the curriculum. One student summarized the result as "really not a drastic change after all!"

In observing some of the negotiations between students and faculty in colleges and high schools, I have noted two themes that have characterized many of the encounters:

1. Frequently, the students' demands are voiced in such belligerent and intimidating terms that faculty members quickly yield. For a while, all seems fine, but a restlessness in both parties soon manifests itself. The faculty members, feeling they have been "taken," become punitive, and the students often complain later about having "too much responsibility!"

2. The students are told to abandon their plans immediately and leave the school. Both sides get more belligerent and bricks and police arrive. The power struggle goes on for some time.

In neither of these two types of situations are the students used as advisers. In the first instance, the students become anxious because their mentors appear too weak and they feel that they have too much responsibility. The second situation is almost self-explanatory—when the students find no one is listening to them, their anger grows more intense and a battle royal ensues.

My experience with the casework students suggests that the use of students as consultants in the full exploration of facts and issues can obviate battles and power struggles. Neither side appears weak so both retain their integrity.

A WARNING

One of the dangers of using young people as consultants is that the adult may utilize the procedure to abdicate his real adult responsibility, which the young person wants and needs him to fulfill. The following example from my own family addresses itself to this point.

Experiencing a great deal of ambivalence about sending our 7-year-old son, Richard, to Sunday school, my wife and I asked his opinion about whether he should attend. After he asked many questions about the curriculum, which we answered directly, his response to our question of whether he would like to attend mirrored our own ambivalence. Several conversations took place in which all of us listed the pros and cons, yet a decision was not being made.

Finally, our son said to us, "This is a thing you should decide for me. I'm not sure of the right answer."

Our use of Richard as a consultant in this instance helped us realize just when and where the adult's knowledge and experience had to be asserted. While children and adolescents are not always as direct as Richard was, they do give clues through restlessness, tension, and failure to come to a decision as to when the time is ripe for adult intervention.

Because children and young people are able to express their psychosocial needs spontaneously, it is incumbent on the adults in their lives to be vigilant to these needs and to meet them as quickly and as well as they can. While children do not directly verbalize their needs at every developmental phase, their needs are always communicated to adults in some way.

Children and young people are frequently ambivalent about submitting to the direction and counsel of adults, at least initially. Permitting the youngsters to be consultants to the adult can diminish their negativism and resistance so that the real issues can be faced—whether the issues be at home, school, or in psychotherapy.

REFERENCES

1. Erikson, Erik H.: Identity and the life cycle (monograph), *Psychological issues*, Vol. 1. International Universities Press, New York, N.Y. 1959.

2. Hartmann, Heinz: Ego psychology and the problems of adaptation. International Universities Press, New York, N.Y. 1958.

3. Alexander, Franz; Ross, Helen: Dynamic psychiatry. The University of Chicago Press, Chicago, Ill. 1952.

4. Freud, Anna: The ego and mechanisms of defense. International Universities Press, New York, N.Y. 1955.

5. Cloward, Richard A.; Ohlin, Lloyd E.: Delinquency and opportunity. Free Press, New York, N.Y. 1960.

6. Davis, C. M.: Self-selection of diets: an experience with infants. *The trained nurse and hospital review,* Vol. 86, No. 5, 1931.

7. Lewin, Kurt: Group decision and social change. *In* Readings in social psychology (G. E. Swanson, T. M. Newcomb, E. L. Hartley, eds.). Holt, Rinehart & Winston, New York, N.Y. 1952.

8. Lennard, Henry L.; Bernstein, Arnold: The anatomy of psychotherapy. Columbia University Press, New York, N.Y. 1960.

9. Strean, Herbert S.: Role theory, role models, and casework: a review of the literature and practice applications. *Social Work,* April 1967.

49.

Sex differences in the school: problem and proposed solution

GARY L. PELTIER

Peltier makes a good case for the contention that the elementary school really is a woman's world. Even though boys are handicapped by a slower maturity rate than girls, they are pressured to keep up and devalued when they cannot. It is not surprising that negative sets toward learning are established in boys which must be overcome or lead to dropping out of school later. Even if boys' more frequent learning difficulties are a true sex difference, should they be handled by comparison and "standards"?

Here, let us reemphasize the importance of early learning. More than three-fourths of one's mental capacity may have developed before the age of twelve years. Probably, basic attitudes, methods of problem solving, and styles of learning also are fairly well established by that time. How much these affect later learning, of course, only can be speculated. Certainly learning rates and styles cannot be expected to improve without specific planning and design.

Phi Delta Kappan, 50:182–185, 1968. Gary L. Peltier, Professor of Education, University of Nevada.

> *By the late high school and college years, academic achievement differences between the sexes tend to disappear. At least they do for those youngsters still in school. Again, speculation is necessary to assess the effect of the female-dominated elementary school upon dropout rates for male high school students.*

ONE OF the most interesting paradoxes in American life is the fact that although males traditionally take on the mantle of leadership in our society, it is the female who more often finds success in our educational system. More girls than boys graduate from high school (in the ratio of about 51 to 49). And although more boys attend college than do girls, girls often are more successful academically.

It appears that the Darwinian adage that the female of the species is more deadly than the male and thus more capable of survival also applies to humans. A female born in 1961 has a life expectancy of 73 years; a male only 67 years. The longevity of women partially explains why they control so much of the world's wealth.

In many ways, young males start life's struggle with gross handicaps. Boys mature less rapidly than girls: Physically they are a year behind at the age of six, 18 months behind at age nine, and a full two years less mature upon entrance to high school. Boys are also more susceptible to physical stress and trauma, as indicated by their higher death and illness rates.[1]

In addition, the prevalence of infantile autism and idiot savants among boys is clearly larger than among girls, as is the incidence of childhood schizophrenia and school adjustment and behavior problems. Indeed, as Sarason has noted, "Up until puberty it is extremely difficult to find a pathologic or problem condition in which the incidence among girls is greater than among boys."[2]

In school, teachers often find that girls excel in mental and educational achievement: Nearly two-thirds of all grade repeaters are boys; more boys than girls, by a huge margin, are underachievers and poor readers; three times as many boys as girls develop stuttering problems.

Although girls appear to be more successful in school, the question of significant and consistent sex differences in scholastic achievement is still unanswered. Some research has indicated that boys are inferior to girls in scholastic performance in the elementary grades. A study involving 13,000 pupils found that on the average girls of ages 8–11 surpass boys in reading ability at the same age.[3] However, a well-controlled study done by the California Test Bureau found no basic difference between the sexes in reading and arithmetic achievement, but in the basic skill areas of language (mechanics of English and spelling), the performance of girls was superior to that of boys even after differences that can be attributed to chronological age and mental age were controlled.[4]

In a more recent study, Wozencraft used a stratified sampling technique and found a real sex difference in favor of girls for total groups and for average ability groups in the third and sixth grades, when they were tested with the Stanford Achievement Test. At the third-grade level, girls in the total and average groups were superior in all four areas tested; at the sixth-grade level, girls in the total group excelled in average scores in reading, arithmetic computation, and the arithmetic composite. In the average ability group, the significant differences existed only in arithmetic computation and in the arithmetic composite. Wozencraft concluded that, in general, girls start off at an advantage in school work, but boys tend to catch up as they progress through the school grades.[5]

Parsley, Powell, and O'Connor analyzed results of the California Achievement Test Battery administered to an entire school population, grades 4–8, and found that significant sex differences did exist within three achievement levels for various I.Q. groups. In general, the results indicated that girls excelled in reading achievement and in arithmetic fundamentals, whereas boys tended to excel in arithmetic reasoning.[6] Other authors have also concluded that in most areas boys achieve as well as girls and in some cases, particularly mathematics, do even better.[7]

Achievement data for secondary students is found in the Project Talent report, *The American High School Student.* Flanagan and his co-authors noted the following general findings on sex differences in achievement: 1) On a test of information, girls in grades 9–12 did finish slightly more items on the average than did boys; 2) almost all the variables for which the reliability coefficient was markedly lower for one sex than for the other involved subject matter in which there were marked sex differences in amount of interest; 3) little difference between boys and girls existed throughout the middle and top of the distribution of scores on a test in reading comprehension, although toward the bottom of the distribution boys scored lower than girls; 4) girls exceeded boys on a test in arithmetic computation at grade nine, but by grade 12 there was little difference; 5) sex differences in a test concerned with arithmetic reasoning and in an achievement test covering intermediate high school mathematics were not significant, although by grade 12 scores for the boys were substantially higher; and 6) boys obtained higher scores on tests of vocabulary at all grade levels.

If sex differences in scholastic achievement await conclusive evidence, there is general agreement that boys do receive lower grades and thus a lower rank in class standing. A 1954 study found that high school girls were given higher rankings than boys in both teacher acceptance and marks, ". . . notwithstanding relative equivalence in actual attainment as measured by tests."[8] A study of Connecticut high schools found that the bottom 10 percent of rank in class was composed 64 percent of boys. In the top 10 percent, by rank in class, boys accounted for only 28 percent.[9] Coleman's data for adolescents provides further evidence of the discrepancy in grading between the sexes.[10] Similar marking practices appear to be prevalent on the elementary school level. A considerably higher failure rate for boys was found in grades one and two, in an NEA study of 532 school districts.[11] Such evidence seems to support the thesis that inequalities in grading between boys and girls do exist.

There is also some evidence to suggest that boys will do well in those academic subjects in which they are expected to be interested, such as mathematics and science. Rarely does a girl outshine a boy in these "masculine" subjects, partly because great interest and correspondingly high grades in science and mathematics are to some extent an invasion of a traditionally male-dominated area. In like fashion boys may feel uncomfortable in traditionally "feminine" subjects such as typing, stenography, art, and literature.

Thus girls appear to get a head-start in the academic race, thanks to a generally faster growth pattern. Although there are no significant differences in intelligence between the sexes which would help to explain the success of girls in school,[12] there are several social, psychological, and institutional factors which hinder the hapless boy in American education.

SOCIALIZATION

First of all, the socialization process in contemporary America is so organized that expectations toward girls' behavior tend to be more clearly defined and more consistent than is the case for boys of ages nine to 15. Although boys are expected to be more rebellious and aggressive, such behavior is unacceptable in many social situations. Also, access to appropriate adult identification models and opportunities for playing portions of their sex roles tend to favor girls. In the family, girls often have more opportunities to interact with their mothers than boys do with their fathers. The pattern is about the same in the school. For boys, the most accessible adult models, such as mothers and teachers, are often inappropriate. Too much interaction with mother, for example, tends to be disapproved as "sissy." In the school situation, "teacher's pet" is a label corresponding to "mama's boy" at home. At the same time, boys are often blocked from taking on significant portions of what is socially defined as appropriate male behavior, such as being aggressive, dominant, or exercising authority. A boy is not regarded as "all boy" unless he exhibits some overt aggression, although the opportunities for him to do so are few and the limitations of these opportunities are often ill-defined.[13]

PSYCHOLOGICAL DIFFERENCE

Psychological differences between the sexes are also soon apparent. Boys usually learn to be more aggressive, independent, and outspoken and to avoid displays of emotion, befitting their traditional sex roles. Boys generally are superior in analytical thinking, problem solving, and scientific pursuits.

Girls, however, are quickly nudged toward conformity and passivity. They tend to be more sensitive to human relations and are usually permitted to express emotions more fully. Female sensitivity often spurs artistic expression and an edge over boys in music and literature. There is further evidence that boys and girls develop different thinking styles, conditioned in part by their sex roles.[14] These thinking styles are further explored in the following discussion of the school's role in sex differences.

THE SCHOOL'S ROLE

The role of the school as an institution further complicates the problem of sex differences. Obviously, sex differences complicate teaching, yet schools have been essentially sex-neutral institutions, treating unequals as equals. We expect first-grade boys to write as well as their girl classmates, in spite of the fact that boys' small-muscle coordination is less well-developed. We also expect boys to progress through school at the same pace as girls in spite of their acknowledged slower rate of maturation.

Boys must also come to terms with conflicting expectations of how they should behave in school. Socially accepted role behavior such as male aggressiveness or dominance in school brings a boy into direct conflict with the teacher's role as the authority figure maintaining order in the classroom. Thus, although boys are expected to behave "like boys," to allow them to do so may upset classroom decorum and result in a loss of status on the part of the teacher. For most teachers such a loss is intolerable.

The large number of female teachers in the elementary schools also seems to work to the disadvantage of boys.[15] By being more analytical, boys may create difficulties for themselves by making too many decisions on their own rather than responding to suggestions and directions from the teacher. Several studies have indicated that elementary school girls receive significantly greater approval from teachers than do boys.[16] It is also true that girls perceive themselves as being more accepted and valued by parents than do boys.[17]

Women teachers scold disorderly boys much more often and much more harshly than they do girls, but this often only leads to greater aggressiveness by the boys.[18] Partly because of this, at least twice as many boys are reported to principals for learning problems and behavior disorders. Women teachers also tend to ask test questions that favor feminine ways of thinking. A girl, for example, is more likely to recall the details of how an organization like NATO works, while a boy could more likely generalize about the purpose of such defense treaties.[19]

Professors Jean Grambs and Walter Waetjen of the University of Maryland argue that "women literally do not know that they use words differently, structure space differently, perceive persons and reality differently from men." Women teachers may not even be aware that they "value neatness and cleanliness above intellectual initiative," and tend to be "not only more prejudiced" than men but "more dogmatic about their prejudices."[20] It is apparent that young boys who attempt to act in conformity with what they have learned as acceptable role behavior will be troubled and confused by the female-dominated classroom. If Grambs and Waetjen are correct, boys are handicapped by their different thinking styles, their inability to comprehend female language completely, and their unwillingness to conform to a feminine value system. For boys, the classroom may well be perceived as a place in which they must be quiet, neat, and think like girls—all of which appear to be contrary to their embryonic ideas of what a boy should be.

School is not apt to be an inviting place for boys. For example, Timmy, a six-year-old who was experiencing difficulty in school, told his father how his teacher had asked him to get some dirt for a planting project from the school yard. Said Timmy, "I was out there all alone, Daddy. I could have escaped."

PROPOSED SOLUTIONS

One often-discussed suggestion is to admit boys to school six months or so later in age than girls.[21] This would enable the slower-maturing boys to begin formal schooling on more equal terms with the girls with whom they must compete. Although this solution appears logical, no major school systems have tried it, probably because of anticipated parental opposition.

Another often considered but rarely tried method of handling sex differences is that of separate classes for boys and girls. Although many European countries have traditionally segregated the sexes, American educators have generally rejected either separate classes or separate schools, at least in modern times. We apparently assume that the social learning that takes place in the classroom is as important as the subject matter under study. It is also argued that segregated classes lessen the school's ability to simulate and reflect real life, although there is little evidence to support this argument.

Recently, however, the Wakefield Forest Elementary School in Fairfax County, Virginia, conducted a pilot program in instructional grouping by sex to investigate the possibility that separate classes for boys and girls might help to minimize the difficulties that boys so often face in school. During the six years that the program has been in operation, studies have indicated that the boys taught in separate classes made better progress in language arts and mathematics than boys in control classes, but the differences were not statistically significant.

Some other advantages of the single-sex classes at Wakefield Forest were a decline in discipline problems and the facts that students were happier, that attendance was better, and that the students were more willing to ask questions and participate in class activities. Motivation was more easily developed by gearing instruction to the interests of the particular sex being taught. Both boys and girls stated that they liked school better with sex grouping (parents also supported the program), and the vast majority of the teachers were in favor of the segregated classes.[22]

Single-sex classes are not the only innovative approach advocated. Some writers tend to favor grouping on the basis of maturational readiness for learning as opposed to grouping by sex,[23] while others have suggested that in view of the superiority of girls in the language area, additional instructional time may need to be given to boys in these subjects.[24]

Nearly everyone agrees on the need for more men teachers in the elementary school. Men are needed to provide appropriate role models, particularly in schools in areas where the divorce rate is high or where many families are fatherless. Grambs and Waetjen advocate male teacher-reseachers for elementary schools so that the men could avoid the usual female stereotype of the elementary teacher.

Other possible male jobs in elementary schools are those of counselor, psychologist, and principal. It has also been suggested that unemployed young men of good character and masculine image could be hired and assigned playground, lunchroom, and school bus duties. The use of sixth-grade boys as tutors and companions for first- and second-grade boys may also have some merit.[25]

A DIRECTION

Further research is obviously necessary before any mandate for major educational change is in order. In the meantime elementary schools would do well to experiment with special classes for boys in those areas in which boys appear to have a maturational and academic disadvantage, such as writing, spelling, and reading. Such classes should be more masculine in tone, more exploratory in nature, and more activity-oriented. Curriculum suggestions could well be garnered from those remedial reading texts which attempt to capture the interest of boys.

Integrated classes could be retained for the social studies, science, music, art, and mathematics, so that social, coeducational learning would not be slighted.

The problem of attracting men teachers to elementary schools is a formidable one. Prospective male teachers seem to be deterred from becoming elementary teachers by the female stereotype attached to the job, the generally lower prestige accorded to the elementary teacher as opposed to the secondary teacher, and, in some areas, lower salaries paid to elementary teachers.

Colleges of education, school administrators, and local school boards must work to make elementary teaching more attractive to pre-service teachers. Educating the public to the demanding tasks an elementary teacher performs would be a significant step toward upgrading the prestige of elementary teachers in general. Allowing PTA members to be the teacher for one day would be an enlightening experience for the public. Opportunities for prospective men teachers to serve as aides in elementary schools during their college years could serve to awaken them to the challenges and rewards of teaching in the elementary school as well as provide male images and language in elementary schools. School systems may wish to provide extra pay for male elementary teachers. This could be justified as additional salary for extra duties such as club sponsorship, directing physical fitness programs, or sponsorship of the school newspaper. Even "hazardous duty" pay for men in the female-dominated elementary school may be called for!

It also seems certain that junior and senior high schools should encourage students to explore various academic areas which have been traditionally taboo because of societal demands for appropriate sex-role activities and classes in the school. With today's need for talented young people, we can ill afford to nurture these stereotypes. Planning science classes from a female point of view could interest more talented girls in the sciences. Boys certainly should be allowed and even encouraged to take home economics, in view of the increasing number of working wives and mothers. Stenography and typing as study skills should be learned by both sexes.

American educational planners thus have several alternatives available to meet the problem of sex differences, including the usual one of ignoring it. But it seems unlikely that our schools will continue to overlook sex differences while our society is so sex-conscious and sex-structured. Using known sex differences as one consideration in organizing for instruction will become a further step toward the final goal of fully individualized instruction.

REFERENCES

1. Frances Bentzen, "Sex Ratios in Learning and Behavior Disorders" *National Elementary Principal,* November, 1966, pp. 13–17.
2. Sarason, *Psychological Problems in Mental Deficiency,* Third Edition. New York: Harper & Brothers, 1959.
3. Arthur I. Gates, "Sex Differences in Reading Ability," *Elementary School Journal,* May, 1961, pp. 431–34.
4. Willis W. Clark, "Boys and Girls: Are There Significant Ability and Achievement Differences?" *Phi Delta Kappan,* November, 1959, pp. 73–76.
5. Marian Wozencraft, "Sex Comparisons of Certain Abilities," *Journal of Educational Research,* September, 1963, pp. 21–27.
6. Kenneth M. Parsley, Marvin Powell, and Henry A. O'Connor, "Further Investigation of Sex Differences in Achievement of Under-, Average-, and Over-

Achieving Students Within Five I.Q. Groups in Grades Four Through Eight," *Journal of Educational Research,* January, 1964, pp. 268–70.

7. Pauline S. Sears and David Feldman, "Teacher Interactions with Boys and with Girls," *National Elementary Principal,* November, 1966, pp. 30–35.

8. Trevor Hadley, "A School Mark—Fact or Fancy?" *Educational Administration and Supervision,* December, 1954, pp. 305–12.

9. Arwood S. Northby, "Sex Differences in High School Scholarship: A Study of Connecticut High Schools in 1956," *School and Society,* February, 1958, pp. 63–64.

10. James Coleman, *The Adolescent Society.* New York: The Free Press, 1961, pp. 252–53.

11. "Pupil Promotion Policies and Rates of Promotion." Washington, D.C.: NEA, AASA, Education Research Service Study, Circular No. 5, 1958.

12. Clark, *op. cit.*

13. Eugene A. Weinstein, "An Analysis of Sex Differences in Adjustment," *Child Development,* December, 1960, pp. 721–28.

14. Sears and Feldman, *op. cit.*

15. Kagan, Jerome, "The Child's Sex Role Classification of School Objects," *Child Development,* December, 1964, pp. 1,051–56.

16. W. J. Meyer and George G. Thompson, "Teacher Interactions with Boys as Contrasted with Girls," in Raymond G. Kuhlen and George G. Thompson (eds.), *Psychological Studies of Human Development.* New York: Appleton-Century-Crofts, 1963; and Robert L. Spaulding, "Achievement, Creativity and Self-concept Correlates of Teacher-Pupil Transactions in Elementary Schools," Cooperative Research Project No. 1352. Washington, D.C.: Office of Education, 1963.

17. Walter Waetjen, "Is Learning Sexless?" *Education Digest,* September, 1962, pp. 12–14.

18. Sears and Feldman, *op. cit.,* p. 34.

19. Jean B. Grambs and Walter Waetjen, "Being Equally Different: A New Right for Boys and Girls," *National Elementary Principal,* November, 1966, pp. 59–67.

20. *Ibid.*

21. "Let's Give the Boys a Break!" *Phi Delta Kappan,* April, 1959, pp. 281–83.

22. Thomas B. Lyles, "Grouping by Sex," *National Elementary Principal,* November, 1966, pp. 38–44.

23. Bentzen, *op. cit.*

24. Clark, *op. cit.*

25. Grambs and Waetjen, *op. cit.*

50.

The concept readiness and several applications

E. KUNO BELLER

*Beller's article possesses relevance for any of the various sections deal-
ing with teaching and learning. It is placed here because it brings pertinent research on the subject into focus and because it points up the
strong relationship between emotional and cognitive readiness. We
believe that one does not learn so well, think so clearly, or choose so
intelligently when he feels threatened. We are glad to know of research that supports our beliefs.*

*Professor Beller, by reviewing research data and adding insights
from his own investigations, shows that readiness is a complex phenomenon and that it includes much more than physical maturity. He
confirms what most teachers know but do not consistently observe:
that one does not simply wait for readiness—it is an outcome of culture, family relationships, learning style, and requisite prior learning.
Some teachers might find it difficult to accept the fact that they themselves are part of the readiness complex, inasmuch as their behaviors
elicit or inhibit trust.*

*It also is commonly known that readiness is in part dependent
upon materials and subject matter; but the matter of pupils' styles of
learning is almost totally overlooked. And it is precisely for this reason that the editors liked the presentation. We believe that, to the extent that varied learning styles are recognized and respected, we will
see some gigantic strides made in teaching effectiveness. Appreciation
of readiness is an important first step in recognition of style.*

THE FIRST PART of this article will deal with a review of the concept of
readiness and a proposed formulation, the second part with the application
of this formulation to recent research on cognitive processes and the teaching of cognitive operations. The third part will deal with implications of
research on emotional and motivational factors for readiness in disadvantaged children.

Reading, per se, is not discussed in this article. Learning, language
development and training, and certain disturbances of readiness are pre-

The Reading Teacher, 23(No. 8):727–737, May, 1970. Reprinted with permission of
E. Kuno Beller and the International Reading Association. E. Kuno Beller, Professor of
Psychology, Temple University.

The discussion of applications is based in part on research carried out by the author with
support from the Ford Foundation through a grant to the Philadelphia Council of Community Advancement and with the support from the Head Start Evaluation and Research Center at Temple University.

sented. A major question to be answered by the reader, therefore, would be: "Is this not information which should be interpreted to parents anxious to aid their children in mastering the reading process?"

THE CONCEPT READINESS

Few concepts in education have been surrounded with more controversy than the concept readiness. Nevertheless, the question of whether the child is ready to learn and to be taught anything new in the cognitive, social or emotional realm remains a vital issue to many educators. Rousseau's (1964) viewpoint of two centuries ago, which is well reflected by his statement, "Regard all delays in teaching as so much time gained; it is already a great gain to have reached this stage without loss: let childhood ripen in children. On the other hand, are certain lessons unavoidable? If so, be careful not to administer them today, if they can safely be put off until tomorrow," has continued to the present day. Underlying Rousseau's concept of readiness was a concept of maturation. One of his major criticisms of education in his day was that educators did not wait for the necessary faculties to ripen in the child. He advised educators to make maximum use of sensory-motor functions which are well developed in the child and suggested a series of activities which the child could carry out and which would go a long way in preparing him for more complex intellectual activities later on in his development. Rousseau's ideas were formalized into a pedagogic system by Pestalozzi (1767) and Montessori (1914). The elaboration of Rousseau's ideas of a sensory-motor phase of development as part of a cognitive development had to wait for the genius of Piaget two centuries later. It is important to keep in mind that, whereas Rousseau and his followers emphasized the concept of readiness, they labored hard to specify the activities which the young child was ready to carry out in preparation for later stages of development. Some of these specifications will be discussed in the context of Piaget.

A different school of readiness which bears some superficial resemblance to that of the thinkers discussed above is represented by Gesell and his associates. Gesell continued the tradition of Darwin, Galton, and Hall (Kessen, 1965) and was more interested in biological speculations about developmental changes in behavior than in the interactions of organism environment and experience and the effects of this interaction on development. He considered maturation as the basic principle for development and maturation was conceived as developmental change due to inner forces. Environmental factors may influence these developmental sequences but the basic course is laid down by biological factors (Gesell, 1954). So, we find Ilg and Ames (1964) of the Gesell Institute, who developed an elaborate battery of tests for school readiness, write:

"The need for accommodation of the environment to both age and individual differences becomes evident from the moment of the child's birth . . . as hard as the mother may try to impose a rigid schedule on some infants, she is not successful unless she responds to the individual demands . . .", and ". . . the greatest single contribution which can be made towards guaranteeing that each individual child will get the most possible out of his school experience is to make certain that he starts that school experience at what is for him the 'right' time. This should be the time when he is truly ready . . ." (1964, P. 6, 14)

For Ilg and Ames, true readiness is based on careful records of what children actually do under normal circumstances. Environmental factors such as ethnic background, social class or any other system of environmental influences are not given any systematic place in the determination of readiness. Biological speculations are offered in the place of psychological theory to account for developmental change. The same viewpoint is reflected by others who are much more concerned with education and curriculum than were Gesell and his associates, e.g., Hymes (1958). "As surely as the baby sat and crawled and stood and walked, always in his own good time, the power on which reading instruction can build will also develop. Maturation and living make this inevitable."[1]

At the opposite extreme, are statements such as those made by Watson earlier in the century: "Give me a dozen healthy infants, well-formed, and my own specified world to bring them up in and I'll guarantee to take any one at random and train him to become any type of specialist I might select—doctor, lawyer, artist, merchant-chief and yes, even beggar-man and thief, regardless of his talents, penchants, tendencies, abilities, vocations, and race of his ancestors," and more recently by Bruner (1960): "The foundations of any subject may be taught to anybody at any age in some form." Such statements provide useful information concerning attitudes underlying educational policies in a broad sense, but they hardly qualify as propositions of knowledge, especially in the empirical sense.

The concept readiness is too complex to lend itself to simplistic generalizations. Statements concerning readiness become more meaningful, in the sense of being testable in some ways, when the criteria of readiness are pinned down to specific activities or operations in such a way that their relationship to the rate of learning and level of achievement of new activities or operations can be ascertained and in some way predicted. Even more important for the concept of readiness to be meaningful is the requirement that the activities and operations which define readiness relate in some logical way to new activities and operations which are to be learned or to the educational method by means of which the new operations are to be taught. This approach to the problem of readiness poses greater difficulties, especially for studies dealing with developmental change in complex psychological processes.

COGNITIVE FACTORS IN READINESS

Fruitful beginnings in this direction of the proposed formulation of readiness have recently appeared in the research literature. Gagne's (1961, 1962) research on the role of learning sets in the acquisition of knowledge, particularly his study of readiness for learning various steps in the hierarchical sequence of mathematical operations, meets some of the requirements which are being proposed in this paper for the study of readiness to learn complex cognitive operations. Gagne proposes a hierarchical system within which certain operations such as "counting," "addition," "subtraction," "multiplication," and "division" are the elementary steps which have to be mastered by an individual to be ready for an understanding and for the mastery of more complex steps such as the solving of equations.

Piaget's formulations of cognitive development have opened up new horizons for the establishment of successive criteria of readiness as a propensity to move from isolated, less coherent mental operations to increasingly more interrelated and complex cognitive operations. For example, in Piaget's (1952) system of sensory-motor development, vision and prehension start out as isolated reflexes. The integration and eventually the dominance of vision over prehension not only moves a child to a higher level of development, but changes altogether the child's experience. Passive reflexity changes into voluntary and eventually into goal-directed behavior. This and other formations described in great detail by Piaget, lay the foundation for further intellectual development such as intentional cognition. At this point, Piaget shows how the next step in cognitive development depends heavily upon experience. While engaging in goal-directed behavior and encountering obstacles in the path towards the goal, the child develops notions of temporal sequence, causality, and the relationship between objects other than himself. Confrontation and interaction with peers forces the child to question the validity of his egocentric views and to revise them. Piaget shows how each stage in development makes a child ready for the next step. Most importantly for meanings of readiness, Piaget makes explicit the logic of developmental progression and shows how operations on one stage prepare the child for operations on the next stage. Piaget's concept of conservation is a case in point. He defines clearly the mental operations, e.g., decentration, multiple classification, and reversibility, which a child must be able to carry out so as to be ready for the operation of conservation, which requires the synthesis of these operations. Sigel (1969) has carried out a series of pioneer studies in this area. These investigators have trained children who could not conserve in the prerequisite operation of multiple classification, multiplicative relations, reversibility and seriation. They found that such training of prerequisite operations made the child more ready to carry out the operation of conservation. It becomes clear that Piaget's system of cognitive development provides a meaningful model of progression in which mastery of certain operations meets the criteria of readiness which appear most meaningful to this writer. Research such as that carried out by Sigel and his associates promises to provide experimental verification of such criteria of readiness in cognitive development.

The discussion so far has been limited to a consideration of readiness in relation to the development of cognitive abilities and skills. The concept of "cognitive styles" does not refer to an ability or skill but rather to a disposition which may influence a child's readiness to benefit more from one type of instruction than from another. In other words, cognitive style may function as a readiness factor in the individualization of instruction. To illustrate such a relationship, the author will discuss a study which he has carried out recently (Beller, 1967). To begin with, a child may order the world he experiences or what he perceives in a variety of ways. One of the ways in which a child may accomplish this is by grouping or classification. There are different types of classification. Kagan, *et al.* (1963) and Sigel (In press) have referred to this process as "cognitive style" and have distinguished several different styles. They have developed first a set of pictures (Kagan, *et al.*) and later a set of objects (Sigel) to determine the preferred style of any individual. Sigel has distinguished three major styles: a descriptive-analytic or part-whole style; a contextual-relational style; and a categorical-inferential style. The term descriptive-analytic or part-whole cognitive style refers to the classification of objects in terms of their objective characteristics such as color, size, or form. The contextual-relational style refers to the classification of objects in terms of their functional use and relation to each other. The term categorical style refers to the classification of objects in terms of some inferred characteristics which are not directly observable.

It is assumed that children form such preferred dispositions or styles of experience early in their life and that these remain stable characteristics, in other words, offer an experiential typology. In a recent study (Beller, 1967), the author has investigated the possibility that methods of language training may correspond to one or another of these cognitive styles and that this common core might make a method of training more or less effective, depending upon its correspondence with the child's preferred style. Such a study was indicated because of the nature of certain types of language instruction. For example, phonetic training, the training of vocabulary and classification consist largely of teaching a child to associate letters or sounds with words, words with objects, words with words, and objects with objects. The association between words and between objects is achieved through the use of criteria for grouping objects as belonging together or as not belonging together. Moreover, objects can be associated in a variety of ways. This association may be based on a shared characteristic such as color, size, and shape which both objects have in common, on a functional relationship between two objects, or on an inferred characteristic shared by both objects. For example, if you consider a (building) block and a box, the two may be together because both share a common color such as brown, or because both start with a "b" (i.e., descriptive, part-whole style), because the block can be put into the box (i.e., relational style), or because both are toys or are made out of wood (categorical style). Thus, in the process of teaching phonetics, vocabulary, and further characteristics of objects which have become part of the child's vocabulary, the child learns to use certain categories for associating the reference objects, e.g., "block" and "box." The criteria of association correspond exactly to the cognitive styles described earlier, namely descriptive-analytic, relational, and categorical.

The relevance of this study for readiness was that it controlled experimentally the logical relationship between operational criteria of readiness, namely cognitive styles and the methods of language training. Readiness in this case was not conceived of as an ability, but rather as a disposition which might make it possible to individualize language instruction and thereby make language training more efficient. Specifically, by varying the correspondence between the child's preferred cognitive style and the method of language training, it was possible to determine the effects of the child's cognitive style (i.e., readiness) on learning (regardless of the method of teaching), the effect of method of language training on learning (regardless of the child's cognitive style), and thirdly, the interreacting effects on learning of both the child's cognitive style and the method with which he is being trained. The outcome of the study demonstrated that readiness in the form of cognitive style and teaching method affected learning or language acquisition both separately and in interaction with one another. Children with a dominantly descriptive style achieved better recognition memory of vocabulary regardless of the methods with which they were taught. Conversely, the descriptive method of language training produced better recognition memory regardless of the child's initial cognitive style. In contrast, children who had a predominantly relational style improved most in their associative memory regardless of the method with which they were taught. Again, the same applied to the relational method of training, regardless of the child's cognitive style. Finally, there was a consistent trend for children to achieve better recognition and associative memory wherever the method of training corresponded with the child's cognitive style or readiness. These findings emerged on a paired associate learning test which was especially constructed to evaluate the effects of cognitive styles (readiness, method of language training, and the interaction between the two).

Another set of findings in the study was obtained from the use and comparison of performance on the *Illinois Test of Psycholinguistic Abilities* before and after language training. A major finding relevant for readiness was that matching the child's cognitive style with the method of language training was clearly more effective than non-matching. The second major finding was found in a group of children who could not sufficiently verbalize to be classified with regard to cognitive styles. It was found that these children who were most backward in language development benefited generally more than other children from the functional-relational method of language training.

As indicated earlier, this study was discussed here to illustrate research on readiness in which it can be shown that a meaningful relationship exists between the operation of readiness and the method of instruction. A conclusion to be drawn from that study is that individualization of instruction has positive effects on language acquisition.

EMOTIONAL AND MOTIVATIONAL FACTORS IN READINESS

The interrelationship between readiness and method of teaching as well as the need for individualization of instruction can also be found in the case of non-cognitive factors such as emotion, motivation, and interpersonal relationships. With regard to the non-cognitive variables of readiness, it should be pointed out that it is often the non-cognitive aspects of teaching or educational methods which must be modified in order to maximize the effectiveness of instruction. In the case of the child who is not ready because of a lack of motivation to learn, it is, of course, indicated first to search for the causes which conflict with the motivation to learn or to be taught. When such factors cannot be found, or cannot be altered, special incentives, contingencies, and other non-cognitive factors are introduced into the teaching process to increase motivational readiness for learning. However, when the particular motivational or emotional factors effecting readiness are unclear, then the theoretical or logical basis for introducing special techniques in the educational process remains also obscure. When that happens, the procedure is similar to the use or prescription of drugs which bring about desired changes without an adequate understanding of the processes responsible for the change. Motivational and emotional factors in certain disturbances of readiness to learn, such as "underachievement" and "school phobia" are still too unclear to permit a logical relationship between readiness and individualization of instruction. However, this problem does not exist in all cases of emotional disturbances in readiness. For example, if the problem is one of low self-confidence on the part of the child which results in a poor reaction to the learning situation, it is possible to maximize opportunities for success so as to let the child gradually build up his self-confidence. The problem here is that in spite of the frequent use of the term "self," especially in relation to the disadvantaged child, it is often difficult to assess, let alone measure, self-image, and self-confidence.

Considerable progress has been made in the area of interpersonal relationships and their effect on readiness. It has been generally known that lower-class, deprived children approach the formal education situation and the educator with a great deal of fear and mistrust which in turn affects their readiness to learn and perform in this situation. This condition has a similar depressing effect as test anxiety on cognitive performance (Sarason, 1960). The author has carried out a study (Beller, 1968) in which, among other things, the effects of this initial apprehensiveness of the disadvantaged child on cognitive performance were investigated. The major purpose of this study was to evaluate the effect of timing of educational intervention in deprived, lower-class children. One group of children began school with nursery at four, a second group began schooling in kindergarten at five, and a third group entered first grade without any prior pre-school experience. These three groups have been compared in a longitudinal study on cognitive and motivational factors and on the interrelationship between these variables. The initial level of intellectual functioning was assessed at the outset for each group. In order to reduce the adverse effects of a new and unfamiliar situation, children were given an opportunity to become familiar with the school environment for several months before the initial testing was carried out. It was found that child's initial I.Q. score did not vary as a function of the time at which educational intervention was started. In other words, the level of intellectual achievement of nursery children, kindergarten children, and first graders in Get Set and ghetto schools as measured by several tests did not differ at the outset when they entered school. Because of uncontrollable circumstances, the same battery of tests had to be given to a group of children immediately after they entered school, that is, within the first three weeks after school entry. This group differed from the other two groups by having a significantly lower performance score on one of the tests; namely, the Stanford Binet tests. The inference was made that this deviant finding was due to heightened undissipated apprehensiveness over the new situation. This inference was tested subsequently by selecting a comparable group in the same classroom and giving them the same test several months after they entered the first grade. The new group performed significantly better than the group which was tested immediately after school entry.

The relevance of this study for readiness was twofold: first, a child's initial level of intellectual performance served as a base line for measuring the effectiveness of educational intervention; thus an artificially depressed initial base line could distort in a variety of ways the obtained change (from pre- to post-testing). Secondly, the emotional component of readiness greatly affected the child's intellectual performance. At least during the initial phase after entering school, the disadvantaged child is apprehensive and this tended to depress his performance. This initial apprehensiveness and its effect on the pre-test, the measure of readiness, dissipated after a relatively short time and with it, the child's intellectual performance rose significantly. Thus, the logic of the relationship between emotional readiness and cognitive functioning was borne out: the apprehensiveness of the child in reaction to a new and strange situation, which represents threatening authority, produces generally inhibiting effects, which extends not only into interpersonal behavior, but also to the cognitive realm, at least insofar as performance is concerned.

The same study which yielded the finding described above explored in greater depth the effects of a child's mistrust towards the adult environment and the relationships of such mistrust with other motivational as well as cognitive factors. Mistrust of adults was defined in this study as conflict over turning to the adult for help and emotional support such as praise and affection. The term used for this measure was Dependency Conflict. A meaning of this conflict is that the child is conflicted over making use of the help and nurturing available to him from the adult environment. It is to be expected that such mistrust and conflict will affect behaviors of the child which are expected of him from the teacher. For example, it was found that a heightening of mistrust or dependency conflict in a child was associated with both lower motivation to achieve and with lower level of actual achievement. Parenthetically, it should be noted that measures of motivation to achieve and of actual achievement were obtained from entirely separate sources.

Since this finding was based on several hundred disadvantaged lower-class children enrolled in nursery, kindergarten, and first grade, and since the study extended throughout the entire school year, it would seem safe to conclude that mistrust of the teacher and conflict over turning to the teacher for help and emotional support affects not only the child's readiness to perform but also his readiness to benefit from the educational experience. Whatever the causal relationship might be, it is clear from this set of findings that the disadvantaged child who is not ready to trust the educational situation and the adult educator is also handicapped in other ways, such as in his motivation to achieve and in his readiness to exhibit his abilities when asked to do so in a test situation. Moreover, these readiness factors influence a child not only at the moment of entrance into school, but appear to persist over time in some children as they continue their educational experience in school. This conclusion is not inconsistent with the findings reported earlier; namely, that as a group, children are more apprehensive when they enter a new situation than several months later, after they have had the opportunity to become familiar with the new situation.

Another finding in the same study is of interest. In comparisons of three groups of children by the end of the first grade, i.e., Group A which had been in school since nursery (three years); Group B, since kindergarten (for two years); and Group C, since first grade (for one year), found that length of time in school was associated with decreasing dependency conflict or mistrust of the educational environment. In other words, by the end of the first grade, the group of children who had been in school for only one year manifested the highest dependency conflict or mistrust of the teacher. The implications of this finding for readiness to benefit from educational experience and the meaning of the relationship between dependency, motivation to achieve and actual intellectual achievement have been discussed earlier. The child who mistrusts the helper and is conflicted over making use of the help available to him is less ready to benefit from the educational process. These findings offer an example of the role and interpersonal factors as an important part of readiness. A crucial next step for research in this area would be to investigate various modifications in the teaching process that might counteract and overcome the child's mistrust of the educational setting and his conflict over expressing his need for help and support in that situation. Such investigations would appear to be important, not only for the sake of facilitating cognitive development in the child, but also for socialization in other areas. For example, it was found that children who were high in dependency conflict also tended to have greater problems than other children in impulse control, particularly in the control of aggression. These continued problems may reflect a lack of readiness on the part of the child to respond to the socializing agent. Thus it would seem that the same forces, both internally and externally, which interfere with the child's readiness to respond to educational processes aimed at developing cognitive functioning also interfere with the child's readiness to respond to the socializing efforts of the educator on impulse control in general and on aggression in particular. However, it should be pointed out that the failure of socialization is often a two-way process. The teacher is no more "ready" to help the child cope with unacceptable impulses and behavior than the child is "ready" to respond favorably to attempts by the teacher to help him. This author has experienced considerable reluctance in a good many nursery and kindergarten teachers of disadvantaged children to recognize and permit the expression of even moderate aggression in the classroom. Thus, one is likely to find less overt expression of aggression in pre-school classes of the disadvantaged child than in pre-school classes of middle-class children. Of course, this does not result in socialization of the child's aggression and other undesirable behaviors; it simply keeps the undesirable behavior out of the classroom. The adult who does not permit the child to express undesirable behavior and does not help the child to cope differently with frustration and tension does not remove the instigation to such behavior but increases the child's mistrust of himself and adult authority. In a broader sense, the teacher as a socializer has achieved a minor success and a major failure. When the same child who continues to live in the ghetto, under many frustrations, approaches adolescence, aggressive and other undesirable impulses come to the fore again, both in the classroom and away from the classroom. But at that point, the child is less ready to be socialized than he was in pre-school.

The author has not attempted to give specific suggestions to school personnel in dealing with communication with parents. It is hoped that the concepts and research findings presented will be shared with parents in a meaningful way. This is impossible until adults working with children understand the concepts and are able, therefore, to help guide parents in the understanding of children and how they learn.

REFERENCES

Beller, E. K. Cognitive styles and methods of language training. Paper presented at the American Educational Research Association, New York, February, 1967.

Beller, E. K. The evaluation of effects of early educational intervention on intellectual and social development of lower-class, disadvantaged children. Paper presented at a colloquium for Head Start, Washington, D.C. October 9, 1968.

Bruner, J. S. *The process of education.* (Part 4) Cambridge: Harvard University Press, 1960. P. 12.

Fowler, W. Cognitive learning in infancy and childhood. *Psychological Bulletin,* 1962, *59,* 116–152

Gagne, R. M., and Paradise, N. E. Abilities and learning sets in knowledge acquisition. *Psychological Monographs,* 1961, *75* (14), 1–23.

Gagne, R. M., Major, J. R., Garstens, H. L., and Paradise, N. E. Factors in acquiring knowledge of a mathematical task. *Psychological Monographs,* 1962, *76* (7), 1–21.

Gesell, A. The ontogenesis of infant behavior. In L. Carmichael (Ed.) *Manual of child psychology.* New York: John Wiley & Sons, Inc., 1954. Pp. 355–356.

Hymes, J. L., Jr. *Before the child reads.* Evanston, Illinois: Row, Peterson & Co., 1958. P. 28.

Ilg, F. L., and Ames, L. B. *School readiness behavior test used at the Gesell institute.* New York: Harper & Row, 1964. P. 6, 14.

Kagan, J., Moss, H. A., and Sigel, I. E. The psychological significance of styles of conceptualization. *Monograph of the Society for Research in Child Development,* 1968, *28* (2).

Kessen, W. *The child.* New York: John Wiley & Sons, Inc., 1965.

Montessori, M. *Dr. Montessori's own handbook.* New York: Frederick H. Stokes Co., 1914.

Heafford, R. M. *Pestalozzi.* London: Methuen & Co., Ltd., 1967.

Piaget, J. *The origins of intelligence in children.* New York: International Universities Press, 1952.

Rousseau, J. J. *Emile ou de l'education.* Paris: Farnier Freres, 1964. P. 83.

Sarason, S. B., et al. *Anxiety in elementary school children.* New York: John Wiley & Sons, Inc., 1960.

Sigel, I. E. The Piagetian system and the world of Education. In D. Elkind and J. H. Flavell (Eds.) *Studies in cognitive development: essays in honor of Jean Piaget.* New York: Oxford University Press, 1969. Pp. 465–489.

Sigel, I. E., and Olmsted, P. Modification of classification, competence, and level of representation among lower-class Negro kindergarten children. In H. A. Passow (Ed.) *Reaching the disadvantaged learner.* New York: Columbia Teachers College Press. (In press)

Tyler, F. T. Issues related to readiness to learn. In E. Hilgard (Ed.) *National Society for the Study of Education*, Part I. Chicago: University of Chicago Press, 1964. Pp. 210–239.

NOTE

1. For an informative discussion of the ambiguity surrounding the concept of maturation, the reader is referred to Tyler (1964). For an interesting discussion of the implications of the concept readiness with regard to the age at which a child can be taught cognitive skills, the reader is referred to an extensive review by W. Fowler (1962).

51.

Social and biological deprivation influences on learning and performance

JAMES E. BIRREN
ROBERT D. HESS

What answers can research offer concerning differences in the cognitive and educational abilities that may be attributed to socioeconomic status? This article does a good job of answering that question. Its authors cite a number of studies on the subject, summarize relative findings, and draw some pertinent conclusions. They do most of the work for the reader, but they don't do it all. This is not an easy article to read. It covers a myriad of topics, and a great deal of information is condensed into comparatively few lines.

The editors suggest that Kagan's idea be kept in mind—that effective learning depends upon home environments in which maximally distinctive stimuli are possible. Also Hess' article dealing with the linguistic-interactional style of mothers may make this reading more meaningful. The editors were particularly impressed by the concept of "cumulative deficit phenomena" as applied to culturally different children. Youngsters who do not learn easily fall further and further behind as they progress through school. The gap between them and their more adept fellows grows wider and wider. This process does not end when school ends. Automation and modern technology accentuate the differences as never before. This happens because of the increased accessibility to sources of power provided by computers and intricate

Part II of Chapter 2, *Perspectives on Human Deprivation—Biological, Psychological, and Sociological,* Washington, D.C.: U.S. Department of Health, Education, and Welfare, 1968, pp. 116–138.

machines. *These add to and continue to increase the power differential between those people who can gain the expertise necessary to control them and those who cannot. Hence, the problem posed by the culturally different is cumulative.*

SOCIOECONOMIC STATUS DIFFERENCES IN COGNITIVE AND EDUCATIONAL ABILITY[1]

THE CURRENT body of research is replete with studies that describe children from socio-economically deprived areas as possessing characteristics which limit their school achievement:

1. Restricted and limited knowledge of their environment;
2. Concretistic in their thought rather than conceptualistic (Sigel & Olmsted, 1967);
3. Using language for communication but not as a tool for reflective and introspective thought (John, 1963);
4. Reading and learning disability in terms of school tasks (Deutsch, 1963);
5. Presenting a high potential of school failure;
6. Time orientation in the present with short-time perspective for planning (Miller, Riessman & Seagull, 1965);
7. Difficulty in dealing with representational material, imagery, etc. (Sigel & McBane, 1967).

The repeatedly documented association between abilities and socioeconomic and cultural variables provides a useful but limited framework for identifying gross differences in the effects of environment upon abilities. At this level of analysis, the lack of information about both developmental and environmental variables leaves genetic and experiential factors confounded and precludes effective manipulation of the conditions of learning. In contrast, variables such as child-rearing (Baldwin, *et al.,* 1945; Bronfenbrenner, 1958), communication modes (Hess & Shipman, 1965), and the general learning atmosphere and degree of language focus in the home (Dave, 1953) have not only been shown to be more potently related to abilities, but they can be conceptualized in terms which bear more directly on the learning processes themselves.

A specialized contemporary development is the interest in analytic, integrative, scanning, and other processes of cognitive style (Fowler, 1966; Kagan, *et al.,* in press; Gardner, *et al.,* 1959, 1960), which appear to function on a level intermediate between general intelligence and specific, area-linked abilities. They bear some resemblance to functions in earlier faculty psychology, which foundered on questions of transfer of learning (Grose & Birney, 1963). Yet, their anchorage, both in trait characteristics of personality and in properties of stimulus organization and perception, which find modest inter-situation reliability in other contexts, suggest an important dimension of information-processing and learning. In fact, there is evidence which directly links variations in representational (pictorial), analytic, and verbal abstract modes of functioning with ability and absence of social deprivation (Hess & Shipman, 1965; Sigel, Jerman & Hanesian, 1967).

Another important line of research activity which has important implications for the differentiation of abilities and for the deprived child is the study of curiosity motivation and stimulus complexity and incongruity (Berlyne, 1960; Fiske and Maddi, 1961; Hunt, 1965). Findings in these areas indicate that the optimal conditions of arousal to perform and thus to learn probably vary according to how well the stimulus patterns dovetail with the already acquired perceptual-cognitive patterns and expectations of the subject. These findings would suggest that many of the difficulties of socially (perceptually-cognitively) deprived children in school systems reflect grossly discrepant matches between program structures and the cognitive structures with which the deprived child is equipped. These studies also serve to reinforce the value of current movements toward programmed learning.

There are other significant motivational characteristics which have been more or less identified in deprived children. Among these are a greater difficulty in delaying gratification, in working for longer range goals, and both greater apathy and withdrawal on one side, and hyperactivity, and low impulse control on the other (Ausubel, 1963). These may reasonably be seen as responses to the character of lower-class environments, but they may also be more persisting response patterns of the individual. There is evidence that under conditions that insure tighter, continuing matches between the curriculum and the child, some of these (gross) motivational problems are dissipated (e.g., Bereiter, 1967; Fowler & Burnett, 1967; Sprigle, 1967).

One of the additional constraints upon the earlier attempts to relate social-environmental factors to ability arose from the fact that the major instrument employed to assess intellectual development was the IQ test. As with sociological variables, IQ test scores provide information largely at the most general level of population trends. The single, linear index minimizes the patterning and organization of abilities through the elimination of items which do not correlate highly with one another (Meyers and Dingman, 1960). This kind of assessment furnishes little data on learning and other cognitive functions. It also makes it difficult to analyze the relations between specific environmental sources and types of deprivation and stimulation (even if they have been adequately measured) on the one hand, and the development of abilities on the other. Moreover, the frequent and large individual IQ shifts are partly due to shifts in test composition relative to age.

Based on Piaget's (1952) observations and theories of cognitive development, there is a movement to measure cognitive development in terms of sequential scales of a variety of stage-linked cognitive operations (e.g., causality, intentionality, object identity, etc.). One study of infants shows a correlation of an object permanence scale with the Griffith Intelligence Scale of .916 (Decarie, 1965). This high correlation supports the view that Piaget's concepts of cognitive processes concentrate on intelligence at the most general and abstract level possibly to the neglect of many of the language-content, task-linked, and cognitive style characteristics which are later found to account for and explain more focally many individual differences in learning ability. Significant trend differences between advantaged and disadvantaged infants as early as eleven months of age on some Piaget type scales (Hunt, Wachs & Uzgiris, 1967), however, suggest that these more logically identified cognitive operations may define ability characteristics more functionally than the traditional global and linear mental (IQ) tests. The latter instruments generally show no social class or other group differences until after two years of age, except on some motor items which favor Negro children regardless of class (Bayley, 1965).

A further important problem emerging in current efforts to explore and develop more varied measures of cognitive processes and other skills is the question of creativity. In the opinion of some, traditional IQ measures are composed mainly of tasks which place a premium upon memory and closed systems of problem-solving and upon producing a specific predefined product (Getzels & Jackson, 1962; Guilford, 1967; Wallach & Kogan, 1965; Sigel, 1963). Measures are being developed which appear to be distinct from IQ measures and which measure more open-system, constructional forms of cognitive activity. There is evidence that certain forms of highly controlled child-rearing techniques in some phases of middle-class family life may be defined as forms of stimulus deprivation. The child is deprived of opportunities to explore, to ask broader questions, and to be exposed to varying stimulus situations. These child-rearing patterns make him bright but less creatively productive than the child reared in a still highly intellectually-oriented, but more interactive open-ended fashion (e.g., D'Heurle & Haggard, 1959; Datta & Parloff, 1967).

Against this overview of relationships between social background and cognitive activities, it may be useful to summarize some research bearing on social class and ethnic differences in cognitive behavior and educational attainment.

1. *Socio-economic Status Differences in Global Estimates of Behavior*[2]

Correlation coefficients between IQ or percentile ranks and the socio-economic status scores of white children summarized across many studies (Eells *et al.,* 1951) are moderate in size but statistically significant. The magnitude of correlation varies with the test used and the age level tested, half range between .25 and .50. In Eells' study, using standard group tests and age levels of 9, 10, 13 and 14 years, correlations ranged between .20 and .40 and were linear for the two older groups but non-linear for the two younger groups (where the relationship was linear only for groups below upper-middle class). The mean IQ differences between high and low SES groups ranged from 8 to 23 IQ points, the amount of IQ difference varying from test to test and by age level of the subjects. This study also confirmed previous results indicating a large amount of over-lapping at all SES levels. Many high SES subjects received low scores and many low SES subjects obtained high scores.

2. Socio-economic Status Differences in the Profile of Cognitive Operations

An item analysis of the IQ test differences between SES groups might be expected to be informative about the environmental conditions which might have been responsible for the differences, but findings that bear on this question are not entirely consistent. Evidence was provided in studies reported by Binet (1911), Stern (1914), Weintrob and Weintrob (1912), Bridges and Coler (1917), Burt (1922), Stoke (1927), Long (1935), Saltzman (1940), and Murray (1947). Eells et al. (1951), reporting on these studies, concluded that despite many inadequacies of procedure and some inconsistency of results, there appears to be a common tendency in the findings indicating that "test items which are essentially linguistic or scholastic in nature show comparatively large differences in favor of children from high socio-economic backgrounds, while test items which are primarily perceptual or 'practical' in nature show either smaller differences or differences in favor of children from the lower socioeconomic backgrounds." Havighurst and Breese (1947) compared the test scores of 13-year olds in terms of Primary Mental Abilities (Thurstone & Thurstone, 1943, 1958) and found that while high status children scored higher on all variables, social class differences were greatest for the Verbal, Word-Fluency, and Number variables and less pronounced for Space, Reasoning, and Memory. Roberts and Robinson (1952) and Mitchell (1956), studying the factorial organization of mental abilities of high and low SES children aged 11 and 12, found the same factors (Number, Verbal Meaning, Space, Word Fluency, Reasoning and a general Test Factor) for both SES groups. The organization of mental abilities was, however, much less differentiated for the low status children, whose pattern reflected a larger general intellective factor (Spearman's g) and less differentiation of the other factors. On the assumption that SES differences in IQ are primarily verbal, Mitchell suggested that this result was partly attributable to the greater saturation of the general factor with verbal components. The lower class child does not have the necessary verbal competence to perform, without a particular effort, the verbal tasks involved even in the non-verbal tests. Therefore, all mental tests, whether verbal or non-verbal in form, are more verbally weighted for the lower class than for the middle class child. This point has been elaborated more recently by Jensen.

There is a limited amount of information about the intelligence test performance of ethnic groups (other than Negro) in this country. On performance tests, American-Indian children are closer to the norms of white children but do less well on verbal tests (Anastasi & Foley, 1949). They may equal or exceed whites on tests of drawing ability (Dennis, 1942; Russell, 1943; Havighurst, Gunther & Pratt, 1946). Although it seems plausible, there is little evidence on the possibility of differences among American-Indian tribes. A similar pattern has been found for Mexican-American children (Garth, Elson, & Morton, 1936) and for Italian-American children (Held, 1941). Differences have been found between the pattern of abilities of Japanese-American children and white children, with Japanese groups earning higher scores on tests of visual perception, spatial orientation, and sustained attention, but lower on verbal tests and arithmetic (Darsie, 1926).

In a study significant for both design and substantive findings, Lesser *et al.*, (1965) designed a project to analyze the relative impact of social class and ethnicity on intellective functioning. Using tests and testing conditions devised to minimize bias, they examined four mental abilities (verbal ability, reasoning, number facility, space conceptualization) of 320 first-grade children from four ethnic groups, Chinese, Jewish, Negro, and Puerto Rican, with each ethnic group divided into middle and lower class.

The major findings of the study were that both social class and ethnic group membership have strong but different effects upon performance on the tests covering the four mental abilities. Ethnicity affects the pattern or profile of performance; social class affects the level of achievement. Among the four ethnic groups, the rankings on the four test areas were as follows: *Verbal Ability:* Jews, Negroes, Chinese, Puerto Ricans; *Reasoning:* Chinese, Jews, Negroes, Puerto Ricans; *Numerical Ability:* Jews, Chinese, Puerto Ricans, Negroes; *Space:* Chinese, Jews, Puerto Ricans, Negroes. Social class differences were greatest for the Negro group, suggesting relatively greater socio-economic disadvantage for the lower class Negroes. In interpreting their data, Lesser and his associates concluded that the natural selection argument for social class effects upon mental abilities "seems weakened by the fact that, once the ethnic pattern of mental abilities emerges, no further alteration in the pattern occurs under the influence of differing social class conditions." They also argued that other explanations of social class effects upon mental abilities (motivation, impulse control, problem solving tactics) gain greater credence from their results.

In other studies the most extensive ethnic comparisons are between Negro and white children. Intelligence test scores of Negro children are typically lower, on the average, than those of white children. Shuey (1958) surveyed the research literature of approximately 240 studies, including roughly 60 tests and thousands of children and adults from all sections of the country. Most of these studies have serious methodological flaws. In only 17 of the studies is social class position of the subjects taken into consideration in some way. The distribution of SES within the U.S. Negro population is very different from that of Caucasians. At this point in history, there is a disproportionate number of Negroes at low SES levels. Social class and race are thus confounded in many comparisons. Shuey (1958) reported that investigators agree that Negroes do "relatively well in tests that are purposeful, practical, concrete and those that involve rote memory; and perform less efficiently in tests that are relatively abstract in nature and in tests involving certain perceptual-motor functions (e.g., Kohs Block Design)." There is disagreement between investigators as to the difficulty Negroes have with verbal as compared with non-verbal test material. Shuey (1958) reports that on the Wechsler-Bellevue, the WISC, and the California Test of Mental Maturity, Negro children and adults achieved higher scores or IQs on the verbal than on the performance sections and that Negro school children scored no higher on the average on the non-verbal than on the verbal group tests. Coleman's report (1966) shows a similar pattern. Also, Lesser (1965) found that Negro children performed better on *verbal* than on *reasoning, number* and *space* sections of the tests he administered.

Comparing Negro and white children of first and fifth grade divided into three social class levels, Deutsch and Brown (1964) found (by using the Lorge-Thorndike Intelligence Test) a linear relationship between SES and performance level for both Negro and white groups; within this linear relationship, the absolute increase in IQ is greater for the white group than it is for the Negro. Deutsch and Brown concluded that the influence of race tends to increase as the social class level rises and interpreted these results as indicating less participation in the cultural mainstream by the middle-class Negro, while the lowest class status operates similarly for the white as well as for the Negro. Deutsch and Brown argue: "It is more difficult for the Negro to attain identical middle or upper-middle class status with whites, and that the social class gradations are less marked because Negro life in a caste society is considerably more homogeneous than is life for the majority group." The mean IQ (102) of the upper-middle class Negro group in Deutsch's study may be atypically low in view of the higher mean (109) reported by Hess and his colleagues for upper-middle class Negro preschool children on the Stanford-Binet. They also found the WAIS IQ of the upper-middle class Negro mothers to be 109. In their data, there was no mean difference between middle class mothers and children in IQ, while the mean scores of children from working class groups exceeded the mean IQ of their mothers by 13 points (Hess & Shipman, 1967).

3. *Socio-economic Status Differences in Educational Achievement*

The distinction between IQ tests and scholastic achievement or aptitude tests is not clear, particularly when one recalls that Binet originally devised tests to predict school success. In this sense, school achievement tests are the criteria and IQ tests are estimates. As in IQ tests, SES differences in school performance are well known. It is not feasible or useful to review all the research bearing on SES disparity in educational attainment as indicated by tests. Several examples will serve to document the difference and indicate its magnitude. The correlation between scholastic ability and IQ scores would in itself be expected to produce differences in educational achievement among different SES levels.

The extent of this divergence is shown by a survey of the school system of Chicago (Havighurst, 1964). The 21 districts were ranked by an index which combined the median family income and median level of education of adults in the area, based on census data, and a gross index, based on combined scores on two reading tests and two arithmetic tests at grade six. The top third of districts in the SES ranking ranged from achievement at grade level to achievement one grade above norms. The bottom third, with one exception, were all about one year below expected grade level. A similar pattern was apparent from reading readiness scores for first-grade children. In the bottom third of ranking, only 40 per cent were up to standard in this crucial set of skills. These differences also apply to socio-economic differentials between the districts with substantial numbers of middle-class Negroes and those with predominately working class Negro populations. The technique for assigning SES ranking is, of course, gross: differentials would probably have been greater if more individualized SES information had been available.

A summary of research data, giving more differentiation among scholastic skills, is reported as the result of a study of socio-economic status and school achievement (California Elementary School Administrators Association, 1962). This study covered 26 schools in Alameda County, California. Using Hollingshead's Two-Factor Index of Social Position, four SES groups of both Negro and white pupils were included; the scholastic measures were the Sequential Tests of Educational Progress (STEP) covering *reading, writing, social studies, mathematics, science* and *listening*. Subjects were asked to request their parents to fill out the forms needed for assigning social status. The response of parents and, perhaps, their acceptance of the goals of the school are themselves of interest; only 62 per cent of parents in low SES schools returned the questionnaires while 85 per cent of parents in highest SES levels did so. In terms of the children's achievement scores, the differences among the four SES groups varied considerably from one subject to another. The greatest discrepancies occurred in science where the percentile range was from 83 for the highest SES group to 14 for the lowest. The smallest difference between high and low SES groups was in writing (75 and 37) with differences in reading scores showing next smallest range.

A third study, the most comprehensive, was that supervised by Coleman (1966). This major national study, commissioned by the U.S. Office of Education, was directed particularly to the analysis of scholastic achievement of minority groups and the factors which contributed to educational attainment. The sample was not divided by social class. Therefore, comparisons of ethnic groups with the majority group do not permit analysis of variability among social class levels within each ethnic group. Comparisons between ethnic groups and whites are confounded with SES, since the proportion of lower and middle class within each ethnic group differs. The comparison, for example, of the average test scores of the Negro and the "majority" group is questionable as a measure of the effect of ethnicity alone, since the proportion of lower class is significantly higher among Negroes than among the white group. Such differences in proportion of lower and middle class probably exist for other ethnic groups as well.

The data reported by Coleman indicate that, with the exception of the Oriental American, minority groups, i.e., Negroes, Indian Americans, Mexican Americans, and Puerto Ricans, score distinctly lower on the standard achievement tests than the average white pupils. Their scores are approximately one standard deviation below the majority pupils' scores in the first grade. At grade 12, the scores of minority groups on tests of the same types of skills, verbal and non-verbal, are farther below the majority group than at grade one. Comparison between the groups' average scores for the five achievement tests used at grade 12 showed that Negroes differed from the majority group most, followed by Puerto Ricans, Mexican Americans, Indian Americans, and Oriental Americans (who showed the least difference from the majority groups). Coleman concluded that "whatever may be the combination of nonschool factors—poverty, community attitudes, low educational level of parents—which put minority children at a disadvantage in verbal and non-verbal skills when they enter the first grade, the fact is the schools have not overcome it."

Regional differences also appear in the Coleman data. In the South, both white and Negro 12th graders scored lower than their age mates in the North. This regional difference was more pronounced for Negroes than for whites, Southern Negroes scoring farther below Southern whites than Northern Negroes did below Northern whites. This regional difference did not exist at the beginning of schooling. However, Coleman points to the fact that "in the metropolitan North and West, 20 per cent of the Negroes of ages 16 and 17 are not enrolled in school—a higher dropout percentage than in either the metropolitan or nonmetropolitan South." If some or many of the Northern dropouts performed poorly when they were in school, Negro achievement in the North may be higher only because some of those who performed poorly have left school.

As already noted, data on achievement scores were not differentiated by social class within each minority group. However, a number of background variables of the pupils were used in computing their contribution to the total variance as compared to school variables. These background variables of the pupils were: urbanism of background (for students of grades 9 and 12), migration (for 6th graders), parents' education, structural integrity of the home, size (smallness) of the family, items in the home indicating its economic standing, reading material at home (such as encyclopedia, etc.), parental interest (talking about school matters with the pupils, reading to them when they were small, etc.), and parents' educational desires for their children. Coleman found that at grade 6, economic level of the family (based on the child's report) had the highest relationship to achievement scores for all the minority groups, while the parents' educational level had the highest relation to achievement scores for the majority group of whites. In later years, however, parents' education had the highest relation to achievement scores of the pupils for nearly all groups.

For Negroes of grade 12, the length of time in an urban environment and the (small) size of their families had approximately the same importance as their parents' education. The structural integrity of the home (presence or absence of the father) showed very little relation to achievement for Negroes. It had, however, a strong relation to achievement for other minority groups.

The position that social class–linked family experience heavily influences subjects' performance on reading tests receives support from the findings of Weiner & Feldman (1963; 1964) who reported that two reading tests in a standard battery yielded distinctly different score distributions by social class within the same school. The scores of lower-class children of grades 3 through 8 on the Gates Advanced Primary Reading Test were spread over a substantially wider range than were their scores on the Gates Basic Reading Test, Level of Comprehension; the opposite was true for the scores of middle-class children. Negative effects of social and emotional impoverishment on school attainments of lower-class Negro and white children have also been described by Deutsch (1960). The performance of both racial groups on the Stanford Achievement Test was significantly lower than the national norms for this test. Academic retardation of both groups increased with age. For the Negro children, this retardation was, however, significantly more pronounced than for white children. Deutsch suggested that this difference between Negro and white lower class subjects may stem from the negative feelings that Negro children develop toward themselves, partly in response to the low expectations of their teachers. The detrimental effects of racial segregation and other school qualities upon the scholastic achievement of Negro students have been documented by Hansen (1960) who reported that in an integrated school system the scores of Negro pupils on the Stanford Achievement Test increased steadily. Stallings (1960) reported similar results for five years following integration, with most marked progress in the scores of Negro pupils appearing in areas related to reading.

One of the most specific and dramatic statements of the relatively low educational achievement of Negro pupils in northern urban areas is found in a report on education in Harlem, *Youth in the Ghetto* (Haryou, 1964). The pupils in Harlem schools are almost all Negroes, primarily from low socio-economic backgrounds. More than half of the students in academic high schools and over 60 per cent of those in vocational schools dropped out

TABLE 2. Median Achievement Scores

	Reading Comprehension			Word Knowledge			Arithmetic		
Grade	Harlem	NYC	USA	Harlem	NYC	USA	Harlem	NYC	USA
3	2.5	3.6	3.7	2.7	3.6	3.7	x	x	x
6	4.1	6.1	6.2	4.1	6.1	6.2	5.0	6.4	6.5
8	6.0	8.1	8.5	6.0	8.1	8.5	5.8	8.1	8.5

without receiving a diploma. The performance of children in Harlem schools, at the time of the report, showed substantial decline with increase in grade. As shown in the following table, Harlem pupils were two and one-half years or more behind national norms in reading comprehension, word knowledge, and arithmetic. IQ scores following a similar pattern, with average ranging from 91 at grade three to 88 at grade eight for Harlem school pupils, compared to roughly 100 from New York City and, presumably, the rest of the nation. Such data have made the problem of education of minority pupils a matter of national concern.

4. Socio-economic Status Differences in Other Cognitive Operations

Some recent studies have provided more detailed information about SES differences in cognitive functioning. Cynthia Deutsch and McArdle (1967) are investigating the hypothesis that there are SES differences in auditory discrimination for white and Negro children. If such a difference is found, however, it will be relevant to recall the findings of Lesser et al. (1965) of SES differences in four ethnic groups regardless of the differences in profile of performance, a caution that applies, of course, to much of the current work on SES and ethnic differences in cognitive functions. Deutsch (1960) found lower class children to be less able than a comparable group of middle class children on tasks requiring concentration and persistence, and to display a tendency to ignore difficult problems. Differences between low and middle class children also appear on techniques designed to assess developmental changes in drawing characteristics (Eisner, 1967).

Recent information on the relationship between aspects of cognitive development and maternal behavior as well as other features of the social and cultural environment (Getzels & Jackson, 1961; Kagan & Moss, 1962; Bing, 1963; Hunt, 1964; Dyk & Witkin, 1965; Busse, 1967) has created keen interest in the degree to which manipulation of the learning situation might affect the relative performance of children from different SES levels.

5. *The Quest for Linkages and Contingencies Between Culture and Cognition*

In more recent years, laboratory studies focus with increased frequency on specific variables which affect development of cognitive processes underlying the performances of children on more global intelligence tests and in scholastic achievement tests.

The studies conducted by Bernstein, Caldwell, Deutsch & Deutsch, Gray, Hess, Jensen, John, and Osler represent more recent efforts on the part of these investigators to use refined laboratory and sampling techniques to tease out the background variables related to working class children's cognitive styles and processes.

The more significant theoretical and research problem, however, is to specify contingencies between the environment and the developing cognitive styles and operations of the child and the degree to which these styles can be modified by intervention of some sort (Caldwell, 1968; Deutsch & Deutsch, 1968; Gray & Klaus, 1968; Glick, 1968; Hess & Bear, 1968). Deutsch (1963, 1965) has suggested that environmental and developmental factors interact and effect intellectual maturation through their influences on the development of the child's perceptual abilities and his language. Interrelationships between language measures and selected demographic variables, based upon the assessments of 292 children of first and fifth grades, led Deutsch to argue that environmentally deprived children are susceptible to a "cumulative deficit phenomenon," which affects both linguistic and cognitive development by inhibiting the development of "abstract and categorical" use of language.

The research of Hess and his colleagues (1965, 1967, in press) pursues the argument that early social experiences which are part of the mother-child interaction shape thought and cognitive styles of problem solving. Studying mother-child interaction styles on the basis of data gathered from 163 Negro families representing four social status levels, ranging from families with mother on public welfare to families with college-educated fathers, they attempted to identify the cognitive environment to which lower status children are exposed. Of particular relevance for the development of cognitive functioning in the child are the mother's strategies for orienting the child toward selected cues in the environment, the types of regulatory or control techniques she uses, and her patterning of stimuli to organize information for the child. The control techniques call attention to status or normative components in the situation, paraphrased as "You should do this because someone in authority has told you to do it: It is a rule" or "It is the way someone your age or sex should behave." Or the control techniques refer to subjective personal status, in which the appeal is to how one's actions will make other people feel, or to the consequences of action apart from rules or feelings. These different techniques of control evoke different cognitive responses on the part of the child and are based on dissimilar reinforcement patterns. The orientation of adults from working class backgrounds toward external control and authority, discussed earlier in the chapter, are congruent with Hess' findings that working class mothers use normative control to a greater extent than do mothers from the middle class and that this type of control is related negatively to the development of verbal behavior, performance on cognitive tasks, and to reading readiness, as measured by standard tests (Hess *et al.,* in press). The ability of mothers to organize and sequence material for their children in face-to-face teaching of simple tasks by appropriate orientation and pretask information feedback, motivating specificity of language and monitoring behavior, are also related both to the mother's social class and to the child's performance in cognitive and school-related tasks.

CONTINGENCY-LEARNING AND ANALYSIS OF THE EFFECTS OF DEPRIVATION UPON LEARNING

The focal point of basic research and of theory with respect to deprivation is the mediation or translation of environmental press (variables) into individual behavior (Hess and Shipman, 1965; Hess, 1968). These processes are not clearly conceptualized in the available literature. They follow, to some degree, the principles of learning and behavior acquisition already known to students of human behavior. The application of some of these principles was summarized for this Task Force by Gewirtz.

1. *The Conceptual Milieu*

Empirical work to date shows that it is both reasonable and profitable to conceive of social behavior as following the general laws of behavior, but with the relevant stimuli mediated by the behavior of persons rather than by other environmental sources. On this basis, our study of human social behavior proceeds in the same way as learning-based studies of other behavior classes: by analysis of the variables in the environment, both present and past, that *control* behavior. Such concepts generally provide a flexible model for ordering the complex development patterns characterizing the child's socialization by detailing the changing conditions of environmental stimulation accompanying his development. The changing capacities of the child through developmental processes, such as those indexed in naturalistic approaches (e.g., Piaget, 1951) by the terms "organismic maturation," "stages," "critical periods," and the like, might qualify this approach but would hardly change its essential features.

2. Definition of the (Social) Environment

The terms *environment* and *stimulation* occur often in everyday discourse. Characterized as "wholesome" or "rich," these terms are frequently invoked as causes of certain patterns of development, and occasionally as labels for experimental or remedial treatments. However, these are neither universal definitions nor consensually defined operational indices of environment and stimulation, nor of "love" or "warmth." Without behavioral-outcome criteria these concepts are essentially useless for understanding both human social development and behavior technology, and may be best suited to literary ventures.

To be useful in an analysis of the impact of the cumulative experience of the child on his current and future behavior, the concept of environment must have a basis in functional criteria, specifically the control of or impact on behavior by stimuli. Emphasis must be placed simultaneously on the environment and the behavior of the organism, and there can be no fruitful independent definition either of stimuli or of behavior. Under our definition, environment is restricted to those stimuli impinging upon the organism that affect his behavior in some way. As such, stimuli can play a number of roles defined by their temporal relation to the response (contingency): they may function to evoke, cue, or reinforce behavior. Before the immediate or long-term response outcome of a stimulus can be predicted, the role of the stimulus in the particular situation must be specified. It is axiomatic that no *acquisition* (equivalent to reinforcement, conditioning, or learning) can occur in the absence of stimuli, and the limiting case of prediction of acquisition therefore occurs when there are no stimuli available. Further, when reinforcing stimuli are available, their effects on behavior are qualified by such factors as temporal gradients of delay between response and stimulus schedules of reinforcement, and the program or temporal sequence of application, as well as by whether or not there are background events present that mask (or change) either the stimuli presented or competing responses to those stimuli. Thus, when environmental events do not occur in such a way as to be discriminable for behavior or immediately contingent upon it, they are not *functional* insofar as they do not constitute stimuli for the organism (Gewirtz, 1968a and b). Under this conception, therefore, a large number of physical events that have no detectable effect on the organism's behavior would not be considered part of his environment; and, similarly, movements by the organism are not considered responses until they are observable and are shown to be under the control of stimuli. Thus, emphasis must be on the stimulus-response unit; a response can only be defined in terms of the preceding and following stimuli that control it, and a stimulus can be defined only in terms of the responses it controls.

The *social environment* consists of those functional stimuli which are provided by people; and *adaptive behaviors* (for the most part termed *social*) are those under the actual or potential control of (for the most part) social stimuli, in either their acquisition, maintenance, or both. The term social learning simply defines a category of learning that involves stimuli provided by people but that follows the same principles as nonsocial learning.

In a sense, concepts of learning belong to every theorist who studies systematic effects of recurring environmental conditions on behavior. This is true whatever the theoretical approach, its degree of development, the particular phenomena ordered by the theory, its language, the level of analysis and detail employed, and the particular heuristic tone given to the concepts (e.g., behavioristic, cognitive, or even animistic). Learning concepts are at issue whether a theory refers to "ego enhancement, growth or changes," to the "growth of self-awareness," or to the "development of a substitute interpersonal attachment." In the same sense, concepts ordinarily grouped under such headings as "ethology," "perception," or "intelligence," which have evolved to order environmental phenomena effecting changes in behaviors, *overlap* learning concepts at various levels as well as each other.

3. *The Facilitation of Valued Behavior Outcomes*

Socially desirable behaviors can be made more likely to occur in unified groups as a result of the application of equivalent environmental processes to all of them. This holds particularly for attempts to raise the incidence of socially desirable behavior classes from zero to low initial rates. To facilitate the emergence and strengthening of valued adaptive and coping behavior outcomes as well as behaviors that are under the control of a variety of social events and combinations (e.g., attachments) and to effect early dimensional and contextual learnings, operations of several types can be applied—reinforcement, extension, shaping, etc.

4. *Implications of the Analysis*

In relation to the concepts for environmental control over behavior, the present analysis has emphasized the learning *contingencies* provided to the infant by his parent-caretaker and the valued behavior outcomes achieved through the control of these contingencies. These contingencies are the basis for the infant's acquisition of patterns of social behavior which are under the control of social discriminative and social reinforcing stimuli. Instead of stressing which or how many of a given class of stimuli are provided to the infant, this analysis has emphasized whether or not stimuli available to the infant are functional for him and whether or not these stimuli, paired with his responses, comprise effective contingencies for learning.

5. Specific Implications of the Provision of Complex Stimuli

The stimuli which can lead to the acquisition of valued behaviors by the developing child can be referred to as "abstract stimulus complexes" (e.g., stimulation, love, mothering). The following are some specific implications of assumptions of stimulus provision and control outlined here:

a. The components of these stimulus complexes can be dispensed only as physical stimuli. This is, they must be visual, auditory, tactile, or olfactory, or combinations of these types of stimuli. From the earliest phases of an infant's development, the component elements of these stimuli may operate as *unconditioned* evoking or reinforcing stimuli for the infant. These same stimuli cease to be functional for the infant as his responses to them habituate.

b. An abstract stimulus complex has functional significance for the infant only to the extent that it has involved effective learning contingencies for him. (Component elements of the stimulus complex may also provide unconditioned stimuli for the infant's responses.)

c. The infant's responsiveness to stimuli (in this case, social stimuli) appears to be established and maintained by unconditioned and conditioned reinforcing stimuli dispensed by people in his environment. In terms of this working assumption underlying the present approach, the proposition that the human infant has certain *innate* needs for social stimuli (such as mothering and love) appears only remotely useful heuristically. Under the learning model, the infant cannot thrive in an environment devoid of stimuli to establish and support his behavior and learning. Also, in the context of this model, if an originally neutral stimulus is provided by the infant's caretakers as discriminative for reinforcement, it will acquire reinforcing value for him.

d. It is apparent that there will be differences among children in the composition and importance of a stimulus complex as a result of the differing conditions existing in the early establishment and maintenance of such stimulus complexes. Stimulus complexes presented by the child's parent or main caretaker can be most effective as reinforcers. These complexes are usually composed of the particular stimuli which are salient in the acquisition of reinforcing value by the stimulus complexes. However, if an identical stimulus complex is offered to the child by others, its reinforcing value for the child may differ, until he learns the functional equivalence of the diverse stimulus sources.

Various stimulus complexes intended by the dispenser to represent stimulation or love to the child will not be efficient as reinforcing stimuli because they have not been conditioned as such in behavior settings different from the ones in which the child's basic learnings occurred. Children will also differ in regard to the relative importance these conditioned reinforcing stimuli have for them. They will differ, too, in regard to the amount of the stimulus considered sufficient and the rate at which they have learned to receive it.

e. There is a fallacy in the proposition that simply giving a child "enough" stimulation, attention, or love can compensate for an earlier "inadequate" supply of these stimuli. A sudden change to a higher rate of stimulus provision, whether or not the stimuli are provided contingent upon behavior, can bring about abrupt disruptive changes in many interrelated behaviors, including social behaviors, and can lead to new behavior patterns which may differ greatly from those that might have been adopted otherwise. This disorganization, actually created by the child's transition to the new caretaking setting, may be used under a long-term deficiency-hunger model as an index of the inadequacy of the supply of these stimuli received by the earlier setting. Changes in existing habit systems toward valued patterns of more social and mature behaviors may occur when the stimuli in the new setting are repeatedly presented to the child in effective contingencies with valued behaviors, when this was not the case in the prior setting. These newly established behavior patterns may, in turn, serve under the deficiency model to indicate that the child has become more "secure," since he no longer *appears* to need so much attention and love and it is thus often concluded that the "hunger" for these stimuli has been reversed. Also, if it is assumed that the conditioned-reinforcer class dispensed is the most effective one for the child, different discriminative stimuli can control the occurrence of behaviors for that reinforcing stimulus in a new setting (e.g., a move to a new home or into a therapeutic setting).

f. Environmental events which have no unconditioned stimulus value and have not been previously paired with any positive or negative reinforcement will not, even when associated with intense affect responses, have any effect on the child's behaviors.

The final assumption brings all the earlier ones into focus:

g. A child's social learning is characterized by his acquisition of social-behavior patterns which are under the control of social discriminative and reinforcing stimuli. This process is dependent upon the contingencies with his behaviors that are constituted by the stimuli provided to the child in his behavior setting. In this context, caretakers can be pivotal in providing efficient conditions (contingencies) for optimal social learning. Unfortunately, this is rarely the case. The approach often taken by parents, as well as by many theorists in this area, is to stress only the provision of a commodity (as food or love) and not the circumstances under which these commodities are given. More specifically, the question is how do these potential discriminative and reinforcing stimuli influence the child's behavior? It is important to consider this latter point, which is compatible with the approach to adaptive behavior in general psychology, for it is the key factor in the child's social learning.

It is thus almost a corollary of the conceptions summarized here that the efficiency of research and engineering endeavors could be greatly increased simply by attending under an instrumental-learning conception to the stimulus events that can affect behavior, rather than by using gross analyses of the impact of relatively unspecified stimuli on relatively unspecified behaviors. A major projection of the preceding analysis is therefore that approaching contexts for systematic behavior change with articulate conditioning concepts and a focus on selected stimuli and behavior can provide considerable leverage on the technological details required for bringing out the potentialities of children of all types.

LINGUISTIC FUNCTIONING IN CHILDREN

1. *Earlier Approaches to the Program*

Throughout the nineteenth century, the United States provided an excellent opportunity for the study of the process by which ethnic groups learned English and lost their original language. Linguistic assimilation proceeded more or less rapidly, but the opportunity to study the process was lost. The educational and social problems of the large cities were qualitatively similar to those now current. In 1865, the underprivileged and "dangerous" classes of New York City were the Irish and Germans; after 1890, they were more apt to be Italians and Jews; and in the 1950's, Negroes and Puerto Ricans. The older groups moved regularly at various rates, but upward, in the socio-economic scale; their antagonisms faded and they joined with the previous residents in their opposition to the new immigrants.

There are several groups of Americans in the United States today for whom this pattern has not prevailed. The Spanish-speaking "Mexican-Americans" of the Southwest seem to have established a more stable bilingualism; this may be true of the Puerto Ricans as well. There is a clear tendency for the second generation to follow the shift to English, but it is held back by a number of factors. Many of the indigenous Indians have lost their native language. Others have kept it, but the shift to the value system associated with the American schools has not taken place. The largest group, the Negroes, has no foreign language to cope with, although their linguistic differences are subtle and complex. These four groups are affected, in one way or another, by the color-bar which prevails in our society. There is a fifth group which is not affected by the physical barriers to upward social mobility nor by language problems—Southern whites of Appalachia. In the ghetto areas of Cleveland and other midwestern cities, they occupy the same low position as the other groups considered here. Clearly, cultural and historical factors are more important with this group than the immediate effects of language and color discrimination.

Finally, it is worth noting that there is a group which is separated from the main body of citizens by both color and language—the Chinese and the Japanese—who have not found it difficult to make use of the American educational system.

Before the 1960's the only relevant research was carried on in the classrooms by educators. Loban's longitudinal studies of California school children (1965; 1966) compare Negro children with other groups; but from a linguist's viewpoint, the information is very scant. All data are given as numbers of deviations from standard English; so that one knows neither whether a regular rule is involved on the part of the non-standard dialect nor what the underlying system is. Hunt's studies of the written compositions of school children (unpublished 1966) give data on some over-all measures of sentence form and length, but the problem remains of relating this information to the linguistic competence of the students and ultimately to their verbal skills.

Recently, linguists have become interested in the language used by Negroes in the United States. McDavid and Austin (1966) traced the traditional dialect markers in the forms elicited from Negroes in Chicago. Shuy (1967) included the Negro population in his study of sociolinguistic stratification in Detroit, and Levine and Crockett are now supplementing their study of the speech of residents of Hillsboro, N.C., with an examination of the responses of Negro speakers. One assumption behind this work has been that exact knowledge of the differences between the speech of Negro speakers and of others will be helpful in solving educational problems. Much of the interest in the details of dialect patterns has been on the part of those interested in the improvement of speech, although it has not been established that closer approximation to standard English speech will significantly change employment opportunities. Other work has had a more general educational orientation. Bailey examined the speech of Tougaloo college students (unpublished 1966) with an eye to developing educational methods. The Urban Language Study at the Center for Applied Linguistics, now under Shuy, is currently oriented toward applying cultural and linguistic information directly to educational problems.

Of the various educational problems, it appears that reading is the most urgent and the most critical. Project Literacy (1964–1967) has attempted to involve linguists as well as psychologists in basic research on reading, and it was felt that data on the linguistic patterns of the deprived groups in the urban ghettos would be essential. The work of Labov and others (1966, 1968), centered in New York City, is concerned with structural differences between non-standard Negro English and the standard English of the classroom, and provides data indicating that reading problems are directly related to differences in linguistic structures.

Some work has also been done on the broader question of the verbal culture in which the linguistic structures are embedded. One part of Labov's studies is explicitly concerned with this aspect; Hannerz (1967) at the Center for Applied Linguistics has produced several anthropological studies of verbal culture; and recent work of Kochman in Chicago (1968) has amplified our knowledge of this area.

Comparatively little work has been done on the language of the other groups discussed above. Gumperz, Fishman, et al. (1967) have been engaged in studies of Spanish-American bilinguals in New York City, and the earlier work of Barker (1947) dealt with Mexican-Americans. Enough is known about the linguistic problems of certain Indian groups in the Southwest to suggest that imperfect ability to read and write standard English is a serious impediment to educational advancement.

Any discussion of class differences in the use of language must take into account the ideas put forward by Bernstein (1964) that there are two fundamentally different "codes" used by speakers of a language—a "restricted" code employed among those who know each other quite well and share a great deal of common information, and an "elaborated" code in general use by the middle class and in schools, which is more explicit and presupposes less shared information. Bernstein suggests that lower socioeconomic groups are handicapped in not having access to or practice with the elaborated code. There have been many proposals for applying Bernstein's ideas to concrete situations in the United States, but again there has been little connection between the general notions and the linguistic concepts of system and structure.

The most influential work on class and ethnic differences in verbal behavior has been that of psychologists who have not had access to linguistic information (Deutsch 1967).[3] In general, work along these lines has helped to establish the concept of "cultural deprivation" as embodied in the planning for Operation Headstart. Negro and lower-class children regularly score lower on a whole range of tests of verbal behavior. However, there have also been many investigations of class differences which report the same rate of development for children of different backgrounds; for example, the development of "paradigmatic" responses in word-association tests has been taken as a measure of verbal development and Baltimore slum children actually surpass suburban children in the first grade, according to the index (Entwistle 1968). A great deal of the testing of children's verbal abilities has taken place in the same environment as the school situation itself, and such tests therefore register the child's reaction to the social context primarily and only secondarily to his actual verbal skills.

2. *Our Present Knowledge of the Verbal Abilities of Underprivileged Groups*

The area in which one can speak with more certainty concerns the effect of differences in linguistic structure which interfere with learning of standard English in school. This type of linguistic interference follows the general patterns outlined by Weinreich in *Languages in Contact* (1951); although our knowledge is not yet precise enough to allow us to predict that a particular kind of interference will in fact take place, we can say in what direction interference will take place if it does occur and trace certain effects directly to the contact language. We can, for example, trace the interference of Puerto Rican Spanish with English in the substitution of final *-ng* for *-m* or *-n,* or the confusion of *seen* and sin. Our analysis of non-standard Negro English (NNE) is now far enough advanced that we can explain the occurrence of *-s* in *I gots to do it* or *He can gets hurt:* NNE has no third singular *-s* at all, and the rule for placing it in standard English (SE) has to be learned entirely from outside the child's basic grammar. The same can be said for *I don't know who book it is,* since there is no possessive *-s* in attributive constructions. We also find, for example, that Negro children preserve the order of direct questions in embedded questions, as in *I ax him did he do it,* for the special rule for placing *if* and re-reversing subject and tense marker is also absent. Negro children have great difficulty learning the standard rules for negatives: *He don't never do it* follows an obligatory rule of negative concord in NNE, which is optional in white non-standard dialects.

Such knowledge can be extremely helpful for teachers of English, for they can direct their efforts efficiently at the most general rule which must be learned or unlearned. But none of the points mentioned above will show any misunderstanding of the teacher's language by the student. Repetition tests show that children have the capacity to perceive and understand the SE forms, even when they cannot reproduce them in speech. Misunderstanding takes place, but not at the level of fundamental grammatical structures such as these. It is far more likely that the teacher will misunderstand the student. One point where such misunderstanding has been noted is the verb *be* meaning 'habitual, general condition' in NNE, which has no SE counterpart. Thus a Negro child who says to a teacher *I be good* may mean that he is habitually good, but may be understood by the teacher to mean that he will be good in the future. The most likely source of misunderstandings occurs when a Negro or Spanish-speaking child reads aloud; there are many homonyms in their speech which may give the teacher the impression that they have read incorrectly, and the teacher may give an incomprehensible correction to the child without realizing that it is a matter of pronunciation rather than reading. Thus a teacher may hear *He like me* for *He liked me* and automatically disapprove: but a child who rarely pronounces the *-ed* in this position may have great difficulty in understanding the teacher's correction. Thus it becomes crucially important to distinguish between mistakes in reading and differences in pronunciation, a distinction which has not been made explicit in previous texts on the teaching of reading. We now have the knowledge necessary to teach such a principle effectively.

However, such linguistic interference recedes in importance when we consider that children in the ghetto show across-the-board deficiencies, and they do not do relatively worse in reading than in arithmetic. It has been pointed out above that IQ tests, reading tests, and perception tests are affected by the over-all setting in which they are given. Sociolinguistic studies of the effect of topic, language, and speakers upon speech forms (Ervin-Tripp 1964) allow us to understand how remote such tests may be from the actual competence of the children tested. Until psycho-linguistic tests in school-room situations are controlled by comparable tests in environments more favorable to children in the ghetto, they will not give us the fundamental data we need on the underlying abilities of the children concerned. However, there is some data now available which points to limitations on children's learning abilities stemming from parent-child interaction. Observations of parents instructing children now being carried on (Baldwin, Hess, and Shipman, 1965, Kamii and Radin, 1967) in semi-laboratory settings do show considerable differences in the way in which parents transmit information to children. Further, direct observations of peer group behavior in the ghetto show that the vernacular culture does limit certain explicit types of verbal inquiry. We do not find members of such peer groups asking for the meanings of words, nor asking for spellings. The underlying forms of certain vernacular words which are never spelled (such as *lodee,* a game, or *war-lord,* a status) are not clear, and such words undergo rapid evaluation. But this is also true of any words confined to pre-adolescent white culture as well.

There is also some evidence to support the notion of a restricted code or form of communication. As noted in an informal study of Schatzman and Strauss of accounts given after a disaster (1955), less-educated, lower-class speakers are less able to take the point of view of the listener; they are apparently more used to communication with those who share the same body of knowledge. Their accounts are more centered around the first person and are more concrete than those of middle-class speakers. But even though there are some comparable indications for school children, most of this data is tentative, sketchy, and in unpublished form. It is possible that such observations are the product of the stimulus—that the questions asked are those most congenial to, or most often answered by, middle-class speakers.

More solid and reproducible data are available on the norms, values, and expectations in regard to verbal behavior. The work of Lambert and his associates (1960, 1967) has established the existence of values associated with the use of particular languages or dialects—values shared by those on both sides of the ledger. Thus, both French-Canadians and English-Canadians agree that speakers of French are apt to be less intelligent, trustworthy, successful, etc., as shown by their uniform reactions to the "matched guise" tests. Similar values cluster around the use of Canadian French vs. Continental French. In New York City, it was found that there is a uniform set of subjective reactions in which those who use a stigmatized feature the most in their own casual speech are quickest to stigmatize others for the use of this feature. Furthermore, it appears that there are opposing sets of values attributed by most speakers to certain forms or dialects, e.g., suitability for a hierarchy of job classifications shows high ratings for the speakers rated lowest on an estimate of their physical toughness or skill in fighting. Such values are apparently acquired in late adolescence, and both values seem to be held most clearly by the middle class. The indications are that such stereotypes are imposed upon all members of a society as part of the view of the dominating sub-group. Thus it is likely that the self-hatred characteristic of many minority groups is reinforced by these social values attributed to their speech forms. Tucker and Lambert's work in Tougaloo (1966) showed that Negro college students follow the same pattern as New York City residents in attributing the highest social values to the "network" style of English heard in the mass media. It follows that most lower-class citizens acquire these values at a point in life where their own style is relatively fixed, and they are reinforced in a low opinion of their own speech.

Within any formal interview or test situation, such middle-class values will be dominant in American society. The positive values which support the speech forms of the dominated groups will not emerge. Folklorists have been aware for some time that urban culture was richer than casual observers would assume. Recent studies of peer groups in spontaneous interaction in Northern ghetto areas show that there is a rich verbal culture in constant use. Negro children in the vernacular culture cannot be considered "verbally deprived" if one observes them in a favorable environment—on the contrary, their daily life is a pattern of continual verbal stimulation, contest, and imitation. The speech event known as "sounding," "the dozens," "signifying," and by many other names, occupies a great deal of time for adolescent Negro children: it is a system of ritualized or abstract insults, directed against the opposite party's parents, or ritualized personal traits, in which each effort is evaluated by spectators and usually with a definite outcome. A large repertoire is prized, but only if accompanied by the ability to make original changes, and to use modified forms appropriately in the immediate context. There is also a large body of rhymed epics in the oral literature, known as "toasts" or "jokes"—works of high poetic quality in which certain modifications and new combinations are admired and permitted. Such toasts, which may run to fifty, a hundred, or even two hundred rhymed couplets, are known in whole or in part by many boys who would be considered nonverbal in a school situation. There is now developing in the ghetto areas, a body of cult mythology and ideology associated with black nationalism, and a new cultural set which prizes book learning, reading, history, and science, as long as it is not associated with white culture. There are many other speech events associated with the vernacular culture of the ghetto: jokes, songs, narratives, and of course the hip vocabulary itself. All of these reflect the value system of the vernacular, and because it is opposed in many ways to the standard culture of the school, it does not appear in school contexts. The bars against obscenity, violence, and aggression are sufficient to keep most of this verbal culture well out of sight; the growing hostility to white culture and preference for separate values complete the division. Most white teachers simply do not know of the existence of the ghetto culture, except in the diluted and bowdlerized form of "folk songs" current in the white urban milieu, such as John Henry spirituals or gospel singing.

Some of the most important findings in the New York City work relate to the difference between the school performance of isolated boys, not personally involved in the vernacular culture, and full peer group members. The former show reading scores which are only one or two years behind grade with several individuals ahead of grade; the latter show records which are much poorer, with no tendency to follow a regular pattern of learning. The verbal leaders of the peer groups are not necessarily good readers in school—in general there is no connection between verbal skill in the street culture and verbal skill in school (Labov and Robins 1968). Thus any educational testing which does not distinguish these two groups in the classroom (and there are no programs which do) will not show the problem in its sharpest form.

Finally, it should be noted that the stereotypes mentioned above are also held by teachers. There is research which indicates that teachers' beliefs about the intelligence of their students affect the performance of these children. It follows that teachers' pre-formed expectations about the performance of underprivileged students will contribute to the educational failure discussed here.

BIBLIOGRAPHY

Anastasi, A., and Foley, J. P., Jr.: *Differential Psychology.* New York, Macmillan, 1949.

Ausubel, D. P.: Teaching strategy for culturally deprived pupils: Cognitive and motivational considerations. *Scholastic Rev.* 71:454–463, 1963.

Bailey, B. L.: Studies in Tougaloo in 1966. Unpublished.

Baldwin, A. L., Kalhorn, J., and Breese, F. H.: Patterns of parent behavior. *Psychol. Monogr.* 58(3): Whole No. 268, 1945.

Barker, G.: Social functions of language in a Mexican-American community. *Acta. Amer.* 5:185–202, 1947.

Bayley, N.: Comparisons of mental and motor test scores for ages 1–15 months by sex, birth order, race, geographical location, and education of parents. *Child Develop.* 36:379–411, 1965.

Bereiter, C.: Acceleration of intellectual development in early childhood. Final Report. Project No. 2129, Office Educ., Department of Health, Education, and Welfare. Urbana, Illinois, University of Illinois, 1967.

Berlyne, D. E.: *Conflict, Arousal and Curiosity.* New York, McGraw-Hill, 1960.

Bernstein, B.: Elaborated and restricted codes. *Amer. Anthro.* 66(6): Part 2, 55–69, 1964.

Bing, E.: Effect of childrearing practices on development of differential cognitive abilities. *Child Develop.* 34:631–648, 1963.

Bridges, J. W., and Coler, L. E.: The relations of intelligence to social status. *Psychol. Rev.* 24:1–31, 1917.

Bronfenbrenner, U.: Socialization and social class through time and space. In *Readings in Social Psychology,* E. E. Maccoby, et al., editors. New York, Holt, 1958.

Burt, C.: The influence of sex and social status. *Mental and Scholastic Tests.* London, P. S. King and Sons, 1921, pp. 190–199.

Busse, T.: Child rearing correlates of flexible thinking. Unpublished doctoral dissertation, University of Chicago, 1967.

Caldwell, B. M.: The fourth dimension in early childhood education. In *Early Education,* R. D. Hess and R. Bear, editors. Chicago, Aldine, 1968, pp. 71–82.

California Elementary School Administrators Association: *The Neighborhood and the School: A Study of Socio-economic Status and School Achievement.* Burlingame, California, Author, 1962.

Coleman, J. S., et al.: *Equality of Educational Opportunity.* U.S. Department of Health, Education, and Welfare, USGPO, 1966.

Darsie, M. L.: Mental capacity of American-born Japanese children. *Comparative Psychol. Monogr.* 3: Serial No. 15, 1926.

Datta, L., and Parloff, M. B.: On the relevance of autonomy: Parent-child relationships and early scientific creativity. *Proc. 75th Ann. Conven. Amer. Psychol. Assoc.,* 1967, pp. 149–150.

Dave, R. H.: The identification and measurement of environmental process variables that are related to educational achievement. Unpublished doctoral dissertation, University of Chicago, 1963.

Decarie, T. G.: *Intelligence and Affectivity in Early Childhood.* New York, Internat. Univer. Press, 1965.

Dennis, W.: The performance of Hopi children on the Goodenough Draw-a-Man Test. *J. Comp. Psychol.* 34:341–348, 1942.

Deutsch, C. P.: The development of auditory discrimination: Relationship to reading proficiency and to social class. *Project Literacy Reports,* No. 8. Ithaca, New York, Cornell University, 1967, pp. 92–100.

Deutsch, C. P., and Deutsch, M.: Brief reflections on the theory of early childhood enrichment programs. In *Early Education,* R. D. Hess and R. Bear, editors. Chicago, Aldine, 1968, pp. 83–90.

Deutsch, M.: Minority group and class status as related to social and personality factors in scholastic achievement. *Monogr. Soc. Appl. Anthrop.,* 1960, No. 2.

Deutsch, M.: The disadvantaged child and the learning process. In *Education in Depressed Areas,* H. A. Passow, editor. New York Teachers College, Columbia University Press, 1963.

Deutsch, M.: The role of social class in language development and cognition. *Amer. J. Orthopsychiat.* 25:78–88, 1965.

Deutsch, M.: *The Disadvantaged Child.* New York, Basic Books, Inc., 1967.

Deutsch, M., and Brown, B.: Social influences in Negro-white intelligence differences. *J. Soc. Issues* 20(2):24–35, 1964.

Dyk, R. B., and Witkin, H. A.: Family experiences related to the development of differentiation in children. *Child Develop.* 36:21–55, 1955.

Eells, K., et al.: *Intelligence and Cultural Differences.* Chicago, University of Chicago Press, 1951.

Eisner, E. W.: A comparison of the developmental drawing characteristics of culturally advantaged and culturally disadvantaged children. (Project No. 3086) Final Report. Stanford, Stanford University, 1967.

Entwistle, D. R.: Developmental Sociolinguistics: A comparative study in four subcultural settings: *Sociometry* 29:67–84, 1966.

Fiske, D. W., and Maddi, S. R.: *Functions of Varied Experience.* Homewood, Illinois, Dorsey, 1961.

Fowler, W.: Dimensions and directions in the development of affectocognitive systems. *Human Develop.* 9:18–29, 1966.

Fowler, W., and Burnett, A.: Models for learning in an integrated pre-school. *Elem. Sch. J.* 67:428–441, 1967.

Gardner, R. W., et al.: Cognitive controls: A study of individual consistencies in cognitive behavior. *Psychol. Issues* 1(4): 1959.

Gardner, R. W., et al.: Personality organization in cognitive controls and intellectual abilities. *Psychol. Issues* 2(4): 1960.

Garth, T. R., Elson, T. H., and Morton, M. M.: Administration of non-language intelligence tests to Mexicans. *J. Abn. Soc. Psychol.* 31:53–58, 1936.

Getzels, J. W., and Jackson, P. W.: *Creativity and Intelligence: Explorations with Gifted Students.* New York, John Wiley, 1962.

Getzels, J. W., and Jackson, P. W.: Family environment and cognitive style: A study of the sources of highly intelligent and highly creative adolescents. *Amer. Sociol. Rev.* 26:351–359, 1961.

Glick, J.: Some problems in the evaluation of pre-school intervention programs. In *Early Education,* R. D. Hess and R. Bear, editors. Chicago, Aldine, 1968, 215–221.

Gray, S. W., and Klaus, R. A.: The early training project and its general rationale. In *Early Education,* R. D. Hess and R. Bear, editors. Chicago, Aldine, 1968, pp. 63–70.

Grose, R. F., and Birney, R. C.: *Transfer of Learning.* New York, Van Nostrand, 1963.

Guilford, J. P.: *The Nature of Human Intelligence.* New York, McGraw-Hill, 1967.

Gumperz, J. J.: On the linguistic markers of bilingual communications. *J. Soc. Issues* 23(2):58–67, 1967.

Hannerz, U.: Another look at lower-class Negro sex roles. Paper given at AAA meeting, 1967.

Hansen, C. F.: The scholastic performances of Negro and white pupils in the integrated public schools of the District of Columbia. *Harvard Educational Review* 30:216–236, 1960.

Harlem Youth Opportunities Unlimited, Inc.: *Youth in the Ghetto*. New York, Century Printing Company, 1964.

Havighurst, R. J.: *The Public Schools of Chicago*. Chicago, The Board of Education of the City of Chicago, 1964.

Havighurst, R. J., and Breese, F. H.: Relation between ability and social status in a midwestern community. III. Primary mental abilities. *J. Educ. Psychol.* 38:241–247, 1947.

Havighurst, R. J., Gunther, M. K., and Pratt, I. E.: Environment and the Draw-a-Man Test: The performance of Indian children. *J. Abn. Soc. Psychol.* 41:50–63, 1946.

Held, O. C.: A comparative study of the performance of Jewish and Gentile college students on the American Council Psychological Examination. *J. Soc. Psychol.* 13:407–411, 1941.

Hess, R. D., and Bear, R.: *Early Education*. Chicago, Aldine, 1968.

Hess, R. D., and Shipman, V.: Early experience and the socialization of cognitive modes in children. *Child Develop.* 36:869–886, 1965.

Hess, R. D., and Shipman, V. C.: Cognitive elements in maternal behavior. In *Minnesota Symposia on Child Psychology, Vol. I*, J. P. Hill, Editor. Minneapolis, University of Minnesota Press, 1967.

Hess, R. D., Shipman, V. C., Brophy, J., and Bear, R.: Cognitive environments of urban preschool Negro children. Report to the Children's Bureau, Social Security Administration, DHEW, (in press).

Hunt, J. McV.: The psychological basis for using preschool enrichment as an antidote for cultural deprivation. *Merrill-Palmer Quart.* 10:209–248, 1964.

Hunt, J. McV.: Intrinsic motivation and its role in psychological development. In *Nebraska Symposium on Motivation*, D. Levine, editor. University of Nebraska Press, 1965, pp. 189–282.

Hunt, K. W.: Unpublished Research Project, CRP 1998–5–0313.

John, V.: The intellectual development of slum children: Some preliminary findings. *Amer. J. Orthopsychiat.* 33:813–822, 1963.

Kagan, J., and Moss, H. A.: *Birth to Maturity: A Study in Psychological Development*. New York, Wiley, 1962.

Kagan, J., Yando, R., and Stagman, T.: Individual variation in cognitive processes. In *Manual of Child Psychology* (3rd ed.), P. H. Mussen, editor (in press).

Kamii, C. K., and Radin, N. L.: Class differences in the socialization practices of Negro mothers. *Journal of Marriage and the Family* 29:302–310, 1967.

Kochman, T.: *Language Behavior in the Negro Ghetto*. Chicago, Northeastern Illinois State College, Center for Inner City Studies, 1968 (mimeographed).

Labov, W., et al.: A preliminary study of the structure of English used by Negro and Puerto Rican speakers in New York City, Cooperative Research Project Report No. 3091, 1968.

Lambert, W., et al.: Evaluational reactions to spoken languages. *J. Abn. Soc. Psychol.* 60:44–51, 1960.

Lesser, G. S., Fifer, G., and Clark, D. H.: Mental abilities of children from different social-class and cultural groups. *Monogr. Soc. Res. Child Develop.* 30 (Whole No. 102): 1965.

Long, H. H.: Test results of third-grade Negro children selected on the basis of socio-economic status. *Journal of Negro Education* 4:192–212, 523–552, 1935.

McDavid, R. I., and Austin, W. M.: O. E., CRP 2107. No. ED 010052, 1966, 179 pgs.

Meyers, C. E., Dingman, H. F., Orpet, R. E., Sitkei, E. G., and Watts, C. A.: Four ability-factor hypotheses at three preliterate levels in normal and retarded children. *Monogr. Soc. Res. Child Develop.* 29: Serial No. 96, 1964.

Miller, S. M., Riessman, F., and Seagull, A. A.: Poverty and self indulgence: A critique of the non-deferred gratification pattern. In *Poverty in America,* L. A. Ferman, J. L. Kornbluh and A. Haber, editors. Ann Arbor, University of Michigan Press, 1965.

Mitchell, J. V.: A comparison of the factorial structure of cognitive functions for a high and low status group. *J. Educ. Psychol.* 47:397–414, 1956.

Murray, W.: The intelligence-test performance of Negro children of different social classes. Unpublished doctoral dissertation, University of Chicago, 1947.

Piaget, J.: *Play, Dreams and Imitation in Childhood,* New York, Norton, 1951.

Piaget, J.: *The Origins of Intelligence in Children.* New York, International University Press, 1952.

Roberts, S. O., and Robinson, J. M.: Intercorrelations of the Primary Mental Abilities Tests for ten-year olds by socioeconomic status, sex, and race. *Amer. Psychol.* 7:304–305, 1952.

Russell, R. W.: The spontaneous and instructed drawings of Zuni children. *J. Comp. Psychol.* 35:11–15, 1943.

Saltzman, S.: The influence of social and economic background on Stanford Binet performance. *J. Soc. Psychol.* 12:71–81, 1940.

Schatzman, I., and Strauss, A.: Social class and modes of communication. *Amer. J. Sociol.* 60:329–338, 1955.

Shuey, A. M.: *The Testing of Negro Intelligence.* Lynchburg, Virginia, J. P. Bell, 1958.

Shuy, R.: Linguistic correlates of social stratification in Detroit speech. Final Report, Cooperative Research Project No. 6–1347. East Lansing, Michigan State University, 1967.

Sigel, I. E.: How intelligence tests limit understanding of intelligence. *Merrill-Palmer Quart.* 9:39–56, 1963.

Sigel, I. E., and McBane, B.: Cognitive competence and level of symbolization among five-year old children. In *The Disadvantaged Child,* Vol. 1, J. Hellmuth, editor. Seattle, Washington, Special Child Publications, 1967.

Sigel, I. E., and Olmsted, P. P.: Styles of categorization among lower-class kindergarten children. Paper presented at the American Educational Research Association annual meeting, New York, New York, 1967.

Sprigle, H., et al.: *A Fresh Approach to Early Childhood Education and a Study of Its Effectiveness.* Jacksonville, Florida, Learning to learn school. 1967.

Stallings, F. H.: Atlanta and Washington racial differences in academic achievement. Southern Regional Report No. L-16. Atlanta, Georgia, The Council, Feb. 1960.

Stern, W.: Children of different social strata. *The Psychological Methods of*

Testing Intelligence. Translated by G. M. Whipple. Baltimore, Warwick and York, 1914, pp. 50–57.

Stoke, S. M.: Occupational groups and child development. *Harvard Monogr. Educ.* Cambridge, Harvard University Press, 1927.

Tucker, G. R., and Lambert, W. E.: White and Negro Listeners' Reactions to Various American-English Dialects, 1966 (unpublished).

Wallach, M. A., and Kogan, N.: *Modes of Thinking in Young Children.* New York, Holt, Rinehart and Winston, 1965.

Weiner, M., and Feldman, S.: *Measurement of Reading Skills in Lower Socioeconomic Status Children.* New York, New York University School of Education, 1963.

Weintrob, J., and Weintrob, R.: The influence of environment on mental ability as shown by Binet-Simon tests. *J. Educ. Psychol.* 3:577–583, 1912.

NOTES

1. The literature on cognitive behavior and SES, both theoretical and empirical, is increasing rapidly as a result of large government appropriations and foundation grants for research on U.S. lower class populations. In addition, major research programs have been established by Project Head Start, Office of Economic Opportunity, & The National Laboratory on Early Education of the U.S. Office of Education, which are oriented toward more intensive examination of many of the issues discussed in this section. These studies and programs encompass many different ethnic groups, thousands of white and non-white children, use many existing and newly developed tests, and attempt, among other goals, to relate teacher and parent behavior and characteristics to pupil behavior. There is a growing body of evidence on the effects of integration on school achievement and experimental studies of attempts to alter the deleterious effects of SES and racial bias. A study of educational attainment of American Indian children is underway, and several national testing programs are accumulating data which will yield more definitive information on SES and test scores.

2. The textual material in this section includes excerpts and restatements of material in "Social Class and Ethnic Influences Upon Socialization" by Robert Hess, to appear in *Carmichael's Manual of Child Psychology,* Paul Mussen, editor.

3. The tests often used unfortunately include some contrasts which are not perceived normally by Negro children, such as *Ruth-roof;* or *pin-pen,* so that Negro subjects who score lower do not necessarily suffer from impaired perception of the sounds of language.

52.

The lessons of poverty

FRANK RIESSMAN

Youth from the lower socioeconomic class suffer a disadvantage not because they are without culture, but because their behavior patterns and culture do not fit with prevailing middle class values and attitudes. Their inability to adapt to the middle class mold is not a result of their inability to learn but a result of their already having learned so well to meet another set of requirements.

Differences due to cultural environments are a matter of degree. They are learned behaviors and they can be modified. Differences are universal. They exist between one family and another and between one campus and another. If we reject those who are culturally different, we limit the diffusion that anthropologists say makes for cultural richness and we limit our own personal growth.

Riessman believes that other cultures should be understood by teachers and their contributions recognized. A teacher who rejects and condemns the behavior, speech patterns, and social interaction processes of a youngster tends to trigger a rejection in the child of the system the teacher represents. Recognizing another as having a contribution of value imparts status and importance to him. Interpersonal transaction then may progress as between equals with mutual learning and growth. The editors agree that the teacher who does not expect to learn and to gain a richer and more meaningful existence from interacting with students is missing most of what teaching is all about: so, too, are the students of such a teacher.

WHEREVER WE look in the United States today, we see criticism of the school system, of the curriculum, of the teachers and administrators. The conformity of the system and the lack of real learning are constantly being attacked. At the same time the middle class in our country is being sharply criticized. Middle-class people are being portrayed as conformists who have lost their spontaneity, their convictions.

These criticisms are widespread. But there is one time when they seldom arise, and this is when the teaching of disadvantaged children is discussed. Suddenly, when we talk about these youngsters, we have a much more idealized picture of our schools and of middle-class life, and suddenly these children are to be made to conform to our suddenly wonderful ways.

I think that some important changes are beginning to take place in

American Education, 1:21–23, February, 1965. Frank Riessman, Department of Psychiatry, Columbia University.

the schools and in the middle class. But a great deal has to be done, and I believe that these disadvantaged youngsters, with their own culture and their own style and their own positives, can help us change the middle class, the school system, and the society.

Before they can help, however, these children do need education. Most particularly they need teachers who take a new approach to teaching; and it is tremendously encouraging that the Federal Government, recognizing this, will next summer support several institutes for the training of teachers of the disadvantaged. These institutes, which were authorized by the 88th Congress when it added Title XI to the National Defense Education Act, will be conducted by colleges and universities, under contract with the Office of Education.

If I were to recommend one thing to the people who will be conducting these institutes, it would be this: Show teachers how to meet the disadvantaged on their own ground.

By this I emphatically do not mean that a teacher should compromise his standards or that he should condescend to his pupils. I mean that he should recognize that the culture from which these pupils spring has its own standards and its own sense of values and that he must work within these standards, in fact turn them to educational profit.

Specifically, I believe that the training of teachers for the disadvantaged should do four things for each trainee:

1. Develop in him a genuine interest in these children and a respect for them rather than simply have him acquire some knowledge about them.

2. Expose him carefully and thoroughly to the disadvantaged so that he can free himself of any negative preconceptions he may have had about these people.

3. Show him how to use teaching methods adapted to the learning style of the disadvantaged.

4. Develop in him an effective teaching *style*, as distinguished from method.

In naming these four objectives I am thinking of disadvantaged children who will be taught in integrated, multi-class schools and classrooms. Although my suggestions may be especially suited to low-income children, they should work well also with middle-class children by improving their styles of learning and broadening their general outlook.

Let us consider each of the four in order.

It is extremely important to respect disadvantaged children. It is the key to winning them to education. But in order to respect someone it is necessary to know something positive about him, and I find that too many of the people who talk about respecting these youngsters really see nothing in them to respect. This is why I think we should stress the good things in the culture, behavior, and style of the disadvantaged. We should stress, for instance, the freedom the disadvantaged enjoy from the strain that accompanies competitiveness; the equalitarianism, informality, and humor; the freedom from self-blame and parental over-protection; the children's enjoyment of each other's company; and the enjoyment of music, games, sports, and cards.

However, it is not enough to give people respect and knowledge; it is necessary also to change the *attitude* of teachers. You may think that this is a very difficult thing to do, but actually it may not be so difficult. The way to do it, I think, is by arousing the *interest* of the teacher in disadvantaged people and their culture.

Generally, teachers and other members of the school staff have not been especially interested in the makeup of these youngsters. They have seen the poor, for the most part, as an undifferentiated drab mass. In order to create interest, I would introduce considerable controversy and ferment about the poor and their psychology. The current proposals for providing teachers with a sociological analysis of disadvantaged groups, while valuable, are not sufficient for developing deep interest in and excitement about these people.

The time has come for teacher preparation to include reading of novels, seeing films, viewing art and dance, and hearing music of various low-income groups, particularly the Negro and Spanish-speaking groups. So I would recommend, for example, that discussions take place around books like *The Cool World* by Warren Miller and movies such as *Nothing But A Man*. I think also a good deal of discussion about Negro history and Negro contributions in science, art, and engineering should take place in this kind of teacher training.

My second point is that we ought to take more thought in planning the "laboratory" programs we have for teachers. Many preparatory programs tend to stress visits to the homes and neighborhoods of the poor, visits which can actually reinforce existing stereotypes about the disadvantaged. The simple and obvious reason is that teachers, like everyone else, see what they want to see, what they have been prepared by their training to see.

What I am suggesting here is a carefully directed, prepared exposure that will help teachers know how to look at the culture of the low-income groups. They won't see simply a family that is broken, for instance, but rather an extended female-based family which is in many ways highly organized, although organized very differently from the traditional family. They will learn to see the way in which functions are delegated and organized in this family, how child rearing is handled, how cooking is assigned, how members of the family take care of the house, and the way responsibility is divided.

The teachers will also have to be taught not to confuse the normal and the pathological. The normal female-based family is not pathological. But pathology does occur in some families. In some middle-class strata, child rearing may have strong traces of parental overprotection, overindulgence, and the like. This may be the norm, just as less direct, less intensive loving is the norm in lower socioeconomic groups. But neither pattern by itself is abnormal, even though the pathologies in both classes may well be related to the normative pattern.

Nor should the focus be on the environment as such—on the crowdedness, the lack of privacy, the lack of economic security. Rather, the focus should be on how these people struggle with this environment, how they have forged a culture in doing this, and how this culture and style can be utilized in the school situation. This calls for much more than "tours" and home visits.

The third point in my suggested program has to do with teaching methods. A number of techniques may have special value for low-income children, but I shall confine myself to discussion of two—namely, role playing and the use of "hip" language.

Before I discuss these two techniques, however, let me simply list a few others that seem to hold promise for the disadvantaged:

1. The "organics" technique of Sylvia Ashton Warner (*The Teacher*) should be especially valuable in building upon the interests and potentialities of the youngsters, and should guard against their being "acted upon." (The latter is the current trend in many programs designed for the disadvantaged, who are supposedly "deficit" ridden.)

2. The Montessori System, which places much emphasis on sensory materials and on order, should be particularly congenial to low-income youngsters.

3. Various game techniques—"In the Manner of the Adverb," for example, and Robbins' "Auditory Set" game—may be valuable.

4. Lawrence Senesh's techniques for teaching economics to first and second-graders seem promising.

The technique we call role playing owes a good deal of its success to the fact that participants feel free of tension. They act out various types of problems. A caseworker interviews a withdrawn client, say; or the manager of a housing project for low-income families interviews a tenant or a prospective tenant. Since they are "only acting," they can safely express their opinions about the situations they are dramatizing and safely try out new solutions to problems.

My own experience indicates that low-income people make an exceptionally positive response to role-play technology. For one thing it is physical, action-oriented. It is *do* vs. *talk,* and low-income people tend to work out mental problems best when they can do things physically.

The verbal performance of deprived children improves markedly in the discussion period following a role-playing session. Ask a juvenile delinquent who comes from a disadvantaged background what he doesn't like about school or the teacher, and you will get an abbreviated, inarticulate reply. But have a group of these youngsters act out a school scene in which someone plays the teacher, and you will start a stream of verbal consciousness that is almost impossible to shut off.

Role playing can have various beneficial results in the teaching of academic material in the school. If an inquiring student should wonder, for example, what Abraham Lincoln would think of our present civil rights policy, let "Lincoln" and "President Lyndon Johnson" stage a debate! The impossibilities of time and space are eliminated, and the civics lesson will be well-remembered.

The second technique I am recommending here, the careful use of "hip" language, sometimes combined with role playing can be highly effective in teaching the disadvantaged. An article in the Syracuse, N.Y., *Herald-Journal* last November told how such a combination was put to good use in a ninth-grade English class at Madison Junior High School, which is participating in a program for the disadvantaged called the Madison Area Project.

A teacher had complained to Gerald Weinstein, the project curriculum coordinator, that her students "practically fell asleep" when she read a poem titled "The Magic Carpet" from a standard anthology. Weinstein went to the class armed with copies of the poem "Motto," by the Negro writer, Langston Hughes. It goes:

> I play it cool and dig all jive.
> That's the reason I stay alive.
> My motto, as I live and learn
> Is: Dig and be dug in return.

The students read the poem. After a long moment of silence—
"Hey, Mr. Weinstein, this cat is pretty cool."
"It's written in our talk."

Discussion centered on the phrase "dig all jive." Weinstein asked the students how many kinds of jive they understood. They claimed that of course they understood all kinds, but when he launched into an abstract essay on the nature of truth, using all the big words he could find, they looked blank.

He asked them to try him with their jive. They threw six expressions at him, and he got five. "According to Hughes, who has the better chance of staying alive?" Weinsten asked, "You or I?" The class had to concede that he did because he dug more than one kind of jive.

The enthusiasm of that class session led the students into more of Hughes' poetry. Later they moved into other kinds of literature in more conventional language.

But the students, the newspaper article pointed out, were not the only ones learning from that exciting class. Weinstein learned, too. He learned the advantage of being familiar with the language of the children he was teaching, the advantage of establishing rapport with them.

I am not suggesting that teachers employ "hip" language in normal conversation with the underprivileged youngster, as a device for attempting to be friendly with the child. This would indeed be patronizing and dangerous. But the use of hip material in a formal lesson plan can become an excellent avenue to the style and interests of the disadvantaged.

There is great need for curriculum materials for use with disadvantaged youngsters. Both the Bank Street College of Education in New York City, through its proposed Educational Resources Center, and New York's Mobilization for Youth project have been developing laboratories in which such materials are created and tested.

Such laboratories should be closely related to the federally supported teacher institutes and should contain not only materials but also reports and films of positive experiments in the teaching of the disadvantaged.

The project conducted by Superintendent Samuel Shepard in the Banneker District of St. Louis is especially noteworthy as an experiment of this sort. He has demonstrated that disadvantaged youngsters at the elementary and junior high school levels can be quickly raised to their proper grade level. More comprehensive efforts than Shepard's might produce even more startling results.

Finally, teaching style—

We tend to assume that good teachers ought to be healthy, well-adjusted people. I am not sure it is that simple. I am not suggesting, of course, that we look for sick people and make them into teachers. I am suggesting that we think about the development of individual teacher style and that some of these individual styles may have significant non-healthy components.

In visits to schools in over 35 cities I have found at least one teacher in each school who according to all—children, parents, colleagues, and administrators—was a "good" teacher. These teachers differed vastly from one another in method and point of view. What I am saying is that there is no one best style.

Teachers attending NDEA institutes should have opportunities to observe teachers using various effective styles and to see films of them in action. They should even role play the classroom, the different problems that arise, the discipline problem, the disorder problem. Out of this role play, each will develop his own repertoire.

Only as he works at it—through such methods and procedures as I have suggested here—can a teacher learn to meet the disadvantaged on their own ground. And only as we meet them on their own ground can we hope to realize the contribution which, as I said at the start, the disadvantaged can make to our schools, our middle class, and society.

53.

Challenge of the poor to the schools

JAMES OLSEN

Olsen's article does more than "view with alarm"; it is a "what to do" and "how to do it" approach.

Because the lower class child is "on his own" early in life, he is in many ways more adequate, self-sufficient, socially experienced, and mature than his middle class counterpart. This may fit him for life on the streets, but it often operates against the authority-directed conformity required by middle class schools and middle class teachers. Furthermore, his opposition is more apt to be overt, acted out, physical, and confrontive, while that of the middle class youngster, although just as real, is more subtle and does not provoke the open conflict which Olsen says often takes eighty per cent of teacher time for keeping order.

The solution this author proposes basically is similar to that advanced by Riessman in the preceding selection. One cannot reject another's behavior and attitudes as being wrong and hope to teach him very much. Furthermore, stimuli for learning, as Birren and Hess emphasize, which are not contingent upon previous reinforcement may have no effect upon a child's behavior. Teaching must have associations with what the learner already knows.

The editors also would like to voice hearty agreement with what is said concerning discipline. Strict routines that establish clear limits are absolutely necessary. Teachers of the culturally different need to be more authoritative in this respect and less authoritarian in their insistence that the middle class culture is the only one of value.

THE DEEPENING concern with educating the children of the poor grows out of fundamental problems in our society. The civil rights movement, youth unemployment, the continued migration of the poor to the great cities, and the need for trained manpower have forced educators to reexamine curriculum content and school practices. Many new programs have come out of this reexamination. The major goal of these programs is to reverse the educational handicaps that result from economic deprivation.

Martin Deutsch's preschool and kindergarten program, for example, attempts to make up for the negative effects of poverty on learning by giving three-, four-, and five-year-old children a rich preschool experience.[1] Provisions are made for block building, easel and finger painting, dramatic and outdoor play, collecting things, receiving and entertaining guests, cook-

Phi Delta Kappan, 47 (No. 2):79–84, 1965. James Olsen, Editor, Special Adult Education Division, McGraw-Hill Book Company.

ing, etc. Activities which increase authority and visual perception and discrimination, concept development, and the meaningful use of language are stressed. In this kind of program, children have an opportunity to develop the cognitive and sensory motor skills they need for successful participation in the later grades.

Mobilization for Youth's Homework Helper Program is another project designed to help students from lower-class homes overcome the academic handicaps that come out of poverty. In this program, high school sophomores and juniors from low-income families are hired for after-school employment as tutors of elementary school students who are retarded in reading or arithmetic. In this way, pupils are helped to acquire the academic skills they need to do their basic school work successfully; at the same time, the tutor who is doing well in high school is financially rewarded. Thus aspirations for school success are strengthened in this group.

Many more programs could be cited as examples of the efforts educators are making to upgrade educational opportunities for the children of the poor. But all of them, however different they may be in their content or approach, have one central characteristic in common: They emphasize the environmental limitations of the slum and the bad effects of those limitations on learning. The fact is that we are building our educational programs almost exclusively around the weaknesses and deficits of low-income people.[2]

While it is unquestionably true that deprivation is one major aspect of lower-income culture, its significance, I believe, has been overemphasized. We have yet to face the fact that lower-class children are socialized in ways that are quite different from those of the middle class. We have yet to take full account of the differing value patterns, attitudes, and beliefs with which the lower-class child comes to school. The child brings the reality of his own life into the classroom, and to be effective the school must admit that reality. I suggest that the central challenge that the slum child presents to the school is not only the disadvantages that he brings with him. His challenge to us is much more profound than this. His ambitions, his hopes, his desires, his attitudes toward authority, education, success, and school, his fears, his habits, his hates—in short, his basic orientation toward life— are, in many ways, so different from ours that we do not understand him nor does he understand us.

In other words, the child born and raised in a lower-class cultural milieu derives his basic perceptions and values from that milieu. He comes to school with a culture—that is, with a way of perceiving and behaving— that is distinctly different from the school culture.[3] The school is a middle-class institution, not only in its attitudes and value orientations, but also in its controls and rewards, its teaching materials, its personnel, and in its administrative practices.[4] The classroom then becomes the battleground of the culture conflict between the child and the teacher. Perhaps this is the major reason why the school experience of most lower-class children remains remote and substantially irrelevant to them and their concerns. We may subject the lower-class street-corner boy to school for ten years of his life, but psychologically he is still out there on the street corner with the boys where academic achievement, diplomas, and degrees are truly unimportant.

How is this child different from his peers in the middle class? First, his basic psychological responses of anger and sex are expressed very directly. Fighting, for example, is part of his life. He fights with his brothers and sisters. He fights with his enemies. He fights with his friends for fun. He fights with "outsiders" from other blocks and neighborhoods. He is physically disciplined by his parents. Since physical aggression is part of his everyday life, he is not intimidated very easily.[5]

Second, the lower-class child grows up very quickly. This is partly because he is on his own early in life and partly because he comes in direct contact with the fruits of unemployment, desertion, crime, and the like. While he may have a negative image of himself as a learner in school, on the streets he develops a sense of rugged independence that he needs for survival. (Unfortunately, because of his repeated failure in school and his alienation from much of the school curriculum, he does not exhibit the same independence in the classroom.) Since he is not supervised very closely by his parents, he has earlier experiences with sex. He also takes on the responsibility of the care of younger siblings quite soon and by the time he becomes fifteen or sixteen he is looked upon as a man.

This precocious maturity makes much of his school reading, for instance, unpalatable. The middle-class bias of our textbooks, which has been well documented elsewhere,[6] makes them meaningless to this youngster. They are "phony" and the child quickly learns that this kind of material will not help him to understand life. The unreality of *Little Men, Little Women,* and *Anne of Green Gables* reminds him of little in his own experience.

Third, the lower-class child has a different idea of social advancement—and this point is crucial for him in school. Since lower-class social organization is characterized by the extended family and reciprocity, there is a very strong emphasis on cooperation and mutual aid. If there is competition, it is physical in nature. But there is little competition in the sense the middle-class child knows it. Therefore, the lower-class child does not respond to the traditional test format.[7]

For the middle-class child, how one does on a test determines one's mark and that determines promotion and the likelihood of future academic success. When a teacher threatens a middle-class child with a failing grade, he is really threatening the basis of that student's personal worth. If the middle-class student suffers the humiliation of failure in school, his parents feel he has "let them down." Thus the middle-class person regards it as perfectly natural for people to strive to be bright, and the belief that one should spend sixteen years of his life in school before beginning adult work goes unquestioned. For the middle-class parent, the diploma and the degree become symbols of his children's successful performance of the initiation rites for entrance into adult life.

PENALTIES FOR VALUING COOPERATION

Since lower-class children are relatively insouciant concerning the independent achievement that the test stresses, they are liable to be apathetic in the test situation. And since so great a part of our educational system is based upon I.Q. tests, standardized tests, school tests, quizzes, exams, College Boards, scholarship tests, talent tests, and the like, the lower-class child finds himself penalized for valuing cooperation and not competition.

Not only this, but the lower-class child has not been trained to value the behaviors implicit in the test situation. He does not especially value speed—a crucial element in test taking. On the contrary, there is some evidence which indicates that the culturally different student tends to become involved in a problem and stick with it.[8] This can be disastrous in a test situation. As we have already pointed out, he does not value this kind of competition. Nor is he familiar with many of the different kinds of test items.[9]

The point here is that the test situation is not a congenial context for the culturally different. Here the student cannot readily project his drives for assertion and achievement and his repeated exposure to tests only reinforces his alienation from the middle-class culture of the school. This is not to say, as have so many in the past, that the lower-class student is a "slow learner." You cannot equate the culturally different with the slow learner. Lower-class children, like middle-class children, present a spectrum of abilities from the very low to the intellectually gifted. The research indicates, moreover, that our low economic groups include more pupils with high I.Q.'s than do middle-class groups.[10] The reason is that most of our pupils come from the lower socioeconomic groups. In our large industrial cities, only 30 per cent of the school population comes from the white-collar and professional family.[11] As the middle-class exodus to the suburbs and the in-migration of the poor to the cities continue, we can expect to have schools that are almost entirely made up of the culturally different.[12]

Fourth, the culturally different do not have the same time orientation that we do. Our schools stress the future. We see elementary school as a preparation for high school. In high school we get ready for college. In college we get ready for either graduate school or a profession. If a youngster does not exhibit this concern for the future, teachers tend to regard him as lacking in ambition and intelligence.

Thus lower-class people do not value education *in the same way* that we do. This does not mean that they do not value education *at all*. Rather, the lower-class person has a kind of "bread and butter" approach to education. He does not especially value going to school *for itself*. Nor does he especially value intellectual activity *per se*. But he does want vocational improvement through education because he knows that such improvement will give him a better consumer life.[13] Education helps get a better house, a larger automobile, nicer clothing. Thus while he does not share the middle-class emphasis on *academic* achievement, the lower-class person is interested in *vocational* goals. He is not so much concerned with "getting ahead" as he is in earning money so that he can have a good standard of living.

As we might expect, then, low-income groups, and Negroes in particular, have very positive attitudes toward education even though academic success is not their major source of status and prestige. (They value education but they also have very negative attitudes toward the school.) In one research study, for example,[14] when lower-class dropouts were asked what their biggest "gripe" about school was, they said that they resented the fact that they hadn't been prepared for a *specific* job. More than half of them wanted to return to school but said that they would want *job training* in school. Certainly, one of the major areas for curriculum reform is here. For many lower-class students attending our secondary schools, academic skills will have to be related to functional job situations. Otherwise we cannot expect to keep these students in school. As in Russia, pre-vocational courses closely integrated with work experience programs should be an accepted part of our high school curriculum.

Fifth, the attitudes of the culturally different and middle-class student toward authority figures are, in many important ways, dissimilar. The culturally different likes a strong leader who is male. (Working-class culture is essentially male-centered.) The working-class student comes from a home in which his father is the boss. His authority is backed up by physical force. When the middle-class teacher appeals to "goodness," "reason" and "social acceptability," his words fall on deaf ears, with the result that the teacher spends most of his time trying to keep order in the classroom so that he can conduct a lesson.

A MAJOR PROBLEM: KEEPING DISCIPLINE

For the teacher in the slum school, this is probably the major difficulty: keeping discipline. Teachers who succeed learn to set up strict routines from which they do not deviate, establish clear limits from the first day, and make it clear to the students that they are there to learn. The working-class student needs a strong authority figure who can maintain discipline in the class in a climate of informality.

One study of a deprived-area school concluded that as much as 80 per cent of a teacher's school day is spent in trying to keep order.[15] Even with the best teachers this figure never fell below 50 per cent. Thus the amount of instruction time in a slum school is severely limited, with the result that the students who need this time the most receive the least. Unlike middle-class children, the lower-class child rarely responds to moral exhortations which are intended to evoke feelings of guilt or shame. The expectation of the culturally different child is that the authority figure will set up fair rules and enforce them without deviation. At the same time, the teacher lets the students know that he likes and respects them. He knows they can —and will—do the work, because this is why they are in school to begin with: to learn. Above all, the ground rules of classroom routines are not discussed; they are followed.[16]

Given these basic differences and other differences which have been explored elsewhere,[17] we can see deep and striking conflicts between the working-class child and the middle-class school. In the best of faith, the middle-class person has a great deal of trouble understanding many of the value orientations of the poor because he unconsciously uses middle-class yardsticks to evaluate another culture. Most middle-class people, and teachers in particular, see lower-class life not as a separate "culture" with its own special viewpoints and values but as a chaotic and disorganized blob filled with deprivation and desperation.

With this point of view, we will not be able to make the changes we need in our schools. Our continued failure to change our curriculums constitutes a striking form of educational inequality. The fact is that our curriculums are organized in such a way as to favor children who are socialized one way rather than another.

AN INTOLERABLE SITUATION

One ludicrous and tragic instance of our inflexibility is well illustrated by those large numbers of pupils we have in our schools today who cannot, even in high school, read at a fourth-grade level, write a few simple, straightforward grammatical sentences, and make simple calculations involving multiplication and division. Yet those same students are "studying" geometrical theorems, Elizabethan drama, and irregular French verbs.[18] Can we continue to tolerate this situation?

We cannot. As long as the curriculum is primarily the embodiment of middle-class values, only middle-class children will tend to do well with it. While education and community programs which attempt to uplift the poor are all to the good, we cannot realistically expect to change the unconscious values of the great mass of working-class youngsters. What we really want to do in programs like Higher Horizons is to change our students' lower-class ways of behaving so that they can aspire to and adopt an essentially middle-class pattern of life. In short, we want them to become like us.

Even if this were desirable—and I am not at all sure that it is—how realistic a goal is this? Lower-class values have grown out of a firm matrix of economic and cultural patterns. These values are transmitted from the parents to the child. Unless we are prepared to change the way in which the family socializes the child—a power only dictatorships have—we cannot expect to convert most of the culturally different to a middle-class way of life.

It seems much more reasonable to reduce the social distance between the school and its students by finding out what the content of lower-class culture is and then modifying or changing some of what we teach and how we teach it.

I therefore make the following recommendations:

1. Since group intelligence tests reflect our middle-class criteria of achievement and success generally, we should not use the existing tests as a means of ability grouping. The latter practice tends to segregate lower-class children to an inferior scholastic status in the school and also lower teacher expectations of their academic potentialities. There should be less emphasis in our schools on *identifying* talent and greater emphasis on *developing* it.

Failure on tests does not generally inspire students with confidence anyway. The culturally different student does not respond well to test situations and repeated failure simply reinforces his negative self-image as a learner and his hostility toward the school. The research clearly indicates that non-promotion does not result in better work. Rather, there is abundant evidence to indicate that there is no consistent relationship between achievement, non-promotion, and ability.[19]

Flexible grouping plans like the ungraded primary school look promising, then, because they are more clearly based on the maturation and achievement patterns of the child and because the child who learns more slowly is not stigmatized as a "slow learner." Such grouping plans will also help us to individualize instruction for *all* children. Thus when a child is not doing the quality of work he is capable of, we can find out what's wrong and then give him the extra help he needs to do better.

2. The pre- and in-service training teacher programs have to be severely revamped so that middle-class teachers learn the content and style of lower-class life. Since 95 per cent of teachers in the United States are recruited from the middle class,[20] we need to acquaint teachers with the social values and mores of lower-class children. In this way teachers can learn to exploit the positive strengths the culturally different have and to fight their weaknesses.

However, the weaknesses of the culturally different are well-known; their strengths are not. You do not change a person's behavior, attitudes, and values by telling him what's wrong with him. That only antagonizes him. If the culturally deprived were in charge of our school systems, they might try to "lower-classize" by telling us that our language lacks the color and vitality of their language; that our absurd emphasis on academic achievement and material affluence leads to divorce, alcoholism, and neurosis; that we neglect the present for the sake of the future, and then learn one day that we have not been really living at all; that we are more impressed by a person's title—Dr. So and So—that is, by the social position a person occupies rather than by the kind of person he is, etc., etc. Such statements about the middle class would not prepare the ground for our acculturation to a lower-class style of life. Nor do similar statements by us about them generate feelings of brotherly love.

Rather, let us act on the sensible assumption that the lower-class child is probably rather bright or at least of normal intelligence and that we have been trapped by the generic problems of our schools, that is, oversized classes, split shifts, teacher shortages, a dearth of specialized services, inadequate staffing, a shortage of classrooms, and a lack of money, as well as by our own ignorance about and indifference to lower-class culture. We can no longer afford to lose the talents and skills of 150,000 able youths a year from the lower-income levels. This amounts to three-quarters of all the talented lower-class students who do not go on to college.[21]

3. Reorganize our school practices so that they are more in line with working-class life. Working-class parents do not, as a rule, attend school functions like PTA meetings. This is not because they are not interested in their child's success in school. They are simply much more comfortable with a few people in an informal atmosphere.[22] Formal presentations by school officials are less likely to bring parents into the school than short, informal, casual meetings. Every attempt should be made to change the impersonal, bureaucratic organization of the school so that the social distance between the school and community is reduced.

There is ample evidence to indicate that most teachers working in slum schools feel alien to the community in which they work and leave the school as soon as they can transfer to a better one. For example, one study of the career patterns of Chicago public school teachers documents how teachers begin their teaching careers in slum schools and then move out.[23] Therefore, teachers must be brought into closer contact with the families of the children they teach. The teacher can hold his conferences with the parent in the parent's home. Three or four other parents can be invited to attend also. In this way, the parents and the teacher can talk informally about the student's school work over a cup of coffee. Then teachers can enlist the aid of parents in creating a more effective learning environment by seeing to it that students do their homework, study for tests, and so on. If the teacher visits the parent, the parent will be more likely to visit the teacher in school.

4. Instructional materials, and especially reading materials, must be changed. Reading selections from modern writers like Steinbeck and Hemingway are much more appropriate for the high school student than

the currently used material. Book learning must be made functional, practical, and germane to the interests of the student.

Also nonverbal materials and audio-visual aids must be used extensively and frequently.[24] In this way, some of the roadblocks to greater verbalization on the part of the culturally different can be overcome.

5. Since our success in reaching the children of the poor depends upon our understanding more fully the *strengths* of working-class persons, let us build our educational programs on those strengths. We can use, for example, the cooperation that characterizes lower-income people by encouraging older siblings to help younger brothers or sisters with their school work. We can restructure our school schedules so that once students become involved in a lesson they can continue that involvement for a period of time. Also, we can relate the vocational interests of the culturally different student to the social studies and English curriculum by providing many applications of these skills in work contexts. We can exploit his precocious maturity by giving him realistic reading materials that relate to his life interests. In this way, he will be encouraged to talk about what really matters to him.

We are at the threshold of a revolution in our educational thinking in this country. The major part of this revolution lies in our realization that *all* children in the United States do not have the same opportunities to develop and exploit their capacities and talents. Since cultural and economic differences among groups profoundly influence how a child sees himself as a person and as a learner, what he hopes to get out of school, what he wants to do—or not do—after he leaves school, the people he values as models to be emulated, and perhaps even how he learns, educators need to study class differences and then translate the insights they gain from that study into curricular and organizational modifications.

NOTES AND REFERENCES

1. Martin Deutsch, *Descriptive Statement of the Institute for Developmental Studies.* New York: New York Medical College, 1960.

2. Frank Riessman, *Action Approaches to Low Income Culture.* New York: Mobilization for Youth, September, 1962.

3. Frank Miller, "Implications of Urban Lower Class Culture for Social Work," *The Social Service Review,* September 30, 1959.

4. This assertion has been well documented by a number of writers. See especially August Hollingshead, *Elmtown's Youth.* New York: John Wiley, 1949.

5. Allison Davis, "Society, School, and the Culturally Deprived Student," in *Improving English Skills of Culturally Deprived Youth.* Washington: U.S. Office of Education, 1964.

6. Abraham T. Tannenbaum, "Family Living in Textbook Town," *Progressive Education,* 31:130–40, 1954.

7. Frank Riessman, *The Culturally Deprived Child.* New York: Harper, 1962.

8. Riessman, *Action Approaches to Low Income Culture, op. cit.*

9. Allison Davis, "Socioeconomic Influences Upon Children's Learning." Speech delivered at the Midcentury White House Conference on Children and Youth, 1950.

10. Kenneth Eells, *et al., Intelligence and Cultural Differences.* Chicago: University of Chicago Press, 1951, pp. 120–61.

11. Robert Havighurst, "Metropolitan Development and the Educational System," *School Review,* 69:251–69, 1961.

12. Robert Havighurst, "Metropolitan Development and Its Implications for American Education," in *A Seminar on Dimensions of American Society.* Washington: American Association for Teacher Education (in press).

13. *Ibid.,* Chap. 2.

14. James A. Jones, "Attitudes Toward Education," a paper delivered for the School-Community Relations Course, Mobilization for Youth, New York, November 15, 1962.

15. Martin Deutsch, *Minority Group and Class Status as Related to Social and Personality Factors in Scholastic Achievement.* New York: The Society for Applied Anthropology, 1960, Monograph No. 2, p. 23.

16. Miriam Goldberg, "Adopting Teacher Style to Pupil Differences," a paper delivered for Teachers College, Columbia, Conference on Disadvantaged Children, July, 1963, p. 9.

17. For a summary of twenty-five years of the research on psychological effects of social class differences in child rearing, see Urie Bronfenbrenner, "Socialization and Social Class Through Time and Space," in E. E. Maccoby, *et al., Readings In Social Psychology.* New York: Holt, 1958.

18. James B. Conant, *Slums and Suburbs, A Commentary on Schools in Metropolitan Areas.* New York: McGraw-Hill, 1961.

19. John I. Goodlad, "Research and Theory Regarding Promotion and Non-Promotion," *Elementary School Journal,* 53:150–53, 1952.

20. James T. Olsen, "The Verbal Ability of the Culturally Different," *Educational Forum,* in press.

21. Rexford G. Moon Jr., quoted in *New York Times,* April 15, 1959.

22. Miller, *op. cit.*

23. Howard Becker, "The Career of the Chicago Public School Teacher," *American Journal of Sociology,* 57:423–26, 1952.

24. James T. Olsen, "The Coming Revolution in Textbooks," *A.V. Communication Review,* Fall, 1964.

section **xiii**

Group influences and communication

54.

Sense about sensitivity training

MAX BIRNBAUM

Sensitivity is a current and pertinent topic. Societies and groups of people are not different from individuals in the sense that when a need arises, ways of meeting it also tend to develop. Sensitivity groups are a good example. Representative of some of the words and phrases used to describe existence in this automated, massed society are materialistic, thing-not-people oriented, personal anonymity and loneliness, alienation, anomie, and lack of identity. The current trend and almost preoccupation with such groups in some circles appears to have evolved as a counter to these kinds of feelings. Sensitivity experiences for the most part are designed to bring people closer together, to help them to identify with and to relate and communicate meaningfully with others on an emotional level.

Most of the time sensitivity groups accomplish these purposes to some degree. But occasionally, and frequently enough to suggest caution, the effect is almost the opposite of the expected interpersonal closeness and increased psychological and personal well-being. Emotional reactions and feelings sometimes are surfaced which are not dealt with and which then make psychiatric treatment necessary. This is unfortunate, both for those so affected and for its influence upon public attitude. Limitations upon the responsible as well as the irresponsible use of groups could result. It would be too bad if this happened, for there is much potential for increasing personal effectiveness here. The very potency and impact that groups have and the fact that they do exert powerful influences upon people can contribute to public disillusion and rejection as well as to use and acceptance. Far too many of those conducting sensitivity groups are inadequately prepared to do so. Enthusiasts would be well advised to bear this in mind.

DURING THE 1960s, public education discovered the emotions. Cognitive learning and skill training, the traditional components of education, no

Saturday Review, 52(No. 46):82–83, 96–98, November 15, 1969. Copyright 1969 Saturday Review, Inc. Max Birnbaum, Director, Human Relations Laboratory, and Professor of Human Relations, Boston University.

longer satisfied the needs of a generation that had experienced the civil rights revolt, the widening generation gap, and the increasing confusion of teachers, administrators, and school board members about ends and means in education. The result was a growing interest in various approaches to affective learning that assigns to the emotional factor in education a role as important as—or, perhaps, more important than—the traditional substantive content and skills. Among these approaches the most enthusiastically embraced has been the so-called sensitivity training.

The term is used loosely to include a wide range of laboratory training approaches in human relations, group dynamics, organizational development (or, as I prefer, applied human relations training), as well as a number of verbal and non-verbal experiences that seek to increase awareness and release human potential. It is an unfortunate term because of its vagueness, but it appears that its very impreciseness and beguiling simplicity are the qualities that have helped it gain wide currency.

By whatever name it is known, however, human relations training is capable, if properly employed, of producing substantial educational change. It holds tremendous potential for improving education by dealing with its affective components, reducing the unnecessary friction between generations, and creating a revolution in instruction by helping teachers to learn how to use the classroom group for learning purposes.

The pity is that this promising innovation may be killed before its unique properties have a fair chance to demonstrate their worth. The opposition to its serious exploration is strong and is apt to grow. But it is not those who oppose sensitivity training because it smacks of therapy, which to a very small degree it does, nor even the members of the renascent John Birch Society, who would equate it with brainwashing, who pose the major challenge. Rather, the most serious threat to sensitivity training comes first from its enthusiastic but frequently unsophisticated school supporters, and second from a host of newly hatched trainers, long on enthusiasm or entrepreneurial expertise, but short on professional experience, skill, and wisdom.

WHAT is needed today is a clearer sense of how sensitivity training developed, the varied forms it may take, and the results that can be anticipated in any given situation. Unfortunately, not all of the "experts" agree on the many issues raised by this kind of training, and there will be those who disagree strongly with many of the judgments presented here. But clearer definition of the issues, wider discussion, and more careful analysis of results should help schoolmen toward more effective use of training for fundamental improvement in the schools.

Contrary to the impression given by some recent popular writing on the subject, it was neither the author of *Joy* nor the devoted creators of Esalen who were responsible for the development of human relations training. Rather, it was Leland Bradford, then director of the Adult Education Division of the National Education Association, together with his old friends and collaborators Ronald Lippitt, now of the University of Michigan, and Kenneth Benne, now of the Boston University Human Relations Center, who were primarily responsible. Drawing on the work of the great social psychologist Kurt Lewin, they established the first training center more than two decades ago at Bethel, Maine, and founded the National Training Laboratories (NTL). And it was Bradford's tough and dogged fight against strong opposition within education that finally won sanction and support for human relations training, first from industry, then from the social and behavioral scientists, and finally from the education hierarchy itself. Now, as he is about to retire as director of NTL, Lee Bradford has the satisfaction of seeing human relations training widely embraced by the education world.

As the field developed, the T-group (Training group) became the heart of any laboratory or workshop that is devoted to the study of group dynamics or human relations. The traditional T-group consists of a small group of people—ideally ten to sixteen—who meet in a residential setting (the laboratory) for approximately two weeks. Although only one part of this educational experience (theory, interpretation, and skill development are also included), the T-group is, because of its intense emotional impact, by far the most significant aspect of any human relations lab. The objectives of the T-group are to help individual participants become aware of why both they and others behave as they do in groups—or, in the jargon of the professional, become aware of the underlying behavior dynamics of the group. This is accomplished, with the help of a trainer, by creating an atmosphere in which the motivations for typical human behavior, of which individuals are often unaware, are brought to the surface in an exaggerated form. Once they are made clear and explicit, they can be discussed and analyzed. Thus, the individual participant can observe both his own behavior and that of others in the group, discover sources of different kinds of behavior, and identify the effect they have upon the functioning of the group. The effort to stimulate exaggerated behavior in order to get at the motivation behind it more explicitly is an uncomfortable experience for many people, but the feeling is usually transitory. The emotional component of the experience makes it appear to verge on therapy, but there is a significant difference between therapy that is focused on the problems of emotionally disturbed people and training that aims at the improvement of human relations skills of normal people.

In the early years of the movement, the T-group emphasis was primarily on the sociology of groups rather than on their psychology—that is, on the roles and functions of leadership and membership, rather than on the individual personality and personal development. (Bradford, Benne, and Lippitt came from adult education, philosophy, and social psychology.) The trend toward a psychological emphasis appeared in the early 1950s when the movement began to attract a larger number of people trained in clinical psychology or psychiatry. And it was at that point the T-group emerged as a new social invention that bears some rough resemblance to a combination of seminar and therapy group, but it actually is neither.

Recognition of the power of the T-group, as well as its limitations, has led to wide experimentation with other applications. Laboratory sessions of varying length and widely differing objectives have been developed, ranging from a single day or weekend to two or three weeks, and having as their purpose varying kinds of individual and organizational change. Much of the confusion in the field stems from the lack of clearly defined purposes, and guidelines that indicate the kind of training session most effective in achieving a particular objective. Most specifically, confusion results from the failure to differentiate between those training experiences that are designed to improve an individual's capacity to work effectively as a manager or member of a group for educational or reeducational purposes, and those that are designed to stimulate the individual's personal growth and so are clearly in a domain that might be labeled paratherapy, in the sense that it is parallel to therapy, rather than therapy itself. Therefore, it is necessary to look at the varying kinds of training that are becoming popular today to see what purposes each is best designed to serve.

Organizational development is a general term that includes a variety of approaches that combine affective and intellectual components in the use of small groups as a medium for consultation, problem solving, and reeducation of individuals in both public and private organizations. It developed primarily out of the earlier, sociologically oriented focus of the T-group that emphasized organizational change rather than personal development. My experience with school systems and other organizations with a process that I term applied human relations training probably falls within this definition. (See Thomas Cottle's "Strategy for Change" [*SR*, Sept. 20] for a description of one application of this process to the resolution of intergroup problems in a single school system.)

Encounter groups, confrontation sessions, and *marathon labs* are usually short term—most often twenty-four-hour or weekend—experiences where the emphasis is on the direct exposure of beliefs and feelings that usually are not put on public display by individuals. The term "encounter group" derives from the phrase "basic encounter group" that Carl Rogers, the noted exponent of non-directive counseling, coined to differentiate a new kind of experience from the traditional T-group. Trainers in these sessions usually encourage participants to explore in some depth their own feelings and motivations, as well as those of other group members. The objective is to stimulate an exchange that is inhibited by a minimum of reserve and defensiveness in order to achieve a maximum of openness and honesty. Marathons differ from encounter groups primarily in the unremitting intensity of the experience that seeks to achieve a significant break-through in normal defenses and so attain what many practitioners believe is a new level of open behavior. Confrontation sessions are usually contrived racial encounters in which militant blacks literally "confront" members of the white community (teachers, police, industrial management, etc.) with their angry reaction to white racism, discrimination, and prejudice. The theoretical basis for this type of experience is that the social conditions requiring this form of learning demand a maximum dose of aggression and hostility in order to convince the targets—the whites— of the seriousness of the personal situation. (Because most confrontation sessions of this kind are not part of a plan for organizational change, they usually end as paratherapeutic experiences rather than training.)

Non-verbal exercises have invaded the training field with a vengeance in recent years. The techniques employed are numerous and range from simple exercises with a minimum of body contact to physically intimate and emotionally revealing designs of the kind most often associated with Esalen and its derivatives. (It should be noted that the explorations of Esalen, on the West Coast, are making major contributions to the field of therapy, but it is less clear how the techniques developed there can contribute to education.) Non-verbal techniques derive their theoretical justification from theories of personality that stress the possibility of achieving greater honesty and authenticity through bodily expression that can become uninhibited more quickly than can verbal communication. Thus, participants can reach deeper levels of consciousness more quickly.

Each of these varied approaches to sensitivity training is designed to serve specific purposes. Undoubtedly each can be immensely beneficial to certain individuals—and provide little help, or have negative results, for others. What must be made clear is the purpose to be achieved, and the kind of training best designed to serve that purpose.

Clearly, organizational development—or applied human relations training—that is focused on organizational change, problems of human relations, and morale within an organization belongs in the training area. These experiences may bring to participants great personal insights and lead to new ways of relating to family and friends, but these are *accidental* consequences of the experience that is directed toward increasing individual effectiveness as a member of the organization. Marathons, personal growth labs, encounter groups, and non-verbal exercises belong in the paratherapeutic area. These are frankly concerned primarily with individual growth and development, the achievement of authenticity, or "therapy for normals." In some cases, labs of this kind assume that there will be an organizational payoff from the experience, but others do not. The original T-group, from which all the forms of sensitivity training developed, can serve either purpose. It can provide the basis for a lab devoted primarily to personal growth, or one that rigorously relates all personal learning to an organizational context. But experience teaches that, unless a lab is consciously dedicated to the latter, the high degree of personal involvement inevitably pulls the focus toward individual growth.

When lab organizers are unable or unwilling to differentiate between various kinds of training, the results can be disastrous. There are many tales, some maliciously embellished, but many all too true, of school systems and communities where bad situations have been made worse by the unintelligent application of inappropriate forms of sensitivity training. Some examples of such misuse of training may help to clarify the point.

The T-group that aims at personal growth, for instance, is an experience that has tremendous validity for school people as long as it takes place in a setting away from home where the individual can be relatively anonymous—a summer laboratory or workshop, for example. But trouble comes when it is applied uncritically within a school system where the participants are co-workers. The result in this case is either impossible resistance, or, even worse, the revelation of intimate personal information that is so highly charged that it makes continuing work relationships very difficult, if not impossible.

Similarly, encounter groups or confrontation sessions between blacks and whites in the same school or community may lead to problems. In the past, such sessions have sometimes had useful shock value in revealing quickly the crucial problems that are polarizing the races today. Under skillful management, with careful control over degrees of resistance and levels of anxiety, and a systematic effort to relate the encounter experience to specific educational issues so that it can lead to follow-up plans for action and change, such training labs can be quite useful. Unfortunately, it appears that too often difficulty arises as a result of routine application of what are basically gimmicks to an involved and highly charged area.

In one large city school system an encounter group recently included teachers, most of whom were white, and students, most of whom were black, from the same school. The result was the opposite of what was sought—increased physical and verbal hostility of students to the teachers in the school. Carefully managed, however, the encounter between teachers and students, away from the school setting, has enormous possibilities for re-educating both teachers and students for a needed revolution in their relationships. But even at its most effective, the encounter session is a shocking and bruising experience. And because of the failure to follow through with concrete plans for specific action, it too often remains a memorable experience, but not one that produces change.

Non-verbal exercises also are susceptible to both effective and inappropriate use. In one recent case at a conference of foundation executives, a trainer was employed to lead the group in several non-verbal exercises designed to stimulate greater openness and trust—two attributes much to be desired in any conference. The result, however, was unexpected. The initially surprised and then outraged participants displayed an enormous amount of openness—all of it hostile—toward both the trainer and the conference sponsors. The simple exercises that may be effective in settings where people are clearly experimenting with behavior are often completely inappropriate in another context. Similarly, young school teachers, after an enthusiastic lab experience, return to the classroom to lead their students into such "games." No harm is done, but because some of these exercises involve body contact of a quasi-intimate nature, it is questionable whether students, especially teenagers, should be so encouraged. Under normal circumstances, teenagers do not need the sanction of the school to become so engaged.

There are, however, cases where non-verbal experiences are very much to the point. In police-community relations training sessions, simple physical contact exercises—a hand shake or, in special circumstances, a hug or touching another person's face—can be helpful. Where ghetto residents have never felt a policeman as a human being, such contact can be a wholesome revelation. For the white police, the personal experience that the black on the skin will not rub off has been equally salutary.

Two kinds of sensitivity training are particularly susceptible today to exploitation by the enthusiastic amateur or the enterprising entrepreneur: the area of non-verbal experience, and the confrontation session. Each requires a minimum of experience and knowledge to stimulate an initial response among participants, but in each case a maximum of expert knowledge and sophistication is required to extract a positive educational outcome. The most damning judgment that can be made about the non-verbal field is that a small bag of easily learned exercises, plus several $33\frac{1}{3}$ rpm records, makes anyone a trainer. As for confrontation sessions, it is not difficult to evoke profound guilt feelings among participants by employing the tactics of staged aggression, but it requires great skill and understanding to follow through to a positive learning experience.

Despite all the possible pitfalls, however, it is necessary today to recognize the affective aspect of the educational process, and to train both teachers and administrators for mastery of the area. Too many of today's teaching-learning problems—in the suburbs as well as the inner city—are in the emotional rather than the cognitive or the skill areas. Change is imperative. But changing individual behavior and organizational structure are extraordinarily difficult and thorny objectives. All too often new superintendents come along with prescriptions for innovation and reform that falter long before their efforts get off the ground. The longer one works in the field of planned change, the more difficult the task appears.

By chance, however, two unusually powerful forces for change in educational systems appeared during the 1960s. The first was the civil rights revolution, the second the extraordinary wave of student unrest that, according to a recent survey, has affected three-fourths of all secondary schools in the country. Although the civil rights movement has been fraught with bitter tension and physical violence, the student rebellion promises to be the more global in its effects on the schools. The former forces schools to examine racial attitudes, curriculum priorities, school culture, hiring and promotion policies, and other fundamental relationships in school administration. But the latter strikes directly at the heart of student-teacher and student-administration relationships that have endured with only minor modifications since the turn of the century. These relationships, which determine who makes significant decisions within the schools, may in the long run prove the most troublesome, but also the most decisive stimulus for change. Schools, after all, have long been one of the most hierarchically organized institutions in our society—only the army and the quasi-military police are more authority-centered. To effect a significant change in the nature of the school and classroom authority, then, is a problem of the first magnitude involving both organizational and human change.

THE devilish seductivity of human relations training stems from the fact that it can reduce individual resistance to change more effectively than any other known means. It promises the wishful decision-maker, therefore, that his desires for school reform can be fulfilled. This is the trap that awaits all school executives interested in using human relations training for planned change experiments.

The superintendent, then, who wants to set about planning for effective change in his school system, must be aware of the variety of training opportunities available for his staff members. He must also make a clear decision about the type of training he wants his staff to experience. If he decides that certain key personnel could benefit themselves—and the school system—by undergoing a personal growth experience that will help to decrease individual defensiveness and the tendency most humans share to ascribe value by status rather than by individual worth, then by all means he should send these individuals to labs away from home in the summer. It may be that both the schools and the participants' wives or husbands will benefit, and both may be legitimate objectives.

If, however, school personnel are to begin the long and complicated process of applying group procedures to organizational meetings, problem solving, or classroom learning, then laboratory training that focuses primarily on personal growth is likely to be minimally productive. Organizational development laboratories or applied human relations workshops focusing on intergroup or community-school problems may be more useful, because the emphasis is on problem solving. But human relations training labs differ not only in their overall emphasis, but often within the same laboratory trainers may run the gamut from exclusively personal growth-oriented sessions to the older concept of the T-group that is designed to help participants to function more effectively on the job.

School systems now infatuated with training will have to learn, as industry has, that not all sorts of training are functional for all personnel. They may also have to learn that under certain conditions a school system would be wasting money by investing in human relations training. When morale is poor—not because of organizational or human impediments to communication, but because decision-making is handled in an authoritarian fashion, or pay is poor and working conditions are worse—instead of training, the school system should opt for higher salaries or elimination of the authoritarian administrator. Similarly, if the middle echelon administrator —the principal—is fearful and unsure of his position, large-scale training for teachers, under the superintendent's sponsorship, can generate intolerable pressures upon him. For example, an effective human relations training program can result in increased enthusiasm among faculty, more demands for help in curriculum, introduction of new ways of class management, greater degree of experimentation, and demands for a larger voice in decision making. These demands can be fearfully unsettling for a principal who has always run a "tight ship" where everything was under his control. Unless he himself is ready for change, it would be wisest to forget training—or forget him.

The serious question remains, of course, of how a superintendent or school board can determine whether a trainer or training organization is capable and experienced. There is no bureau of standards or licensing agency for human relations trainers. NTL has some three or four levels of affiliation, but it is very cautious about claiming universal virtuosity for members of its network. As increasing numbers of psychologists become interested in the field, it is likely that school systems will be assured of securing individuals with reputable academic credentials, but these will provide no assurance of effectiveness in human relations training. Training, like teaching or therapy, is largely an art—based, to be sure, on a conceptual framework and multiple skills, but still a highly individual affair. Therefore, at this point in the development of the field, the school administrator's best bet is to check the length of the trainer's experience as well as his knowledge of schools and school systems, and to talk with his fellow superintendents who have already ventured into the field.

Whatever the difficulties, however, the promise that human relations training holds for fundamental improvement and reform in the schools cannot be denied. The need of school personnel for training in the affective area is great for several reasons. First, in an era of increasing tension and alienation, both teachers and administrators must develop more fully the qualities of empathy and human objectivity—the essential hallmarks of the helping professions. Placed in a role where they are often the target of juvenile hostility—directed at them either personally or as parental substitutes —teachers more than most require a resilient personality that can absorb aggression, and that can also remain open and sympathetic to students and their problems without becoming personally involved with adolescent hang-ups.

Second, training in the affective area can help to reduce attitudinal blocks and group resistance to needed educational change. Normal resistance to significant change is no less for teachers than for other human beings; the trouble lies in the fact that the institution of which they are a part is the most beleaguered of any in society today. The need for change to meet the multiple dissatisfactions and pressures that plague the schools wants little documentation here. But if needed change is to be achieved, the individuals involved will themselves have to be prepared to change.

WE must remember, however, that attention to the emotions in the learning process derives from an educational model, not a therapeutic one. Despite the assumption by many people that attention to the emotional dimensions of learning demands a therapeutic model, teachers cannot, and should not, be therapists.

Third, human relations training can make it easier for school personnel to "hang loose" during these revolutionary changes in teacher-student relationships so that both they and their students can survive. Moreover, the experience school systems will acquire in integrating the emotions and group process into classroom instruction will surely make for improvement in social intelligence that is so necessary for effectiveness in the helping professions. This capacity for dealing effectively with other humans individually or in groups that, for want of a more precise term, is called social intelligence has largely been ignored or taken for granted as the schools have focused on stimulating and rewarding cognitive learning. But as the abrasion of human existence increases in our crowded world, it can no longer be ignored.

Finally, appropriate human relations training should begin to equip teachers with a new teaching technology that is based on a learning group of peers, in contrast to the traditional classroom with the teacher as an authority figure and the students as a group of charges. The capacity to be a group process teacher is undoubtedly the most difficult of all goals for human relations training. But the ability to make a classroom into a learning group where peers share in the teaching-learning transaction holds the greatest promise for overcoming the all too familiar pattern—in the suburbs as well as the inner city—of sullen and disaffected children mobilizing to impede the educational process. The objective of making use of the emotional factor in teacher training, school reorganization, and classroom learning is an extraordinarily difficult one, but the revolution in education that this will achieve makes it imperative that school systems begin now.

55.

Adolescent choices and parent-peer cross-pressures

CLAY V. BRITTAIN

The research reported in this selection should be of value to the reader for two reasons. First, the information gained about the effect of peer versus parental pressures upon the choice of alternatives by high school girls may help in understanding these kinds of youngsters. Second, the manner in which this study is organized, the findings are presented, and the conclusions are drawn is sufficiently typical so that learning to interpret and to understand other studies of a similar nature may be facilitated.

In order to understand the significance of the differences between the experimental and control groups in studies like this, it is necessary to examine Tables 1 and 2, and especially the right-hand columns labelled Chi Square. *Notice the asterisks to the right of the quantities listed in this column. Now look at the bottom of the tables where the asterisks are used to denote the statistical terms, $p < .1$; $p < .05$; $p < .01$; $p < .001$. The meaning of these terms refers to the number of times, or the probability, that a difference of this magnitude can be expected to occur by chance. Since they show how significant the differences are, they are referred to as levels of significance. Hence, in the term, $p < .1$, p is an abbreviation for probability; $<$ shows a relationship of less than, or more than; and .1 indicates that if there were 100 repetitions of this study, differences in choice patterns would occur because of chance, or in a random fashion, less than ten times, or conversely that similar results probably would be obtained more than 90 times. Similarly the term $p. < .05$ or the "oh five" level of significance means it is probable that a difference of this magnitude could be expected to occur at least 95 times in every 100 replications. The .01 or "oh one" level of significance expresses a confidence that similar results can be expected 99 out of 100 times and the .001 level indicates a probability of 999 in every 1000 repetitions.*

For example, the data in item one, Table 1, show that fifty-two per cent of the subjects in the experimental group shifted responses from the first to the second testing to correspond with changes in problem form, whereas only twenty-three per cent of control subjects, responding twice to the same form, did so. The difference of .29 with a chi square value of 15.60 is probable, because of random or chance factors, in less than one out of every 1000 repetitions.

American Sociological Review, 28:385–391, 1963. Clay V. Brittain, Teacher Education, Emory University, Atlanta.

From "Parents and Peers as Competing Influences in Adolescence" (unpublished Ph.D. dissertation, University of Chicago, 1959). The writer gratefully acknowledges the guidance of Professors Robert D. Hess, Jacob W. Getzels, and Robert J. Havighurst.

As THEY are commonly portrayed, adolescents confronted with parent-peer cross-pressures tend to opt in favor of the peer-group. But to what extent and under what circumstances does this image square with reality?[1] Does the tendency toward peer-conformity vary as a function of the type of choice to be made by the adolescent?

The concept of reference group is useful in attacking this problem. Following Shibutani's[2] formulation that a reference group is one whose perspective constitutes the frame of reference of the actor, both peers and parents might be thought of as reference groups; i.e., as groups each provides perspectives in terms of which adolescents make choices. Does the extent to which adolescents tend to adopt these different perspectives vary systematically across situations? We hypothesized that in making certain kinds of choices, adolescents are inclined to follow peers rather than parents; in making certain other types of choices, the opposite is true.

PROCEDURE

Situations involving conflict between parent-peer expectations were described to the subjects—girls in grades 9 through 11. Each situation was structured around an adolescent girl who was trying to choose between two alternatives, one of which was favored by her parents and the other by her friends. The following item illustrates the procedure:

> A large glass in the front door of the high school was broken. Jim broke the glass. But both he and Bill were seen at the school the afternoon the glass was broken and both are suspected. Bill and Jim are friends and they agree to deny that they know anything about the broken glass. As a result, the principal pins the blame on both of them. Nell is the only other person who knows who broke the glass. She was working in the typing room that afternoon. She didn't actually see the glass broken, but she heard the noise and saw Jim walking away from the door a few moments later. Nell is very much undecided what to do. The three girls she goes around with most of the time don't think Nell should tell the principal. These girls hate to see an innocent person punished. But they point out to Nell that this is a matter between Jim and Bill and between Jim and his conscience. Nell talks the matter over with her mother and father. They felt that Jim is unfairly using Bill in order to lighten his own punishment. Her parents think Nell should tell the principal who broke the glass.
>   Can you guess what Nell did when the principal asked her if she saw who broke the glass?
>   She told him that she didn't see it broken.
>   She told him who broke the glass.[3]

Two versions of 12 items each were constructed to make up two forms (A and B) of the present instrument, which will be called the Cross-Pressures Test, or CPT. The two forms were identical in all respects except for the opinions and preferences attributed to parents and friends.

These were reversed from one form to the other. The parent-favored alternatives on Form A were the peer-favored alternatives on Form B, and vice versa.[4] The instructions accompanying the CPT were:

> The following stories are about young people like your friends and the people you know. These people are in situations where they are not sure what to do. We would like to have you read each story carefully and tell us which one of the two things the person in the story is more likely to do. Do *not* tell us what the person should do, but what she is *likely* to really do. We hope you will enjoy doing this.

The CPT was administered to an experimental group and a small control group. The experimental group responded to one form and then to the other; the control responded twice to the same form. Both were divided into subgroups and tested as follows:

Experimental Group	First Testing	Second Testing
Group AB	Form A	Form B
Group BA	Form B	Form A
Control Group		
Group A	Form A	Form A
Group B	Form B	Form B

One to two weeks intervened between the testing dates. The subjects were not told that they were to be tested a second time.

As can be seen from the specimen item, the dilemmas described on the CPT were double-barreled (as well as double-horned). There is the dilemma embodied in the content of the alternatives (e.g., telling who broke the glass in the door of the high school versus not telling; or going steady with a boy having certain personal qualities versus going steady with a boy having other personal qualities), and, on top of this, the dilemma posed by the cross-pressures from parents and friends. The subjects could respond to either dilemma or to both. We anticipated that they would respond to both; i.e., the tendency to choose the parent-favored or the peer-favored alternative would depend upon what the dilemma was about. Hence, there would be marked inter-item variation in the frequency of parent-conforming and peer-conforming choices.

The experimental group data were analyzed for differential preferences for the parent-favored and peer-favored alternatives. In response to each item there were three possibilities: (1) The subject, responding to the content of the dilemma, chooses the same content alternative on both forms of the CPT. (2) The peer-favored alternative is selected on both forms. (3)

The parent-favored alternative is selected on both forms. In event of 2 or 3, the choice of content alternative shifts from the first testing to the second. The data, then, were analyzed for shifts in choice of content alternatives from one form of the CPT to the other.[5] The control group was used to help establish that the shifts in the experimental group were due to differences in the forms of the test and not simply to the tendency to respond randomly.

Items on which peer-conforming response shifts were more frequent and those on which parent-conforming shifts were more frequent were identified. From the content of these items inferences were drawn about the bases of preferences for peer-favored and parent-favored alternatives.

Following the second testing 42 girls in grades 9 and 10 were individually interviewed.[6] The interview data help to clarify the above analysis of responses to the CPT.[7]

SUBJECTS

The subjects were girls[8] from high schools in Alabama and Georgia. The 280 girls in the experimental group came from an urban high school, a high school in a small city, and three small rural high schools. Analysis of the data did not reveal any rural-urban differences. The 58 control respondents were from a high school in a small town and a rural high school.

RESULTS

Comparison of the experimental and control groups indicates that the findings reported below were not due to the tendency to respond randomly, but that changes in form did elicit changes in choice of content alternatives. The data are given in Table 1. On item one, for example, 23 per cent of the control subjects, who responded twice to the same form, shifted content alternatives from the first testing to the second as compared to 52 per cent in the experimental group. On each of the 12 items, shifts in choice of content alternative occur more frequently in the experimental group. On 11 of the items the experimental control differences were significant at the .01 level or better.

An analysis of the experimental group is given in Table 2. The responses to each item were first broken down in terms of the following two categories: (1) The choice of content alternatives did not shift from one form to the other. (2) The content choice did shift; i.e., the peer-favored or parent-favored alternative was consistently chosen. (See columns NS and S.) The second category was then broken down into peer-conforming and parent-conforming choices. (See columns P and F.) As can be seen from this break-down, items 1, 6, and 8 tended more strongly to elicit peer-conforming choices; items 3, 4, 5, 7, 9, 11, and 12 tended to elicit parent-conforming choices. All of these differences except that for item 4 are significant at the .05 level or better. Parent-conforming and peer-conforming choices were distributed equally on item 2.

Before interpreting these findings, note the following observations. They suggest the results were not dictated simply by the method.

(1) The subjects responded naively. Of the 42 girls individually interviewed soon after the second testing, only two were able to tell how the two forms of the CPT differed.

(2) Responding to the CPT seemed to be accompanied by anxiety. In informal group discussions immediately following the second testing there

TABLE 1. PROPORTION OF CONTROL GROUP AND EXPERIMENTAL GROUP SHIFTING RESPONSES

Item	Experimental Group $N = .280$	Control Group $N = 58$	Difference $P_k - P_o$	Chi Square[a]
1. Which course to take in school	.52	.23	.29	15.60**
2. Which boy to go steady with	.50	.28	.22	12.71**
3. How to get selected for a school honor	.33	.28	.05	.94
4. Whether to report boy who damaged school property	.35	.14	.21	13.57**
5. Whether to enter beauty contest or be cheerleader	.44	.16	.28	22.52**
6. How to dress for football game and party	.51	.19	.32	26.42**
7. Whether to be beauty contestant or appear on TV program	.39	.14	.25	18.56**
8. Which dress to buy	.58	.19	.39	39.39**
9. Which one of two boys to date	.49	.16	.33	29.00**
10. Which part-time job to take	.34	.16	.18	10.66*
11. Whether to report adult who damaged public property	.38	.19	.19	10.23*
12. How to let boy know she is willing to date him	.36	.21	.15	6.66*

[a] Chi square computed from frequencies, df = 1. *p < .1; **p < .001.

TABLE 2. FREQUENCY OF SHIFTS IN CHOICE OF CONTENT ALTERNATIVES FROM ONE FORM TO THE OTHER

Item	Not Shifting Content Alternatives (NS)	Total (S)	Shifting Content Alternatives		Chi Square[a]
			Alternative Selected		
			Parent (P)	Peer (F)	
1. Which course to take in school	135	145	48	97	16.56***
2. Which boy to go steady with	141	139	70	69	.01
3. How to get selected for a school honor	187	93	63	30	11.70***
4. Whether to report boy who damaged school property	182	98	58	40	3.30
5. Whether to enter beauty contest or to be cheerleader	156	124	93	31	28.26***
6. How to dress for football game and party	138	142	47	95	16.22***
7. Whether to be beauty contestant or appear on TV program	170	110	83	27	31.00***
8. Which dress to buy	118	162	59	103	11.92***
9. Which one of two boys to date	143	137	81	56	4.56*
10. Which part-time job to take	184	96	69	27	18.37***
11. Whether to report adult who damaged public property	174	106	73	33	15.09***
12. How to let boy know she is willing to date him	180	100	64	36	(7.84)**
Column totals	1908	1452	808	644	

[a] Chi square for differences between columns P and F computed on the basis of 50/50 assumption. df 1. *p < .05; **p < .01; ***p < .001.

were expressions of irritability at having to make the choices called for. This suggests that the subjects did tend to become emotionally involved in the hypothetical situations themselves.

(3) Groups of subjects differentiated on the basis of their responses to the CPT were also differentiated on the basis of sociometric data. For example, subjects who most frequently chose peer-favored alternatives tended not to be well accepted by their peers.

(4) At least some of the response trends were consistent with what informal observation of adolescent behavior would lead one to expect. For example, choices relating to dress were especially likely to be peer-conforming.

DISCUSSION

The findings, as reported in Table 2, are consistent with the hypothesis that responses of adolescents to parent-peer cross-pressures are a function of the content of the alternatives and that peer-conformity in adolescence, rather than being diffuse, tends to vary systematically across situations. The response variation across items supports the hypothesis.

More specific interpretations of the response trends are now in order. Why were the peer-favored alternatives more commonly selected in response to some of the hypothetical situations and parent-favored alternatives in response to others? This question relates to the more general problem of understanding the processes involved in coming to terms with conflicting pressures, which, as Merton has pointed out,[9] is salient for reference group theory.

From the content of the hypothetical dilemmas, viewed against the response trends shown in Table 2, the following hypotheses are offered:

1. The responses reflect the adolescent's perception of peers and parents as competent guides in different areas of judgment.

The general social orientation of adolescents is of a dual character. Choices tend to derive meaning from either of two general reference groups, or both: the peer society in which many status and identity needs are gratified, and the larger society in which the status positions which one can aspire to as an adult are found. When choices pertain to the latter, parents are perceived as the more competent guides. In response to the hypothetical situation involving choice of part-time jobs (item 10), for example, preferences commonly were for the parent-favored rather than the peer-favored alternatives.

2. The responses reflect concern to avoid being noticeably different from peers. Two of the items to which responses showed clear-cut peer-conforming trends involved a choice of dress; i.e., item 6—how to dress for a football game and party, and item 8—which one of two dresses to buy.

3. The responses reflect concern about separation from friends. Peer-conforming choices were predominant in response to item 1—which one of two courses to take in school, where the consequence of a peer-defying choice would have been some degree of separation from friends.[10]

4. A fourth hypothesis overlapping but different from those above is that the choices reflect perceived similarities and differences between self

and peers and self and parents. Adolescents, for example, perceiving themselves to be more like peers in regard to tastes in clothes and in regard to feelings about school, find peer-favored alternatives in these areas psychologically closer and more acceptable. But in other areas the greater perceived similarity is between self and parents. For example, with respect to values involved in the difficult choice whether to report a person who has destroyed property (items 4 and 11), the parent-favored alternatives are closer and more acceptable.[11]

The interviews referred to above provided a source for further inferences. According to one hypothesis derived from the interview data, responses to the CPT were a function of the perceived difficulty of the content choices. Parent-conformity was more prevalent in response to dilemmas posing what were perceived to be the more difficult choices. The 42 subjects interviewed soon after the second testing were asked to rank the content choices according to difficulty. The items from the CPT, with the parent-versus-peer aspect deleted, were typed on small cards; the subjects were asked to select from among them, first the situation in which the girl would have the greatest difficulty making up her mind, then the situation in which she would have the least difficulty. This was repeated until the choices were ordered from most to least difficult. Median ranks were computed. The items eliciting predominantly peer-conforming trends fell at the least difficult end of the resulting rank order. Hence, the tendency toward parent-conformity was directly related to the perceived difficulty of the choice.

A second inference was suggested by a discrepancy between the interview data and CPT responses. Interviewees were asked to select from among the content dilemmas, as presented on the cards, the two about which a girl would most likely talk to her friends rather than her parents. Neither of the two items most frequently selected had elicited predominantly peer-conforming CPT response shifts. Choices in response to one of them (item 9—which one of two boys to date) were more frequently parent-conforming; while in response to the other (item 2—which one of two boys to go steady with) parent-conforming and peer-conforming choices were equally frequent. No such discrepancy was found when the girls were asked to select the two dilemmas about which a girl was most likely to talk to her parents rather than her friends. The three items most commonly selected (i.e., 4, 10, and 11) had all elicited predominantly parent-conforming response shifts.

This divergence of interview and test data may indicate that the latter lead to an overestimate of parent-conformity. But it also suggests a device used by adolescents in coping with parent-peer cross-pressures, namely, avoiding communication with parents. This would be likely to occur in areas in which parent-peer conflict is most acute. If this is the case, such discrepancies as those reported here could be used to identify points at which adolescents tend to be most disturbed by cross-pressures from parents and peers.

Let me note one other aspect of the data. Despite the greater overall incidence of parent-conformity, there was greater convergence relative to peer-conforming choices. As shown in Table 2, a majority of the items elicited a preponderance of parent-conforming over peer-conforming choices. On each of the items where there was a reversal of this trend (i.e., items 1, 6, and 8) there were, however, more peer-conforming choices than parent-conforming choices on any single item. This suggests the following possibility: Analogous trends in the social behavior of adolescents create the impression that peer-conformity in adolescence is more diffuse than actually is the case. Lack of parent-adolescent communication about certain types of choices contributes to this impression.

SUMMARY AND FURTHER APPLICATIONS

The study explored the hypothesis, suggested by reference-group theory, that adolescent choices in response to parent-peer cross-pressures are dependent upon the character of the content alternatives presented. Hypothetical dilemmas were described to adolescent girls. In each dilemma a girl was confronted with a complex choice where one course of action was favored by parents and another by peers. The respondents were asked in each case to indicate what the girl would probably do. With the situations remaining otherwise unchanged, peer-favored and parent-favored alternatives were interchanged and the hypothetical dilemmas again presented to the respondents. Comparison of responses to the two forms of the test revealed that peer-conforming choices were more prevalent in response to certain of the dilemmas and parent-conforming choices in response to others. These results were taken to support the hypothesis.

The content of the items suggested additional specific hypotheses as partial explanations of the trends toward peer-conforming and parent-conforming responses: (1) The responses reflect the adolescent's perception of peer and parents as competent guides in different areas of judgment. (2) The responses reflect a concern to avoid being noticeably different from peers. (3) The responses reflect concern about separation from peers. (4) The choices reflect perceived similarities and differences between self and peers and self and parents.

Additional data were collected by interviewing a number of the respondents. From the interview data and from discrepancies between test and interview it was hypothesized that: (1) The tendency toward parent-conformity is directly related to the perceived difficulty of the choices. (2) Adolescents attempt to come to terms with parent-peer cross-pressures by simply not communicating with parents.

The present study argues the value of the approach exemplified here in exploring an important facet of adolescence. What considerations predispose adolescents toward peer-conformity in situations where they are confronted with parent-peer cross-pressures? What are the persisting cognitive schemata against which choices in such situations are made? We believe that through applications of the present method or adaptations of it, hypotheses relating to these questions could be investigated. For example:

1. Stability of social values: Adolescents are more strongly given to peer-conformity in making choices in areas in which social values are changing rapidly, than making choices in areas in which social values are relatively stable.

2. Time perspective: Adolescents are more strongly disposed toward peer-conformity in making choices where immediate consequences are anticipated than in making choices where the emphasis is on long term effects.

In addition, the present procedure might be used to assess individual differences in predispositions toward peer- versus parent-conformity. Although the study did not deal with the problem, the subjects were found to differ from one another in their tendencies to make parent-conforming or peer-conforming choices. At the extremes four groups were identified: (1) subjects manifesting relatively strong tendencies toward parent-conformity; (2) subjects manifesting relatively strong tendencies toward peer-conformity; (3) a mixed-conformity group composed of subjects making parent-conforming choices and peer-conforming choices with relatively great and about equal frequency; and (4) subjects making very few responses of either type; i.e., subjects whose responses were mostly consistent by content. The stability of these response biases and their possible correlates remain a problem for further study.

NOTES AND REFERENCES

1. There is controversy about the legitimacy of this image. For contrasting views see Frederick Elkin and William A. Westley, "The Myth of the Adolescent Peer Culture," *American Sociological Review,* 20 (December, 1955), pp. 680–684; and James S. Coleman, *The Adolescent Society,* New York: The Free Press, 1961, Ch. 1.

2. Tamotan Shibutani, "Reference Groups as Perspectives," *American Journal of Sociology,* 60 (May, 1955), pp. 562–569.

3. Item number 4 on the instrument used in the study.

4. The alternate version of the item given above read as follows: "The three girls she goes around with most of the time feel that Jim is unfairly using Bill in order to lighten his own punishment. They think that Nell should tell the principal who broke the glass. Nell talks the matter over with her

mother and father. They don't think Nell should tell the principal. Nell's parents hate to see an innocent person punished. But her father points out to Nell that this is a matter between Jim and Bill and between Jim and his conscience." There are obviously many situations for which this type of reversal would not be plausible.

5. Biases toward parent-favored or peer-favored alternatives showed up also as differences in first test responses between experimental subgroups AB and BA. A comparison of these groups, not reported here, reveals substantially the same trends as shown in the present analysis.

6. Both the interviewing and the testing were done by the writer.

7. Sociometric data were collected in one of the schools included in the study, but only brief reference is made to them in this paper.

8. This imposes an important qualification in generalizing the findings. If a sample of adolescent boys were studied in similar manner, the findings would undoubtedly diverge at some points from those presented here.

9. Robert K. Merton, *Social Theory and Social Structure.* Revised and Enlarged Edition, New York: The Free Press, 1957, p. 244.

10. An example identical on both forms concerned which one of two high schools to attend. Responses to it were predominantly peer-conforming.

11. This hypothesis holds, in effect, that there is a close interrelationship between what Merton refers to as normative type and comparison type reference groups. Merton, *op. cit.,* p. 283.

56.

Effects of a personal growth group on a measure of self-actualization

MELVIN L. FOULDS

This article by Foulds is an example of the attempt to bridge the gap between impressionistic material and experimental data. Sensitivity groups, T-groups, basic encounter groups, interpersonal process groups are to some persons a great social invention that promises much for optimum human development. To others, to state it bluntly, such groups are anathema. Such groups should be outlawed because they are so destructive! For those at the extremes of these views, Foulds' article will be lightly discarded. It will be regarded as being unnecessary (we knew it already) or inconsequential (even the author admits procedural limitations).

For the reader whose mind is not made up, Foulds provides some

Journal of Humanistic Psychology, 10:33–38, Spring, 1970. Melvin L. Foulds, Counseling Psychologist, Bowling Green State University.

tangible data. But what we especially like about the article is the emphasis on dealing with feelings *and* attitudes *that exist* now *among those present; i.e., "psychological archeology" was discouraged. Before and after measures indicate that "for this group" personal growth was facilitated and mental health was fostered by the group process.*

We should like to underline an important point about groups of this kind, whatever they are called: Trained facilitators are needed. See the first paragraph under "Procedure" in the article.

THE GROWTH center model has been advocated by the author for the provision of counseling services in educational institutions (Foulds & Guinan, 1969). On the college or university campus, the growth center is a proactive agency that provides a wide variety of educative, developmental, and remedial services designed to foster increased levels of self-actualization and human effectiveness, expansion of human awareness and experience, and maximum development of human potentials. A description of various activities designed to achieve these goals has been offered (Foulds & Guinan, in press), and the present paper is a report of a study that attempted to evaluate the effectiveness of one activity, the weekly personal growth group, in facilitating the increased self-actualization of "normal," relatively healthy, growth-seeking college students. The personal growth group is a form of experiential learning that focuses on expanded awareness, authenticity, and more effective interpersonal communication.

Shostrom (1964, 1966) has constructed the Personal Orientation Inventory (POI), a diagnostic instrument designed to assess the values and self-percepts believed to be associated with self-actualization. Significant positive changes in mean scores on several scales of this inventory have been reported for groups of college students following sensitivity training (Culbert, Clark, & Bobele, 1968), and a weekend marathon group (Guinan & Foulds, in press). The present study was conducted to test the hypothesis that an experimental group of college students who participated in a personal growth group experience of nine weekly sessions would demonstrate significant positive changes in POI scores while a nontreatment group controlled for pretest scores would not.

METHOD

Subjects

The experimental group consisted of 20 undergraduate college students (10 males and 10 females), ranging from freshmen to seniors and from 18 to 22 years of age, who had contacted the university counseling center and requested to participate in a growth group experience. Since these groups are intended to be a growth and learning experience for "normal" students, each prospective participant was interviewed by the author in order to screen for severe pathology, to assess motivation for change and personal growth, and to prepare the individual for the experience. The goals of the group (Foulds & Guinan, 1969) were stated to the subject, and he was encouraged to explore and express his feelings and expectations concerning the upcoming event. The subjects were then divided into two subgroups of equal size. One male withdrew from the university prior to the end of the group experience; consequently, data were available for only 19 subjects.

An equal number of subjects were selected for a nontreatment group controlled for sex and pretest scores on the Inner Direction plus Time Competence scales of the POI (all 150 items in the inventory). Control subjects were selected from a population of 164 students who completed the POI while enrolled in a course in educational psychology, and pretest scores differed by no more than four points for each pair of subjects included in the study.

Procedure

The author, an experienced psychotherapist and group leader with an experiential-Gestalt orientation, served as facilitator in the growth groups. Nine weekly sessions of 4 hours each were held in the evening at the counseling center for each subgroup.

The personal growth group was a semistructured group experience with emphasis on the exploration and expression of "here-and-now" feelings concerning self and other group members. Psychological "archeology" was discouraged, and group members were encouraged to live as fully as possible in the present, to stay in the continuum of awareness, and to relate authentically "in the now." The facilitator attempted to create a psychological climate of safety and trust in which each person might feel increasingly free to risk being transparently real, to trust his feelings, to communicate his needs and preferences openly and honestly, and to be more aware of his personal freedom and the responsibility associated with this. Participants were urged to "talk straight" at all times (with directness, clarity, and congruence), to become aware of their manipulative behaviors, and to discover ways in which their intended "helpfulness" sometimes inhibits growth and change in another person. They were encouraged to become increasingly aware of internal sensations and the reflexive muscle movements associated with these (and also the antagonistic muscle movements that prevent bodily movement and the release of inner tensions). They were also encouraged to develop behavioral flexibility (to learn to respond behaviorally to feelings in a variety of ways so that the probability of releasing tension in an appropriate, nondestructive, and satisfying manner can be increased) and to develop closer contact with the external environment through sharpened sensory awareness. Subjects were invited to remove their social masks, to reduce their phony game-playing, and to begin communicating openly and authentically. At appropriate times the group facilitator used a variety of techniques (including sensory awareness exercises, nonverbal exercises, Gestalt awareness training, psychodrama, guided fantasy, directed daydreams, and psychomotor experiences) to help group members experience more fully in awareness (in the foreground) what had previously been in the background of unawareness. Special emphasis was placed on awareness of one's decision-making process, on the importance of choosing in awareness, and on accepting personal responsibility for one's choices.

Experimental subjects responded to the POI at the beginning of the first group session, and posttests were administered 1 week following the last group session. Control subjects also completed the pre- and posttests 9 weeks apart during regular class periods of a course in educational psychology. Group means, standard deviations, and t tests of significance of differences between correlated means were then computed.

RESULTS AND DISCUSSION

Table 1 presents the results of the statistical analysis of the data. Experimental group mean scores changed in a positive direction following the group experience on all 12 POI scales, and statistically significant changes ($p < .05$) were observed on 8 of 12 scales. No significant changes occurred in control group mean scores. The pretest mean scores of the subjects in the present study were higher than those of the normative group of college students reported by Shostrom (1966); thus, the prediction that the subjects would be "normal," relatively healthy individuals was confirmed.

Following the personal growth group, experimental subjects scored significantly higher scores on the scales of the POI that purport to assess the following personality characteristics: (1) feelings or attitudes of personal freedom or independence and internal direction based upon inner motivations rather than upon external expectations and influences (I); (2) flexibility in the application of values and reduced compulsivity and dogmatism, as well as increased ability to situationally or existentially react without blind or rigid adherence to principles (Ex); (3) awareness of and sensitivity to one's own needs and feelings (Fr); (4) the ability to be open and disclosing of one's authentic being and to express feelings in spontaneous action (S); (5) acceptance of self in spite of weaknesses and deficiencies (Sa); (6) ability to transcend dichotomies and to see opposites in life as meaningfully related (Sy); (7) ability to accept one's natural aggressiveness (A); and (8) ability to develop intimate relationships with other human beings that are unencumbered by expectations and obligations (C). Changes in the I, Ex, Fr, S, Sa, and C scale scores were significant beyond the .001 level. Thus, the personal growth group appears to be one effective method for fostering increased self-actualization and the personal growth process in normal college students.

TABLE 1. MEANS AND *t* TESTS OF DIFFERENCES BETWEEN MEANS ON POI PRE-
AND POSTTESTS

POI Scale	Experimental Group			Control Group		
	Pre M	Post M	t	Pre M	Post M	t
Time Competence (Tc)	15.78	16.22	.80	15.72	15.67	− .12
Inner Direction (I)	83.61	89.17	4.27***	83.33	83.39	.06
Self-Actualizing Values (SAV)	19.94	20.17	.43	19.44	19.17	− .60
Existentiality (Ex)	22.22	24.78	4.46***	19.72	19.28	−1.46
Feeling Reactivity (Fr)	15.67	18.11	7.08***	15.22	14.56	−1.27
Spontaneity (S)	12.11	13.56	3.97***	12.56	11.78	−1.69
Self-Regard (Sr)	10.72	11.17	1.03	12.22	12.39	.36
Self-Acceptance (Sa)	14.78	17.39	7.20***	15.72	15.89	.31
View of the Nature of Man (Nc)	12.22	12.33	.57	12.11	12.22	.36
Synergy (Sy)	7.05	7.44	2.36*	7.00	6.83	−1.14
Acceptance of Aggression (A)	16.05	17.61	2.89**	15.39	15.06	−1.00
Capacity for Intimate Contact (C)	18.44	21.33	7.82***	17.67	17.44	− .48

* $P < .05$, one-tailed test.
** $P < .01$, one-tailed test.
*** $P < .001$, one-tailed test.

The findings of the present study are highly consistent with those of a previous investigation (Foulds, 1969) in which a group of 15 subjects demonstrated significant positive changes on the same 8 POI scales following a growth group experience of 8 weekly sessions. The results of these two studies provide empirical validation of claims made by advocates of growth groups that such experiences can assist persons to achieve positive personality changes and increased levels of personal functioning. The reader should be aware, however, that all growth groups may not provide the same set of experiences leading to identical results, for group facilitators provide differential stimuli for group members and initiate different forms of group process that may yield differential outcomes. The present findings are the result of a specific form of group process facilitated by a specific group leader, and thus the generalization of results is necessarily limited.

Future investigations should attempt to compare the results of outcome studies of growth groups with differential time structures, group facilitators, and forms of group process in order to vary these independent variables to determine which factors seem to be associated with the constructive personality and behavior change of group members. Also, followup investigations would be helpful in determining the permanency of change, the transfer of learning to real-life situations, and group members' perceptions of the value of a growth group experience (Foulds, Wright, & Guinan, in press).

One possible weakness in the present study is that both the experimental and control groups did not consist of subjects who had volunteered to participate in a growth group and were then randomly assigned to treatment and nontreatment groups. A service agency has considerable difficulty justifying this type of research design, particularly when control subjects would be denied a service for weeks or months. Also, LeMay and Christensen (1968) have demonstrated that the research design of randomly assigned subjects to experimental and control groups is not free of contamination, for control subjects who request assistance in increasing their levels of personal functioning and then are denied help while they serve as control subjects in a research study frequently seek out some alternate form of assistance that is unknown to the investigator, thus invalidating their nontreatment control status and distorting experimental evidence.

In summary, the present study was designed to investigate the effects of a personal growth group on a measure of self-actualization, and the results indicate that this group experience seems to be an effective method for fostering positive mental health and the process of personal growth and learning in relatively healthy, growth-seeking college students.

REFERENCES

Culbert, S. A., Clark, J. V. & Bobele, H. K. Measures of change toward self-actualization in two sensitivity training groups. *Journal of Counseling Psychology*, 1968, *15*, 53–57.

Foulds, M. L. & Guinan, J. F. The counseling service as a growth center. *Personnel and Guidance Journal*, 1969, *48*, 111–118.

Foulds, M. L. & Guinan, J. F. On becoming a growth center. *Journal of College Student Personnel*, 1970, *11*, in press.

Foulds, M. L., Wright, J. C. & Guinan, J. F. The marathon group: A six month follow-up. *Journal of College Student Personnel*, 1970, *11*, in press.

Guinan, J. F. & Foulds, M. L. The marathon group: Facilitator of personal growth? *Journal of Counseling Psychology*, 1970, *17*, in press.

LeMay, M. L. & Christensen, O. C. The uncontrollable nature of control groups. *Journal of Counseling Psychology*, 1968, *15*, 63–67.

Shostrom, E. L. A test for the measurement of self-actualization. *Educational and Psychological Measurement*, 1964, *24*, 207–218.

Shostrom, E. L. *Manual, Personal Orientation Inventory*. San Diego: Educational and Industrial Testing Service, 1966.

57.

When are feelings communicated inconsistently?

ALBERT MEHRABIAN

Mehrabian presents a data-based article that arouses many speculations—at least on the part of the editors. Verbal communication is one of the three or four uniquely human characteristics. Prior to the last decade, problems of communication were pretty much ivory tower concerns of the academicians. But the present "younger generation" is much concerned with the communication process, and the literature in human development is responding with numerous books and articles. Although Mehrabian does not present a complete summary of the topic of communication, his paper is challenging to thought and helpful in behavior.

A person does not like to be criticized directly, but he prefers that over ambiguity (inconsistency in Mehrabian's terminology). A critic who praises with his words but censures with his tones may puzzle the person he is judging because communication is not clear. The person would rather have it straight and know what the situation is than to wonder whether he is facing friend or foe. You may discover from the article why sarcasm is proscribed for teachers. You may learn some propositions for your own behavior from the data presented. The article is an excellent example of science as a base for speculations about one's own behavior.

WHEN DOES a communicator choose to express an attitude inconsistently rather than consistently? Why does he select sarcasm, for instance, a message in which he uses negative intonation with positive content (e.g., "I really like that!"), thereby communicating a negative attitude to the addressee? In that case, he might also have communicated negative attitude in both the verbal and vocal channels. One question, then, is what function an inconsistent message can serve that a consistent one cannot.

There are no available experimental studies of this problem although there are some studies of inconsistent communications which attempt to relate attitudes communicated in various channels to the attitude transmitted by a total communication. Mehrabian and Wiener (1967) investigated the decoding of consistent and inconsistent vocal-verbal communications. Three

Journal of Experimental Research in Personality, 4:198–212, June, 1970. Albert Mehrabian, University of California, Los Angeles.

This research was supported by Grant MH 13509 from the United States Public Health Service. The author is thankful to Jerry Brennan, Robert Law, Stanley Sue, and Charles West for their assistance in the preparation of materials and for running the subjects.

degrees of attitude in the verbal component were combined with three degrees of attitude in the vocal component, thus yielding nine types of communications. The results indicated that the vocal component is dominant in determining the attitude inferred from a combined vocal-verbal message; that is, whenever the vocal component is inconsistent with the verbal one, the total attitude communicated is determined by the vocal portion. For example, if the speaker says, "That's just great," with intonation which is independently judged as negative, a negative attitude is inferred. In a similar vein, an experiment by Mehrabian and Ferris (1967) studied combined vocal and facial communications involving all possible combinations of three degrees of attitude in the facial component and three degrees of attitude in the vocal component. The results indicated that the facial component is more important than the vocal one in determining the total attitude that is inferred. Mehrabian and Ferris (1967) proposed a linear model as a first-order approximation for conceptualizing multichannel attitude communications: simultaneous verbal, vocal, and facial attitude cues received the coefficients .07, .38, and .55, respectively. In other words, according to the model, the verbal component of inconsistent attitude communications contributes least to the overall attitude that is inferred from the three-channel communication; the vocal component contributes moderately, and the facial component contributes the most. It was also noted that procedures outlined by Anderson (1962, 1964) can be used to investigate possible nonlinear contributions to such judgments made by any one individual.

The preceding model suggests that inconsistent attitude communications can be readily classified into two categories—one where the total impact is positive and another where it is negative. Positive inconsistency is evidenced when someone verbally insults a friend while smiling. An irritated facial expression accompanied by positive vocal and verbal expressions exemplifies negative inconsistency. These two categories can in turn be distinguished from consistent attitude communications, in which all components are judged as either positive or negative in quality.

Given these distinctions, the problem can be restated in two parts: (1) When are inconsistent negative attitude communications preferred more, with preferences for consistent negative attitude communications of the same degree used as a baseline? (2) When are inconsistent positive communications preferred, using consistent positive attitude communications as the base of comparison? In the following experiments, two channels of communication, verbal and vocal, were employed. The inconsistent positive communications involved a positive vocal component and a negative verbal component, and the inconsistent negative communications involved negative vocal components and positive verbal components. The control stimuli for these two sets of messages consisted of moderately positive verbal and vocal communications on one hand and moderately negative verbal and vocal communications on the other.

All of the following experiments employed the same set of verbal-vocal communications. Several instances of each of the four types of communication were recorded on tape. Subjects listened and indicated preferences for these while imagining a variety of social situations.

The study constituted an explanatory search for relationships. In the absence of any experimental literature bearing directly on the problem, it was possible only to elaborate a general tentative hypothesis: inconsistent communications are less formal or more intimate expressions of attitude than consistent ones. Further, since reservations about the expression of negative attitude were assumed to be determiners of the preference for consistent versus inconsistent messages, several of the factors involved the elicitation of negative feelings from the communicator by the addressee.

The choice of factors for the study was guided by the preceding tentative considerations and included negative affect-arousing cues in combination with social situations varying in formality. One group of factors was: (1) liking of the addressee, (2) degree of conflict and irritation between the communicator and addressee, and (3) pleasantness of the addressee's behavior toward the communicator. A second group of factors related to the formality of communication situations: (4) the degree of formality of the communication setting, (5) the status of the communicator relative to the addressee, (6) the presence versus absence of bystanders at the time when the communication was directed at the addressee, (7) the ability of the addressee to accept unambiguous expressions of dislike toward himself, and (8) the implicit versus explicit quality of a negative message from the addressee to the communicator.

The two personality variables explored in the study were communicator social approval-seeking tendency, as measured by the Crowne and Marlowe (1960) Social Desirability Scale, and communicator anxiety as measured by the Mandler and Sarason (1952) Test Anxiety Questionnaire. These two variables were selected because higher degrees of social approval-seeking tendency and anxiety were expected to be associated with greater difficulty in the overt expression of negative feelings.

METHOD

Verbal Stimuli Used in All the Experiments

The audio-taped communications employed in all the experiments were prepared as follows: A group of 30 University of California undergraduates were initially presented with written sentences such as, "I hate it when you do things like that," or "I really don't care for that," and were asked to indicate, using a -3 to $+3$ scale, how much positive attitude was communicated by each statement. From these ratings, the following set of statements was selected to represent four categories of affect for male communicators and male addressees: "I really like that," "Now, that's great," and "That was really very nice of you," for strong positive affect; "That makes me feel terrible," "I hate it when you do things like that," and "That's disgusting," for strong negative affect; "That was clever," "I think that's all right," and "That's okay," for moderate positive affect; and "I really don't care for that," "Don't you think that's ridiculous," and "How do you ever get the gall to do such things?" for moderate negative affect.

The following set was selected for female communicators and female addressees: "That was really very nice of you," "That's great," and "I really like that," for strong positive affect; "I hate it when you do things like that," "That's disgusting," "That makes me feel terrible," and "Why do you have to be so irritating?" for strong negative affect; "That's okay," "I think that's all right," and "That was clever," for moderate positive affect; and "I really don't care for that," "Don't you think that's ridiculous," and "How do you ever get enough gall to do such things?" for moderate negative affect.

Next, a second set of 15 male and 15 female University of California undergraduates was asked to communicate a strong positive content with negative intonation, a strong negative content with a positive intonation, a moderately positive content with moderately positive intonation, and a moderately negative content with moderately negative intonation. Informal observation of subjects trying to communicate negative content with positive intonation indicated that it was difficult and required a larger number of trials than stimuli in the other categories. From these audio-tape recordings, a preliminary selection was made, reducing the stimuli to a more manageable set. This set was subsequently administered to a third group of University of California undergraduates, two separate groups of 30 males and 30 females, with the following instructions:

> For each of the comments which you will hear, please imagine the following situation. You and another person of the same sex and approximately the same age are together. You do something, and the other person makes a comment. For each of the comments, use the scale below to indicate how much preference, liking, or positive evaluation for your action is indicated by the other person's comment.

A scale ranging from +3 (extreme liking, preference, and evaluation) to −3 (extreme dislike, lack of preference, and low evaluation) was inserted at this point, and spaces were provided for subjects to rate their judgments of each recorded communication.

Analysis of the judgments of attitude from these recordings yielded the final set of inconsistent and consistent communications. There were six communications which had positive contents spoken with negative intonation (i.e., inconsistent negative) and six with moderately negative contents spoken with moderately negative intonation. Each of the latter was equated in overall level of attitude communication to each of the first set of six inconsistent negative communications. Thus, for example, for the statement, "That's great!" spoken with negative intonation and rated as −.60, there was a control negative communication ("How do you ever get the gall to do such things?") which was rated −.53. Similarly, there was another set of six negative content-positive intonation (i.e., inconsistent positive) communications with a corresponding set of six control statements which were moderately positive in content and intonation. For example, there was the statement, "I hate it when you do things like that," spoken with positive intonation and rated as +.95 and the control statement, "I think that's all right," spoken with moderately positive intonation and rated as +.89.

In sum, two sets of 24 statements were obtained, one for male communicators and male addressees, the other for female communicators and female addressees. The 24 communications of male speakers were recorded in four random sequences on audiotape, as were the 24 communications of females.

Experiment I

The factors investigated in this experiment were two levels of attitude toward the addressee, like versus dislike; two degrees of conflict between communicator and addressee, resolved versus unresolved; and the pleasantness of the addressee's behavior which elicited a communication from the communicator, pleasant versus unpleasant. In addition, the Crowne and Marlowe (1960) Social Desirability Scale and the Mandler and Sarason (1952) Test Anxiety Questionnaire were administered to the subjects before they listened to the tapes. Thus, two additional factors in the experiment were the high versus low social approval-seeking tendency of the communicator and the high versus low anxiety level of the communicator.

Subjects. Forty-eight male and 48 female University of California undergraduates were paid to participate as subjects in the experiment.

Procedure. In separate group administrations, male and female subjects judged and indicated their preference for each of the 24 communications under the following four within-subject conditions: Liked addressee and resolved conflict, liked addressee and unresolved conflict, disliked addressee and resolved conflict, disliked addressee and unresolved conflict. The instructions for each condition were presented to the subject in a four-page booklet (one condition on each page). For instance, in the liked addressee, resolved conflict and pleasant addressee behavior condition, the subject read the following instructions:

> Think of someone of the same sex and about the same age as you whom you know reasonably well and whom you like. Imagine the following situation involving yourself and this person. You have been irritated with this person for some time and have just discussed the source of your irritation with him to your mutual satisfaction.

Right now, the two of you are together, and this person is doing something which both of you know is quite pleasant for you.

I am going to play some tape-recordings of different statements which you are to imagine yourself as possibly making in this situation. First please try, as best you can, to get into the mood of the above situation so as to be able to indicate what kinds of statements you would prefer to make in the situation and what kinds of statements you would not prefer to make in the situation.

At this point instructions for the recording of responses were provided to the subject. For each statement he indicated a preference score ranging from zero ("I would have no preference at all for making the statement") to 6 ("I would have extremely high preference for making the statement").

The instructions for the remaining conditions were identical to the preceding, with these exceptions:

"Whom you like," was replaced by "whom you dislike," in the negative attitude condition. ". . . you have just discussed the source of your irritation with him to your mutual satisfaction," was replaced by ". . . you have not discussed the source of your irritation," in the unresolved conflict condition. ". . . which both of you know is quite pleasant for you," was replaced by ". . . which both of you know is quite unpleasant for you," in the negative addressee behavior condition.

The sequence of four within-subject conditions in the booklets was counterbalanced over all subjects. After reading each condition (i.e., each page of instructions in the booklet), subjects listened to a random presentation of the 24 verbal stimuli and recorded their preferences.

Experiment II

In this experiment the effects of the following variables on the differential preference for inconsistent versus consistent communications were explored: two degrees of addressee status relative to the communicator, high versus low; two degrees of formality of the communication situation, formal versus informal; and pleasant versus unpleasant addressee behavior. In addition to these variables, the Social Desirability Scale and the Test Anxiety Questionnaire were administered to the subjects prior to their hearing of the tapes.

Subjects. Forty-eight male and 48 female University of California undergraduates participated as paid subjects in the experiment.

Procedure. In several group sessions, each subject received a four-page booklet, each page containing instructions for one of the four within-subject conditions: formal situation and pleasant addressee behavior, formal situation and unpleasant addressee behavior, informal situation and pleasant addressee behavior, informal situation and unpleasant addressee behavior.

Each subject was assigned to either a high or low status of addressee condition and received all possible combinations of the remaining two conditions, formality and pleasantness. The order of presentation to the subjects of these four conditions was counterbalanced, and since there were 24 possible sequences of these four conditions, multiples of 24 subjects were employed.

Instructions for the high social status of addressee, formal condition and pleasant addressee behavior condition were:

> Think of someone of the same sex as you who has a higher social status than you. (A person of higher social status might be an employer, a teacher, or some other person in a position of authority over you; a person of lower social status might be someone whom you have authority over.) Imagine the following situation involving yourself and this person. You are in a situation with this person where it would be very awkward and socially inappropriate for the two of you to have an argument or disagreement. Right now the two of you are together and this person is doing something which both of you know is quite pleasant for you.
>
> Now I am going to play some tape recordings . . . [the remaining instructions were as in preceding experiments].

The instructions for the remaining seven conditions were identical with the following exceptions:

"Higher social status," was replaced by "lower social status"; "quite pleasant for you," was replaced by "quite unpleasant for you"; finally, "it would be socially appropriate for the two of you to have a disagreement or argument," was the replacement in the informal condition.

This experiment was replicated (Experiment III) with, however, only 24 male and 24 female subjects.

Experiment IV

In this experiment the effects of the following factors on the differential preference for inconsistent versus consistent communications were explored: the addressee's negative attitude communication, explicit versus implicit, as indicated by the phrase, "This person has just expressed a negative and cutting remark toward you in a very open and obvious way," versus ". . . very subtle and sly way"; the level of the addressee's tolerance for criticism, as indicated by, "This person is the kind of person who can accept frank and unambiguous expressions of dislike toward himself without getting upset," versus ". . . who cannot accept frank and unambiguous expressions of dislike toward himself without getting terribly upset"; and finally the size of the audience, that is, bystanders who observe the interactions of the communicator and addressee, as indicated by, "Imagine the following situation involving yourself and this person with no one else being present," versus ". . . with three of your mutual acquaintances present." Once again, social approval-seeking tendency and anxiety level were two additional factors in the experiment.

Subjects. Forty-eight male and 48 female University of California undergraduates were paid to participate in this experiment.

Procedure. The procedure in this experiment was similar to those in preceding ones. The instructions for one of the experimental conditions were as follows:

> Think of someone of the same sex and same age as you who you know reasonably well and you neither like nor dislike. Imagine the following situation involving yourself and this person, with no one else being present. This person has just expressed a negative and cutting remark toward you in a very open and obvious way. He is the kind of person who can accept frank and unambiguous expressions of dislike toward himself without getting upset.
>
> Now, I'm going to play some tape recordings . . . [the instructions continued at this point as in the preceding experiments.]

The instructions for all conditions were identical to the preceding except for the changes already noted. Each subject was initially assigned to either the explicit or implicit addressee remark condition and received all four combinations of two degrees of addressee tolerance for criticism and two degrees of audience size. The sequence of the four conditions was counterbalanced over the group of subjects.

RESULTS

Experiment I

In each condition, 24 preference scores were obtained from a subject for each of four categories of verbal stimuli: inconsistent positive, inconsistent negative, and control statements for these categories, consistent positive and consistent negative, respectively. The six preference scores obtained from a subject in each of these four categories were summed, thus yielding four composite scores for each category.

The preferences for inconsistent negative messages were analyzed using a multiple regression technique described by Cohen (1968). He detailed the procedures whereby multiple regression can be used as a substitute for the analysis of variance or the analysis of covariance. These procedures allow the expression of the dependent measure (preference for inconsistent negative messages) as a function of the significant effects from the following set: the covariate (preference for consistent negative messages), the independent effects (pleasantness of addressee behavior, communicator approval-seeking tendency, liking of the addressee, and conflict between communicator and addressee), and all possible interactions among the independent effects.

Some reasons for the use of multiple regression in the present study are, (1) a single equation readily summarizes all the effects of a complex factorial design, (2) the coefficients in the equation provide information about the relative magnitudes of the various significant effects, and (3) comparisons of the results from several experiments are facilitated when presented in equation form. The results from the regression analysis of the preferences for inconsistent negative messages are given in equation 1 of Table 1. A second regression analysis was done for the same dependent measure to explore the possible contribution of communicator anxiety (the substitute for commu-

---

TABLE 1. Results of the Regression Analyses for All Experiments[a]

Results for Experiment I

$$N_i = 10.43 + 1.02N_c + 1.10P - 0.76L + 0.58AL + 0.55AP + 0.60APL \quad (1)$$
$$P_i = 8.77 + 0.76L - 0.73AP \quad (2)$$

Results for Experiment II

$$N_i = 9.11 + 2.05N_c - 0.93F + 0.78PS \quad (3)$$
$$P_i = 8.00 - 1.59P - 1.27F - 0.77A + 1.12AS \quad (4)$$

Results for Experiment III

$$N_i = 8.09 + 3.03N_c + 1.84P + 0.84AF + [-0.96X - 1.28XS] \quad (5)$$
$$P_i = 6.72 - 1.07P + 1.07PS - 1.03XS \quad (6)$$

Results for Experiment IV

$$N_i = 8.14 + 2.69N_c + 0.44E - 0.65A + [-1.04X + 0.54XE] \quad (7)$$
$$P_i = 6.79 + 1.76P_c - 0.49BE + 0.63AE + [0.94X - 0.53XB - 0.42XET] \quad (8)$$

Notation

N_i = preference for inconsistent negative messages
N_c = preference for consistent negative messages—a normalized variable
P_i = preference for inconsistent positive messages
P_c = preference for consistent positive messages—a normalized variable

Independent effects		Values in preceding equations	
		1.0	−1.0
A = communicator approval-seeking tendency		High	Low
B = presence of bystanders		Present	Absent
E = explicitness of negative message from addressee		Explicit	Implicit
F = formality of setting		Formal	Informal
L = liking of addressee		Like	Dislike
P = pleasantness of addressee behavior		Pleasant	Unpleasant
S = addressee status		High	Low
T = addressee tolerance for criticism		High	Low
X = communicator anxiety		High	Low

[a] Note: Since, for each of the preceding independent effects, there were equal numbers of the two conditions (i.e., equal numbers of conditions assigned values of 1.0 and −1.0), these effects had mean values of zero and standard deviations of unity. As a consequence, and due to the factorial arrangement of the conditions, all the significant effects in the various equations (e.g., P or APL in equation 1) have mean values of zero and standard deviations of unity. Thus, the coefficients in each equation indicate the relative strengths of the various effects in that equation.

nicator social approval-seeking tendency in the first analysis). This second analysis did not yield any significant effects for communicator anxiety or any of its interactions with the other independent effects. Therefore, equation 1 of Table 1 summarizes all the significant determiners of preferences of inconsistent negative messages in Experiment I. For all the effects in equation 1, significance of the F values was assessed at the .01 level.

Equation 1 of Table 1 indicates that the covariate (N_c = preference for consistent negative communications) is a significant correlate of the dependent variable (N_i = preference for inconsistent negative communications). Equation 1 provides predicted values for the adjusted cell means, and those actually obtained are reported in Table 2. In Table 2, as well as all subsequent tables of means, arrows connect .05 level significant simple effects.

The predicted adjusted cell means can be computed from equation 1 by transferring the term involving the covariate to the lefthand side of the equation.

$$N_i - 1.02N_c = 10.43 + 1.10P - 0.76L + 0.58AL + 0.55AP +$$
$$0.60APL \quad (1b).$$

For instance, to predict the two cell means for the first effect in Table 2, average values of all variables on the right side of equation 1b except those of pleasantness of addressee behavior, P, are first computed. This is simple since average values of all variables and interaction effects equal zero. Therefore, $N_i - 1.02N_c = 10.43 + 1.10P$. Thus, when addressee behavior is pleasant (i.e., $P = 1$) the predicted mean = 11.53, and when addressee behavior is unpleasant (i.e., $P = -1$) the predicted mean = 9.33. The predicted means for the liking of addressee effect are given by (10.43 − 0.76L) and equal 9.67 when the addressee is liked ($L = 1$) and 11.19 when he is disliked ($L = -1$).

The four means for the AL effect are predicted from 10.43 − 0.76L + 0.58AL. Thus, for a high approval-seeking communicator and a disliked addressee ($A = 1$, $L = -1$), the predicted adjusted cell mean equals 10.43 − 0.76 × (−1) + 0.58 × (1) × (−1) = 10.61, as compared to the actual value of 10.80. Finally, the eight means for the APL effect are predicted from the entire right side of equation 1b.

A second pair of regression analyses was carried out for the preference of inconsistent positive communications, in which the preferences for consistent positive communications served as the covariate. The results of the first regression analysis which included communicator approval-seeking tendency as a factor are given in equation 2 of Table 1. The second regression analysis which included communicator anxiety as the personality factor showed no significant effects for anxiety or its interactions with the remaining independent effects. Thus, equation 2 summarizes all the sig-

TABLE 2. Significant Determiners of the Preference for Inconsistent Negative Communications in Experiment I[a]

1. Pleasantness of addressee behavior   Pleasant: 11.67   Unpleasant: 9.18

2. Liking of addressee   Addressee liked: 9.76   Addressee disliked: 11.10

3. Liking of addressee × Communicator social approval-seeking tendency

	Liked addressee	Disliked addressee
High approval-seeking communicator	10.65	10.80
Low approval-seeking communicator	8.86	11.39

4. Pleasantness of addressee behavior × Communicator social approval-seeking tendency

	Pleasant addressee behavior	Unpleasant addressee behavior
High approval-seeking communicator	12.66	8.80
Low approval-seeking communicator	10.68	9.57

5. Pleasantness of addressee behavior × Liking of addressee × Communicator social approval-seeking tendency

	Liked addressee	Disliked addressee
Addressee behavior pleasant		
High approval-seeking communicator	13.17	12.15
Low approval-seeking communicator	8.67	12.70
Addressee behavior unpleasant		
High approval-seeking communicator	8.14	9.45
Low approval-seeking communicator	9.05	10.08

[a] For all the significant effects in this table, $df = 1/91$, $MS_e = 16.1$, and $p < .01$. t-tests were used to assess the significance of simple effects, and arrows connect cell means which differed significantly at the .05 level.

nificant determiners of preferences for inconsistent positive communications in Experiment I. In this, as in some other instances (e.g., equations 4 or 6 of Table 1) the covariate was not significantly correlated with the dependent variable. The obtained cell means for the effects of equation 2 are given in Table 3.

TABLE 3. SIGNIFICANT DETERMINERS OF THE PREFERENCE FOR INCONSISTENT POSITIVE COMMUNICATIONS IN EXPERIMENT I[a]

1. Liking of addressee   Addressee liked: 9.52   Addressee disliked: 8.01

2. Pleasantness of addressee behavior × Communicator social approval-seeking tendency

	Pleasant addressee behavior	Unpleasant addressee behavior
High approval-seeking communicator	7.56 ⟷	9.96
Low approval-seeking communicator	9.04	8.50

[a] For all the significant effects in this table, $df = 1/91$, $MS_e = 16.3$, and $p < .01$. t-tests were used to assess the significance of simple effects, and arrows connect cell means which differed significantly at the .05 level.

In addition to the cell mean values reported in Tables 2 and 3, it is helpful to briefly note the absolute preferences for the various communication stimuli over all experimental conditions. The mean preference was 8.77 for inconsistent positive communications, 10.43 for inconsistent negative communications, 14.00 for consistent positive communications, and 14.02 for consistent negative communications. It is thus seen that preferences for the inconsistent messages were significantly less than those for the consistent messages, over all the experimental conditions. Furthermore, preferences for inconsistent positive messages were significantly less than for inconsistent negative messages.

Experiments II and III

For Experiment II, preferences for inconsistent negative messages were analyzed as a function of the covariate (preferences for consistent negative messages) and two levels each of communicator approval-seeking tendency (or communicator anxiety in a second regression analysis), relative status of the addressee, formality of the communication setting, and pleasantness of addressee behavior. The regression analyses also tested for all possible interactions among the independent effects. The results are reported in equation 3 of Table 1, and the corresponding results from the replication experiment (Experiment III) are given in equation 5 of Table 1. The added terms within brackets in equation 5 are those obtained from the second regression analysis in which communicator anxiety (X) replaced communicator approval-seeking tendency (A). The obtained adjusted cell means for the effects predicted by equations 3 and 5 are given in Table 4.

The results of similar regression analyses for preferences of inconsistent positive communications, with preferences of consistent positive communications serving as the covariate, are given in equations 4 and 6 of Table 1.

TABLE 4. SIGNIFICANT DETERMINERS OF THE PREFERENCE FOR INCONSISTENT NEGATIVE COMMUNICATIONS IN EXPERIMENTS II AND III[a]

Results for Experiment II
1. Formality of setting   Formal: 8.35   Informal: 9.86
2. Pleasantness of addressee behavior × Addressee status

	Pleasant behavior	Unpleasant behavior
High status addressee	9.99 ⟷	7.32
Low status addressee	9.20	9.93

Results for Experiment III
1. Pleasantness of addressee behavior   Pleasant: 10.06   Unpleasant: 6.13
2. Formality of setting × Communicator social approval-seeking tendency

	Formal	Informal
High approval-seeking communicator	9.01	8.11
Low approval-seeking communicator	6.41 ⟷	8.85

3. Communicator anxiety   High anxious: 7.06   Low anxious: 9.13
4. Addressee status × Communicator anxiety

	High status	Low status
High anxious communicator	5.85 ⟷	8.26
Low anxious communicator	10.41 ⟷	7.85

[a] For all the significant effects of Experiment II, $df = 1/91$, $MS_e = 19.7$, and $p < .01$. For Experiment III, $df = 1/43$, $MS_e = 20.9$, and $p < .05$. t-tests were used to assess the significance of simple effects, and arrows connect cell means which differed significantly at the .05 level.

The corresponding obtained adjusted cell means are given in Table 5.

Once again, it is helpful to consider the absolute values of mean preferences for the four categories of communication. In Experiment II, mean preference for inconsistent positive communications was 8.0, that for inconsistent negative communications was 9.11, that for consistent positive communications was 13.17, and that for consistent negative communications was 12.33.

TABLE 5. SIGNIFICANT DETERMINERS OF THE PREFERENCE FOR INCONSISTENT POSITIVE COMMUNICATIONS IN EXPERIMENTS II AND III[a]

Results for Experiment II

1. Pleasantness of
   addressee behavior　　　Pleasant: 6.57　　　　　　　　Unpleasant: 9.43

2. Formality
   of setting　　　　　　　Formal: 6.77　　　　　　　　　Informal: 9.23

3. Communicator social approval-seeking tendency
   　　　　　　　　　　　High: 7.20　　　　　　　　　　Low: 8.80

4. Communicator social approval-seeking tendency × Addressee status

	High status addressee	Low status addressee
High approval-seeking communicator	8.31 ⟷	6.10
Low approval-seeking communicator	7.54 ⟷	10.06

Results for Experiment III

1. Pleasantness of
   addressee behavior　　　Pleasant: 5.64　　　　　　　　Unpleasant: 7.80

2. Pleasantness of addressee behavior × Addressee status

	High status addressee	Low status addressee
Pleasant addressee behavior	6.12	5.16
Unpleasant addressee behavior	6.14 ⟷	9.46

3. Addressee status × Communicator anxiety

	High status addressee	Low status addressee
High anxious communicator	5.71 ⟷	8.95
Low anxious communicator	6.54	5.67

[a] For all the significant effects of Experiment II, $df = 1/91$, $MS_e = 19.7$, and $p < .01$. For experiment III, $df = 1/43$, $MS_e = 13.4$, and $p < .05$. t-tests were used to assess the significance of simple effects, and arrows connect cell means which differed significantly at the .05 level.

Experiment IV

Preferences of inconsistent negative communications were analyzed as a function of the covariate (i.e., preferences for consistent negative communications) and two levels of each of the following: explicitness of the negative communication from the addressee, communicator approval-seeking tendency (or anxiety level, in the second regression analysis), addressee tolerance for criticism, and audience size. The results of the regression analyses are given in equation 7 of Table 1, and the adjusted cell means are given in Table 6.

TABLE 6. SIGNIFICANT DETERMINERS OF THE PREFERENCE FOR INCONSISTENT NEGATIVE COMMUNICATIONS IN EXPERIMENT IV[a]

1. Communicator social approval-seeking tendency

	High: 7.70	Low: 8.59

2. Explicitness of negative addressee message (behavior)

	Explicit: 8.64	Implicit: 7.64

3. Communicator anxiety   High: 7.51   Low: 8.78

4. Explicitness of negative addressee message (behavior) × Communicator anxiety

	Explicit	Implicit
High anxious communicator	8.53 ← → 6.49	
Low anxious communicator	8.76	8.80

[a] For all the significant effects in this table, $df = 1/91$, $MS_e = 8.5$, and $p < .01$. t-tests were used to assess the significance of simple effects, and arrows connect cell means which differed significantly at the .05 level.

A similar pair of regression analyses were performed on preferences for inconsistent positive messages, with preferences for consistent positive messages serving as the covariate. The adjusted cell means from these analyses are given in Table 7, with the corresponding regression results being summarized in equation 8 of Table 1.

The absolute mean value for preference of inconsistent positive messages was 6.79, that for preference of inconsistent negative messages was 8.14, that for consistent positive messages was 11.09, and finally that for consistent negative messages was 11.10.

TABLE 7. Significant Determiners of the Preference for Inconsistent Positive Communications in Experiment IV[a]

1. Communicator anxiety   High: 7.77   Low: 5.81

2. Explicitness of negative addressee message × Bystander presence

	Explicit	Implicit
Bystanders present	6.29	6.55
Bystanders absent	8.07 ←——————————→ 6.25

3. Explicitness of negative addressee message × Communicator social approval-seeking tendency

	Explicit	Implicit
High approval-seeking communicator	8.37 ←——————————→ 6.12
Low approval-seeking communicator	5.99	6.68

4. Bystander presence × Communicator anxiety

	Present	Absent
High anxious communicator	6.96 ←——————————→ 8.58
Low anxious communicator	5.88	5.74

5. Explicitness of negative addressee message × Addressee tolerance for criticism × communicator anxiety

	High tolerance	Low tolerance
Explicit		
High anxious communicator	8.16	7.79
Low anxious communicator	7.00	5.76
High anxious communicator	8.41 ←——————————→ 6.70
Low anxious communicator	4.60	5.88

[a] For all the significant effects in this table, $df = 1/91$, $MS_e = 10.6$, and $p < .01$. t-tests were used to assess the significance of simple effects, and arrows connect cell means which differed significantly at the .05 level.

DISCUSSION

Each experiment indicated that consistent communications of attitude are preferred over inconsistent ones, and that among inconsistent communications, positive ones are less preferred than negative ones. These findings corroborate informal observations made during the preparation of the stimuli, where it was noted that subjects had greater difficulty producing the inconsistent messages than the consistent ones. This difficulty was even more pronounced when the inconsistent messages were positive. The implication here is that, due to their less frequent use, inconsistent messages are more difficult to produce and that less frequent use reflects a lower preference for them. Another observation was that inconsistent communications of attitude frequently rely on facial expressions. For instance, when subjects were instructed to say something negative with positive intonation, they actually spoke with neutral intonation but assumed a negative facial expression, so that audiotape recordings of their statements did not reflect substantial inconsistency. It thus seems that a more general exploration of preferences for inconsistent messages should include facial as well as verbal and vocal expressions.

The first generalization that emerges from the data is that inconsistent communications are preferred more in less formal situations. The experiments included a series of factors for various aspects of the formality of a communication setting. In some conditions, the situation was simply described as formal versus informal; in others formality was implied by indicating that the addressee was of a higher rather than lower status. A third manipulation involved the presence versus absence of bystander observers, the assumption being that the presence of observers in the situation tends to increase formality. A fourth manipulation involved an explicit versus implicit insult from the addressee as a cue to which the communicator responded. Here the expectation was that a situation in which the addressee was explicitly insulting would be more informal than one in which an insult was implicit. A final manipulation involved the addressee's tolerance for criticism, based on the assumption that persons who can tolerate criticism would tend to elicit more informal interaction than those who cannot.

Experiment I contained none of these formality factors, but Experiments II and III both contained two such factors: formality of the setting, F, and status of the addressee relative to the communicator, S. The two main effects in equations 3 and 4 of Table 1 indicate that both the positive inconsistent and the negative inconsistent communications were preferred less in more formal situations. The cell mean values for the remaining interaction effects involving the formality and addressee status factors in equations 3 through 6 are given in Tables 4 and 5. Of the eight relevant significant simple effects in these tables, only the following two are contrary to the general trend. The more approval seekers of Experiment II preferred inconsistent positive communications more with their higher-than lower-status addressees. The less anxious communicators of Experiment III preferred inconsistent negative messages more with the higher- than the lower-status addressees.

Experiment IV contained three factors relating to the formality of the communication setting. These were the presence of bystanders, the implicit rather than explicit insults from the addressee, and the lower addressee tolerance for criticism. There is only one significant main effect for these factors: equation 7 shows that negative inconsistent messages were preferred more when the insulting behavior of the addressee had been more explicit. The cell means corresponding to the various interactions in equations 7 and 8 are given in Tables 6 and 7. In these tables, all the significant simple effects involving the three formality factors show greater preference for inconsistent messages when the situation was more informal. For instance, the second effect of Table 7 shows that inconsistent positive messages were preferred more only when the addressee's insulting behavior had been explicit and when bystanders were absent. In other words, in this case, both of the informality cues were required for communicators to have greater preference for the inconsistent positive messages.

In sum, the results relating to various aspects of formality in a communication situation show 16 effects in support and two opposed to the following generalization: inconsistent communications are preferred more in the more informal communication settings.

The remaining results from all four experiments constitute a considerable list of quite distinct findings. The integration of most of these findings within a coherent framework is nevertheless possible with a detailed consideration of the task presented to subjects in each experimental condition.

Subjects were to indicate preferences for each of the following four kinds of messages: (1) inconsistent positive message involving a positive nonverbal and a negative verbal component; (2) consistent positive message involving moderately positive verbal and nonverbal components; (3) inconsistent negative message involving a negative nonverbal and a positive verbal component; and (4) consistent negative message involving moderately negative verbal and nonverbal components. Type 2 messages were matched with type 1 messages for the degree of preference, liking, or positive evaluation for an action which each indicated. Type 4 messages were matched with type 3 in a similar way. Despite such average matching of the inconsistent and consistent pairs of messages over all experimental conditions, when subjects had to respond evaluatively to the addressee in a specific experimental condition, one or the other of the matched pair of messages was clearly the more appropriate response. For instance, when subjects were faced with a choice between a consistent positive and an inconsistent positive message for an addressee who was behaving in an unpleasant way, the inconsistent positive message, which at least included a negative verbal component referring to an action, was more appropriate. In contrast, given the same messages and an addressee who was behaving in a pleasant way, the consistent positive message which included a positive verbal component referring to an action was more appropriate.

In sum, even with the statistical controls, preferences for inconsistent positive messages (relative to preferences for consistent positive messages) were to be correlated with the unpleasantness of addressee behavior. Similarly, preferences for inconsistent negative messages (relative to preferences for consistent negative ones) were to be correlated with the pleasantness of addressee behavior.

A second aspect of the subjects' task was that, for all the messages, the verbal contents referred to the action of the addressee; thus, evaluative attitudes toward the person of the addressee could only be expressed with the nonverbal portion of the messages. That is, when the liking of the addressee was the determiner of message choice, the nonverbal portions of the messages carried the burden. In these instances, the stronger nonverbal components of the inconsistent messages (relative to those of the consistent messages) could serve as a basis for their selection for liked-disliked addressees. Thus, despite statistical controls, preference for inconsistent positive messages (relative to preferences for consistent positive messages) were to be correlated with the liking of the addressee. Further, preferences for inconsistent negative messages were to be correlated with the degree of dislike of the addressee.

The statements in the preceding two paragraphs are completely supported. The relevant data for the first interpretation is available from Experiments I, II, and III. The main effects in equations 1 and 5 indicate that inconsistent negative communications were preferred more when addressee behaviors were more pleasant. The main effects in equations 4 and 6 indicate that inconsistent positive communications were preferred less when the addressee behaviors were more pleasant. Additional interaction effects involving pleasantness of addressee behavior in equations 1, 2, 3, and 6 are readily considered in terms of the cell means given in Tables 2 through 5. In Tables 2 and 4 all relevant significant simple effects indicate that inconsistent negative communications were preferred more when addressee behaviors were more pleasant. In Tables 3 and 5 all relevant significant simple effects indicate that inconsistent positive communications were preferred more when addressee behaviors were more unpleasant.

The results from Experiment I given in equations 1 and 2 of Table 1 bear on the second interpretation relating to message preference as a function of addressee liking. The main effect in equation 1 indicates that negative inconsistent messages were preferred less when the addressee was liked more. The main effect in equation 2 shows that positive inconsistent messages were preferred more when the addressee was liked more. Further, the interaction terms involving addressee liking (L) in equation 1 can be readily considered in terms of the cell means given in Table 2. Both relevant significant simple effects of this table show that inconsistent negative messages were preferred more when the addressee was disliked more.

Without exception, then, the significant effects were consistent with the following general conclusions: (1) The verbal component of an inconsistent message conveys evaluative attitudes toward the action of the addressee and therefore is the basis for selecting a message when the addressee behaves in pleasant versus unpleasant ways. (2) The nonverbal component of an inconsistent message conveys evaluative attitudes toward the person of the addressee and therefore is the basis for selecting a message when the addressee is liked versus disliked.

It is now possible to proceed to a discussion of the findings involving communicators' approval-seeking tendency and anxiety levels. These two measures were included in the study because it seemed that the more anxious or the more approval-seeking communicators are less willing to express dislike, and more willing to express liking, to others. In relation to this assumption, Zaidel and Mehrabian (1969) had found that high social approval seekers were less able to communicate variations in negative affect, either facially or vocally. Although no special hypotheses had been proposed for these two personality variables, findings are already available from this study which allow the statement of a hypothesis. As noted in the preceding paragraph, the nonverbal component of an inconsistent message conveys evaluative attitudes toward the person of the addressee.[1] Therefore, it is expected that communicator anxiety or approval-seeking tendency is a positive correlate of preferences for positive inconsistent messages and a negative correlate of negative inconsistent messages.

Without exception, the main effects in equations 5, 7, and 8 and all the significant simple effects in Tables 4 through 7 indicate that the more anxious subjects had more preference for positive inconsistent messages and less preference for negative inconsistent messages. In sharp contrast to these results for communicator anxiety, the results relating to communicator approval-seeking tendency are inconsistent. The two main effects in equations 4 and 7 show that more approval-seeking persons have less preference for both positive and negative inconsistent messages. However, this pattern is not maintained with the significant simple effects involving communicator approval-seeking tendency, and these results cannot be interpreted at present. The individual difference measures included in this study were selected to reflect a communicator's unwillingness to express negative feelings to others. Since a measure of sensitivity to rejection was not available when this study was designed, measures of communicator anxiety and approval-seeking tendency were used; however, it was felt that a direct measure of sensitivity to rejection (e.g., Mehrabian, 1970) would be more appropriate since such persons would be more hesitant about communicating negative feelings to others.

An overview of the results shows that only part of the findings relating to formality and informality of communication settings had been anticipated. In addition, several consistent lines of evidence emerged from the study which had not been anticipated. For the verbal-vocal stimuli of the present study, the verbal components of the inconsistent messages served to convey evaluative attitudes toward the actions of the addressees. In contrast, the nonverbal (vocal) portions of these messages conveyed evaluative attitudes toward the addressees themselves. Thus, positive inconsistent messages (which included positive nonverbal and negative verbal components) were preferred more when the addressee was liked and when his actions were disliked. In contrast, negative inconsistent messages (which included negative nonverbal and positive verbal components) were preferred more when the addressee was disliked and when his actions were liked. In this context, it was not surprising to find that the more anxious communicators showed a very consistent preference for positive inconsistent messages and a lack of preference for the negative inconsistent messages.

The definition of inconsistent negative messages in this study corresponds closely to the concept of sarcasm, but there does not seem to be a term in English which would correspond to instances of positive inconsistency. Some forms of teasing involve positive inconsistency, such as a girl saying "No," to a boy's sexual advances while she nonverbally communicates, "I am attracted to you." The findings of the present study have provided a tentative basis for identifying the conditions under which both types of inconsistent messages are likely to occur and also those under which one type of message is preferred over the other. It would be of interest to explore the implications of these findings for positive and negative inconsistent communications involving more than just verbal and vocal channels (e.g., when the facial or postural channel [Mehrabian, 1969] communicates positive affect and the verbal-vocal channels communicate negative affect, or vice versa).

The research cited in the introductory comments has shown that different nonverbal cues exhibit similar relationships to verbal cues, when they accompany the latter. Thus, one extrapolation of the findings of the present study is that even when other nonverbal cues are also involved and contribute to inconsistency, the preceding interpretations of the findings still hold: verbal components of inconsistent messages convey evaluative attitudes toward another's actions, whereas the nonverbal (e.g., facial or postural) components convey evaluative attitudes to the person himself. In general, then, positive inconsistent messages should be more likely with liked than disliked addressees, and when the addressee's actions are unpleasant. In contrast, negative inconsistent messages should be more likely with disliked than liked addressees and when the addressee's actions are pleasant.

In closing, we should note the humorous aspect of positive inconsistent messages, which was not explored. If humor occurs more in informal situations it would not be unexpected to find that positive inconsistent messages (which were found to be preferred more in more informal settings) are also used as a form of humor. One type of experimental paradigm which might explore such humor would involve inconsistent messages referring to incongruous situations. For example, one friend says to another, "Dig the suave cat in the combat boots," when they observe a third person who is dressed in a coat and tie but has old Army boots on. Here the amusement in the intonation and facial expression of the speaker is positive and the contents are, at best, mixed positive and negative. Thus, in addition to being humorous, the communication expresses a negative attitude toward the third person's "unacceptable" combination of clothing and shoes.

REFERENCES

Anderson, N. H. Application of an additive model to impression formation. *Science*, 1962, **138**, 817–818.

Anderson, N. H. Note on weighted sum and linear operator models. *Psychonomic Science*, 1964, **1**, 189–190.

Cohen, J. Multiple regression as a general data-analytical system. *Psychological Bulletin*, 1968, **70**, 426–443.

Crowne, D. P., & Marlowe, D. A new scale of social desirability independent of psychopathology. *Journal of Consulting Psychology*, 1960, **24**, 349–354.

Mandler, G., & Sarason, S. B. A study of anxiety and learning. *Journal of Abnormal and Social Psychology*, 1952, **47**, 166–173.

Mehrabian, A. Significance of posture and position in the communication of attitude and status relationships. *Psychological Bulletin*, 1969, **71**, 359–372.

Mehrabian, A. Measures of affiliative tendency and sensitivity to rejection. *Educational and Psychological Measurement*, 1970, in press.

Mehrabian, A., & Ferris, Susan R. Inference of attitudes from nonverbal communication in two channels. *Journal of Consulting Psychology*, 1967, **31**, 248–252.

Mehrabian, A., & Wiener, M. Decoding of inconsistent communications. *Journal of Personality and Social Psychology*, 1967, **6**, 108–114.

Zaidel, Susan R., & Mehrabian, A. The ability to communicate and infer positive and negative attitudes facially and vocally. *Journal of Experimental Research in Personality*, 1969, **3**, 233–241.

NOTE

1. The examination of the tasks that were presented to the subjects has already shown how it was possible for them to use inconsistent messages and convey evaluative attitudes toward the action or the person of the addressee, despite the statistical controls.

section **xiv**

The problem is man

58.

Classification of behavior problems of children

RICHARD L. JENKINS

Labelling, naming or substituting a verbal symbol for an activity or an object, appears to be a necessary part of reasoning or dealing with the item in question. In order for human beings to manipulate and to test an idea and to minimize errors, they engage in a process of mental grasping, sorting, combining, and recombining. They check for possible contingencies and workability through the use of symbols and intellectual manipulation before risking an actual trial. By means of this process they avoid the necessity of acting out mistakes and trial-and-error behavior and learning.

The author of this selection provides some labels, classifications, or ways of thinking about the behavior problems of children. But he carries the process further than describing categories. He lists some causes and he suggests some remedies. In reading the article, however, it is important to realize that much of the behavior described is merely an exaggeration of normal ways of acting. All average youngsters withdraw and daydream at times. Some aggressive behavior and tendencies to rebel against society can be expected from any child. It is only when these kinds of reactions become habitual and self-defeating and clearly exceed usual limits that there may be cause for concern.

The editors are apprehensive that well-meaning adults, in their urge to help youngsters, tend sometimes to apply labels, to diagnose inappropriately, and to generate a self-fulfilling prophecy with their expectations. People are inclined to become as they are treated. It may be as possible that individuals come to act like delinquents because they are regarded in that manner as it is that behaving like a delinquent causes the perception. Behaviors may be limiting or facilitating, depending upon how they are used.

American Journal of Psychiatry, 125(No. 8):1032–1039, 1969. Copyright 1969, the American Psychiatric Association. Richard L. Jenkins, Chief, Child Psychiatry Service, State Psychopathic Hospital, Iowa City, Iowa, and Professor of Child Psychiatry, Department of Psychiatry, the University of Iowa.

Based on a paper read at the 124th annual meeting of the American Psychiatric Association, Boston, Mass., May 13–17, 1968.

THE SECOND EDITION of the *Diagnostic and Statistical Manual of Mental Disorders* (*DSM-II*) of the American Psychiatric Association utilizes the category *behavior disorders of childhood* from the eighth revision of the International Classification of Diseases. Since childhood is commonly conceived to include adolescence and yet the symptoms prone to occur in these two phases of immaturity may be perceptibly different, *DSM-II* permits the separation of behavior disorders of childhood and behavior disorders of adolescence. Each of these categories is subdivided into seven groups, the *hyperkinetic reaction,* the *withdrawing reaction,* the *overanxious reaction,* the *runaway reaction,* the *unsocialized aggressive reaction,* the *group delinquent reaction,* and *other reaction.* The last, of course, is a miscellaneous group without further definition which is included to avoid forcing cases into groups which they do not fit.

The manual states that this major category of behavior disorders "is reserved for disorders occurring in childhood and adolescence that are more stable, internalized, and resistant to treatment than *Transient situational disturbances* but less so than *Psychoses, Neuroses,* and *Personality disorders.* This intermediate stability is attributed to the greater fluidity of all behavior at this age."

This subdivision of behavior disorders of children takes its origin from groupings which appear repeatedly in statistical clusterings of large numbers of children brought to child psychiatry services and child guidance clinics (1, 3–8, 10–12, 17). These same groupings are recognizable in the clinical study of individual children (2).

Although these groupings are arrived at by a purely descriptive clustering of cases with similar behavior, an examination of the family backgrounds in which these different disorders of behavior develop reveals contrasting types of family situations more or less specifically associated with five of these types of behavior disorder. A consideration of the behavior disorder in relation to the background factors makes it evident that each of these five groupings embodies a faulty way of endeavoring to cope with the world. One behavioral grouping, the *hyperkinetic reaction,* resembles the results of an organic handicap (5, 11).

THE HYPERKINETIC REACTION

The hyperkinetic or hyperactive reaction is widely recognized in child psychiatry. It is disproportionately frequent before the age of eight years and tends gradually to become less frequent and less prominent thereafter. It usually disappears by the middle teens.

The traits distinguishing this group are overactivity, restlessness, distractibility, and short attention span. Poor concentration, excitability, impulsiveness, mischievousness, and changeable moods are often present.

These children tend to be socially immature and uninhibited. They are likely to talk incessantly. There is usually some general overreactivity and lack of self-control. Usually they do not appear anxious except as their hyperactivity may at times be interpreted as evidence of anxiety.

When organic brain damage can definitely be diagnosed, the diagnosis should fall under *mental disorders not specified as psychotic associated with physical conditions*. However, this reaction is certainly intensified in circumstances in which the child is under tension. This implies a functional element, and there is no present justification for assuming that all cases are due to organic brain damage.

When hyperkinetic children develop in a strong, understanding, and stable home, they usually become adequately trained and socialized, although their training requires more than the usual amount of patience, repetition, firmness, and consistency. In an unstable, inconsistent home they tend to develop increasing conflict with their parents and to get out of control.

Paradoxically, cerebral stimulants such as the amphetamines or methylphenidate characteristically have a quieting effect on these children, reducing their hyperactivity and distractibility and increasing their attention span. This often makes them tolerable in regular school classes when they have not previously been tolerable and typically increases their rate of school progress. This result appears to be obtained by improving their attention span and application. It does not typically improve their intelligence test performance, at least in individual testing.

Some clinicians consider a favorable response to cerebral stimulants and an unfavorable response to phenobarbital as clinical evidence of organic brain dysfunction.

There is particular need for patience, steadiness, understanding, restraint, and kindly repetition in the training of the hyperkinetic child. One should not expect to check the hyperkinesis but should rather seek to channel the activity constructively and to avoid unnecessary distracting stimuli and situations.

THE WITHDRAWING REACTION

The withdrawing reaction is characterized by "seclusiveness, detachment, sensitivity, shyness, timidity, and general inability to form close interpersonal relations. This diagnosis should be reserved for those who cannot be classified as having schizophrenia and whose tendencies toward withdrawal have not yet stabilized enough to justify the diagnosis of schizoid personality."

The reaction of withdrawal and detachment has long been recognized as a defensive device utilized by the individual who is convinced he cannot win and who finds involvement too painful. It is one of the patterns which repeatedly emerge from cluster analysis of children's behavior traits(5, 8) and is quite common in the age range of five to seven years.

There are enormous differences among individuals in their tendencies toward the reaction of autistic withdrawal. It is not easy to produce such withdrawal either in vigorous persons who seem wedded to life or in dependent persons who have developed confidence in others and actively seek the support of others as a way of coping with life. However, at a certain point of hurt and frustration even hitherto dependent persons may, in emotional desperation, turn away from others, detach themselves emotionally, and defensively tell themselves that it really does not matter or that there is no help whatever to be had from turning to others.

The traits shown by the withdrawing children include seclusiveness, daydreaming, listlessness and apparent apathy(8), and an absence of close friendships or, indeed, of close relationships of any kind(5). Having given up hope of satisfaction in the human world and the real world, these children turn to daydreaming, fantasies, unrealistic thinking, or autistic thinking as a compensation. Impulsive destructiveness is not infrequent, apparently as an expression of frustration.

In turning away from objective reality, these children turn away from the normal practice of constantly checking their expectations against experience. With such turning away, their capacity to distinguish fact from fancy tends to deteriorate. They function inefficiently and fail to develop effective patterns of behavior. As they fail to check their thinking against the thinking of others, their own thinking becomes more and more idiosyncratic, and they are increasingly regarded as queer.

It is natural enough that this reaction of withdrawal and detachment is prone to occur when the child's relationship to his parents is unsatisfactory and lacking in warmth. Maternal ill health in the form of psychosis, instability, withdrawal, chronic illness, serious crippling, or physical impairment are disproportionately frequent(5). The mother is likely to report alcoholism or chronic illness or disability in her parental home. In any event, she has often failed to give the child any clear, consistent, understandable relationship. She is likely to be overly permissive toward the child, infantilizing and overprotective, and yet is frequently punitive in her attitude. If the child does not feel rejected by the mother, neither does he feel adequately supported or directed. He has no consistent relationship to a parent. He does not know what to expect and he has no confidence in human relations. The father's reaction to the child's problem is likely to be indifferent, detached, or minimizing. The parents may be suspicious and jealous of each other, but overt sexual conflict between them is not characteristic.

The problem of treating the withdrawn child involves developing a relationship or encouraging others to develop a relationship with him through which he can gradually be drawn out of his autistic fantasies and into the real world, and gradually helping him to deal more and more successfully with the real world until autistic withdrawal no longer effectively competes with living in the real world(2). While such withdrawal still may occasionally occur, it is used only for an occasional vacation from the hard realities of the real world.

One aspect of treating the withdrawn child is illustrated by Aesop's fable of the contest between the north wind and the sun as to which could make the traveler remove his cloak. The protective covering of the withdrawn child cannot be commanded away or torn away. It must be melted away.

THE OVERANXIOUS REACTION

Children showing the overanxious reaction are "characterized by chronic anxiety, excessive and unrealistic fears, sleeplessness, nightmares, and exaggerated autonomic responses. The patient tends to be immature, self-conscious, grossly lacking in self-confidence, conforming, inhibited, dutiful, approval-seeking, and apprehensive in new situations and unfamiliar surroundings"(1, 4, 8, 10, 11). Parents often describe these children as worrisome, sensitive, shy, nervous, and discouraged. They cry easily, often feel inferior, and may show disturbed sleep, being particularly prone to nightmares(5, 6, 17). They are likely to be submissive.

This is the pattern of the anxious, fearful child who feels inadequate and consequently feels very dependent upon others. He feels keenly a need to meet the expectations of others, particularly his parents, and so to please them, for this is his source of security(1, 10). Sometimes the child's anxiety is stimulated by an overanxious mother(6, 17). Sometimes illness of the child has contributed to his insecurity(1, 10). In general, the overanxious reaction tends to occur particularly in middle-class families with parents who are educationally ambitious(11) and who expect much of their children and hold them to high standards of behavior and achievement(1, 10, 14). The child is not freely given security for his position as a member of the family, but from an early age is made to feel he must earn his acceptance in the family by his conformity and his performance. Love, affection, and emotional support are made to seem conditional to the child. He is held to an exacting standard and comes to feel that his place in the family is dependent upon very controlled behavior and very superior performance. He incorporates severe standards for himself and becomes overly exacting and overly critical of himself. This results in an overinhibited, overdutiful adjustment to life which becomes his way of coping with the world.

The overanxious individual is in general responsive to those methods of individual psychotherapy which have been derived from psychoanalytic theory and which increase self-understanding and self-tolerance(1, 2, 4, 10). He needs initially a feeling of support and human warmth in the treatment relationship. Then, as he is asked to trace back in his own history and experience the elements which have led to his overanxious, overdutiful, self-critical tendencies, he finds the focus of his attention shifted from his severe and critical judgments of himself to a consideration of how these tendencies have developed in him through the experiences to which he has been subjected.

Such a shift of frame of reference involves a shift from his looking at himself as villain toward looking at himself as a victim of circumstances. When we are dealing with a person whose judgment of himself is unduly harsh and guilt-ridden, this shift in emphasis may have a very constructive, salutary, and therapeutic effect. The uncovering or exploratory methods of psychotherapy, if skillfully handled, commonly have a constructive and therapeutic effect in such cases, particularly if some more reasonable integration of objectives and values is encouraged in the latter stages of this process. A general anxiety and self-critical judgment tends to be replaced with a measure of self-tolerance and more discriminating self-judgment, with positive benefits.

It may be stated that one of our major problems in child psychiatry is that psychoanalytic thinking has attained such a dominance in our field that the psychoneurotic model has been overextended and that the treatment appropriate for the overanxious child has tended automatically to be extended to all types of children regardless of whether or not it is appropriate for their needs. Unfortunately, it is inappropriate to five of our six groups and thus leads to many poorly conceived treatment efforts.

THE RUNAWAY REACTION

The children who fall into this group all repeatedly run away from home overnight. They are timid and furtive and are inclined to stealing, particularly stealing in the home(7). Often the child will steal money in the home and then run away. These children are unhappy in their homes and stay out late at night. They tend to be discouraged. Frequently they are seclusive and apathetic. Often they seek the protection of peers whom they regard as stronger and more adequate than themselves. They may become involved in passive homosexuality, sometimes as a means of seeking a protector. In any event, they tend to associate with companions whom the community regards as undesirable and may become hangers-on of the delinquent gang(12), but they lack the loyalty or adequacy necessary to make or be accepted as good members of a well-knit delinquent gang. They are more furtive and more deceptive than most delinquents.

The home background of the chronic runaway children is typically one of parental rejection from birth or before birth(7) and one of parental severity and inconsistency. As a group these children do not show the muscular development that is fairly characteristic of children who develop a truly aggressive adjustment to life. As a consequence, any aggressiveness is less likely to be successful and is less likely to meet any reward than is the case with the unsocialized aggressive child. Typically there is a gross lack of self-confidence and a very poor self-image. The unwanted illegitimate child is very common in this group, and only child status is extremely common(7). This child has lacked socializing experiences with siblings as well as with parents.

The treatment of these children is difficult. Treatment of the home is essential. If the parents cannot be successfully encouraged toward a more accepting attitude than is usually present, at least temporary removal from the home is necessary. These children usually have conspicuously poor self-images(18), and the development of some sense of personal value is necessary.

If management in the home cannot be effectively and constructively modified, they will need a relatively prolonged period of treatment and training in a foster home or treatment institution. Even then, these children cannot be returned home successfully without very substantial modification of the home atmosphere and home management.

THE UNSOCIALIZED AGGRESSIVE REACTION

Unsocialized aggressive children are characterized by "overt or covert hostile disobedience, quarrelsomeness, physical and verbal aggressiveness, vengefulness, and destructiveness. Temper tantrums, solitary stealing, lying, and hostile teasing of other children are common"(1, 2, 4–12, 17). They are sexually uninhibited and inclined to be sexually aggressive (7, 9). There appears to be a basic defect in socialization, and the aggressive behavior itself appears to be in the nature of a frustration response. The work of Norman Maier(15) has demonstrated that in rats, at a certain level of frustration, adaptive behavior is replaced by what he calls frustration behavior. Frustration behavior is maladaptive, stereotyped, repetitive, and is typically increased by punishment. All of these characteristics are evident in the behavior of the unsocialized aggressive child(4, 16).

It is clear that the home life of the unsocialized aggressive child has typically been very frustrating. The parents are themselves typically unstable in their marital relationship(4, 11) and have never given the child any consistent acceptance or affection. The mother in particular has been immature and not ready for motherhood. Thus, rejection is not a product of his behavior for it predates it—in fact it commonly predates the birth of the child(1, 10). The most typical contributing factor in the background of such a child is that he was never wanted and knows it(1, 10). He has never experienced consistent acceptance, and he has never had a basis for developing trust in an adult(14). Because of family instability he is very likely to have a stepparent(6, 17). These children may be only children and are not likely to have many siblings.

A good musculature and male sex both show a significant association with the unsocialized aggressive reaction. Although rejected, these children are also often somewhat overprotected by their parents(7). These types of maternal behavior, rejection and overprotection may, in fact, be complementary, as David Levy pointed out 25 years ago(13). The rejecting mother may seek to redeem herself in her own and the public's eye by going through the gestures of maternity, but she may do so resentfully and in a way which actually restricts and frustrates the child. These parents not infrequently shield their children from the natural consequences of their delinquent acts. Such actions, and an inconsistent and unpredictable severity of punishment which may relate more to how the parent feels at the moment than to what the child has done, are characteristic. These parents are likely to alternate severity with bribery in the effort to control the child. They are unlikely to agree with each other and unlikely to support each other in discipline.

Persistent enuresis is a common problem(11).

Successful treatment of the unsocialized aggressive child is not possible without altering his management. The younger the age at which this can be undertaken, the better, for the longer it goes on the more hostility and distortion are produced in the personality of the child. Many women are not able to be maternal when overburdened in an unhappy marriage. Yet the maternal instinct is deeply rooted, and a combination of emotional support and guidance will improve the maternal behavior of most of these women. Some cases call for removal from the home. This ordinarily requires the intervention of a court. Sometimes a combination of some treatment in a hospital or other treatment institution and return to the home after a period of work with the parents is indicated.

When the child is hospitalized, he needs an environment that is warm, kindly, and accepting, yet firm and patient in its refusal to be bullied or blackmailed into making concessions to his aggressiveness. The limitations and the reasons for these limitations must be explained again and again and must be maintained effectively. The child's immediate response to a limitation is typically: "You don't like me!" The adult must reassure the child of his accepting attitude and give evidence of it as the occasion arises, while still maintaining the limits. Care must be taken to begin with first things first and not to try to bring on too many points at once, but rather to follow a step-by-step procedure at a gradual pace. Meanwhile, the family must be worked with and helped to show their acceptance of the child while maintaining a reasonable and consistent program of control. The extreme of the unsocialized aggressive reaction develops into the antisocial or psychopathic personality(3).

THE GROUP DELINQUENT REACTION

The groups of behavior disorders we have described to this point represent individual types of maladaptations. By contrast, the socialized delinquent represents group rebellion against the structure and limitations of our society. This group behavior is largely learned behavior and represents social group conflict more than individual psychopathology. Viewed from the short range, it is functional, adaptive, motivated, understandable behavior which has a goal.

This group of delinquents averages a bit older than the groups of children we have heretofore discussed. These delinquents are distinguished by group rebellion, with cooperation (and often loyalty) among the members of the group. They have typically been involved in group or gang delinquency, stealing (particularly cooperative stealing), and truancy from school(1, 3–12, 17).

Most socialized delinquents are boys. Girls are less prone to group rebellion, are not prone to "gang up," and when they relate to more or less organized delinquent gangs it is typically as the girl friends of gang members, although not infrequently girls may cooperate in shoplifting.

The socialized delinquent is distinguished from the unsocialized aggressive child and the runaway by his greater basic socialization, particularly by his capacity for loyalty. Usually he has experienced more or less normal mothering in his infancy and early childhood, but there has been a lack of parental supervision and particularly of paternal supervision during his later development(5). Group delinquency is a phenomenon that is more common in the impoverished and disadvantaged areas of our cities. The large family in poor housing on the wrong side of the railroad tracks, the working mother, the absent or alcoholic father, the broken home, the step-father who has conflict with his adolescent stepson—these are all elements that appear with disproportionate frequency in this group(5).

The socialized delinquent represents not a failure of socialization but a limitation of loyalty to a more or less predatory peer group. The basic capacity for social relations has been achieved. What is lacking is an effective integration with the larger society as a contributing member.

The socialized delinquent needs to become a functioning and productive part of this larger society. He needs first of all a tie, a loyalty, to one or more socialized adults who can help him integrate himself to school and to the job-world of adults(2). Elements which interfere with this integration are very important. Reading disability is an extremely common contributing factor to school maladjustment. Opportunities for earning money and for gaining status thereby are very important, and limitations of these opportunities because of minority status or educational deficiencies make major contributions to delinquency. Although employment of the juvenile appears constructive, periods of high employment tend to be accompanied by more delinquency than periods of low employment. This is presumably because in periods of high employment the children are more likely to be unsupervised.

Prevention is generally more successful than treatment and involves effective leadership in neighborhood youth activities. Juvenile delinquency tends to develop in a hiatus between effective schooling and integration with the adult society and may be combated by furthering such integration. The development of a personal relationship with a strong, interested, socialized man is most important in bridging the gap. Increasing maturity, interest in marriage, the establishment of family life all create powerful pressures tending to make the socialized delinquent give up his delinquency and get a job, thereby becoming a productive member of society. For the individual with an aptitude for it and who has really developed group loyalty, military service may offer an alternative route.

SUMMARY

The six reactions listed under behavior disorders of childhood and adolescence represent clinically recognizable symptomatic clusters supported by different studies using different clustering methods.

The hyperkinetic reaction resembles the behavior seen in children with minimal brain damage.

The withdrawing reaction is prone to occur when real life offers too little satisfaction to the child, as may be the case for the child with inadequate parents who are detached, overly permissive in behavior, and yet punitive in attitude.

The overanxious reaction tends to occur particularly in middle-class, educationally ambitious families in which children are held to high standards of behavior and achievement and may come to feel that their acceptance in the family is dependent upon maintaining these standards.

The unsocialized aggressive reaction tends to occur as a reaction to parental rejection coupled with some parental overprotection.

The runaway reaction tends to occur as a reaction to simple undiluted parental rejection.

The group delinquent reaction tends to occur as a result of group rebellion in the adolescent years and in the absence of parental, and particularly in the absence of paternal, supervision.

Consideration is given to the problems of treating children falling in each of these groups. While the treatment of all children must be individualized, it can with advantage be individualized from a general pattern appropriate to the child's general type of problem. The widespread present tendency to generalize the treatment of all cases from the psychoneurotic model is self-defeating and humanly wasteful.

REFERENCES

1. Hewitt, C. E., and Jenkins, R. L.: Fundamental Patterns of Maladjustment: The Dynamics of Their Origin. Springfield: State of Illinois, 1946.

2. Jenkins, R. L.: Breaking Patterns of Defeat. Philadelphia: J. B. Lippincott Co., 1954.

3. Jenkins, R. L.: The Psychopathic or Antisocial Personality, J. Nerv. Ment. Dis. 131:318–334, 1960.

4. Jenkins, R. L.: Diagnoses, Dynamics and Treatment in Child Psychiatry, Psychiat. Res. Rep. Amer. Psychiat. Ass. 18:91–120, 1964.

5. Jenkins, R. L.: Psychiatric Syndromes in Children and Their Relation to Family Background, Amer. J. Orthopsychiat. 36:450–457, 1966.

6. Jenkins, R. L.: The Varieties of Children's Behavioral Problems and Family Dynamics, Amer. J. Psychiat. 124:1440–1445, 1968.

7. Jenkins, R. L., and Boyer, A.: Types of Delinquent Behavior and Background Factors, Int. J. Soc. Psychiat. 14:65–76, 1967.

8. Jenkins, R. L., and Glickman, S.: Common Syndromes in Child Psychiatry: I. Deviant Behavior Traits, II. The Schizoid Child, Amer. J. Orthopsychiat. 16:244–261, 1946.

9. Jenkins, R. L., and Glickman, S.: Patterns of Personality Organization Among Delinquents, Nervous Child 6:329–339, 1947. Reprinted in Gorlow, L., and Katkovsky, W., eds.: Readings in the Psychology of Adjustment. New York: McGraw-Hill, 1959.

10. Jenkins, R. L., and Hewitt, L.: Types of Personality Structure Encountered in Child Guidance Clinics, Amer. J. Orthopsychiat. 14:84–94, 1944.

11. Jenkins, R. L., NurEddin, E., and Shapiro, I.: Children's Behavior Syndromes and Parental Responses, Genet. Psychol. Monogr. 74:261–329, 1966.

12. Kobayaski, S.; Mizushima, K., and Shinohara, M.: Clinical Groupings of Problem Children Based on Symptoms and Behavior, Int. J. Soc. Psychiat. 13:206–215, 1967.

13. Levy, D.: Maternal Overprotection. New York: Columbia University Press, 1943.

14. Lewis, H.: Deprived Children. London: Oxford University Press, 1954.

15. Maier, N. R. F.: Frustration: The Study of Behavior Without a Goal. New York: McGraw-Hill, 1949.

16. Saksida, S.: Motivation Mechanisms and Frustration Stereotypes, Amer. J. Orthopsychiat. 29:599–611, 1959.

17. Shamsie, S. J., ed.: Adolescent Psychiatry. Pointe Claire, Quebec: Schering Corp., 1968.

18. Shinohara, M., and Jenkins, R. L.: MMPI Study of Three Types of Delinquents, J. Clin. Psychol. 23:156–163, 1967.

59.

Interacting factors in juvenile delinquency

ERDMAN B. PALMORE
PHILLIP E. HAMMOND

Many things become obvious after they are pointed out. Like the cuff link under the husband's nose that he cannot see until he calls his wife, they are there but they remain unnoticed until someone brings them to our attention. This appears to be the case with many of the factors connected with juvenile delinquency which are indicated by the authors of this article. One agrees. He thinks: "Just as I would expect," but he would not have thought of these things by himself. Once the points are brought to mind, however, he may add to them from his own ideas and experience and he may go on to develop new and different conclusions.

It may be thus with many worthwhile reading experiences. They may not present startlingly new ideas, but they may cause us to think differently and perhaps more productively about relatively familiar situations. For example, one would expect such factors as sex, race, and school performance to have some connection with juvenile delinquency. But he might be gratified, as the editors were, to add the concept that while these factors have an additive effect upon delinquency, the two variables represented by blocked legitimate avenues on the one hand and illegitimate avenues on the other tend to exert a multiple effect. As the author indicates, if one term has a value of zero, deviance is not increased by the other term. Think about this. There may be more difference than you have realized between additive and multiple effect relationships.

SOCIAL SCIENTISTS' understanding of delinquency is reasonably advanced in two respects. First, they have identified with fair accuracy the social structures that contain high rates of juvenile crime. And second, they have developed a number of theories regarding the social-psychological processes that lead youth to delinquency. The literature attests to the importance on the one hand of age, sex, race, social rank, and neighborhood, and, on the other hand, to alienation, guilt, frustration, and aspiration, as factors in explaining juvenile delinquency.[1]

One recent attempt to integrate both these aspects of knowledge about

American Sociological Review, 29:848–854, 1964. Erdman B. Palmore, Social Security Administration; Phillip E. Hammond, Yale University.

We gratefully acknowledge the aid of the Ford Foundation, who supported the research reported here, and we thank Hubert M. Blalock and Elton F. Jackson for their critical reading of the manuscript.

delinquency is Cloward and Ohlin, *Delinquency and Opportunity*.[2] The authors present a theoretical argument to explain the development and content of patterns of juvenile deviance or delinquent subcultures. Put briefly, their argument is that discontent or alienation develops from restricted access to legitimate avenues, while the *likelihood* and *direction* of actual criminal behavior depend on access to illegitimate avenues. Thus, an explanation of delinquency must take into account not only the impoverishment of legal paths of behavior but the "richness" and kind of illegal paths as well.

As Cloward and Ohlin note, a theory of delinquent subcultures need not explain every delinquent act; in their essay they restrict their attention to "those forms of delinquent activity which result from the performance of social roles specifically provided and supported by delinquent subcultures."[3] But much research into delinquency (including that reported here) is based on police and court records, and it is not always clear whether the delinquent acts result from subcultural forces or represent instead the extra-role behavior of individuals. Since "delinquency is normally an activity carried on in groups,"[4] however, the theory of delinquent subcultures may be relevant to the explanation of delinquency.[5] We shall assume its relevance in the following analysis of an implication of the Cloward-Ohlin theory regarding interacting factors in juvenile delinquency. Here we present an *ex post facto* illustration of this interaction. Although we make no effort to investigate delinquency as a subcultural phenomenon, our analysis is guided by the question: what results would be expected if the theory in *Delinquency and Opportunity* were adequate to the explanation of different rates of delinquent acts?

THE DATA

The study reported here investigated every youth in Greater New Haven born in 1942–44 whose supervising relative—most often the mother —was on the rolls of Aid to Dependent Children (ADC) in 1950.[6] The record of each youth was followed from his sixth birthday to his 19th, so that the age span would be the same for all subjects. Data were taken from the welfare office records and from school and police records in all cases. Socio-economic characteristics of the neighborhoods were derived from a 1950 study of New Haven,[7] and neighborhood delinquency rates were calculated from recent statistics of the New Haven Police Youth Bureau.

We concentrated on ADC cases for two reasons. First, social casework records were available for the years they were on ADC. Our information on family characteristics, for example, was obtained from these records. Second, this group is relatively homogeneous with respect to social class and home conditions. It is by definition in a deprived stratum, since neither the parents nor other relatives could support the children. Furthermore, the records show that virtually all these cases not only were economically deprived in 1950 but also came to ADC with a history of such deprivation. All but one of these ADC families were broken by death of a parent, divorce, separation, or desertion. This state of affairs tends to be chronic: 74 per cent of the sample were still on ADC rolls after five years, and 63 per cent were still receiving aid after 10 years.

At the outset, then, this population is at least grossly homogeneous in terms of social class, broken homes, and age span. Since lower-class youth from broken homes are known to have high delinquency rates, it is not remarkable that by 1962, 34 per cent of the sample had become known to the police or juvenile court.[8] Interest thus shifts to *which* third of this deprived group became delinquent, and why.

THE FINDINGS

Three rather powerful factors associated with delinquency are race, sex, and school performance.[9] Table 1 summarizes the simultaneous effects

TABLE 1. The Effects of Race, Sex, and School Performance on Delinquency

| | Percentage with one or more arrests or court referrals (Numbers in parentheses are base N's) | | | |
School Performance	Negro Males	White Males	Negro Females	White Females
Success	43(14)	38(37)	24(25)	0(75)
Failure	71(38)	61(61)	40(25)	23(44)

of these factors. Each of the three factors has an independent effect, i.e., influences the delinquency rate when the other two factors are held constant. The range in these rates, from zero to 71 per cent, indicates that a considerable portion of the variation in delinquency in this population can be predicted, if not theoretically explained, by race, sex, and school performance.

The introduction of two more variables, however, not only increases the range in rates but also reveals a different pattern. Unlike race, sex, and school performance, whose effects generally are additive, "family deviance" and "neighborhood deviance" have non-additive or interaction effects; their influence on delinquency is differentially felt.[10]

One of the overwhelming impressions one gets from reading the case work records is the different *degree* to which these broken homes are "deviant." At one extreme are families that are relatively stable even though one parent is dead, deserted, or disabled. At the other extreme are units deviating grossly from societal norms: one or both parents are in prison or mental hospital, or the parent has had a series of marriages, separations, multiple illegitimacies, or "cut and run" affairs.[11] Negroes are more likely to live in one of these unstable or grossly deviant families (57 per cent, vs. 28 per cent of whites), and family deviance is somewhat related to delinquency (in the sample as a whole, 41 per cent from deviant families, vs. 31 per cent from non-deviant families were delinquent). The surprising observation is that family deviance influences the delinquency of Negroes but not that of whites, as Table 2 indicates.

TABLE 2. The Effect of Family Deviance
on Delinquency among Negroes and Whites

Percentage with one or more arrests or court referrals

Family	Negroes	White
Deviant	55(58)	27(60)
Non-deviant	39(44)	29(157)
Difference	16	−2

These data, which apply equally to males and females, lead one to infer that race and family deviance have an interactive effect on delinquency. A possible explanation, to be discussed presently, is suggested by the next table, where the impact of family deviance on Negro delinquency is concentrated among those failing in school.

Table 3 indicates that family deviance influences Negroes performing

TABLE 3. The Effect of Family Deviance
on Delinquency among Negroes Failing or
Succeeding in School

Percentage with one or more arrests or court referrals

Family	School Failure	School Success
Deviant	71(34)	33(24)
Non-deviant	45(29)	27(15)
Difference	26	6

badly in school but has much less effect on those doing well. One could just as easily phrase the point this way: school failure has more effect on those from deviant families. Thus, school success seems to play a compensating role, protecting persons from the impact of a surrounding force that otherwise encourages delinquency.[12]

Another relevant variable is deviance of the neighborhood environment. The great majority, of course, live in areas of great poverty. But some do not, and even the lower-class neighborhoods differ in the rates of crime and delinquency that occur year after year. Subjects were classified as living in a deviant neighborhood when their area was both of the lowest class and characterized by high delinquency rates.[13] Again, Negroes are more likely than whites to live in deviant neighborhoods (54 vs. 26 per cent), and neighborhood deviance is somewhat related to delinquency rates (42 vs. 30 per cent). But again, the impact of neighborhood deviance is restricted—this time to boys. (See Table 4.)

TABLE 4. THE EFFECT OF NEIGHBORHOOD DEVIANCE ON DELINQUENCY, AMONG BOYS AND GIRLS

Percentage with one or more arrests or court referrals

Neighborhood	Boys	Girls
Deviant	71(55)	14(56)
Non-deviant	47(95)	16(113)
Difference	24	−2

This pattern, which holds for both Negroes and whites, is another example of interacting factors: neighborhood deviance influences the delinquency of boys but not girls. And once more, this influence is further restricted almost entirely to boys failing in school; boys doing well in school appear to be little influenced by a deviant neighborhood. The protective or compensating role of adequate school performance is once again observed.[14]

INTERPRETATION

We have presented an uncomplicated notion several times—the notion that a factor has a "protective role" or differential effect, or that two factors have an interacting effect on a third. In summary: (1) A deviant family background increases Negro, but not white, delinquency. (2) A deviant neighborhood increases male, but not female, delinquency. (3) Either kind of deviant influence increases delinquency more among those failing in school than among those succeeding. Taken together, these findings illustrate an implication of Cloward and Ohlin's theoretical work in which illegitimate as well as legitimate opportunity structures are related to delinquency.

The youths in this research are lower-class, both in origin and by present circumstance. They also are or have been on welfare rolls. For those reasons alone, then, their life chances, their range of alternatives or "effective scope" is relatively narrow. Unable to avoid some contact with society's general value system, they too are confronted by a goal of success, self-esteem, or dignity.[15] Yet the probability that they will achieve this goal, whatever its particular form, is less than the probability for youths not from lower-class, welfare families.

We can specify this generalization, however, because the chances for "success" are not equally low throughout the lower class. For example, Negroes systematically have more difficulty than whites reaching comparable goals, and they know it. "The last hired and first fired," reflects in both belief and reality the different probabilities of getting and keeping a steady job. Correlatively, among lower-class youth the sexes differ in their chances of achieving "success." Girls typically can anticipate a future of marriage and motherhood, however imperfect, and regardless of hardships in performing the role, most will meet some acceptable criterion of success. For lower-class boys, on the other hand, aspirations of marriage and fatherhood are not enough. In the eyes of society a job and income are further criteria they must meet. And ironically, lower-class women can frequently find employment more readily than can men.

Reworded in Cloward and Ohlin's terms, our assertions are that lower strata generally, and Negroes and boys especially, face more barriers to legitimate goals. Their situation is more anomic. Similarly, school failure can be conceived of as another barrier to legitimate opportunity. Whether school failure stems from low intelligence or lack of motivation or deprived cultural background, it is clear that a youth failing or dropping out of school will find more obstacles to the legitimate goals of our society than will other youths.

As different indicators of the variable "legitimate opportunity," therefore, these measures might be expected to have an *additive* effect on the degree of delinquency. That is, the more legitimate opportunities a person has, the less likely he is to engage in illegitimate behavior. Table 1 generally shows that this is the case—persons who have the least access to legitimate avenues (i.e., Negro boys failing school) are most likely to engage in illegitimate behavior (their delinquency rate is 71 per cent); persons who have most opportunity to learn and fulfill legitimate avenues (i.e., white girls succeeding in school) are least likely to engage in illegitimate behavior (their delinquency rate is 0 per cent). Other categories differ in delinquency rates depending on the extent of their legitimate opportunity.

Cloward and Ohlin make an important theoretical specification, however. Social structural conditions account not only for differential barriers to *legitimate* avenues but also, they argue, for differential opportunities to

learn and execute *illegitimate avenues*.[16] If deviance, or illegitimate behavior, is to be explained, both kinds of opportunity should be incorporated
in the analysis.

Stated in extreme terms, the theory says that irrespective of the degree
to which legitimate avenues are unavailable, patterned deviance can
occur only when deviant avenues (illegitimate means) are available.[17] We
can infer, then, that the level of deviant behavior is predicted not by the
sum of blocked legitimate opportunity plus illegitimate opportunity, but
rather by the *multiplied* effect of the two variables. Thus, if one of the
terms has a value of zero, deviance would not be increased by the other
term.

We repeat, this is the *extreme* form of an inference from the Cloward-
Ohlin theory. No research could claim to have adequate measures ranging
from zero to maximum opportunity. Nor are these two variables the
only ones required for an adequate explanation of delinquency. Motivation,
or the extent to which "societal" goals are indeed goals for given subjects,
for example, is obviously important in understanding the vigor with which
any avenue will be tried and thus the strength of reaction upon finding that
avenue blocked. The theory nevertheless implies that, since "each individual occupies a position in both legitimate and illegitimate opportunity
structures,"[18] the likelihood that he will pursue a deviant path is the
product of his position in both structures. In short, illegitimate avenues
will be *disproportionately* utilized by those whose legitimate opportunities
are more restricted.[19]

Family deviance and neighborhood deviance can be conceived as
measures of opportunity to learn and to execute illegitimate means. It
seems reasonable to assume that children brought up in grossly deviant
homes or in slum neighborhoods with high delinquency rates have more
opportunity to observe and learn disregard for law, to learn how to reduce
the visibility of illegal activities, and to find gang support and organized
crime to facilitate delinquent behavior. If this is the case, then the simultaneous effect of family deviance and neighborhood deviance on delinquency
might well be additive,[20] since both are measures of the same variable—
illegitimate opportunity—but the simultaneous effect of one or more
measures of *legitimate* opportunity, coupled with one or more measures of
illegitimate opportunity, ought to be interactive.[21] And indeed Tables 2–5
reveal just that pattern: availability of illegitimate opportunities (family
deviance or neighborhood deviance) has greater impact on the deviance of
those with fewer legitimate opportunities (Negroes, or boys, or school
failures).

If two measures of each variable are used, the result is to sharpen the
differential effect of illegitimate opportunity, as Table 6 shows. Table 6,
of course, simply synthesizes data already shown, but it does show concisely that illegitimate opportunity has greater impact on persons with
fewer legitimate avenues to legitimate goals (46 percentage points) than

TABLE 5. The Effect of Neighborhood Deviance on Delinquency among Boys Failing or Succeeding in School

Percentage with one or more arrests or court referrals

Neighborhood	School Failure	School Success
Deviant	82(39)	44(16)
Non-deviant	53(60)	37(35)
Difference	29	7

TABLE 6. The Effect of Illegitimate Opportunity on Delinquency among Youths with Varying Degrees of Legitimate Opportunity

Percentage with one or more arrests or court referrals

	Degree of Legitimate Opportunity			
	Low		High	
	School Failure		School Success	
Degree of Illegitimate Opportunity	Negroes	Whites	Negroes	Whites
High: Both Family Deviance and Neighborhood Deviance	82(17)	63(8)	21(14)	0(4)
Medium: Either Family Deviance or Neighborhood Deviance	56(32)	39(46)	42(19)	15(46)
Low: Neither Family Deviance nor Neighborhood Deviance	36(14)	47(51)	17(6)	11(62)
Difference Attributed to Illegitimate Opportunity	46	16	4	−11

on those with many (11 percentage points). The number of cases is too small to permit refinements in Table 6, but the pattern of differences remains the same when, instead of race and school performance, any two of the three measures of legitimate opportunity are paired. A reasonable, if tentative, conclusion is that legitimate and illegitimate opportunities have an interacting effect on juvenile delinquency.

SUMMARY

We have investigated the effect on delinquency of two basic variables: (1) legitimate opportunity as indicated by race, sex, and school success, and (2) illegitimate opportunity as indicated by family deviance and neighborhood deviance. We have used our data to illustrate an implication of Cloward and Ohlin's theory of delinquent gangs, that delinquency is proportional to barriers to legitimate opportunity *times* illegitimate opportunity.

Any measure of one of the opportunity variables, coupled with any measure of the other opportunity variable, should produce an interaction effect on delinquency. In the discussion above, four such effects were shown in tabular form. The probabilities[22] of finding the observed differences (between percentage differences) by chance are:

Family Deviance and Race	.13
Family Deviance and School Performance (for Negroes)	.30
Neighborhood Deviance and Sex	.01
Neighborhood Deviance and School Performance (for Boys)	.20

According to the theory, four other pairs of variables, which combine alternative measures of *either* legitimate *or* illegitimate opportunity, need not have differential impact on delinquency. Note that the following probabilities are higher:

Neighborhood Deviance and Family Deviance	.52
Sex and School Performance	.76
Sex and Race	.28
Race and School Performance	.68

These tests of significance are meant, of course, only as bench-marks. In addition to reservations about the test's applicability to these data, several other qualifications must be noted. First, these results should not be construed as a test of Cloward and Ohlin's theory. The latter is chiefly concerned with the nature or content of delinquent subcultures, rather than rates of delinquent acts; in addition, the relation between the measures used here and the *concepts* of legitimate and illegitimate opportunity is tenuous. School success, for example, reflects not only a legitimate means to respectability but probably indicates a higher level of aspiration as well. Sex, as another example, no doubt measures differential access to legitimate means, but in addition taps the difference between male and female socialization in families; therefore, the finding that family deviance has more effect on female delinquency comes as no surprise though it is contrary to the theory discussed here.[23]

Put briefly, these data, taken entirely from records compiled for other purposes, cannot adequately confirm the theoretical implication regarding interaction effects. Further investigation will require sharper measures of avenues to opportunity structures, both legitimate and illegitimate. It would also benefit from measures of frustration, resentment, and so on, thus providing the social-psychological links between opportunity and delinquency that necessarily cannot be provided here.

To explain away unconfirmed predictions by claiming they have been tested with impure measures is to admit that the propositions that *were* upheld are open to question. Certainly no deception is warranted or intended, given these conditions. Our data, however, convincingly suggest that interaction effects of legitimate and illegitimate opportunity structures are worth looking for: either variable taken singly might leave out a significant portion of the story.

NOTES AND REFERENCES

1. For reviews of this literature, see any text on juvenile delinquency, e.g., Herbert A. Bloch and Frank T. Flynn, *Delinquency,* New York: Random House, 1956, pp. 60 ff. For a succinct outline and appraisal of delinquency theory see Albert K. Cohen and James F. Short, Jr., "Juvenile Delinquency," in Robert K. Merton and Robert A. Nisbet, *Contemporary Social Problems,* New York: Harcourt, Brace and World, 1961, pp. 89–112.

2. Richard A. Cloward and Lloyd E. Ohlin, *Delinquency and Opportunity,* Glencoe, Ill.: The Free Press, 1960.

3. *Ibid.,* p. 9.

4. Cohen and Short, *op. cit.,* p. 103.

5. This is especially true when the delinquents are persons of similar age living in a limited number of neighborhoods, and when many of the acts with which they are charged are acts typically engaged in by gangs. Both of these conditions apply to the data reported here.

6. A total of 353. Of this number 34 were eliminated because they died or moved from the area, or because insufficient data were available; therefore $N = 319$.

7. See August B. Hollingshead and Frederich C. Redlich, *Social Class and Mental Illness,* New York: John Wiley, 1958.

8. In contrast, a "control" group (all youths of the same age as the welfare group, and included in the 1950 New Haven Study as Class 5, the lowest class) had a delinquency rate of 18 per cent. Though the two groups were similar with respect to age, sex, type of neighborhood lived in, and performance in school, they did differ radically on attributes associated with welfare cases. Compared with the control group, our sample contained twice as many persons living in public housing, twice the number who had moved three or more times during the 11-year period, three times the number of Negroes, and over ten times the number from broken homes. For further comparisons of these two groups see Erdman B. Palmore "Factors Associated with School Dropouts and Juvenile Delinquency Among Lower-Class Children," *Social Security Bulletin,* 26 (October, 1963), 4–9. Of course, we recognize that reported delinquency is not necessarily equivalent to actual delinquency.

9. School success is operationally defined as a grade average of A, B, or C; all others are defined as failure.

10. An interaction effect occurs when the relation between two variables is not additive, that is, when the relationship differs under various conditions of a third variable. In much survey research, identifying interaction effects is thus analysis by "specification." See Paul F. Lazarsfeld and Morris Rosenberg (eds.), *The Language of Social Research,* Glencoe, Ill.: The Free Press, 1955, pp. 115–126.

11. Any person whose family displayed one or more of these gross deviations is characterized as being from a deviant family. Most of these deviant families had multiple illegitimate births and a series of illegitimate "affairs."

12. This pattern does not emerge among the whites.

13. The delinquency rate of the neighborhood is not completely independent of the percentage in our sample from that neighborhood who are delinquent, since the delinquents in our sample contribute to the over-all delinquency rate. This interdependence is insignificant, however, because our delinquents constituted only a small fraction of the total delinquents from any given neighborhood.

14. This pattern emerges also among the girls.

15. Data that we do not have, on what values these persons in fact hold, would obviously improve this statement. As it stands it is an assumption, the same assumption central to the theoretical tradition being applied here. See Robert K. Merton, *Social Theory and Social Structure* (rev. ed.), Glencoe, Ill.: The Free Press, 1957, chs. 4–5; Albert K. Cohen, *Delinquent Boys,* Glencoe, Ill.: The Free Press, 1955; and Cloward and Ohlin, *op. cit.* Herbert Hyman, in "The Value Systems of Different Classes," in Reinhard Bendix and Seymour M. Lipset (eds.), *Class, Status and Power,* Glencoe, Ill.: The Free Press, 1953, pp. 426–442, has investigated this assumption and shown its potential importance to delinquency theory.

16. Cloward and Ohlin, *op. cit.,* ch. 6.

17. We say "in extreme terms" because, of course, social survey research is not in a position to measure, or hold constant, every avenue, legitimate and illegitimate. It is possible, though, to imagine true experiments on a variable such as school performance, where other factors are randomized.

18. Cloward and Ohlin, *op. cit.,* p. 150.

19. And correlatively, a point for which we have no illustrative data: an increase in legitimate avenues will be disproportionately utilized by those with more restricted illegitimate opportunities.

20. Though not shown in tabular form, the data clearly indicate that these two variables do have an additive effect on delinquency.

21. Specifically it ought to be a particular form of interaction, a multiplicative effect. Were it possible to measure opportunity precisely, one could examine the implication in its strict form: illegitimate opportunity has no effect on persons whose legitimate avenues for success are adequate but has an increasing impact as legitimate avenues are less and less adequate.

22. The test is Goodman's test of the difference between the differences in two proportions (Leo A. Goodman, "Modifications of the Dorn-Stouffer-Tibbetts Method for 'Testing the Significance of Comparisons in Sociological Data,'" *American Journal of Sociology,* 66 (January, 1961), pp. 355–359. Since many of the cells in the tables contain fewer than 100 cases, and since the subjects are not strictly a random sample but constitute a universe of local ADC cases of their ages for those years, the appropriateness of the test is debatable. Its

use (two-tailed here) does provide a basis for contrasting patterns of results, however.

23. This reversal of the general prediction is understandable on other theoretical grounds: girls are more influenced by their homes and more likely to pattern their behavior after adults in their families. See Jackson Toby, "The Differential Impact of Family Disorganization," *American Sociological Review, 22* (October, 1957), pp. 502–512, and F. Ivan Nye, *Family Relationships and Delinquent Behavior,* New York: John Wiley, 1958.

The theory anticipates three more multiplicative effects, one of which we observed: neighborhood deviance has greater impact on the delinquency of school failures: The other two (family deviance and school performance; neighborhood deviance and race) do not conform to the theory.

60.

The fantastic if

ISAAC ASIMOV

You are about to read a speculative argument replete with provocative statistics and provocative phrases. Will the "unchanged rabbit power of mankind" really subject our grandchildren to a "perpetual dignity-destroying crowdedness"? Some readers may be able to tune in with that generation to find out. Indeed, the time may be sufficiently close that the dignities of many present readers will be among those ruffled.

If the thesis advanced in this article is true, man's rate of reproduction soon will result in such crowded conditions that no meaningful and satisfactory existence will be possible for anyone. Science, by continuing to make life possible for more people and by extending their life span, in effect, will operate to create such crowded conditions that human life, at least as we know it, will be impossible. Paradoxically, it may be that the greatest hazard to development is that so many hazards to development have been eliminated. As the editors pointed out in introducing an earlier selection, the instigation of one control almost always brings about conditions that require further regulation. The process is endless.

The question may not be whether or not people will develop some means of population control but how long they will procrastinate before they do so. How stringent and limiting this control will be may depend directly upon how long it is avoided and how critical the situation gets before something is done.

SUPPOSE YOU were asked to decide what mankind's most dangerous delusion was. Let me tell you my own candidate.

It is simply this: Science can solve everything.

Long Island Newsday, April 15, 1967. Isaac Asimov, Associate Professor of Biochemistry, Boston University Medical School.

Science can't, and that's the way it is. There are some problems that are insoluble in the future, no matter how far and how fast science progresses.

I might suggest, as examples, that scientists will never learn how to go faster than the speed of light, or how to travel in time, or how to build an antigravity device. But there might be room for argument there.

Let's try something else to make my point clear. Let's pose a problem that science can't solve *ever*, for reasons so clear that there can be no argument at all from anybody, and where the delusion that science can solve it may destroy civilization—perhaps humanity.

Here's the problem: If the present birth and death rates do not change, can science take care of the earth's increasing population?

When civilization first began—say, in 6000 B.C.—the total population of the earth, according to some estimates, was roughly 8,000,000, a figure about equal to the population of a single modern city such as New York or Tokyo. By the time the Roman Empire was at its height at 100 A.D., the total population of the earth was perhaps 150,000,000.

In 6,000 years, the population had risen from 8,000,000 to 150,000,000. Population doubled every 1,400 years. But why should it take so long for population to double? Surely one could do better than that if one were reasonably fertile.

The trouble is that most of the children died young. Indeed, virtually nobody lived to be very old, and the average life expectancy in uncivilized conditions was probably no more than 25 years. Even in highly civilized areas, such as the Roman Empire of 100 A.D., average life expectancy was probably not more than 35 years.

But Civilization kept spreading and agricultural methods slowly improved. The danger of famine dropped somewhat, even if disease remained as terrifying as ever. By 1600 the world population is estimated to have been 500,000,000, and by 1800 it had reached 900,000,000. Thus between 100 and 1600, population was doubling, on the average, every 900 years; between 1600 and 1800, the doubling rate was every 250 years.

The death rate was still an important control, however. As late as 1850, the average life expectancy in even the most advanced areas was not more than 40 years. But then came the germ theory of disease, the development of antitoxins, the discovery of vitamins, the coming of antibiotics. Down went the death rate in Europe and North America. Up went the average life expectancy to 50, then to 60, finally to 70.

The population reached the 1-billion mark soon after 1800. By 1900, the population stood at 1.6 billion; by 1950 it was 2.5 billion; and in 1967 it stands at an estimated 3.2 billion. During the 19th Century, the world population showed a doubling rate of 90 years; in the first half of the 20th Century, it stood at 75 years. The population is now increasing at such a rate it may be expected to double every 47 years.

You might take the attitude that science is making more rapid progress than ever, too.

Half the population is crowded into southern and eastern Asia and western Europe with a total area of less than one-tenth of the earth's land surface. Scientific advance will surely make it possible to live in Greenland and Antarctica, in the mountains and deserts, even under the sea.

Food? Water? Minerals? Man has only begun to scratch the surface. We scarcely use the food resources of the ocean; we haven't begun to use our rainwater efficiently, to say nothing of the possibility of using the icecaps in Greenland and Antarctica, and the desalinization of ocean water. As for minerals, the sea-bottom is loaded with all kinds of metallic nodules.

And yet, man's growing numbers and the machines and industries he insists on having to serve him, are already producing problems quite beyond such matters as room and resources.

We have millions of cars belching smog-forming molecules into the air, and thousands of industrial plants adding their wastes to air and water. Our technology is already dirtying the planet at a rate faster than the cleansing abilities of rain and microorganisms can keep up with.

And even if the technical problems involved in cleaning up the world can be solved for now and the next century, that would still leave the matter of psychological well-being.

Experiments on rats and other animals have shown that crowding, if made severe enough, produces clear signs of behavioral derangement. How much of the nastiness of city life today is due to the increasing incidence of mental sickness arising from nothing more than general crowding?

You might feel that there are natural safeguards against unlimited population increase that will come into play automatically. It is often stated that the birth rate goes down as the standard of living goes up. So it does, but not fast enough. In 1940, the population of the United States was 130,000,000; now it is just about 200,000,000. The doubling rate is 30 years, so that at this rate the population of the United States will be 400,000,000 by 2000.

Or you might take the other tack and say that with increasing population there will be increasing misery and therefore a lower birth rate. During the depression the American birth rate dropped, for instance, and experiments with animals show that overcrowding actually upsets the maternal instincts of rats and reduces their abilities to raise young in the normal manner.

This reliance on misery to redress the balance is, however, inhumane. Worse still it wouldn't work.

The human misery in such nations as India and Egypt would be hard to match, yet India's population has risen from 330,000,000 in 1948 to 450,000,000 now; Egypt's has risen from 19,000,000 in 1948 to 28,000,000 now.

Shall we wait for a downturn in the birth rate as a result of a misery even deeper than that of the Indian and Egyptian peasants?

And if we wait for that, what side effects will we have to endure first? Already, the United States—the richest and most powerful nation on earth, sits on a powder-keg made up of its own submerged portion of the population than seems helpless to do anything about it.

The unrest in the cities and the crime in the streets is something that cannot be removed merely by disapproving of it or by increasing the police force or by hardening the judicial system. As long as human beings are condemned to live in perpetual dignity-destroying crowdedness that unrest will continue. And as population increases, the number of people subjected to that dehumanizing process will grow.

Let us, however, suppose we will solve the problem of pollution and we will greatly increase agricultural efficiency and tap the sea, find minerals everywhere, and develop fusion power to give us all the energy we want.

In that case, how many people can the earth support? Five billion? Ten billion? Fifty billion? And how long will it take to reach that figure at the present rate of increase?

Suppose we decide the earth can support 50 billion people in ease and comfort—something like 16 times its present population. We are now doubling in population every 47 years. Suppose that continues, too.

The earth's population, which is 3.2 billion now, will be 6.4 billion in 2014; 12.8 billion in 2061; 25.6 billion in 2108; and 51.2 billion in 2155. In other words, in less than two centuries, that 50 billion population figure will have been reached, and we'll still be going up.

Do you want to assume a bigger figure? Then let's consider the three boroughs of Manhattan, the Bronx and Brooklyn. They are crowded enough, certainly. The combined area of these three boroughs is 145 square miles and the combined population is 5,500,000.

Suppose all the earth were as thickly packed with human beings as those boroughs; *all* the earth: Greenland, Antarctica, the top of Mount Everest, Death Valley, and every bit of the floor of the ocean. In that case, the total population of the earth would be 7,300 billion people, more than 2,300 times as many people as there are now.

If we continued doubling our population every 47 years, how long would it take to cover the entire surface of the earth and make every bit of it on land and under the sea a single, great Brooklyn? The answer is 520 years.

Of course, you may argue that we won't have to stay on earth. Some of us can go to other worlds by spaceship. But can they? The earth's population will increase by 3.2 billion in 47 years. How many people do you think we can put on the moon in that period of time?

Suppose that instead of the airless, waterless moon, we had another earth out there, as rich and fertile as our own. And suppose we could transport people there as easily as snapping our fingers. By 2014, that second earth would be as full as ours is now and our own earth would be no less full.

Let's go further. Our galaxy has about 100 billion stars in it and there may be as many as 100 billion other galaxies in the universe. Let's suppose that every one of the stars in every one of the galaxies has 10 planets just as rich and beautiful as our earth. That would be 10,000,000,000,000,-000,000,000 planets altogether. And suppose we could transport people to any one of those planets just by snapping our fingers.

How long do you suppose it would take, at our present rate of increase, to fill all those planets? I don't mean to fill them merely to our present population, but to make every bit of the surface of every bit of those planets as crowded as the boroughs of New York. The answer—4,000 years.

Are you satisfied? Do you agree that science cannot possibly solve the population problem if birth rate and death rate continue unchanged? Nothing science can do—NOTHING—can keep up with the unchanged rabbit-power of mankind indefinitely.

Of course, we can't really expect to use up the universe in 6,500 years or fill all the surface of all the planets in 4,000 years. We can't even expect to fill up the earth's own surface in 520 years. Something will have to give—and within the next century at most.

There are two possibilities: Either the death rate will go up, or the birth rate will go down. It would be much easier for us to raise the death rate. If we just sit back and take it easy, the death rate will go up without our having to lift a finger, just through the press of population increase.

I think, though, it would be better to lower the birth rate. Since there is no way short of mass death, to keep large numbers of people from indulging in sexual activity, we'll just have to work out methods of preventing conception.

In short, we need some efficient and cheap method of birth control quickly, or we are doomed. It is absolutely as simple as that.

61.

Leaving the drug world behind

RONALD MOSKOWITZ

Why do young people use drugs? The answers are as numerous as the people who write and talk about it. It's the speed of living. It's population pressure and increasing anonymity. It's parental hypocrisy. It's the decline of morality. It's the Spock permissiveness child-rearing atmosphere. However, finding a cause, or scapegoat, only provides am-

American Education, 6(No. 1):3–6, January–February, 1970. Ronald Moskowitz, Education Reporter, San Francisco Chronicle.

munition for further rationalization of a hazardous experiment or an escape from the frying pan into the fire.

The real question is not Why? but What can be done about it? While Moskowitz may not have the answer for every young person and every school and every community, the approach he describes was effective in one instance. The article says in effect: Destroy the rationalizations and clarify concepts of self and life. Latch on to life and let loose of drugs. "Turn on" to a personal meaning and involvement. We think there is another crucial element—adults who can become concerned without becoming judgmental. An excellent article can, we think, become additionally meaningful if the readers will discuss it.

SOMETHING WAS wrong at Fort Bragg High School. Strangely wrong. The 5,000 residents of the tough, isolated, California coastal milltown that lies some 200 miles north of San Francisco wouldn't have readily noticed the difference. But school counselor Bryce Brooks did. Still, he couldn't put his finger on it.

For a place where 550 young people were gathered, the school was ominously quiet. The happy chatter of normal teenagers was gone. In its place, a lethargy fastened many of the students drowsily to their seats, as if someone had let loose a tsetse fly.

Some teachers blamed it on "the times." Others said the students were just living too high on weekends, and this seemed somewhat plausible because the apparently contagious apathy reached its peak on Monday mornings. Brooks might have accepted these explanations if some students hadn't walked into his office one day and asked for advice on how to help "friends" who were on "speed." Brooks didn't know what speed was. But he soon found out. The "friends" angle didn't fool him. He knew the kids were asking for help for themselves.

The soft-spoken counselor helped as much as he could, considering he knew little if anything about the problem. He began boning up on drug abuse, and the word got around that Brooks was an all-right guy who could be trusted. He wouldn't get you busted, or even turn you in to your parents.

Other students came. Brooks soon found out the school's drug problem was too big for one man to handle.

"We had hints that there was a problem late in the fall of 1967," Brooks says. "We really realized it, though, the following April when we took a survey that showed 50 percent of the senior class had experimented with drugs, 35 percent of them heavily. We thought we were isolated from the evils of the big city. We were shocked when we found out that such a large percentage of our high school kids were users.

"We got the community together and told them we had a problem. First we had to talk them out of calling in the law. That would have been playing right into the kids' hands, because they love to play cops and robbers. Besides, emptying the schools and filling the jails would have only ruined a lot of lives.

"We looked around for someone or some program to help. We found no one could. There were some drug programs in other schools, but they were based on trying to scare the students. The kids are too smart to believe a completely negative approach. That doesn't work. Then we heard about the 'family' program at Mendocino State Hospital."

The program combines techniques used by Esalen Institute and the Synanon Foundation which try to increase or awaken a person's awareness of himself and of others. The Mendocino program centers around self-help—with addicts helping other addicts. Brooks decided to try extending the theory into the schools, using Mendocino's ex-addicts to help Fort Bragg High School's potential addicts.

Two young Mendocino "graduates," Ed Lasher and Jim Gibson, were hired by the school district as counselor aides. Until enough money could be raised to pay for a new office location on what Brooks calls neutral ground, the counselor offered his own home for any students who needed help.

The first to seek aid were two senior girls who described themselves as "speed freaks," meaning they were taking amphetamines like Benzedrine. Later they brought along a 17-year-old boy who had been "dropping acid" (LSD), and before long there were eight students coming regularly. Lasher and Gibson used the tactics they had been steeped in at Mendocino which seemed to be working. "The idea is involvement," explains Gibson, "to turn on to life with people instead of turning on to drugs. The cure for drug addiction is a meaningful life."

Then summer approached and the students began to get panicky. They had been on and off drugs during the sessions, and they were afraid that without help through the summer they'd be hooked for good.

The eight made a contract with one another to avoid all their old friends and to give one another moral support. Meanwhile, Brooks searched desperately for money. The State department of education came through with $1,400 for a summer drug-abuse workshop. A psychologist, a psychiatrist, and a psychiatric social worker, along with Lasher and Gibson, all donated their pay. This, together with a $1,000 donation from the city, made enough money to rent a Main Street bungalow and open the first Awareness House.

"After the end of summer, we found that something had happened," Brooks says. "Kids who had been against drug abuse but had kept their mouths shut were now speaking out against it. In effect, a peer group antidrug culture had begun. Such a thing had been totally unknown before."

During the 1968–69 school year Brooks, Lasher, and Gibson launched their full-scale program, concentrating on speed users in the high school. Lasher and Gibson talked to large groups, small classes, and individual students—in school and at Awareness House. Both users and nonusers were encouraged to attend group sessions at the house.

"We knew that in a small town we wouldn't have a prayer with a program just for drug kids," Brooks explains. "The kids couldn't cop out on themselves."

The students came. They enjoyed the confrontation tactics which were the heart of the games played in the house. The games got students to challenge other students to tell the truth. In doing so everyone helped others and was, in turn, helped himself to knock down his own wall of rationalization about drug usage. For both users and potential users, the sessions helped the kids turn on to each other and learn how to communicate with themselves and with adults.

As the drug crisis began abating, the mood of the town began changing and support for the program grew. During their off hours the two ex-addicts became diplomats, selling themselves and their program to coffee klatches, sewing circles, and civic groups. Townspeople, who at first mistrusted the idea of ex-addicts in close contact with their children, finally realized the two men were no threat. Most of them quit being uptight. Brooks is sorry they ever were.

"They should remember that, for an addict, it takes real strength to become an ex-addict," he says. "People worry about their kids associating with former drug users when they should realize that their kids are associating with drug users every day—sometimes in their own living rooms. In many, many places nowadays if a kid has two friends, the chances are that one of them is a drug user."

During the school year, application was made for a special projects training grant from the U.S. Office of Education to prepare more ex-addicts "who dress and think more like teenagers than the establishment, who give a believable message because they speak from their own lives, who substitute for drugs their natural antidote—personal and interpersonal discovery."

The 12 additional ex-addicts—to be trained as counselor specialists under the Education Professions Development Act—were to work with some 20,000 high school students in the rest of Mendocino County and three neighboring North Coast counties. A Federal training grant was awarded in April. But in the last six months Brooks has not exactly been besieged with requests from neighboring counties, although letters, phone calls, and visitors come daily from other parts of the country.

"There is resistance because of fear of ex-addicts being involved," Brooks explains. "But most resistance comes from the large number of people who don't want to admit there is a problem. Then too, all four of these counties are poor and really couldn't afford to do much, even if they wanted to."

The program insists on the city providing a meetingplace on neutral ground. And such places cost money. To raise money, there has to be community support. And to have community support, there must first be a recognition that a problem exists.

There has been some response from the neighbors. A program has been established and is operating well in Sonora, which has established its own Awareness House called "In-Site," staffed by three graduates of Brooks' training program. A group in Ukiah is attempting to start a program. South Fork near the Oregon border has requested help, as have individual churches in Eureka and Arcata. But it was Tucson, Ariz., that really wanted the program.

"My wife and I took three of the eight original kids who came to us for help down to Pacific Palisades so they could tell their story to a conference on drug abuse," Brooks says.

"The Reverend Comer M. Alden, Jr., of Tucson's St. Paul's United Methodist Church, brought a committee there that listened to what the kids said. The committee toured programs throughout California and then decided that ours was the one they wanted to lick their problem. We were leery because they were so far away.

"But we're responsive to people who want to do something. We found they have an unbelievable, frightening nightmare of a problem. Tucson may have as many as 3,000 heroin users—down to 13- and 14-year-olds—that have come to the attention of the police. Imagine how many there are who haven't. The Tucson Awareness House Committee estimates 80 percent usage of some illegal or dangerous drugs in some east side schools—the upper-middle-class schools—and 20 percent usage in the chicano schools. So we decided to help them.

"They have white-middle-class heroin addicts. There is lots of heroin. We're not even sure we can deal with this, but we are determined to try."

Last October 24, Tucson opened its first Awareness House with great fanfare. The old mansion, given rent-free for the project by a supermarket chain, nestles with its bold Spanish architecture, stables, shops, and crafts buildings on 14 acres. The house director is Mrs. William Jacquin, a social worker whose husband is majority leader in the Arizona State Senate.

"Before the opening, Mrs. Jacquin was laying brick," Brooks says. "The Senator and two other men were working on the roof. A society matron who hadn't lifted a dust rag in her own home in years was cleaning inside. So were 100 kids. The people of Tucson are putting more than their money into Awareness House; they are putting in their hearts."

Brooks stresses that Awareness House is Tucson's program, not his. And he feels that's the way it should be. It is the community that must get involved before such a program can work, he says, and Tucson has done just that. Brooks supplied two supervisors—Lasher and Gibson—to be paid out of his own budget until the program could get going. He also supplied four trained ex-addict counselors, but their salaries are paid by the Tucson program. They, in turn, are busy training other ex-addicts to help.

THE Tucson program has seemed to touch off a chain reacton. Requests for help and advice have now become an almost daily occurrence for

Brooks. Recently a subcommittee of the Georgia State Legislature dropped in on Awareness House in Fort Bragg to look over the program.

"I told them it was nice of them to visit on their tour of other facilities," Brooks says. "Their leader replied, 'Don't you know we flew 2,500 miles to Fort Bragg because it is the only place we could get help?' Yesterday a woman called from Los Angeles and said she would like to move here with her son. He has had 100 known injections of speed and is now on heroin. She said if she can get him released from the courts, she'll move up.

"We have a lion by the tail. If we can hang on and survive, maybe we can help the kids and save scores of ex-addicts by giving their lives some meaning and purpose as counselors."

Brooks' formula has worked well for Lasher and Gibson. Ed Lasher, 29, started using drugs when he was 15.

"First it was Benzedrine, then pot," he says. "I've used about everything. I had my first fix when I was about 18 and I've had the habit from the time I was 21 until two years ago. I got a bachelor's degree from California State College at Los Angeles in 1963 by using addiction as a carrot to study. I'd use drugs as a kind of reward. When my work was taken care of, I got high. But later when the heroin got to me, I had to have it to get going in the morning."

Lasher supported his habit by a number of legitimate part-time jobs while in school. But after graduation he decided to quit the habit and enroll in the University of California's Hastings College of Law in San Francisco.

"I began law school after I had been using heroin for two years," he says. "I had been thinking I wouldn't use drugs, but I couldn't take the grind of that much work and no heroin. I think it was then I decided to make drugs my full-time job. I threw school out the window and started drifting. I went to Chicago, then to Los Angeles."

As his habit got more and more expensive Lasher turned to a variety of criminal activities: He jimmied pay telephones, "boosted" clothing from stores and sold it or demanded refunds, and even held up dope dealers—the most dangerous game an addict can play.

"Finally I had enough. I left Los Angeles because I wanted to stop using, but the only people I knew there were users. I went to San Francisco and before long I became a "burn artist" in Haight-Ashbury, selling saccharin for acid."

Trying again to quit, Lasher heard about San Francisco General Hospital's methadone withdrawal program for heroin addicts. He enrolled in it and withdrew from heroin after two weeks. A social worker suggested he enroll in the family program at Mendocino. He stayed six months, then had the chance to go with Brooks. After a year with Awareness House, he had an opportunity to enroll in doctoral programs at the

University of California or the University of Massachusetts. He chose to stay at Fort Bragg.

"Awareness House has given me a chance to turn on to people," he explains. "I forgot that I was trying not to shoot dope by getting immersed in these kids who are shooting speed. When I got into college, I felt I had to do something worthwhile, apart from just making money. Economics—my major—wasn't it. What I'm doing now is. I have a sense of power here. I can see things happen and know it's because I'm helping make them happen.

"I think if VISTA or the Peace Corps had been available at the time I was in college and someone had steered me in that direction, things would have turned out differently for me.

"Before, my feeling was 'No hope without dope.' You see that slogan carved on the walls of every jail you'll ever go into. I learned that wasn't true, and I've developed a pride in knowing that."

LASHER understands well how easy it is when you're in your early teens to allow yourself to experiment with drugs, especially if the offer comes from a trusted friend your own age. After all, that's how he got into it. With Gibson, 28, it was much the same. In his case, the trusted friend was his older brother.

"If they look back to when they were teenagers, most people will have to admit it is a pretty miserable time," says Brooks. "You don't know who you are or where you're going. You think you are the only one in the whole world with your particular problems. We should expect that kids will want to grab on to the drug thing during that time.

"Kids can't communicate today, either with adults, or with each other. This is the first generation that has used television as a baby-sitter from the cradle. A whole generation has turned its kids over to the idiot box and then wonders why they are alienated, why they can't communicate. When we got Awareness House in Tucson, five color television sets were donated. The first thing we made them do was take away every last one of them.

"My position is that kids don't need education about drug abuse as much as parents, teachers, ministers, and doctors do. How many adults are actually making a positive effort to be a real part of the lives of their children? Drugs are only used to fill a void. Why must there be a void to fill?"

Where does the program go from here? Wherever it is called.

"We are trying to get 'family programs' established in hospitals wherever we can," says Brooks. "Then our program could be a natural extension of their program."

62.

Psychology as a means of promoting human welfare

GEORGE A. MILLER

The last selection ended with the conclusion that people can, and must, be enlisted in creating conditions which can lead to their becoming more affectionate, intimate, cooperative, honest, and intelligent. The editors and the author of the present selection agree. He sees the task of psychologists as one of giving psychology or psychological expertise away. He believes that the practice of valid psychology by nonpsychologists inevitably will change people's concepts of themselves and what they can do. In other words, psychologists should teach what they know about controlling behavior to all behavers.

The allocation of the management and responsibility for a person's actions could pass from sources outside himself to an interior, or self, control. Despite the behavioristic, stimulus-response orientation of American psychology, this may prove to be one of the soundest of behavioral science principles; the dignity of mankind has seldom been increased by dictators. Positive, self-accepting attitudes are not achieved by the puppet status imposed by exterior direction and string-pulling.

The dilemma of helping is this: If a person is helped too much, a lack of confidence in him is indicated and his own feelings of worthlessness are confirmed. So it is that the harder we try in this respect, the more we are apt to fail. The more we defeat others with injudicious help, the more we defeat ourselves if we really want them to become more effective. Parents, teachers, politicians, and members of the helping professions need to become acutely aware of this paradox. They need to learn how to renounce the gratification of being the powerful, influential, and controlling helper in the interest of others' welfare. Help that results in dependency is not the generous, self-sacrificing gesture we have come to accept it as being. It is insidiously selfish. Both parties are diminished by it.

THE MOST urgent problems of our world today are the problems we have made for ourselves. They have not been caused by some heedless or malicious inanimate Nature, nor have they been imposed on us as punishment by the will of God. They are human problems whose solutions will require us to change our behavior and our social institutions.

As a science directly concerned with behavioral and social processes, psychology might be expected to provide intellectual leadership in the

American Psychologist, 24:1063–1075, 1969. Copyright 1969 by the American Psychological Association, and reproduced by permission.

Presidential Address to the American Psychological Association in Washington, D.C., September 1969.

search for new and better personal and social arrangements. In fact, however, we psychologists have contributed relatively little of real importance—even less than our rather modest understanding of behavior might justify. We should have contributed more; although our scientific base for valid contributions is far from comprehensive, certainly more is known than has been used intelligently.

This is the social challenge that psychologists face. In the years immediately ahead we must not only extend and deepen our understanding of mental and behavioral phenomena, but we must somehow incorporate our hard-won knowledge more effectively into the vast social changes that we all know are coming. It is both important and appropriate for us, on occasions such as this, to consider how best to meet this social challenge.

In opening such a discussion, however, we should keep clearly in mind that society has not commissioned us to cure its ills; a challenge is not a mandate. Moreover, there is nothing in the definition of psychology that dedicates our science to the solution of social problems. Our inability to solve the pressing problems of the day cannot be interpreted as an indictment of the scientific validity of our psychological theories. As scientists we are obliged to communicate what we know, but we have no special obligation to solve social problems.

Our obligations as citizens, however, are considerably broader than our obligations as scientists. When psychological issues are raised in this broader context, we cannot evade them by complaining that they are unscientific. If we have something of practical value to contribute, we should make every effort to insure that it is implemented.

I believe that the majority of American psychologists have accepted this broader interpretation of our responsibilities and have been eager—perhaps, sometimes, overly eager—to apply our science to social problems. We have not been aloof or insensitive; the bulk of our profession works full time on exactly such problems. And I do not wish to discount the many and often successful efforts toward application that we have made already. Yet I cannot escape the impression that we have been less effective than we might have been. "Why" and "what more might be done" are questions that have troubled me increasingly in recent years.

First, however, I would like to raise a somewhat parochial question.

ROLE OF THE AMERICAN PSYCHOLOGICAL ASSOCIATION

If we accept this challenge to use psychology to solve social problems, what role should we expect the American Psychological Association to play? I raise this question because my experience as an officer of APA has taught me that many of our members look to their national organization for leadership in insuring that our scientific and professional activities have greater social relevance.

Psychologists have been well represented among those who sign petitions of political protest (Ladd, 1969), and they have not failed to make their opinions heard in their own national headquarters. Scarcely a meeting of the Board of Directors in recent years has not featured one or more petitions from concerned members, committees, boards, divisions, or state associations requesting some action related to public affairs. These matters range all the way from the proper use of psychological tests, where APA usually has something to say, to the endorsement of particular political candidates, where APA usually does not.

These demands have imposed considerable strain on the Association, which was not created to be an instrument for social action and which responds hesitantly to any suggestion that it should become something more than a scientific and professional organization. But it does respond. I was surprised to discover how seriously APA regards any legitimate request from its membership, and how sensitive it is to the social implications of its actions, policies, and communications. Some members wish APA would do more, some less. On balance, I think APA has reflected reasonably accurately the general consensus of its members with respect to its role in public affairs.

It is not my intention to raise here any of the specific issues of public policy that have concerned the Board of Directors and the Council of Representatives, or even to offer a general formula for deciding what the public role of the APA should be. Procedurally, I am willing to stand on the thoughtful recommendations of the ad hoc Committee on Public Affairs (Tyler, 1969).

A point of general interest, however, and one that relates more directly to the theme I wish to discuss, is the frequently heard argument that APA should take some action or other because the first article of our Bylaws states that the Association shall have as its object to promote human welfare, a goal that is echoed in our statement of the *Ethical Standards of Psychologists*.

This argument is usually made by those who recommend that APA should publicly advocate some particular social reform. When these recommendations are appropriate, the action is adopted—the necessary letters are written, public statements are released to the press, etc. But not every recommendation is acceptable. It has been my impression that the less related the issue is to the scientific and professional interests of our membership, the greater is the likelihood that the promotion of human welfare will be invoked in the course of the discussion.

In most cases this argument has not persuaded me; I have traced my skepticism to two sources.

First, even the most cursory study of welfare economics will show that human welfare has never been operationally defined as a social concept. If there is such a thing as human welfare in the general sense, it must be some kind of weighted average. In difficult cases, where disagreement is most probable, something that advances the welfare of one group may disadvantage another group. The problem is to decide whose welfare we wish to promote. The APA is committed to advancing the welfare of psychologists, of course, but we dare not assume blindly that whatever is good for psychology must always be good for humanity.

Vague appeals to human welfare seldom answer specific questions because we seldom have sufficient information to decide which actions will have the desired result. And even when we do have sufficient wisdom to know in advance which actions will promote human welfare most effectively, we still face the ethical question of whether such actions are morally permissible.

My first reason for distrusting appeals to human welfare, therefore, is that they do little to clarify the logical, informational, or ethical bases for making difficult decisions. Something more is required than a sincere declaration that our heart is in the right place.

My second reason has to do with the fact that the phrase is usually quoted out of context. At the risk of losing your attention, therefore, I would like to state Article I of our Bylaws in full:

> The objects of the American Psychological Association shall be to advance psychology as a science and as a means of promoting human welfare by the encouragement of psychology in all its branches in the broadest and most liberal manner; by the promotion of research in psychology and the improvement of research methods and conditions; by the improvement of the qualifications and usefulness of psychologists through high standards of professional ethics, conduct, education, and achievement; by the increase and diffusion of psychological knowledge through meetings, professional contacts, reports, papers, discussions, and publications; thereby to advance scientific interests and inquiry, and the application of research findings to the promotion of the public welfare [APA, 1968, xii].

As I understand Article I, our corporate aim is to promote psychology. We justify that aim by our belief that psychology can be used for the public good. I do not understand Article I as a general license to endorse social actions or positions, however meritorious on other grounds, that do not advance psychology as a science and as a means of promoting human welfare. The APA is our own creature, of course; we can change our Bylaws any way we like. As presently conceived, however, APA does not have a charter to intervene on behalf of every good cause that comes along.

There are many things of social value that APA can do, and many that it has already done. If your officers have not always seemed hungry for innovation, eager to reshape APA to meet every new social issue, they have certainly been open to constructive change within the scope of our charter. I believe they have reflected the wishes of the bulk of the membership, and I feel no need to apologize for what has been accomplished. The APA has been doing what its membership wanted to do, and doing it rather well.

Of course, the membership has been far from unanimous in these matters. For example, there has been a running debate in recent years concerning the proper role for individual psychologists to play in the initiation of social reforms. We have been divided as to whether psychologists should remain expert advisers or should take a more active, participatory responsibility for determining public policy. An adviser is expected to summarize the arguments pro and con, but to leave the policy decisions to others; a participant wants to make the policy decisions himself.

Those who favor more active participation by individual psychologists tend to argue that APA should also become directly involved in advocating particular social policies. This whole debate seems to presuppose, however, that social reforms can occur only as a result of policy decisions by government or industry. This presupposition should not go unchallenged. Perhaps our options for promoting human welfare are broader than this debate would suggest.

It was E. G. Boring who first impressed on me the importance of a clear distinction between Psychology with a capital P and psychology with a small p. Capital-P Psychology refers to our associations, departments, laboratories, and the like. Small-p psychology refers to the discipline itself. Capital-P Psychology can do little to promote human welfare, outside of its faithful promotion of small-p psychology. We should not, through impatience or bad judgment, try to use capital-P Psychology where only small-p psychology could succeed. Let us by all means do everything we can to promote human welfare, but let us not forget that our real strength in that cause will come from our scientific knowledge, not from our national Association.

In my opinion, our Association can never play more than a supporting role in the promotion of social change. I do not conclude from this that APA has become irrelevant or useless, or, even worse, that it has tacitly endorsed a political bureaucracy that presides over the inequitable distribution of health, wealth, and wisdom in our society. The fact that APA has not reformed society does not mean that it approves the status quo; it means simply that there is relatively little such an association can do. When one considers the magnitude and urgency of the problems mankind faces, the question of what positions APA takes is, after all, a minor matter.

The important question, to my mind, is not what APA is doing, but what psychologists are doing. What Psychology can do as an association depends directly on the base provided by psychology as a science. It is our science that provides our real means for promoting human welfare.

So let me turn now to broader aspects of my topic.

REVOLUTIONARY POTENTIAL OF PSYCHOLOGY

I will begin by stating publicly something that I think psychologists all feel, but seldom talk about. In my opinion, scientific psychology is potentially one of the most revolutionary intellectual enterprises ever conceived by the mind of man. If we were ever to achieve substantial progress toward our stated aim—toward the understanding, prediction, and control of mental and behavioral phenomena—the implications for every aspect of society would make brave men tremble.

Responsible spokesmen for psychology seldom emphasize this revolutionary possibility. One reason is that the general public is all too ready to believe it, and public resistance to psychology would be all too easy to mobilize. Faced with the possibility that revolutionary pronouncements might easily do more harm than good, a prudent spokesman finds other drums to march to.

Regardless of whether we agree that prudence is always the best policy, I believe there is another reason for our public modesty. Anyone who claims that psychology is a revolutionary enterprise will face a demand from his scientific colleagues to put up or shut up. Nothing that psychology has done so far, they will say, is very revolutionary. They will admit that psychometric tests, psychoanalysis, conditioned reflexes, sensory thresholds, implanted electrodes, and factor analysis are all quite admirable, but they can scarcely be compared to gunpowder, the steam engine, organic chemistry, radio-telephony, computers, atom bombs, or genetic surgery in their revolutionary consequences for society. Our enthusiastic spokesman would have to retire in confused embarrassment.

Since I know that rash statements about the revolutionary potential of psychology may lead to public rejection and scientific ridicule, why do I take such risks on this occasion? My reason is that I do not believe the psychological revolution is still pie in the sky. It has already begun.

One reason the psychological revolution is not more obvious may be that we have been looking for it in the wrong place. We have assumed that psychology should provide new technological options, and that a psychological revolution will not occur until someone in authority exercises those options to attain socially desirable goals. One reason for this assumption, perhaps, is that it follows the model we have inherited from previous applications of science to practical problems. An applied scientist is supposed to provide instrumentalities for modifying the environment—instrumentalities that can then, under public regulation, be used by wealthy and powerful interests to achieve certain goals. The psychological revolution, when it comes, may follow a very different course, at least in its initial stages.

Davis (1966) has explained the difference between applied social science and applied natural science in the following way:

> Applied science, by definition, is instrumental. When the human goal is given, it seeks a solution by finding what effective means can be manipulated in the required way. Its function is to satisfy human desires and wants; otherwise nobody would bother. But when the science is concerned with human beings—not just as organisms but as goal-seeking individuals and members of groups—then it cannot be instrumental in this way, because the object of observation has a say in what

> is going on and, above all, is not willing to be treated as a pure instru-
> mentality. Most so-called social problems are problems because people
> want certain things or because there is a conflict of desires or interests
> [p. 26].

Davis goes on to argue that once conflicts of interest have developed, applied social science is helpless; that it is only when people are agreed on
their goals that our information can be usefully applied.

Although I agree with Davis that behavioral and social sciences cannot be applied to people and institutions in the same way physical and biological sciences are applied to objects and organisms, I do not agree with
his view that we must remain impotent in the face of conflict. We know
a great deal about the prevention and resolution of conflicts, and that information could certainly be put to better use than it has been. Indeed,
sometimes what is needed is not to resolve conflict but to foster it, as when
entrenched interests threaten segments of the public that have no organizational identity. And there, in turn, we know a great deal about the creation
of appropriate constituencies to defend their common interests. Behavioral
and social scientists are far from helpless in such situations.

More important, however, I believe that the real impact of psychology
will be felt, not through the technological products it places in the hands
of powerful men, but through its effects on the public at large, through a
new and different public conception of what is humanly possible and what
is humanly desirable.

I believe that any broad and successful application of psychological
knowledge to human problems will necessarily entail a change in our conception of ourselves and of how we live and love and work together. Instead of inventing some new technique for modifying the environment, or
some new product for society to adapt itself to however it can, we are proposing to tamper with the adaptive process itself. Such an innovation is
quite different from a "technological fix." I see little reason to believe that
the traditional model for scientific revolutions should be appropriate.

Consider, for example, the effect that Freudian psychology has already
had on Western society. It is obvious that its effects, though limited to certain segments of society, have been profound, yet I do not believe that one
can argue that those effects were achieved by providing new instrumentalities for achieving goals socially agreed upon. As a method of therapy, psychoanalysis has had limited success even for those who can afford it. It has
been more successful as a method of investigation, perhaps, but even there
it has been only one of several available methods. The impact of Freud's
thought has been due far less to the instrumentalities he provided than to
the changed conception of ourselves that he inspired. The wider range of
psychological problems that Freud opened up for professional psychologists
is only part of his contribution. More important in the scale of history has
been his effect on the broader intellectual community and, through it, on
the public at large. Today we are much more aware of the irrational com-

ponents of human nature and much better able to accept the reality of our unconscious impulses. The importance of Freudian psychology derives far less from its scientific validity than from the effects it has had on our shared image of man himself.

I realize that one might argue that changes in man's conception of himself under the impact of advances in scientific knowledge are neither novel nor revolutionary. For example, Darwin's theory changed our conception of ourselves, but not until the past decade has it been possible to mount a truly scientific revolution based on biological science. One might argue that we are now only at the Darwinian stage in psychology, and that the real psychological revolution is still a century or more in the future. I do not find this analogy appropriate, however.

To discover that we are not at the center of the universe, or that our remote ancestors lived in a tree, does indeed change our conception of man and society, but such new conceptions can have little effect on the way we behave in our daily affairs and in our institutional contexts. A new conception of man based on psychology, however, would have immediate implications for the most intimate details of our social and personal lives. This fact is unprecedented in any earlier stage of the Industrial Revolution.

The heart of the psychological revolution will be a new and scientifically based conception of man as an individual and as a social creature. When I say that the psychological revolution is already upon us, what I mean is that we have already begun to change man's self-conception. If we want to further that revolution, not only must we strengthen its scientific base, but we must also try to communicate it to our students and to the public. It is not the industrialist or the politician who should exploit it, but Everyman, every day.

The enrichment of public psychology by scientific psychology constitutes the most direct and important application of our science to the promotion of human welfare. Instead of trying to foresee new psychological products that might disrupt our existing social arrangements, therefore, we should be self-consciously analyzing the general effect that our scientific psychology may have on popular psychology. As I try to perform this analysis for myself, I must confess that I am not altogether pleased with the results.

I would like now to consider briefly some of the effects we are having and where, in my view, our influence is leading at the present time. Let me begin with a thumbnail sketch of one major message that many scientific psychologists are trying to communicate to the public.

CONTROL OF BEHAVIOR

One of the most admired truisms of modern psychology is that some stimuli can serve to reinforce the behavior that produces them. The practical significance of this familiar principle arises from the implication that if you can control the occurrence of these reinforcing stimuli, then you can control the occurrence of adaptive behavior intended to achieve or avoid them. This contingency between behavior and its consequences has been demonstrated in many studies of animal behavior, where environmental conditions can be controlled, or at least specified, and where the results can be measured with some precision.

Something similar holds for the human animal, of course, although it is complicated by man's symbolic proclivities and by the fact that the disparity between experimenter and subject changes when the subject is also a man. Between men, reinforcement is usually a mutual relation and each person controls the other to some extent. This relation of mutual reinforcement, which man's genius for symbols has generalized in terms of money or the promise of money, provides the psychological basis for our economic system of exchange. Psychologists did not create this economic system for controlling behavior, of course. What we have tried to do is to describe its psychological basis and its limits in terms sufficiently general to hold across different species, and to suggest how the technique might be extended to educational, rehabilitative, therapeutic, or even political situations in which economic rewards and punishments would not normally be appropriate. Once a problem of behavior control has been phrased in these terms, we may then try to discover the most effective schedule of reinforcements.

My present concern has nothing to do with the validity of these ideas. I am concerned with their effect on the public at large, for it is there, if I am right, that we are most likely to achieve a psychological revolution.

In the public view, I suspect, all this talk about controlling behavior comes across as unpleasant, if not actually threatening. Freud has already established in the public mind a general belief that all behavior is motivated. The current message says that psychologists now know how to use this motivation to control what people will do. When they hear this, of course, our scientific colleagues are likely to accuse us of pseudoscientific claims; less scientific segments of the public are likely to resent what they perceive as a threat to their personal freedom. Neither reaction is completely just, but neither is completely unjustifiable.

I believe these critics see an important truth, one that a myopic concentration on techniques of behavior control may cause us to overlook. At best, control is but one component in any program for personal improvement or social reform. Changing behavior is pointless in the absence of any coherent plan for how it should be changed. It is our plan for using control that the public wants to know about. Too often, I fear, psychologists have implied that acceptable uses for behavior control are either self-evident or can be safely left to the wisdom and benevolence of powerful men. Psychologists must not surrender the planning function so easily. Humane applications of behavior control must be based on intelligent diagnosis of the personal and social problems we are trying to solve. Psychology has at least as much, probably more, to contribute to the diagnosis of personal and social problems as it has to the control of behavior.

Regardless of whether we have actually achieved new scientific techniques of behavior control that are effective with human beings, and regardless of whether control is of any value in the absence of diagnosis and planning for its use, the simple fact that so many psychologists keep talking about control is having an effect on public psychology. The average citizen is predisposed to believe it. Control has been the practical payoff from the other sciences. Control must be what psychologists are after, too. Moreover, since science is notoriously successful, behavior control must be inevitable. Thus the layman forms an impression that control is the name of the road we are traveling, and that the experts are simply quibbling about how far down that road we have managed to go.

Closely related to this emphasis on control is the frequently repeated claim that living organisms are nothing but machines. A scientist recognizes, of course, that this claim says far more about our rapidly evolving conception of machines than it says about living organisms, but this interpretation is usually lost when the message reaches public ears. The public idea of a machine is something like an automobile, a mechanical device controlled by its operator. If people are machines, they can be driven like automobiles. The analogy is absurd, of course, but it illustrates the kind of distortion that can occur.

If the assumption that behavior control is feasible in some precise scientific sense becomes firmly rooted in public psychology, it could have unfortunate consequences, particularly if it is coupled with an assumption that control should be exercised by an industrial or bureaucratic elite. Psychologists must always respect and advocate the principle of *habeas mentem*—the right of a man to his own mind (Sanford, 1955). If we really did have a new scientific way to control human behavior, it would be highly immoral to let it fall into the hands of some small group of men, even if they were psychologists.

Perhaps a historical analogy would be appropriate. When the evolution of species was a new and exciting idea in biology, various social theorists took it up and interpreted it to mean that capitalistic competition, like the competition between species, was the source of all progress, so the great wealth of the new industrialists was a scientifically necessary consequence of the law of the survival of the fittest. This argument, called "social Darwinism," had unfortunate consequences, both for social science and for society generally (Hofstadter, 1944).

If the notion should now be accepted that it is a scientifically necessary consequence of the law of reinforcement that industrialists or bureaucrats must be allowed the same control over people that an experimenter has over his laboratory animals, I fear that a similar period of intolerable exploitation might ensue—if, indeed, it has not already begun.

The dangers that accompany a science of behavior control have been pointed out many times. Psychologists who study motivation scientifically are usually puzzled by this widespread apprehension that they might be successful. Control is not something invented by psychologists. Everyone is "controlled" all the time by something or other. All we want is to discover how the controls work. Once we understand that, society can use the knowledge in whatever manner seems socially advantageous. Our critics, on the other hand, want to know who will diagnose our problems, who will set our social goals, and who will administer the rewards and punishments.

All that I have tried to add to this familiar dialogue is the observation that the social dangers involved need not await the success of the scientific enterprise. Behavior control could easily become a self-fulfilling prophecy. If people generally should come to believe in the scientific control of behavior, proponents of coercive social programs would surely exploit that belief by dressing their proposals in scientific costumes. If our new public conception of human nature is that man's behavior can be scientifically controlled by those in positions of power, governments will quickly conform to that conception. Thus, when I try to discern what direction our psychological revolution has been taking, some aspects of it disturb me deeply and lead me to question whether in the long run these developments will really promote human welfare.

This is a serious charge. If there is any truth to it, we should ask whether any other approaches are open to us.

Personally, I believe there is a better way to advertise psychology and to relate it to social problems. Reinforcement is only one of many important ideas that we have to offer. Instead of repeating constantly that reinforcement leads to control, I would prefer to emphasize that reinforcement can lead to satisfaction and competence. And I would prefer to speak of understanding and predictions as our major scientific goals.

In the space remaining, therefore, I want to try to make the case that understanding and prediction are better goals for psychology than is control —better both for psychology and for the promotion of human welfare— because they lead us to think, not in terms of coercion by a powerful elite, but in terms of the diagnosis of problems and the development of programs that can enrich the lives of every citizen.

PUBLIC PSYCHOLOGY: TWO PARADIGMS

It should be obvious by now that I have somewhere in the back of my mind two alternative images of what the popular conception of human nature might become under the impact of scientific advances in psychology. One of these images is unfortunate, even threatening; the other is vaguer, but full of promise. Let me try to make these ideas more concrete.

The first image is the one I have been describing. It has great appeal to an authoritarian mind, and fits well with our traditional competitive ideology based on coercion, punishment, and retribution. The fact that it represents a serious distortion of scientific psychology is exactly my point. In my opinion, we have made a mistake by trying to apply our ideas to social problems and to gain acceptance for our science within the framework of this ideology.

The second image rests on the same psychological foundation, but reflects it more accurately; it allows no compromise with our traditional social ideology. It is assumed, vaguely but optimistically, that this ideology can be modified so as to be more receptive to a truer conception of human nature. How this modification can be achieved is one of the problems we face; I believe it will not be achieved if we continue to advertise the control of behavior through reinforcement as our major contribution to the solution of social problems. I would not wish to give anyone the impression that I have formulated a well-defined social alternative, but I would at least like to open a discussion and make some suggestions.

My two images are not very different from what McGregor (1960) once called Theory X and Theory Y. Theory X is the traditional theory which holds that because people dislike work, they must be coerced, controlled, directed, and threatened with punishment before they will do it. People tolerate being directed, and many even prefer it, because they have little ambition and want to avoid responsibility. McGregor's alternative Theory Y, based on social science, holds that work is as natural as play or rest. External control and threats are not the only means for inspiring people to work. People will exercise self-direction and self-control in the service of objectives to which they are committed; their commitment is a function of the rewards associated with the achievement of their objects. People can learn not only to accept but to seek responsibility. Imagination, ingenuity, and creativity are widely distributed in the population, although these intellectual potentialities are poorly utilized under the conditions of modern industrial life.

McGregor's Theory X and Theory Y evolved in the context of his studies of industrial management. They are rival theories held by industrial managers about how best to achieve their institutional goals. A somewhat broader view is needed if we are to talk about public psychology generally, and not merely the managerial manifestations of public psychology. So let me amplify McGregor's distinction by referring to the ideas of Varela, a very remarkable engineer in Montevideo, Uruguay, who uses scientific psychology in the solution of a wide range of personal and social problems.

Varela (1970, in press) contrasts two conceptions of the social nature of man. Following Kuhn's (1962) discussion of scientific revolutions, he refers to these two conceptions as "paradigms." The first paradigm is a set of assumptions on which our social institutions are presently based. The second is a contrasting paradigm based on psychological research. Let me outline them for you very briefly.

Our current social paradigm is characterized as follows: All men are created equal. Most behavior is motivated by economic competition, and conflict is inevitable. One truth underlies all controversy, and unreasonableness is best countered by facts and logic. When something goes wrong, someone is to blame, and every effort must be made to establish his guilt so that he can be punished. The guilty person is responsible for his own misbehavior and for his own rehabilitation. His teachers and supervisors are too busy to become experts in social science; their role is to devise solutions and see to it that their students or subordinates do what they are told.

For comparison, Varela offers a paradigm based on psychological research: There are large individual differences among people, both in ability and personality. Human motivation is complex and no one ever acts as he does for any single reason, but, in general, positive incentives are more effective than threats or punishments. Conflict is no more inevitable than disease and can be resolved or, still better, prevented. Time and resources for resolving social problems are strictly limited. When something goes wrong, how a person perceives the situation is more important to him than the "true facts," and he cannot reason about the situation until his irrational feelings have been toned down. Social problems are solved by correcting causes, not symptoms, and this can be done more effectively in groups than individually. Teachers and supervisors must be experts in social science because they are responsible for the cooperation and individual improvement of their students or subordinates.

No doubt other psychologists would draw the picture somewhat differently. Without reviewing the psychological evidence on which such generalizations are based, of course, I cannot argue their validity. But I think most of you will recognize the lines of research on which McGregor's Theory Y and Varela's second paradigm are based. Moreover, these psychologically based paradigms are incompatible in several respects with the prevailing ideology of our society.

Here, then, is the real challenge: How can we foster a social climate in which some such new public conception of man based on psychology can take root and flourish? In my opinion, this is the proper translation of our more familiar question about how psychology might contribute to the promotion of human welfare.

I cannot pretend to have an answer to this question, even in its translated form, but I believe that part of the answer is that psychology must be practiced by nonpsychologists. We are not physicians; the secrets of our trade need not be reserved for highly trained specialists. Psychological facts should be passed out freely to all who need and can use them. And from successful applications of psychological principles the public may gain a better appreciation that is emerging from our science.

If we take seriously the idea of a peaceful revolution based on a new conception of human nature, our scientific results will have to be instilled in the public consciousness in a practical and usable form so that what we know can be applied by ordinary people. There simply are not enough psychologists, even including nonprofessionals, to meet every need for psychological services. The people at large will have to be their own psychologists, and make their own applications of the principles that we establish.

Of course, everyone practices psychology, just as everyone who cooks is a chemist, everyone who reads a clock is an astronomer, everyone who drives a car is an engineer. I am not suggesting any radical departure when I say that nonpsychologists must practice psychology. I am simply proposing that we should teach them to practice it better, to make use self-consciously of what we believe to be scientifically valid principles.

Our responsibility is less to assume the role of experts and try to apply psychology ourselves than to give it away to the people who really need it —and that includes everyone. The practice of valid psychology by nonpsychologists will inevitably change people's conception of themselves and what they can do. When we have accomplished that, we will really have caused a psychological revolution.

HOW TO GIVE PSYCHOLOGY AWAY

I am keenly aware that giving psychology away will be no simple task. In our society there are depths of resistance to psychological innovations that have to be experienced to be believed (Graziano, 1969).

Solving social problems is generally considered to be more difficult than solving scientific problems. A social problem usually involves many more independent variables, and it cannot be finally solved until society has been persuaded to adopt the solution. Many who have tried to introduce sound psychological practices into schools, clinics, hospitals, prisons, or industries have been forced to retreat in dismay. They complain, and with good reason, that they were unable to buck the "System," and often their reactions are more violent than sensible. The System, they say, refuses to change even when it does not work.

This experience has been so common that in my pessimistic moments I have been led to wonder whether anything less than complete reform is possible.

Deutsch (1969) has made an interesting case that competitive and cooperative social relationships tend to be mutually exclusive. He summarizes the result of considerable research in the following terms:

> The strategy of power and the tactics of coercion, threat, and deception result from and also result in a competitive relationship. Similarly, the strategy of mutual problem solving and the tactics of persuasion, openness, and mutual enhancement elicit and also are elicited by a cooperative orientation [p. 4].

Each orientation has its own internal consistency; elements of one are not easily injected into the other.

Perhaps a similar pressure toward internal coherence lies at the root of public resistance to many of our innovative suggestions. It often seems that any one of our ideas taken alone is inadequate. Injected into the existing social paradigm it is either a foreign body, incompatible with the other presuppositions that shape our social institutions, or it is distorted and trivialized to fit the preexisting paradigm.

One of the most basic ideas in all the social sciences is the concept of culture. Social anthropologists have developed a conception of culture as an organic whole, in which each particular value, practice, or assumption must be understood in the context of the total system. They tell terrible tales about the consequences of introducing Western reforms into aboriginal cultures without understanding the social equilibria that would be upset.

Perhaps cultural integrity is not limited to primitive cultures, but applies also to our own society here and now. If so, then our attempts at piecemeal innovation may be doomed either to fail or to be rejected outright.

I label these thoughts pessimistic because they imply a need for drastic changes throughout the whole system, changes that could only be imposed by someone with dangerous power over the lives of others. And that, I have argued, is not the way our psychological revolution should proceed.

In my more optimistic moments, however, I recognize that you do not need complete authority over a social organization in order to reform it. The important thing is not to control the system, but to understand it. Someone who has a valid conception of the system as a whole can often introduce relatively minor changes that have extensive consequences throughout the entire organization. Lacking such a conception, worthwhile innovations may be total failures.

For example, if you institute a schedule of rewards and punishments in the psychiatric ward of a Veterans Hospital, you should not be indignant when the American Legion objects on the grounds that you cannot withhold food and clothing from veterans. If you had had a more adequate understanding of the hospital as a social system, you would have included the interests and influence of the American Legion in your diagnosis of the problem, and you would have formulated a plan to gain their endorsement as part of your task as a social engineer. You should not demand inordinate power just because you made an inadequate diagnosis of the problem. Understanding must come first.

In my optimistic moments I am able to convince myself that understanding is attainable and that social science is already at a stage where successful applications are possible. Careful diagnosis and astute planning based on what we already know can often resolve problems that at first glance seemed insurmountable. Many social, clinical, and industrial psychologists have already demonstrated the power of diagnosis and planning based on sound psychological principles.

Varela has illustrated such applications by his work in Uruguay. Diagnosis involves not only a detailed analysis of the social organization and of the perceptions and goals of all the people caught up in the problem, but also the description of their abilities and personalities. Planning involves the explicit formulation of a series of steps that will lead these people to consider the problem together and will help them to discover a solution that respects everyone's hopes and aspirations. If, in the course of this plan, it becomes necessary to persuade someone, this is not to be accomplished by coercion or by marshaling facts, but by a gradual, step-by-step process that enables him to reduce his reactance little by little as he convinces himself of the virtues of the alternative view and broadens his conception of the range of acceptable solutions (Zimbardo & Ebbeson, 1969, pp. 114–121). This is not the place and I am not the person to describe the ingenuity with which Varela has constructed such plans and carried them out, but such applications give me some reason for optimism.

Diagnosing practical problems and developing detailed plans to deal with them may or may not be more difficult than solving scientific problems, but it is certainly different. Many psychologists, trained in an empiricist, experimental tradition, have tried to serve two masters at once. That is to say, they have tried to solve practical problems and simultaneously to collect data of scientific value on the effects of their interventions. Other fields, however, maintain a more equitable division of labor between scientist and engineer. Scientists are responsible for the validity of the principles; engineers accept them and try to use them to solve practical problems.

Although I recognize the importance of evaluating an engineer's product, in this domain it is no easy thing to do. Assessing social innovations is a whole art in itself, one that we are only beginning to develop. Economic considerations are relevant, of course, but we must also learn to evaluate the subtler psychological and social implications of our new solutions (Bauer, 1966). Technological assessment in this sense will not be achieved by insisting that every reform should resemble a well-designed experiment. In particular, the need for assessment should not be allowed to discourage those who enjoy and have a talent for social engineering.

We are in serious need of many more psychological technologists who can apply our science to the personal and social problems of the general public, for it is through them that the public will eventually discover the new paradigm that psychologists are developing. That is to say, it is through the success of such practical applications that we have our best hope for revolutionizing public psychology.

Obviously, we must avoid the evils of superficiality; we must continue as scientists to refine, clarify, and integrate our new paradigm. Most importantly, we must self-consciously recognize that it *is* a new and revolutionary conception that we are working toward, so that isolated discoveries can be related to and evaluated in terms of that larger context. But all that would be futile, of course, if the general public did not accept it, or if public psychology were not altered by it.

There is no possibility of legislating the changes I have in mind.

Passing laws that people must change their conceptions of themselves and others is precisely the opposite of what we need. Education would seem to be our only possibility. I do not mean only education in the schoolroom, although that is probably the best communication channel presently at our disposal. I have in mind a more ambitious program of educating the general public.

It is critically important to shape this education to fit the perceived needs of the people who receive it. Lectures suitable for graduate seminars are seldom suitable for laymen, and for a layman facing a concrete problem they are usually worse than useless. In order to get a factory supervisor or a ghetto mother involved, we must give them something they can use. Abstract theories, however elegant, or sensitivity training, however insightful, are too remote from the specific troubles they face. In order to get started, we must begin with people where they are, not assume we know where they should be. If a supervisor is having trouble with his men, perhaps we should teach him how to write a job description and how to evaluate the abilities and personalities of those who fill the job; perhaps we should teach him the art of persuasion, or the time and place for positive reinforcement. If a ghetto mother is not giving her children sufficient intellectual challenge, perhaps we should teach her how to encourage their motor, perceptual, and linguistic skills. The techniques involved are not some esoteric branch of witchcraft that must be reserved for those with PhD degrees in psychology. When the ideas are made sufficiently concrete and explicit, the scientific foundations of psychology can be grasped by sixth-grade children.

There are many obvious and useful suggestions that we could make and that nonpsychologists could exploit. Not every psychological problem in human engineering has to be solved by a professional psychologist; engineers can rapidly assimilate psychological facts and theories that are relevant to their own work. Not every teaching program has to be written by a learning theorist; principles governing the design and evaluation of programmed materials can be learned by content specialists. Not every personnel decision has to be made by a psychometrician; not every interview has to be conducted by a clinical psychologist; not every problem has to be solved by a cognitive psychologist; not every reinforcement has to be supervised by a student of conditioning. Psychological principles and techniques can be usefully applied by everyone. If our suggestions actually work, people should be eager to learn more. If they do not work, we should improve them. But we should not try to give people something whose value they cannot recognize, then complain when they do not return for a second meeting.

Consider the teaching of reading, for example. Here is an obviously appropriate area for the application of psychological principles. So what do we do? We assemble experts who decide what words children know, and in what order they should learn to read them; then we write stories with those words and teachers make the children read them, or we use them in programmed instruction that exploits the principles of reinforcement. But all too often the children fail to recognize the value of learning these carefully constructed lessons.

Personally, I have been much impressed with the approach of Ashton-Warner (1963), who begins by asking a child what words he wants. Mummy, daddy, kiss, frightened, ghost, their own names—these are the words children ask for, words that are bound up with their own loves and fears. She writes each child's word on a large, tough card and gives it to him. If a child wants words like police, butcher, knife, kill, jail, and bomb, he gets them. And he learns to read them almost immediately. It is *his* word, and each morning he retrieves his own words from the pile collected each night by the teacher. These are not dead words of an expert's choosing, but words that live in a child's own experience. Given this start, children begin to write, using their own words, and from there the teaching of reading follows naturally. Under this regimen, a word is not an imposed task to be learned with reinforcements borrowed from some external source of motivation. Learning the word is itself reinforcing; it gives the child something he wants, a new way to cope with a desire or fear. Each child decides where he wants to start, and each child receives something whose value he can recognize.

Could we generalize this technique discovered by an inspired teacher in a small New Zealand school? In my own thinking I have linked it with something that White (1959) has called competence motivation. In order to tap this motivational system we must use psychology to give people skills that will satisfy their urge to feel more effective. Feeling effective is a very personal thing, for it must be a feeling of effectiveness in coping with personal problems in one's own life. From that beginning some might want to learn more about the science that helped them increase their competence, and then perhaps we could afford to be more abstract. But in the beginning we must try to diagnose and solve the problems people think they have, not the problems we experts think they ought to have, and we must learn to understand those problems in the social and institutional contexts that define them. With this approach we might do something practical for nurses, policemen, prison guards, salesmen—for people in many different walks of life. That, I believe, is what we should mean when we talk about applying psychology to the promotion of human welfare.

If you tell me that such a program is too ambitious or too foreign to our conception of ourselves as scientists and practitioners, I must agree that I do not know where to place our fulcrum to move the world. My goal is to persuade you that this is the problem we face, and that we dare not leave it for bureaucrats or businessmen to solve. We will have to cope with it however we can, and I hope that someone has better ideas than I about how to do it.

I can see some promise for innovations in particular subcultures. If we apply our new paradigm in particular institutions—in schools, hospitals, prisons, industries—we can perhaps test its validity and demonstrate its superiority. Many such social experiments are already in progress, of course. And much of the recent surge of interest in community psychology (Bennett, 1966) has been stimulated by the realization that we really do have something to contribute to community life. Perhaps all this work will eventually have a cumulative effect.

One trouble, of course, is that we are trying to reverse the natural direction of influence. Ordinarily, an institution or a community models its own subculture more or less automatically after the larger culture in which it is embedded, and new members require little indoctrination in order to understand the tacit assumptions on which the institution is based. Whether the new paradigm will be powerful enough to reverse this direction is, I suppose, a matter for pure speculation at the present time. It seems unlikely that we will succeed, however, if each application of the new paradigm is viewed as unrelated to every other, and no attempt is made to integrate these experiments into a paradigm for society as a whole.

It is possible, however, that our society may not be quite as resistant as we anticipate. The demand for social relevance that we have been voicing as psychologists is only one aspect of a general dissatisfaction with the current state of our society. On every hand we hear complaints about the old paradigm. People are growing increasingly alienated from a society in which a few wise men behind closed doors decide what is good for everyone. Our system of justice based on punishment and retribution is not working. Even those most blessed by economic rewards are asking for something more satisfying to fill their lives. We desperately need techniques for resolving conflicts, and for preventing them from becoming public confrontations from which reasonable retreat is impossible. Anyone who reads the newspapers must realize that vast social changes are in the making, that they must occur if civilized society is to survive.

Vested interests will oppose these changes, of course, but as someone once said, vested interests, however powerful, cannot withstand the gradual encroachment of new ideas. If we psychologists are ready for it, we may be able to contribute a coherent and workable philosophy, based on the science of psychology, that will make this general agitation less negative, that will make it a positive search for something new.

I recognize that many of you will note these ambitions as little more than empty rhetoric. Psychologists will never be up to it, you will say. We should stay in our laboratories and do our own thing. The public will work out its own paradigms without us. Perhaps such skepticism is justified.

On the other hand, difficulty is no excuse for surrender. There is a sense in which the unattainable is the best goal to pursue. So let us continue our struggle to advance psychology as a means of promoting human welfare, each in our own way. For myself, however, I can imagine nothing we could do that would be more relevant to human welfare, and nothing that could pose a greater challenge to the next generation of psychologists, than to discover how best to give psychology away.

REFERENCES

American Psychological Association. Bylaws of the American Psychological Association. *1968 Directory*. Washington, D.C.: Author, 1968.

Ashton-Warner, S. *Teacher*. New York: Simon & Schuster, 1963.

Bauer, R. A. (Ed.) *Social indicators*. Cambridge: M.I.T. Press, 1966.

Bennett, C. C. *Community psychology*. Report of Boston Conference on the Education of Psychologists for Community Mental Health. Boston: Boston University, 1966.

Davis, K. The perilous promise of behavioral science. In, *Research in the service of man: Biomedical knowledge, development, and use*. A conference sponsored by the Subcommittee on Government Research and the Frontiers of Science Foundation of Oklahoma for the Committee on Government, Operations of the U.S. Senate, October 1966. Washington, D.C.: U.S. Government Printing Office, 1967.

Deutsch, M. Reflections on some experimental studies of interpersonal conflict. Presidential Address to the Eastern Psychological Association, New York, April 11, 1969.

Graziano, A. M. Clinical innovation and the mental health power structure: A social case history. *American Psychologist*, 1969, **24**, 10–18.

Hofstadter, R. *Social Darwinism in American thought*. Philadelphia: University of Pennsylvania Press, 1944.

Kuhn, T. *The structure of scientific revolutions*. Chicago: University of Chicago Press, 1962.

Ladd, E. C., Jr. Professors and political petitions. *Science*, 1969, **163**, 1425–1430.

McGregor, D. *The human side of enterprise*. New York: McGraw-Hill, 1960.

Sanford, F. H. Creative health and the principle of *habeas mentem*. *American Psychologist*, 1955, **10**, 829–835.

Tyler, L. An approach to public affairs: Report of the ad hoc Committee on Public Affairs. *American Psychologist*, 1969, **24**, 1–4.

Varela, J. A. *Introduction to social science technology*. New York: Academic Press, 1970, in press.

White, R. W. Motivation reconsidered: The concept of competence. *Psychological Review*, 1959, **66**, 297–333.

Zimbardo, P., & Ebbeson, E. *Influencing attitudes and changing behavior*. Reading, Mass.: Addison-Wesley, 1969.

Author index

Subject index